Assessment of Malingered Neuropsychological Deficits

Assessment of Malingered Neuropsychological Deficits

Edited by
Glenn J. Larrabee

OXFORD
UNIVERSITY PRESS

2007

OXFORD
UNIVERSITY PRESS

Oxford University Press, Inc., publishes works that further
Oxford University's objective of excellence
in research, scholarship, and education.

Oxford   New York
Auckland   Cape Town   Dar es Salaam   Hong Kong   Karachi
Kuala Lumpur   Madrid   Melbourne   Mexico City   Nairobi
New Delhi   Shanghai   Taipei   Toronto

With offices in
Argentina   Austria   Brazil   Chile   Czech Republic   France   Greece
Guatemala   Hungary   Italy   Japan   Poland   Portugal   Singapore
South Korea   Switzerland   Thailand   Turkey   Ukraine   Vietnam

Copyright © 2007 by Oxford University Press, Inc.

Published by Oxford University Press, Inc.
198 Madison Avenue, New York, New York 10016

www.oup.com

Oxford is a registered trademark of Oxford University Press

Library of Congress Cataloging-in-Publication Data
Assessment of malingered neuropsychological deficits /
edited by Glenn J. Larrabee.
    p. ; cm.
Includes bibliographical references and index.
ISBN 978-0-19-518846-2
1. Neuropsychological tests.   2. Malingering.   I. Larrabee, Glenn J. [DNLM:
1. Malingering—diagnosis.   2. Malingering—psychology.   3. Psychological Tests.
W 783 A846 2008]
RC386.6.N48A87 2008
616.8'0475—dc22   2007001084

9 8 7 6 5 4 3 2

Printed in the United States of America
on acid-free paper

Lovingly dedicated to my wife, Jan, and our son, Zack.

Preface

Malingering, the exaggeration and/or fabrication of deficits in the pursuit of some external incentive, is a common risk in persons with compensable neurological claims following accidental injury or malpractice, or in those claiming impaired competency or diminished responsibility when facing criminal charges. Estimates of malingering prevalence (base rate) in both civil and criminal contexts approach and even exceed 50%, as reviewed in the first chapter of the present volume.

Forensic neuropsychology in general, and malingering in particular, are leading areas of research from 1990 to 2000 (Sweet, King, Malina, Bergman, & Simmons, 2002). The neuropsychological evaluation is multivariate and dependent upon symptom report measures, as well as upon performance on a range of tasks of language, perception, sensorimotor, attention, processing speed, verbal and visual learning and memory, and intellectual and problem-solving skills (Lezak, Howieson, & Loring, 2004). Not surprisingly, data are accumulating showing that malingering is also multivariate, occurring across a variety of measures of ability including perception, motor function, attention, memory, and problem-solving (Larrabee, 2003a; Mittenberg, Aguila-Puentes, Patton, Canyock, & Heilbronner, 2002). Three general patterns of malingering can occur, including: 1) underperformance or neuroanatomically implausible performance on measures of cognitive or perceptual-motor abilities, 2) exaggeration of symptom report, and 3) underperformance or atypical performance on measures of ability, in combination with exaggeration on measures of symptom report (Iverson & Binder, 2000; Larrabee, 2005). Assessment of malingering on measures of ability can take the form of

using freestanding measures of response bias and effort, referred to as symptom validity tests (SVTs), or depend upon atypical or derived measures of symptom validity based on standard measures of basic neuropsychological abilities such as motor function or attention.

The present volume is designed to fulfill the need for a comprehensive review of the procedures available for assessment of malingered neuropsychological deficits. The introductory chapter by Larrabee defines malingering, discusses research designs for evaluation of malingering, and provides data on the base-rate or frequency of occurrence of malingering. The second chapter by Larrabee and Berry considers diagnostic classification statistics in relation to the diagnosis of malingering using data from two published studies of the Fake Bad Scale of the MMPI-2 (Lees-Haley, English & Glenn, 1991; Larrabee, 2003b; Ross, Millis, Krukowski, Putnam, & Adams, 2004). The third chapter by Boone and Lu reviews freestanding SVTs that do not depend upon the use of two-alternative forced choice testing. The fourth chapter by Grote and Hook covers SVTs that depend upon the use of two-alternative forced choice testing, which has become a popular paradigm for freestanding measures of effort. The fifth chapter by Larrabee discusses SVT procedures that have been derived from statistical analysis of patterns of performance on subtests comprising measures such as the Wechsler Adult Intelligence Scale-III and Wechsler Memory Scale-III (Wechsler, 1997a,b). The sixth chapter by Greiffenstein reviews SVT procedures that have been derived for standard clinical measures of perception and sensorimotor function. The seventh chapter by Suhr and Barrash covers SVT procedures which have been derived for measures of attention, processing speed and memory. Greve and Bianchini consider SVT procedures derived from standard clinical measures of executive function in chapter eight. Chapter 9 by Berry and Schipper, and chapter 10 by Larrabee review the evaluation of exaggerated psychiatric, and exaggerated health and injury symptoms, respectively. In Chapter 11, Suhr and Gunstad cover research on the effects of coaching on the detection of feigned impairments. Chapter 12 by Albers and Schiffer discusses the detection of non-credible performance on the neurological examination. In chapter 13, Larrabee, Greiffenstein, Greve, and Bianchini review the diagnostic criteria for malingering proposed by Slick, Sherman and Iverson (1999) and subsequent research supporting these criteria. Larrabee and colleagues then provide empirically-derived suggestions for improvements to the Slick et al. criteria.

In view of the problems associated with coaching, reviewed by Suhr and Gunstad in chapter 11, discussion of SVT procedures in the present volume followed the guideline of not disclosing information that was not already available in standard publicly available texts on assessment such as Lezak, et al. (2004) or Strauss, Sherman, and Spreen (2006), or available in public domain research journals in the field of neuropsychology. Information was not taken directly from test manuals, and the reader of this book is advised that should requests for copies of test manuals be made in the context of

litigated matters, guidelines for dealing with such requests are found in the position papers by the National Academy of Neuropsychology on test security, found at nanonline.org (also see National Academy of Neuropsychology, 2000).

I gratefully acknowledge the assistance of several individuals whose contributions have been extremely helpful in the completion of this book. First, I acknowledge the assistance of Holly Strader and Bridgette Rees, who helped read and proof the contents of the entire volume. Their attention to detail was invaluable. Next, I am grateful to Patricia Reynolds of the Bishopric Medical Library at Sarasota Memorial Hospital in Florida, for providing articles for the chapters I prepared for the current volume. Last, I am grateful to my editors: Fiona Stevens, who was editor on my first book, *Forensic Neuropsychology: A Scientific Approach*, and who helped me prepare a successful proposal for the current volume, and Shelley Reinhardt, for her assistance in seeing this volume through to publication.

References

Iverson, G. L., & Binder, L. M. (2000). Detecting exaggeration and malingering in neuropsychological assessment. *Journal of Head Trauma Rehabilitation, 15*, 829–858.

Larrabee, G. J. (2003a). Detection of malingering using atypical performance patterns on standard neuropsychological tests. *The Clinical Neuropsychologist, 17*, 410–425.

Larrabee, G. J. (2003b). Detection of symptom exaggeration with the MMPI-2 in litigants with malingered neurocognitive dysfunction. *The Clinical Neuropsychologist, 17*, 54–68.

Larrabee, G. J. (2005). Assessment of malingering. In G. J. Larrabee (Ed.), *Forensic neuropsychology: A scientific approach* (pp. 115–158). New York: Oxford University Press.

Lees-Haley, P. R., English, L. T., & Glenn, W. J. (1991). A Fake Bad Scale for the MMPI-2 for personal injury claimants. *Psychological Reports, 68*, 203–210.

Lezak, M. D., Howieson, D. B., & Loring, D. W. (2004). *Neuropsychological assessment* (4th ed.). New York: Oxford University Press.

Mittenberg, W., Aguila-Puentes, G., Patton, C., Canyock, E. M., & Heilbronner, R. L. (2002). Neuropsychological profiling of symptom exaggeration and malingering. *Journal of Forensic Neuropsychology, 3*, 227–240.

National Academy of Neuropsychology (2000). Test security. *Archives of Clinical Neuropsychology, 15*, 383–386.

Ross, S. R., Millis, S. R., Krukowski, R. A., Putnam, S. H., & Adams, K. M. (2004). Detecting probable malingering on the MMPI-2: An examination of the Fake-Bad Scale in mild head injury. *Journal of Clinical and Experimental Neuropsychology, 26*, 115–124.

Slick, D. J., Sherman, E. M. S., & Iverson, G. L. (1999). Diagnostic criteria for malingered neurocognitive dysfunction: Proposed standards for clinical practice and research. *The Clinical Neuropsychologist, 13*, 545–561.

Strauss, E., Sherman, E. M. S., & Spreen, O. (2006). *A compendium of neuropsychological tests* (3rd ed.). New York: Oxford University Press.

Sweet, J. J., King, J. H., Malina, A. C., Bergman, M. A., & Simmons, A. (2002). Documenting the prominence of forensic neuropsychology at national meetings and in relevant professional journals from 1990–2000. *The Clinical Neuropsychologist, 16,* 481–494.

Wechsler, D. (1997a). *WAIS-III. Administration and scoring manual.* San Antonio, TX: Psychological Corporation.

Wechsler, D. (1997b). *WMS-III. Adminstration and scoring manual.* San Antonio, TX: Psychological Corporation.

Contents

Contributors

James W. Albers, MD, PhD Professor, Department of Neurology, University of Michigan

Joseph Barrash, PhD Associate Professor of Clinical Neurology, Department of Neurology, University of Iowa Carver College of Medicine

David T. R. Berry, PhD Professor, Department of Psychology, University of Kentucky

Kevin J. Bianchini, PhD Clinical Assistant Professor, Department of Psychology, University of New Orleans

Kyle B. Boone, PhD Professor-in-Residence, Department of Psychiatry and Biobehavioral Sciences, David Geffen School of Medicine at the University of California, Los Angeles

Manfred F. Greiffenstein, PhD Psychological Systems, Inc.

Kevin W. Greve, PhD Professor, Department of Psychology, University of New Orleans

Christopher L. Grote, PhD Associate Professor and Associate Chair, Department of Behavioral Sciences, Rush Medical College

John Gunstad, PhD Assistant Professor, Department of Psychology, Kent State University

Julie N. Hook, PhD Assistant Professor, Department of Behavioral Sciences, Rush Medical College

Glenn J. Larrabee, PhD Independent Practice, Sarasota, Florida

Po H. Lu, PsyD Assistant Professor, Department of Neurology, University of California–Los Angeles

Randolph Schiffer, MD Chair and Professor, Department of Neuropsychiatry, Texas Tech University Health Sciences Center

Lindsey J. Schipper, MA Doctoral Candidate, Department of Psychology, University of Kentucky

Julie A. Suhr, PhD Associate Professor, Department of Psychology, Ohio University

Assessment of Malingered
Neuropsychological Deficits

1

Introduction

Malingering, Research Designs, and Base Rates

Glenn J. Larrabee

Neuropsychological evaluation depends upon an accurate symptom report by the examinee and requires that the examinee exert full effort during neuropsychological testing. Persons in adversarial circumstances such as personal-injury litigation or criminal prosecution may be tempted to modify their symptom reporting and test performance in order to achieve an external incentive such as monetary compensation or mitigation of responsibility for an alleged criminal act. With the expansion of neuropsychology into the legal arena, the fact that symptom report and effort on testing are under the control of the examinee has led to a veritable explosion in research on malingering in the past 10 years. Thus forensic neuropsychology became a leading area of research in the 1990s, and malingering was the most widely investigated topic in this area (Sweet, King, Malina, Bergman, & Simmons, 2002). In 2005 the National Academy of Neuropsychology published a position paper on symptom validity assessment that concluded that, "When the potential for secondary gain increases the incentive for symptom exaggeration or fabrication and/or when neuropsychologists become suspicious of insufficient effort or inaccurate or incomplete reporting, neuropsychologists can, and must, utilize symptom validity tests and procedures to assist in the determination of the validity of the information and test data obtained" (Bush et al., 2005, pp. 425–426).

Definitions of Malingering

Malingering has been defined in various manners. The *Diagnostic and Statistical Manual* of the American Psychiatric Association (*DSM-IV-TR*, 2000) defines malingering as the intentional production of false or grossly exaggerated physical or psychological symptoms that are motivated by external incentives such as avoiding work or military duty, obtaining drugs or financial compensation, or evading criminal prosecution. Malingering must be distinguished from factitious disorder, in which the volitional production of symptoms is motivated by the need to assume a sick or disabled role rather than the achieving of a specific external incentive. Malingering must also be distinguished from the somatoform disorders, in which the motivation for symptom production derives from a psychological need or conflict that is outside the patient's conscious awareness. The *DSM-IV* suggests that malingering should be strongly suspected if any combination of the following is noted: (a) medicolegal context, (b) marked discrepancy between the person's claimed stress or disability and the objective findings, (c) lack of cooperation during the diagnostic evaluation and in complying with the prescribed treatment regimen, and (d) the presence of antisocial personality disorder.

Rogers (1997a) proposes a definition of malingering similar to that found in the *DSM-IV*, but it eliminates psychopathology and antisocial personality disorder as factors. He advocates moving away from a "mentally disordered" or "bad" (criminological) conceptualization of malingering to a definition that recognizes malingering as an adaptational behavior (Rogers, 1990a, 1990b). In this adaptational model, would-be malingerers are viewed as engaging in a cost-benefit analysis when confronted with an assessment perceived as indifferent or in opposition to their needs. Rogers notes that malingering is more likely to occur when the context is adversarial, the personal stakes are high, and no other viable alternatives are perceived. The *DSM-IV* also indicates that malingering may represent adaptive behavior (for example, feigning illness while a captive during wartime).

Slick, Sherman, and Iverson (1999) have proposed diagnostic criteria for malingered neurocognitive dysfunction (MND), which is defined as the volitional exaggeration or fabrication of cognitive dysfunction for the purpose of obtaining substantial material gain (e.g., compensation for injury) or avoiding or escaping legally obligated formal duty (e.g., prison sentence, military service) or responsibility (e.g., competency to stand trial). Slick et al. provide specific criteria for response bias (B criteria) and symptom magnification or misreporting (C criteria), which are used in combination with rule-out conditions (D criteria) for other disorders that fully account for the B or C criteria (e.g., developmental, neurological, or psychiatric abnormalities). The B criteria are as follows:

1. definite negative response bias; below-chance performance ($p < .05$) on one or more forced-choice measures of cognitive function

2. probable response bias; performance consistent with feigning on one or more *well-validated* psychometric tests or indices designed to measure exaggeration or fabrication of deficits
3. discrepancy between test data and known patterns of brain dysfunction (e.g., severely impaired performance on attention tests with normal performance on memory tests)
4. discrepancy between test data and observed behavior (e.g., significantly impaired performance on two or more measures of memory function in persons who show no memory difficulties when relating details about how they suffered their injuries, their medical history, and other history subsequent to their accident)
5. discrepancy between test data and reliable collateral reports (e.g., a patient handles all of the family finances but is unable to perform simple calculations during formal testing)
6. discrepancy between test data and documented background history (e.g., a patient with no loss of consciousness or posttraumatic amnesia [PTA] performs in the severely impaired range at levels seen in persons with more than 1 month of coma)

The following are the C criteria:

1. Self-reported history is discrepant with documented history.
2. Self-reported symptoms are discrepant with known patterns of brain functioning (e.g., extensive autobiographical amnesia).
3. Self-reported symptoms are discrepant with behavioral observations (e.g., reporting severe memory impairment but showing little difficulty relaying one's clinical history or details of the accident leading to the claimed injury).
4. Self-reported symptoms are discrepant with information obtained from a reliable informant (claims of severe memory impairment but no evidence of memory dysfunction in the home).
5. There is evidence of exaggerated or fabricated psychological dysfunction. Self-reported dysfunction is substantially contradicted by behavioral observation, reliable collateral information, well-validated validity scales, and/or indices on self-report measures of psychological adjustment (e.g., the MMPI-2) that strongly suggest exaggerated or fabricated symptom report.

The Slick et al. criteria are used to identify definite, probable, or possible MND when these behaviors occur in the context of a substantial external incentive (criterion A) and are not fully accounted for by psychiatric, neurologic, or developmental factors (D criteria). Definite MND is defined by criterion B1 (significantly worse-than-chance performance on a two-alternative forced-choice test). Probable MND is defined by two of B2–B6 criteria or one of B2–B6 plus one of C1–C5 criteria. Possible MND is defined by C1–C5 or when the criteria for probable MND are met, except that D criteria (psychiatric,

neurologic, or developmental conditions that fully account for B and C criteria) cannot be ruled out.

By developing specific criteria for response bias, symptom fabrication/exaggeration, and exclusionary criteria, Slick et al. (ibid.) operationalize the diagnosis of malingering and avoid issues regarding direct assessment of intent. Rather, the presence of intent is inferred by the diagnostic criteria; in other words, *if there are substantial external incentives, negative response bias, and symptom exaggeration that are not fully accounted for by neurologic, psychiatric, or developmental disorders, then what else could this pattern be other than malingering?* Slick et al. argue that inferred intent is no different from the inferences clinicians make regarding assessment of phenomena such as hallucinations. The Slick et al. criteria have been modified and adapted for the assessment of malingered pain-related disability (Bianchini, Greve, & Glynn, 2005).

Although most researchers in malingering accept the various response-bias criteria proposed by Slick et al. for assessment of the validity of neuropsychological test data, some are still hesitant to use the term "malingering." Rather, they prefer terminology such as "suspect effort" (Babikian, Boone, Lu, & Arnold, 2006) or "incomplete effort" (Axelrod, Fichtenberg, Millis, & Wertheimer, 2006). Hesitance to use the term "malingering" appears to derive from continuing concerns about the need to establish intent and to differentiate somatoform disorders (caused by unconscious motivational factors outside volitional control) from the motivated and volitional production of symptoms characteristic of factitious disorders or malingering (Boone, in press). Nonetheless, researchers and clinicians who use terminology such as "noncredible symptoms" or "incomplete effort" rather than "malingering" are looking at the same phenomenon that others are identifying as evidence of "malingering" (i.e., multiple-symptom validity-test failure in persons with substantial external incentives; ibid.). In this vein, Boone (ibid.) has advocated changing the terminology for the Slick et al. (1999) criteria from "diagnosis of malingered neurocognitive function" to "determination of noncredible neurocognitive function."

Research Designs in Malingering

Historically, interest in malingering dates back many centuries in the military (Palmer, 2003). Palmer cites Glueck (1915), who noted that Ulysses feigned insanity to escape the Trojan War by yoking a bull and horse together and plowing the seashore, sowing salt instead of grain.

Rey (1964) and Benton and Spreen (Benton & Spreen, 1961; Spreen & Benton, 1963) addressed issues of simulated memory impairment more than 40 years ago. One of the landmark investigations of malingering was conducted by Heaton, Smith, Lehman, and Vogt (1978), who demonstrated that

experienced clinicians could not reliably distinguish noninjured subjects simulating neurologic injury from patients with severe traumatic brain injury (TBI) by relying on subtests from the Wechsler Adult Intelligence Scale (WAIS; Wechsler, 1955), Halstead-Reitan Battery (HRB; Reitan & Wolfson, 1993), and the MMPI (Hathaway & McKinley, 1983). By contrast, the simulators could be significantly differentiated from the TBI patients by a discriminant function analysis that statistically weighted the atypical performances of the simulators in contrast to the performance patterns characteristic of actual traumatic brain injury.

Despite the findings of Heaton et al. (1978), research on malingering lagged until the late 1980s, when Pankratz, Binder, and Wilcox (1987) and Hiscock and Hiscock (1989) began their work on two-alternative forced-choice testing. As noted earlier, the period from 1990 to 2000 reflected a logarithmic expansion of research on malingering (Sweet et al., 2002). This research has taken the assessment of malingering far beyond earlier procedures such as the Rey 15-Item test, as well as beyond the use of the F scale on the MMPI/MMPI-2.

The expanding research on malingering has been accompanied by advances in research designs for the evaluation of malingering. Rogers (1997b) has reviewed these research designs, which include the case study approach, differential prevalence designs, simulation, and known-group research designs. The case study approach was used by Pankratz, Fausti, and Peed (1975) in the evaluation of hysterical deafness using forced-choice methodology. Hiscock and Hiscock (1989) also employed forced-choice methodology in their case study of malingered memory impairment. These case studies led to the development of the Multi-Digit Memory procedure (Prigatano & Amin, 1993) and the Portland Digit Recognition Test (PDRT; Binder, 1993). As Rogers (1997a) has observed, the primary value of the case study approach is that it allows for the generation of additional hypotheses to be studied using more rigorous methodology. Although case studies are obviously limited in terms of generalizability, they may be the only practical design for the investigation of rare syndromes such as Munchausen-by-proxy syndrome.

Simulation studies (also known as analogue research on dissimulation) allow for a quasi-experimental design, whereby subjects can be randomly assigned to dissimulating versus nondissimulating conditions. However, if the investigation is based on normal subjects attempting a task and giving an honest effort versus other normal subjects attempting a task while intentionally attempting to portray impairment, one weakness is the lack of a clinical comparison group. Of course, once a nonmalingering clinical comparison group is employed, one loses the ability to randomly assign subjects. Obviously, one has full control over the nonclinical dissimulating group but no control over the nonmalingering clinical group and no assurance that the dissimulators will perform as would actual patients who are attempting to dissimulate. This limits generalizability to real-world settings. To improve the generalizability of research results, Rogers (ibid.) has suggested that

simulation studies include clinical patients who are randomly assigned to either honest effort or dissimulating conditions. Examples of simulation designs in neuropsychology include the Heaton et al. (1978) investigation, as well as the work of Mittenberg and colleagues on patterns of malingering on the Wechsler Adult Intelligence Scale-Revised and III (WAIS-R; Wechsler, 1981; WAIS-III; Wechsler, 1997; Mittenberg, Theroux, Zielinski, & Heilbronner, 1995; Mittenberg, Theroux, Aguila-Puentes, Bianchini, Greve, & Rayls, 2001), Wechsler Memory Scale-Revised (WMS-R; Wechsler, 1987; Mittenberg, Azrin, Millsaps, & Heilbronner, 1993), and HRB (Mittenberg, Rotholc, Russell, & Heilbronner, 1996).

Known-groups comparisons have two discrete and independent stages: (a) establishment of the criterion groups of bona fide patients and malingerers and (b) systematic analysis of the similarities and differences between the criterion groups (Rogers, 1997b). Although the main problem is the reliable and accurate classification of the criterion groups, known-groups comparisons fully address the clinical relevance for two reasons: (a) the research is conducted in settings in which dissimulation is expected to occur, and, more important, (b) the persons engaging in dissimulation are doing so for real-world reasons (ibid.). Unlike with simulation designs, the investigator loses the capability to randomly assign subjects to the malingering and nonmalingering groups. The use of known-groups designs in neuropsychology has increased due to the use of operationally defined groups of persons with suspect effort (Greiffenstein, Baker, & Gola, 1994). Since 1999, studies have begun to appear using applications of the Slick et al. (1999) criteria for MND (Greve, Bianchini, Mathias, Houston, & Crouch, 2002; Larrabee, 2003a).

Last, the weakest research design discussed by Rogers (1997b) is the differential prevalence design. In this design, the researcher assumes that two samples will have different proportions of dissimulating individuals; for example, a group of clinical patients without evidence of external incentive are assumed to have lower rates of dissimulation than a group of clinical patients who have external incentives such as Workers' Compensation or personal injury litigation. One problem of the differential prevalence design is that the differences in prevalence rates are inferred and not directly measured. A more significant problem is determining who or how many in each group are dissimulating. In neuropsychology, differential prevalence designs are represented by the financial effect size investigations of Binder and colleagues on TBI and chronic pain (Binder & Rohling, 1996; Rohling, Binder, & Langhinrischen-Rohling, 1995).

Although these studies are limited in terms of identifying who and how many in each group are malingering, the studies are quite important for demonstrating the average effects associated with financial compensation, which can then be directly compared to effect sizes associated with severity of injury. For example, the Binder and Rohling (1996) financial effect size of .49

for compensation effects in traumatic brain injury is nearly five times the overall effect size for mild traumatic brain injury (Binder, Rohling, & Larrabee, 1997) and equivalent to the injury severity effect associated with 2–5 days of time-to-follow commands/coma at 1 year following traumatic brain injury (Dikmen, Machamer, Winn, & Temkin, 1995).

Base Rates of Malingering

The expansion of research on malingering has yielded important information on the base rate or frequency of occurrence of malingering. Mittenberg, Patton, Canyock, and Condit (2002) surveyed American Board of Clinical Neuropsychology (ABCN) diplomates who did forensic work and found that 29% of personal injury, 30% of disability, 19% of criminal, and 8% of general medical cases involved probable malingering and symptom exaggeration. The highest base rate of malingering was in personal injury litigants alleging mild head injury, 38.5% (41.24% adjusted for referral source). The 38.5–41.24% of mild head-injury cases found to be malingering in the Mittenberg et al. survey closely matches the value of 40% that I determined following a review of 11 studies encompassing 1,363 consecutively evaluated mild traumatic brain-injury litigants (Larrabee, 2003a). The Mittenberg et al. (2002) and Larrabee (2003a) base rate figures are quite similar to the results of an investigation by Carroll, Abrahamse and Vaiana (1995), who found that 35–42% of all medical costs submitted in support of automobile injury claims were excessive. Mittenberg et al. (2002) have reasoned that the base rate of malingering in mild traumatic brain injury could even be as high as 88%, given the 5% prevalence of actual persisting deficit in mild traumatic brain injury estimated by Binder et al. (1997; note that if 5% have true deficit and 38% have malingered deficit, the ratio of malingered deficit to true deficit plus malingered deficit is 38/43 or 88%; also note that this only applies to persons presenting with neuropsychological deficits following mild traumatic brain injury, and does not apply to those injured persons reporting symptoms but performing normally on testing).

Malingering also occurs frequently in claims for disability. Chafetz and Abrahams (2005) found that 13.8% of adults seeking Social Security disability met criteria for definite malingering (worse-than-chance performance) and 58.6% met criteria for probable malingering (two or more failed validity indicators), for a combined definite/probable base rate of malingering of 72.4%. Miller, Boyd, Cohn, Wilson, and McFarland (2006) found that 54% of Social Security disability applicants failed either the Computerized Assessment of Response Bias (CARB; Conder, Allen, & Cox, 1992) or the Word Memory Test (Green, 2003). The potential economic impact of these base rates that exceed 50% in Social Security disability applicants is substantial, according to

Chafetz and Abrahams (2005), who note that the total expenditure for Social Security disability insurance in 2004 was $80.3 billion.

More recently, Ardolf, Denney, and Houston (in press) have determined the base rate of malingering in a criminal forensic setting. In defendants undergoing pretrial, presentencing neuropsychological evaluation, 32.4% met criteria for probable malingering, and 21.9% met the criteria for definite malingering, for a combined probable/definite base rate of malingering of 54.3%. This rate is substantially higher than the 19% base rate of malingering in criminal defendants reported by Mittenberg et al. (2002) but likely reflects the fact that the Ardolf et al. data were derived from direct assessment of a consecutive series of examinees, whereas the Mittenberg et al. data were derived from a survey of American Board of Clinical Neuropsychology diplomates, who were involved in providing forensic neuropsychological services.

These data show base rates of malingering that approach or exceed 50% for a range of civil and criminal settings. Clearly, malingering is a significant problem in forensic settings, underscoring the recommendations for symptom validity testing by the National Academy of Neuropsychology (Bush et al., 2005) and substantiating the need for a comprehensive review of this area.

References

American Psychiatric Association. (2000). *Diagnostic and statistical manual of mental disorders* (4th ed.). Washington, DC: Author.

Ardolf, B. R., Denney, R. L., & Houston, C. M. (in press). Base rates of negative response bias and malingered neurocognitive dysfunction among criminal defendants referred for neuropsychological evaluation. *The Clinical Neuropsychologist.*

Axelrod, B. N., Fichtenberg, N. L., Millis, S. R., & Wertheimer, J. C. (2006). Detecting incomplete effort with Digit Span from the Wechsler Adult Intelligence Scale (3rd ed.). *The Clinical Neuropsychologist, 20,* 513–523.

Babikian, T., Boone, K. B., Lu, P., & Arnold, G. (2006). Sensitivity and specificity of various Digit Span scores in the detection of suspect effort. *The Clinical Neuropsychologist, 20,* 145–159.

Benton, A. L., & Spreen, O. (1961). Visual memory test: The simulation of mental incompetence. *Archives of General Psychiatry, 4,* 79–83.

Bianchini, K. J., Greve, K. W., & Glynn, G. (2005). On the diagnosis of malingered pain- related disability: Lessons from cognitive malingering research. *Spine Journal, 5,* 404–417.

Binder, L. M. (1993). Assessment of malingering after mild head injury with the Portland Digit Recognition Test. *Journal of Clinical and Experimental Neuropsychology, 15,* 170–182.

Binder, L. M., & Rohling, M. L. (1996). Money matters: A meta-analytic review of the effects of financial incentives on recovery after closed-head injury. *American Journal of Psychiatry, 153,* 7–10.

Binder, L. M., Rohling, M. L., & Larrabee, G. J. (1997). A review of mild head trauma. Part I: Meta-analytic review of neuropsychological studies. *Journal of Clinical and Experimental Neuropsychology, 19,* 421–431.

Boone, K. B. (in press). A reconsideration of the Slick et al. (1999) criteria for malingered neurocognitive dysfunction. In K. B. Boone (Ed.), *Assessment of feigned cognitive impairment. A neuropsychological perspective.* New York: Guilford.

Bush, S. S., Ruff, R. M., Troster, A. I., Barth, J. T., Koffler, S. P., Pliskin, N. H., et al. (NAN Policy and Planning Committee). (2005). Symptom validity assessment: Practical issues and medical necessity. NAN position paper. *Archives of Clinical Neuropsychology, 20,* 419–426.

Butcher, J. N., Graham, J. R., Ben-Porath, Y. S., Tellegen, A. T., Dahlstrom, W. G., & Kaemmer, B. (2001). *Minnesota Multiphasic Personality Inventory-2: Manual for administration, scoring, and interpretation* (Rev. ed.). Minneapolis, MN: University of Minnesota Press.

Carroll, S., Abrahamse, A., & Vaiana, M. (1995). *The costs of excess medical claims for automobile personal injuries.* Santa Monica, CA: RAND.

Chafetz, M., & Abrahams, J. (2005, October). *Green's MACT helps identify internal predictors of effort in the Social Security disability exam.* Paper presented at the annual meeting of the National Academy of Neuropsychology, Tampa, FL.

Conder, R., Allen, L., & Cox, D. (1992). *Computerized assessment of response bias test manual.* Durham, NC: CogniSyst.

Dikmen, S. S., Machamer, J. E., Winn, H. R., & Temkin, N. R. (1995). Neuropsychological outcome at 1-year post head injury. *Neuropsychology, 9,* 80–90.

Glueck, B. (1915). The malingerer: A clinical study. *International Clinics, 3,* 200–251.

Green, P. (2003). *Green's Word Memory Test for Windows: Manual.* Edmonton, Alberta, Canada: Green's Publishing.

Greiffenstein, M. F., Baker, W. J., & Gola, T. (1994). Validation of malingered amnesia measures with a large clinical sample. *Psychological Assessment, 6,* 218–224.

Greve, K. W., Bianchini, K. J., Mathias, C. W., Houston, R. J., & Crouch, J. A. (2002). Detecting malingered performance with the Wisconsin Card Sorting Test: A preliminary investigation in traumatic brain injury. *The Clinical Neuropsychologist, 16,* 179–191.

Hathaway, S. R., & McKinley, J. C. (1983). *Minnesota Multiphasic Personality Inventory.* New York: Psychological Corp.

Heaton, R. K., Smith, H. H., Jr., Lehman, R. A., & Vogt, A. J. (1978). Prospects for faking believable deficits on neuropsychological testing. *Journal of Consulting and Clinical Psychology, 46,* 892–900.

Hiscock, M., & Hiscock, C. K. (1989). Refining the forced-choice method for the detection of malingering. *Journal of Clinical and Experimental Neuropsychology, 11,* 967–974.

Iverson, G. L., & Binder, L. M. (2000). Detecting exaggeration and malingering in neuropsychological assessment. *Journal of Head Trauma Rehabilitation, 15,* 829–858.

Larrabee, G. J. (2003a). Detection of malingering using atypical performance patterns on standard neuropsychological tests. *The Clinical Neuropsychologist, 17,* 410–425.

Larrabee, G. J. (2003b). Exaggerated pain report in litigants with malingered neurocognitive dysfunction. *The Clinical Neuropsychologist, 17,* 395–401.

Larrabee, G. J. (2005). Assessment of malingering. In G. J. Larrabee (Ed.), *Forensic neuropsychology: A scientific approach* (pp. 115–158). New York: Oxford University Press.

Lees-Haley, P. R., English, L. T., & Glenn, W. J. (1991). A Fake Bad Scale for the MMPI-2 for personal-injury claimants. *Psychological Reports, 68,* 203–210.

Main, C. J. (1983). The Modified Somatic Perception Questionnaire (MSPQ). *Journal of Psychosomatic Research, 27,* 503–514.

Miller, L. S., Boyd, M. C., Cohn, A., Wilson, J. S., & McFarland, M. (2006, February). *Prevalence of sub-optimal effort in disability applicants.* Paper presented at the 34th annual meeting of the International Neuropsychological Society, Boston.

Mittenberg, W., Azrin, R., Millsaps, C., & Heilbronner, R. (1993). Identification of malingered head injury on the Wechsler Memory Scale-Revised. *Psychological Assessment, 5,* 34–40.

Mittenberg, W., Patton, C., Canyock, E. M., & Condit, D. C. (2002). Base rates of malingering and symptom exaggeration. *Journal of Clinical and Experimental Neuropsychology, 24,* 1094–1102.

Mittenberg, W., Rotholc, A., Russell, E., & Heilbronner, R. (1996). Identification of malingered head injury on the Halstead-Reitan Battery. *Archives of Clinical Neuropsychology, 11,* 271–281.

Mittenberg, W., Theroux, S., Aguila-Puentes, G., Bianchini, K., Greve, K., & Rayls, K. (2001). Identification of malingered head injury on the Wechsler Adult Intelligence Scale (3rd ed.). *The Clinical Neuropsychologist, 15*(4), 440–445.

Mittenberg, W., Theroux, S., Zielinski, R. E., & Heilbronner, R. L. (1995). Identification of malingered head injury on the Wechsler Adult Intelligence Scale-Revised. *Professional Psychology: Research and Practice, 26*(5), 491–498.

Palmer, I. P. (2003). Malingering, shirking, and self-inflicted injuries in the military. In P. W. Halligan, C. Bass, & D. A. Oakley (Eds.), *Malingering and illness deception* (pp. 42–53). New York: Oxford University Press.

Pankratz, L., Binder, L. M., & Wilcox, L. (1987). Evaluation of an exaggerated somatosensory deficit with symptom validity testing. *Archives of Neurology, 44,* 798.

Pankratz, L., Fausti, A., & Peed, S. (1975). A forced-choice technique to evaluate deafness in a hysterical or malingering patient. *Journal of Consulting and Clinical Psychology, 43,* 421–422.

Prigatano, G. P., & Amin, K. (1993). Digit memory test: Unequivocal cerebral dysfunction and suspected malingering. *Journal of Clinical and Experimental Neuropsychology, 15,* 537–546.

Reitan, R. M., & Wolfson, D. (1993). *The Halstead-Reitan neuropsychological test battery. Theory and clinical interpretation* (2nd ed.). Tucson, AZ: Neuropsychology Press.

Rey, A. (1964). *L'examen clinique en psychologie.* Paris: Presses Universitaires de France.

Rogers, R. (1990a). Development of a new classificatory model of malingering. *Bulletin of the American Academy of Psychiatry and Law, 18,* 323–333.

Rogers, R. (1990b). Models of feigned mental illness. *Professional Psychology: Research and Practice, 21,* 182–188.

Rogers, R. (1997a). Introduction. In R. Rogers (Ed.), *Clinical assessment of malingering and deception* (2nd ed., pp. 1–19). New York: Guilford.

Rogers, R. (1997b). Researching dissimulation. In R. Rogers (Ed.), *Clinical assessment of malingering and deception* (2nd ed., pp. 398–426). New York: Guilford.

Rogers, R., Bagby, R. M., & Dickens, S. E. (1992). *Structured Interview of Reported Symptoms (SIRS) and professional manual.* Odessa, FL: Psychological Assessment Resources.

Rohling, M. L., Binder, L. M., & Langhinrischen-Rohling, J. (1995). Money matters: A meta-analytic review of the association between financial compensation and the experience and treatment of chronic pain. *Health Psychology, 14,* 537–547.

Slick, D. J., Sherman, E. M. S., & Iverson, G. L. (1999). Diagnostic criteria for malingered neurocognitive dysfunction: Proposed standards for clinical practice and research. *The Clinical Neuropsychologist, 13,* 545–561.

Spreen, O., & Benton, A. L. (1963). Simulation of mental deficiency on a visual memory test. *American Journal of Mental Deficiency, 67,* 909–913.

Sweet, J. J., King, J. H., Malina, A. C., Bergman, M. A., & Simmons, A. (2002). Documenting the prominence of forensic neuropsychology at national meetings and in relevant professional journals from 1990 to 2000. *The Clinical Neuropsychologist, 16,* 481–494.

Wechsler, D. (1955). *WAIS manual.* New York: Psychological Corp.

Wechsler, D. (1981). *WAIS-R manual.* New York: Psychological Corp.

Wechsler, D. (1987). *Wechsler Memory Scale-Revised manual.* San Antonio: Psychological Corp.

Wechsler, D. (1997). *WAIS-III: Administration and scoring manual.* San Antonio: Psychological Corp.

2

Diagnostic Classification Statistics
and Diagnostic Validity
of Malingering Assessment

Glenn J. Larrabee and David T. R. Berry

The *diagnostic validity* of a test refers to the test's ability to differentiate persons with and without a specified disorder (Smith, Cerhan, & Ivnik, 2003). Diagnostic validity is dependent on classification accuracy statistics, including sensitivity, specificity, positive and negative predictive power, and likelihood ratios (Baldessarini, Finklestein, & Arana, 1983; Glaros & Kline, 1988; Grimes & Schulz, 2005; Ivnik et al., 2001; Smith, Cerhan, & Ivnik, 2003; Meehl & Rosen, 1955). These statistics can be considered to be *individual statistics* in contrast to the *group statistics* such as ANOVA and *t*-test procedures characteristic of group comparison research designs. In an example relevant to malingering, group statistics would be applied to differential prevalence designs: A significant difference tells us that the litigation and nonlitigation groups differ but not *which subjects* are contributing to the group difference. By contrast, classification accuracy statistics allow us to determine (at a given degree of probability) which subjects are identified as malingering as a function of the base rate (frequency) of malingering in the population of interest.

Sensitivity, Specificity, and Related Diagnostic Statistics

The following section illustrates diagnostic statistics using pooled data from two studies on the use of the Fake Bad Scale (FBS) of the MMPI-2 (Lees-Haley, 1992; Lees-Haley, English, & Glenn, 1991) to discriminate persons with definite or probable malingered neurocognitive dysfunction (MND;

Slick, Sherman, & Iverson, 1999) from patients with moderate or severe traumatic brain injury (TBI; Larrabee, 2003b; Ross, Millis, Krukowski, Putnam, & Adams, 2004). Table 2.1 displays these pooled data for the FBS for 85 patients with definite or probable MND (26 from Larrabee, 2003b; 59 from Ross et al., 2004) and 88 patients with bona fide moderate or severe TBI (29 from Larrabee, 2003b; 59 from Ross et al., 2004). The actual number of MND subjects at or above a given FBS score is recorded, as well as the actual number of TBI patients at or above a particular FBS score. In Table 2.1, *sensitivity* refers to the cumulative proportion of MND at or above a particular FBS score, and *specificity* refers to the cumulative proportion of TBI patients below a given FBS score.

Table 2.2 shows a fourfold table of data for evaluation of the classification accuracy of a cutting score of 22 or higher on the FBS (Baldessarini et al., 1983; Kraemer, 1992). Sensitivity (SN) is the probability of a positive test result in persons who have the condition or characteristic of interest, in this case, malingering, defined as a/(a + c), or 73/(73 + 12) = .859 (Table 2.2). In other words, sensitivity is the ratio of true positives (a) to true positives plus false negatives (a + c). By contrast, specificity (SP) is the probability of a negative test result in patients who do *not* have the condition or characteristic of interest, in this case, legitimate moderate or severe traumatic brain injury, defined in Table 2.2 as d/(b + d), or 79/(9 + 79) = .898. In other words, specificity is the ratio of true negatives (b) to true negatives plus false positives (b + d). The *base rate* is the frequency of the disorder or condition of interest and is defined as (a + c)/(a + b + c + d), or (73 + 12)/(73 + 9 + 12 + 79) = .491.

Kraemer (1992) uses P to represent the base rate, .491, and P' to represent 1 – base rate or 1 – .491 = .509. Kraemer also defines the *level* of the test, also referred to as the *positive sign rate* (percentage of the sample with a positive test sign) as (a + b)/(a + b + c + d), or (73 + 9)/(73 + 9 + 12 + 79) = .474. Kraemer maintains that the *level* of the test can be referred to as Q, with Q' representing 1 – *level*, or 1 – .474 = .526. *Overall diagnostic power*, also defined as the *hit rate* of the test, describes the total proportion of accurately classified cases (true positives + true negatives)/n or (a + d)/(a + b + c + d) or (73 + 79)/(73 + 9 + 12 + 79) = .879 (Table 2.2). The hit rate is the same as the efficiency of the test (i.e., the probability that the test and the diagnosis agree; ibid.).

Last, Kraemer (ibid.) defines *quality sensitivity* (QSN) and *quality specificity* (QSP). She contends that QSN and QSP are essentially weighted kappa statistics, which may take values ranging from 0 to 1, with 0 representing a chance level of agreement and increasing values representing greater superiority over chance levels of agreement relative to the maximum value possible, 1.0. Both QSN and QSP provide standardized indices of test parameters that are more comparable across different samples and tests than the classic diagnostic accuracy statistics. First, $QSN = (SN - Q)/Q'$ or the increment in sensitivity beyond the *level/positive sign rate* of the test (Q), standardized relative to the negative rate of the test (Q'). Per Table 2.2, QSN is .859 – .474/

Table 2.1

FBS Distribution for Definite/Probable Malingerers and Moderate/Severe Traumatic Brain Injury

	Malingerers		Moderate–Severe Traumatic Brain Injury	
FBS	n	Sensitivity	n	Specificity
4	85	1.00	88	.000
5	85	1.00	87	.011
6	85	1.00	87	.011
7	85	1.00	87	.011
8	85	1.00	82	.068
9	85	1.00	81	.080
10	85	1.00	77	.125
11	85	1.00	67	.239
12	85	1.00	63	.284
13	85	1.00	59	.330
14	85	1.00	51	.420
15	85	1.00	42	.523
16	85	1.00	38	.568
17	84	.988	36	.591
18	83	.976	28	.682
19	82	.965	21	.761
20	80	.941	15	.830
21	74	.871	10	.886
22	73	.859	9	.898
23	70	.824	7	.920
24	66	.776	5	.943
25	62	.729	3	.966
26	56	.659	2	.977
27	52	.612	1	.989
28	46	.541	1	.989
29	41	.482	1	.989
30	35	.412	1	.989
31	32	.376	0	1.00
32	24	.282	0	1.00
33	15	.176	0	1.00
34	11	.129	0	1.00

(continued)

Table 2.1
(*continued*)

FBS	Malingerers n	Sensitivity	Moderate–Severe Traumatic Brain Injury n	Specificity
35	10	.118	0	1.00
36	6	.071	0	1.00
37	4	.047	0	1.00
38	2	.024	0	1.00
39	2	.024	0	1.00
40	0	.000	0	1.00

Note. FBS: Fake Bad Scale.

$.526 = .732$. Moreover, $QSP = (SP - Q')/Q$, or the increment in specificity beyond 1 minus the level/positive sign rate of the test, standardized relative to the level/positive sign rate of the test. Thus, $QSP = .898 - .526/.474 = .785$ (Table 2.2).

Due to the fact that the distributions of scores on a diagnostic indicator overlap for groups with the condition and those without it, there is no one cutoff point that perfectly separates the groups; rather, a range of sensitivity (true positive) and specificity (one minus false positive) values exists for various cutoffs. By plotting the sensitivities and their corresponding false positive rates (one minus specificity) for different cutting scores on a particular test, the *receiver operating characteristic* (also known as the *relative*

Table 2.2.
Contingency Table for Diagnosis of Malingering Based on FBS Scores of 22 or Higher

Test Result FBS	Diagnosis Malingering +	TBI −
Malingering +	a 73	b 9
Not Malingering −	c 12	d 79

TBI: traumatic brain injury
FBS: Fake Bad Scale

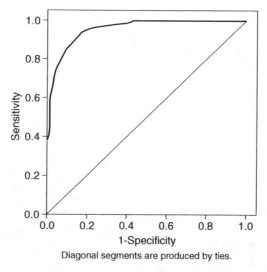

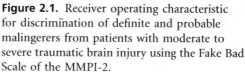

Diagonal segments are produced by ties.

Figure 2.1. Receiver operating characteristic for discrimination of definite and probable malingerers from patients with moderate to severe traumatic brain injury using the Fake Bad Scale of the MMPI-2.

operating characteristic) of the test can be determined (Hsaio, Bartko, & Potter, 1989; Swets, 1973).

The sensitivity and one minus specificity values for different cutting scores on the FBS, based on the data in Table 2.1, have been used to generate Figure 2.1, which displays the receiver operating characteristic (ROC) for these data. The greater the area under the ROC curve (AUC), the greater the overall diagnostic power of the test. Any ROC scores that fall on the diagonal are no better than chance, 50%, whereas "perfect" diagnostic power would encompass 100% of the area in Figure 2.1. Thus, an AUC score of 0.5 reflects no discrimination by the diagnostic test, whereas values greater than 0.5 reflect increasing degrees of discrimination. All AUC of 0.7 to <0.8 have been characterized as *acceptable;* 0.8 to <0.9 as *excellent,* and =0.9 as *outstanding* (Hosmer & Lemeshow, 2000; Ross et al. 2004). For the data in Figure 2.1, the AUC is .958, reflecting outstanding discrimination of definite/probable malingerers from patients with moderate/severe TBI.

Vickery, Berry, Inman, Harris, and Orey (2001) have published a review of diagnostic research conducted on the Digit Memory Test, Portland Digit Recognition Test, Rey 15-Item Test, 21-Item Test, and Dot Counting Test. The average sensitivity, collapsed across these different tests/investigations was .56, and the average specificity was .96, with an average hit rate (overall

diagnostic power) of .77. These data show findings characteristic of most tests of malingering: The specificity is set at a high value to minimize the occurrence of false-positive errors, that is, misidentifying someone as a malingerer who is not truly malingering. The consequence of setting specificity high is that sensitivity is low; that is, according to Vickery et al. (ibid.), on average 44% of those who truly are malingering go undetected. *Thus, at cutoffs associated with high specificity but low sensitivity, tests of symptom validity are good at providing information that can rule in malingering but poor at providing information to rule it out.* Again, this general statement is moderated by the base rate of malingering (see the discussion in the following section of positive and negative predictive power, which shows that negative predictive power associated with ruling out malingering is higher at very low base rates of malingering, whereas positive predictive power associated with ruling in malingering is higher at very high base rates of the condition).

The problem of low sensitivity with high specificity can be overcome by using multiple diagnostic indicators that are not highly correlated or, preferably, are weakly correlated in nonmalingering samples. Use of multiple indicators increases sensitivity by not appreciably altering specificity (Iverson & Franzen, 1996; Larrabee, 2003a; Martens, Donders, & Millis, 2001). For example, using standard neuropsychological tests, Larrabee (2003a) employed a known-groups design using the Slick et al. (1999) criteria to derive cutoff scores for discrimination of definite MND from moderate or severe traumatic brain injury. The sensitivity and specificity of the individual tests, respectively, were .48 and .93 for the Visual Form Discrimination Test (VFD; Benton, Sivan, Hamsher, Varney, & Spreen, 1994), .40 and .94 for the Finger Tapping Test (FT; Reitan & Wolfson, 1993), .50 and .94 for the Reliable Digit Span (RDS; Greiffenstein, Baker, & Gola, 1994), .48 and .87 for failure to maintain set on the Wisconsin Card Sorting Test (FMS, WCST; Heaton, Chelune, Talley, Kay, & Curtiss, 1993), and .81 and .86 for the FBS of the MMPI-2. Evaluating all of the possible pairwise combinations of test failure (e.g., VFD and FT; RDS and FBS) yielded a sensitivity of .88 and a specificity of .89. Evaluating all of the possible three-way test failure patterns yielded a sensitivity of .54 at a perfect specificity of 1.00 (better than that achieved by any individual test). Use of multiple indicators is further discussed in chapter 13, by Larrabee, Greiffenstein, Greve, and Bianchini.

Positive and Negative Predictive Power

Frequently, when they are derived to define sensitivity, specificity, and hit rate (overall diagnostic power), cutting scores are based on equal sample sizes of persons with a given disorder (e.g., litigants who are malingering) and those without it (e.g., nonlitigating severe traumatic brain-injury patients).

This effectively sets the base rate of the condition at 50%, which may not reflect the actual base rate in the total population (Baldessarini et al., 1983). *Predictive value* (also referred to as *predictive power*) takes into account the base rate of the condition of interest.

Predictive power can be considered as two different probabilities. *Positive predictive power* (*PPP*) is the probability of the presence of the disorder or condition of interest given a *positive* test finding (in this case the probability of malingering, given an FBS = 22) and per Table 2.2 is defined as a/(a + b), or the ratio of true positives to all positive scores (i.e., true positives plus false positives): 73/(73 + 9) = .890. *Negative predictive power* (*NPP*) is the probability of the *absence* of the disorder or condition of interest given a *negative* test finding (in this case the probability of not malingering, given an FBS < 22). Per Table 2.2 this is defined as d/(d + c), or the ratio of true negatives to all negative scores: 79/(79 + 12) = .868.

The preceding computation of *PPP* and *NPP* only applies to the base rate for the data in Table 2.2, which is .491. Both *PPP* and *NPP* will change with a change in the base rate. Baldessarini et al. (ibid.) provide the formula for computing *PPP* and *NPP*. Sensitivity is represented as x; specificity is represented as y; base rate (prevalence) is represented as p:

$$PPP = [(p)(x)]/[(p)(x) + (1 - p)(1 - y)].$$
$$NPP = [(1 - p)(y)][(1 - p)(y) + (p)(1 - x)].$$

As already computed, the base rate of malingering in Table 2.2 was .491, resulting in *PPP* of .890 and *NPP* of .868. Mittenberg, Patton, Canyock, and Condit (2002) provide data on the base rate of malingering for cases with an opportunity for external incentive (e.g., civil and criminal litigation) and clinical cases in which there are no apparent external incentives (e.g., medical and/or psychiatric cases seen in a university-affiliated hospital or medical center). The base rate for malingering in litigating mild TBI was .38 and for medical/psychiatric cases was .08. Also, Mittenberg et al. (ibid.) argue that the base rate of malingering in mild TBI litigants who demonstrate continuing deficits (excluding those with continuing symptoms who have normal test results) could be as high as .88, given the base rate of .38 they determined, divided by .38 plus the .05 base rate of persistent deficit following mild TBI determined by Binder, Rohling, and Larrabee (1997). Table 2.3 shows the effects on *PPP* and *NPP*, using the data in Table 2.2, an FBS cutting score of = 22, and malingering base rates of .08, .38, and .88.

The data in Table 2.2 demonstrate what Baldessarini et al. (1983) highlighted in their own article: A reciprocal relationship exists between *PPP* and *NPP* as a function of prevalence/base rate, with sensitivity and specificity held constant. At a low prevalence/base rate, a negative test result is more likely to be correct than a positive one, resulting in higher values of *NPP* compared to *PPP*. The converse is true with high prevalence/base rates, where

Table 2.3.
Positive and Negative Predictive Power for the FBS at Sensitivity of .859 and Specificity of .898

Base rate of malingering (Mittenberg et al., 2002)	PPP[a]	NPP[b]
.08	.420	.987
(Nonlitigating medical/psychiatric)		
.38	.838	.912
(Litigating mild TBI)		
.88	.984	.465
(Hypothetical maximum mild TBI)		

Note. [a]PPP: positive predictive power.
[b]NPP: negative predictive power.

a positive test result is more likely to be correct than a negative one, resulting in higher values of *PPP* compared to *NPP*.

Likelihood Ratios

Likelihood ratios reflect the percentage of people with the diagnostic condition of interest identified by a given test result divided by the percentage of people not having that characteristic but who have the same test result (Grimes & Schultz, 2005). The positive likelihood ratio, LR+, is defined as sensitivity/(1 − specificity). The reader should note that sensitivity and (1 − specificity) are the values used to plot the ROC curve in Figure 2.1; indeed, each point on the curve can be used to generate a unique LR+. Moreover, LR+ can also be defined as the true-positive percentage divided by the false-positive percentage. The negative likelihood ratio, LR−, is (1 − specificity)/specificity. LR− can also be defined as the false-negative percentage divided by the true-negative percentage.

Multiplying the LR+ by the pretest odds (i.e., the base rate odds of having the condition of interest) yields the posttest odds, which can be converted to the probability of a positive result for the cutting score derived for a particular test, or the *PPP*. Likelihood ratios between 0 and 1 reduce the probability of the condition. Likelihood ratios of 1 are unhelpful since the percentage of persons with the condition equals the percentage without the condition. By contrast, likelihood ratios greater than 1 increase the probability of the condition, such that the more the likelihood ratio rises above 1, the greater is the probability for the presence of the condition.

Obviously, exact probabilities can be computed for various increases in LR+, but Grimes and Schultz (2005) have review a mnemonic suggested by McGee (2002) that applies to pretest probabilities between 10% and 90% and works well for demonstrating the effects of changes in magnitude of likelihood ratios on posttest probabilities. The diagnostician needs to remember only three benchmark likelihood ratios: 2, 5, and 10, which correspond to the first three multiples of 15%. For LR+, a likelihood ratio of 2 increases the pretest probability by about 15%, a ratio of 5 increases the posttest probability by 30%, and 10 increases the posttest probability by 45% (Grimes & Schultz, 2005).

In the example provided by Grimes and Schultz (ibid.), using a pretest probability of 40% and a likelihood ratio of 2, the posttest probability is 40% + 15% or 55%, which is quite close to the actual probability of 57% when calculated by formula. Extending this example, a likelihood ratio of 5 results in a probability estimate of 40% + 30% or 70%, and a likelihood ratio of 10 results in a probability estimate of 40% + 45% or 85%. For likelihood ratios less than 1, the rule works in the opposite direction; thus, the reciprocal of 2 is 0.5, that of 5 is 0.2, and that of 10 is 0.1, such that a likelihood ratio of 0.5 reduces pretest probability by 15%, 0.2 reduces pretest probability by 30%, and 0.1 reduces pretest probability by 45%.

For the data in Table 2.2, representing an FBS cutting score of ≥ 22, sensitivity is .859 and specificity is .898. Thus, LR+ is .859/(1 − .898) or 8.42. At a pretest base rate of .38 in litigating mild TBI (MTBI), the pretest odds are .38/(1 − .38) or .613. Thus, the posttest odds of malingering are (.613)(8.42) or 5.161 to 1. These odds can be converted to obtain a posttest probability, odds/1 + odds, 5.161/6.161, or .838. This is the probability of malingering for an FBS score of 22 or more for the data displayed in Tables 2.1 and 2.2 at a base rate of malingering of .38, and matches the PPP for this base rate in Table 2.3.

If tests of response bias are independent from one another, the LR+ can be "chained" (Straus, Richardson, Glasziou, & Haynes, 2005). Thus, the posttest odds obtained by multiplying the LR+ by the pretest odds (determined from the base rate of malingering by the formula: base rate/ 1 − base rate) become the new prettest odds which are multiplied by the LR+ for the next test, to yield new posttest odds. As already cited, Vickery et al. (2001) reported an average sensitivity of .56 and specificity of .96 for the tests they reviewed. For ease of computation, if we set base rate at .40, sensitivity at .50 and specificity at .95, prettest odds then become .67, which are multiplied by .5/.05 or 10, to yield posttest odds of 6.7, yielding a probability of malingering of 6.7/7.7 or .87 following failure of a single test. These new posttest odds of 6.7 can then be multiplied by the LR+ of a new test, 10, to yield a new posttest odds of 67.0, consistent with a probability of malingering of 67 /68 or .99, when two independent tests, each with sensitivity of .50 and specificity of .95, are failed in a population wherein the base rate of malingering is .40. Per Straus et al. (2005), the probabilities computed by chaining LR+ are over-

estimated if the tests are not independent. The relationship of chained LR+ using multiple indicators to increased probability of malingering will be discussed further in Chapter 13.

Additional Diagnostic Considerations

The preceding text has reviewed diagnostic classification statistics with a specific example related to the diagnosis of malingering. Most malingering tests fit under the definition of measures of response bias as defined by Slick et al. (1999) in their article on diagnostic criteria for malingered neurocognitive dysfunction (MND). According to them and consistent with current thinking on assessment of malingering (Iverson & Binder, 2000; Larrabee, 2005; Mittenberg et al., 2002; Sweet, 1999), the diagnosis of malingering is based on multiple sources of evidence, with the goal of keeping false-positive diagnosis of malingering at a low rate (i.e., high specificity). Thus, to meet a Slick et al. (1999) diagnosis of probable MND, a person must have an obvious external incentive and also show evidence of two B criteria for response bias (other than worse-than-chance performance) or one B criterion for response bias and one C criterion for symptom exaggeration, with the D specifier of no other condition that can reasonably account for the abnormal response bias and/or symptom exaggeration. Of course, studies such as those by Larrabee (2003a) and Greve, Bianchini, Mathias, Houston, and Crouch (2002), which employ the Slick et al. (1999) criteria for MND, yield actual probabilities of malingering based on individual measures of response bias *for the samples they have investigated*. As Greve and Bianchini (2004) have observed, the key to improving the diagnostic accuracy of malingering tests is to improve the *PPP*. Although *PPP* is partly dependent on sensitivity, it is actually more dependent on specificity (Baldessarini et al., 1983).

Improving specificity requires that specific measures of response bias and symptom exaggeration be evaluated across multiple samples of patients who have no external incentives for restriction of effort or for symptom exaggeration during neuropsychological assessment. This gives the clinician greater confidence that the specific measure of response bias or symptom exaggeration is unlikely to be affected by factors such as bona fide neuropsychological dysfunction secondary to conditions such as severe traumatic brain injury, stroke, or dementia and that the specific measure of bias/exaggeration is not affected by other common clinical conditions such as depression or pain.

Larrabee (2005) has previously argued that since *PPP* represents a probability of malingering, scores associated with no false positives yield a *PPP* of 1.00 (true positives/true positives + 0 false positives) and are arguably equivalent, on a statistical basis, to significantly worse-than-chance performance. By contrast, such scores associated with a *PPP* of 1.00 (but not

significantly worse than chance) are not readily interpreted as consistent with evidence of deliberate response distortion since they cannot be viewed as providing evidence of active avoidance of the correct answer, an interpretation that fits well the pattern of significantly worse-than-chance performance on forced-choice testing. In other words, to perform significantly worse than chance on forced-choice testing, an examinee has to actively avoid the correct response. As the following paragraph explains, a score of 29 on Test of Memory Malingering (TOMM) Trial 2 associated with 1.00 *PPP* actually falls slightly above chance (25) and consequently does not provide the same evidence of conscious intent that would apply to scores falling at 18 or below on the TOMM. As a result, scores associated with 1.00 *PPP* provide extremely strong evidence of deliberate response distortion but are not conceptually identical to significantly worse-than-chance performance.

My earlier argument equating scores associated (on a statistical basis) with 1.00 *PPP* with definite malingering depends on extensive cross-validation of the response bias test across a wide range of samples of clinical patients without external incentives. To date, these data exist for two procedures that we are aware of: the Test of Memory Malingering (Tombaugh, 1996) and the FBS. Scores on the TOMM Trial 2 of less than 29 are exceeded by 100% of patients with neurologically caused cognitive impairment, 100% of patients with aphasia, 100% of patients with TBI, 100% of patients with dementia (ibid.), 100% of depressed patients (Ashendorf, Constantinou, & McCaffrey, 2004; Rees, Tombaugh, & Boulay, 2001), and 100% of research subjects undergoing laboratory-induced pain (Etherton, Bianchini, Greve, & Ciota, 2005). On the FBS, scores greater than 30 are *higher* than those obtained by 100% of non-compensation-seeking moderate/severe TBI (Larrabee, 2003b; Ross et al., 2004), 100% of nonlitigating chronic pain patients (Meyers, Millis, & Volkert, 2002), and 100% of traumatic stress patients (Greiffenstein, Baker, Axelrod, Peck, & Gervais, 2004).

References

Ashendorf, L., Constantinou, M., & McCaffrey, R. J. (2004). The effect of depression and anxiety on the TOMM in community-dwelling older adults. *Archives of Clinical Neuropsychology, 19,* 125–130.

Baldessarini, R. J., Finklestein, S., & Arana, G. W. (1983). The predictive power of diagnostic tests and the effect of prevalence of illness. *Archives of General Psychiatry, 40,* 569–573.

Benton, A. L., Sivan, A. B., Hamsher, K. deS., Varney, N. R., & Spreen, O. (1994). *Contributions to neuropsychological assessment: A clinical manual* (2nd ed.). New York: Oxford University Press.

Binder, L. M., Rohling, M. L., & Larrabee, G. J. (1997). A review of mild head trauma. Part I: Meta-analytic review of neuropsychological studies. *Journal of Clinical and Experimental Neuropsychology, 19,* 421–431.

Etherton, J. L., Bianchini, K. J., Greve, K. W., & Ciota, M. A. (2005). Test of Memory Malingering is unaffected by laboratory-induced pain: Implications for clinical use. *Archives of Clinical Neuropsychology, 20,* 375–384.

Glaros, A. G., & Kline, R. B. (1988). Understanding the accuracy of tests with cutting scores: The sensitivity, specificity, and predictive value model. *Journal of Clinical Psychology, 44,* 1013–1023.

Greiffenstein, M. F., Baker, W. J., Axelrod, B., Peck, E. A., & Gervais, R. (2004). The Fake Bad scale and MMPI-2 F-family in detection of implausible psychological trauma claims. *The Clinical Neuropsychologist, 18,* 573–590.

Greiffenstein, M. F., Baker, W. J., & Gola, T. (1994). Validation of malingered amnesia measures with a large clinical sample. *Psychological Assessment, 6,* 218–224.

Greve, K. W., & Bianchini, K. J. (2004). Setting empirical cutoffs on psychometric indicators of negative response bias: A methodological commentary with recommendations. *Archives of Clinical Neuropsychology, 19,* 533–541.

Greve, K. W., Bianchini, K. J., Mathias, C. W., Houston, R. J., & Crouch, J. A. (2002). Detecting malingered performance with the Wisconsin Card Sorting Test: A preliminary investigation in traumatic brain injury. *The Clinical Neuropsychologist, 16,* 179–191.

Grimes, D. A., & Schulz, K. F. (2005). Epidemiology 3: Refining clinical diagnosis with likelihood ratios. *Lancet, 365,* 1500–1505.

Heaton, R. K., Chelune, G. J., Talley, J. L., Kay, G. G., & Curtiss, G. (1993). *Wisconsin Card Sorting Test manual.* Odessa, FL: Psychological Assessment Resources.

Hosmer, D. W., & Lemeshow, S. (2000). *Applied logistic regression.* New York: Wiley InterScience.

Hsaio, J. K., Bartko, J. J., & Potter, W. Z. (1989). Diagnosing diagnoses: Receiver operating characteristic methods and psychiatry. *Archives of General Psychiatry, 46,* 664–667.

Iverson, G. L., & Binder, L. M. (2000). Detecting exaggeration and malingering in neuropsychological assessment. *Journal of Head Trauma Rehabilitation, 15,* 829–858.

Iverson, G. L., & Franzen, M. D. (1996). Using multiple objective memory procedures to detect simulated malingering. *Journal of Clinical and Experimental Neuropsychology, 18,* 38–51.

Ivnik, R. J., Smith, G. E., Cerhan, J. H., Boeve, B. F., Tangalos, E. G., & Peterson, R. C. (2001). Understanding the diagnostic capabilities of cognitive tests. *The Clinical Neuropsychologist, 15,* 114–124.

Kraemer, H. C. (1992). *Evaluating medical tests: Objective and quantitative guidelines.* Newberry Park, CA: Sage.

Larrabee, G. J. (2003a). Detection of malingering using atypical performance patterns on standard neuropsychological tests. *The Clinical Neuropsychologist, 17,* 410–425.

Larrabee, G. J. (2003b). Detection of symptom exaggeration with the MMPI-2 in litigants with malingered neurocognitive dysfunction. *The Clinical Neuropsychologist, 17,* 54–68.

Larrabee, G. J. (2005). Assessment of malingering. In G. J. Larrabee (Ed.), *Forensic neuropsychology: A scientific approach* (pp. 115–158). New York: Oxford University Press.

Lees-Haley, P. R. (1992). Efficacy of MMPI-2 Validity scales and MCMI-II Modifier scales for detecting spurious PTSD claims: F, F–K, Fake Bad Scale, Ego Strength, Subtle-Obvious subscales, DIS, and DEB. *Journal of Clinical Psychology, 48,* 681–688.

Lees-Haley, P. R., English, L. T., & Glenn, W. J. (1991). A Fake Bad Scale for the MMPI-2 for personal-injury claimants. *Psychological Reports, 48,* 203–210.

Martens, M., Donders, J., & Millis, S. R. (2001). Evaluation of invalid response sets after traumatic head injury. *Journal of Forensic Neuropsychology, 2,* 1–18.

McGee, S. (2002). Simplifying likelihood ratios. *Journal of General Internal Medicine, 17,* 646–649.

Meehl, P. E., & Rosen, A. (1955). Antecedent probability and the efficiency of psychometric signs, patterns, or cutting scores. *Psychological Bulletin, 52,* 194–216.

Meyers, J. E., Millis, S. R., & Volkert, K. (2002). A validity index for the MMPI-2. *Archives of Clinical Neuropsychology, 17,* 157–169.

Mittenberg, W., Patton, C., Canyock, E. M., & Condit, D. C. (2002). Base rates of malingering and symptom exaggeration. *Journal of Clinical and Experimental Neuropsychology, 24,* 1094–1102.

Rees, L. M., Tombaugh, T. N., & Boulay, L. (2001). Depression and the Test of Memory Malingering. *Archives of Clinical Neuropsychology, 16,* 501–506.

Reitan, R. M., & Wolfson, D. (1993). *The Halstead-Reitan Neuropsychological Test Battery: Theory and clinical interpretation* (2nd ed.). South Tucson, AZ: Neuropsychology Press.

Ross, S. R., Millis, S. R., Krukowski, R. A., Putnam, S. H., & Adams, K. M. (2004). Detecting incomplete effort on the MMPI-2: An examination of the Fake Bad scale in mild head injury. *Journal of Clinical and Experimental Neuropsychology, 26,* 115–124.

Slick, D. J., Sherman, E. M. S., & Iverson, G. L. (1999). Diagnostic criteria for malingered neurocognitive dysfunction: Proposed standards for clinical practice and research. *The Clinical Neuropsychologist, 13,* 545–561.

Smith, G. E., Cerhan, J. H., & Ivnik, R. J. (2003). Diagnostic validity. In D. S. Tulsky, D. H. Saklofske, G. J. Chelune, R. K. Heaton, R. J. Ivnik, R. Bornstein, et al. (Eds.), *Clinical interpretation of the WAIS-III and WMS-III* (pp. 273–301). San Diego: Academic Press.

Straus, S. E., Richardson, W. S., Glasziou, P., & Haynes, R. B. (2005). *Evidence-based medicine. How to practice and teach EBM* (3rd ed.). Edinburgh, UK: Elsevier Churchill Livingstone.

Sweet, J. J. (1999). Malingering: Differential diagnosis. In J. J. Sweet (Ed.), *Forensic neuropsychology* (pp. 255–285). Lisse, the Netherlands: Swets and Zeitlinger.

Swets, J. A. (1973). The relative operating characteristic in psychology. *Science, 182,* 990–1000.

Tombaugh, T. N. (1996). *Test of Memory Malingering: TOMM.* North Tonawanda, NY: Multi-Health Systems.

Vickery, C. D., Berry, D. T. R., Dearth, C. S., Vagnini, V. L., Baser, R. E., Cragar, D. E., et al. (2004). Head injury and the ability to feign neuropsychological deficits. *Archives of Clinical Neuropsychology, 19,* 37–48.

Vickery, C. D., Berry, D. T. R., Inman, T. H., Harris, M. J., & Orey, S. A. (2001). Detection of inadequate effort on neuropsychological testing: A meta-analytic review of selected procedures. *Archives of Clinical Neuropsychology, 16,* 45–73.

3

Non-Forced-Choice Effort Measures

Kyle B. Boone and Po H. Lu

During the past 15 years there has been an explosion of empirical research to develop and validate measures to detect noncredible cognitive symptoms. The most common effort test paradigm has utilized a forced-choice recognition memory format in which subjects are presented a set of stimuli and then are shown pairs of stimuli (one target, one foil) and requested to select the item in each pair that was previously seen in the stimulus selection. Individuals who have never viewed the stimuli can be expected to perform at chance on the recognition trial (i.e., correctly recognize approximately 50% of the items), given that, for each trial, the test taker has a 50% chance of guessing correctly. Forced-choice paradigms have utilized words (Word Memory Test; Warrington Recognition Memory Test for Words), numbers (Computerized Assessment of Response Bias; Hiscock Procedure; Portland Digit Recognition Test; Victoria Symptom Validity Test), and pictures (Test of Memory Malingering [TOMM]). Dozens of publications support the accuracy of these measures (for reviews, see Bianchini, Mathias, & Greve, 2001; Millis & Volinsky, 2001; Vickery, Berry, Inman, Harris, & Orey, 2001) and recent surveys of neuropsychological test usage have shown that forced-choice measures such as the TOMM and the Word Memory Test are among the most frequently administered effort tests (Sharland, Gfeller, Justice, Ross, & Hughes, 2005).

However, there are several pitfalls in relying solely on forced-choice measures. First, the current recommended practice is to administer several effort indicators throughout a test battery to continuously sample effort

(Bush et al., 2005; Lynch, 2004). However, if the effort indices employed are substantially intercorrelated, then the information they provide is redundant and cannot be used as converging evidence of poor effort (Rosenfeld, Sands, & van Gorp, 2000). We could not locate any studies in which correlations between forced-choice measures were reported, but it can be assumed that the associations might be large, given that the same test format is employed.

Second, forced-choice measures tend to be rather time consuming to administer (e.g., $\geq$ 20 minutes), and if several are included in a test battery, overall test administration time is substantially lengthened. To the extent that multiple-effort indicators are incorporated in a battery, it is preferable that they be brief and/or serve "double duty," that is, measure both effort and discrete types of cognitive ability (e.g., digit span; Babikian, Boone, Lu, & Arnold, 2006).

Third, forced-choice paradigms appear to be particularly sensitive to feigned memory impairment, but it is less clear whether they detect other types of feigned cognitive symptoms. For example, there is little reason to suggest that a malingerer who is intent on showcasing deficient processing speed, poor math calculation ability, or impaired reading skill would choose to underperform on a forced-choice measure. Osmon, Plambeck, Klein, and Mano (2006) in fact observed that a reading test specifically developed to detect feigned learning disability outperformed a verbal memory forced-choice measure in identifying learning disability simulators. Thus, various types of effort tests that measure a range of approaches to symptom feigning need to be employed.

Finally and perhaps most important, due to their popularity, forced-choice tests are the effort measures that examinees are the most likely to be knowledgeable about and coached on. Some investigations have indicated that forced-choice measures can be found on Internet sites frequented by individuals interested in learning about malingering (Bauer & McCaffrey, 2006; Ruiz, Drake, Marcotte, Glass, & van Gorp, 2000). Lezak, Howieson, and Loring (2004) describe a testing session in which a plaintiff spontaneously commented, "Oh, the TOMM," when one of the authors started to administer the test. In fact, the publisher of the TOMM issued a notice instructing examiners to shield the test acronym from view by examinees due to evidence that individuals were being educated about the test. Unfortunately, all that an unscrupulous attorney would have to say to a malingering plaintiff to ensure a passing performance on every forced-choice measure would be to "do well on every memory test in which you are given a choice of two options."

Thus, for these various reasons, the field of clinical neuropsychology cannot rely solely on forced-choice effort indices. In this chapter we review four freestanding, brief, non-forced-choice effort measures and provide new cross-validation data for two of them. These measures have been found to be only modestly correlated with each other (e.g., 3–36% shared variance; Nelson, Boone, Dueck, Wagener, Lu, & Grills, 2003), suggesting that it is appropriate to use them in concert. We also refer the reader to the other chapters in this

book that describe non-forced-choice effort indices embedded in existing neuropsychological measures.

Rey 15-Item Test Plus Recognition Trial

The Rey 15-Item Test in its original format utilizes a 10-second presentation of a single page that contains 15 items grouped in overlearned sequences (Lezak, Howieson, & Loring, 2004). After the page is removed, the patient is required to reproduce as many of the items as possible on a blank sheet of paper. The Rey 15-Item has historically been the most widely used malingering test (e.g., between 1987 and 1992 it was the only effort test to appear on a listing of the most commonly administered neuropsychological tests; Lees-Haley, Smith, Williams, & Dunn, 1995); however, beginning primarily in the 1990s, research began appearing that illustrated the substantial shortcomings of the Rey test, including poor sensitivity and a high false positive rate in select populations (e.g., persons with mental retardation; Goldberg & Miller, 1986; and those with dementia; Philpott, 1992; Schretlen, Brandt, Krafft, & van Gorp, 1991). Using a cutoff of < 9, sensitivity typically hovers slightly below 50%, although specificity is high (e.g., 97–100%) in patient and control populations that exclude individuals with mental retardation and dementia (Boone, Salazar, Lu, Warner-Chacon, & Razani, 2002).

In an attempt to raise sensitivity while maintaining adequate specificity, Boone, Salazar, et al. (2002) added a recognition paradigm to the standard administration while still restricting the overall test administration time to less than 5 minutes. The recognition trial consists of a page containing the 15 items from the original stimulus interspersed with 15 foils similar to the target items. The following summary score was derived from the free recall and recognition trials:

$$Combination\ score = recall\ correct + [recognition\ correct$$
$$- false\ positive\ errors]$$

In the original validation study (ibid.), a sample of 49 litigating/disability-seeking patients who also scored below the cutoffs on at least two independent effort measures and met at least one behavioral criterion (e.g., implausible self-reported symptoms such as "cannot see through glass") scored significantly more poorly on this equation than 36 neuropsychology clinic referrals with no motive to feign (i.e., not in litigation or attempting to obtain disability compensation), 33 college students with a learning disability, and 60 older controls. Use of a cutoff score of <20 resulted in a sensitivity rate of 71.4% with overall specificity of 91.7%. False positive identifications on the recognition trial ≥4, while associated with a sensitivity of only 10%, occurred in only ≤ 7% of comparison patients and controls, suggesting that, when this response pattern is present, it is highly suspicious for poor effort.

In addition, tabulation of the frequencies of recognition for individual foils revealed that no comparison subjects circled an upper- or a lowercase *F* or a 6. These responses were also rare in the noncredible group (4–6% occurrence), but because they did not occur in credible subjects, their presence may be almost pathognomonic for suspect effort.

Test performance was only minimally related to age (<8% shared variance) and education (<14% shared variance), which suggests that test performance is relatively unaffected by older age and lower education levels. Interestingly, the performance of the sample of persons with a learning disability was comparable to that of the older controls, arguing that a learning disability does not appear to compromise performance, although persons with learning disability in college settings may not be representative of the entire LD population.

Cross-Validation Data

Since the original publication, we have collected additional data on 90 noncredible patients and 105 clinic comparison patients who met the same inclusion and exclusion criteria as in the initial study (with the exception that an overall *b* Test E score of ≥ 90 was employed rather than cutoffs for 4 separate *b* Test scores, and no comparison patient had dementia, FSIQ < 70, or failed >1 of the criterion effort tests). Descriptive statistics for age, education, and gender distribution for the two study groups are shown in Table 3.1. The clinic comparison patients had significantly more years of education, and the suspect effort group had a higher proportion of men, while the clinic comparison group was overrepresented by women.

Statistical examination (Kolmogorov-Smirnov Test of Normality) of the distribution of the combination score revealed that it was not normally distributed within each group, necessitating the use of nonparametric statistics. Age was not significantly related to test performance in either the suspect

Table 3.1.
Comparisons of Demographic Characteristics and Combination Scores of the Two Study Groups

	Suspect Effort ($N=90$)	Clinic Patients ($N=105$)		
	Mean (SD)	Mean (SD)	Statistical Tests	P Value
Age, years	40.7 (11.9)	43.7 (14.0)	$t=-1.59$	.11
Education, years	12.1 (2.7)	12.9 (3.0)	$t=-2.02$	.04
Gender, m/f	57/33	46/59	$\chi^2=7.41$	.006
Combination score	17.8 (7.0)	24.5 (5.0)	$U=2067.5$	.0001

effort group or the clinical comparison group; however, educational level was significantly correlated with test performance in both groups (Spearman rho = .381, $p = .0001$ in suspect effort; Spearman rho = .241, $p = .04$ in clinical comparison), although the degree of test score variance accounted for by education was relatively small (≤ 15%). Within each group, no significant difference in test performance between men and women was observed.

Due to the modest amount of test score variance accounted for by demographic variables, no attempt was made to adjust group comparisons for demographic variables. Analyses using the Mann-Whitney U Test showed that the suspect effort patients obtained significantly worse scores compared to the clinic comparison patients (Table 3.1).

Examination of specificity and sensitivity values, as reproduced in Table 3.2, showed that the use of the previously published cutoff of < 20 was associated with a specificity of 85.7%, which reflects a relatively small drop from the original specificity of ≥ 92% obtained in the original study. However, the decline in sensitivity was somewhat more substantial; 55.6% of noncredible subjects were identified in the cross-validation sample as compared to the 71% in the original study.

While some loss in classification accuracy is generally found upon cross-validation, the decrease in combination score sensitivity is greater than expected. It is possible that a growing sophistication of malingerers regarding effort tests may have played a role. The data from the original study were collected over a 15-year span ending approximately 5 years ago, while the current data were accrued in the last 5 years. Given the widespread use of the original Rey 15-Item Test over many years by professionals in various disciplines (e.g., psychology, neuropsychology, psychiatry, neurology), some compromise in test security may have occurred. On at least one occasion we have observed a noncredible patient smirk when presented with the 15-item stimulus page in an apparent indication of recognition of the test (the patient "passed" the 15-Item Test plus recognition trial but was identified as noncredible on other indices).

Table 3.2.
Classification Accuracy for a Range of Rey 15-Item Plus Recognition Combination Scores

	Suspect Effort	Clinic Patients	Base Rate of 30%	
	Sensitivity	Specificity	PPV	NPV
Cutoff scores	$N = 90$	$N = 105$		
< 18	42.2	87.6	59.5	77.8
< 19	53.3	86.7	62.3	80.8
< 20	**55.6**	**85.7**	**63.5**	**81.8**
< 21	61.1	80.0	57.1	82.6

Examination of the 15 cases that were incorrectly identified as noncredible showed that 3 spoke English as a second language and 1 was bilingual (English as first language) and that 11 were non-Caucasian. In terms of diagnosis, 6 had symptoms of psychosis, 2 had a seizure disorder, 2 had histories of drug and/or alcohol abuse, 1 had experienced a severe head injury with a 30-day coma, 1 had a history of special education placement, 1 exhibited mild cognitive impairment (often considered a precursor to Alzheimer's disease), 1 was somatoform, and 1 had depression. Thus, it appears that presence of psychosis, nonwhite ethnicity, and ESL status places patients at particular risk for misidentification as noncredible on the Rey 15-Item combination score.

In conclusion, while admittedly the Rey 15-Item combination score sensitivity may not be optimal, specificity is relatively high, and given that the test is brief to administer, it appears to still have value in the measurement of effort; the clinician needs to keep in mind that while a failed performance is informative, a passing score may not be.

Dot Counting Test

The Dot Counting Test, also originally developed by Rey (Lezak, Howieson, & Loring, 2004), consists of 12 cards, each containing a varying number of dots. On the first 6 cards, 7–27 dots are randomly arranged, but on the latter 6 cards, the 8–28 dots are grouped into units that facilitate the use of multiplication tables. Subjects are instructed to count the dots as quickly as possible with answers and response time recorded for each card; administration time is typically less than 5 minutes. Subjects can be provided with a pointer (such as the back end of a pencil) to facilitate counting (and the use of such an aid helps to document the counting of grouped dots individually, an atypical behavior that is suggestive of suspect effort).

Original interpretation of the test scores focused on noting whether the individual counted grouped dots more quickly than ungrouped dots (Lezak, 1995). Subsequently, some researchers also examined the number of errors (Beetar & Williams, 1995; Binks, Gouvier, & Waters, 1997; Hayes, Hale, & Gouvier, 1997; Lee et al., 2000; Martin, Hayes, & Gouvier, 1996; Paul, Franzen, Cohen, & Fremouw, 1992; Rose, Hall, & Szalda-Petree, 1998), as well as grouped dot counting time in isolation (Back et al., 1996; Greiffenstein, Baker, & Gola, 1994; Lee et al., 2000; Paul et al., 1992; Rose et al., 1998), ungrouped dot counting time in isolation (Greiffenstein et al., 1994; Lee et al., 2000; Paul et al., 1992; Rose et al., 1998), the slopes of the ungrouped and grouped response latency curves (Binks et al., 1997), and the ratio of ungrouped dot to grouped dot counting time (Back et al., 1996).

Empirical studies on the Dot Counting Test have been equivocal, with some suggesting that the measure was effective in documenting poor effort (Beetar & Williams, 1995; Binks et al., 1997; Hayes et al., 1997; Martin et al.,

1996; Paul et al., 1992; Youngjohn, Burrows, & Erdal, 1995) and others questioning its utility (Greiffenstein et al., 1994; Hiscock, Branham, & Hiscock, 1994; Rose et al., 1998). In a meta-analysis of Dot Counting Test studies, Vickery et al. (2001) concluded that group means were separated by a standard deviation of only .75 and that the test was comparable in effectiveness to the original Rey 15-Item Test.

However, Boone, Lu, Back, and colleagues (2002) suspected that the unimpressive performance of the Dot Counting Test in some previous studies may have been an artifact of the failure to identify the most sensitive scores (or combination of scores), as well as examination of test performance in simulators rather than in actual malingerers. Dot Counting Test data were collected on two noncredible groups: 85 litigating or compensation-seeking patients as defined by failure on at least two independent effort tests and who met at least one behavioral criterion (e.g., implausible self-reported symptoms such as "cannot see through glass"), and 14 inpatient prisoners determined to be feigning by a staff consensus.

In addition, data were obtained on nine normal effort groups: older controls ($n = 51$), older depressed patients ($n = 64$), patients with schizophrenia ($n = 28$), patients with moderate to severe brain injury in rehabilitation ($n = 20$), right stroke patients in rehabilitation ($n = 9$), left stroke patients in rehabilitation ($n = 9$), college students with learning disabilities ($n = 31$), and subjects with mild ($n = 16$) or moderate dementia ($n = 21$). None of the comparison subjects were in litigation or attempting to obtain disability.

Dot Counting Test time and error data were found to be only modestly correlated with each other, which suggested that the use of this information in tandem would be more effective in identifying individuals with poor effort than either type of data in isolation. In fact, the following combination effort index score (E score), incorporating both time and error variables, was more sensitive than individual scores:

$$E \; score \; = \; mean \; ungrouped \; time + mean \; grouped \; time$$
$$+ \; total \; number \; of \; errors$$

The two noncredible groups performed significantly poorer on the E score than all of the comparison groups with the exception that the patients in civil litigation or attempting to obtain disability did not perform significantly differently from patients with moderate dementia. The civil suspect effort subjects obtained an average E score of 35, while the criminal suspect effort individuals averaged an E score of over 80; the average scores for the comparison groups were typically < 18 with the exception of the patients with moderate dementia, who obtained a mean score of 25. Use of an E score cutoff ≥ 17 yielded a sensitivity value in the civil litigant/disability-seeking group of 78.8% while achieving a specificity value of 90.4% for a

combined normal effort group (excluding moderate dementia). In the prison noncredible group, an E score of 32 was associated with 100% sensitivity, at 99.1% specificity. Additional specificity tables were generated for each comparison group separately to allow for the selection of cutoffs appropriate for specific differential diagnoses (i.e., actual versus feigned depression, schizophrenia, head injury, stroke, learning disability, or mild dementia).

In addition to using the combination E score, the clinician can also examine individual test performance parameters. For example, 92% of the combined comparison groups (excluding moderate dementia) made no more than 4 errors (no patients with depression committed >3 errors; no subjects with head injury or learning disability made >4 errors), and only 7% averaged ≥6 seconds to count grouped dots (no patients with depression averaged >4 s, no subjects with a learning disability averaged >6 seconds, and no head-injured patient averaged >7 seconds), thus rendering such findings highly specific to noncredible subjects. Again, scores were only modestly related to age and education (<4% test score variance), which suggests that the test is appropriate for use across differing age and education levels.

Cross-Validation Data

Since the original publication, we have collected additional data on 91 civil litigation/disability-seeking suspect effort patients who met the same inclusion criteria as in the original study (with the exception that an overall b Test E score of ≥90 was employed rather than cutoffs for four separate b Test scores, and no comparison subject failed more than one of the effort criterion measures) and on 111 heterogeneous neuropsychology clinic comparison patients with no motive to feign and who did not meet criteria for dementia or obtain a Full Scale IQ (FSIQ) <70. Descriptive statistics for age, education, and gender distribution for the two study groups are shown in Table 3.3. The clinic comparison patients averaged significantly more years of education, and the suspect effort group had a higher proportion of men, while the clinic comparison group was overrepresented by women.

Statistical examination (Kolmogorov-Smirnov Test of Normality) of the distribution of the Dot Counting E score revealed that it was not normally distributed within each group, necessitating the use of nonparametric statistics. Age was not significantly related to test performance in either the suspect effort group or the clinical comparison group, and education was not significantly correlated with test performance in the clinic group; however, a significant negative association between education and E score was present in the suspect effort group (Spearman rho = .367, p = .0001), although the degree of test score variance accounted for by education was relatively small (<14%). Within each group, no significant difference in test performance between men and women was observed.

Table 3.3.
Comparisons of Demographic Characteristics and E Scores of the
Two Study Groups

	Suspect Effort ($N=91$)	Clinic Patients ($N=111$)		
	Mean (SD)	Mean (SD)	Statistical Tests	P Value
Age, years	41.2 (12.3)	44.3 (14.4)	$t=-1.64$	.10
Education, years	11.9 (2.4)	12.7 (2.9)	$t=-2.12$	.04
Gender, m/f	57/34	50/61	$\chi^2=6.21$	.01
E score	25.7 (14.6)	12.2 (7.3)	$U=1316.5$	.0001

Due to the modest amount of test score variance accounted for by demographic variables, no attempt was made to adjust group comparisons for demographic variables. Analyses using the Mann-Whitney U Test showed that the suspect effort patients performed significantly worse than the clinic comparison patients (Table 3.3).

Examination of specificity and sensitivity values revealed that use of the previously published cutoff of ≥ 17 was associated with a specificity of 89.2%, which reflects a minimal drop from the original specificity of $\geq 91\%$ obtained in the original study. Sensitivity was slightly lowered to 72.5%, as compared to the 75% documented previously.

Examination of the 12 cases that were incorrectly identified as non-credible showed that 4 spoke English as a second language, 1 was bilingual (English as first language), and 7 were non-Caucasian. In terms of diagnosis, 3 had symptoms of psychosis, 2 had had strokes, 2 were depressed, 1 had a history of drug abuse, 1 had experienced a severe head injury, 1 had a history of special education placement, 1 exhibited mild cognitive impairment (considered a precursor to Alzheimer's disease), and 1 had a panic disorder.

Table 3.4.
Classification Accuracy for a Range of DCT Combination Scores

Test and Cutoff Scores	Suspect Effort Sensitivity	Clinic Patients Specificity	Base Rate of 30% PPV	NPV
DCT	$N=91$	$N=111$		
≥ 19	64.8	92.8	80.0	86.2
≥ 18	68.1	91.0	82.4	87.4
≥ 17	72.5	89.2	78.6	88.4

Thus, it would again appear that presence of psychosis, nonwhite ethnicity, and ESL status may place patients at particular risk for misidentification as noncredible on the dot counting E score.

In conclusion, available cross-validation data continue to demonstrate the efficacy of the dot counting test in detection of suspect effort.

b Test

The *b* Test (Boone et al., 2000; Boone, Lu, & Herzberg, 2002) had its genesis in the observation that some noncredible patients, when queried as to chronic symptoms following mild traumatic brain injury, reported that they had become "dyslexic" (i.e., now saw letters "upside down and backward"). However, this symptom is not reported by actual patients with significant brain injury in whom overlearned information, such as letter discrimination, is typically preserved.

The *b* Test consists of 15 pages of lowercase *b*'s interspersed with lowercase *d*'s, *p*'s, and *q*'s, as well as *b*'s with diagonal stems or extra stems. The same three sets of pages are reproduced in a progressively smaller font; the letters on the first three pages are seven-eighths of an inch, while the letters on the last three pages are one-eighth of an inch. Patients are instructed to work through the booklet, circling just the letter *b* as quickly as possible; they are also told that they may find that the test becomes progressively more difficult, and that they should try to do their best. Most cooperative individuals complete the task in 7 minutes; if a patient is markedly slow, the test can be discontinued if commission or omission errors have exceeded cutoffs (discussed below).

When patients indicate that they have finished the test, the examiner should check to see whether all of the pages have been completed; if any have been skipped, patients should be encouraged to complete the remaining pages (the examiner then adds these times to the total time). Occasionally patients will ask whether a diagonal *b* or a *b* with extra stems should be circled; in these situations, the examiner should redirect them to the cover page and instruct them that the *b*'s they circle should look "just like" the target reproduced there. It is also useful to document any spontaneous comments the patients make about the test; many somatoform patients complain about the arduousness of the test (e.g., "I have to do all these?!" "These letters are making me dizzy!," "This is putting my eyes out!") when in fact it is a preschool-level activity.

The *b* Test (Boone, Lu, & Herzberg, 2002) was administered to 91 litigating or disability compensation–seeking real-world noncredible patients as determined by failure on at least two independent effort indices and at least one behavioral criterion. It was also administered to six normal effort groups (older controls [$n = 26$], older depressed [$n = 38$], patients with

schizophrenia [$n = 28$], patients with moderate to severe brain injury in rehabilitation [$n = 20$], right stroke patients in rehabilitation [$n = 9$], left stroke patients in rehabilitation [$n = 9$], college students with learning disabilities [$n = 31$]). None of the comparison subjects were in litigation or attempting to obtain disability.

Data on total time to complete the task, omission errors, and commission errors (including a separate tabulation of "d errors" in isolation) were collected. The suspect effort group committed significantly more commission errors, was slower than all comparison groups except stroke patients, and displayed more omission errors than all groups except patients with right stroke. Commission errors in the noncredible group were particularly characterized by the circling of d's, apparently due to the misperception in the general public that dyslexia is synonymous with perceiving letters backward. The following combination score, utilizing both types of error scores (as well as double weighting of d errors) and a time score, achieved the highest sensitivity:

$$E\ score = [(number\ of\ commission\ errors$$
$$+\ number\ of\ d\ commission\ errors) \times 10]$$
$$+\ number\ of\ omission\ errors + mean\ time\ per\ page$$

The noncredible group performed significantly worse on the E score than all of the comparison groups; the suspect effort group obtained an average E score of 601, with mean scores for all other groups well below 100 with the exception of the patients with schizophrenia and right stroke patients, who averaged less than 130. The use of an E score cutoff ≥ 90 resulted in 77% sensitivity and 90% specificity in the head-injury group; comparable specificity was obtained in the learning disability and depression groups by raising the cutoff to ≥ 140 (66% sensitivity). However, to limit false positive identifications to around 10% in the groups with stroke and schizophrenia, the cutoffs had to be substantially raised (≥ 170 and ≥ 190), respectively), which resulted in significantly lowered sensitivity (54–56%). The observation of poor performance on the b Test in the psychotic group is not particularly unexpected given that the b Test is a continuous performance task; psychotic individuals tend to perform poorly on such measures (Braver, Barch, & Cohen, 1999; Nelson, Sax, & Strakowski, 1998; Pigache, 1999). Thus, these findings suggest that the b Test may not be the best measure for identifying actual versus feigned psychosis or stroke.

In addition to using the combination E score for identifying suspect effort, the clinician can also examine individual test performance parameters. For example, no patient in any clinical comparison group committed more than four d errors, only 3% of comparison subjects made more than eight commission errors, no head-injured patient committed ≥ 50 omission

errors, and only 8% of comparison patients required ≥850 seconds to complete the task; thus, performance beyond these cutoffs is highly specific to noncredible subjects.

Scores were unrelated to age and education, with the exception that age was associated with time scores in the combined clinical comparison group (15% shared variance), and no significant gender effects were found. These findings suggest that the test is appropriate for use across differing age and education levels and that the same cutoffs are appropriate for men and women. The cutoff associated with specificity ≥90% in the learning disability sample showed comparable specificity in the comparison groups as a whole, indicating that, although the test involves rapid letter identification, actual learning disability does not substantially interfere with task performance.

Thus, available data support the use of the *b* Test in clinical practice.

Rey Word Recognition Test

The Rey Word Recognition Test has been the least investigated of the three effort measures developed by Andre Rey (1941; Lezak, 1983). In the task, the examinee is asked to remember a list of 15 words that are read aloud; after a 5-second delay, the individual is handed a page with the 15 target words interspersed with 15 foils and instructed to circle the words spoken by the examiner; administration time is typically less than 2 minutes.

The Rey Word Recognition Test was originally designed to be interpreted in tandem with the first trial of the Rey Auditory Verbal Learning Test (RAVLT). Given that recognition is easier than free recall, if a patient recognized the same or fewer words than recalled on the first trial of the RAVLT, performance would be judged to be suspect (Lezak, 1983). However, published sensitivity rates for this comparison have ranged widely—from a low of 4% in 177 college student simulators and 7% in actual patients with motive to fake (Frederick, Saraty, Johnston, & Powel, 1994), to 60% of probable malingerer persistent postconcussive patients (Greiffenstein, Baker, and Gola, 1996) and 70% of 17 forensic psychiatric patients (Frederick et al., 1994). In contrast, Greiffenstein and colleagues (1994, 1995, 1996) documented relatively high sensitivity values (59–81%) for the recognition score (with or without subtracting false positives) in isolation. Despite these promising findings, the Rey Word Recognition Test has been essentially ignored in clinical practice.

In a recent study (Nitch, Boone, Wen, Arnold, & Alfano, 2006), Rey Word Recognition task data were obtained on 92 litigating or disability compensation–seeking real-world noncredible subjects as determined by failure on at least two independent effort measures and one behavioral criterion. Comparison subjects were 31 college students with learning disability and 51 fluent English-speaking neuropsychology clinic referrals with no motive to feign (i.e., not in litigation or attempting to get disability), who failed <2

effort indicators and did not meet criteria for dementia or have FSIQ <70. Number of words correctly recognized, number of false positive recognitions, and recognitions minus false positive recognitions were examined. No significant correlations with age or education were observed; however, a significant gender effect was observed in the suspect effort group, with men performing worse than women. Group comparisons conducted for men and women separately showed that noncredible men and women scored worse than their clinic comparison and learning disabled counterparts in recognition correct and recognition minus false positive errors, in contrast, the noncredible groups did not commit significantly more false positive errors. Clinic patients and those with a learning disability did not significantly differ from each other in test scores, and thus the groups were collapsed for the purpose of developing cut scores.

Using a cut score of ≤ 7 correctly detected 81% of noncredible women while maintaining specificity in the female comparison group to >90%. However, use of this same cut score in men resulted in nearly 20% false positive identifications, although sensitivity was 88%. Lowering the cutoff to achieve ≥90% specificity in the men required the use of a cut score of ≤ 5, with a resultant drop in sensitivity to 63%. Not unexpectedly (given that the noncredible group did not circle significantly more foils), subtracting false positives did not increase sensitivity. A cut score of ≤ 6 words recognized minus false positive errors preserved 90% specificity in women and detected 73% of suspect effort women. However, the cutoff had to be lowered to ≤ 3 words correctly recognized minus false positive errors to achieve specificity of ≥90% in the men, which dropped sensitivity to only 53%. No patient committed >6 false positive errors, suggesting that scores above this cutoff may be virtually pathognomonic for suspect effort.

Given that some research has shown that noncredible patients may fail to show a primacy and recency effect on word list learning tasks (Suhr, 2002), the frequency of correct recognitions of individual words in each group was tabulated. In fact, examination of recognition frequencies showed that credible patients displayed a higher rate of recognizing words from the first half of the list (72–75% versus 53–59%), while the noncredible patients recognized the two sets of words with equal frequency (38% versus 33%). The following combination score was developed to provide double weighting of the first half of the list:

$$Combination\ score = recognition\ minus\ false\ positives$$
$$+ total\ words\ recognized\ from\ the$$
$$first\ eight\ words\ of\ the\ list$$

This equation produced slightly higher sensitivity values in men than recognition total (67% versus 63%), although sensitivity in women actually dropped from 81% to 68%. However, in the subset of noncredible patients claiming symptoms in the context of traumatic brain injury (the majority of

whom were mild; $n = 38$), sensitivity for a cut score of ≤ 9 was 81.6% with an associated $\geq 90\%$ specificity (sensitivity was 71.7% in the noncredible group as a whole). Due to the relatively small sample size, the traumatic brain-injury subgroup was not divided by gender.

Subjects with a learning disability scored comparably to clinic patients and significantly higher than noncredible patients, indicating that the Rey Word Recognition Test may be appropriate for use in the differential diagnosis of actual versus feigned learning disability.

In conclusion, available data suggest that the Rey Word Recognition Test, despite its brevity, is effective in identifying noncredible cognitive performance, although gender-specific cutoffs need to be employed.

Discussion

Detection of feigned or exaggerated cognitive impairment and suspect effort should rely on a multidimensional approach that integrates multiple sources of evidence to identify inconsistencies that can surface in the test data or through behaviors exhibited during or outside the testing session. Administration of effort tests, such as those described in this chapter, should be standard clinical practice particularly in, but not isolated to, settings where examinees have obvious external incentives to fabricate or exaggerate cognitive dysfunction. Among the tests specifically designed to measure effort, the forced-choice paradigm remains the most popular format for assessing the veracity of a patient's cognitive complaint. However, with the growing sophistication of attorneys and unparalleled access to information provided by the Internet, patients are being coached on or are researching strategies for circumventing various effort tests, thus compromising test security and the validity of test data. In this regard, it is imperative for neuropsychologists to continue to develop novel and creative methods for capturing suspect effort and noncredible symptoms. This chapter focuses on four non-forced-choice tests found to be reliable and valid methods for detection of suspect effort. The advantages of these tests include brevity (less than 30 minutes to administer all four tests) and the ability of these tests to complement each other by sampling a variety of approaches to the feigning of cognitive deficits (e.g., mental slowness, loss in simple math skills, poor free recall and recognition memory for overlearned information, deficient letter recognition) rather than memory alone.

References

Babikian, T., Boone, K., Lu, P., & Arnold, G. (2006). Sensitivity and specificity of various digit span scores in the detection of suspect effort. *The Clinical Neuropsychologist, 20,* 145–159.

Back, C., Boone, K. B., Edwards, C., Parks, C., Burgoyne, K., & Silver, B. (1996). The performance of schizophrenics on three cognitive tests of malingering: Rey 15-Item Memory Test, Rey Dot Counting Test, and Hiscock Forced-Choice Method. *Assessment, 3,* 449–457.

Bauer, L., & McCaffrey, R. J. (2006). Coverage of the Test of Memory Malingering, Victoria Symptom Validity Test, and Word Memory Test on the Internet: Is test security threatened? *Archives of Clinical Neuropsychology, 21,* 121–126.

Beetar, J. T., & Williams, J. M. (1995). Malingering response style on the Memory Assessment scales and symptom validity tests. *Archives of Clinical Neuropsychology, 10,* 57 72.

Bianchini, K. J., Mathias, C. W., & Greve, K. W. (2001). Symptom validity testing: A critical review. *The Clinical Neuropsychologist, 15,* 19–45.

Binks, P. G., Gouvier, W. D., & Waters, W. F. (1997). Malingering detection with the Dot Counting Test. *Archives of Clinical Neuropsychology, 12,* 41–46.

Boone, K. B., Lu, P., Back, C., King, C., Lee, A., Philpott, L., et al. (2002). Sensitivity and specificity of the Rey Dot Counting Test in patients with suspect effort and various clinical samples. *Archives of Clinical Neuropsychology, 17,* 625–642.

Boone, K. B., Lu, P., & Herzberg, D. (2002). *The b Test manual.* Los Angeles: Western Psychological Services.

Boone, K. B., Lu, P., Sherman, D., Palmer, B., Back, C., Shamieh, E., et al. (2000). Validation of a new technique to detect malingering of cognitive symptoms: The *b* Test. *Archives of Clinical Neuropsychology, 15,* 227–241.

Boone, K. B., Salazar, X., Lu, P., Warner-Chacon, K., & Razani J. (2002). The Rey 15-Item Recognition Trial: A technique to enhance sensitivity of the Rey 15-Item Memorization Test. *Journal of Clinical and Experimental Neuropsychology, 24,* 561–573.

Braver, T. S., Barch, D. M., & Cohen, J. D. (1999). Cognition and control in schizophrenia: A computational model of dopamine and prefrontal function. *Biological Psychiatry, 46,* 312–328.

Bush, S. S., Ruff, R. M., Troster, A. I., Barth, J. I., Koffler, S. P., Pliskin, N. H., et al. (NAN Policy and Planning Committee). (2005). Symptom validity assessment: Practice issues and medical necessity. NAN position paper. *Archives of Clinical Neuropsychology, 20,* 419–426.

Frederick, R. I., Saraty, S. D., Johnston, J. D., & Powel, J. (1994). Validation of a detector of response bias on a forced-choice test of nonverbal ability. *Neuropsychology, 8,* 118–125.

Goldberg, T. O., & Miller, H. R. (1986). Performance of psychiatric inpatients and intellectually deficient individuals on a task that assesses the validity of memory complaints. *Journal of Clinical Psychology, 42,* 792–795.

Greiffenstein, M. F., Baker W. J., & Gola, T. (1994). Validation of malingered amnesia measures with a large clinical sample. *Psychological Assessment, 6,* 218–224.

Greiffenstein, M. F., Baker, W. J., & Gola, T. (1996). Comparison of multiple scoring methods for Rey's malingered amnesia methods. *Archives of Clinical Neuropsychology, 11,* 283–293.

Greiffenstein, M. F., Gola, T., & Baker, W. J. (1995). MMPI-2 Validity scales versus domain-specific measures in detection of factitious traumatic brain injury. *The Clinical Neuropsychologist, 9,* 230–240.

Hayes, J. S., Hale, D. B., & Gouvier, W. D. (1997). Do tests predict malingering in defendants with mental retardation? *Journal of Psychology, 131,* 575–576.

Hiscock, C. K., Branham, J. D., & Hiscock, M. (1994). Detection of feigned cognitive impairment: The two-alternative forced-choice method compared with selected conventional tests. *Journal of Psychopathology and Behavioral Assessment, 16,* 95–110.

Lee, A., Boone, K. B., Lesser, I., Wohl, M., Wilkins, S., & Parks, C. (2000). Performance of older depressed patients on two cognitive malingering tests: False positive rates for the Rey 15-Item Memorization and Dot Counting tests. *The Clinical Neuropsychologist, 14,* 303–308.

Lees-Haley, P. R., Smith, H. H., Williams, C. W., & Dunn, J. T. (1995). Forensic neuropsychological test usage: An empirical study. *Archives of Clinical Neuropsychology, 11,* 45–51.

Lezak, M. D. (1983). *Neuropsychological assessment* (2nd ed.). New York: Oxford University Press.

Lezak, M. D. (1995). *Neuropsychological assessment* (3rd ed.). New York: Oxford University Press.

Lezak, M. D., Howieson, D. B., & Loring, D. W. (2004). *Neuropsychological assessment* (4th ed.). New York: Oxford University Press.

Lynch, W. (2004). Determination of effort level, exaggeration, and malingering in neurocognitive assessment. *Journal of Head Trauma Rehabilitation, 19,* 277–283.

Martin, R. C., Hayes, J. S., & Gouvier, W. D. (1996). Differential vulnerability between postconcussion self-report and objective malingering tests in identifying simulated mild head injury. *Journal of Clinical and Experimental Neuropsychology, 18,* 265–275.

Millis, S. R., & Volinsky, C. T. (2001). Assessment of response bias in mild head injury: Beyond malingering tests. *Journal of Clinical and Experimental Neuropsychology, 23,* 809–828.

Nelson, E. B., Sax, K. W., & Strakowski, S. M. (1998). Attentional performance in patients with psychotic and nonpsychotic major depression and schizophrenia. *American Journal of Psychiatry, 155,* 137–139.

Nelson, N. W., Boone, K., Dueck, A., Wagener, L., Lu, P., & Grills, C. (2003). Relationships between eight measures of suspect effort. *The Clinical Neuropsychologist, 17,* 263–272.

Nitch, S., Boone, K. B., Wen, J., Arnold, G., & Alfano, K. (2006). The utility of the Rey Word Recognition Test in the detection of suspect effort. *The Clinical Neuropsychologist, 20,* 873–887.

Osmon, D. C., Plambeck, E., Klein, L., & Mano, Q. (2006). The Word-Reading Test of effort in adult learning disability: A simulation study. *The Clinical Neuropsychologist, 20,* 315–324.

Paul, D. S., Franzen, M. D., Cohen, S. H., & Fremouw, W. (1992). An investigation into the reliability and validity of two tests used in the detection of dissimulation. *International Journal of Clinical Neuropsychology, 14,* 1–9.

Philpott, L. M. (1992). *The effects of severity of cognitive impairment and age on two malingering tests: An investigation of the Rey Memory Test and Rey Dot Counting Test in Alzheimer's patients and normal middle-aged/older adults.* Unpublished doctoral dissertation, California School of Professional Psychology, Los Angeles.

Pigache, R. M. (1999). Vigilance in schizophrenia and its disruption by impaired preattentive selection: A disintegration hypothesis. *Cognitive Neuropsychiatry, 4,* 119–144.

Rey, A. (1941). Psychological examination of traumatic encephalopathy. *Archives de Psychologie, 28,* 286–340; sections translated by J. Corwin, & F. W. Bylsma. *The Clinical Neuropsychologist, 1993,* 4–9.

Rose, F. E., Hall, S., & Szalda-Petree, A. D. (1998). A comparison of four tests of malingering and the effects of coaching. *Archives of Clinical Neuropsychology, 13,* 349–363.

Rosenfeld, B., Sands, S. A., & van Gorp, W. G. (2000). Have we forgotten the base rate problem? Methodological issues in the detection of distortion. *Archives of Clinical Neuropsychology, 15,* 349–359.

Ruiz, M., Drake, E., Marcotte, D., Glass, A., & van Gorp, W. G. (2000, November). *Trying to beat the system: Misuse of the Internet to assist in avoiding the detection of neuropsychological symptom dissimulation.* Poster presented at the annual conference of the National Academy of Neuropsychology, Orlando, FL.

Schretlen, D., Brandt, J., Krafft, L, & van Gorp, W. G. (1991). Some caveats in using the Rey 15-Item Memory Test to detect malingered amnesia. *Psychological Assessment, 3,* 667–672.

Sharland, M. J., Gfeller, J. D., Justice, L., Ross, M., & Hughes, H. (2005, October). *A survey of neuropsychologists' beliefs and practices with respect to the assessment of effort.* Paper presented at the annual meeting of the National Academy of Neuropsychology, Tampa, FL.

Suhr, J. A. (2002). Malingering, coaching, and the serial position effect. *Archives of Clinical Neuropsychology, 17,* 69–77.

Vickery, C. D., Berry, D. T., Inman, T. H., Harris M. J., & Orey, S. A. (2001). Detection of inadequate effort in neuropsychological testing. *Archives of Clinical Neuropsychology, 15,* 45–73.

Youngjohn, J. R., Burrows, L., & Erdal, K. (1995). Brain damage or compensation neurosis? The controversial postconcussion syndrome. *The Clinical Neuropsychologist, 9,* 112–123.

4

Forced-Choice Recognition Tests
of Malingering

Christopher L. Grote and Julie N. Hook

Forced-choice recognition tests are increasingly used methods in the detection of insufficient effort or malingering. Many of these tests share a common characteristic in that the initial presentation of a stimulus (such as a five-digit number) is followed successively by a brief delay (e.g., blank computer screen) and then by the simultaneous presentation of both the original stimulus and a wrong answer (the foil). The patient is asked to identify which of the two stimuli had just been presented.

The original impetus for forced-choice testing was its suitability for application of the binomial theorem to answer the question "How likely is this response to occur by chance alone?" Of course, patients blinded to the original presentation of the stimulus (i.e., truly unaware or with "zero ability") would be expected to answer about half of the questions correctly by random guessing, which is the same level of success as the occurrence of "heads" in a series of tosses of an unbiased coin. If a large enough series of such trials is presented to the patient, bias might be inferred as a patient's score deviates from chance levels. A patient who correctly answers more than chance levels might be thought of as making at least a sporadic effort to do well on the test, whereas a patient who scored significantly less than chance might be considered to be someone who was intentionally avoiding the correct answer.

Perhaps one of the chief advantages of forced-choice recognition testing is that it may detect levels of performance that are significantly below chance. For example, if a patient completes 24 trials of forced-choice recognition testing, seven or fewer correct answers would be expected to occur less than

5% of the time ($p<.05$) by chance alone, per application of the normal approximation to the binomial:

$$Z = \frac{x - np}{\sqrt{npq}}$$

In this formula, x is the person's obtained score (7), n is the number of trials (24), p is the probability of success (.50), and q is the probability of failure (.50). The value np is the mean of the binomial distribution, and npq represents the variance of the binomial distribution. Finally, Z represents the z score generated for the obtained score. For better approximation to the normal curve, a correction factor of .5 is added when x falls below the mean and subtracted when it falls above the mean.

Thus, below-chance scores would seem to offer rather definitive evidence of an intentional (i.e., nonchance) attempt to perform poorly on the test by active avoidance of the correct response. This behavior could be construed as meeting the *DSM-IV* criteria for malingering, which includes "the intentional production of false or grossly exaggerated physical or psychological symptoms, motivated by external incentives." It is the word "intentional" that is difficult to operationalize in most cases. How does a clinician know that a patient's poor test performance is intentional and is calculated to suggest impairment? Such an inference might be made on the basis of clinical acumen, but this does not lend itself to the actuarial methods pursued by most neuropsychologists. Therefore, a patient who scores significantly below chance seems to offer the clearest evidence of an intention to appear impaired and therefore potentially to meet the *DSM* criteria for malingering. Indeed, Pankratz (Pankratz & Erickson, 1990) has characterized worse-than-chance performance as "the smoking gun of intent." In the diagnostic criteria for malingered neurocognitive dysfunction (MND) proposed by Slick, Sherman, and Iverson (1999), significantly worse-than-chance performance is identified as providing evidence for "definite negative response bias."

However, research on forced-choice recognition tests (Binder, 2002; Grote et al., 2000; Loring, Larrabee, Lee, & Meador, in press) shows that very few litigating patients achieve scores that are significantly below chance levels. Thus, authors and test publishers have increasingly turned their attention to the use of simulation studies and known-groups research to identify empirically derived cutoffs that discriminate simulators or probable malingerers from nonlitigating or compensation-seeking clinical patients. Simulation studies typically ask noninjured patients, often college undergraduates, to feign cognitive deficits in anticipation of a monetary reward. Some studies will coach the research subjects on the best way to avoid detection of insufficient effort. Results of coached or uncoached simulators are then compared against a group of nonlitigating or compensation-seeking patients, who themselves may be screened on a measure of symptom validity other than the test being

validated. Rogers (1997) and others have criticized the use of simulation studies as they may not be generalized to other populations. That is, do college students perform the same way as real-world malingerers? Research by De-makis (2004) suggests that the results of college student simulators may be more generalizable to patient samples than was once believed, but alternate methods of studying malingering tests have been proposed.

A "differential prevalence" design usually involves comparison of effort test scores between two types of groups (Rogers, 1997). The first of these is a group of patients known to have neurological impairment but who are ex-plicitly known to not be seeking compensation at the time of evaluation. An example of this would be a group of epilepsy surgery candidates who specif-ically deny that they are in the midst of personal-injury litigation or a dis-ability application. The second type would be of a group of compensation-seeking patients who may or may not have objective evidence of neurologic dysfunction. Previous research has usually included patients with mild trau-matic brain injury in this second type of group, where few or none of the patients have MRI, EEG, or other objective evidence of brain damage. It is assumed that certain persons in this group will be exaggerating and or ma-lingering deficits due to the presence of an external incentive. The problem with this design is that the researcher does not know which patients in the litigating/compensation-seeking group are actually malingering.

The third type of research design, the known-groups approach (ibid.), compares a group of nonlitigating/compensation-seeking clinical patients who may also be screened for good effort and who are contrasted with a group of litigating/compensation-seeking claimants independently identified as probable malingerers. An important part of this method is the specifica-tion of the criteria for the malingering group, such as failure on one or more well-standardized measures of symptom validity (other than the measure under investigation). The criteria published by Slick et al. (1999), which take a multiple evidence approach to identification of possible, probable, and definite MND have been employed in many recent known-groups investi-gations of malingering.

Sharland & Gfeller (in press) show that the most frequently used measure of effort is the Test of Memory Malingering (TOMM; Tombaugh, 1996). Other forced-choice tests endorsed as used by those surveyed included the Word Memory Test (WMT; Green, Lees-Haley, & Allen, 2002), Validity In-dicator Profile (VIP; Frederick & Crosby, 2000), Portland Digit Recognition Test (PDRT; Binder, 2002), and Victoria Symptom Validity Test (VSVT; Slick, Hopp, Strauss, and Spellacy, 1996). Moreover, a meta-analysis by Vickery, Berry, Inman, Harris, & Orey (2001) shows that forced-choice procedures (Hiscock Digit Memory, PDRT, and the 21-item test of Iverson, Franzen, & McCracken, 1991) yielded larger effect sizes in a comparison of simulation/ known groups with clinical samples than did more traditional symptom va-lidity procedures such as the 15-item test and dot-counting procedures (Lezak, Howieson, & Loring, 2004). Hence, forced-choice measures of symptom

validity are widely used and sensitive measures of effort and are applicable for use in settings where external incentives are prominent.

The rest of this chapter reviews some of the more commonly used and researched malingering tests that utilize forced-choice recognition methodology. These include the Test of Memory Malingering, Victoria Symptom Validity Test, Letter Memory Test, Medical Symptom Validity Test, Word Memory Test, Computerized Assessment of Response Bias, Portland Digit Recognition Test, and Validity Indicator Profile. A general description is given of how each of these is administered and scored. Standardization and cross-validation studies are reviewed, with an emphasis on their research design, and the cut scores that seem to be most effective are discussed. Brief commentary is also provided on the authors' impressions of the perceived strengths and weaknesses of each test.

Test of Memory Malingering

The Test of Memory Malingering is one of the earlier-developed measures of effort using forced-choice methodology. During the TOMM, the patient is shown 50 line drawings, one at a time. Following this, the patient is shown 50 more pages, each containing two line drawings, one of which had previously been shown. The patient must identify the previously shown drawing and is given feedback on the correctness of the response. The Trial 1 score, which can range between 0 and 50, is not considered of interest in interpretation, although significantly worse-than-chance performance on Trial 1 provides meaningful data regarding validity of effort. Following Trial 1, the original 50 line drawings are presented again, although in a different order. The patient then is shown another 50 pages, each containing a target stimulus, as well as a new foil. The patient again indicates which item looks familiar. Research by Rees, Tombaugh, Gansler, and Moczynski (1998) indicates that patients who are making a good effort are expected to score at least 45 correct on Trial 2.

An optional Retention Trial can also be given 15 minutes after Trial 2. The target pictures are not readministered, but the patient is again expected to correctly answer at least 45 items. Greve and Bianchini (2006b) found that early termination of the TOMM (i.e., not giving the optional Retention Trial) resulted in 3% of malingering patients going undetected by the TOMM. The authors recommended that the Retention Trial could be eliminated as long as at least one other symptom validity measure was given.

Normal Controls, Mixed Neurological Illness, Simulators, and at Risk for Malingering

The initial standardization study included 405 normal controls ranging in age from 16 to 84, with an average age of 54.8 years, and an average educational

level of 13.1 years. The average score for Trial 2 was 49.8, and for the Retention Trial was also 49.8. Multiple regression analyses revealed that age and education accounted for only 7.5% of the variance for Trial 1 and less than 2% of the variance for Trial 2. Of note, patients in this early study used an earlier version of the TOMM, one in which three distractors were present, not one. Also, subjects were not given explicit feedback about their performance after each trial. A phase 2 study with only one distractor then followed, and subjects received feedback after each trial. The 70 subjects in this study ranged in age from 17 to 73, with a mean age of 37.8 years, with an average of 12.7 years of education. The average score of Trial 2 was 49.9 and for Retention, 49.9.

Tombaugh and colleagues then obtained data from 138 consecutive inpatients and outpatients seen at the Boston VA Medical Center, who were described as having either "no cognitive impairment" ($n = 13$), "cognitive impairment" ($n = 42$), "aphasia" ($n = 21$), "traumatic brain injury" ($n = 45$), or "dementia" ($n = 40$). Patients in the dementia group averaged 45.7 on Trial 2 and 47.0 on the Retention Trial. The other four groups obtained even higher average ranges, with all 13 of the "no cognitive impairment" subjects obtaining a perfect score of 50 on both Trial 2 and the Retention Trial.

Twenty-seven undergraduates were asked to simulate the test performance of an individual seeking compensation for a head injury following a motor vehicle accident. Another 22 control subjects were asked to do their best on the TOMM. The controls averaged 49.9 correct on Trial 2, and all 50 obtained a perfect score on the Retention Trial. In contrast, the simulators obtained an average score of 35.3 on Trial 2 and 30.9 on the Retention Trial.

The final standardization study referred to in the TOMM manual indicates that 11 litigating or compensation-seeking subjects "at risk" for malingering, all of whom had a traumatic brain injury, averaged only 32.8 correct on Trial 2 and 35.1 on the Retention Trial.

Patients With Depression

Yanez, Fremouw, Tennant, Strunk, and Coker (2006) found 20 patients who had high scores on the Beck Depression Inventory (2nd ed.) and met the *DSM* criteria for major depressive disorder and compared them to normal controls on the TOMM. There was not a significant difference between the groups in terms of TOMM performance. Two of the patients scored below 45 on Trial 2, and 1 scored below this cutoff point on the Retention Trial. None of the normal controls scored below 45 on Trial 2 or the Retention Trial. The authors concluded that the TOMM can be used even with participants with severe depression with only slight caution. Rees, Tombaugh, and Boulay (2001) and Ashendorf, Constantinou, and McCaffrey (2004) also found that depression did not affect TOMM scores.

Children

Donders (2005) administered the TOMM to a sample of 100 consecutively referred 6- to 16-year-old children with a wide range of clinical diagnoses. Of these, 97 scored 45 or higher on Trial 2 and the Retention Trial. Two children were correctly identified as having given suboptimal effort, and only one case was a possible false positive. Performance on the second trial of the TOMM did not vary with gender, ethnicity, parental occupation, or length of coma. It was concluded that the TOMM is a potentially useful measure of effort in the clinical neuropsychological evaluation of school-age children.

Constantinou and McCaffrey (2003) also found that the TOMM was an easy test for children. For example, 7 children who were 5 years of age averaged 49.7 correct on Trial 2.

Pain Patients

Etherton, Bianchini, Greve, and Ciota (2005) studied 60 subjects assigned to take the TOMM under one of three conditions: with normal instructions ($n = 20$), with instructions to simulate pain-related memory deficits in pursuit of personal-injury litigation ($n = 20$), or while experiencing cold-induced pain as brought on by a cold-pressor test. Results indicated that TOMM performance was unaffected by laboratory-induced moderate to severe pain and support the TOMM's use in evaluating clinical patients with pain.

Forensic and Psychiatric Patients

Using a differential prevalence design, Gierok, Dickson, and Cole (2005) administered the TOMM to subjects in two groups (20 men in each). The first group, referred to as forensic, was composed of inpatients from a forensic psychiatric facility who were referred for pretrial evaluation and were predicted to do less well on the TOMM for reasons related to secondary gain. The psychiatric group was composed of male inpatients who had no pending legal involvement. As hypothesized, the psychiatric group performed significantly better than the forensic group on all TOMM trials. Only one member of the psychiatric group scored below 45 on the TOMM, compared to 7 of those in the forensic group.

In an epidemiological exploration, Greiffenstein and Baker (2006) used the TOMM as part of a validity test battery to examine the prevalence of simulation in persistent postconcussion claimants. Their sample consisted of 750 persons representing a broad range of cervicocranial injury severity and claiming subjective disability for more than 6 months. Greiffenstein and Baker found a reversed dose-response association between initial head-injury severity and TOMM scores. In other words, those with cervical strain (whiplash) made the most TOMM errors, followed by those with minor concussion

and mild closed-head injury. Persons with moderate–severe brain injury produced the fewest TOMM errors. A fair conclusion is that the TOMM represents a continuous measure of test-taking effort.

Dementia

Teichner and Wagner (2004) found a high rate of misclassification among patients with dementia who took the TOMM. While all of the normal controls and 93% elderly patients without dementia but with cognitive impairment were able to pass the TOMM, an unacceptably high number of patients with dementia failed the TOMM even when the "pass" criterion was reduced to 40 on Trial 2. The authors concluded that the TOMM is a useful test for detecting the malingering of memory deficits, but only when dementia could be ruled out.

Impressions of the TOMM

The TOMM is inexpensive and easy to administer and also seems to be a good screening measure of effort. However, it has been criticized as being too easy in that its hit rate appears to be lower than that found with other tests of effort (Tan, Slick, Strauss, & Hultsch, 2002; Gervais, Rohling, Green, & Ford, 2004). On the other hand, the TOMM has the advantage of showing expected normal scores from a large number of clinical populations (with the exception of elevated failure rate in dementia). However, because of concerns that it may be insensitive to malingerers, the TOMM might be paired with other tests of effort during evaluations where a patient's motivation is suspect.

Portland Digit Recognition Test

The Portland Digit Recognition Test (PDRT) is one of the earliest applications of forced-choice recognition testing. On this test, the examiner reads aloud a five-digit number at 1-second intervals for 72 trials. After various time intervals, the patient is asked to visually differentiate the target from a foil. Thirty-six trials are referred to as "easy," whereas the next 36 are "hard," based on apparent difficulty. The initial validation study (Binder & Willis, 1991) compared six groups of adults: nonpatient simulators, nonpatient controls, patients with affective disorders not seeking compensation, patients with brain dysfunction not seeking compensation, patients with well-documented brain dysfunction seeking financial compensation, and mild head trauma patients seeking compensation. This study did not include a clinical group of patients diagnosed as malingering.

According to a review of this study conducted by Binder (2002), the data showed that the brain dysfunction non-compensation-seeking group was significantly superior to all three compensation-seeking groups in total

PDRT score. This review examined previous studies by other investigators (Vickery et al., 2001; Ju & Varney, 2000; Greiffenstein, Baker, & Gola, 1994) and found that sensitivity (the proportion of examinees who are malingering that are correctly identified) ranged from 39% for nonpatient simulators to 56% for traumatic brain injury (TBI) patients instructed to simulate to 77% for patients with external evidence of malingering. Sensitivity in these studies was probably attenuated in that cutoff scores were used that ensured 100% specificity, so that none of the non-compensation-seeking brain-injured patients were identified as malingerers. Binder's review points out ways in which the PDRT met Daubert criteria regarding its admissibility as scientific evidence, as well as the fact that several versions of the PDRT are available. He indicates that these alternative tests are different from the original 72-item version and maintains that in cases of suspected incomplete effort it may be preferable to administer the original version given its wider validation.

The PDRT includes a distraction test during the delay interval, leading to a criticism by some (Lezak et al., 2004) that this then incorporates a working-memory component into the procedure, making it possible that patients with frontal-lobe injuries would do poorly but might nevertheless be judged as having malingered cognitive deficits. Binder (2002) has countered this assertion by illustrating that the PDRT was not sensitive to brain injury in the absence of external incentives for poor performance.

Head Injury and Probable Malingerers

Greve and Bianchini (2006a) have reviewed the classification accuracy of the PDRT using a known-groups design. The authors point out that a relatively small number of PDRT cutoff scores had been examined for sensitivity and specificity and that only one study of the PDRT using the known-groups design had been published (Bianchini, Mathias, Greve, Houston, & Crouch, 2001). In their study, Greve and Bianchini (2006a) included 262 persons referred for neuropsychological evaluation after having an apparent traumatic brain injury, whose severity was rated using objective criteria. These patients were categorized on the basis of the Slick et al. (1999) criteria for malingered neurocognitive dysfunction (MND). That is, patients with mild or moderate–severe TBI were subdivided as to whether they were judged likely to be malingering cognitive deficits, and cumulative percentages of patients from each subgroup were calculated for their PDRT easy, hard, and total scores. The authors conclude that the originally established PDRT norms were too conservative in view of the fact that they detected only between 20 and 50% of malingering TBI patients. By keeping the false positive rate to 5% in their sample, the authors found that a higher cutoff score increased the sensitivity to as high as 70%. Therefore, the authors recommended increasing the PDRT cutoff scores, which they contend increases sensitivity without sacrificing specificity.

Greve and Bianchini (2006a) comment that surveys have shown that the TOMM is a more commonly used test than the PDRT despite some evidence that the PDRT may be a more sensitive test when specificity is set at 99%. Further, the PDRT may be more sensitive to the detection of definite response bias among test-takers. Binder (1993b) found that 17% of the 103 compensation-seeking mild head trauma subjects in his study achieved scores that were significantly-below-chance levels. This rate of below chance performance has not been confirmed in other studies, but does appear to be significantly higher than that of other forced choice symptom validity tests.

The reason for the TOMM's more widespread use may be secondary to the length of time it takes to administer (15–20 minutes), without the Retention Trial. In contrast, it has been reported that the PDRT takes 40–60 minutes to administer. Binder (1993a) has developed an abbreviated form of the PDRT to avoid a lengthy task for well-motivated patients. This short form has been cross-validated by Doane, Greve, and Bianchini (2005), who demonstrated little risk of false-negative errors using the abbreviated PDRT. Length of administration still remains an issue for examinees failing the PDRT.

Impressions of the PDRT

The PDRT is the forerunner of other tests such as the Victoria Symptom Validity Test but might be considered less advantageous than its successors. The primary reason for this is the amount of time required of the psychometrician to administer the test (sometimes as much as an hour but usually closer to 40 minutes). In contrast, the VSVT is computer administered, allowing the psychometrician to attend to other matters for that interval, such as scoring other tests. Also, the PDRT has been studied primarily by its author, but this comment can be made about most other tests of its type. Otherwise, it has demonstrated good ability to differentiate patients making an acceptable effort from those who are not.

Victoria Symptom Validity Test (VSVT)

The VSVT arises from Symptom Validity Technique (Pankratz, 1979) and the Portland Digit Recognition Test (Binder, 1993b) in that it presents a five-digit number for the patient to study and remember (Slick, Hopp, Strauss, & Hunter, 1994; Slick et al., 1996). After an interval of either 5, 10, or 15 seconds, the patient has to say which of two stimuli—the correct five-digit number or a five-digit foil—had just been presented.

The VSVT differs from earlier versions of digit memory tests in at least three ways. First, it is computer administered. Second, response latencies are recorded and referred to in the interpretive report. Finally, two different types of foils are presented. One type is referred to as "easy" because all

of the digits contained within the foil differ from those in the correct answer. For example, if "12345" had been presented, the foil might be "67890." The patient ostensibly needs to recognize only one digit of the presented stimulus to correctly answer the item. The second type of foil is referred to as "hard" since it contains exactly the same digits as the presented stimuli, but the order of two of them has been switched. That is, if the presented stimulus were "12345," the hard foil might be "12435."

The 48 trials on the VSVT are equally divided (16 each) among the 5-, 10-, and 15-second delay blocks. Similarly, the test has an equal number (24 each) of easy and hard trials. These are also evenly distributed across the time blocks, so that in the first part of the test the subject completes 8 easy and 8 hard trials with a 5-second delay, and so on. Interpretation of VSVT scores is based on the binomial probability theory, in that patients who respond randomly should still be expected to perform at random levels. The authors originally considered that patients at above-chance levels (16 to 24 of 24 easy or hard items correct) would be considered as examples of "valid" effort. Scores at "chance" levels (8 to 15 of 24 correct) would be considered "questionable." Finally, "invalid" scores would be those at below-chance levels (0 to 7 correct).

Control, Simulation, Compensation Seeking, and Non–Compensation Seeking

The standardization manual (Slick et al., 1997) refers to an initial study including 95 controls (college undergraduates), 43 feigning subjects (college undergraduates), 205 compensation-seeking patients (traumatic brain-injury patients seen in a private practice secondary to litigation), and 20 non-compensation-seeking patients (seizure patients). It was found that the hard item score was the most sensitive measure of effort. With a maximum possible score of 24, the control subjects averaged 23.4 correct on the hard items, and the seizure patients (non-compensation-seeking) averaged 22.6 correct. In contrast, the compensation-seeking patients averaged only 20.1 correct, and the feigning subjects averaged 10.9.

Epilepsy Patients

Grote and colleagues (2000) compared VSVT results of 30 non-compensation-seeking patients (NCS) who were epilepsy surgery candidates against a group of 53 compensation-seeking (CS) patients, most of whom were classified as having had a mild traumatic brain injury. All 30 of the epilepsy surgery candidates scored at least 18 correct (of the maximum 24) on the hard items. In contrast, only 27 of the 53 CS patients (50.9%) scored 18 or better on the VSVT difficult items. This study supports the work of Guilmette, Hart, and Guiliano (1993) in suggesting that the application of binomial probability theory to forced-choice recognition testing does not result in the most efficient

cutoff scores for memory performance, in that only 3 of the 53 CS patients (5.7%) obtained VSVT difficult memory scores that were significantly below chance. Instead, this study (Grote) supports the idea that even those with mild to moderate cognitive impairment should be able to correctly select at least 90% of the items on forced-choice recognition testing. That is, patients should be expected to correctly answer at least 90% of the 24 difficult VSVT items, or about 21. More than 2.5 times as many NCS patients scored 21 or better in comparison to the CS sample (93.3%/35.8%).

Studies by Loring, Lee, and Meador (2005) somewhat substantiate the findings of Grote et al. (2000) but also suggest a higher rate of VSVT failure in NCS samples. They studied a much larger ($n = 120$) sample of epilepsy patients, most of whom had a focal seizure onset (with or without secondary generalization). Eighty-six of these patients (71.6% of the sample) scored at least 21 correct on the VSVT hard items. When examining scores of 18 and higher, they found that 106 patients (88.3%) of the sample scored at such a level, compared to all (100%) of the 30 epilepsy surgery patients in the sample studied by Grote et al. (ibid.). Loring and colleagues (2005) found that poorer cognitive test performance and being older than age 40 were associated with a poorer VSVT score.

Dementia, Cerebrovascular, Multiple Sclerosis, and Memory Complaints

In a second study by this group (Loring, Larrabee, Lee, & Meador, in press), the VSVT scores of 374 patients who underwent neuropsychological assessment were retrospectively reviewed. Patients were classified as either neurological (but not traumatic brain injured; $n = 297$), traumatically brain injured with no known financial incentive ($n = 49$), or compensation seeking ($n = 25$). Three other patients did not meet the criteria for any of these groups and were considered separately. The authors further divided the neurological group into subgroups based on the patient's primary diagnosis (dementia [$n = 50$], cerebrovascular [$n = 38$], multiple sclerosis (MS) [$n = 19$], or mixed [$n = 27$]) or on their having "memory complaints," but no neurologic entity was suggested from neurologic evaluation or based upon neuropsychological test findings ($n = 163$).

A relatively high number of patients in the neurologic group failed to score at least 18 correct on the VSVT difficult memory items. This ranged between 11% of both the mixed and MS groups and 22% of the group with dementia. Of course, an even higher percentage of these groups failed to score at least 21 correct, ranging between 22% of the memory complaints group and 38% of the dementia group. Overall, approximately 16% of the sample of clinical referrals failed to achieve a score of at least 18/24 compared to 12% in their other published study of epilepsy surgery patients (Loring et al., 2005). As high as the failure rate for those clinical groups appears to

be (at least in comparison to the Grote study), it pales in comparison to the rate for the compensation-seeking patients. Forty-four percent of the 25 compensation-seeking patients failed to score at least 18 correct, and 60% failed to score at least 21 correct. Loring and colleagues noted in both studies that below-chance scores were extremely rare among all groups, but when they do occur, they are almost exclusively found among compensation-seeking patients.

Why did Loring and colleagues find a higher rate of failure on the VSVT among non-compensation-seeking patients than did Grote? At least three explanations seem possible. First, Grote's study was prospective in that those authors specifically asked the epilepsy surgery candidates whether they were in the midst of any compensation-seeking activity, such as a current application for Social Security disability. A number answered affirmatively and thus were not included in the study. The number of such replies was not recorded but is retrospectively estimated to have been about 10%.

Since Loring and colleagues did not specifically ask all of their clinically referred patients about their compensation-seeking status, it is possible that they inadvertently included such patients in their study and that these patients represented a disproportionately high number of VSVT failures. A second possible explanation is cited by Loring and colleagues: because they administered the VSVT last in their battery, they speculate that some of the patients may have been tired or bored by the time they took the VSVT and perhaps were not able or motivated to give their best effort. A third possibility seems the most likely to account for at least some of the differences between the Loring and Grote studies, which is that tests of effort are not immune to significant cognitive dysfunction. Although none of the epilepsy surgery candidates in the Grote study scored lower than 18/24 on the VSVT difficult items, it is not reasonable to think it impossible for a brain-injured or brain-diseased patient to do poorly on this test. Such a possibility seems to be borne out in the studies by Loring, which had the advantage of much larger sample sizes in comparison to Grote. It would seem self-evident that as the number of patients with moderate to severe brain damage increases in a sample, so do the chances of finding cognitive deficits of sufficient magnitude as to interfere with VSVT performance.

Patients With Profound Memory Impairment

Slick, author of the VSVT, has published a follow-up study of the VSVT performance of six nonlitigating patients shown to have severe memory impairments (Slick, Tan, Strauss, & Mateer, 2003). Neurological diagnoses included aneurysm of the anterior communicating artery, Korsakoff's, anoxia, and epilepsy. Three of these patients scored 24/24 on the VSVT difficult items; the other three score 22 or 23 correct. Slick concluded that confirmed neurologic illness or injury cannot be uncritically accepted as the source of

subnormal litigant VSVT scores but also noted that the small sample size limited generalizability.

Impressions of the VSVT

Much of the research done on the VSVT has been done by the authors, and one of the independent studies (Grote et al., 2000) was not strongly confirmed by the two analyses done by Loring (Loring et al., 2005; in press), who found that about 15% of clinical patients scored 17 or lower on the difficult items. It is difficult to know whether these failures are solely attributable to Loring's use of a much larger number of subjects or whether it is because they assumed (and were not able to confirm) that none of the clinical patients were seeking compensation at the time of evaluation.

Another shortcoming of the VSVT is that there seem to be no studies of the test in pediatric samples. Nonetheless, the VSVT does offer some advantages. It is very easy to administer, although it necessitates the use of a computer. It also varies the perceived difficulty of the stimuli, which increasingly seems to be an important factor in demonstrating suboptimal performance among patients not inclined to always give their best effort. A third positive factor associated with this test is the fact that the failure rate has been demonstrated for a number of clinical populations, and it has been consistently shown that this rate is substantially lower than that of compensation-seeking samples in differential prevalence designs.

Medical Symptom Validity Test

Designed for use by physicians, the Medical Symptom Validity Test (Richman et al., 2006) is a computer-administered test that takes about 5 minutes of patient time. Reading the instructions aloud, a nurse or psychologist asks the person to watch the screen while a list of word pairs is presented twice (at a rate of 6 seconds per pair), and the person is required to select the word shown previously in the original list. This produces a total of 20 test items on the immediate recognition (IR) trial. After a delay of 10 minutes, a delayed recognition (DR) trial is performed, again using different word foils. A consistency score (CNS) calculates how well the person performs on both trials.

Simulators

In a German study (Merten, Green, Henry, Blaskewitz, & Brockhaus, 2005), 18 healthy experimental malingerers were compared with 18 controls. The simulators were instructed in how they might appear 2 years after a car accident in the context of ongoing litigation. The scenario contained a strong element of coaching about looking impaired while "not overdoing symptom presentation or else the litigant might fail testing done by an experienced

neuropsychologist using effort tests" (p. 722). The controls were asked to make their best effort. Raw score analysis showed that the controls answered correctly about 99% of the pairs on both the immediate and the delayed recall; in contrast, the simulators correctly answered only about 65% of the pairs across these two trials. The authors point out that one limitation of their study is that these German-speaking volunteer subjects were very well educated (mean level of education was 17.4 years) and that less educated patients may not do so well, creating the need for clinical validation studies. Additionally, a normal subject comparison group does not provide a meaningful contrast; in other words, the more important contrast is simulators versus actual clinical patients.

Disability Claimants

Richman and colleagues (2006) gave the MSVT to 106 patients who were undergoing an independent medical evaluation. The majority of the claimants (68) were classified as having soft-tissue injury or fibromyalgia, while the remaining patients represented a number of other presenting problems. These 106 claimants were selected from a larger sample of 296 persons presenting to an independent medical evaluation (IME) clinic, but the majority did not take the MSVT for a variety of reasons. A control group consisted of child and adult volunteers, but it is otherwise quite difficult to understand its composition. Some of the controls spoke French, others spoke English, some were adults, some were children, some were asked to try their best, others were asked to simulate impairments, and so on. These samples were ones of convenience, each collected by one of the seven authors at various clinics or private-practice operations in either Canada or the United States. Overall, it is quite difficult to comprehend the rationale for these various groups, as well as how many subjects of which type were in each one.

Further, the way in which Richman et al. have analyzed the data is somewhat confusing. Their Table 1 lists scores from nine groups, but these are not necessarily the groups listed in the participants section. Instead, the groups in the table refer to adult outpatients who passed the oral or computer-based versions of the WMT. It is difficult to understand the groups as listed in this table as compared to those described in other parts of the article. Although the authors comment that data from this and other tables are based on data published in their test article, their statement does not make the information easier to follow, nor does it reassure the reader that the authors used a programmatic series of guidelines to clearly establish a series of known groups from which to collect data.

After reviewing the outcomes of this disparate series of groups, Richman et al. conclude that the only people found to have genuine difficulty with the MSVT recognition subtests were patients with dementia sufficient to render them incapable of living independently. They point out that non-French-speaking subjects, who were tested in French, showed near-perfect

performance on the effort subtests, but 42% of the IME patients failed the tests in their native English. These particular data alone provide compelling evidence for the simple level of difficulty of the MSVT (i.e., persons who are tested in a language they do not know can achieve a nearly perfect score, compared to compensation-seeking claimants who fail the test in their native language).

Impressions of the MSVT

As mentioned earlier, the test authors have shown impressive differentiation of scores among various groups, but it is difficult to understand some of their findings. It would be of benefit for researchers other than the test authors to examine the utility of this test in a prospective study using known-group designs including suspected malingerers and programmatically defined comparison groups.

Letter Memory Test

The Letter Memory Test (LMT) was developed on the basis of a literature review that suggested that a key feature of many motivational tests is a discrepancy between face difficulty level and actual difficulty level for genuine neurological patients (Inman et al., 1998). The LMT is a computerized test wherein 45 trials are presented to the patient, each asking the patient to select the stimulus that had just been presented. The presented stimuli are letters of the alphabet, constructed from the first 10 consonant letters (e.g., *B*, *G*, *F*). Either 3, 4, or 5 letters are presented at a time, with an interval of 5 seconds before either two, three, or four choices are presented. Five consecutive trials are presented within each of the nine cells (three levels of letter length by three levels of number of foils), again for a total of 45 trials.

Standardization Studies

Inman and colleagues used four groups in their first validation study. Most of the 32 patients in the neurologic control group had sustained a moderate to severe head injury but were not involved in any compensation-seeking behavior. A control group comprised 151 college students who were randomly assigned to either a naïve or a coached malingering group. Patients in both the neurological and student control groups answered more than 99% of the items in the LMT trials correctly. In contrast, only 59% of the naïve malingering students and 65% of the coached malingering students answered the items correctly.

A second validation study consisted of five groups. These included 28 neurologic patients who were not seeking compensation, 26 patients with depression, and three groups (totaling 101 subjects) randomly assigned to

the three conditions used in Condition 1. Results showed that more than 99% of the LMT trials were passed by patients in three groups: neurologic, depressed, and normal control. The naïve malingering group averaged only 55% correct, and the coached malingering averaged only 68% correct.

The third validation study comprised two samples: a suspected motivationally impaired group ($n = 19$) and a neurologic group ($n = 21$). Patients in the suspect group had all been referred for a neuropsychological evaluation as part of a personal-injury lawsuit or disability evaluation, had not passed another test of effort, and had no other objective evidence of neurologic injury. Most of the neurologic group were patients with moderate or severe brain injuries. Again, the neurologic group averaged 99% correct, compared to only 69% in the suspect group. The authors concluded that the LMT is sensitive to feigning, shown by simulation studies using either college students or community volunteers, as well as by a group of patients seeking compensation who were suspected of poor motivation.

Compensation-Seeking Patients

Vagnini, Sollman, and Berry (2006) conducted a cross-validation study of the Letter Memory Test with a new sample of 122 compensation-seeking patients, most of whom were being evaluated secondary to an alleged traumatic head injury. All of the patients received the VSVT, TOMM, and LMT. On the basis of performance on various components of the TOMM, VSVT, or WAIS-III Digit Span tests, the patients were assigned a motivational impairment (MI) score, ranging from 0 to 5, reflecting the number of motivational indicators they had failed. Those who scored 0 had no objective evidence of inadequate effort and were classified as honest ($n = 37$). Those who failed one measure were classified as inadequate ($n = 32$), in that there was insufficient effort to place them in the honest (HON) or probable cognitive feigning (PCF) group. Fifty-three participants were classified as PCF if they scored 2 or higher on the MI index. Patients in the HON group averaged 97.0% correct on the LMT, while patients in the PCF group averaged only 79.9% correct.

The authors found that the HON and PCF groups were comparable on demographic, estimated premorbid level of function, and injury-severity parameters with the exception of significantly higher rates of disability in the PCF group and of documented loss of consciousness in HON TBI patients. Using the LMT's recommended cutting score resulted in a sensitivity rate of .640 and a specificity rate of .984 with positive predictive power at .968 and negative predictive power at .784. The authors point out the threat of the Internet, as well as coaching by attorneys and others, on other well-established measures of malingering, and suggest that the LMT may be a viable option for the detection of insufficient effort.

Other studies by Berry and colleagues include one (Inman & Berry, 2002) that shows that the Letter Memory Test and the Digit Memory Test attained higher hit rates for the detection of malingering when compared to

the 15-item test, the 21-item test, and several other measures of cognitive ability. Another study (Graue et al., in press) found the LMT to be useful in the detection of feigned mental retardation but added that new cutting scores may need to be used and validated for this purpose.

Simulated Malingering

Only one LMT study could be identified that was not conducted by the test author or his university colleagues. Greub and Suhr (2006) used a group of university undergraduate students to replicate the standardization study of the LMT and to explore the effects of coaching on the effectiveness of the LMT and then compared these results to the 15-item test. Students were quasi-randomly assigned to groups of simulated head injury (with or without malingering detection warning) or to a group instructed to give their best effort. Using the 93% cutoff, the LMT correctly identified both 76% of the simulators and 96% of the best-effort participants. Positive predictive accuracy was 95%, and negative predictive accuracy was 81%. In comparison, the 15-item test showed limited sensitivity to malingering (17%), but with 100% specificity. The authors concluded that the LMT yielded adequate indices of accuracy in multiple comparisons of groups, did not show order effects, and was generally robust to coaching.

Impressions of the LMT

The LMT has the advantage of varying its perceived difficulty along two dimensions: apparent stimulus difficulty (number of letters presented) and number of foils. It has also been shown to discriminate well between simulators or suspected malingerers on the one hand and clinical populations or well motivated normals on the other. This test also has the advantage of being relatively new (therefore not as well known) and thus perhaps more resistant to attempts by others to coach or be coached on how to pass it. There appears to be only one publication on this test from a group not connected to the test authors. Thus, it would be helpful to obtain further independent confirmation of the utility of this test, as well as its application to other groups of patients, including children.

Computerized Assessment of Response Bias

The Computerized Assessment of Response Bias (CARB; Conder, Allen, & Cox, 1992) is a test of effort that uses a digit recognition paradigm. The basic design of the CARB follows the Hiscock and Hiscock (1989) procedure and Binder's Portland Digit Recognition Test (Binder, 1990). However, the CARB has been cited as distinguishing itself from its predecessors by having only easy items and briefer delays (Green & Iverson, 2001b). The CARB is a

computerized test that presents the respondent with 111 two-second presentations of five-digit numbers, each of which is followed by a delay (as described in ibid.). For each series of 37 items, delays for the task are 3, 6, and 9 seconds, respectively. During each delay, the respondent is asked to count backward from 20. After the delay, the respondent is presented with the original number and a foil and is asked to select the original. The CARB yields the percentage of correct scores for each of the 37-item blocks and an overall percent-correct score. Response latency is also reported. In one of the first validation studies, Conder et al. (1992) reported that a percent-correct score at or below 89% is suggestive of limited effort because this score fell below two standard deviations of their standardization sample of severely brain-injured persons.

A review of the published literature on the CARB reveals at least three different forms of the test. The original version, which was described earlier, appears to be the most commonly used. The second, the CARB-97 (Allen, Conder, Green, & Cox, 1997), has the same basic structure as the original CARB but offers an additional feature: when a participant responds to a test item correctly, a pleasant tone is emitted, and an unpleasant tone is emitted if the response is incorrect. The CARB-97 also includes only 75 trials (versus the original 111). The third form (called the revised version) appears to maintain the same basic structure as the original CARB but implements shorter delays (1.5, 2.5, or 3.5 seconds) between trials (as described in Green & Iverson, 2001a).

CARB Studies

The original validation study for the CARB consisted of a small number of severely brain-injured patients ($n = 8$) who obtained 96.8% correct (SD = 3.6%) on the task (Conder et al., 1992). Since its development, a handful of published studies have validated the test in mostly head-injury, compensation-seeking patients. The following section offers a review and critique of several of these studies.

Head Injury
One of the first published studies on the CARB (Green & Iverson, 2001b) examined 119 compensation-seeking patients who were undergoing a neuropsychological evaluation due to a reported head injury. The sample was divided into three groups: (a) the alleged mild head-injury (AMHI) group, which included 45 persons who reported no loss of consciousness or posttraumatic amnesia and no significant medical attention as a result of the head injury; (b) the mild head-injury (MHI) group, which included 49 persons with no neuroradiological evidence of head injury but who reported a positive loss of consciousness and/or had posttraumatic amnesia with Glasgow Coma Scale (GCS; Teasdale & Jennett, 1974) between 13 and 15 (for those with this information); and (c) the TBI group, which included 25 persons

reporting a mean duration of loss of consciousness of 6.9 days and a mean posttraumatic amnesia of 11.7 days. These groups did not differ in age, education, or verbal IQ (as measured by the Wechsler Adult Intelligence Scale-Revised; Wechsler, 1981). Though not reported in the study, the gender distribution per group may have significantly differed from those of the AMHI group (44% women), the MHI group (73% women), and the TBI group (8% women).

Green and Iverson (2001b) reported that the AMHI group received a total score of 89.2% correct, the MHI group had a total score of 90.1% correct, and the TBI group had a total score of 97.5% correct. The TBI group scored significantly better on the CARB than did either of the other two groups. Using a proposed cutoff score of 89% or lower for classification of less than optimal effort (as reported by Conder et al., 1992), one person in the TBI group fell below the cutoff; however, 13 persons in the AMHI group scored below the cutoff, as did 12 persons in the MHI group. With regard to latency of response, the TBI group responded significantly faster to test items than did the AMHI and MHI groups. Furthermore, there was a significant negative correlation between response latency and the percent-correct total score, indicating that the longer participants took to respond, the lower was their total score on the CARB.

With these findings in mind, performance on the CARB does not appear to be unduly influenced by degree of head trauma (Green & Iverson, 2001b). However, if one uses the reported cutoff of 89% or below, then 28% of the AMHI group and 24% of the MHI group were found to be putting forth less than optimal effort. These percentages are lower than the reported base rate of malingering in compensation-seeking people with mild head injury, which has been estimated at 39% (Mittenberg, Patton, Canyock, & Condit, 2002). These findings may be reflective of the sample, such that this sample of mild head-injury litigants was unique in that only a few persons were putting forth less than optimal effort, or it may be reflective of characteristics of the test.

In another study (Slick, Iverson, & Green, 2000), the CARB was used as a measure of test-taking effort in conjunction with the California Verbal Learning Test (CVLT; Delis, Kramer, Kaplan, & Ober, 1987) to examine the efficacy of particular CVLT indicators of limited effort. Included in this study were 193 persons who were seeking neuropsychological assessment due to a reported head injury resulting in cognitive impairment. All of the patients were seeking compensation as a result of the reported head injury. These persons were divided into two groups. The first consisted of 131 persons who were deemed to have negligible or possible mild brain injuries (NMBI) and were classified as such by having brief or no loss of consciousness (0–30 minutes) and brief or no posttraumatic amnesia (0–24 hours). The other group comprised 62 persons who were classified as having moderate to severe brain injury (MSBI) based on documentation from one or more historical or outside sources (e.g., neuroradiological evidence, GCS scores of 12 or less).

The groups were not significantly different with regard to age but did differ in years of education and gender (the MSBI group was significantly less educated and had more men).

A review of findings from the Slick et al. (2000) article is presented, particularly as they relate to the CARB. The results were in the expected direction for the CARB such that persons in the MSBI group tended to perform above the cutoff score for suboptimal effort (i.e., scoring total percent correct at or above 90%), compared to the NMBI group. This finding suggests that the CARB is less sensitive to bona fide deficits. Examining the concordance rates between the CVLT indices and the CARB, the authors note that the CVLT indices may be more sensitive than the CARB. Specifically, a number of additional cases of possible feigning (2–24%) were detected by the CVLT indices that the CARB did not detect. However it is difficult to determine whether these additional cases were false positives.

Simulators

Dunn, Shear, Howe, and Ris (2003) used a sample of 125 undergraduate students to assess the effects of coaching on the Word Memory Test (WMT; Green, Allen, & Astner, 1997) and the CARB-97. The participants were first administered the North American Adult Reading Test (NAART; Blair & Spreen, 1989) as an estimate of their intellectual functioning. After blocking for NAART scores, the participants were randomly assigned to either a control group or one of four feigning groups. The participants in the control group were told they were in a memory study and were asked to do their best on testing. All four of the feigning groups were first given a vignette to read that asked each participant to pretend that he or she was a paramedic who was assaulted while on duty. The instructions for the four feigning groups differed: (1) A naïve group was asked to feign injury but was given no information from the examiners on how to respond; (2) an informed group was asked to feign injury and given information about the behavioral symptoms of head injuries; (3) a coached group was asked to feign injury and given information about ways to cheat the test of effort but no information about behavioral symptoms; and (4) an informed and coached group was given information about head-injury symptoms, as well as ways to cheat on tests of effort. The examiners were blind to participant-group inclusion.

The results showed that coaching significantly improved the participants' responses such that those who were given advice on how to cheat on the tests scored at greater-than-chance levels on both the CARB-97 and the WMT. However, none of the feigning groups (i.e., informed-coached, informed-uncoached, uninformed-coached) performed as well as the naïve group, and most of the feigning groups scored below the cutoffs for each measure (Dunn et al., 2003). In addition, providing information on brain-injury symptoms only (i.e., informed group) did not improve the feigners' scores; rather, this group seemed to exaggerate their symptoms to a greater degree.

Impressions

The CARB is a test of effort that employs a digit recognition paradigm. It reportedly differs from previous tests that use similar paradigms by having briefer delays between stimulus presentation and response, as well as by employing only easy test items (Green & Iverson, 2001b). The test appears to be fairly noncomplex in administration, with only computer requirements limiting its ability to be administered. The CARB has been validated using primarily head-injury compensation-seeking patients, though it has also been used with the WMT in other samples (see the WMT section of this chapter). The CARB also seems to fare well against coaching for the test (Dunn et al., 2003). However, as Slick et al. (2000) have noted, the CARB is limited by its negative predictive power; consequently, false negatives may be common. Certainly, one way to attempt to guard against this would be to employ more than one test of effort, which Lynch (2004) has advised.

Future research with the CARB should compare the different versions of this test, including the CARB, the CARB-Revised, and the CARB-97. It would seem helpful to the users of the test to better understand the nuances between these measures. In addition, much research has been done comparing and/or employing the CARB and the WMT. As these are reported to be distinct rather than companion measures, it would seem advisable to continue to compare the CARB against other measures of symptom validity to better understand its psychometric properties and ability to detect those putting forth limited effort.

Word Memory Test

The Word Memory Test (WMT; Green, 2005) uses a word recognition paradigm to assess both test-taking effort and verbal memory. The test can be orally administered by an examiner but also has a computerized version requiring less examiner involvement. A publication by Allen and Green (2002) shows that the two different administrations are fairly similar. During the administration of this test, the respondent is shown two learning trials of 20 semantically related word pairs (as described in Green et al., 2002). Next, the respondent is presented with an immediate recognition task and is asked to select target words from foils. After a 30-minute delay, the respondent is asked again to select target words from distractors. This results in both immediate recognition and delayed recognition scores. A consistency score is calculated by comparing the number of words recognized during both the IR and the DR trials. That is, the CNS score is based on the number of words recognized consistently across both trials (Green, Iverson, & Allen, 1999). Scores at or below 82.5% correct are considered as exceeding the cutoff (e.g., Iverson, Green, & Gervais, 1999).

As described in the published literature (e.g., Green et al., 2002), four memory trials are administered after the DR trial. The first two are cued memory tests, including multiple choice and paired associates tasks. The third is a free recall task, administered after the paired associates task, and the fourth is a free recall task, administered 20 minutes after the third recall task.

WMT Studies

The WMT has been studied primarily by its developers in a number of populations, including both simulators and a variety of patient samples (e.g., head injury, psychiatric samples). A review and critique of a selection of these studies follows.

Head Injury

In one of the first published validation studies of the WMT using a patient sample, Green et al. (1999) assessed 298 patients referred for a neuropsychological assessment in connection with head-injury litigation. Sixty-four of the patients were termed definite traumatic brain injury, and 234 cases were termed mild head injury, based on the results from one or more of the following indicators: length of posttraumatic amnesia, Glasgow Coma Scale, neuroimaging results, and length of loss of consciousness. For example, the participants in the definite traumatic brain-injury group were described as having an average posttraumatic amnesia of 16.4 days (SD = 24), and those in the mild head-injury group had posttraumatic amnesia for less than one day (or not at all). The authors reported that there were no differences between the mild and definite brain-injury groups in terms of verbal IQ or years of education. Both groups were described as being of about average intelligence and having around 12 years of education. The participants were administered the computerized WMT in conjunction with a larger neuropsychological test battery that also included the Computerized Assessment of Response Bias (Allen et al., 1997), another test of effort.

Results were reported to show that persons in the definite brain-injury litigation group performed at or above 90% correct on the IR, DR, and CNS, which was statistically significantly better than the mild head-injury litigation group, whose mean scores ranged from 84.8% to 88.0% correct on these indices (Green et al., 1999). The authors then eliminated those from their statistical analyses who failed the CARB in order to examine what would happen to the percentage of correct scores on the WMT. The results showed that, when these people were eliminated, the WMT percent-correct scores rose to 89.3% correct or above on IR, DR, and CNS across both groups. When using the CARB as the standard for less than optimal effort, two persons from the definite brain-injury group were identified as putting forth limited effort (though their IR and DR scores were above 90% correct on the WMT), and 56 persons from the mild head-injury group were eliminated

whose mean percent-correct scores on the IR, DR, and CNS were 73.3%, 68.6%, and 70.5% correct, respectively. In sum, Green et al. (ibid.) described these results as constituting evidence that the WMT is "relatively insensitive to brain damage" (p. 817) but sensitive to limited test-taking effort.

Examining the results of this study, one might conclude that only 56 persons from the mild head-injury group were definitely feigning symptoms, as identified by the CARB independently of the WMT. However, one could argue that these were the same subjects who were the least sophisticated at exaggerated symptom presentation; other more sophisticated feigners may have been present in the sample but were perhaps harder to detect. As Slick et al. (1999) have noted, there are various levels of diagnostic certainty when examining malingered neurocognitive disorders (e.g., definite, probable, and possible). Furthermore, when looking at the range of scores for the IR, DR, and CNS in the mild head-injury group presumed to be putting forth adequate effort (i.e., as identified by their CARB scores), at least some of the subjects scored below 90% correct. For example, Green et al. (1999) report a mean score of 89.3% correct for the CNS with a standard deviation of 11.9, which raises the possibility that someone scored 77.4. An analysis of those who pass the CARB but fail some aspect of the WMT or vice versa would perhaps give us a better understanding of the sensitivity and specificity of both of those tests, particularly when compared to independent measures of symptom validity so that there is no contamination of predictor with criterion.

Neurological and Psychiatric Patients

Green, Rohling, Lees-Haley, and Allen (2001) assessed 904 patients, of whom 470 had a head injury, 80 had another neurological diagnosis, 107 had psychiatric complaints, and 246 reported medical problems (the article listed 246 for this last group, but this number should likely be 247). Of the 904 patients, 889 were seeking external incentives, such as disability. With regard to tests of effort, the participants were given the CARB, the WMT (version not specified), and a measure of effort calculated from the patients' California Verbal Learning Test score (see Millis & Volinsky, 2001). The patients were administered up to 43 measures of neuropsychological functioning, with a mean number of 34 measures per person. An overall test battery mean was computed by converting the patients' raw scores into z scores using normative data (Green et al., 2001).

According to Green and colleagues (ibid.), the results indicated that overall neurobehavioral performance (as measured by the overall test battery mean) was significantly worse in people who failed the WMT across all patient groups (ibid.). In addition, patients with less neurological impairment (e.g., no loss of consciousness with head injury) performed worse on the overall test battery mean compared to severely injured persons. When those who failed the WMT were eliminated, performance was in the expected direction. That is, more severe neurological impairment was associated with more impaired neurobehavioral functioning (ibid.).

Although Green et al. (ibid.) present an interesting study showing the use of the WMT as a test of effort in a primarily compensation-seeking sample, the study employs some computations that are difficult to follow. For example, the authors cite Heaton norms (Heaton, Grant, & Matthews, 1991) as a type of normative data used in the computation of z scores (for the test battery overall mean), but it is unclear whether all of the normative data used in the calculation of z scores were age and education corrected. Green and colleagues (2001) also note that an average of 34 out of a total of 43 measures were given per patient, but they provide no further explanation as to which measures were not administered.

Simulators

Green and colleagues have published a number of studies on the efficacy of the WMT as a measure of effort. Using four case examples, Iverson, Green, and Gervais (1999) have reported that consistent impairments on the IR and DR scales are not easily feigned. In addition, the WMT has been examined using both community-dwelling and patient simulators; the results were reported to show that simulators (even those described as sophisticated) scored below 90% correct on IR, DR, and CNS measures, while those putting forth maximal effort scored above 90% on these scales (Green et al., 2002).

Children

Green and Flaro (2003) have examined the WMT with children (ages 7 to 18 years), and the preliminary results suggest that those with at least a third-grade reading level should be able to complete the WMT effort measures at 90% correct or higher.

Comparison to Other Tests of Effort

Litigation

Only a handful of studies have investigated the effectiveness of the WMT in comparison to other tests of effort. Gervais et al. (2004) compared the Test of Memory Malingering (TOMM; Tombaugh, 1996), the WMT, and the CARB in a sample of 519 patients referred for personal injury or disability assessments. Of these patients, 35% failed at least one test of effort, and the authors noted that few if any of the participants performed at below-chance levels on any of the tests. Failure rates varied per measure, with 32% failing the WMT, 17% failing the CARB, and 11% failing the TOMM. Gervais et al. (ibid.) examined the likelihood that the WMT may be prone to false positives by examining the performance on cognitive testing (using the overall test battery mean, a computation described earlier in this text). The overall test battery mean was significantly lower in the WMT group when compared to those who passed all three effort measures. These authors suggest that this finding lends credibility to the notion that the WMT is more sensitive to exaggerated cognitive deficits.

Simulators

Using undergraduate controls ($n = 25$) and simulators ($n = 27$), Tan et al. (2002) compared participants' performance on the TOMM, the Victoria Symptom Validity Test (VSVT; Slick, Hopp, Strauss, & Thompson, 1997), and the WMT. First, the participants were told to imagine having been involved in a car accident 6 months prior to their involvement in the study. Then it was explained that they would come back to complete the cognitive testing later. The controls were told to do as well as they could on the upcoming tests, while the simulators were told to feign cognitive deficits but to try not to be detected. Both groups were encouraged to look up materials that might be helpful to them in deciding how to perform on the testing before returning to complete the experiment.

Upon their return, the participants from both groups reported that they used the Internet most frequently as a resource, and the majority of the simulators listed memory complaints as the strategy most often employed to feign brain injury. The results of logistic regression analyses showed that the VSVT (easy and hard items) appeared to be the best at classifying persons into their respective groups and the TOMM was the least effective. Using the cutoffs listed by the respective test manuals, Tan et al. found that the TOMM was the least effective in classifying the participants and the WMT was the most. Compared to the TOMM and the VSVT, the WMT was rated as the least face-valid test of effort, with approximately one third of the participants believing it to be a test of memory.

According to the study by Tan et al. (ibid.), people may use the Internet as a way to learn how to change their performance on cognitive testing, possibly to feign greater impairment. Bauer and McCaffrey (2006) have examined the information available on the Internet pertaining to the TOMM, the VSVT, and the WMT, using Google as the search engine. Of these three measures, the WMT was rated as having the least information available to assist someone in becoming a more sophisticated feigner on this test.

Impressions

As with any test of neurobehavioral functioning, the psychologist needs to be an educated consumer of the psychometric properties of the test and the situations in which it would be most applicable. With this in mind, the WMT appears to have definite strengths. First, it was found to have the least information available on the Internet to assist in coaching on the test (ibid.). With regard to validation samples, the WMT has more than 2,800 persons with a range of diagnoses and ages as reported in the test manual (Green, 2005; Green & Flaro, 2003). The WMT also appears to have good sensitivity in comparison to other forced-choice symptom-validity tests (Gervais et al., 2004; Tan et al., 2002). However, with good test sensitivity, test specificity may be questioned (i.e., false positives). This issue has been addressed in part in an article by Gervais et al. (2004).

Other areas also warrant further clarification or study. For example, in reviewing the available published studies on the WMT and its test manual, we have found it difficult to determine whether the study samples overlap and which participants, if any, are included only in the test manual or the published studies. Further clarification and delineation of these points would be helpful for users of the test. In addition, the WMT has been researched primarily by the developers of the test, who used the CARB as its primary comparison measure. A reasonable next step would be for researchers from outside laboratories to continue to examine the construct validity of the WMT in comparison to other measures of effort, using known-groups designs.

Validity Indicator Profile

The Validity Indicator Profile (Frederick, 1997; Frederick & Crosby, 2000) comprises both nonverbal (VIP-NV) and verbal (VIP-V) subtests that can be administered separately or as companion measures. Both subtests use a two-alternative forced-choice response paradigm and are designed to be fairly self-administering. The VIP-NV contains 100 nonverbal abstraction problems (or picture-matrix problems, as described by Fredrick, 2002), in which the user selects either a correct answer or a foil. The stimuli for the VIP-NV are modified items from the Test of Nonverbal Intelligence (Brown, Sherbenou, & Johnsen, 1982). The VIP-V contains 78 word definition items. The respondent is presented with a stimulus word and then must decide which of two choices is more similar semantically to the stimulus word. In both the VIP-NV and the VIP-V subtests, the items are not arranged in order from hardest to easiest but rather are varied in their presentation of difficulty (Frederick & Crosby, 2000).

Scoring of both subtests is typically done by computer since advanced statistical analyses are employed (e.g., Lezak et al., 2004). A brief overview of the terms and process used in the analyses is provided here (for a more detailed review see Frederick, 1997; Frederick, Crosby, & Wynkoop, 2000). One of the first steps is to score each item as either $1 =$ correct response or $0 =$ incorrect. Then the items are reordered by degree of difficulty (Frederick, 2002). Next, they are averaged in terms of *running means,* which are representations of average test performance on runs of 10 consecutive test items (ordered by degree of difficulty). For example, the first running mean would be the proportion of correct answers achieved on the ten easiest items (Frederick et al., 2000). The second running mean is calculated by dropping the score for the easiest item and adding the score from the next most difficult item. This process continues until the most challenging item is used in the calculation.

For the VIP-NV, which has 100 items, 91 running means would be calculated. These are plotted with item difficulty on the x-axis and the proportion correct on the y-axis, resulting in a performance curve (Frederick & Crosby,

2000). The responses of those who exert optimal effort and know the correct response would generate a running mean at or near perfect (values 1.0 to 0.8); when performance is random (possibly indicating a ceiling item for the respondent), the running mean value is at chance levels (value 0.5). The shape of the performance curve of compliant responders should remain fairly consistent despite different ceiling items. That is, the shape should remain fairly similar across different ability levels (ibid.).

The calculations also utilize several measures of consistency (ibid.), including (a) the consistency ratio (CR), which indicates how frequently the respondent answered items of the same difficulty correctly; (b) the norm conformity index (NCI), which determines the extent to which the respondent's correct answers were made before incorrect ones and is based on normative data; and (c) the individual consistency index (ICI), which calculates an individual's average responses across five parallel-item sets.

The measure also examines interaction scores, including the score by correlation (SCC) and the slope by consistency ratio (SLCR). These validity measures are used in the decision rules for classification into VIP types. Specifically, the VIP offers a fourfold classification system for response validity based on motivation (i.e., motivation to fail or excel) and effort (i.e., low or high; Fredrick et al., 2000). Of the four possible classifications, three are indicative of invalid responding: (a) the careless response style, which is based on low effort but decent motivation; (b) the irrelevant response style, which is marked by a low effort to exhibit failure; and (c) the malingered response style, which represents a high effort to fail. Fredrick et al. (2000) state that the VIP offers a conservative classification of malingering by reserving the term for only those who have no other explanation for their poor performance. The last classification category—the compliant response style— is the only classification for valid responding and is characterized by high effort and motivation to excel.

VIP Studies

Only a limited number of peer-reviewed publications about the psychometric properties and efficacy of the VIP are available (most of the existing publications have been authored primarily by the developer of the test). Lezak and colleagues (2004) have commented on this point as well, citing the cost of scoring each profile as a limiting factor for studying this measure. With this in mind, we offer a review and critique of the available published articles.

Clinical, Nonclinical Controls, and Nonclinical Simulators

Frederick and Crosby (2000) have published two companion studies as part of the development phase of the VIP. In the first study, they assessed both clinical ($n = 104$) and nonclinical ($n = 944$) participants. The nonclinical group consisted of college students and the employees of a computer

company; the nonclinical sample was predominantly female, 18–25 years of age, caucasian, and had some college or technical school education. These individuals were divided into "compliant" (those putting forth effort) and "noncompliant" (those asked to feign believable impairment). Of the noncompliant or simulator group, some of the participants were provided strategies on how to avoid detection of malingering, and some were offered $20 if their performance was believable.

The clinical group consisted of 104 patients, some of whom were litigating, while others were seeking assessment as part of their clinical care. In total, the clinical sample appeared to have slightly more men than women; most were 26–45 years of age, white, and high school educated. The clinical group was also broken into compliant and noncompliant respondents, based on their performance on the Rey 15-Item Test (Rey, 1958), the Word Recognition Test (Rey, 1941), the Dot Counting Test (ibid.,), and clinical ratings. It is not clear from the article, however, how many people were in each subgroup (e.g., clinical noncompliant). In addition, it is unclear whether the groups had underlying demographic differences. For example, qualitatively, the clinical group appeared to be older than the nonclinical group, but the text provided no quantitative analysis.

Based on a priori classifications of these participants, Frederick and Crosby (ibid.) developed decision rules for the VIP's primary validity indicators (CR, NCI, curvature, SCC, and SLCR) that would correctly classify 90% of the compliant participants' performance as valid. They stated that they were equally concerned about false negatives and false positives and thus determined this cutoff score (i.e., setting the false-positive rate to 10%; 1.0 minus specificity of 90%).

After determining the decision rules for the primary validity indicators, Frederick and Crosby (ibid.) sought to cross-validate these decisions rules by using five different assessment groups. The first group comprised participants with traumatic brain injury (TBI; $n = 61$). All of the TBI group members had sustained a closed-head injury within 36 months of participation, had documented injury from neuroimaging or electroencephalogram, and had a Glasgow Coma Scale of less than 13 at the time of admission. There was no mention of whether these participants were seeking compensation, though presumably they were not. These patients were paid for their participation.

The second group consisted of patients at risk for malingering cognitive deficits ($n = 49$) who participated as part of a clinical evaluation, were seeking compensation, and claimed cognitive deficits but had normal findings on medical examination. These patients were not reimbursed for inclusion in the study. The third group was composed of 100 compliant (putting forth maximal effort) community-dwelling participants, and the fourth group was made up of 52 community-dwelling coached simulators. The simulators were given detailed information about the nature and symptoms of brain injury, watched a video on the topic, and were told that they would

receive extra money for a fundraiser if they could fake symptoms in a believable manner. In addition, all of the community-dwelling participants earned money for a fundraiser for their participation in the study. The fifth comparison group contained 50 VIP response sets that were randomly generated by the computer and entered into the analyses as noncompliant participants. There was no report as to whether demographic characteristics significantly differed across the four participant groups.

The participants in the cross-validation study completed the VIP, the Rey malingering tests (listed earlier), and the Portland Digit Recognition Test (Binder, 1993b). For the validation study, the rate of false positives was set at 10% for the VIP-V and the VIP-NV. In the cross-validation study, the VIP-NV false-positive rate reportedly increased to 14%, and for the VIP-V, it rose to 17%. Frederick and Crosby (2000) also found that the VIP had greater incremental validity and sensitivity than either the Rey tests or the PDRT, but they stated that the latter two tests had better specificity.

The results were also reported to show that the VIP-NV correctly classified 79.8% of participants, with 73.5% sensitivity and 85.7% specificity (ibid.). The VIP-V's classification rate was reported to be 75.5%, with 67.3% sensitivity and 83.1% specificity. The rate of agreement, kappa, between VIP-V and VIP-NV was significant ($p < 0.001$). For the VIP-NV, the number of persons identified as responding in a valid manner ranged from 93% (compliant, honest normals) to 0% (noncompliant, computer-generated, random responders). For the VIP-V, the number of persons selected as responding in a valid manner ranged from 95% (compliant, honest normals) to 100% (noncompliant, computer-generated, random responders). The largest discrepancy between the VIP-NV and the VIP-V occurred with the noncompliant, suspected malingering group, where the VIP-NV classified 55% of these persons as valid responders, and the VIP-V classified 73% as valid responders. For the simulator group, the VIP-NV classified 27% as valid responders, and the VIP-V classified 25% as valid responders.

These results raise several questions. For example, the number of suspected malingerers and simulators classified as valid responders raises concerns about the psychometric properties of the test. Another question has to do with the discrepancy between valid and invalid responses in the VIP-NV and the VIP-V scales. In addressing these issues, Frederick and Crosby (ibid.) propose that some variability in the performance of the simulators and the suspected malingerers may be attributed to what symptoms these individuals wanted to feign or how compliant they were in feigning symptoms. They also state that the suspected malingering group may have been contaminated by persons who were putting forth more effort. In any event, further study seems warranted.

Criminal Defendants

Frederick et al. (2000) conducted another study of the VIP-NV by examining the responses of 737 male pretrial defendants referred for a mental health

evaluation. The majority of participants were white (56.2%) and had a mean age of 36.6 (SD = 10.9) and mean years of education of 10.7 (SD = 3.3). The reasons for referral varied, but most of the participants ($n = 522$) were referred to assess competency to stand trial. In addition to the VIP-NV, the participants completed the Rey malingering tests (described earlier in this section), and a portion also completed the Minnesota Multiphasic Personality Inventory-2 (MMPI-2; Butcher, Dahlstrom, Graham, Tellegen, & Kaemmer, 1989).

Classification of performance using the VIP-NV resulted in 415 compliant participants, 223 careless, 91 irrelevant, and 8 malingering. These results suggest that slightly more than half the population of defendants were putting forth valid effort on the test. This finding may be related to characteristics of the sample, or it may speak to the psychometric properties of the test.

Frederick and colleagues (2000) performed a series of advanced statistical analyses to assess the VIP-NV performance curve characteristics. In the first set of analyses, they established two groups called the "motivated to perform well" group (composed of people classified as compliant and careless) and the "motivated to perform poorly" group (composed of people classified as irrelevant and malingering). For the Rey malingering tests, they noted a large effect size.

Next they examined the two classification groups with presumed low effort, the irrelevant and the careless groups, and found moderate effect sizes on the Rey malingering tests. Frederick et al. (ibid.) also assessed those participants who were classified as careless responders and showed that, compared to the compliant group, this group had significantly higher scores on the MMPI-2 scales of F, Fb, and VRIN (as well as other measures of consistency on the MMPI-2). In sum, the authors felt that their research confirmed the notion that motivation and effort are two distinct constructs, therefore adding further support to the classification system for the VIP-NV.

Impressions

The VIP conceptually distinguishes itself from other symptom validity tests (SVTs) by assessing nonverbal reasoning and word definitions. This clearly adds to the existing pool of SVTs, which frequently employ recognition paradigms or memory tests. The VIP has also been cited as one of the more sophisticated tests of effort (Lynch, 2004) and offers more classifications of test-taking behaviors than other SVTs. Specifically, the VIP offers three categories for invalid responders and one for valid responding, while other measures typically categorize respondents into two groups, valid or invalid.

The test, however, has some drawbacks. The advanced statistical analyses in the computations of the fourfold classification system and in the

published studies are somewhat difficult to fully understand. In addition, the VIP seems to have a low rate of classifying malingerers, which the authors suggest may be due to the conservative nature of the test. Moreover, a limited number of studies have assessed the characteristics of this test, although few, if any, have been published by authors other than its developer. This may in part be due to the cost of scoring each respondent's profile. A reasonable next step in the study of the VIP would be to assess the measure against more tests of validity (rather then the Rey tests and the PDRT) and to encourage researchers in other settings to investigate the test.

Summary

In this chapter we have reviewed the major forced-choice symptom validity tests, including the CARB, PDRT, TOMM, VSVT, MSVT, Letter Memory Test, WMT, and VIP. The methodology of these procedures has a long history in symptom validity testing, including data on early work on functional vision loss (Theodor & Mandelcorn, 1973) that demonstrated the utility of forced-choice testing in the detection of functional visual impairment. Later adaptations of this technique to the evaluation of noncredible memory impairment led to the prototype forced-choice memory symptom validity tests, the Hiscock and Hiscock Digit Memory Test (Hiscock & Hiscock, 1989), and the PDRT (Binder, 1990). Forced-choice SVTs are widely utilized in the evaluation of test performance validity (Sharland & Gfeller, in press) and appear to be among the most sensitive freestanding measures of symptom validity (Vickery et al., 2001).

References

Allen, L. M., Conder, R. L., Green, P., & Cox, D. R. (1997). *CARB-97 manual for the computerized assessment of response bias.* Durham, NC: CogniSyst.

Allen, L. M., & Green, P. (2002). Equivalence of the computerized and orally administered Word Memory Test effort measures. *WebPsychEmpiricist.* Retrieved February 21, 2007, from http://www.wpe.info/papers_table.html

Ashendorf, L., Constantinou, M., & McCaffrey, R. J. (2004). The effect of depression and anxiety on the TOMM in community-dwelling older adults. *Archives of Clinical Neuropsychology, 19,* 125–130.

Bauer, L., & McCaffrey, R. J. (2006). Coverage of the Test of Memory Malingering, Victoria Symptom Validity Test, and Word Memory Test on the Internet: Is test security threatened? *Archives of Clinical Neuropsychology, 21,* 121–126.

Bianchini, K. J., Mathias, C. W., Greve, K. W., Houston, R. J., & Crouch, J. A. (2001). Classification accuracy of the Portland Digit Recognition Test in traumatic brain injury. *The Clinical Neuropsychologist, 15,* 461–470.

Binder, L. M. (1990). Malingering following minor head trauma. *The Clinical Neuropsychologist, 4,* 25–36.

Binder, L. M. (1993a). An abbreviated form of the Portland Digit Recognition Test. *The Clinical Neuropsychologist, 7,* 104–107.

Binder, L. M. (1993b). Assessment of malingering after mild head trauma with the Portland Digit Recognition Test. *Journal of Clinical and Experimental Neuropsychology, 15,* 170–182.

Binder, L. M. (2002). The Portland Digit Recognition Test: A review of validation data and clinical use. *Journal of Forensic Neuropsychology, 2,* 27–41.

Binder, L. M., & Willis, S. C. (1991). Assessment of motivation after financially compensable minor head trauma. *Psychological Assessment, 3,* 175–181.

Blair, J. R., & Spreen, O. (1989). Predicting premorbid IQ: A revision of the national adult reading test. *The Clinical Neuropsychologist, 3,* 129–136.

Brown, L., Sherbenou, R. J., & Johnsen, S. K. (1982). *Test of Nonverbal Intelligence.* Austin, TX: Pro-Ed.

Butcher, J. N., Dahlstrom, W. G., Graham, J. R., Tellegen, A., & Kaemmer, B. (1989). *MMPI-2: Manual for administration and scoring.* Minneapolis: University of Minnesota Press.

Conder, R., Allen, L., & Cox, D. (1992). *Computerized Assessment of Response Bias test manual.* Durham, NC: CogniSyst.

Constantinou, M., & McCaffrey, R. (2003). Using the TOMM for evaluating children's effort to perform optimally on neuropsychological measures. *Child Neuropsychology, 9,* 81–90.

Delis, D. C., Kramer, J. H., Kaplan, E., & Ober, B. A. (1987). *California Verbal Learning Test: Adult version.* San Antonio: Psychological Corp.

Demakis, G. (2004). Application of clinically derived malingering cutoffs on the CVLT and the WAIS-R to an analog malingering study. *Applied Neuropsychology, 15,* 220–226.

Doane, B. M., Greve, K. W., & Bianchini, K. J. (2005). Agreement between the abbreviated and standard Portland Digit Recognition Test. *The Clinical Neuropsychologist, 19,* 99–104.

Donders, J. (2005). Performance on the Test of Memory Malingering in a mixed pediatric sample. *Child Neuropsychology, 11,* 221–227.

Dunn, T. M., Shear, P. K., Howe, S., & Ris, M. D. (2003). Detecting neuropsychological malingering: Effects of coaching and information. *Archives of Clinical Neuropsychology, 18,* 121–134.

Etherton, J., Bianchini, K., Greve, K., & Ciota, M. (2005). Test of Memory Malingering is unaffected by laboratory-induced pain: Implications for clinical use. *Archives of Clinical Neuropsychology, 20,* 375–384.

Frederick, R. I. (1997). *Validity Indicator Profile manual.* Minnetonka, MN: NCS Assessments.

Frederick, R. I. (2002). Detection of response bias in forensic neuropsychology. *Journal of Forensic Neuropsychology, 2,* 125–145.

Fredrick, R. I., & Crosby, R. D. (2000). Development and validation of the Validity Indicator Profile. *Law and Human Behavior, 24,* 59–82.

Fredrick, R. I., Crosby, R. D., & Wynkoop, T. E. (2000). Performance curve classification of invalid responding on the Validity Indicator Profile. *Archives of Clinical Neuropsychology, 15,* 281–300.

Gervais, R. O., Rohling, M. L., Green, P., & Ford, W. (2004). A comparison of WMT, CARB, and TOMM failure rates in non-head-injury disability claimants. *Archives of Clinical Neuropsychology, 19,* 475–487.

Gierok, S., Dickson, A., & Cole, J. (2005). Performance of forensic and nonforensic adult psychiatric inpatients on the Test of Memory Malingering. *Archives of Clinical Neuropsychology, 20,* 755–760.

Graue, L., Berry, D., Clark, J., Sollman, M. J., Cardi, M., Hopkins, J., et al. (in press). Identification of feigned mental retardation using the new generation of malingering detection instruments. *The Clinical Neuropsychologist.*

Green, P. (2005). *Green's Word Memory Test for Microsoft Windows: User's manual.* Seattle: Green's Publishing.

Green, P., Allen, L. M., & Astner, K. (1997). *The Word Memory Test: A user's guide to the oral and computer-administered forms.* Durham, NC: CogniSyst.

Green, P., & Flaro, L. (2003). Word Memory Test performance in children. *Child Neuropsychology, 9,* 189–207.

Green, P., & Iverson, G. L. (2001a). Effects of injury severity and cognitive exaggeration on olfactory deficits in head-injury compensation claims. *NeuroRehabilitation, 16,* 237–243.

Green, P., & Iverson, G. L. (2001b). Validation of the Computerized Assessment of Response Bias in litigating patients with head injuries. *The Clinical Neuropsychologist, 15,* 492–497.

Green, P., Iverson, G. L., & Allen, L. (1999). Detecting malingering in head-injury litigation with the Word Memory Test. *Brain Injury, 13,* 813–819.

Green, P., Lees-Haley, P. R., & Allen, L. M., III. (2002). The Word Memory Test and validity of neuropsychological test scores. *Journal of Forensic Neuropsychology, 2,* 97–124.

Green, P., Rohling, M. L., Iverson, G. L., & Gervais, R. O. (2003). Relationships between olfactory discrimination and head-injury severity. *Brain Injury, 17,* 479–496.

Green, P., Rohling, M. L., Lees-Haley, P. R., & Allen, L. M. (2001). Effort has a greater effect on test scores than severe brain injury in compensation claimants. *Brain Injury, 15,* 1045–1060.

Greiffenstein, M. R., & Baker, W. J. (2006). Miller was (mostly) right: Head-injury severity inversely related to simulation. *Legal and Criminological Psychology, 11,* 131–145.

Greiffenstein, M. R., Baker, W. J., & Gola, T. (1994). Validation of malingered amnesia measures with a large clinical sample. *Psychological Assessment, 6,* 218–224.

Greub, B., & Suhr, J. (2006). The validity of the Letter Memory Test as a measure of memory malingering: Robustness to coaching. *Archives of Clinical Neuropsychology, 21,* 249–254.

Greve, K., & Bianchini, K. (2006a). Classification accuracy of the Portland Digit Recognition Test in traumatic brain injury: Results of a known-groups analysis. *The Clinical Neuropsychologist, 20,* 816–830.

Greve, K., & Bianchini, K. (2006b). Should the retention trial of the Test of Memory Malingering be optional? *Archives of Clinical Neuropsychology, 21,* 117–119.

Grote, C., Kooker, E., Garron, D., Nyenhuis, D., Smith, C., & Mattingly, M. (2000). Performance of compensation-seeking and non-compensation-seeking samples on the Victoria Symptom Validity Test: Cross-validation and extension of a standardization study. *Journal of Clinical and Experimental Neuropsychology, 22,* 709–719.

Guilmette, T., Hart, K., & Guiliano, A. (1993). Malingering detection: The use of a forced-choice method in identifying organic versus simulated memory impairment. *The Clinical Neuropsychologist, 7,* 59–69.

Hartman, D. E. (2002). The unexamined lie is a lie worth fibbing: Neuropsychological malingering and the Word Memory Test. *Archives of Clinical Neuropsychology, 17*, 709–714.

Heaton, R. K., Grant, I., & Matthews, C. G. (1991). *Comprehensive norms for an extended Halstead-Reitan Battery.* Odessa, FL: Psychological Assessment Resources.

Hiscock, M., & Hiscock, C. K. (1989). Refining the forced-choice method for the detection of malingering. *Journal of Clinical and Experimental Neuropsychology, 11*, 967–974.

Inman, T., & Berry, D. (2002). Cross-validation of indicators of malingering: A comparison of nine neuropsychological tests, four tests of malingering and behavioral observations. *Archives of Clinical Neuropsychology, 17*, 1–23.

Inman, T., Vickery, C., Berry, D., Lamb, D., Edwards, C., & Smith, G. (1998). Development and initial validation of a new procedure for evaluating adequacy given during neuropsychological testing: The Letter Memory Test. *Psychological Assessment, 10*, 128–139.

Iverson, G., Franzen, M., & McCracken, L. (1991). Evaluation of an objective assessment technique for the detection of malingered memory deficits. *Law and Human Behavior, 15*, 667–676.

Iverson, G., Green, P., & Gervais, R. (1999, March/April). Using the Word Memory Test to detect biased responding in head-injury litigation. *Journal of Cognitive Rehabilitation*, 2–6.

Ju, D., & Varney, N. (2000). Can head-injury patients simulate malingering? *Applied Neuropsychology, 7*, 201–207.

Larrabee, G. (2005). Assessment of Malingering. In G. Larrabee (Ed.), *Forensic neuropsychology: A scientific approach* (pp. 115–158). New York: Oxford University Press.

Lezak, M. D., Howieson, D. B., & Loring, D. W. (2004). *Neuropsychological assessment* (4th ed.). New York: Oxford University Press.

Loring, D., Larrabee, G. J., Lee, G. P. & Meador, J. (in press). Victoria Symptom Validity Test performance in a heterogeneous clinical sample. *The Clinical Neuropsychologist*.

Loring, D., Lee, G., & Meador, J. (2005). Victoria Symptom Validity Test performance in nonlitigating epilepsy surgery candidates. *Journal of Clinical and Experimental Neuropsychology, 27*, 610–617.

Lynch, W. J. (2004). Determination of effort level, exaggeration, and malingering in neurocognitive assessment. *Journal of Head Trauma Rehabilitation, 19*, 277–283.

Merten, T., Green P., Henry, M., Blaskewitz, N., & Brockhaus, R. (2005). Analog validation of German-language validity tests and the influence of coaching. *Archives of Clinical Neuropsychology, 20*, 719–726.

Millis, S. R., & Volinsky, C. T. (2001). Assessment of response bias in mild head injury: Beyond malingering tests. *Journal of Clinical and Experimental Neuropsychology, 23*, 809–828.

Mittenberg, W., Patton, C., Canyock, E., & Condit, D. (2002). Base rates of malingering and symptom exaggeration. *Journal of Clinical and Experimental Neuropsychology, 24*, 1094–1102.

Pankratz, L. (1979). Symptom validity testing and symptom retraining: Procedures for the assessment and treatment of functional sensory deficits. *Journal of Clinical and Consulting Psychology, 47*, 409–410.

Pankratz, L., & Erickson, R. D. (1990). Two views of malingering. *The Clinical Neuropsychologist, 4*, 379–389.

Rees, L., Tombaugh, T., & Boulay, L. (2001). Depression and the Test of Memory Malingering. *Archives of Clinical Neuropsychology, 16*, 501–506.

Rees, L., Tombaugh, T., Gansler, D., & Moczysinski, N. (1998). Five validation experiments of the Test of Memory Malingering. *Psychological Assessment, 10*, 10–20.

Rey, A. (1941). L'examen psychologique dans les cas d'encephalopathie traumatique. *Archives de Psychologie, 28*, 286–340.

Rey, A. (1958). *L'examen clinique de psychologie*. Paris: Universitaires de France.

Richman, J., Green, P., Gervais, R., Flaro, L., Merten, T., Brockhaus, R., et al. (2006). Objective tests of symptom exaggeration in independent medical examinations. *Journal of Occupational and Environmental Medicine, 48*, 303–311.

Rogers, R. (1997). Researching dissimulation. In R. Rogers (Ed.), *Clinical assessment of malingering and deception* (2nd ed., pp. 398–426). New York: Guilford.

Sharland, M. J., & Gfeller, J. D. (in press). A survey of neuropsychologists' beliefs and practices with respect to the assessment of effort. *Archives of Clinical Neuropsychology*.

Slick, D. J., Hopp, G., Strauss, E., & Hunter, E. (1994). Detecting dissimulation: Profiles of simulated malingerers, traumatic brain-injured patients, and normal controls on a revised version of Hiscock and Hiscock's forced-choice memory test. *Journal of Clinical and Experimental Neuropsychology, 16*, 472–481.

Slick, D. J., Hopp, G., Strauss, E., & Spellacy, F. (1996). Victoria Symptom Validity Test: Efficiency for detecting feigned memory impairments and relationship to neuropsychological tests and MMPI-2 validity scales. *Journal of Clinical and Experimental Neuropsychology, 18*, 911–922.

Slick, D. J., Hopp, G., Strauss, E., & Thompson, G. (1997). *Victoria Symptom Validity Test: Professional manual*. Odessa, FL: Psychological Assessment Resources.

Slick, D. J., Iverson, G. L., and Green, P. (2000). California Verbal Learning Test indicators of suboptimal performance in a sample of head-injury litigants. *Journal of Clinical and Experimental Neuropsychology, 22*, 569–579.

Slick, D. J., Sherman, E., & Iverson, G. (1999). Diagnostic criteria for malingered neurocognitive dysfunction: Proposed standards for clinical practice and research. *The Clinical Neuropsychologist, 13*, 545–561.

Slick, D. J., Tan, J., Strauss, E., & Mateer, C. (2003). Victoria Symptom Validity Test scores of patients with profound memory impairment: Nonlitigant case studies. *The Clinical Neuropsychologist, 17*, 390–394.

Tan, J. E., Slick, D. J., Strauss, E., & Hultsch, D. F. (2002). How'd they do it? Malingering strategies on symptom validity tests. *The Clinical Neuropsychologist, 16*, 495–505.

Teasdale, G., & Jennett, B. (1974). Assessment of coma and impaired consciousness: A practical scale. *Lancet, 2*, 81–84.

Teichner, G., & Wagner, M. (2004). The Test of Memory Malingering: Normative data from cognitively intact, cognitively impaired, and elderly patients with dementia. *Archives of Clinical Neuropsychology, 19*, 455–464.

Theodor, L. H., & Mandelcorn, M. S. (1973). Hysterical blindness: A case report and study using a modern psychophysiological technique. *Journal of Abnormal Psychology, 82*, 552–553.

Tombaugh, T. N. (1996). *Test of Memory Malingering (TOMM)*. New York: Multi-Health Systems.

Vagnini, V. L., Sollman, M., & Berry, D. (2006). Known-groups cross-validation of the Letter Memory Test in a compensation-seeking mixed neurologic sample. *The Clinical Neuropsychologist, 20,* 289–304.

Vickery, C. E., Berry, D. T. R., Dearth, C. S., Vagnini, V. L., Baser, R. E., Crager, D. E., et al. (2004). Head injury and the ability to feign neuropsychological deficits. *Archives of Clinical Neuropsychology, 19,* 37–48.

Vickery, C. D., Berry, D. T. R., Inman, T. H., Harris, M. J., & Orey, S. A. (2001). Detection of inadequate effort on neuropsychological testing: A meta-analytic review of selected procedures. *Archives of Clinical Neuropsychology, 16,* 45–73.

Yanez, Y., Fremouw, W., Tennant, J., Strunk, J., & Coker, C. (2006). Effects of severe depression on TOMM performance among disability-seeking outpatients. *Archives of Clinical Neuropsychology, 21*(2), 161–165.

Wechsler, D. (1981). *Wechsler Adult Intelligence Scale-Revised manual.* San Antonio, TX: Psychological Corp.

5

Identification of Malingering by Pattern Analysis on Neuropsychological Tests

Glenn J. Larrabee

Noncredible or malingered neuropsychological test performance can be detected by the use of freestanding symptom validity tests (SVTs) such as the Portland Digit Recognition Test (Binder, 1993; see chapter 4, by Grote and Hook in the present volume), the Rey 15-Item Test or *b* Test (see chapter 3, by Boone and Lu in the present volume), and by the use of atypical patterns of performance on standard neuropsychological test procedures. There are many advantages of using procedures derived from standard neuropsychological tests. First, there is a time savings, for these procedures can do "double duty," both as measures of core neurobehavioral functions (e.g., attention, memory, and problem solving) and as measures of validity of test performance. Second, they are useful when evaluating data from a previous examination in which freestanding SVTs were not administered. Finally, procedures derived from standard neuropsychological tests are useful in cases wherein the examinee detects the purpose of freestanding SVTs, either through coaching (see chapter 11, by Suhr and Gundstad in this volume) or self-guided research and modifies performance so as to "pass" the SVTs, while exerting suboptimal effort on the other tasks in the battery.

Two major approaches exist in which standard neuropsychological tests are employed to yield derived measures of response bias or malingering. The first derives scores from a single test that are atypical for neurological dysfunction, either by determining errors that are rarely made by persons with a bona fide disorder such as excessive failure-to-maintain-set errors on the Wisconsin Card Sorting Test (Larrabee, 2003; Suhr & Boyer, 1999) or by identifying atypically low performance relative to persons with true neurological

disorder, such as an unrealistically low level of performance on the Finger Tapping Test (Arnold et al., 2005; Larrabee 2003). These atypical derived patterns are reviewed by Greiffenstein, in chapter 6 on malingered sensori-motor performance; Suhr and Barrash, in chapter 7 on malingering on measures of attention, processing speed, and memory; and by Greve and Bianchini, in chapter 8 on malingering on measures of executive function. The second approach is to determine atypical patterns of performance on a battery or group of tests. This is the focus of the present chapter.

Patterns of performance characteristic of intentionally poor performance or malingering have been derived for general neuropsychological test batteries such as the Halstead-Reitan Battery (HRB; Reitan & Wolfson, 1993) and the Luria-Nebraska Neuropsychological Battery (LNNB; Golden, Purisch, & Hammeke, 1985), as well as for the Wechsler Memory Scale-Revised (WMS-R; Wechsler, 1987), Wechsler Memory Scale III (WMS-III; Wechsler, 1997b), Memory Assessment Scales (MAS; Williams, 1991), Wechsler Adult Intelligence Scale-Revised (WAIS-R; Wechsler, 1981), and Wechsler Adult Intelligence Scale-III (Wechsler, 1997a). Typically, these atypical patterns have been derived via discriminant function analysis applied to battery test scores produced by noninjured persons trying to simulate impairment from an imagined injury and have been contrasted with battery test scores produced by patients with bona fide neurological disorder, typically moderate and severe traumatic brain injury (TBI), who are not being examined in the context of presence of external incentives (i.e., nonlitigating, non-compensation-seeking clinical patients). This chapter shows that the patterns that discriminate feigned from legitimate performance are easily understood as "atypical" (e.g., presence of normal memory with impaired attention; presence of impaired immediate memory, as measured by Digit Span, but with normal memory and normal intellectual function); in other words, the patterns do not make "neuropsychological sense" (Larrabee, 1990; 2005).

In the following sections I first review malingering pattern formulae derived for the HRB and the LNNB. The 2006 survey by Sweet, Nelson, and Moberg shows that the use of batteries such as the HRB and LNNB by neuropsychologists has been in decline over the past 20 years and now represents a minority approach (7%) compared to the 93% who use flexible batteries or purely flexible approaches. Nonetheless, research on batteries such as the HRB is of historical importance, given the landmark investigation by Heaton, Smith, Lehman, and Vogt (1978), who demonstrated discrimination of non-injured simulators from severe TBI patients on the HRB using discriminant function analysis (DFA), contrasted with the general inability of skilled neuropsychologists to make this discrimination on a clinical interpretive basis. The test battery section is followed by sections on the Wechsler Scales of Memory and Intelligence and the Memory Assessment Scales and concludes with a brief review of approaches that utilize aggregation of malingering indices derived from independent tests.

Malingering on Neuropsychological Test Batteries

Identification of Malingered Head Injury
on the Halstead-Reitan Battery

Heaton et al. (1978) contrasted the ability of 10 neuropsychologists to discriminate the HRB test performance of 16 noninjured persons who were simulating impairment they imagined they would have suffered as a result of head injury and for which they were pursuing litigation from that of 16 nonlitigating patients who had suffered significant head injury. In addition to the standard HRB measures, the neuropsychologist judges were provided with WAIS IQ and subtest scores and the MMPI profiles. The neuropsychologist judges correctly classified from 50.0% to 68.8% of the subjects.

By contrast, stepwise DFA using the WAIS and HRB subtests correctly classified 100% of the cases, and a second stepwise DFA using the MMPI scales alone correctly classified all but one subject in each group. Table 1 of Heaton et al. (ibid.) shows that the simulating malingerers performed significantly *worse* on Digit Span compared to the TBI subjects; the malingerers performed significantly *better* than the TBI subjects on Category total errors and better on Trail Making B errors and the Tactual Performance Test (TPT; time per block, memory, and location). However, they performed significantly *worse* on Speech Sounds Perception, Finger Tapping, Finger Agnosia errors, Grip Strength, and number of suppressions. On the MMPI, the simulating malingerers showed significantly higher elevations on *F, Hs, Hy, Pa, Pt, Sc,* and *Si*. In a cross-validation using real cases, DFA correctly identified 64.3% of subjects involved in litigation and/or judged to show evidence of malingering; moreover, it correctly distinguished 73.8% of nonlitigating patients who were rated as putting forth full effort.

Thompson and Cullum (1991) performed a cross-validation of the Heaton et al. (1978) DFA by comparing 19 subjects judged to not have put forth good effort to 17 subjects judged to have put forth good effort. All of the subjects had sustained mild TBI, and all were in litigation or seeking disability compensation or benefits. The Heaton et al. DFAs for both the neuropsychological variables (HRB and WAIS) and MMPI failed to cross-validate in this sample. Significantly, the Thompson and Cullum subjects all had mild TBI and external incentives, contrasted with the Heaton et al. (1978) comparison of noninjured simulators with nonlitigating/compensation-seeking patients with severe TBI.

Mittenberg, Rotholc, Russell, and Heilbronner (1996) contrasted the performance of 80 noninjured persons simulating the effects of head trauma with that of 80 subjects who had suffered mild, moderate, or severe TBI and who were not in litigation or seeking compensation. The DFA equations were derived from a validation sample of 40 simulators and 40 TBI and cross-validated on the remaining 80 subjects. In contrast to Heaton et al. (1978), the Mittenberg

et al. (1996) simulators performed *worse* than the TBI subjects on the Category test. On the other hand, results that were similar to those of Heaton et al. were noted for TPT total time and Trail Making B (simulators *better* than TBI), Speech Sounds Perception, Finger Tapping, Grip Strength, suppressions, and Finger Agnosia (simulators *worse* than TBI). In addition, Mittenberg et al. (ibid.) found that simulators performed *worse* than TBI on Seashore Rhythm and Fingertip Number Writing.

In addition, the DFA based on the derivation sample correctly identified 88.75% of the subjects, with 92.5% true positives and 85% true negatives. On cross-validation, 83.75% of the simulators were correctly identified, with 80% true negatives. When the derivation and cross-validation samples were combined, the overall hit rate was 88.75%, with 83.8% true positives and 93.8% true negatives. Ten variables contributed to the DFA: Category Test, TPT time and memory, Seashore Rhythm, Speech Sounds Perception, Trails A and B, Finger Tapping, sensory suppressions, and Fingertip Number Writing. When Mittenberg et al. (ibid.) applied their DFA to the original Heaton et al. (1978) data, the simulating and TBI samples from this study were correctly classified. The Mittenberg et al. DFA also correctly identified the one malingering subject from Faust, Hart, Guilmette, and Arkes (1988), the three malingering subjects from Cullum, Heaton, and Grant (1991), and eight malingering and eight TBI patients from Trueblood and Schmidt (1993; the eight questionable malingerers were not correctly classified). Last, Mittenberg et al. used the DFA to correctly identify three cases they had directly examined and that had been identified by methods independent of the HRB as probable malingerers.

McKinzey and Russell (1997) evaluated the specificity of the Mittenberg et al. (1996) DFA using HRB profiles of 796 persons. Of these subjects, 158 had normal neurological diagnoses. The overall false positive for this sample (assumed to contain no malingerers) was 27%; for TBI, 22.5% were false positive. Of the 65 subjects with moderate/severe average impairment ratings, 40 (62%) had positive Mittenberg DFA scores. McKinzey and Russell recommended further research on the Mittenberg DFA.

In a review of the HRB formulae, Mittenberg, Aguila-Puentes, Patton, Canyock, and Heilbronner (2002) suggested that the findings of McKinzey and Russell (1997) were affected by including neurologically normal subjects, as well as subjects with neurological conditions other than TBI. They urged restriction of the formula to cases of TBI. Recently, another potential explanation of the McKinzey and Russell false positives is viable: Some of the subjects assumed not to have been malingering, may have actually been malingering. Larrabee, Millis, and Meyers (2007) selected subjects from the Halstead Russell Neuropsychological Evaluation System (HRNES; Russell & Starkey, 1993; data provided courtesy of Elbert W. Russell) to compare the sensitivity to brain dysfunction of the HRB and an ability-focused core flexible battery. Since the HRNES data were collected in the Veterans Administration Hospital System, secondary gain is a potential factor (i.e., disability

payments). In this vein, symptom validity testing was not conducted with the HRNES sample (note that this sample was collected through 1989, prior to the subsequent explosion in malingering research). Larrabee et al. (2007) applied two screening procedures to the data: (a) omitting subjects with an age-corrected scaled score of 5 or less on Digit Span, or (b) omitting subjects with an age-corrected scaled score difference of 5 or greater between vocabulary and digit span, which resulted in the exclusion of 16% of the neurologically normal sample and 50% of the neurologically impaired sample. Thus, a substantial number of the presumed false positives in the McKinzey and Russell (1997) investigation of the Mittenberg DFA may not have been actual false positives.

Luria-Nebraska Neuropsychological Battery

McKinzey, Podd, Krehbiel, Mensch, and Trombka (1997) derived a malingering formula for the Luria-Nebraska Neuropsychological Battery (LNNB) by contrasting item endorsement patterns that discriminated between 34 noninjured normal subjects instructed to feign brain impairment and 34 nonlitigating neurologically impaired patients, with all of the subjects matched on age, education, and severity of impairment on the LNNB. A contrast of 26 items (13 correlated with the simulator group, 13 correlated with the patient group) had an overall hit rate of 94%. This 26-item formula was cross-validated in 51 noninjured normal subjects simulating impairment and 202 nonlitigating, neurologically impaired subjects, yielding a cross-validated hit rate of 88%. McKinzey et al. characterized the LNNB items that correlated with malingerer status as "simple" tasks and those that correlated with patient status as "complex" tasks. This item characterization follows the general inconsistency principle of better performance on more complex than on easier tasks for persons feigning impairment (Larrabee, 1990, 2005).

There have been no cross-validations of the McKinzey et al. (1997) LNNB malingering formula by independent investigators. This is likely the consequence of the small number of practitioners (3.3%) who currently use the LNNB (Rabin, Barr, & Burton, 2005).

Memory Test Batteries

Wechsler Memory Scale-Revised

Various procedures have been developed for the Wechsler Memory Scale-Revised (WMS-R). Bernard, McGrath, and Houston (1993) derived a DFA for the discrimination of 41 noninjured normal subjects simulating brain injury from 24 TBI patients on the basis of their WMS-R scores, obtaining an overall hit rate of 85%, with 85% sensitivity and 83% specificity. On cross-validation employing 47 simulators and 20 TBI patients, the overall hit rate

was 79%, with 79% sensitivity and 80% specificity. The variables contributing to the DFA were Visual Paired Associates I and II, Visual Reproduction I and II, Digit Span, Visual Memory Span, and Logical Memory II. The authors also derived a DFA based on all 12 WMS-R variables that had a 78% overall hit rate but did not report the DFA weighting of the individual items. Bernard et al. interpreted their data as consistent with malingerers performing better on relatively more difficult tests (Logical Memory II, Visual Paired Associates II, Visual Reproduction II) than on easier ones (Visual Reproduction I and Visual Memory Span).

In the same year as the Bernard et al. (1993) article, Mittenberg's group published what has become the more widely studied DFA for the identification of malingering on the WMS-R. Mittenberg, Azrin, Millsaps, and Heilbronner (1993) compared the WMS-R performance of 39 noninjured normal subject simulators with that of 39 nonlitigating or compensation-seeking TBI patients who had a median loss of consciousness (LOC) of 48 hours (range: no LOC to 1 month or more). The DFA correctly identified 91% of the subjects, with a sensitivity of 89.7% and a specificity of 92.3%. On jackknife cross-validation, the overall hit rate was 87.2% with a sensitivity of 84.6% and a specificity of 89.7%.

Mittenberg et al. (ibid.) also compared the simulating and TBI groups on the difference between the General Memory (GM) Index and Attention/Concentration (AC) Index, noting the common finding of preserved attention but impaired memory in severe TBI (Levin, Benton, & Grossman, 1982). The TBI subjects in Mittenberg et al. had the expected pattern of higher attention/concentration ($m = 95.9$) than general memory ($m = 85.26$), whereas the malingerers had an attention/concentration ($m = 70.95$) that was *lower* than their general memory ($m = 85.33$) and *lower* than the attention/concentration mean of the TBI group. Using the General Memory minus Attention/Concentration index scores, the DFA correctly identified 83% of the cases, with a sensitivity of 76.9% and a specificity of 89.7%. There was minimal shrinkage on the jackknife cross-validation, given the subject-to-variable ratio of 78:1, with an overall hit rate of 82%. Mittenberg et al. present the probability of malingering for various General Memory minus Attention/Concentration scores and for various values of the weighted score produced by the DFA (based on Mental Control, Verbal Paired Associates I and II, Digit Span, Visual Memory Span, Visual Paired Associates I and II, and Logical Memory II).

There have been three partial cross-validations of the Mittenberg et al. (ibid.) formulae, using various nonlitigating, non-compensation-seeking patient groups. Iverson, Slick, and Franzen (2000) found that using a General Memory Index minus Attention/Concentration Index (GM−AC) difference >21 points (probability of malingering of .80 per Mittenberg et al. [ibid.]) yielded an 8% false positive rate in a sample of 332 inpatient substance-abuse program attendees. Per Table 2 of Iverson et al. (2000) a GM−AC difference

of >19 points had a specificity of 89.8%. Iverson et al. did not study the DFA based on the WMS-R subtests.

Slick, Hinkin, van Gorp, and Satz (2001) found that GM – AC difference scores above 18 points had a specificity of 93% in non-compensation-seeking men infected with HIV-1. Moreover, they demonstrated that the overall level of GM was an important mitigating factor, with more numerous false-positive errors in patients who had above-average GM scores. Even when GM–AC was >29, the false positive rate was 18.2% in patients with above-average GM (i.e., >109).

Hilsabeck et al. (2003) evaluated the specificity of the Mittenberg et al. (1993) WMS-R indices in 200 nonlitigating neurologic and psychiatric patients. Hilsabeck et al. selected DFA scores and GM – AC differences associated with a .85 probability of malingering in the Mittenberg et al. (1993) investigation (DFA = 1.39; GM – AC = 25). The specificity was 93.5% for the DFA and 91.5% for the GM–AC difference score. Patients with lower IQ scores were more likely to be classified as malingering. Misclassification was also more likely in Alzheimer-type dementia and stroke/vascular groups.

Wechsler Memory Scale-III

In 1997 the WMS-R was replaced by the WMS-III. Studies have identified subtest patterns indicative of poor effort and malingering, in particular, on subtests requiring recognition memory such as the recognition items for Logical Memory (Kilgore & DellaPietra, 2000; Langeluddecke & Lucas, 2003), Paired Associate Learning (Langeluddecke & Lucas, 2003), and Faces I (Glassmire et al., 2003). Only two studies have investigated WMS-III patterns of performance potentially indicative of noncredible performance: Lange, Iverson, Sullivan, and Anderson (2006) and Mittenberg, Patton, and Legler (2003).

Lange et al. (2006) evaluated the WMS-III performance of 145 litigating or compensation-seeking persons who were divided into two groups on the basis of their performance on the Test of Memory Malingering (Tombaugh, 1996) and the Warrington Recognition Memory Test word trial (Warrington, 1984; Iverson & Franzen, 1998): a poor-effort group ($n = 19$, primarily mild TBI) and an adequate-effort group ($n = 126$, primarily mild TBI although also including 29.4% of moderate and severe TBI). The WMS-III Working Memory Index (WMI) was subtracted from the Auditory Immediate Index (AII) and the Auditory Delayed Index (ADI), as well as from the Immediate Memory Index (IMI) and the General Memory Index (GMI) to create four memory WMI discrepancy scores.

Significant differences were found on all five of the indices, with the poor-effort group performing more poorly than the adequate-effort group. Significant differences were also found on all four memory WMI discrepancy scores, with larger discrepancies found for the poor-effort contrasted with the adequate-effort group. Further analysis with the DFA showed significant

discrimination of the poor-effort from adequate-effort groups on the basis of the GMI alone with an 82% combined hit rate; the various memory index and WMI difference scores produced much lower combined hit rates, ranging from 60% (ADI–WMI) to 63.4% (IMI–WMI). Utilizing base rates of memory minus WMI difference scores of 5% or less (derived from the WMS-III standardization sample) yielded very good specificity (range of .95 to .98 for the adequate-effort group) but very low sensitivity (range of .00 to .11 for the poor-effort group) and very low positive predictive power (range of .00 to .40).

Lange et al. (2006) concluded that the memory WMI difference scores did not appear useful for identifying poor effort in their sample of personal-injury litigants. The authors considered three possible explanations for their negative results: (a) a change in the WMS-III subtests in reference to the WMS-R, noting that for the WMS-III the Digit Span subtest no longer contributed to the WMI, whereas it had contributed to the Attention/Concentration Index on the WMS-R (also note that the Mental Control subtest also does not contribute to the WMI Index but did contribute to the AC Index); (b) the fact that the WMS-R pattern analysis research was based on analog (simulating) malingerers rather than clinical samples with poor effort; and (c) the low base rate of malingering in Australian (their sample) vs. North American samples, on which the WMS-R DFAs were derived.

Mittenberg et al. (2003) conducted pattern analyses using DFA, simulating, and head-injury comparison groups that were partially cross-validated using a known-groups design employing probable and definite malingerers. These authors contrasted the WMS-III performance of 60 noninjured normal subjects simulating the effects of TBI to the performance of 60 nonlitigating TBI patients (primarily moderate/severe TBI; 90% had CT or MRI abnormalities). Mittenberg et al. also administered the Digit Span subtest (an optional measure on the WMS-III). The simulating malingerers performed less well than the TBI patients on Visual Delayed and the Working Memory indexes and less well on the Spatial Span, Faces, and Digit Span subtests.

The DFA derived a Logical Memory I minus Spatial Span difference score that differentiated 78.3% of malingerers and 73.3% of the TBI group. Including the Digit Span resulted in a four-test DFA (Logical Memory I, Spatial Span, Digit Span, and Letter-Number Sequencing) that correctly identified 81.7% of the malingerers and 83.3% of the TBI group. Applying both DFAs correctly identified 72.1% of the probable malingering group (litigating subjects who showed evidence of multiple SVT failure). For the definite malingering group (litigating subjects who performed significantly worse than chance on forced-choice testing), 88.9% of the subjects were identified by the Logical Memory I minus Spatial Span difference score, with this value improving to 94.4% for the four-subtest DFA. Mittenberg et al. provide a table for both the difference score and the four-subtest DFAs that shows various probabilities of malingering at a malingering base rate of 40%. These data show the importance of including Digit Span in the WMS-III malingering formulae and suggest that the failure of Lange et al. (2006) to

detect poor effort on the WMS-III was largely secondary to the omission of this subtest.

Memory Assessment Scales

The Memory Assessment Scales (MAS; Williams, 1991) are available as an alternative to the Wechsler scales of memory but not as widely used (Rabin et al. [2005] found that 1.4% of those surveyed used the MAS, contrasted with 42.7% who used the WMS-R/III). Beetar and Williams (1995) contrasted the MAS performance of 30 noninjured normal subjects instructed to perform poorly (but not with instructions related to a personal-injury or compensation scenario) with that of 30 noninjured normal subjects who were instructed to perform their best. The poor-performance group performed less well than the normal-performance group on all of the subtests except the recall component of the Letters and Numbers subtest. Interestingly, on the recognition component of Letters and Numbers, the poor-effort group demonstrated a response pattern characterized by intentionally wrong answers (although not significantly worse than chance). Beetar and Williams noted the ability of the poor-effort and normal-effort groups to perform alike on the recall component of Letters and Numbers, but the demonstration of differences on the recognition trial of this test suggested that it was easier to choose rather than to construct an incorrect answer.

Ross, Krukowski, Putnam, and Adams (2003) compared the MAS performance of 21 litigation or compensation-seeking persons with mild TBI who performed within chance or below chance on the Warrington Recognition Memory test to the performance of 21 nonlitigating patients with moderate to severe TBI. They found that a logistic regression employing MAS Verbal and Visual Span subtests correctly identified 90.5% of the probable malingering group and 81.0% of the nonlitigating TBI group, with an overall correct classification rate of 86%. Contrary to findings by Mittenberg et al. (1993) regarding the utility of the WMS-R GM−AC difference scores, the difference score based on the MAS counterparts, Short-Term Memory and Global Memory, failed to yield decision rules predicting group membership beyond chance.

Wechsler Scales of Intelligence

Wechsler Adult Intelligence Scale-Revised

Mittenberg, Theroux-Fichera, Zielinski, and Heilbronner (1995) compared the WAIS-R performance of 67 nonlitigating or compensation-seeking TBI patients (most of whom had loss of consciousness beyond 20 minutes, and two thirds of whom had CT or MRI abnormalities) to the performance of

67 noninjured normal persons who simulated exaggerating or faking the effects of TBI. The subjects were matched on the basis of age, IQ, and occupation. The DFA derived an equation including Digit Span, Vocabulary, Arithmetic, Comprehension, Similarities, Picture Completion, and Digit Symbol that had a sensitivity of 76% and a specificity of 82%, with an overall correct classification of 79%. On jackknife cross-validation, sensitivity was 70% and specificity was 78%, with an overall correct classification of 74%. A DFA using the Vocabulary minus Digit Span age-scaled score difference yielded a sensitivity of 63%, a specificity of 79%, and an overall correct classification of 71%, which was essentially unchanged on jackknife cross validation (70%). Mittenberg et al. (ibid.) provide a table that lists the probability of malingering as a function of the Vocabulary minus Digit Span difference score and the DFA score. They also cross-validated their procedures (DFA and Vocabulary minus Digit Span) on published data from six independent studies of malingering and head trauma and on six clinical cases found to be probable malingerers on the basis of independent SVT information.

Millis, Ross, and Ricker (1998) cross-validated the Mittenberg et al. (1995) DFA using a known-groups design. They contrasted the WAIS-R performance of 50 nonlitigating, non-compensation-seeking moderate and severe TBI patients with that of 50 litigating/compensation-seeking mild TBI claimants who also showed chance or worse-than-chance performance on Warrington's Recognition Memory Test. The TBI patients had significantly smaller scores on the DFA, as well as on the Vocabulary minus Digit Span difference scores, than did the probable malingerers, with large effect sizes (DFA Cohen's d of 2.10; Vocabulary minus Digit Span difference, Cohen's d of 1.48).

Employing receiver operating characteristic (ROC) curve analysis, a DFA cutoff score of .10536 yielded a sensitivity of 88% and a specificity of 92%, with 90% of all subjects correctly classified. Employing the Mittenberg et al. (1995) DFA cutoff of 0 or higher yielded a slightly lower specificity, 86%, with an identical sensitivity, 88%. A Vocabulary minus Digit Span cutoff score of 2 yielded a sensitivity of 72% and a specificity of 86%, with an overall correct classification of 79%. Additional analyses demonstrated that the DFA was statistically superior to the Vocabulary minus Digit Span difference score and was not significantly correlated with education. Millis et al. point out that their research supports the generalizability of the Mittenberg et al. (1995) equations since Mittenberg et al. used an analog (simulation) design as opposed to their own clinical (known-groups) design.

Wechsler Adult Intelligence Scale-III

Mittenberg et al. (2001) demonstrated the generalizability of the WAIS-R DFA and the Vocabulary minus Digit Span formulae to the WAIS-III. They compared the WAIS-III performance of 36 nonlitigating, non-compensation-seeking TBIs (81% moderate/severe, with CT abnormalities on 92% of all cases) with that of 36 noninjured normal subjects simulating impairment and

36 litigating/compensation-seeking persons characterized as probable malingerers on the basis of WAIS-III full-scale IQ scores that were at least
15 points below the estimated premorbid level of function. The DFA from
Mittenberg et al. (1995), when applied to the WAIS-III, yielded a specificity of
83.3%, a sensitivity (to the simulated malingerers) of 72.2%, and a sensitivity
(to the probable malingerers) of 44.4%. The Vocabulary minus Digit Span
difference score yielded a specificity of 86.1%, a sensitivity (to simulated
malingerers) of 55.6%, and a sensitivity (to probable malingerers) of 25%.
The maximum positive predictive power for the DFA, 87%, was found for a
DFA score of +.2 and a malingering base rate of .5. The maximum positive
predictive power for the Vocabulary minus Digit Span, 94%, was found for a
difference score of 4 at a base rate of .5.

Greve, Bianchini, Mathias, Houston, and Crouch (2003) compared the
WAIS-R or WAIS-III performance of 37 nonlitigating/compensation-seeking
TBI patients (57% with moderate or severe injury)—none of whom had failed
the Portland Digit Recognition Test (Binder, 1993) or the TOMM (Tom-
baugh, 1996)—to the performance of 28 litigating/compensation-seeking
TBI claimants (79% with mild injury) who met the Slick, Sherman, and
Iverson (1999) criteria for probable ($n = 23$) or definite ($n = 5$) malingered
neurocognitive dysfunction.

Since there were no WAIS-R vs. WAIS-III differences for the DFA scores
or the Vocabulary minus Digit Span difference, the data were collapsed across
both versions of the Wechsler scales. Using a DFA score >0 resulted in a
sensitivity of 53% and a specificity of 83%. Increasing the DFA to $>.212$ kept
the sensitivity at 50% but improved the specificity to 89%. Using a Vocabulary
minus Digit Span difference score of 2 resulted in a sensitivity of 32% and a
specificity of 81%. The sensitivity decreased to 14%, whereas the specificity
improved to 86% using a Vocabulary minus Digit Span difference score of 4.

Greve et al. (2003) also investigated the results of using the DFA score
and the Vocabulary minus Digit Span in combination at a malingering base
rate of 30%. Requiring positive scores on *both* the DFA (>0, $>.212$) and the
Vocabulary minus Digit Span ($= 2$, 3, or 4) resulted in sensitivities ranging
from 14% to 32% and specificities that all fell at 92%. Requiring positive
scores on *either* the DFA or the Vocabulary minus Digit Span resulted in a
sensitivity ranging from 50% to 54% and a specificity ranging from 73% to
83%. Greve et al. concluded that their results indicated that a positive finding
in the presence of substantial external incentive is associated with malingering, particularly if the IQ is below expectation, based on premorbid estimated function. By contrast, a positive finding in the absence of external
incentive requires further scrutiny of the case, particularly when the IQ is
near expected premorbid level of function.

Miller, Ryan, Carruthers, and Cluff (2004) conducted a specificity study
of the Vocabulary minus Digit Span difference score, as well as the Rarely
Missed Index (Killgore & DellaPietra, 2000). These authors identified the
WAIS-III and WMS-III protocols from a nonlitigating/compensation-seeking

VA sample and a private practice. The Vocabulary minus Digit Span mean difference for 30 patients with alcohol abuse was −.63; for 43 cases with poly-substance abuse this mean was −.77; and for 27 cases of traumatic brain injury (severity not described), this mean difference was 0. A conservative Vocabulary minus Digit Span cutoff score of ≥6 misclassified only one subject with polysubstance abuse and no subjects with alcohol abuse or TBI, for an overall specificity of 99%. More liberal cutting scores were not investigated, but if the data in Table 1 of Miller et al. (2004) are pooled and the Vocabulary minus Digit Span difference scores are normally distributed, 90% specificity is reached at a Vocabulary minus Digit Span difference of 4 or more.

Iverson and Tulsky (2003) investigated the distribution of several Digit Span measures, including the Vocabulary minus Digit Span difference score, for the WAIS-III standardization sample and for the clinical groups studied as part of the WAIS-III standardization. Across all ages (16–89) for the stan-dardization group, a difference score of 5 occurred in 7.1%, and a difference score of 4 occurred in 12.5%. For the clinical groups (TBI, chronic alcohol abuse, Korsakoff's syndrome, left and right temporal lobectomy, and Alz-heimer's disease) combined, a Vocabulary minus Digit Span difference of 5 occurred in 2.8%, a difference score of 4 occurred in 6.9%, and a score of 3 occurred in 13.8%. Iverson and Tulsky suggested suspecting the possibility of malingering when the Vocabulary minus Digit Span difference score was 5 or 6 (or greater) since the base rate of occurrence in the general and clinical populations was approximately 5% or less.

Mittenberg, Roberts, Patton, and Legler (2005) compared the Vocabu-lary minus Digit Span difference scores of 59 probable malingerers (identified on the basis of failure of multiple SVTs at levels lower than the lowest score of any TBI patient in standardization studies) who were claiming mild TBI (median GCS = 15; median coma = <1 hour) to the performance of 59 nonlitigating, non-compensation-seeking patients with primarily moderate to severe TBI (median GCS = 9; median coma = 18 hours). The DFA based on the Vocabulary minus Digit Span difference score yielded a sensitivity of 76.3% and a specificity of 74.6%. The DFA score was significantly correlated with the TOMM Trial 2 (r = −.50) and with the Victoria Symptom Validity Test Total (r = −.70). Cross-validation of the DFA in independent groups of 68 nonlitigating/compensation-seeking TBI and 108 noninjured normals who were instructed to simulate malingering yielded a sensitivity of 76.9% and a specificity of 70.7%.

Aggregation of Multiple Independent Measures of Malingering

The preceding sections have reviewed malingering detection based on pat-tern analysis on neuropsychological test batteries, memory batteries, and the Wechsler scales of intelligence. Detection of malingering has also been

evaluated on the basis of using multiple independent measures of malingering derived from standardized tests. While these approaches do not represent a true pattern analysis, the data are reviewed here because they illustrate how aggregating across multiple independent indicators can improve diagnostic accuracy, a point that is key to current diagnostic models of malingering such as the criteria proposed by Slick et al. (1999).

Meyers and Volbrecht (2003) investigated the rate of failure on nine measures of response validity, eight of which were derived from standard measures of neuropsychological ability (one measure was a forced-choice procedure). Tests from which the validity measures were derived included the Rey Complex Figure Test (RCFT; Meyers & Volbrecht, 1998), Reliable Digit Span (Greiffenstein, Baker, & Gola, 1994), a 20-item forced-choice test (Brandt, Rubinksy, & Lassen, 1985), Judgment of Line Orientation, Dichotic Listening, and the Token Test (Meyers, Galinsky, & Volbrecht, 1999), Sentence Repetition and the Auditory Verbal Learning Test (Meyers, Morrison, & Miller, 2001), and finger tapping (a derived formula reported in Meyers & Volbrecht [2003] that predicts finger tapping on the basis of the RCFT, WAIS Digit Symbol, and Block Design and analyzes the discrepancy between the actual finger-tapping score and that predicted by the derived formula). The cutting scores on these nine measures were set to minimize false positives (based on prior research) and were then analyzed for failure rate across several hundred clinical cases.

Nonlitigating, non-compensation-seeking subjects with TBI (grouped by less than 1 hour LOC, 1–24 hours LOC, 1–8 days LOC, and 9 or more days LOC), chronic pain, and depression did not fail more than one of the validity indicators. By contrast, patients in litigation showed increased failure rates up to and including failure of eight out of nine indicators. Of 21 noninjured persons simulating deficit, 17 failed two or more indicators. Meyers and Volbrecht also studied a variety of nonlitigating, non-compensation-seeking patients with severe disorders and found that failure of more than two indicators was rare in noninstitutionalized patients. They concluded that their multiple indicator method was probably not appropriate for (a) persons who are untestable or under 24-hour institutional care, (b) patients with large (easily identified) CVAs that affect the ability to understand even simple directions, and (c) patients with advanced dementia or moderate to severe mental retardation.

I (Larrabee, 2003) investigated patterns of failure on embedded/derived measures of symptom validity in four groups of subjects: litigants identified as definite malingerers based on worse-than-chance performance on the PDRT; litigants identified as probable malingerers based on failure of multiple SVTs but at levels that were not significantly worse than chance; patients with moderate/severe TBI (some litigating, some not, but none with performance inconsistent with injury severity); and mixed neurologic and psychiatric samples, none of whom were litigating/compensation seeking. Five

variables were investigated, including Visual Form Discrimination (VFD; Benton, Sivan, Hamsher, Varney, & Spreen, 1994), combined (dominant and nondominant) finger tapping (FT) speed, Reliable Digit Span (RDS; Greiffenstein et al., 1994); Wisconsin Card Sorting Test Failure to Maintain Set (WCST FMS; Heaton, Chelune, Talley, Kay, & Curtiss, 1993); and the Fake Bad scale (FBS) of the MMPI-2 (Lees-Haley, English, & Glenn, 1991).

Optimal cutting scores for each of these tests were derived, contrasting performance of the definite malingerers with that of the moderate/severe TBI that kept specificity at 86% or better. For VFD, sensitivity was 48%, with specificity of 93.1%; for FT, sensitivity was 40%, with specificity of 93.5%; for RDS, sensitivity was 50%, with specificity of 93.5%; for WCST FMS, sensitivity was 48%, with specificity of 87.1%; and for FBS, sensitivity was 80.8%, with specificity of 86.2%. When the data were aggregated across the different indicators, the sensitivity improved to 87.5%, with specificity at 88.9%, for failure of *any two* indicators. The overall hit rate of 88.2% correctly identified was quite similar to the overall hit rate of 82.4% obtained by considering the five indicators as continuous variables and employing logistic regression. When failure of *any three* indicators was used as the criterion, sensitivity dropped to 54.2%, but specificity was 100%. In the probable malingerer vs. mixed neurologic and psychiatric cross-validation, failure of *any two* indicators was associated with sensitivity of 88.2%, and specificity of 100%, whereas failure of *any three* indicators had a sensitivity of 47% and specificity of 100%.

Combining the derivation and cross-validation samples (definite and probable malingerers, moderate/severe TBIs, mixed neurologic, and psychiatric samples) yielded a sensitivity of 87.8% and a specificity of 94.4% for failure of *any two* indicators. The most common pairwise failure was on the RDS and the FBS. These data show that aggregating across multiple indicators improves sensitivity of embedded indicators without appreciably altering specificity and supports the practice of relying on multiple indicators of malingering to improve diagnostic accuracy.

Victor, Boone, Serpa, and Buehler (2006) compared a noncredible group of 32 subjects in litigation who met the Slick et al. (1999) criteria for probable malingering with a group of 57 patients not in litigation or attempting to obtain disability on four embedded or derived indicators: RDS, Rey-Osterrieth Complex Figure Test (ROCFT) equation (Lu, Boone, Cozolino, & Mitchell, 2003), ROCFT/AVLT discriminant function (Sherman, Boone, Lu, & Razani, 2002), and finger tapping (Arnold et al., 2005). Cutting scores were set for the individual tests so as to minimize false positives. The sensitivity and specificity for failure of *any two* indicators were 87.5% and 96.1%, respectively. Sensitivity and specificity for failure of *any three* indicators were 54.2% and 98.0%, respectively. These values are essentially identical to the values obtained by Larrabee (2003) in his pooled derivation and cross-validation samples for failure of *any two* or *any three* indicators. Similar to Larrabee (ibid.), Victor et al. found that the two-failure contingency yielded

an overall hit rate of 93.3%, which was quite similar to that obtained by using logistic regression (96.0%), considering the four indicators as continuous variables.

The results found by both Victor et al. (2006) and Larrabee (2003) are consistent with those of Vickery et al. (2004), which show that failure of three or more validity indicators has essentially a zero false-positive occurrence (perfect specificity) in nonlitigating clinical samples (note: Victor et al. [2006] had one false positive [2%], whereas Larrabee [2003] and Vickery et al. [2004] had none). Again, the presence of profound neurological impairment and/or institutionalization is a modifying factor to consider in the evaluation of the rarity of multiple SVT failure, particularly on measures derived from standard neuropsychological tests, according to Meyers and Volbrecht (2003). The increase in sensitivity by aggregating across multiple indicators appears to occur at two positive indicators (Larrabee, 2003; Victor et al., 2006) when these are from multiple domains of function. By contrast, Vickery et al. found that sensitivity *decreased* from 89.1 for one or more indicators, to 65.2 for two or more indicators, likely because the three SVTs they studied were all freestanding, memory paradigm SVTs (TOMM; Digit Memory Test, Hiscock & Hiscock, 1989; Letter Memory Test, Inman et al., 1998) that assessed effort within one domain.

Summary

This chapter has reviewed the use of pattern analysis to identify malingering on the basis of test score profiles that are not credible for bona fide neuropsychological disorder. The majority of this work, that by Mittenberg and colleagues, has employed discriminant function analysis to differentiate the test score profiles produced by noninjured persons who were simulating the effects of traumatic brain injury for the purpose of pursuing unwarranted claims for compensation following accidental trauma from those produced by nonlitigating patients suffering significant traumatic brain injury. Replication of the DFA functions or other discriminating test patterns by independent investigators has been undertaken for the Wechsler scales of intelligence and memory. This replication has shown the generalizability of findings derived from the WAIS-R to the subsequent WAIS-III. Replication from the WMS-R to WMS-III has not occurred due to substantial changes in the nature of the subtests composing the most recent iteration of the Wechsler Memory Scale. Replication is limited for the formulae derived for the Halstead Reitan Battery and for the formula derived for the Luria Nebraska Neuropsychological Battery. This is most likely the consequence of the limited use of the HRB and the LNNB in modern neuropsychological practice (Rabin et al., 2005).

The results for the Wechsler scales of intelligence and memory have been cross-validated with both simulation designs and known-groups comparisons, although the former clearly outweigh the latter. Additional known-groups

investigations will help in further demonstrating the generalizability of the DFAs and related pattern analysis approaches beyond the research that has been conducted contrasting noninjured simulators with nonlitigating clinical patients. Some have urged caution in using DFAs that discriminate noninjured simulators from nonlitigating clinical patients because simulators do not have the same real-world incentives that clinical malingerers have (Bianchini, Mathias, & Greve, 2001). This is certainly a valid point, but this problem is more likely to impact false negative identification (i.e., miss true malingerers) than false positive identification, since nonlitigating clinical patients have been used as the comparison group to rule out clinically valid patterns of performance. If anything, simulators may overplay their hand. Hence, a positive sign on a simulator-derived DFA yields confidence in noncredible performance, whereas a negative sign does not necessarily exclude the possibility of malingering. I have used descriptive language to characterize noncredible performance based on simulator vs. nonlitigating studies such as "this claimant performed in a manner similar to noninjured persons trying to appear impaired in ways that are not characteristic of patients who have severe traumatic brain injury." Of course, the most comprehensively validated SVT (derived from either standard or freestanding neuropsychological tests) would include both simulation and known-groups research designs.

Partial cross-validation using specificity-only studies have played an important role because they demonstrate that the DFA and other atypical pattern scores rarely occur in nonlitigating clinical patients. The specificity-only studies are important, for specificity is the primary driving force in establishing positive predictive power (i.e., true positives divided by true positives plus false positives; when false positives are small, the positive predictive power can be significantly increased; see Greve & Bianchini, 2004; and chapter 2, by Larrabee and Berry in the present volume).

Finally, research on pattern analysis through DFA and, in more recent times, logistic regression provides important empirical confirmation of inconsistencies characteristic of malingering. The work of Mittenberg and others in this area has supported observations derived from clinical experience and logical and scientific reasoning in confirming that, indeed, attention is not substantially lower than memory in bona fide neuropsychological dysfunction, but it is characteristic of the type of noncredible performance typical of malingering. These data support recommendations for consistency analysis in the interpretation of neuropsychological data in forensic settings (Larrabee, 1990; 2005; Slick et al., 1999).

References

Arnold, G., Boone, K. B., Lu, P., Dean, A., Wen, J., Nitch, S., et al. (2005). Sensitivity and specificity of finger-tapping scores for the detection of suspect effort. *The Clinical Neuropsychologist, 19*, 105–120.

Beetar, J. T., & Williams, J. M. (1995). Malingering response styles on the Memory Assessment Scales and symptom validity tests. *Archives of Clinical Neuropsychology, 10,* 57–72.

Benton, A. L., Sivan, A. B., Hamsher, K. deS., Varney, N. R., & Spreen, O. (1994). *Contributions to neuropsychological assessment: A clinical manual* (2nd ed.). New York: Oxford University Press.

Bernard, L. C., McGrath, M. J., & Houston, W. (1993). Discriminating between simulated malingering and closed-head injury on the Wechsler Memory Scale-Revised. *Archives of Clinical Neuropsychology, 8,* 539–551.

Bianchini, K. J., Mathias, C. W., & Greve, K. W. (2001). Symptom validity testing: A critical review. *The Clinical Neuropsychologist, 15,* 461–470.

Binder, L. M. (1993). Assessment of malingering after mild head trauma with the Portland Digit Recognition Test. *Journal of Clinical and Experimental Neuropsychology, 15,* 170–182.

Brandt, J., Rubinsky, E., & Lassen, G. (1985). Uncovering malingered amnesia. *Annals of the New York Academy of Science, 44,* 502–503.

Cullum, C. M., Heaton, R. K., & Grant, I. (1991). Psychogenic factors influencing neuropsychological performance: Somatoform disorders, factitious disorders, and malingering. In H. O. Doerr & A. S. Carlin (Eds.), *Forensic neuropsychology: Legal and scientific bases* (pp. 141–171). New York: Guilford.

Faust, D., Hart, K., Guilmette, T. J., & Arkes, H. R. (1988). Neuropsychologists' capacity to detect adolescent malingerers. *Professional Psychology: Research and Practice, 19,* 508–515.

Glassmire, D. M., Bierley, R. A., Wisniewski, A. M., Greene, R. L., Kenned, J. E., & Date, E. (2003). Using the WMS-III Faces subtest to detect malingered memory impairment. *Journal of Clinical and Experimental Neuropsychology, 25,* 465–481.

Golden, C. J., Purisch, A. D., & Hammeke, T. A. (1985). *Luria-Nebraska Neuropsychological Battery: Forms I and II.* Los Angeles: Western Psychological Services.

Greiffenstein, M. F., Baker, W. J., & Gola, T. (1994). Validation of malingered amnesia measures with a large clinical sample. *Psychological Assessment, 6,* 218–240.

Greve, K. W., & Bianchini, K. J. (2004). Setting empirical cutoffs on psychometric indicators of negative response bias: A methodological commentary with recommendations. *Archives of Clinical Neuropsychology, 19,* 533–541.

Greve, K. W., Bianchini, K. J., Mathias, C. W., Houston, R. J., & Crouch, J. A. (2003). Detecting malingered performance on the Wechsler Adult Intelligence Scale: Validation of Mittenberg's approach in traumatic brain injury. *Archives of Clinical Neuropsychology, 18,* 245–260.

Heaton, R. K., Chelune, G. J., Talley, J. L., Kay, G. G., & Curtiss, G. (1993). *Wisconsin Card Sorting Test manual* (Rev. and exp.). Odessa, FL: Psychological Assessment Resources.

Heaton, R. K., Smith, H. H., Lehman, R. A. W., & Vogt, A. T. (1978). Prospects for faking believable deficits on neuropsychological testing. *Journal of Consulting and Clinical Psychology, 46,* 892–900.

Hilsabeck, R. C., Thompson, M. D., Irby, J. W., Adams, R. L., Scott, J. G., and Gouvier, W. D. (2003). Partial cross-validation of the Wechsler Memory Scale-Revised (WMS-R): General Memory–Attention/Concentration Malingering Index in a nonlitigating sample. *Archives of Clinical Neuropsychology, 18,* 71–79.

Hiscock, M., & Hiscock, C. K. (1989). Refining the forced-choice method for the detection of malingering. *Journal of Clinical and Experimental Neuropsychology, 11,* 967–974.

Inman, T. H., Vickery, C. D., Berry, D. T. R., Lamb, D. G., Edwards, C. L., & Smith, G. T. (1998). Development and initial validation of a new procedure for evaluating adequacy of effort given during neuropsychological testing: The Letter Memory Test. *Psychological Assessment, 10,* 128–139.

Iverson, G. L., & Franzen, M. D. (1998). Detecting malingered memory deficits with the Recognition Memory Test. *Brain Injury, 12,* 275–282.

Iverson, G. L., Slick, D. J., & Franzen, M. D. (2000). Evaluation of a WMS-R malingering index in a nonlitigating clinical sample. *Journal of Clinical and Experimental Neuropsychology, 22,* 191–197.

Iverson, G. L., & Tulsky, D. S. (2003). Detecting malingering on the WAIS-III: Unusual Digit Span performance patterns in the normal population and in clinical groups. *Archives of Clinical Neuropsychology, 18,* 1–9.

Kilgore, W. D., & DellaPietra, L. (2000). Using the WMS-III to detect malingering: Empirical validation of the Rarely Missed Index. *Journal of Clinical and Experimental Neuropsychology, 22,* 761–771.

Lange, R. T., Iverson, G. L., Sullivan, K., & Anderson, D. (2006). Suppressed working memory on the WMS-III as a marker for poor effort. *Journal of Clinical and Experimental Neuropsychology, 28,* 294–305.

Langeluddecke, P. M., & Lucas, S. K. (2003). Quantitative measures of memory malingering on the Wechsler Memory Scale (3rd ed.) in mild head injury litigants. *Archives of Clinical Neuropsychology, 18,* 181–197.

Larrabee, G. J. (1990). Cautions in the use of neuropsychological evaluation in legal settings. *Neuropsychology, 4,* 239–247.

Larrabee, G. J. (2003). Detection of malingering using atypical patterns of performance on standard neuropsychological tests. *The Clinical Neuropsychologist, 17,* 410–425.

Larrabee, G. J. (2005). A scientific approach to forensic neuropsychology. In G. J. Larrabee (Ed.), *Forensic neuropsychology: A scientific approach* (pp. 3–28). New York: Oxford University Press.

Larrabee, G. J., Millis, S. R., & Meyers, J. E. (2007, February). *Sensitivity to brain dysfunction of the Halstead-Reitan vs. an ability-focused neuropsychological battery.* Paper presented at the annual meeting of the International Neuropsychological Society, Portland, OR.

Lees-Haley, P. R., English, L. T., & Glenn, W. J. (1991). A Fake Bad Scale on the MMPI-2 for personal injury claimants. *Psychological Reports, 68,* 203–210.

Levin, H. S., Benton, A. L., & Grossman, R. G. (1982). *Neurobehavioral consequences of closed head injury.* New York: Oxford University Press.

Lu, P. H., Boone, K. B., Cozolino, L., & Mitchell, C. (2003). Effectiveness of the Rey-Osterrieth Complex Figure Test and the Meyers and Meyers Recognition Memory Trial in the detection of suspect effort. *The Clinical Neuropsychologist, 17,* 426–440.

McKinzey, R. K., Podd, M. H., Krehbiel, M. A., Mensch, A. J., & Trombka, C. C. (1997). Detection of malingering on the Luria-Nebraska Neuropsychological Battery: An initial and cross-validation. *Archives of Clinical Neuropsychology, 12,* 505–512.

McKinzey, R. K., & Russell, E. W. (1997). Detection of malingering on the Halstead-Reitan Battery: A cross-validation. *Archives of Clinical Neuropsychology, 12,* 585–589.

Meyers, J. E., Galinsky, A. M., & Volbrecht, M. (1999). Malingering and mild brain injury: How low is too low? *Applied Neuropsychology, 6,* 208–216.

Meyers, J. E., Morrison, A. L., & Miller, J. C. (2001). How low is too low, revisited: Sentence repetition and AVLT recognition in the detection of malingering. *Applied Neuropsychology, 8,* 234–241.

Meyers, J. E., & Volbrecht, M. E. (1998). Validation of memory error patterns on the Rey Complex Figure and Recognition Trial. *Applied Neuropsychology, 6,* 201–207.

Meyers, J. E., & Volbrecht, M. E. (2003). A validation of multiple malingering detection methods in a large clinical sample. *Archives of Clinical Neuropsychology, 18,* 261–276.

Miller, L. J., Ryan, J. J., Carruthers, C. A., & Cluff, R. B. (2004). Brief screening indexes for malingering: A confirmation of Vocabulary minus Digit Span from the WAIS-III and the Rarely Missed Index from the WMS-III. *The Clinical Neuropsychologist, 18,* 327–333.

Millis, S. R., Ross, S. R., & Ricker, J. H. (1998). Detection of incomplete effort on the Wechsler Adult Intelligence Scale-Revised: A cross-validation. *Journal of Clinical and Experimental Neuropsychology, 20,* 167–173.

Mittenberg, W., Aguila-Puentes, G., Patton, C., Canyock, E. M., & Heilbronner, R. L. (2002). Neuropsychological profiling of symptom exaggeration and malingering. *Journal of Forensic Neuropsychology, 3,* 227–240.

Mittenberg, W., Azrin, R., Millsaps, C., & Heilbronner, R. (1993). Identification of malingered head injury on the Wechsler Memory Scale-Revised. *Psychological Assessment, 5,* 34–40.

Mittenberg, W., Patton, C., & Legler, W. (2003, October). *Identification of malingered head injury on the Wechsler Memory Scale (3rd ed.).* Paper presented at the 23rd annual conference of the National Academy of Neuropsychology, Dallas.

Mittenberg, W., Roberts, D. M., Patton, C., & Legler, W. (2005, October). *Identification of malingered head injury with WAIS-3 Vocabulary and Digit Span.* Paper presented at the 25th annual meeting of the National Academy of Neuropsychology, Tampa, FL.

Mittenberg, W., Rotholc, A., Russell, E., & Heilbronner, R. (1996). Identification of malingered head injury on the Halstead-Reitan Battery. *Archives of Clinical Neuropsychology, 11,* 271–281.

Mittenberg, W., Theroux, S., Aguila-Puentes, G., Bianchini, K., Greve, K., & Rayls, K. (2001). Identification of malingered head injury on the Wechsler Adult Intelligence Scale (3rd ed). *The Clinical Neuropsychologist, 15,* 440–445.

Mittenberg, W., Theroux-Fichera, S., Zielinski, R. E., & Heilbronner, R. L. (1995). Identification of malingered head injury on the Wechsler Adult Intelligence Scale-Revised. *Professional Psychology: Research and Practice, 26,* 491–498.

Rabin, L. A., Barr, W. B., & Burton, L. A. (2005). Assessment practices of clinical neuropsychologists in the United States and Canada: A survey of INS, NAN, and APA Division 40 members. *Archives of Clinical Neuropsychology, 20,* 33–65.

Reitan, R. M., & Wolfson, D. (1993). *The Halstead-Reitan Neuropsychological Test Battery: Theory and clinical interpretation* (2nd ed.). South Tucson, AZ: Neuropsychology Press.

Ross, S. R., Krukowski, R. A., Putnam, S. H., & Adams, K. M. (2003). The Memory Assessment Scales in the detection of incomplete effort in mild head injury. *The Clinical Neuropsychologist, 17,* 581–591.

Russell, E. W., & Starkey, R. I. (1993). *Halstead-Russell Neuropsychological Evaluation System (manual and computer program).* Los Angeles: Western Psychological Services.

Sherman, D. S., Boone, K. B., Lu, P., & Razani, J. (2002). Re-examination of a Rey Auditory Verbal Learning Test/Rey Complex Figure discriminant function to detect suspect effort. *The Clinical Neuropsychologist, 16,* 242–250.

Slick, D. J., Hinkin, C. H., van Gorp, W. G., & Satz, P. (2001). Base rate of a WMS-R malingering index in a sample of non-compensation-seeking men infected with HIV-1. *Applied Neuropsychology, 8,* 185–189.

Slick, D. J., Sherman, E. M. S., & Iverson, G. L. (1999). Diagnostic criteria for malingered neurocognitive dysfunction: Proposed standards for clinical practice and research. *The Clinical Neuropsychologist, 13,* 545–561.

Suhr, J. A., & Boyer, D. (1999). Use of the Wisconsin Card Sorting Test in the detection of malingering in student simulator and patient samples. *Journal of Clinical and Experimental Neuropsychology, 21,* 701–708.

Sweet, J. J., Nelson, N. W., & Moberg, P. J. (2006). The TCN/AACN 2005 "salary survey": Professional practices, beliefs, and incomes of U. S. neuropsychologists. *The Clinical Neuropsychologist, 20,* 325–364.

Thompson, L. L., & Cullum, C. M. (1991). Pattern of performance on neuropsychological tests in relation to effort in mild head-injury patients. *Archives of Clinical Neuropsychology, 6,* 231.

Tombaugh, T. N. (1996). *Test of Memory Malingering.* North Tonawanda, NY: Multi-Health Systems.

Trueblood, W., & Schmidt, M. (1993). Malingering and other validity considerations in neuropsychological evaluation of mild head injury. *Journal of Clinical and Experimental Neuropsychology, 15,* 578–590.

Vickery, C. D., Berry, D. T. R., Dearth, C. S., Vagnini, V. L., Baser, R. E., Cragar, D. E., et al. (2004). Head injury and the ability to feign neuropsychological deficits. *Archives of Clinical Neuropsychology, 19,* 37–48.

Victor, T. L., Boone, K. B., Serpa, J. G., & Buehler, M. A. (2006, February). *Using multiple measures of effort.* Paper presented at the 34th annual meeting of the International Neuropsychological Society, Boston.

Warrington, E. K. (1984). *Recognition Memory Test.* Windsor, UK: NFER-Nelson.

Wechsler, D. (1981). *WAIS-R manual.* New York: Psychological Corp.

Wechsler, D. (1987). *Wechsler Memory Scale-Revised manual.* San Antonio: Psychological Corp.

Wechsler, D. (1997a). *WAIS-III: Administration and scoring manual.* San Antonio: Psychological Corp.

Wechsler, D. (1997b). *Wechsler Memory Scale III: Administration and scoring manual.* San Antonio: Psychological Corp.

Williams, J. M. (1991). *Memory Assessment Scales.* Odessa, FL: Psychological Assessment Resources.

6

Motor, Sensory, and Perceptual-Motor Pseudoabnormalities

Manfred F. Greiffenstein

Noncredible neuropsychological performance is multidimensional. Persons feigning neurological disorders for personal or external gain may present with a variety of pseudoabnormalities not reflective of underlying neurological disease (Bianchini, Greve, & Glynn, 2005; Greiffenstein, Baker, & Gola, 1995; Greiffenstein & Baker, 2006). This chapter focuses on the assessment of perceptual-motor pseudoabnormalities in compensable injury. For brevity, the term *perceptual-motor pseudoabnormality* (PMPA) will refer broadly to poor scores on sensory, motor, perceptual-motor integration, visuospatial perception, and/or constructional praxis tasks; further, these scores must be unexplainable on any medical or neurological basis. While PMPA may be evidence of poor effort and malingering, it can also be associated with severe psychopathology and in some cases be comorbid with genuine brain disorder.

Why Consider Perceptual-Motor Pseudoabnormalities?

In legal contexts, test-taking effort is the major threat to neuropsychological validity (Greiffenstein & Cohen, 2005), and PMPA may be overlooked because of an overfocus on feigned cognitive defects. Consideration of PMPA is definitely underrepresented in contemporary simulation and malingering research. Greiffenstein and Baker (2006) found that up to 40% of late

postconcussion claimants produced suspiciously poor grip-strength scores, while Greiffenstein, Baker, and Gola (1996b) found nonorganic motor patterns in 65% of postconcussive claimants; similarly, Peterson (1998) reported 70% of soft-tissue-injury claimants showed nonorganic motor and 56% nonorganic sensory deficits. Despite these studies suggesting a high prevalence of nonphysiological sensory and motor findings, reviews of neuropsychological symptom validity tests (SVTs) are dominated by measures of feigned memory or attention disorders. Sweet's (1999) exhaustive review of neuropsychological SVTs listed 26 measures, 21 of which capture feigned deficits in attention, memory, and problem solving but only 5 that investigate potential PMPA measures. Further, Sweet's compilation listed 126 studies that focus on feigned cognitive signs but only 13 that examine potential PMPA. Larrabee's (2005) work on malingering also describes many studies of cognitive and symptom validity tests but cites only six studies on motor test validity. Such underrepresentation of PMPA studies could be part of a larger bias against studying motor behavior in the psychology literature (Rosenbaum, 2005), or it could represent a collective (but erroneous) intuition that PMPA is not fundamental to noncredible performance.

The purpose of this chapter is to provide comprehensive historical, methodological, and literature reviews of PMPA. The chapter concludes with a theoretical integration, such as implications for the modeling of malingering behaviors and recommendations for best practices in PMPA assessment in forensic examinations.

Predication for Studying PMPA

Brief History

The dearth of contemporary studies of PMPA goes against the historical grain. Taking a broad historical perspective, Shorter (1994) showed that unexplained sensory and motor symptoms dominated medical analysis of "psychosomatic" disorders for centuries. Empirically, the earliest psychological studies of feigned disorders favored measures of PMPA over feigned cognitive problems. Behavioral psychologists demonstrated that operant conditioning principles could bring functional blindness under the control of visual stimuli, both proving the nonorganic basis of the symptom and providing a means of treatment (Brady & Lind, 1961; Theodor & Mandelcorn, 1973; Zimmerman & Grosz, 1966). Loren Pankratz, a psychologist commonly credited with starting the neuropsychology validity-testing movement, first investigated malingering in the context of functional sensory complaints (Pankratz, 1979; Pankratz, Fausti, & Peed, 1975). Pankratz's two-alternative, forced-choice testing model provided the psychometric basis for many of the

cognitive malingering measures in common use today, such as the Test of Memory Malingering (Tombaugh, 1995).

Predication

There are good empirical and epidemiological grounds for focusing research and assessment on PMPA. The neurology literature is replete with small- and large-group literature on nonorganic sensorimotor issues such as psychogenic tremor (Gironell, López-Villegas, Barbanoj, & Kulisevsky, 1997; Koller et al., 1989), unrecognized movement disorders (Kulisevsky, Berthier, Avila, Gironell, & Escartin, 1998; Verdugo & Ochoa, 2000), improbable proprioceptive disturbance (Allum & Shepard, 1999), controversial autonomic reflexes (Ochoa, 1999), and nonanatomic parasthesia (Voiss, 1995). A PubMed (www.ncbi.nlm.nih.gov) search I conducted in August 2006 retrieved 4,797 citations containing the keyword "psychogenic." Pairing this keyword with neurological symptoms produced 66 citations for "psychogenic amnesia" but 80 for "psychogenic sensory," 150 for "motor," and 190 for "movement."

An epidemiological approach similarly suggests that PMPA attracts the attention of more physicians than neuropsychologists. The base rate for functional motor and sensory complaints is high in neurology settings. In one prospective study, 30% of patients had primary symptoms "not" or "somewhat explained" by neurologic disease (Carson et al., 2000). Peterson (1998) reported that 70% of soft-tissue-injury claimants showed nonorganic motor disorders and 56% nonorganic sensory deficits. The most common functional sign in suspect presentations is unexplained pain (12%), while the least common is amnesia (5%) (Lempert, Dieterich, Huppert, & Brandt, 1990). This suggests that prospects for PMPA are more common than noncredible memory deficit. Any time the prevalence of a target symptom or condition exceeds the error rate of a technique designed to detect it, there is good justification for use of the instrument (Gouvier, 1999; Meehl & Rosen, 1955).

Research Design Issues

A precondition for reviewing the PMPA requires understanding validation methods and research design. There are five basic methods for validating SVTs. Each one has strengths and weaknesses to consider in weighing the SVT literature:

- clinical case study
- role-play simulation
- known groups
- differential prevalence
- mixed-group Bayesian approach

Clinical Case Study

Single case studies of malingering come in two forms: (a) anecdotal reports rich in clinical detail showing clear discrepancies between self-report and objective findings and (b) single-case experimental designs. Anecdotal reports can prove that a certain form of malingering exists but gives no clues as to prevalence, for instance, Khan, Fayaz, Ridgley, and Wennberg's (2000) demonstration of nonorganic spatial neglect. Experimental designs in the single case provide unambiguous demonstrations of malingering to support theory. Examples include Binder and Johnson-Greene's (1995) A-B-A-B design, which demonstrates that cognitive malingering varies lawfully as a function of an observer's presence, and Pankratz's (1979) demonstration of below-chance responding in functional sensory loss. The limitation of this approach is not knowing the sensitivity and specificity of a task in larger groups. Below-chance responding is rare, and most probable malingerers score at either chance or near-chance levels (e.g., Tombaugh, 1995), so below-chance responding is probably not representative of how feigned deficits present.

Role-Play Simulation Design

When SVTs are administered to nonlitigating volunteers (typically undergraduates), the subjects are asked to feign brain disorders under various instructional sets. An SVT is said to be validated if coached or naïve volunteers perform worse on the SVT than control volunteers or genuine brain-damage groups. For example, Benton and Spreen (1961) instructed undergraduates to feign closed-head injury on the 10-second recall condition of the Benton Visual Retention Test. The simulators produced lower total correct scores and drew more distortions than a genuine brain-injury group but made fewer omissions, size errors, and perseverations.

Although the value of this design is the nonrandom format in which the experimenter knows who was instructed to fake, a limitation is limited generalizability (Rogers, 1997). Moreover, a laboratory setting cannot replicate the duration or complexity of postincident social influences acting on the typical plaintiff (see Rosen, 1995, for a good example): Undergraduates are of a higher social class than typical litigants and receive only brief exposure to symptom cues, and their financial inducements are minor compared to life-altering consequences in natural groups (Greiffenstein, Baker, Axelrod, Peck, & Gervais, 2004). A second weakness is that SVT validity may be inflated. It is well known that student simulators exaggerate to extreme degrees not seen in applied legal settings (ibid.; Rogers, Sewell, Martin, & Vitacco, 2003). Gola (1994) showed that noncredible litigants produced SVT scores intermediate between student simulators (who were poorest) and genuine patients (who performed best). Role-play simulation is useful for pilot work but not definitive in demonstrating sensitivity in applied settings.

Differential Prevalence Design (DPD)

Differential prevalence design requires a demonstration that SVT failures are more common in populations at high risk for malingering than populations at low risk. When used for comparative research, SVTs with higher failure rates in at-risk populations are said to be more sensitive than SVTs with lower failure rates. Gervais, Rohling, Green, and Ford (2004) showed that more failures occurred on the Word Memory Test than on the Test of Memory Malingering in persons seen for independent medical examinations related to medically unexplained pain. The problem with this approach is the inability to calculate sensitivity and specificity: Without external criteria, it is not clear whether higher test failures in at-risk groups represent better sensitivity or more false positive errors (Rogers, 1997).

Known-Groups Design

Known-groups, a form of concurrent validity, rely on natural samples rather than volunteers. Symptom validity tests are validated if performed worse by pseudoneurological patients preselected for either (a) noncredible performance on standard neuropsychological tests or (b) implausible symptom histories, compared to genuine brain-disease patients. The crucial step is constructing malingering criteria that are completely independent of the dependent SVT measure while simultaneously minimizing the prospects for genuine organic dysfunction. As an example, Greiffenstein, Baker, and Gola (1994, 1996a) preselected minor trauma patients for implausible symptom claims, cognitive scores of $z \leq -3.0$, and self-report discrepant with records. Slick, Sherman, and Iverson (1999) expanded and formalized Greiffenstein et al.'s (1994) criteria into an ordinal ranking system of definite, probable, and possible malingering in cases that present little radiological or other objective evidence for structural brain damage.

The main strength of known groups is generalizability to applied settings: SVTs are validated against current claimants who are socially similar to future litigants making similar brain-damage claims. The use of operational criteria for preselecting definite or probable malingerers allows for replication across laboratories. A weakness of this approach is imperfect confidence in malingering status, but this is a common issue in all inexact sciences, including clinical medicine. This weakness is addressed by (a) using strict exclusionary criteria to lower the prospects for true cerebral dysfunction and (b) choosing claimants who show *numerous* implausible signs and symptoms (Slick et al., 1999). A confession of malingering is no more necessary in a civil case than confession is in a criminal case.

Mixed-Groups Validation (MGV)

The MGV design is a rarely used variant of DPD originally proposed by Dawes and Meehl (1966). This is a Bayesian approach that uses grouped data

to estimate hit rates without knowing the true credibility status of any individual. Adherents such as Frederick (2000) argue that malingering is a probabilistic statement and that the known-groups approach is imperfect because it requires a strict dichotomous classification (p of malingering membership $= 1$) when the category limits may be fuzzy ($0 < p < 1$). However, the advantages of MGV are difficult to ascertain. The design still relies on ordinal rankings of individuals' credibility by clinicians, but such intuitive hunches are examiner dependent and prone to substantial error (Faust, 1995; Heaton, Smith, Lehman, & Vogt, 1978). This makes replication difficult; the known-groups method better supports replication efforts because operational definitions are provided (Greiffenstein et al., 1994). Additional issues include the fact that MGV typically requires enormous samples and the few studies utilizing MGV produce hit rates comparable to concurrent validity designs (Crawford, Greene, Dupart, Bongar, & Childs, 2006; Knowles & Schroeder, 1990).

Methods for Detecting Perceptual-Motor Pseudoabnormalities

Neurological Approaches

Neurologists use physical challenges to elicit motor behaviors or sensory reports discrepant with patterns seen in genuine neurologic disease (Goldberg, 1981). They employ terms such as "nonphysiological," "nonorganic," or "functional" to label findings that imply a voluntary or nonsensical component. Neurological techniques are based on a face valid approach contingent on a shared understanding of sensory and motor nerve innervation. Sensory challenges take advantage of accepted nerve distribution patterns, while motor challenges take advantage of expected reciprocal inhibition/activation patterns in muscle groups in both health and neurological disease.

Table 6.1 summarizes some common physical challenges used to elicit and measure nonorganic signs (refer to chapter 12, by Albers and Schiffer, in this volume for a comprehensive description of neurological methods). However, as in neuropsychology, a face valid approach is not necessarily accurate. For example, midline splitting is a popular means of detecting deception. The cutaneous branches of the intercostal nerves overlap with the contralateral side, so a face valid approach that predicts genuine tactile loss should begin within 1–2 cm of the sternum midline (paramedian). Patients who report numbness beginning at the midline of the sternum (or the forehead) would be labeled as nonorganic. However, thalamic stroke is associated with exact midline splitting reports (Stone, Zeman, & Sharpe, 2002).

Empirical studies of nonorganic signs show mixed findings. Methods for detecting bogus motor complaints are well validated. The Hoover sign (see Table 6.1) has been popular since its introduction in 1908. Sonoo (2004)

Table 6.1.
Neurological Tests for Nonorganic Weakness and Sensory Disturbance

Test Name	Description	Expected Result in Functional Disorder	Rationale and Validity
Hoover's sign	Supine patient is asked to flex hip (lift leg) while neurologist places hand under contralateral heel	Pressure on examiner's hand means contralateral hip is extending. Used in patients claiming unilateral lower limb weakness.	Takes advantage of crossed extensor reflex underlying normal walking; can be seen in brain disease where patient embellishes to get help; empirically validated but validity in multiple sclerosis patients is unknown.
Abductor sign	Supine patient is asked to abduct (move away from midline) either the sound or paretic leg against examiner adduction (examiner pushes legs toward midline).	The paretic leg remains fixed despite examiner's opposing force when sound leg is moved, but both legs are easily adducted by examiner when patient is commanded to move paretic leg.	A variant of the Hoover test; relies on synergistic contraction of muscle groups; failure of sound leg to resist adduction force means no effort by patient. (Introduced by Sonoo, 2004.)
Collapsing weakness or "give-away" tests	Patient is asked to maintain extended or flexed limb against light pressure or just touch	Limb falls rapidly in functional conditions, sometimes even before touched; in true organic disease, limb slowly lowers	Validity affected by joint pain in tested limb, failure to understand instructions, or desire of truly ill patient to persuade.

Arm drop	Examiner drops the claimed paralyzed arms over the supine patient's face	The arm misses the face, or arm moves slowly or erratically.	Hemiparetic patients have no voluntary control so hand would hit face. Useful only when weakness is great, not partial. Face valid; no empirical studies to date. Validated by Lempert et al., 1991.
Psychogenic Romberg	Examiner gently pushes patient who is standing with eyes closed	Functional problems suspected if there is large-amplitude body sway or patient falls away/toward examiner regardless of force vector	
Midline splitting tests	Place tuning fork over midline of skull or sternum; ask what patient feels	Bone carries vibration diffusely, so reports of unilateral numbness beginning exactly at the midline are suspicious	Exact splitting of sensation in the midline not believed to occur because of overlapping nerve distributions or conduction properties of bone; despite this, splitting is seen in some patients with documented thalamic lesions.
Crossed sensory testing	After standard tactile testing, patient is asked to cross hands behind back; single or double simultaneous touch compared to earlier results	Tactile recognition errors of mixed laterality or slower patient responses are not consistent with organic disease.	The complication of crossing causes malingerers to expend time thinking about which response is consistent with their goals. Face valid; no known studies.

reported 100% sensitivity and specificity for the Hoover test and the related "abductor" sign in a small sample of pseudohemiparetic patients. However, physicians' methods for detecting nonorganic sensory and pain complaints have a mixed empirical record. Rolak (1988) examined 100 patients with psychogenic or genuine hemifacial numbness. He found 92.5% specificity and 20% sensitivity for a midline splitting test but 86% false positives when the criterion was reduced vibratory sense. The Waddell signs, used primarily by physiatrists to detect nonphysiological pain reports, have been empirically challenged (Fishbain et al., 2003). Sensory testing relies more on subjective evidence than motor testing, perhaps explaining the divergent literature. For example, Waddell's signs require a physician's evaluation of patient facial expressions during physical maneuvers, a subjective appraisal.

Somatosensory Tests

Sensory-perceptual tests, particularly somatosensory (tactile and proprioception) tests, form a crucial portion of neurology evaluations (Ropper & Brown, 2005). Neuropsychologists began incorporating standardized tactile, visual, and auditory discrimination tests after Bender, Benton, and Semmes's pioneering demonstrations of lawful somatosensory changes following focal brain damage (Spreen & Strauss, 1998). Specific tests include esthesiometry (ibid.), formal two-point discrimination (ibid.), stereognosis, and tactile form recognition (Reitan & Wolfson, 1993). The Klove-Reitan Sensory-Perceptual Examination (ibid.) quantifies hemisomatic field testing (single and double visual, auditory, and tactile simulation) but emphasizes somatosensory perception (finger gnosis, fingertip number writing, and tactile form recognition). Other tests include the face-hand test to examine for somatosensory inattention (Zarit, Miller, & Kahn, 1978). Minor head-neck trauma and toxic exposure, conditions that are often the focus of forensic evaluations, are not expected to cause focal damage to primary sensory pathways and cortex. Hence, excessive errors on sensory discrimination tests are discrepant with etiologic expectation and thus constitute a basis for suspecting malingering (Larrabee, 1990; Slick et al., 1999).

A number of studies have examined sensory test failures as an indicator of PMPA using single case methodology. Pankratz (1979) showed that below-chance performance on two-choice tests specific to a patient's sensory complaints represents proof of functional disability. Pankratz's (ibid., 1983) two-choice approach is a technique rather than a specific test, requires 100 trials of two-choice discriminations (e.g., "Is the pencil red or blue?"), and is adaptable to any sensory deficit claim such as color blindness, tunnel vision, numbness, deafness, and visual loss. Greve, Bianchini, and Ameduri (2003) have demonstrated how simple two-point tactile discrimination (one of two fingers applied to the "affected" area) proved nondermatomal numbness patterns in three patients with suspicious disability claims. Binder (1992)

demonstrated noncredible deficits (e.g., below-chance scores on two-choice memory and tactile sensation tests) in a Social Security disability applicant.

A number of studies have included somatosensory perception and inattention measures as part of larger batteries. These studies show a remarkably consistent pattern: Simulators and atypical patients performed worse on finger agnosia than graphesthesis subtests of the Reitan-Klove Sensory-Perceptual Examination. Trueblood and Schmidt (1993) examined tactile perception in known groups ($n = 16$) and nonlitigating controls ($n = 16$). The malingering groups produced six times the finger agnosia errors and three times the fingertip writing errors produced by controls. Binder and Willis (1991) reported that a minor head trauma group that failed the Portland Digit Recognition Test produced five times more finger localization and graphesthesis errors (mean $= 18$) than those passing it (mean $= 3.6$) and four times the errors on the face-hand tests (mean $= 9$ versus 2.4, respectively). Heaton et al. (1978) reported group effects for finger agnosia errors in a small simulation group (mean $= 7.2$) versus a brain-injury group (mean $= 3.5$) but no effects for fingertip number writing (6.5 versus 6 errors, respectively) or tactile form recognition time.

Mittenberg, Rotholc, Russell, and Heilbronner (1996) replicated Heaton et al.'s (1978) feigned somatosensory pattern and also found group effects for finger agnosia with simulators making twice the errors but no group effect for fingertip writing. However, they also showed striking differences in sensory suppressions, with 10 times more errors in simulators, although with wide variance (25 errors versus 2.5 in patients). Tactile form recognition was not examined. Binder, Salinsky, and Smith (1994) found that finger agnosia errors identified 33% of psychogenic seizure patients with only 4% false positive errors versus genuine seizure. Binder, Kindermann, Heaton, and Salinsky (1998) later found 59% more finger agnosia errors in nonepileptic versus genuine seizure patients, compared to only 9% more fingertip writing errors.

Greve et al. (2005) used esthesiometry as a tactile SVT. Eighty undergraduates (divided into four groups) received instructions to produce sensory loss patterns, including one instruction to fake numbness for personal gain. Forces at 1.25 gm and above were applied to the thenar eminence and provided perfect separation between the feigned numbness versus no-loss and partial-loss groups. Esthesiometry as an SVT has not yet been validated against groups of real-world malingerers or genuine hemianesthesia.

Other Functional Sensory Deficits

There is little research on feigned auditory discrimination deficits. Haughton, Lewsley, Wilson, and Williams (1979) showed that simulators can easily feign believable bilateral hearing-loss patterns when asked to do so. A forced-choice paradigm with binomial probability calculation was effective "but not infallible" in the detection of simulation. Schear, Skenes, and Larson (1988) showed that 24 undergraduates who were asked to simulate a high-frequency

hearing loss produced Speech Sounds Perception Test scores in a range consistent with genuine "central auditory impairment" as defined by Reitan and Wolfson (1993). Skenes, Schear, and Larson (1989) further demonstrated that simulated hearing loss can cause a false positive diagnosis of conduction aphasia by affecting repetition tasks. Otherwise, I was unable to identify any research into auditory single and double simultaneous stimulation as malingering signs. Typically, researchers who utilize the Sensory-Perceptual Examination report global unilateral and double simultaneous scores (see Mittenberg et al., 1996).

Pain is an important sensory function. Despite the prominent role it plays in personal-injury and disability claims (Lempert, Dieterich, Huppert, & Brandt, 1990), little attention has been paid to the objective measurement of pain exaggeration. One difficulty is that pain is a purely private experience that is difficult to falsify; second, ethical considerations severely limit experimental approaches to inducing pain. Third, no reliable methods have yet been developed, and decisions still rest on a physician's judgment of the subjective distance between pain self-report and objective findings (Mendelson & Mendelson, 2004) (see chapter 10, by Larrabee, in this volume for a detailed exploration of noncredible pain and health complaints).

One approach is to give cognitive SVTs to persons with medically unexplained pain in a compensable context. Gervais et al (2004) showed a high prevalence of failed Word Memory Test scores in such pain patients. Other examples of this approach include studies by Meyers, Rohling, Green, and Ford (2002), Vickery, Ranseen, Cooley, and Berry (1999), and Schexnayder, Creveling, Nemeth, and Hannie (2000). However, this approach requires the inferential leap that faking in one symptom domain predicts faking in the pain domain without a direct demonstration that pain is being faked. Greiffenstein et al. (1995) showed that fictitious brain injury is best captured by diagnosis-specific validity tests, not the traditional MMPI-2 validity scales. Moreover, persons with genuine disorders can spontaneously exaggerate their deficits (Boone & Lu, 2003) or simulate worse deficits on experimenter request (Ju & Varney, 2000). Another approach is to compare self-report pain scales in disability applicants with the scores produced by unequivocal clinical pain patients (Bianchini, Etherton, & Greve, 2004; Larrabee, 2003b).

Feigned Visuoperceptual Deficits

Visuoconstructive Peculiarities
Historically, quantitative neuropsychology began with visuoconstructive tasks such as the Bender Visual-Motor Gestalt Test (BG). Based on anecdotal evidence produced by a few volunteer simulators and "confessed" malingerers, Bender (1938) developed qualitative scoring methods to detect feigned psychosis. For example, she believed that inordinately small reproductions were specific to feigned schizophrenia; she offered no signs of feigned organic brain syndromes. Subsequent empirical studies indicate that the BG is ineffective in

detecting feigned psychosis. Blum and Nims (1953) found that role-play simulators could mimic the Bender performances of genuine "neuropsychiatric" patients when a popular scoring system was used. Schretlen, Wilkins, van Gorp, and Bobholz (1992) asked prisoners to simulate psychosis but found the Bender a poor single predictor relative to domain-specific tests scales such as the MMPI-F scale; the BG contributed only modest unique variance when combined with other scales in a regression formula. There are some published BG data on its relevance to feigned brain injury. Bruhn and Reed (1975) found that most judges using the Pascall-Sutter BG scoring system could not reliably differentiate simulators from an "organic" criterion group, although one clinician achieved satisfactory accuracy.

Other visuoconstruction tasks were investigated as potential SVTs. Khan et al. (2000) describe a patient who seemingly demonstrated left spatial neglect during clock drawing. However, true neglect and visuoconstructive deficit were ruled out by normal line bisection, ability to draw mirror images with little error, and nonorganic left-side symptoms. The patient was a vague historian, so the authors could only speculate on how he "knew" that left neglect is associated with right-brain signs. Bernard (1990) asked 86 undergraduates to feign brain injury through the Rey Complex Figure Test (RCFT) under two incentive conditions. Simulators who were given stronger incentives scored 5 units lower than the controls on the copy condition but 8 points lower on the RCFT recall, suggesting that malingerers seize opportunities to show memory but not visuoconstructional deficits. Additional discriminant function analysis showed the RCFT recall score provided greater classification accuracy than the copy score, which did not add unique variance.

Chouinard and Rouleau (1997) compared RCFT copy scores in volunteer and clinical malingerers to patients with either memory disorder or frontal damage. Both simulation groups performed *better* by 6–7 figural units in the RCFT copy condition than the three organic groups, whose mean performance was deep in the impaired range. This suggests that the RCFT copy cannot be used to rule out malingering but may rule in brain problems. Meyers and Volbrecht (1998, 1999) showed large-group differences in RCFT recall/recognition patterns between probable malingerers, undergraduate simulators, and clinical patients; however, the authors did not report the RCFT copy scores in either study. Only Lu, Boone, Cozolino, and Mitchell (2003) reported RFCT copy cut scores showing sensitivity (45–50%) comparable to RCFT memory scores in detecting probable malingering. However, specificity was a problem (71%) when the copy cut score was applied to patients with genuine visual memory disturbance, compared to near-perfect specificity for RCFT delayed-recognition scores.

Visuospatial Deficits

The literature on functional visuospatial deficits is sparse. Iverson and Franzen (1994) examined the Knox Cube Test (KCT) as a response bias measure in undergraduate and inmate simulators. A Knox total correct score

of <3 was more sensitive than span length (72% versus 42%, respectively) relative to brain-injury controls. However, the simulators were equally poor on a small battery of other measures, and the KCT was not validated in a natural litigating group. Given the small battery, the Knox may have been "failed" because of demand characteristics, not because it is fundamental to a false brain-injury claim. Battery size and experimental demand characteristics are areas that require more research.

Meyers, Galinsky, and Volbrecht (1999) calculated the sensitivity and specificity of a battery of 13 tests that included the Benton Judgment of Line Orientation (JOLO). The overall battery was very effective in classifying multifaceted clinical and known groups, but individual JOLO statistics were not reported. Iverson (2001) focused on the JOLO but found limited utility in a large sample of well-defined probable malingerers. Larrabee (2003a) studied diagnostic efficiency by a pairwise combination of four cognitive measures, including the Benton Visual Form Discrimination Test (VFD) and the MMPI-2 Fake Bad Scale. The VFD had a sensitivity of 48% with a specificity of 93.1%. Perfect specificity was reached in combination with the Fake Bad Scale, but the VFD was less sensitive when paired with other measures. Overall, Larrabee (ibid.) found that combinations including the Fake Bad Scale provided the best incremental validity.

The Rorschach inkblots are a special case of visuospatial perception. Although not a visuospatial measure per se, this projective test requires personal interpretation of ambiguous visual stimuli, with a scoring system that incorporates spatial location. Benton (1945; cited in Lezak, Howieson, & Loring, 2004) anecdotally observed that servicemen with pseudoneurologic presentations produced fewer and more unelaborated responses than they would have on intelligence tests. Benton's proposal of fewer responses was shown effective in feigned psychosis (Perry and Kinder, 1990), but Medline and PsychInfo searches I conducted in September 2005 showed no Rorschach studies in the feigned brain-injury literature. Only Brussel, Grassi, and Melniker (1942) discussed Rorschach use in 16 servicemen with a variety of neuropsychiatric issues, but they did not propose specific scoring criteria for malingering of cognitive deficits.

Motor Skills

Quantification of motor function is a fundamental neuropsychological activity. As used in neuropsychology, motor dysfunctions are those that occur in the absence of hemiparesis or other severe neurological abnormality (Lezak et al., 2004). Motor skills are also useful in predicting activities of daily living (Dikmen et al., 1994). In order of increasing complexity, the motor skills of interest to neuropsychologists include simple strength, motor speed, manual dexterity, and multistep skilled movement (apraxia testing). A general law of neuropsychology is that simple motor skills are less affected by cerebral insult than skilled or integrated sensorimotor tasks (Haaland,

Harrington, & Yeo, 1987; Haaland, Temkin, Randahl, & Dikmen, 1994; Lewis & Kupke, 1992). Specific motor tests with the strongest normative base are grip-strength testing with the Smedley dynamometer, mechanical finger tapping (FT), and the Lafayette Grooved Pegboard (Mitrushina, Boone, Razani, & D'Elia, 2005). From a litigant's standpoint, motor skills may have the greatest face validity for measuring one's capacity to provide labor. Judging by the base rates for implausible pain and weakness cited earlier, motor performance may be sensitive to underperformance.

Grip Strength

A frequently studied effort-detection method is grip strength (GS). As a common procedure used in both physical medicine and neuropsychology, GS is typically measured with either the Smedley or the Jamar dynamometer. Grip strength can serve as a rough index of lateralization and handedness (Triggs, Calvanio, Levine, Heaton, & Heilman, 2000) or as an outcome measure in head-injury recovery and rehabilitation (Haaland et al., 1994).

There are many scoring methods for GS. Neuropsychologists use the simple "peak strength" variable, meaning the average highest endpoint readings from a grip device, such as the Smedley Dynamometer (Reitan & Wolfson, 1993). There are more complex GS methods, such as the configural scoring of force-time curves (Gilbert & Knowlton, 1983; Smith, Nelson, Sadoff, & Sadoff, 1989); the coefficient of variation (Fairfax, Balnave, & Adams, 1995); ratios and differences scores; and simultaneous electromyography. Robinson & Dannecker (2004) have extensively reviewed this literature and concluded that complex scoring methods such as the coefficient of variation are time consuming and add little to our understanding of effort in the individual case. Hereinafter, GS will refer to peak strength expressed in pounds or kilograms, unless otherwise indicated. Because GS requires exertion and some physical discomfort, it is motivation dependent. Hence, it is natural to ask whether GS is useful in credibility determinations.

Numerous studies have examined GS using simulation (analogue) designs. Some studies used motor measures embedded in larger batteries to study malingering behavior. In their now classic study, Heaton et al. (1978) compared the neuropsychology protocols of 16 volunteer simulators and 16 brain-injured patients. They reported group effects for GS and FT but not for the grooved pegboard. Mittenberg et al. (1996) revisited Heaton's (1978) protocol in their study of well-educated simulators versus a heterogeneous head-injury group. The simulators pressed an average of 7 kg less than the brain-injured patients, but this was not significant, in contrast to a group effect for finger tapping. Other studies that report group effects in simulators include those by Fairfax et al. (1995); Gilbert and Knowlton (1983); Hagstrom and Carlsson (1996); Hamilton, Balnave, and Adams, 1994; and Lechner, Bradbury, and Bradley (1998).

Only a few concurrent validity (known-groups) studies examined GS performance in mildly injured persons at risk for feigned deficits. Greiffenstein

et al. (1996b) used a configural approach to examine demographically adjusted motor skill profiles in late postconcussion syndrome (LPCS). They found a double dissociation: The LPCS patients showed worse GS than fine motor coordination, while severely brain-injured persons showed worse grooved pegboard than grip strength. The LPCS pattern violated the laws of motor dissolution in organic brain disease (Haaland et al., 1987). Sweeney (1999) examined motor performance in 33 adults who were claiming a disability of more than 2 years following ordinary whiplash and reported mean GS scores >1 SD below historical norms. In a reverse design, Trueblood and Schmitt (1993) used GS as an independent variable for selecting faked head injury. Persons with implausibly low GS scores also showed lower cognitive performances in areas not associated with mild head trauma, which suggests that low GS is associated with other submaximal effort signs. Hagstrom and Carlsson (1996) and Olivegren, Jerkvall, Hagstrom, and Carlsson (1999) also found medically unexplained low GS scores in small whiplash cohorts (1–73 months postinjury).

Table 6.2 summarizes the effect sizes (ES) associated with GS evaluations in simulators and known groups. The ES represent the difference in pooled standard deviation units between group means, allowing standardization and quantification of the difference magnitude across studies using different measures (Cohen, 1988). Any ES of +/−0 to 0.19 are "indeterminate"; 0.20 to 0.49, "small"; 0.50 to 0.79, "medium"; and 0.80+ are "large." This represents an improvement over less meaningful "statistical significance." Seven of the nine simulation studies showed large ES, and four of six known-group comparisons showed large ES. Using the sample-size weighted formulas recommended by Lipsey and Wilson (2001), the large mean ES seen in Table 6.2 imply a 55.4% nonoverlap between groups (Cohen, 1988) in the case of simulators and a 52% nonoverlap in known groups with conditions not reasonably associated with reduced simple motor function. Although ES calculations cannot be used to calculate efficient GS cutting scores, these theoretical nonoverlap figures suggest that GS should provide excellent positive predictive power (few false positive errors) at lower GS readings.

Finger Tapping

Motor speed and control (also known as "finger oscillation") are commonly evaluated with the finger tapper (Greiffenstein et al., 1996a; Reitan & Wolfson, 1993). There are various manual, electronic, and PC-based methods for FT, but this section assumes manual tapping with a counter recording finger depressions > 0.50 inch (Mitrushina et al., 2005), unless otherwise indicated.

Finger tapping is frequently included in studies of feigned brain injury, although it is rarely the sole focus. Table 6.3 summarizes a number of these studies. The first noteworthy feature is the clinical benchmark section of Table 6.3, which summarizes combined (dominant plus nondominant hand) FT in association with various unequivocal brain diseases, some of which are

Table 6.2.
Effects Sizes for Grip Strength in Simulation and Known-Group Research

First Author (Year)	Comparison Groups		
	Simulation Designs	Cohen's d	Magnitude
Smith (1989)	simulators vs. normals, M	−2.2	very large
Smith (1989)	simulators vs. normals, F	−2.1	very large
Niebuhr (1987)	simulators vs. normals, MG	−1.4	large
Fairfax (1995)	simulators vs. normals, MG	−1.4	large
Rapport (1998)	simulators (coached) vs. normals, MG	−1.3	large
Rapport (1998)	simulators (naïve) vs. normals, MG	−1.2	large
Heaton (1978)	simulators vs. TBI, MG	−1.1	large
Gilbert (1983)	simulators vs. normals, MG	−0.7	medium
Mittenberg (1996)	simulators vs. brain injury, MG	−0.2	small
	Mean ES all simulators	**−1.0**	**large**
	Known-Groups Designs		
Sweeney (1999)	whiplash after 2 years vs. norms	−1.66	large
Olivegren (1999)	whiplash vs. normals	−1.37	large
Sweeney (1999)	whiplash (2 years post) vs. historical norms; M	−0.80	large
Hagstrom (1996)	whiplash vs. normals	−0.93	large
Greiffenstein (1996)	minor trauma vs. TBI, M	−0.76	medium
Greiffenstein (1996)	minor trauma vs. TBI, F	−0.47	small
	Mean ES all known groups	**−0.92**	**large**

Note. ES = Effect size, rounded to nearest decile; F = female; M = male; MG = mixed gender but fully crossed; TBI = traumatic brain injury; Sev = severe

defined by movement disorder. Hence, lower FT scores in the context of minor and remote head trauma can be termed noncredible. Among volunteer simulators, Heaton et al. (1978), Mittenberg et al. (1996), Orey, Cragar, and Berry (2000), and Rapport, Farchione, Coleman, and Axelrod (1998) reported combined FT rates in the high 50s to low 60s.

Among studies using improbable disability claimants, the larger samples showed higher but still noncredible pooled means from the mid-60s to the mid-70s depending on the sample size (Arnold et al., 2005; Backhaus, Fichtenberg, & Hanks, 2004; Binder & Willis, 1991; Greiffenstein et al.,

Table 6.3.
Studies Reporting Finger Tapping Rates in Noncredible and Genuine Groups

First Author (Year)	Sample Description	Pooled[a] Mean
Known Groups		
Greiffenstein (1996)	78 female and 53 males, LPCS claimants	68
Larrabee (2003)	26 definite malingerers using Slick et al. (1999) rules	67
Arnold (2005)	33 women and 44 men, persistent subjective disability after minor injury	64
Binder (1991)	10 persons failing PDRT	72
Trueblood (1993)	16 litigants with low grip strength	72
Backhaus (2004)	25 probable malingerers; gender unknown	77
Mean summed finger tapping score, known noncredible		**70**
Simulation		
Heaton (1978)	11 males, 5 females	63
Mittenberg (1996)	11 males, 5 females	63
Rapport (1998)	80 volunteers	63
Orey (2000)	26 undergraduates with remote mild head injury	64
Tanner (2003)[b]	63 undergraduates, 58% women	57
Vickery (2004)	24 undergraduates; 11 simulators and 13 genuine	51
Mean summed finger tapping, volunteer simulators		**60**
Clinical Benchmarks		
Dikmen (1995)	161 mTBI; < 1 h PTA	98
Arnold (2005)	24 mod–severe head injury, mixed gender	85
Dikmen (1995)	37 mild–mod TBI; 1–24 h PTA	97
Golden (1998)	67 brain-injury patients with radiographic confirmed left anterior damage	96
Hom (1990)	20 patients with diffuse cerebrovascular disease	76
Reitan (2000)	18 acute mTBI, 14 days postinjury	93
Orey (2000)	25 mildly injured undergraduates asked to perform best	91
Powell (1991)	50 patients; mostly diffuse brain disease (e.g., anoxia)	85
Butters (1998)	26 MS patients	60
Butters (1998)	18 cortical dementia	62
Butters (1998)	16 Huntington's patients	48
Mean summed finger tapping, genuine brain disease		**81**

Note. All means represent summed dominant and nondominant tapping rates.
[a]Pooled = recalculation of means after combining female and male samples; all means rounded to nearest whole number.
[b]Electronic, not manual tapper.

1996b; Trueblood & Schmidt, 1993). The lower combined tapping in simulation versus known groups supports the hypothesis that volunteer simulators (usually undergraduates) show greater response distortion than probable malingerers from natural samples (Greiffenstein et al., 2004). Of special note is Reitan and Wolfson's (2000) study of Halstead-Reitan performance in classic concussion. Their 18 acutely concussed patients achieved FT rates in the low 90s, comparable to those of normal controls. This implies that poor FT rates long after minor neck-head trauma or even genuine mild TBI can confidently be attributed to low motivation, barring any other medical explanation.

Some studies have offered FT classification accuracy to assist validity decisions in individual cases. Backhaus et al. (2004) used a normative floor-effects strategy to develop cutting scores, based on FT distribution in 95 clinical TBI patients. Dominant and nondominant tapping scores of 38 and 33, respectively, were associated with 100% specificity and 32% sensitivity. This implies that combined FT rates of 71 and below are not associated with false positive diagnosis of PMPA in otherwise neurologically normal persons. Arnold et al. (2005) offered more context-sensitive cutting scores. For example, their Table 6 (p. 114) shows that summed male FT rates of ≤ 65 allowed 38% general sensitivity to malingering with the following specificities: 100% for clinical depression, 100% for normal aging, 94% for head injury, 90% for psychosis, and 71% for dementia. These rates are based on FT rates alone and could be further boosted by considering extratest information, such as the absence of dementing signs on clinical examination. In a poster presentation in 2005, Patton and Black categorized 418 injury claimants according to TOMM pass/fail rates. Those who failed the TOMM produced average dominant FT rates of 35 versus 42 in the credible group.

Small Parts Dexterity
Studies of the Lafayette Grooved Pegboard (LGP) in simulators show generally either nonsignificant or minor group effects. Heaton et al. (1978) reported no group effects for either LGP or static motor function (a measure of resting tremor) in their volunteers. Johnson and Lesniak-Karpiak (1997) observed the effect of forewarning on undergraduate simulators and found that warned simulators improved their LGP completion times by 7 seconds relative to unwarned simulators; however, they remained 10–11 seconds slower than controls. Using a similar design (Wong, Lerner-Poppen, & Durham, 1998) failed to replicate Johnson and Lesniak-Karpiak's (1997) modest LGP findings. Rapport et al. (1998) found that naïve malingerers produced slightly lower scores on the LGP (Binder et al., 1998) than on GS and FT, which is nomothetically similar to genuine organic patients, yet coached malingerers produced better LGP than FT scores. Rapport et al.'s study is further evidence that student simulators behave differently from natural samples.

In this regard, the impact of actual experience in postinjury environments is amply demonstrated by Vickery et al. (2004): Community volunteers who were asked to malinger performed better on the LGP than genuinely injured persons who were asked to malinger deficits. However, the volunteer simulators performed slightly better than a third group—head injury controls who were instructed to do their best. The few known-groups analyses that have addressed dexterity as an SVT showed no group effects or better performance by probable malingerers. Greiffenstein et al. (1996b) found that neurologically abnormal patients performed much worse than persistent postconcussion patients on the LGP. Binder et al. (1998) compared motor-sensory levels in controls (nonepileptic seizures and genuine epileptic patients) and found that genuine and nonepileptic seizure groups were indistinguishable on the LGP.

Feigned Apraxia?

The highest level of skilled movement is praxis. This refers to sequential movements on command or in pursuit of a goal. Disorders of skilled movement in a context of normal movement include ideational apraxia (poor sequencing of movements) and ideomotor apraxia (inability to recall required movements). There is a paucity of data on feigned praxis, which perhaps reflects its extreme rarity. A literature search found only Ballard and Stoudemire (1992), a single case report of inconsistent dyspraxia: inability to carry out movements on command but ability to carry out similar routines when unobtrusively observed. Diagnostic studies ruled out any brain lesion. Others investigated speech-related dyspraxia but did not include an examination of limb movements (Kent, 2000; Schnider, Mattle, & Mumenthaler, 1987).

Differential Diagnostic Issues

A finding of PMPA is the start, not the end, of the diagnostic process. Such findings are combined with extratest data to engage in a full differential diagnosis. Extratest information to consider includes neuroimaging (CT, MRI), electrophysiological (EMG), clinical (e.g., deep tendon reflexes), and historical (severity and symptom evolution) data. A number of conditions need consideration before one settles on a diagnosis of malingering. The collective experience with pseudoseizures reminds us that organic disease can be one risk factor for pseudoneurologic symptoms (Binder et al., 1998).

We can expect to find PMPA in conversion disorder (CD), a mental illness that is characterized by motor and sensory symptoms unexplainable by objective central nervous system findings, according to the *DSM-IV* (American Psychiatric Association, 1994). Unlike malingering, CD is conceptualized as involuntary, and the precipitant is a personally meaningful stressor ("primary gain"), as opposed to external gain. Unfortunately, the *DSM-IV* provides no guidance on how to differentiate unconscious from conscious production.

A patient's self-report of a noncompensable stressor just prior to symptom onset supports CD. Factitious disorder (FD) is conceptually similar to malingering in that its symptoms are voluntarily produced (APA, 1994). It is differentiated from malingering and CD on the basis of assumed motive (sole desire for patient role) and the level of enactment (intentional self-injury to mimic disorders). It is difficult for clinicians to evaluate motives and covert incentives in deceptive patients, and the FD concept fails to recognize the multifactorial nature of sickness behavior (Cunnien, 1997). Why cannot a patient pursue both compensation and a passive patient role at the same time? In contrast to CD's emphasis on sensorimotor signs, there is no reason to expect FD patients to regularly present with PMPA abnormalities. In fact, FD may be considered if PMPA signs are accompanied by evidence of self-inflicted medical problems and the reliable absence of compensability (although it is difficult to prove a negative).

Somatization disorder (SD) is characterized by multisystem physical complaints that are unexplainable on a medical basis, unlike CD and FD, where complaints are more focal or singular (Binder & Campbell, 2004). Unlike CD, the symptom reports are not limited to neurological complaints; SD symptoms are remarkable for their frequency (a minimum of eight required) and multilocation nature (four separate body systems). The validity of SD is controversial for many reasons, including an association with malingering that the *DSM-IV* guidelines explicitly acknowledge; signs of neurocognitive malingering in persons who produce somatoform MMPI-2 profiles (Boone & Lu, 1999; Larrabee, 1998; Youngjohn et al., 1995); and empirical failure to prove that somatization symptoms are the product of psychological distress (Brown, 2004). As with FD, the criteria for SD do not automatically create a reason to look for PMPA. Absent clear secondary gain, the presence of multisystem complaints associated with distress, onset before age 30, clear psychosocial stressors, and at worst negligible PMPA findings (as opposed to grossly deviant PMPA), SD may be considered.

Conclusions

Integration of Literature

The first generalization is that feigned or invalid sensorimotor deficits are often overlooked at both the research and individual assessment levels. One possible reason for this is a bias toward cognitive SVTs (Sweet, 1999). A related reason may be conceptual blindness, which is the failure to consider even the prospect of sensory and motor underperformance. The behavioral neurotoxicology literature often relies on neuromotor tests for medical surveillance of subcortical dysfunction in workers (Lees-Haley, Rohling, & Langhinrichsen-Rohling, 2006); these industrial contexts are rife with

compensability, yet nonorganic motor score patterns are clearly over-looked (Lees-Haley, Greiffenstein, Larrabee, & Manning, 2004). For example, Schmechel and Koltai (2001) have presented neuropsychological data from a laboratory worker who alleged exposure to a biological toxin. The claim-ant's standardized finger-tapping scores were >3 SD below expectation, yet the psychomotor speed (Trail-Making Test, part B) was within normal limits, the neurological examination showed no weakness or coordination problems, mood was euthymic, and an MRI showed an intact motor cortex. However, despite a context of potential compensability, this claimant's compellingly discrepant psychomotor patterns were uncritically accepted as valid indicators of brain injury.

The second generalization from the literature is that the simplest mo-tor and sensory tasks are sufficiently sensitive to implausible disability claims, as large-group effects consistently show. Grip strength, finger agnosia, tactile number writing, and finger tapping are simple tasks that are brief, portable, and easily scorable. Finger tapping is especially well suited for PMPA detection, as it has repeatedly been shown to be slower in both known groups and sim-ulators, and low FT shows good sensitivity and specificity, assuming a normal neurological examination. The clinical and research implication is that time-consuming and complicated formulas (e.g., coefficient of variation) or hun-dreds of sensory discrimination trials have no proven incremental validity.

A third generalization is that complex visuoperceptual and complex sen-sorimotor function tasks appear insensitive to motivational status. Put dif-ferently, noncredible respondents may not choose constructional praxis (e.g., copying) or fine motor tasks to display false signals of impairment. First, studies of faked visuospatial or praxis deficits are rare. Second, a few group studies provide negative evidence for the sensitivity of constructional praxis tasks to feigned status, and third, some studies show a lower sensitivity of such measures to feigned status (see Larrabee, 2003a). For example, scores on con-structional tasks such as the Rey Complex Figure copy and Bender-Gestalt miss many persons who have been instructed to malinger (Bernard, 1990; Chouinard & Rouleau, 1997; Schretlen & Arkowitz, 1990; Schretlen et al., 1992). Fourth, poor RCFT copy scores may indicate real neurocognitive deficits (Chouinard & Rouleau, 1997). Hence, constructional praxis tasks may be highly specific to brain disease; the clinician may more confidently rule out feigned deficit with respect to visuospatial function, whereas the same is not true of poor memory scores (Greiffenstein et al., 1994).

Similarly, dexterity tasks may have value only insofar as organic groups perform worse (Greiffenstein et al., 1996b). Certainly the general lack of studies of visuoconstructional malingering could still reflect insufficient attention by clinicians, as I have argued in the case of noncredible motor deficits. But based on other considerations stated earlier, I believe the dearth of such demon-strations supports a collective intuition that complex visuospatial tasks are really insensitive. A good hypothesis to test is whether compensation-seeking

claimants believe that such deficits are not fundamental to head injury (i.e., visuoconstructional tasks have no face validity for respondents). With regard to the latter, volunteers' cognitive appraisal of brain-injury presentations has rarely been the subject of research (Gunstad and Suhr, 2002).

Directions for Future Research

Embedding and Demand Characteristics

Simulation research that utilizes undergraduates has limitations, but other limitations not addressed to date are the issues of *task embedding* and *demand characteristics*. Because the demand cues are different, a simulator who is given instructions to fake impairment may behave differently when given 1 versus $k > 1$ tests. For example, a single-target SVT that is given to simulators may make it appear more sensitive than when the same SVT is given as part of a larger battery; there is more pressure to fail that single test because the experimenter's intentions are easily inferred. However, the experimenters' interests are less clear in a larger battery. Contrast the simulator studies of Tanner, Bowles, and Tanner (2003), who found groups separated by 2 SD when given only finger tapping (FT), with those of Mittenberg et al. (1996), who found a ½ SD separation when FT was embedded in a large battery. Although many factors could explain these differences, test isolation and the associated demand cues represent a compelling hypothesis to explore. This is not a trivial procedural issue, as belief in the sensitivity of a particular SVT may depend on task embedding in the original validation study.

Diagnostic Efficiency

Many of the studies reviewed here are concurrent validity designs that rely only on statistical significance testing. More studies of diagnostic hit rates and positive predictive power linked to specific cutting scores are necessary to support PMPA determinations in individual cases. For example, many studies indicate higher mean finger agnosia error rates than other tactile-perceptual errors during simulation, but sensitivity and specificity data for known groups is generally lacking (see Binder et al. [1994] for an exception).

Exaggerated Pain

Unlike other sensory behavior, pain is a subjective experience that is almost impossible to falsify, and the study of feigned pain is fraught with many methodological, empirical, and conceptual difficulties. First, the question of feigned pain presentations has rarely been addressed in quantitative terms and is generally ignored. Turk and Melzack's (2001) well-known text does not even mention the term "malingering" in the index. Second, subjective pain is interconnected with many other constructs such as learning history, personality, and medical history; it also has complex localization. In contrast, tactile perception has clearer cerebral localization, making it easier to correlate scores and

behaviors with records and brain neuroimaging studies. Third, experimental and clinical pain induction is complex and ethically challenging. Fourth, inferential issues limit conclusions. Current approaches to pain-based disability claims include giving cognitive SVTs; SVT failures are then generalized to make inferences about pain validity (Bianchini et al., 2004; Etherton et al., 2005; Larrabee, 2003b). However, cognitive SVTs and PMPA measures are not embedded in tasks. Hence, it is not always clear which abnormal scores on genuine tests are invalidated by SVT failure. More research is needed on the generalizability of SVTs to pain and other symptom reports. Early efforts in the generalization question, although not involving pain complaints, include Greiffenstein and Millis (2004) and Constantinou et al. (2005).

Best Practices

Diagnostic conclusions about PMPA should be based on a multistrategy, converging-evidence approach. The evidentiary tripod should include (a) outside records that focus on prior neurological evaluations, (b) injury history that focus on initial severity in quantitative and qualitative terms, and (c) accuracy and/or speed scores on simple sensory and motor tasks. A converging-evidence approach capitalizes on the strengths of each method while minimizing their limitations (Greiffenstein & Cohen, 2005; Larrabee, 2005; Slick et al., 1999). For example, a finding of combined finger tapping <63 (score) is more compelling evidence for PMPA if combined with negative neurological evaluations, an ER report showing that the claimant was only stunned after head trauma, and an acute CT scan that showed a normal pre-Rolandic (motor) cortex. Contrast this outcome with the same tapping score in the context of a claimant of advanced age, outside records that document consistent psychomotor retardation, minimal effort during neurological examinations, rheumatoid arthritis, and recurrent major depression of melancholic proportions.

The best battery composition for detecting PMPA includes the commonly given "motor triad" (GS, FT, and grooved pegboard) and the Klove-Reitan Sensory-Perceptual examination. Finger agnosia has repeatedly been shown to be more sensitive to atypical status than fingertip number writing, with no negative findings reported. The empirical database for somatosensory inattention tests is smaller (e.g., face-hand test), but some studies suggest that sensory inattention measures (double simultaneous stimulation) are promising as PMPA evidence. Although specific cutting scores are beyond the scope of this chapter, the reader should compile clinical benchmark studies that provide sensorimotor means and dispersions for well-defined organic groups. For example, Butters et al. (1998) published FT scores for various movement disorder groups (e.g., persons with Huntington's disease) whose summed FT scores were in the 45–60 range. Tapping scores in this range or lower, produced by persons claiming mild or ambiguous neurological insult, are strong evidence in favor of PMPA.

The highest confidence that PMPA represents a nonorganic or voluntary behavior occurs when objective physical and radiological evidence are blanketly negative. For example, a healthy male who presses less than 20 kg on the Smedley dynamometer in both hands is underperforming if serial neurological examinations show normal strength and movement. Confidence decreases with increasing disease, assuming such diseases are known to affect brute strength. A 60-year-old female plaintiff who is deconditioned and has rheumatoid arthritis should not be called a "somatic malingerer" based on low GS scores. When in doubt, consult with a physician colleague on a disease's functional impact.

References

Allum, J. H., & Shepard, N. T. (1999). An overview of the clinical use of dynamic posturography in the differential diagnosis of balance disorders. *Journal of Vestibular Research, 9,* 223–252.

American Psychiatric Association (APA). (1994). *Diagnostic and statistical manual of mental disorders* (4th ed.). Washington, DC: Author.

Arnold, G., Boone, K. B., Lu, P., Dean, A., Wen, J., Nitch, S., et al. (2005). Sensitivity and specificity of finger-tapping test scores for the detection of suspect effort. *The Clinical Neuropsychologist, 19*(1), 105–120.

Backhaus, S. L., Fichtenberg, N. L., & Hanks, R. A. (2004). Detection of sub-optimal performance using a floor-effect strategy in patients with traumatic brain injury. *The Clinical Neuropsychologist, 18*(4), 591-603.

Ballard, R. S., & Stoudemire, A. (1992). Factitious apraxia. *International Journal of Psychiatry and Medicine, 22*(3), 275–280.

Bender, L. (1938). A visual-motor gestalt test and its clinical use. *Research Monograph 3.* New York: American Orthopsychiatric Association.

Benton, A. L., & Spreen, O. (1961). Visual memory test: The simulation of mental incompetence. *Archives of General Psychiatry, 4,* 79–83.

Bernard, L. C. (1990). Prospects for faking believable memory deficits on neuropsychological tests and the use of incentives in simulation research. *Journal of Clinical and Experimental Neuropsychology, 12*(5), 715–728.

Bianchini, K. J., Etherton, J. L., & Greve, K. W. (2004). Diagnosing cognitive malingering in patients with work-related pain: Four cases. *Journal of Forensic Neuropsychology, 4*(1), 65–77.

Bianchini, K. J., Greve, K. W., & Glynn, G. (2005). On the diagnosis of malingered pain-related disability: Lessons from cognitive malingering research. *Spine Journal, 5,* 404–417.

Binder, L. M. (1992). Malingering detected by forced-choice testing of memory and tactile sensation: A case report. *Archives of Clinical Neuropsychology, 7*(2), 155–163.

Binder, L. M., & Campbell, K. A. (2004). Medically unexplained symptoms and neuropsychological assessment. *Journal of Clinical and Experimental Neuropsychology, 26*(3), 369–392.

Binder, L. M., & Johnson-Greene, D. (1995). Observer effects on neuropsychological performance: A case report. *The Clinical Neuropsychologist, 9*(1), 74–78.

Binder, L. M., Kindermann, S. S., Heaton, R. K., & Salinsky, M. C. (1998). Neuropsychologic impairment in patients with nonepileptic seizures. *Archives of Clinical Neuropsychology, 13*(6), 513–522.

Binder, L. M., Salinsky, M. C., & Smith, S. P. (1994). Psychological correlates of psychogenic seizures. *Journal of Clinical and Experimental Neuropsychology, 16*(4), 524–530.

Binder, L. M., & Willis, S. C. (1991). Assessment of motivation after financially compensable minor head injury. *Journal of Clinical and Consulting Psychology, 3,* 171–181.

Blum, R. H., & Nims, J. (1953). Two clinical uses of the Bender Visual-Motor Gestalt Test. *U.S. Armed Forces Medical Journal, 4,* 1592–1599.

Boone, K. B., & Lu, P. H. (1999). Impact of somatoform symptomatology on credibility of cognitive performance. *The Clinical Neuropsychologist, 13*(4), 414–419.

Boone, K. B., & Lu, P. H. (2003). Noncredible cognitive performance in the context of severe brain injury. *The Clinical Neuropsychologist, 17*(2), 244–254.

Brady, J. P., & Lind, D. L. (1961). Experimental analysis of hysterical blindness: Operant conditioning techniques. *Archives of General Psychiatry, 4,* 331–339.

Brown, R. J. (2004). Psychological mechanisms of medically unexplained symptoms: An integrative conceptual model. *Psychological Bulletin, 130*(5), 793–812.

Bruhn, A. R., & Reed, M. R. (1975). Simulation of brain damage on the Bender-Gestalt Test by college subjects. *Journal of Personality Assessment, 39*(3), 244–255.

Brussel, J. A., Grassi, J. R., & Melniker, A. A. (1942). The Rorschach method and postconcussion syndrome. *Psychiatric Quarterly, 16,* 707–743.

Butters, M. A., Goldstein, G., Allen, D. N., & Shemansky, W. J. (1998). Neuropsychological similarities and differences among Huntington's disease, multiple sclerosis, and cortical dementia. *Archives of Clinical Neuropsychology, 13*(8), 721–730.

Carson, A. J., Ringbauer, B., Stone, J., McKenzie, L., Warlow, C., & Sharpe, M. (2000). Do medically unexplained symptoms matter? A prospective cohort study of 300 new referrals to neurology outpatient clinics. *Journal of Neurology, Neurosurgery, and Psychiatry, 68*(2), 207–210.

Chouinard, M. J., & Rouleau, I. (1997). The 48-Picture Test: A two-alternative forced-choice recognition test for the detection of malingering. *Journal of the International Neuropsychology Society, 3*(6), 545–552.

Cohen, J. (1988). *Statistical power analysis for the behavioral sciences* (2nd ed.). Hillsdale, NJ: Erlbaum.

Constantinou, M., Bauer, L., Ashendorf, L., Fisher, J. M., & McCaffrey, R. J. (2005). Is poor performance on recognition memory effort measures indicative of generalized poor performance on neuropsychological tests? *Archives of Clinical Neuropsychology, 20*(2), 191–203.

Crawford, E. F., Greene, R. L., Dupart, T. M., Bongar, B., & Childs, H. (2006). MMPI-2 assessment of malingered emotional distress related to a workplace injury: A mixed-group validation. *Journal of Personality Assessment, 86,* 217–221.

Cunnien, A. (1997). Psychiatric and medical syndromes associated with deception. In R. Rogers (Ed.), *Clinical assessment of malingering and deception* (2nd ed., pp. 23–46). New York: Guilford.

Dawes, R. M., & Meehl, P. E. (1966). Mixed-group validation: A method for determining the validity of diagnostic signs without using criterion groups. *Psychological Bulletin, 66,* 63–67.

Dikmen, S. S., Machamer, J. E., Winn, H. R., & Temkin, N. R. (1995). Neuropsychological outcome at 1-year post head injury. *Neuropsychology, 9*, 80–90.

Dikmen, S. S., Temkin, N. R., Machamer, J. E., Holubkov, A. L., Fraser, R. T., & Winn, H. R. (1994). Employment following traumatic head injuries. *Archives of Neurology, 51*(2), 177–186.

Etherton, J. L., Bianchini, K. J., Greve, K. W., & Heinly, M. T. (2005). Sensitivity and specificity of reliable digit span in malingered pain-related disability. *Assessment, 12*(2), 130–136.

Fairfax, A. H., Balnave, R., & Adams, R. D. (1995). Variability of grip strength during isometric contraction. *Ergonomics, 38*(9), 1819–1830.

Faust, D. (1995). The detection of deception. *Neurology Clinics, 13*(2), 255–265.

Fishbain, D. A., Cole, B., Cutler, R. B., Lewis, J., Rosomoff, H. L., & Rosomoff, R. S. (2003). A structured evidence-based review on the meaning of nonorganic physical signs: Waddell signs. *Pain Medicine, 4*(2), 141–181.

Frederick, R. I. (2000). Mixed-group validation: A method to address the limitations of criterion group validation in research on malingering detection. *Behavioral Sciences and the Law, 18*(6), 693–718.

Gervais, R. O., Rohling, M. L., Green, P., & Ford, W. (2004). A comparison of WMT, CARB, and TOMM failure rates in non-head-injury disability claimants. *Archives of Clinical Neuropsychology, 19*(4), 475–487.

Gilbert, J. C., & Knowlton, R. G. (1983). Simple method to determine sincerity of effort during a maximal isometric test of grip strength. *American Journal of Physical Medicine, 62*(3), 135–144.

Gironell, A., López-Villegas, D., Barbanoj, M., & Kulisevsky, J. (1997). Psychogenic tremor: Clinical, electrophysiologic, and psychopathologic assessment. *Neurologia, 12*(7), 293–299.

Gola, T. J. (1994). *Investigation of the validity of common methods to detect dissimulation in neuropsychological examination of mild traumatic brain injury.* University Microfilms International.

Goldberg, S. (1981). Principles of neurologic localization. *American Family Physician, 23*(4), 131–141.

Golden, C. J., & van den Broek, A. (1998). Potential impact of age- and education-corrected scores on HRNB score patterns in participants with focal brain injury. *Archives of Clinical Neuropsychology, 13*(8), 683–691.

Gouvier, W. D. (1999). Base rates and clinical decision making. In J. J. Sweet (Ed.), *Forensic neuropsychology: Fundamentals and practice* (pp. 27–38). Lisse, the Netherlands: Swets and Zeitlinger.

Greiffenstein, M. F., & Baker, W. J. (2006). Miller was (mostly) right: Head injury severity inversely related to simulation. *Legal and Criminological Psychology, 11*, 131–145.

Greiffenstein, M. F., Baker, W. J., Axelrod, B., Peck, E. A., & Gervais, R. (2004). The Fake Bad Scale and MMPI-2 F-family in detection of implausible psychological trauma claims. *The Clinical Neuropsychologist, 18*(4), 573–590.

Greiffenstein, M. F., Baker, W. J., & Gola, T. (1994). Validation of malingered amnesia measures with a large clinical sample. *Psychological Assessment, 6*, 218–224.

Greiffenstein, M. F., Baker, W. J., & Gola, T. (1995). MMPI-2 vs. domain-specific measures in the detection of factitious traumatic brain injury. *The Clinical Neuropsychologist, 9*, 230–240.

Greiffenstein, M. F., Baker, W. J., & Gola, T. (1996a). Comparison of multiple scoring methods for Rey's malingered amnesia measures. *Archives of Clinical Neuropsychology, 4*, 283–293.

Greiffenstein, M. F., Baker, W. J., & Gola, T. (1996b). Motor dysfunction profiles in traumatic brain injury and postconcussion syndrome. *Journal of the International Neuropsychological Society, 2*, 477–485.

Greiffenstein, M. F., & Cohen, L. (2005). Principles of productive neuropsychologist-attorney interactions. In G. Larrabee (Ed.), *Forensic neuropsychology: A scientific approach* (pp. 29–91). New York: Oxford University Press.

Greiffenstein, M. F., & Millis, S. R. (2004). The Test of Memory Malingering may be a general effort construct. *The Clinical Neuropsychologist, 18*, 479–480.

Greve, K. W., Bianchini, K. J., & Ameduri, C. J. (2003). Use of a forced-choice test of tactile discrimination in the evaluation of functional sensory loss: A report of 3 cases. *Archives of Physical Medicine and Rehabilitation, 84*(8), 1233–1236.

Greve, K. W., Love, J. M., Heinly, M. T., Doane, B. M., Uribe, E., Joffe, C. L., et al. (2005). Detection of feigned tactile sensory loss using a forced-choice test of tactile discrimination and other measures of tactile sensation. *Journal of Occupational and Environmental Medicine, 47*(7), 718–727.

Gunstad, J., & Suhr, J. A. (2002). Perception of illness: Nonspecificity of postconcussion syndrome symptom expectation. *Journal of the International Neuropsychology Society, 8*(1), 37–47.

Haaland, K. Y., Harrington, D. L., & Yeo, R. (1987). The effects of task complexity on motor performance in left and right CVA patients. *Neuropsychologia, 25*(5), 783–794.

Haaland, K. Y., Temkin, N., Randahl, G., & Dikmen, S. (1994). Recovery of simple motor skills after head injury. *Journal of Clinical and Experimental Neuropsychology, 16*(3), 448–456.

Hagstrom, Y., & Carlsson, J. (1996). Prolonged functional impairments after whiplash injury. *Scandinavian Journal of Rehabilitation Medicine, 28*(3), 139–146.

Hamilton, A., Balnave, R., & Adams, R. (1994). Grip strength testing reliability. *Journal of Hand Therapy, 7*(3), 163–170.

Haughton, P. M., Lewsley, A., Wilson, M., & Williams, R. G. (1979). A forced-choice procedure to detect feigned or exaggerated hearing loss. *British Journal of Audiology, 13*(4), 135–138.

Heaton, R. K., Smith, H. H., Jr., Lehman, R. A., & Vogt, A. T. (1978). Prospects for faking believable deficits on neuropsychological testing. *Journal of Consulting and Clinical Psychology, 46*(5), 892–900.

Hom, J., & Reitan, R. M. (1990). Generalized cognitive function after stroke. *Journal of Clinical and Experimental Neuropsychology, 12*(5), 644–654.

Iverson, G. L. (2001). Can malingering be identified with the judgment of line orientation test? *Applied Neuropsychology, 8*(3), 167–173.

Iverson, G. L., & Franzen, M. D. (1994). The Recognition Memory Test, Digit Span, and Knox Cube Test as markers of malingered memory impairment. *Assessment, 1*(4), 323–334.

Johnson, J. L., & Lesniak-Karpiak, K. (1997). The effect of warning on malingering on memory and motor tasks in college samples. *Archives of Clinical Neuropsychology, 12*(3), 231–238.

Ju, D., & Varney, N. R. (2000). Can head-injury patients simulate malingering? *Applied Neuropsychology, 7*, 201–207.

Kent, R. D. (2000). Research on speech motor control and its disorders: A review and prospective. *Journal of Communication Disorders, 33*(5), 391–427; quiz, 428.

Khan, I., Fayaz, I., Ridgley, J., & Wennberg, R. (2000). Factitious clock drawing and constructional apraxia. *Journal of Neurology, Neurosurgery, and Psychiatry, 68*(1), 106–107.

Knowles, E. E., & Schroeder, D. A. (1990). Concurrent validity of the MacAndrew Alcoholism scale: Mixed-group validation. *Journal of Studies on Alcohol, 51*(3), 257–262.

Koller, W., Lang, A., Vetere-Overfield, B., Findley, L., Cleeves, L., Factor, S., et al. (1989). Psychogenic tremors. *Neurology, 39*(8), 1094–1099.

Kulisevsky, J., Berthier, M. L., Avila, A., Gironell, A., & Escartin, A. E. (1998). Unrecognized Tourette syndrome in adult patients referred for psychogenic tremor. *Archives of Neurology, 55*(3), 409–414.

Larrabee, G. J. (1990). Cautions in the use of neuropsychological evaluation in legal settings. *Neuropsychology, 4*(4), 239–247.

Larrabee, G. J. (1998). Somatic malingering on the MMPI and MMPI-2 in personal-injury litigants. *The Clinical Neuropsychologist, 12*, 179–188.

Larrabee, G. J. (2003a). Detection of malingering using atypical performance patterns on standard neuropsychological tests. *The Clinical Neuropsychologist, 17*(3), 410–425.

Larrabee, G. J. (2003b). Exaggerated pain report in litigants with malingered neurocognitive dysfunction. *The Clinical Neuropsychologist, 17*(3), 395–410.

Larrabee, G. J. (2005). Assessment of malingering. In G. Larrabee (Ed.), *Forensic neuropsychology: A scientific approach* (pp. 115–158). New York: Oxford University Press.

Lechner, D. E., Bradbury, S. F., & Bradley, L. A. (1998). Detecting sincerity of effort: A summary of methods and approaches. *Physical Therapy, 78*(8), 867–888.

Lees-Haley, P. R., Greiffenstein, M. F., Larrabee, G. J., & Manning, E. L. (2004). Methodological problems in the neuropsychological assessment of effects of exposure to welding fumes and manganese. *The Clinical Neuropsychologist, 18*, 449–464.

Lees-Haley, P. R., Rohling, M. L., & Langhinrichsen-Rohling, J. (2006). A meta-analysis of the neuropsychological effects of occupational exposure to manganese. *The Clinical Neuropsychologist, 20*, 90–107.

Lempert, T., Brandt, T., Dieterich, M., & Huppert, D. (1991). How to identify psychogenic disorders of stance and gait: A video study in 37 patients. *Journal of Neurology, 238*(3), 140–146.

Lempert, T., Dieterich, M., Huppert, D., & Brandt, T. (1990). Psychogenic disorders in neurology: Frequency and clinical spectrum. *Acta Neurologia Scandinavia, 82*(5), 335–340.

Lewis, R., & Kupke, T. (1992). Intermanual differences on skilled and unskilled motor tasks in nonlateralized brain dysfunction. *The Clinical Neuropsychologist, 6*(4), 374–382.

Lezak, M. D., Howieson, D. B., & Loring, D. W. (2004). *Neuropsychological assessment* (4th ed.). New York: Oxford University Press.

Lipsey, M., & Wilson, D. (2001). *Practical meta-analysis.* Thousand Oaks, CA: Sage.

Lu, P. H., Boone, K. B., Cozolino, L., & Mitchell, C. (2003). Effectiveness of the Rey-Osterrieth Complex Figure Test and the Meyers and Meyers recognition trial in the detection of suspect effort. *The Clinical Neuropsychologist, 17*(3), 426–440.

Meehl, P. E., & Rosen, A. (1955). Antecedent probability and the efficiency of psychometric signs, patterns, or cutting scores. *Psychological Bulletin, 52,* 194–216.

Mendelson, G., & Mendelson, D. (2004). Malingering pain in the medicolegal context. *Clinical Journal of Pain, 20*(6), 423–432.

Meyers, J. E., Galinsky, A. M., & Volbrecht, M. (1999). Malingering and mild brain injury: How low is too low? *Applied Neuropsychology, 6*(4), 208–214.

Meyers, J. E., Millis, S. R., & Volkert, K. (2002). A validity index for the MMPI-2. *Archives of Clinical Neuropsychology, 17*(2), 157–169.

Meyers, J. E., & Volbrecht, M. (1998). Validation of memory error patterns on the Rey Complex Figure and Recognition Trial. *Applied Neuropsychology, 5*(3), 120–131.

Meyers, J. E., & Volbrecht, M. (1999). Detection of malingerers using the Rey Complex Figure and Recognition Trial. *Applied Neuropsychology, 6*(4), 201–207.

Mitrushina, M., Boone, K., Razani, J., & D'Elia, L. (2005). *Handbook of normative data for neuropsychological assessment* (2nd ed.). New York: Oxford University Press.

Mittenberg, W., Rotholc, A., Russell, E., & Heilbronner, R. (1996). Identification of malingered head injury on the Halstead-Reitan Battery. *Archives of Clinical Neuropsychology, 11*(4), 271–281.

Niebuhr, B. R., & Marion, R. (1987). Detecting sincerity of effort when measuring grip strength. *American Journal of Physical Medicine, 66*(1), 16–24.

Ochoa, J. L. (1999). Truths, errors, and lies around "reflex sympathetic dystrophy" and "complex regional pain syndrome." *Journal of Neurology, 246*(10), 875–879.

Olivegren, H., Jerkvall, N., Hagstrom, Y., & Carlsson, J. (1999). The long-term prognosis of whiplash-associated disorders. *European Spine Journal, 8*(5), 366–370.

Orey, S. A., Cragar, D. E., & Berry, D. T. R. (2000). The effects of two motivational manipulations on the neuropsychological performance of mildly head-injured college students. *Archives of Clinical Neuropsychology, 15*(4), 335–346.

Pankratz, L. (1979). Symptom validity testing and symptom retraining: Procedures for the assessment and treatment of functional sensory deficits. *Journal of Consulting and Clinical Psychology, 47*(2), 409–410.

Pankratz, L. (1983). A new technique for the assessment and modification of feigned memory deficit. *Perceptual and Motor Skills, 57*(2), 367–372.

Pankratz, L., Fausti, S. A., & Peed, S. (1975). A forced-choice technique to evaluate deafness in the hysterical or malingering patient. *Journal of Consulting and Clinical Psychology, 43*(3), 421–422.

Patton, C., & Black, F. W. (2005, October). *Assessment of effort in brain-injured patients using the finger-tapping test.* Poster presented at the meeting of the National Academy of Neuropsychology, Tampa, FL.

Perry, G. G., & Kinder, B. N. (1990). The susceptibility of the Rorschach to malingering: A critical review. *Journal of Personality Assessment, 54*(1–2), 47–57.

Peterson, D. I. (1998). A study of 249 patients with litigated claims of injury. *The Neurologist, 4*(3), 131–137.

Powell, J. B., Cripe, L. I., & Dodrill, C. B. (1991). Assessment of brain impairment with the Rey Auditory Verbal Learning Test: A comparison with other neuropsychological measures. *Archives of Clinical Neuropsychology, 6*(4), 241–249.

Rapport, L. J., Farchione, T. J., Coleman, R. D., & Axelrod, B. N. (1998). Effects of coaching on malingered motor function profiles. *Journal of Clinical and Experimental Neuropsychology, 20,* 89–97.

Reitan, R. M., & Wolfson, D. (1993). *The Halstead-Reitan Neuropsychological Test Battery* (2nd ed.). Tucson: Neuropsychology Press.

Reitan, R. M., & Wolfson, D. (2000). The neuropsychological similarities of mild and more severe head injury. *Archives of Clinical Neuropsychology, 15*(5), 433–442.

Robinson, M. E., & Dannecker, E. A. (2004). Critical issues in the use of muscle testing for the determination of sincerity of effort. *Clinical Journal of Pain, 20*(6), 392–398.

Rogers, R. (Ed.). (1997). *Clinical assessment of malingering and deception* (2nd ed.). New York: Guilford.

Rogers, R., Sewell, K. W., Martin, M. A., & Vitacco, M. J. (2003). Detection of feigned mental disorders: A meta-analysis of the MMPI-2 and malingering. *Assessment, 10*(2), 160–177.

Rolak, L. A. (1988). Psychogenic sensory loss. *Journal of Nervous and Mental Disease, 176*(11), 686–687.

Ropper, A., & Brown, R. (2005). *Adams and Victor's principles of neurology* (8th ed.). New York: McGraw-Hill.

Rosen, G. M. (1995). The *Aleutian Enterprise* sinking and posttraumatic stress disorder: Misdiagnosis in clinical and forensic settings. *Professional Psychology: Research and Practice, 26*, 82–87.

Rosenbaum, D. A. (2005). The Cinderella of psychology: The neglect of motor control in the science of mental life and behavior. *American Psychologist, 60*(4), 308–317.

Schear, J. M., Skenes, L. L., & Larson, V. D. (1988). Effect of simulated hearing loss on speech sounds perception. *Journal of Clinical and Experimental Neuropsychology, 10*(5), 597–602.

Schexnayder, M. M., Creveling, C. C., Nemeth, D. G., & Hannie T. J, Jr. (2000). Consideration of latency/slowed performance rate when malingering and chronic pain are at issue during a neuropsychological evaluation. *Archives of Clinical Neuropsychology, 15*(8), 836.

Schmechel, D. E., & Koltai, D. C. (2001). Potential human health effects associated with laboratory exposures to *Pfiesteria piscicida*. *Environmental Health Perspectives, 109*(5), 775–779.

Schnider, A., Mattle, H., & Mumenthaler, M. (1987). Buccolinguofacial apraxia: A probably psychogenic speech and deglutition disorder. *Schweizerische Medizine Wochenschrift, 117*(48), 1888–1895.

Schretlen, D., & Arkowitz, H. (1990). A psychological test battery to detect prison inmates who fake insanity or mental retardation. *Behavioral Sciences and the Law, 8*(1), 75–84.

Schretlen, D., Wilkins, S. S., van Gorp, W. G., & Bobholz, J. H. (1992). Cross-validation of a psychological test battery to detect faked insanity. *Psychological Assessment, 4*(1), 77–86.

Shorter, E. (1994). *From paralysis to fatigue: A history of psychosomatic illness in the modern era.* New York: Free Press.

Skenes, L. L., Schear, J. M., & Larson, V. D. (1989). Simulated hearing loss and phrase dictation. *International Journal of Neuroscience, 47*(3–4), 287–293.

Slick, D. J., Sherman, E. M., & Iverson, G. L. (1999). Diagnostic criteria for malingered neurocognitive dysfunction: Proposed standards for clinical practice and research. *The Clinical Neuropsychologist, 13*(4), 545–561.

Smith, G. A., Nelson, R. C., Sadoff, S. J., & Sadoff, A. M. (1989). Assessing sincerity of effort in maximal grip-strength tests. *American Journal of Physical and Medical Rehabilitation, 68*(2), 73–80.

Sonoo, M. (2004). Abductor sign: A reliable new sign to detect unilateral non-organic paresis of the lower limb. *Journal of Neurology, Neurosurgery, and Psychiatry, 75*(1), 121–125.

Spreen, O., & Strauss, E. (1998). *A compendium of neuropsychological tests: Administration, norms, and commentary* (2nd ed.). New York: Oxford University Press.

Stone, J., Zeman, A., & Sharpe, M. (2002). Functional weakness and sensory disturbance. *Journal of Neurology, Neurosurgery, and Psychiatry, 73*(3), 241–245.

Sweeney, J. E. (1999). Raw, demographically altered, and composite Halstead-Reitan Battery data in the evaluation of adult victims of nonimpact acceleration forces in motor vehicle accidents. *Applied Neuropsychology, 6*(2), 79.

Sweet, J. J. (1999). Malingering: Differential diagnosis. In J. J. Sweet (Ed.), *Forensic neuropsychology: Fundamentals and practice* (pp. 255–285). Lisse, the Netherlands: Swets and Zeitlinger.

Tanner, B. A., Bowles, R. L., & Tanner, E. L. (2003). Detection of intentional suboptimal performance on a computerized finger-tapping task. *Journal of Clinical Psychology, 59*(1), 123–131.

Theodor, L. H., & Mandelcorn, M. S. (1973). Hysterical blindness: A case report and study using a modern psychophysical technique. *Journal of Abnormal Psychology, 82*(3), 552–553.

Tombaugh, T. (1995). *Test of Memory Malingering.* Toronto: Multi-Health Systems.

Triggs, W. J., Calvanio, R., Levine, M., Heaton, R. K., & Heilman, K. M. (2000). Predicting hand preference with performance on motor tasks. *Cortex, 36*(5), 679–689.

Trueblood, W., & Schmidt, M. (1993). Malingering and other validity considerations in the neuropsychological evaluation of mild head injury. *Journal of Clinical and Experimental Neuropsychology, 15*(4), 578–590.

Turk, D. C., & Melzack, R. (2001). *Handbook of pain assessment* (2nd ed.). New York: Guilford.

Verdugo, R. J., & Ochoa, J. L. (2000). Abnormal movements in complex regional pain syndrome: Assessment of their nature. *Muscle Nerve, 23*(2), 198–205.

Vickery, C. D., Berry, D. T. R., Dearth, C. S., Vagnini, V. L., Baser, R. E., Cragar, D. E., et al. (2004). Head injury and the ability to feign neuropsychological deficits. *Archives of Clinical Neuropsychology, 19*(1), 37–48.

Vickery, C. D., Ranseen, J. D., Cooley, A., & Berry, D. T. (1999). Use of malingering tests in forensic evaluation of pain patients. Vickery, C. D., *Archives of Clinical Neuropsychology, 14*(1), 102.

Voiss, D. V. (1995). Occupational injury: Fact, fantasy, or fraud? *Neurology Clinics, 13*(2), 431–446.

Wong, J. L., Lerner-Poppen, L., & Durham, J. (1998). Does warning reduce obvious malingering on memory and motor tasks in college samples? *International Journal of Rehabilitation and Health, 4*(3), 153.

Youngjohn, J. R., Burrows, L., & Erdal, K. (1995). Brain damage or compensation neurosis? The controversial post-concussion syndrome. *The Clinical Neuropsychologist, 9*(2), 112–123.

Zarit, S. H., Miller, N. E., & Kahn, R. L. (1978). Brain function, intellectual impairment, and education in the aged. *Journal of the American Geriatric Society, 26*(2), 58–67.

Zimmerman, J., & Grosz, H. J. (1966). "Visual" performance of a functionally blind person. *Behaviour Research Archives and Therapy, 4*(2), 119.

7

Performance on Standard Attention, Memory, and Psychomotor Speed Tasks as Indicators of Malingering

Julie A. Suhr and Joseph Barrash

Early research suggested that neuropsychologists who were analyzing traditional neuropsychological measures could not reliably distinguish malingering from brain injury, leading many to the conclusion that these tests would not be useful as indicators of malingering (Faust, Hart, & Guilmette, 1988a, 1988b; Heaton, Smith, Lehman, & Vogt, 1978). As a result, measures specifically designed to detect malingering were developed and have been extensively validated over the past decade or so.

However, researchers have continued to explore the usefulness of standard neuropsychological instruments in the detection of malingering, as they offer many potential advantages. For example, in some cases a clinician may not have access to data from specialized malingering tests, such as when reviewing data from other clinicians who did not include malingering tests in their battery (van Gorp et al., 1999). Knowing the cutoffs for malingering on traditional neuropsychological tests would prove beneficial in this sort of record review. Another advantage is the time efficiency offered by the use of cutoffs on standard neuropsychological tests, as these malingering indices are available for use any time the standard test is administered (Killgore & DellaPietra, 2000). In addition, because standard neuropsychological tests are measures of actual cognitive skills, they have high face validity to the examinee and thus may be less vulnerable to coaching (Glassmire et al., 2003).

The purpose of this chapter is to critically examine some of the malingering indices that have been derived from traditional neuropsychological tests of attention, memory, and psychomotor speed. Our review focuses on cutoff or created scores from standard neuropsychological data rather than

pattern analysis methods that often combine multiple scores into a regression equation (for a review of pattern analysis research, including patterns on the Wechsler tests of memory and intelligence, see chapter 5 of the current volume). While the pattern analysis method may ultimately be more robust to sophisticated and coached malingering, cutoff scores may be more user friendly in that they require less time and effort for a clinician to calculate and interpret. Our focus here is on attention and memory indices, as they are among the most commonly malingered symptoms of neurological injury (Binder & Rohling, 1996; Williams, 1998), but tests of psychomotor speed are also included. We also address the limitations of the existing literature for any given cutoff method, especially the use of diverse samples and research designs. Where data provide some consistency in the interpretation of the suggested malingering scores, we offer our conclusions.

We have chosen to provide sensitivity and specificity indices as an indication of the classification accuracy of the methods we review. In malingering classification, *sensitivity* refers to the proportion of malingerers correctly identified, and *specificity* is the proportion of nonmalingerers who are correctly identified. These numbers will help the reader determine the relative accuracy of the index, regardless of the base rate of malingering, which varies across the studies we discuss (Glassmire et al., 2003; Greve & Bianchini, 2004). Interested readers can calculate the predictive accuracy based on whatever base rates they choose, using formulas provided by Baldessarini, Finklestein, and Arana (1983), and thus determine an index of confidence in their rating using base rates that are appropriate to their setting. These computations are also discussed by Larrabee and Berry in chapter 2 of the current volume. In addition, although some studies report the sensitivity and specificity for multiple cutoffs, we have chosen to concentrate on cutoff scores that obtain at least 90% specificity in comparison samples, as this proved to be the most commonly used limit across all studies and, in our opinion, represents at least adequate specificity.

Attention Measures as Indicators of Malingering

Several researchers have developed malingering cutoffs or calculated scores from traditional measures of attention. One reason for our focus on attention measures is that even patients with severe amnestic disorders do relatively well on Digit Span tests (Baddeley & Warrington, 1970; Butters & Cermak, 1980; Cermak & Butters, 1972; Warrington & Weizkrantz, 1973). Thus, basic attention measures seem relatively insensitive to severe neuropsychological injury and may be particularly useful as malingering detection instruments.

Trueblood and Schmidt (1993) were among the first to examine the use of the standard Digit Span, as found in the Wechsler instruments, as a malingering detection measure. In a review of data from consecutive neuropsy-

chological evaluations in which symptom validity tests were failed, an age-corrected scaled score of <7 correctly identified 15% of their malingering sample. However, Iverson and Franzen (1994) suggested an even lower score (an age-corrected scaled score of <5), which had 90% sensitivity and 95% specificity in their sample of inmates and undergraduates who were asked to malinger, as compared to a small sample of patients with documented memory impairment. Suhr, Tranel, Wefel, and Barrash (1997) reviewed a large archival database of patients who were undergoing neuropsychological evaluation and supported the high specificity of <5 as a cutoff (100% specificity in their sample of individuals with mild head injury but not involved in litigation). Iverson and Tulsky (2003) also provided specificity data for various age-corrected scaled score cutoffs, using the WAIS-III standardization samples. They found that <4 was extremely rare in the normative sample and that <6 was rare in the clinical samples used to validate the WAIS-III. They recommended 5 or less as a cutoff for malingering.

Several very recent studies have provided further support for the age-corrected scaled score cutoff of <5 for malingering on the Digit Span task. Table 7.1 provides a summary of the most recent studies, all of which involved large clinical samples with well-defined probable malingerers and a wide variety of patient groups for analysis of specificity. The results from all four studies suggest that the Digit Span age-corrected scaled score of <5 shows variable but good sensitivity to malingering with generally very high to excellent (94% or above) specificity (but adequate specificity [closer to 90%] in moderate to severe TBI and other clinical control groups).

In another approach to the analysis of Digit Span data, Greiffenstein, Baker, and Gola (1994) introduced the Reliable Digit Span (RDS), which is the sum of the longest string of digits repeated without error over two trials under both forward and backward conditions. They examined data from consecutive referrals for neuropsychological evaluation and divided the sample into head-injured patients and probable malingerers, based on a good clinical definition of probable malingering (which included performance on standard malingering tests). An RDS score of 7 or less had 68% sensitivity and was 89% specific to malingering, while a score of 8 or less had 82% sensitivity but was only 69% specific to malingering. In a second study, also using a known-groups design, Greiffenstein, Gola, and Baker (1995) reported a sensitivity of 86% using a cutoff of <8 but noted significant specificity problems (only 57%). Meyers and Volbrecht (1998) conducted a cross-validation of Greiffenstein et al.'s findings. In their sample of mild head-injury patients (using litigation status to indicate probable malingering), an RDS score of <8 was about 49% sensitive and 96% specific. A small portion of their sample also failed symptom validity tests; of the nine who failed, seven also failed the RDS. Overall, many who failed the RDS did not fail the symptom validity test, although Meyers and Volbrecht speculated that the RDS was simply more sensitive to malingering. Interestingly, they also examined the

Table 7.1.
Recent Studies Assessing Sensitivity and Specificity of Digit Span Age-Corrected Scaled Score < 5 to Malingering

Study	Samples	Sensitivity	Specificity
Babikian et al. (2006)	large clinical sample; PM defined by external criteria, CC, HC	32%	98% in CC, 100% in HC
Heinly et al. (2006)	large TBI clinical sample (varying severity) and other neurological diagnoses (CC); PM defined by Slick et al. (1999) criteria	41% in TBI-M, 25% in TBI-M/S	94% in TBI-M, 92% in TBI-M/S, 90% in CC
Etherton et al. (2006) Study 1	UG SIM pain-related NP problems, UG controls, UG exposed to cold pressor while completing NP tests	30%	100%
Etherton et al. (2006) Study 2	large CP clinical sample, TBI, and mixed neurological patients with documented memory impairment (CC); PM documented by external criteria	47%	100% in CP without evidence of M, 89% in TBI, 92% in CC
Axelrod et al. (2006)	large clinical sample, including TBI; PM defined by Slick et al. (1999) criteria and includes performance on standard malingering tests, cross-validation sample of mild TBI	25%	96.6% in TBI, cross validation data not reported for this cutoff

Note. PM = probable malingering/malingerers, SIM = simulators/simulating, TBI = traumatic brain injury, M = mild severity, M/S = moderate/severe, CC = clinical control group, HC = healthy control group, UG = undergraduates, CP = chronic pain, NP = neuropsychological.

correlation of the RDS with standard neuropsychological tests and found that the RDS was highly correlated with WAIS-R performance. They speculated that RDS failure might be more useful for indicating effort on the WAIS rather than effort on memory tasks.

In the past 5 years, several additional studies have further documented the use of an RDS score of < 8 as an indicator of malingering. Table 7.2 provides a summary of these studies. In all cases, specificity using RDS < 8 was very good, at 93% or greater, with a few exceptions (Babikian, Boone, Lu, &

Table 7.2.
Summary of Recent Studies Validating Reliable Digit Span <8 as an Index of Malingering

Study	Samples	Sensitivity	Specificity
Meyers & Diep (2000)	Patients with CP referred for NP testing; PM defined as seeking compensation	19.6%	96%
Inman & Berry (2002)	UG SIM, HC	27%	100%
Mathias et al. (2002)	Patients with TBI referred for NP evaluation for Workers' Compensation, personal injury, or treatment planning; PM defined by Slick et al. (1999) criteria	67%	93%
Duncan & Ausborn (2002)	Criminals with no history of TBI (archival database); PM diagnosis based on clinical judgment	67.9%	71.6%
Strauss et al. (2002)	UG SIM, HC	53%	95%
Larrabee (2003)	Patients with TBI; PM diagnosis based on failure on symptom validity tests	50%	93.5%
Etherton, Bianchini, Ciota, & Greve (2005a)	UG SIM versus UG subjected to cold pressor task	65%	100%
Etherton, Bianchini, Greve, Heinly (2005b)	Patients with CP; PM defined by Slick et al. (1999) criteria; TBI-M/S comparison group	60%	>90% in both CP and TBI
Babikian et al. (2006)	Large clinical sample; PM defined by Slick et al. (1999) criteria; HC	62%	77% in CC, 87% in HC
Heinly et al. (2006)	Large clinical sample of head-injured patients of varying severity and other clinical patients (CC); PM defined by Slick et al. (1999) criteria	71% in TBI-M, 52% in TBI-M/S	83% in TBI-M, 91% in TBI-M/S, 58% in CC

Note. PM = probable malingering/malingerers, SIM = simulator/simulating, TBI = traumatic brain injury, M = mild severity, M/S = moderate/severe, CC = clinical control group, HC = healthy control group, UG = undergraduates, CP = chronic pain, NP = neuropsychological.

Arnold, 2006; Duncan & Ausborn, 2002; Heinly, Greve, Bianchini, Love, & Brennan, 2006). Interestingly, Duncan and Ausborn's sample consisted of inmates with no history of head injury. In their sample, a score of <7 was more than 90% specific. In Babikian et al.'s sample, a score of <7 was much less sensitive to malingering (45%) but had very good specificity (93–94%). In Heinly and colleagues' large clinical sample, an RDS <8 showed better specificity in the traumatic brain-injury patients (83% in mild traumatic brain injury, 91% in the moderate to severe traumatic brain-injury group) but had poor specificity in a broad clinical group composed of various neurological patients. A score of <7 in their sample showed better specificity (93% in mild traumatic brain injury and 99% in moderate to severe traumatic brain injury but only 74% in the broad clinical group). It is interesting that the specificity was greater in the severe traumatic brain-injury sample, relative to the mild traumatic brain-injury group; one might speculate that at least some of the false positives in the mild traumatic brain-injury group represent individuals who were in fact performing in an invalid fashion but who had not been identified with traditional malingering measures.

Table 7.2 also demonstrates that the sensitivity of the RDS is quite variable, likely due to the nature and size of the sample tested in the individual studies. In any event, the RDS has been well validated in many diverse samples and across different research designs. Thus, a cutoff of <7 seems to be a solid recommendation, although <8 might also indicate malingering, particularly in the presence of other malingering indicators to help minimize false positives and with consideration of the nature and severity of the neurological injury.

The Working Memory Index of the WAIS-III has also been examined for its value as a malingering detection measure in one recent study (Etherton, Bianchini, Ciota, Heinly, & Greve, 2006). Patients with chronic pain were divided into malingering and nonmalingering groups, based on below-chance performance on standard forced-choice malingering instruments. They were also compared to neurological controls. Focusing on a score that would minimize false positives to less than 10%, their data suggest that a score of 70 or less on the Working Memory Index correctly identified 31% of the patient malingerers and 35% of the undergraduate simulators, with 90% specificity in the sample of patients with memory disorders, 92% specificity in the sample of traumatic brain-injury patients, and 96% specificity in the nonmalingering pain patients. Given their promising results, more studies should examine the use of the Working Memory Index in malingering detection, using additional neurological patient groups to further examine specificity.

Another attention task that has been evaluated as a malingering instrument is the Seashore Rhythm test, one of the subtests of the Halstead Reitan Battery, whose format is similar to that of a symptom validity measure. Spector, Lewandowski, Kelly, and Kaylor (1994) found that a score no better than chance on this test had 20% sensitivity to malingering. Trueblood and Schmidt (1993) compared head-injury patients who failed symptom validity

tests ($n = 8$) to those who passed and found that a cutoff of 9 or more errors was 65% sensitive to malingering, with 100% specificity. Gfeller and Craddock (1998) attempted to further validate these scores using undergraduate simulators compared to patients with mild TBI. They found that a score of 6 or more errors was 72.5% sensitive to malingering, with 85% specificity, while a score of 9 or more errors was 47.5% sensitive, with 97.5% specificity. In a simulated malingering study, Inman and Berry (2002) found that a score of 9 or more errors was 27% sensitive to malingering, with 98% specificity. Although these studies suggest that a score of 9 or more errors shows excellent specificity to malingering, a recent study (Ross et al., in press) found that score to be only 86% specific to malingering, using a large clinical sample of individuals with head injury, with some well defined as malingering. In their sample, a score of 10 or more errors was 92% specific, with 59% sensitivity to malingering.

Yet another attention task from the Halstead-Reitan Battery that has received some evaluation as a malingering instrument is the Speech Sounds Perception Test. Trueblood and Schmidt (1993, described in the preceding paragraph) found that a cutoff of > 17 errors was potentially useful in the detection of malingering (63% sensitivity, 94% specificity), although their small sample of malingerers makes this number difficult to interpret. Ross et al. (in press, also described in the preceding paragraph) found that a score of 13 or more errors was 90% specific to malingering, with 70% sensitivity. Overall, the data on these two Halstead-Reitan subtests are limited, and the recommended cutoffs for malingering detection show little consistency.

Cutoffs for Malingering on Tests of Psychomotor Speed

Although the vast majority of studies of malingering indices for standard neuropsychological instruments have focused on attention and memory, some researchers have highlighted psychomotor speed tasks as having potential for malingering detection. Van Gorp and colleagues (1999) observed that, on average, malingerers typically perform much more slowly on timed tasks than do individuals with documented brain damage and speculated that this might be because it is difficult for individuals to accurately judge the speed with which they are completing a task or to understand what might be an expected change in speed of performance after neurological injury.

The Trail-Making Test

Because the Trail-Making Test (TMT) is one of the most commonly administered neuropsychological tests, many have suggested that indices of malingering for this instrument would be especially useful (Guilmette, Faust, Hart, & Arkes, 1990; Lees-Haley, Smith, Williams, & Dunn, 1996). The TMT is a particularly sensitive neuropsychological test known to be influenced by

many neurological and medical conditions and also by factors such as age, education, or general intellect (Lezak, Howieson, & Loring, 2004). In neurological patients, part B of the TMT takes relatively longer to complete than part A, likely due to the increasing cognitive complexity of part B (Lamberty, Putnam, Chatel, Bieliauskas, & Adams, 1994).

Very early studies by Goebel (1983) and Trueblood and Schmidt (1993) suggested that malingerers perform in unrealistic ways on the TMT. Goebel suggested that a lower TMT B/A ratio might be useful as a malingering detection pattern, and Trueblood and Schmidt suggested that extremely long times to completion and an unusual number of errors were characteristic of malingering rather than brain damage. Lamberty, Putnam, Chatel, Bieliauskas, and Adams (1994) were among the first to assess the usefulness of such indicators for malingering detection. They combined data from several clinical and normative samples and found that age, education, and intellect significantly correlated with most TMT indices but not with the B/A ratio. They speculated that a score on B/A of <3 would indicate suspect effort.

Ruffolo, Guilmette, and Willis (2000) reviewed case files of patients with head injuries who had received outpatient neuropsychological evaluations. Malingerers made more errors and took longer on TMT A and B, although no cutoff scores were tested for classification accuracy. Of note, the average score on B/A was less than 3 in all of the groups, regardless of malingering status, thus suggesting a need to review Lamberty et al.'s suggested cutoff. Horton and Roberts (2002) applied cutoffs for TMT A and B, as well as for the ratio score, in a large sample of substance abusers. They found that few patients fell below the cutoffs they used, which were >64 seconds on TMT part A, >201 seconds on TMT part B, and a B/A ratio of ≤1.49. However, their study was significantly limited by the fact that the substance abuse sample was not screened with any other malingering measures; thus, the false positive scores may not actually have been false positives.

Iverson, Lange, Green, and Franzen (2002) used the same cutoffs as Horton and Roberts (2002) in a large sample of patients, including those with known or suspected head injury, all of whom were tested within 1 month of their injury and outpatients seeking evaluation for disability, some of whom passed effort tests and some of whom failed. The TMT A scores correctly identified 15% of malingerers, with >90% specificity across various control groups. The TMT B scores identified 12% of malingerers, with >90% specificity. The ratio score was not sensitive to malingering (4%), and specificity was relatively low (80%). They also examined the use of error scores for malingering detection and found that it was unusual for the nonmalingering groups to demonstrate two or more errors on part A and three or more on part B, suggesting some value in using error scores for malingering detection.

Unfortunately, more recent literature has not tested the diagnostic efficiency of the cutoffs suggested in these earlier studies. For example, O'Bryant, Hilsabeck, Fisher, and McCaffrey (2003) used two discriminant function analyses (one for the ratio score and one for the speed of completion for TMT

A and B) to determine whether they could distinguish litigating patients with traumatic brain injury and failure on standard malingering tests from litigating patients with traumatic brain injury who passed standard malingering tests. The DFA suggested that the ratio score identified 63% of malingerers but was not specific to malingering (44.8% specificity) and also that the DFA (using time to completion of TMT A and B time as predictors of group) suggested 65% sensitivity, with only 85% specificity. These results led them to conclude that the TMT was not useful in malingering detection.

Unfortunately, the authors did not indicate what cutoff scores were identified by the DFA, which makes it difficult to compare their results to those of prior studies. In addition, they did not test alternative cutoffs that may have increased specificity. Martin, Hoffman, and Donders (2003) tested a B/A ratio score of < 2 in their sample of malingerers compared to patients with mild brain injury. This score was not sensitive to malingering, although the base rate of malingering in their sample was quite low. There was also no mean difference in the ratio scores between the two groups, further confirming that the score was not a good discriminator. Finally, Backhaus, Fichtenberg, and Hanks (2004) used data from an archival dataset of brain-injured patients to set a floor for performance on the TMT. Performance at or above the 90th percentile on the TMT A (equal to a score of 63.3 seconds) detected 8% of malingerers, while a score at or above the 90th percentile on the TMT B (equal to a score of 192.6 in their sample) was 24% sensitive to malingering.

In summary, as the TMT studies show little consistency, it is difficult to conclude that the test has value in malingering detection. Early research using the ratio score was promising, but the majority of the literature suggests that the ratio score does not reliably discriminate malingering from valid performance. There is too little information on error scores to draw conclusions about the value of the TMT in malingering detection, although a very high number of errors on either part of the TMT is relatively unusual in clinical samples. Finally, the studies are inconsistent in speed score cutoffs, although it appears that those used by Iverson and colleagues (2002) are at least specific to malingering, relative to mildly injured patient control-group performance.

WAIS-III Processing Speed Index

The WAIS-III Processing Speed Index has been explored for its potential in malingering detection (Etherton, Bianchini, Heinly, & Greve, 2006), using the sample described earlier (Etherton, Bianchini, Ciota, et al., 2006). Processing Speed Index scores that were equal to or fell below a standard score of 70 were rare in the nonmalingering chronic pain group (96% specificity), but 63% of the malingering group fell at or below 70 on this index. Interestingly, specificity rates declined in the neurological comparison group (85% in moderate to severe traumatic brain injury, 84% in patients with documented memory disorder), which highlights the importance of considering patient

variables before interpreting any cutoff score. However, their findings support van Gorp and colleagues' (1999) contention that malingerers may exaggerate impairment by invalidly slowing their performance and suggest further exploration of the value of psychomotor speed indices in the detection of malingering.

Use of Standard Memory Tests as Indicators of Malingering

The most extensive work on the development of malingering indices within standard neuropsychological tests has been conducted on memory tasks, likely in part because memory complaints occur with such a high base rate in litigating/compensation-seeking patients (Binder & Rohling, 1996; Paniak et al., 2002). In addition, patterns of expected performance on different types of memory tasks in neurological illness/injury are well documented, allowing for the development of malingering cutoffs or indices that should be relatively specific to malingering. Recognition tasks have been particularly popular in this literature, as many studies have shown recognition tasks to be relatively robust to memory impairment in neurological injury (Bigler et al., 1996; Freed, Corkin, Growden, & Nissen, 1989; Millis & Dijkers, 1993). However, the complexity of list-learning tasks and the multiple scores they generate have led to extensive evaluation of these measures as malingering indices as well.

The Recognition Memory Test

The Recognition Memory Test (RMT) has been a popular choice as a cost- and time-efficient malingering indicator. One reason is that the RMT's sensitivity to actual memory impairment is low (Hermann, Connell, Barr, & Wyler, 1995; Kneebone, Chelune, & Luders, 1997; Naugle, Chelune, Schuster, Luders, & Comair, 1994; Sweet, Demakis, Ricker, & Millis, 2000). Another reason is that the RMT has a forced-choice format, which allows it to be used in a manner similar to symptom validity tests. However, studies have documented that less than chance performance on the RMT is not particularly sensitive to malingering (Iverson & Franzen, 1998).

Early work on the use of the RMT as a malingering indicator was conducted by Millis and colleagues, in which they demonstrated that RMT scores could differentiate patients with moderate to severe traumatic brain injury from patients in litigation related to mild traumatic brain injury (Millis, 1992; Millis & Putnam, 1994). Millis (1992) suggested a cutoff of less than 32 on the Word subtest as an indicator of malingering.

Iverson and Franzen (1994) compared patients with documented memory impairment to inmates and undergraduates who were asked to malinger on the RMT. They found that a score of < 33 on the Words subtest detected 90% of the malingerers, with 100% specificity, while a score of < 40 had 95% sensitivity, with at least 90% specificity. On the Faces subtest, a score of < 30

showed 80% sensitivity to malingering, with 100% specificity; a score of < 32 caught 92.5% of the malingerers, while still maintaining at least 90% specificity. In addition, they demonstrated that a pattern of better performance on the Faces subtest relative to the Words subtest was seen more often in the malingering subjects (55%) but less often in the memory-impaired group (22.5%). In a replication study (Iverson & Franzen, 1998), they compared patients with and without memory impairment and undergraduate malingerers on the RMT. In this study, a score of < 38 on the Words subtest identified 95% of the malingerers, with 100% specificity, and a score of < 26 on the Faces subtest successfully identified 65% of the malingerers, with 100% specificity. Furthermore, coding performance by Faces subtest higher than Words subtest resulted in an overall classification rate of 96.7%.

Based on the results of their two studies, Iverson and Franzen suggested the following interpretation of RMT scores with regard to malingering status: For the Words subtest, < 38 is a questionable performance, < 32 is suspicious of malingering, < 28 is highly suspicious of malingering, and < 20 is an invalid performance; for the Faces subtest < 30 is a questionable performance, < 28 is suspicious of malingering, < 26 is highly suspicious of malingering, and < 20 is an invalid performance. Using a cutoff of < 32 on either subtest (which falls within the 95% confidence interval for random responding; Millis, 2002), Barrash, Suhr, and Manzel (2004) detected 80% of clinical patients defined as probable malingerers, but the specificity was weak, particularly for their neurologically impaired control group (80%; 94% specificity in the psychiatric control group). Silverberg and Barrash (2005) found 93% specificity in patients with unilateral temporal lobe epilepsy who were candidates for temporal lobectomy, using a cutoff of < 32.

Other studies have provided valuable information on the specificity of RMT cutoffs to malingering by documenting the likelihood of particular scores based on injury severity. Millis (2002) has provided data on the likely scores on RMT subtests based on the severity of traumatic brain injury, using an inpatient rehabilitation sample. Of importance for the present argument, the lowest score on the Words subtest obtained in patients with severe head injury was 28, suggesting that a cutoff of < 28 would have excellent specificity for malingering, while the lowest score on the Faces subtest was 26, suggesting that a cutoff of < 26 would again show excellent specificity.

In summary, the utility of the RMT as a malingering measure has been assessed in multiple studies, using both simulator and patient probable malingerers and with specificity tested in multiple patient samples. Based on the available data, with the goal of maximizing specificity, cutoff scores of < 28 on words and < 26 on faces seem to be strongly supported, although sensitivity to malingering is likely quite low at this level of performance; a score of < 32 on the Words subtest (termed "suspicious" by Iverson and Franzen [1998]) appears to be at least adequately specific in most samples (i.e., 90% or above). However, Millis's (2002) data can be used to determine the likely scores on the RMT subtests based on injury severity. With regard to other

uses of the RMT for malingering detection, Iverson and Franzen's faces/words pattern needs further replication before its use can be recommended. Millis (ibid.) has suggested additional RMT malingering indicators that future researchers might consider examining, including long runs of incorrect responses, which were rare in his sample of traumatic brain-injury patients and thus might be useful as a malingering detection index, as well as the development of a rarely missed index equivalent for the RMT.

Cutoffs From Subtests of the Wechsler Memory Scale-III

The addition of delayed recognition trials to the latest version of the Wechsler Memory Scale prompted the development of malingering indices for two of its subtests. Langeluddecke and Lucas (2003) have examined the recognition trials for immediate and delayed recognition on the Faces subtest, as well as delayed recognition for the Logical Memory and Paired Associate Learning subtests, in patients with traumatic brain injury with malingering status diagnosed according to the Slick et al. (1999) criteria. Scores were selected for 100% specificity in the mild traumatic brain-injury patients with no evidence of malingering. A score of < 24 on Faces I was 32% sensitive to malingering, with 96% specificity in severe traumatic brain injury; a score of < 25 on Faces II was 28% sensitive to malingering, with 98% specificity in severe traumatic brain injury. For Logical Memory delayed recognition, scores of < 19 detected 48% of malingerers, with 91% specificity in the severe traumatic brain-injury comparison group. Finally, for Paired Associate Learning delayed recognition, scores of < 22 detected 69% of malingerers, with 90% specificity in severe traumatic brain injury. Although these results are not directly comparable to the RMT data, they provide further support for the value of recognition memory tests in malingering detection, even when recognition is assessed after a delay.

Other researchers have attempted to develop specific malingering indices within the recognition tasks of the Wechsler Memory Scale, rather than using cutoff scores. In 2000, Killgore and DellaPietra reported on the Rarely Missed Index (RMI), which was developed from the long-term delayed recognition trial for the Logical Memory subtest. Using a sample of 50 healthy volunteers who had never seen the content of the Wechsler Memory Scale-III stories, six long-term delay recognition items were found to be correctly endorsed above chance levels. When comparing the performance of analog malingerers to patients with traumatic brain injury on a weighted combination of these items (derived from a discriminant function analysis), using a cutoff score of less than or equal to 136, they found that they could detect malingering with 97% sensitivity and 100% specificity. Table 7.3 summarizes research studies that have examined the effectiveness of the RMI in malingering detection using this cutoff.

Interestingly, although Table 7.3 demonstrates that the RMI has adequate sensitivity and at least acceptable specificity to malingering, Lange,

Table 7.3.
Studies Validating the Rarely Missed Index in Malingering Detection

Study	Samples	Sensitivity	Specificity
Killgore & DellaPietra (2000)	SIM compared to patients with TBI	97%	100%
Miller et al. (2004)	VA patients with alcohol/ substance abuse or TBI, none in litigation or seeking compensation	not assessed	95%
Lange et al. (2003)	Patients with TBI, some PM, compared to HC	88.9%	90%
Lange et al. (2005)	Patients with TBI given symptom validity measures to judge PM status, CC	25% in PM, 41.7% in borderline PM	90.7% in TBI-M, 94.6% in TBI-M/S, 93.6% in CC

Note. PM = probable malingering/malingerers, SIM = simulator/simulating, TBI = traumatic brain injury, M = mild severity, M/S = moderate/severe, CC = clinical control group, HC = healthy control group, UG = undergraduates, CP = chronic pain, NP = neuropsychological.

Senior, Douglas, and Dawes (2003) and Lange, Sullivan, and Anderson (2005) interpreted their results as suggesting that the RMI is unreliable in view of the fact that the positive predictive power (PPP; the ratio of true positives to true positives plus false positives) was only 57% in their first study. Moreover, in their second study, the symptom validity test identified significantly more individuals as malingerers. The PPP values in their first study were likely due to the extremely low base rate of malingering in the sample; in the second study, the results merely suggest the lower sensitivity of the RMI relative to standard malingering instruments. However, to date only limited data are available on this relatively new malingering measure, and more studies are needed.

In 2003 Glassmire and colleagues attempted to develop a similar index with the WMS Faces subtest. Although the format of this subtest is not truly that of a symptom validity test, they speculated that, given the equal number of yes and no responses in the task as a whole, the format was similar enough to suggest its use as a malingering test. Participants in their study included patients with traumatic brain injury who had passed effort tests and were not in unresolved litigation, as well as a healthy control group. In their within-subjects design, both groups first performed the test under normal conditions and were then asked to malinger.

Using the normal condition data from their traumatic brain-injury patients, they identified five items that 90% of the sample answered correctly. Each item was weighted to create a rarely missed index. Unfortunately, the index did not add significantly to the detection of groups beyond a simple

cutoff score on this subscale and thus was not further examined in their study. A cutoff score of < 18, which would be significantly below chance, was 100% specific to malingering and 30% sensitive to healthy control malingering but was only 13% sensitive to patient malingering. A score of < 24 was also 100% specific but caught more malingerers (33% sensitivity in the patient sample and 63% in the control sample); it is notable that this cutoff would be consistent with data from Landeluddecke and Lucas (2003) reported earlier. Further cross-validation of these cutoffs would increase support for their use in malingering detection.

The Complex Figure Test

The Complex Figure Test (CFT) has been suggested as a potentially useful indicator of malingering, in part because of the nonmemory portion of the task (the copy condition), which tends to be relatively insensitive to general brain dysfunction (Ashton, Donders, & Hoffman, 2005), and also because there are multiple trials that may be more difficult to malinger accurately (Lu, Boone, Cozolino, & Mitchell, 2003). The addition of a recognition trial has also been viewed as useful for malingering detection (ibid.).

However, only a few studies have examined scores other than delayed recall/recognition for their usefulness in malingering detection. Lu and colleagues (ibid.) compared mild head-injured patients (both in litigation and not in litigation) to 10 confirmed patient malingerers and 25 undergraduate simulators. A CFT copy score of < 28 was 50% sensitive to malingering, with 91.4% specificity in their sample. A CFT copy score of < 25 had 44% sensitivity but was 95.7% specific to malingering. Lu and colleagues also examined the value of the immediate recall score as a malingering detection measure. A score of < 10 had 36.2% sensitivity and 91.4% specificity. Finally, they examined the recognition subscale and found that a score of < 4 was 24.1% sensitive to malingering, with 98.6% specificity, while a false positive score of > 4 was only 6.9% sensitive to malingering but with 100% specificity.

Lu and colleagues observed that the copy and recognition scores were not correlated, and yet each was sensitive to malingering; thus, they calculated a combination score in the hope that it would increase sensitivity while remaining specific to malingering. Their formula was copy score + [(true positive recognition score − atypical recognition errors) × 3]. Atypical recognition errors were determined from recognition trial items that were rarely missed by healthy controls or individuals with documented brain damage. A cutoff of < 48 on this combination of scores was 75.9% sensitive to malingering, with > 90% specificity in most clinical control groups, with the exception of those with documented visual memory impairment, where specificity dropped to 82.4%. However, a score of < 46 was still highly sensitive to malingering (74.1%), with 88.2% specificity (the highest specificity reported for this sample in their data). However, as this combination score was developed based on that study, it would need to be cross-validated in an

independent sample in order for it to be sufficiently accurate for use in malingering detection.

Meyers and colleagues (Meyers, Bayless, & Meyers, 1996; Meyers & Volbrecht, 1998) developed and validated memory error patterns (MEPs) as a way to classify performance on the CFT recall and recognition trials. Four memory error patterns were described: attention/encoding, storage, retrieval, and normal patterns; assignment to a pattern was based on overall performance (impaired or not) and the relative pattern of immediate, delay, and recognition scores. These patterns are described more fully in the professional manual for the CFT (Meyers & Meyers, 1995).

Meyers and Volbrecht (1999) examined the use of MEPs in the detection of malingering. Their first experiment assessed the efficacy of these measures by comparing the performance of patients in litigation to those not in litigation. They found that attention and storage MEPs were made by the litigation group but not by the nonlitigation group. In their second study, the litigant patients from their first study were classified as malingerers based on performance on a malingering test; they also administered the CFT to undergraduate simulators. The results suggested that attention and memory MEPs were found only in very severely impaired patients, but all of the malingerers produced either storage or attention MEPs. Thus, they suggested that these scales might be useful in the detection of malingering. Meyers and Diep (2000) also used the MEP system to examine malingering in patients with chronic pain. They gave numerical values to the levels of MEPs (1 = attention, 2 = encoding, 3 = storage, 4 = retrieval, 5 = normal/other) and found that a score of 3 or less was 31.4% sensitive and 100% specific to suspected malingering (as defined by the patients' involvement in litigation).

Overall, relatively few studies have examined the use of the CFT in malingering detection. Cross-validation of cutoff scores suggested by Lu and colleagues is needed before they can be recommended for use. Although MEPs have shown promise, particularly with regard to specificity, further work by other independent research laboratories is necessary.

The Auditory Verbal Learning Test

As malingering investigators began turning their attention to standard neuropsychological tests, it was natural that the Auditory Verbal Learning Test (AVLT) would generate particular interest. Not only is the AVLT one of the most widely used memory tests (Peaker & Stewart, 1989), but it also allows for the quantification of several aspects of memory function and detailed characterization of patterns of performance. Since the first investigation of the potential of AVLT scores to identify malingerers by Bernard in 1990, numerous AVLT variables have been examined. Most widely studied have been standard scores such as immediate recall on Trial 1 and Trial 5; "learning" (total words recalled on Trials 1–5); recall at short delay (Trial 7); and delayed recall, delayed recognition (true positives), and intrusions (false

positive recognition of foils). The findings from these studies are summarized in Table 7.4.

Probable malingerers (i.e., clinical groups, defined variously) or, more often, simulated malingerers almost invariably perform more poorly on each of these measures when compared to healthy control groups. However, because individuals with normal memory can be expected to perform normally, these findings constitute weak support of these measures' diagnostic potential. A different picture is seen when either malingering group is compared to clinical groups with documented brain dysfunction: There is a failure to find significant differences about as often as not for each of the standard AVLT measures and for suggested AVLT patterns of performance, with one notable exception. In all six studies that compared the delayed recognition of probable malingerers to clinical groups, the probable malingerers had significantly lower recognition, and simulated malingerers performed more poorly than clinical groups in most such comparisons.

Studies of the diagnostic accuracy of specific cutoffs on AVLT indices, although fewer in number than those comparing group means, have been appearing more frequently over the past 5 years and have examined an ever-increasing array of variables. Table 7.5 summarizes these findings. As delayed recognition is the score on which probable malingerers differ most reliably from clinical comparison groups, it is not surprising that its diagnostic accuracy has been the most investigated. In approximately a quarter of the reviewed studies, recognition was assessed with words embedded in a paragraph; in most of the studies a recognition word list was employed. The results are highly consistent across paradigms, and we thus consider both methodologies together.

Binder and colleagues (Binder, Kelly, Villanueva, & Winslow, 2003; Binder, Villanueva, Howieson, & Moore, 1993) reported that a cutoff of < 6 on delayed recognition is reasonably specific to malingering (94–95% in TBI in their 1993 study; 92–95% in their 2003 study); others suggest that a higher cutoff is more sensitive while maintaining specificity above 90%. For example, Meyers, Morrison, and Miller (2001) used a cutoff of < 10, which was 100% specific among individuals with mild TBI and not in litigation, although this cutoff was not very sensitive to malingering, at least in their clinical sample of probable malingerers (12%).

While Boone, Lu, and Wen (2005) report multiple sensitivity and specificity values, their cutoff of < 10 was highly sensitive to malingering (67%), with acceptable specificity (92–93% in a mixed neurological sample). Research suggests that, to consistently demonstrate 100% specificity, much more stringent cutoffs are needed; for example, Binder and colleagues (1993, 2003) report a cutoff of 3, and Boone and colleagues (2005) report a similar cutoff. Of note, the sensitivities for cutoffs that achieved 100% specificity ranged from 10% to 15% across studies, demonstrating a significant overlap in the distribution of delayed recognition scores in probable malingerers and clinical controls at the lower end of the latter group's distribution. Taken

Table 7.4.

Summary of Group Difference Findings in Studies of Malingering Detection Using the Auditory Verbal Learning Test[1]

Standard Measures	PM vs. Clinical Controls	SIM vs. Clinical Controls	PM vs. Normal Controls	SIM vs. Normal Controls
Trial 1	1/4 (1)	1/2	1/1	3/4
Trial 5	2/3 (1)	2/4	—	4/4
Learning	1/3	0/2 (1)	—	2/2
Short-delay recall	2/3	1/3	—	2/2
Delayed recall	2/3 (1)	2/4	—	7/7
Delayed recognition[2]	6/6	4/6 (1)	2/2	7/7
Intrusions[2]	0/2 (1)	1/2	—	1/1
Pattern indices				
Primacy	— (1)	2/2 (1)	—	4/4
Recency	0/1	0/2	—	1/2
Serial position	—	—	—	0/1
Learning curve	0/1	—	—	2/2
Difference[3]	1/1	0/1	—	—
Delayed recognition/ delayed recall	—	—	—	1/1
30′ recall/60′ recall	—	—	—	1/1
30′ recognition/ 60′ recognition	—	—	—	0/1
Index 1	—	—	—	—
Index 2	—	—	—	—
Index 3	—	—	—	0/1

Notes. Studies included are Bernard (1990, 1991), Bernard et al., (1993), Binder (1993a), Greiffenstein et al. (1994), Flowers et al. (1996), Chouinard & Rouleau (1997), Suhr et al. (1997), King et al. (1998), Suhr & Gunstad (2000), Haines & Norris (2001), Meyers et al., (2001), Inman & Berry (2002), Sherman et al. (2002), Suhr (2002), Binder et al. (2003), Suhr et al. (2004), Boone et al. (2005).
[1]Number of studies with positive results/total number of studies, with number of studies with mixed results when there are multiple target groups or comparison groups presented in parentheses. When target groups differed from a comparison group with a mild or moderate brain condition but did not differ from a severely injured brain-injured comparison group, this was considered a positive finding.
[2]Included are findings from Chouinard & Rouleau (1997), in which recognition and intrusions were assessed after a short delay rather than at 30′ delay.
[3]Difference = (short delay recognition − Trial 5); Index 1 = failure to recognize words recalled on three or more learning trials; Index 2 = failure to recognize words recalled at 30′ delay; Index 3 = failure to recognize words at 60′ that were recalled
at 30′ delay. PM = probable malingering, SIM = simulated malingering.

Table 7.5.
Studies of Malingering Detection Using the Auditory Verbal Learning Test: Sensitivity and Specificity

Study	Samples	Index and Cutoff	Sensitivity	Specificity
Bincer et al. (1993b)	TBI of varying severity, some well-documented PM	Delayed recognition <6	27%	94% TBI-M, 95% TBI-M/S
Chouinard & Rouleau (1997)	PM in large mixed clinical group (75% TBI-M); HC SIM, CC	Difference score <0	76%	87%
Suhr & Gunstad (2000)	UG SIM, HC	¹Primacy index <25%	16%	97%
Meyers et al. (2001)	TBI of varying severity, some in litigation, HC (some SIM)	Delayed recognition <10	12% TBI-lit, 50% HC SIM	100%
Suhr (2002)	UG SIM (some coached), TBI-M/S, HC	Primacy index <26%	13%	97%
Binder et al. (2003)	TBI sample well defined as PM, TBI of varying severity	Delayed recognition <6	38%	95% TBI-M, 92% TBI-M/S
Barrash et al. (2004)	Study 1: PM, neurological CC, psychiatric CC. Study 2: same groups, independent samples	Exaggeration index >2	72% in Study 1, 59% in Study 2	Study 1: 98% neuro CC, 93% psych CC. Study 2: 97% neuro CC, 92% psych CC

Study	Sample	Measure/Cutoff	Sensitivity	Specificity
Suhr et al. (2004)	Study 1: UG SIM, some coached, HC. Study 2: UG with history of head injury, some SIM, some coached, HC	Exaggeration index >2	Study 1: 19% naïve SIM, 27% coached SIM; Study 2: 33% naïve SIM, 24% coached SIM	Study 1: 100%, Study 2: 96%
Boone et al. (2005)[2]	PM patients, mixed neurological injury sample, HC	Trial 5 <8	48%	90% CC, 96% HC
		Total learning <30	41%	91% CC, 96% HC
		Short-delay recall <4	30%	96% CC, 100% HC
		Delayed recall <3	28%	94% CC, 96% HC
		Primacy recall <11	54%	91% CC, 92% HC
		Recency recall <11	16%	91% CC, 96% HC
		Delayed recognition <10	67%	93% CC, 92% HC
		Intrusions >9	2%	99% CC, 100% HC
		True recognition <8	64%	93% CC, 96% HC
		Primacy recognition <3	44%	97% CC, 92% HC
		Recency recognition <3	54%	91% CC, 96% HC
		Index 1 >3	8%	100%
		Index 2 >2	1%	99% CC, 100% HC
		Stem 2 <5	26%	92% CC, 96% HC
		Stem 2 time (sec) >89	32%	93% CC, 96% HC
		Time difference (sec) >39	15%	92% CC, 96% HC

(continued)

Table 7.5.
(*continued*)

Study	Samples	Index and Cutoff	Sensitivity	Specificity
		Temporal order <5	15%	94% CC
		Implicit memory combination <23	76%	91% CC
		AVLT combination <11	62%	94% CC, 96% HC
Silverberg & Barrash (2005)	Candidates for temporal lobectomy for severe temporal lobe epilepsy	Exaggeration Index >2	N/A	94%

Note. [1]The later analysis of primary index of data from Suhr & Gunstad (2000) was reported in Suhr (2002).
[2]Boon et al. (2005) reported sensitivity and specificity cutoffs across a wide range; here values over 90% specificity for both control groups are reported. PM = probable malingering/malingerers, SIM = simulators/simulating, TBI = traumatic brain injury,
M = mild severity, M/S = moderate/severe, HC = healthy control group, UG = undergraduates.

together, the studies suggest that the sensitivities and specificities for various cutoffs of delayed recognition may vary widely depending on the "purity" of the probable malingerer sample and the severity of the brain-injured comparison group.

In addition to delayed recognition, Boone et al. (ibid.) examined the diagnostic accuracy of several other standard AVLT scores over a range of cutoffs. Although they report data across a range of specificity values, Table 7.5 provides only cutoff scores that generated at least 90% specificity in all of the control groups. As Table 7.5 indicates, a wide range of sensitivities was identified across many potential AVLT indices, with a general pattern suggesting that variables reflecting deficient learning tend to be more sensitive than those associated with poor delayed recall.

Given the limited sensitivity of standard scores other than delayed recognition, the diagnostic accuracy of indices based on patterns of AVLT performance has been receiving increasing attention. In their 1997 study, Chouinard and Rouleau (1997) observed that both probable and simulated malingerers tended to recognize fewer words than they had recalled on Trial 5, a pattern that differed qualitatively from patients with bona fide memory impairment. In a post hoc analysis of the difference score (i.e., recognition minus Trial 5 recall), a cutoff of –1 had 76% sensitivity among clinical probable malingerers (various etiologies, 75% with mild TBI) and 76% among simulated malingerers, with specificities of 89% to mild memory impairment, 100% to severe memory impairment, and 80% to memory impairment among patients with frontal lobe dysfunction.

Several studies have also reported on the diagnostic accuracy of the primacy effect. Suhr and colleagues (1997, 2002) found group differences in the number of words 1–5 recalled, yet findings from other studies (reviewed in Table 7.4) have suggested that the lack of primacy effect is not reliably associated with malingering. In 2002 Suhr described the "primacy index," a refined definition of the relevant pattern of performance: the recall of words 1–5 as a percentage of total learning over the five learning trials. With a cutoff of 25%, the sensitivity of the primacy index among simulated malingerers was 13%, with 97% specificity to moderate–severe TBI. Application of the primacy index to data from an earlier study (Suhr & Gunstad, 2000) yielded virtually identical sensitivity among simulated malingerers (16%) and specificity among normal controls (97%).

Boone et al. (2005) looked at the primacy effect across the five learning trials (not adjusted for level of total learning) and reported that a cutoff of 3 or less identified 10% of the probable malingerers with 100% specificity to brain-damaged controls, while a cutoff of 10 or less identified 54% of the probable malingerers with 91% specificity. These studies raise the question of whether attenuation of the primacy effect might be more pronounced among clinical malingerers than simulated malingerers and, if so, whether it might be more useful diagnostically than studies of simulated malingerers have suggested.

They also raise the question of the optimal definition of the primacy effect for the purpose of identifying malingerers. Although investigators have followed the precedent of Bernard (1991) in defining the effect as the preferential recall of words 1–5, Barrash, Suhr, and Manzel have suggested that it is the preferential recall of words 1–3 that characterizes the primacy effect. Moreover, it is the relative failure in recalling words 1–3 that most effectively discriminates malingering patients from brain-injured patients and a psychiatric comparison group (preliminary analyses reported in Barrash et al., 1998, 2004).

In 1998 Barrash and colleagues described an innovative approach to using the AVLT to detect malingering based on observations that many malingerers demonstrate misconceptions regarding *both* the severity *and* the nature of memory impairment caused by brain dysfunction (Rogers, Harrell, & Liff, 1993), including a steadily progressive loss of information over time, in contrast to neuropathological memory impairment, which is characterized by rapid forgetting followed by relatively stable retention of successfully acquired information (Cohen & Eichenbaum, 1993). Barrash and colleagues (1998) reasoned that sensitivity to malingering or inadequate effort could be increased by adding a second round of delayed recall and recognition at 60 minutes and then examining several aspects of performances across trials. To the extent that malingerers are unable to keep track of which of the *truly remembered* words they had reported recalling or recognizing at earlier trials, their pattern of recall and recognition might reveal inconsistencies that are atypical of brain-damaged individuals.

The guiding principle in developing the "Exaggeration Index" (EI) from the expanded AVLT procedure was to include only variables that would maintain an extremely high level of specificity in the composite measure. Preliminary analyses were conducted with 25 probable malingerers (using the criteria of Greiffenstein et al. [1994], excluding neuropsychological test performance), 43 patients with memory impairment from documented brain damage (BD), and 40 persons referred for evaluation of memory impairment determined to be due to primary psychiatric disturbance (Study 1, Barrash et al., 2004).

These analyses resulted in the inclusion of seven aspects of AVLT performance in the EI: (a) exceedingly poor learning; (b) lack of a primacy effect (words 1–3 constituting the primacy effect); (c) worsening recall (from 30-minute to 60-minute delay); (d) worsening recognition; (e) failure to recognize learned words ("learned words" refers to words recalled on at least four of the five learning trials); (f) failure to recognize recalled words; and (g) exceedingly poor recognition. To maximize specificity, scores on these seven aspects of performance were each scaled along a 4-point scale: 3 = completely outside the range of the BD distribution; 2 = scores rare among BD; 1 = scores very infrequent among BD; 0 = scores not sufficiently infrequent among BD. Scaled scores for the seven variables were then tallied to form the Exaggeration Index score. An EI cutoff score of 3 or higher resulted in 72% sensitivity with 98% specificity for the brain-damaged group and 93% specificity for the psychiatric group.

In a cross-validation study (Study 2, ibid.) the diagnostic accuracy of the EI was assessed in independent samples of 34 probable malingerers, 70 patients with BD, and 40 persons with psychiatric disturbance (as defined in Study 1). With the EI cutoff of 3, sensitivity declined from 72% to 59%, while specificity remained at 97% for the brain-damaged group and was 92% for the psychiatric group. Rather than reducing information from the Exaggeration Index to "pass/fail" with a single cutoff, a probabilistic interpretation of EI scores was encouraged. A score of 4 ("extremely probable malingering") showed 38% sensitivity with a specificity of 100% to brain damage and 98% to psychiatric disturbance. A score of 2 ("probable malingering") yielded 71% sensitivity with a specificity of 92% to brain damage and 88% to psychiatric disturbance. A score of 1 ("possible malingering") had 88% sensitivity with a specificity of 77% to brain damage and 73% to psychiatric disturbance.

Suhr, Gunstad, Greub, and Barrash (2004) hypothesized that the EI, by virtue of its complexity, would be less vulnerable to coaching. Undergraduate simulated malingerers were either naïve to or coached regarding the presence of malingering-detection techniques in a battery of tests. As Table 7.5 shows, EI sensitivity was no lower in the coached malingerers, thus supporting the hypothesis. The specificity was 100%. In Study 2 with independent samples, Suhr et al. found that EI sensitivity was only marginally lower for coached rather than naïve malingerers, and specificity was 96%.

The EI was designed to minimize false positives. A stringent test was provided by Silverberg and Barrash (2005), who examined EI specificity in a consecutive series of 56 Canadian candidates for temporal lobectomy for severe temporal lobe epilepsy. Specificity in this group with severe memory impairment was 94%. It was noted that elevated EI scores were largely the result of very low levels of learning and/or recognition and were rarely due to the five pattern variables. It was concluded that elevated EI scores due to atypical patterns of AVLT performance are almost always associated with inadequate effort or malingering, but when a patient with severe neuropathology has an elevated EI score due solely to a very low level of learning or recognition, it is especially important for clinicians to consider whether independent evidence of malingering is present.

Boone and colleagues (2005) also added tasks onto the standard AVLT administration in an effort to improve sensitivity to malingering. First, after the delayed recognition trial, the examinees performed a word-stem completion task with 12 unrelated three-letter stems. Next, they were presented with a second set of 12 three-letter stems derived from 12 of the 15 AVLT target words. They were instructed to work as quickly as possible on both trials, which were timed. Finally, memory for the temporal order of the AVLT words was assessed. The outcome measures included the number of AVLT words produced on the second word-stem task ("Stem 2"), the time to completion on the second word-stem task ("Stem 2 time"), the time to completion on the second word-stem task minus the time to completion on the first word-stem task ("time difference"), and the number of correct responses

regarding the temporal order of the target words ("temporal order"). For cutoffs with 90–95% specificity in the brain-damaged control group, sensitivities among probable malingerers were 26% and 32%, respectively, for Stem 2 and Stem 2 time but only 14–15% for time difference and temporal order.

An analysis of the data led to the creation of two post hoc composite indices. "Implicit memory combination score" (true memory [delayed recognition minus intrusions] + Stem 2 + temporal order) yielded sensitivities ranging from 76% to 49% for cutoffs associated with specificity among neurologic patients ranging from 91.5% to 98.6%. A second composite index, "AVLT combination score" (true recognition + primacy recognition), yielded sensitivities ranging from 74% to 28% for cutoffs associated, with specificity among neurologic patients ranging from 90% to 99%. A cross-validation of these measures will be critical to examine the degree to which observed sensitivities and specificities are inflated by capitalization on chance.

In summary, there is very little consistency across the studies in cutoff scores on standard AVLT indices, with the possible exception of delayed recognition. However, even for a cutoff of < 10 on delayed recognition, sensitivity was highly variable, although specificity was consistently high. Thus, the generalizability of the diagnostic accuracy reported for specific AVLT cutoff scores remains unknown. The studies of Boone and colleagues and Barrash and colleagues suggest that indices that combine several aspects of performance on the AVLT have considerably greater sensitivity than do individual AVLT variables while maintaining good levels of specificity. It may be that the combined information regarding (a) an exceedingly low level of performance (especially on recognition) and (b) a pattern of performance atypical of bona fide memory impairment enhances sensitivity.

The sole AVLT measure for which the diagnostic accuracy of the scores has been cross-validated in independent clinical samples is the Exaggeration Index. The high specificity that was the primary consideration in its derivation (Barrash et al., 2004, Study 1) has been cross-validated for EI scores of 2 or higher in clinical samples in three different centers (ibid., 2004, Study 2; Silverberg & Barrash, 2005; Suhr et al., 2004, Study 2). Sensitivities associated with EI scores have been cross-validated in only one clinical sample of probable malingerers (Barrash et al., 2004, Study 2), but the levels of sensitivity showed only limited reduction from those observed in the derivation sample (ibid., Study 1), lending some confidence in sensitivities reported for various EI scores.

The California Verbal Learning Test

Not long after the first investigation of malingering detection with the AVLT, Trueblood and Schmidt (1993) reported the first investigation employing the California Verbal Learning Test (CVLT), which examined the performances of very small clinical groups. The findings from this and other

Table 7.6.
Summary of Group Difference Findings in Studies of Malingering Detection
Using the California Verbal Learning Test

Standard Measures	PM vs. Clinical Controls	SIM vs. Healthy Controls
Total learning	5/5	1/1
Delayed recognition	5/5	1/1
Intrusions	0/1	—
Long-delay cued recall	3/3	1/1
Discriminability	3/3	1/1
Slope	—	1/1
Primacy	0/2	—
Recency	0/2	—
Semantic clustering	1/1	—
Recall consistency	0/1	—
Pattern Indices		
Consistency (T1)[1]	—	1/1
Consistency (T2)[1]	—	1/1
CVLT indicators[2]	1/1	—

Note. Studies in this review include the following: Trueblood & Schmidt (1993), Trueblood (1994), Millis et al. (1995), Coleman et al. (1998), Demakis (1999), Slick (2000), & Curtis et al. (in press). PM = probable malingerers, SIM = simulated malingerers.
[1]Consistency is defined as percentage of words recalled on learning trial that were recalled on the subsequent learning trial; in this study (Demakis, 1999) assessment occurred at two different time periods separated by 3 weeks. Two CVLT indicators were the number of indicators that fell below cutoff; indicators included total learning, long-delay cued recall, delayed recognition, and discriminability (Sweet et al., 2000).

CVLT investigations are catalogued in Table 7.6. Across studies, consistent differences emerge in the CVLT total learning score, long-delayed cued recall, delayed recognition, and discriminability, even when clinical comparison groups are used. Table 7.7 summarizes the studies that examined the diagnostic accuracy of cutoffs that have been assessed in CVLT studies. The majority of these studies focused on the replication of cutoffs suggested by Millis, Putnam, Adams, and Ricker (1995) and are included in Table 7.7 with permission. For a total learning score of < 35, sensitivities vary from 39% to 74%, with specificities generally above 90%. However, at least two studies suggested lower specificity (83%) in moderate to severe TBI and in older community-dwelling adults (Sweet et al., 2000; Ashendorf, O'Bryant, & McCaffrey, 2003). For a long-delayed cued recall score of < 7, sensitivities ranged from 48% to 83%, again with specificities generally above 90% (but

Table 7.7.
Studies Using the California Verbal Learning Test (CVLT) to Detect Malingering: Sensitivity and Specificity of Cutoffs

Study	Samples	Index and Cutoff	Sensitivity	Specificity
Trueblood & Schmidt (1993)	Patients with TBI, mostly mild severity; some PM (failure on SV test), some QV (as judged by performance on non-SV test performance)	delayed recognition (<13)	63% PM, 50% QV	72–100%
Trueblood (1994)	Similar to Trueblood and Schmidt (1993)	total learning (<48)	75% PM, 70% QV	92–100%
		delayed recognition (<13)	75% PM, 60% QV	90–92%
		CVLT indicators (>0)	91% PM, 89% QV	89–91%
Millis et al. (1995)	Mild TBI patients diagnosed as PM using RMT; TBI-M/S	total learning (<35)	74%	91%
		LDCR (<7)	83%	91%
		delayed recognition (<11)	83%	96%
		discriminability (<81)	96%	91%
Coleman et al. (1998)	UG SIM, some coached, HC	delayed recognition (<11)	68%	100%
		discriminability (<81)	52%	96%
Sweet et al. (2000)	PM, SIM, TBI-M/S, HC	total learning (<35)	52% PM, 64% SIM	83% TBI-M/S, 100% HC

Study	Group	Measure (cutoff)		
		total learning (<41)	62% PM, 80% SIM	76% TBI-M/S, 100% HC
		LDCR (<7)	48% PM, 56% SIM	83% TBI-M/S, 95% HC
		LDCR (<8)	62% PM, 56% SIM	74% TBI-M/S, 95% HC
		delayed recognition (<11)	48% PM, 76% SIM	90% TBI-M/S, 100% HC
		delayed recognition (<13)	71% PM, 88% SIM	83% TBI-M/S, 95% HC
		discrminability (<81)	57% PM, 60% SIM	86% TBI-M/S, 100% HC
		discriminability (<84)	62% PM, 68% SIM	81% TBI-M/S, 100% HC
		intrusions (>12)	29% PM, 32% SIM	88% TBI-M/S, 100% HC
		recognition-recall (>100)	30% PM, 30% SIM	80% TBI-M/S, 100% HC
Slick (2000)	TBI patients, varying severity, some diagnosed as PM based on SV testing	total learning (<35)	39%	91%
		LDCR (<7)	39%	92%
		delayed recognition (<11)	36%	93%
		discriminability (<81)	36%	96%
		CVLT indicators (>0)	58%	87%
Ashendorf et al. (2003)	HC (healthy community-dwelling adults over age 55)	learning (<35)	83%	
		LDCR (<7)	92%	
		delayed recognition (<11)	90%	
		discriminability (<81)	92%	

(continued)

Table 7.7.
(continued)

Study	Samples	Index and Cutoff	Sensitivity	Specificity
Demakis (2004)	SIM, HC	learning (<35)	54%	100%
		learning (<48)	73%	74%
		LDCR (<7)	50%	96%
		delayed recognition (<11)	46%	96%
		delayed recognition (<13)	69%	96%
		discriminability (<81)	62%	100%
Curtis et al. (2006)	TBI (malingering status diagnosed using Slick et al. criteria) (this study also used psychiatric patients as controls, but they were not screened for malingering status and thus are not included in the data reported in this table)	delayed recognition (<11)	47%	91%
		discriminability (<81)	52%	89%
		LDCR (<7)	56%	83%

Note. PM = probable malingering/malingerers, SIM = simulators/simulating, TBI = traumatic brain injury, M = mild severity, M/S = moderate/severe, HC = healthy control group, CC = clinical control group, UG = undergraduates, SV = symptom validity, QV = questionable validity, RMT = Recognition Memory Test, LDCR = long-delay cued recall.

see Curtis, Greve, Bianchini, and Brennan [2006] for an exception). For a delayed recognition score of < 11, sensitivities ranged from 36% to 83%; in all five studies, specificity was above 90%. For a discriminability score of < 81, sensitivities ranged from 36% to 96%, again generally with specificities above 90%.

Other researchers have explored additional cutoffs for these CVLT indices. The cutoff for recognition used by Trueblood (1993) and Trueblood and Schmidt (1994) is more liberal than the Millis cutoff and results in impressive rates of sensitivity. On replication, however, Millis et al. (1995) found a grossly inadequate specificity (74%) for this cutoff. Similarly, the Trueblood cutoff for learning was evidently set too high; that cutoff has not been replicated with a clinical comparison group, but Demakis (2004) found a grossly inadequate specificity (74%) for the cutoff in a normal control group. More liberal post hoc cutoffs that maximized the correct classification of the Sweet et al. (2000) samples improved the sensitivity of the four frequently studied CVLT indicators (compared to that of the Millis cutoffs), but the generally modest improvement occurred at some cost to specificity, which fell to the 74–83% range.

In a departure from a focus on individual score cutoffs, Demakis (1999) described a procedure similar to the repeated AVLT (Barrash et al., 1998) and also cited the expectation that malingerers would have difficulty remembering their earlier responses and performing consistently across presentations. They administered the CVLT to groups of undergraduates simulating malingering or putting forth normal effort and then readministered the test after a 3-week interval. In addition to standard performance measures, Demakis assessed consistency across learning trials (i.e., the percentage of words recalled on one learning trial that were recalled on the subsequent learning trial). As expected, the simulated malingerers were more inconsistent than normal controls on the initial administration of the CVLT and again 3 weeks later. Diagnostic accuracy was not reported for these two measures but was reported for the change across the two test sessions on learning, short-delay free recall (SDFR), and long-delay free recall (LDFR). Post hoc cutoff scores were determined. Although sensitivities were encouraging (67–81%), the specificities were exceedingly weak (62–71%). The low specificities among normal undergraduates reveal liberal cutoffs, and the high sensitivities observed in the derivation sample would likely be reduced considerably were cutoffs set to achieve more than 90% specificity in a brain-injured population.

Slick, Iverson, and Green (2000) also examined a combination of CVLT variables in patients with brain injuries ranging from negligible to severe. The patients were classified according to their performance on a symptom validity test, and those with an implausibly low performance (i.e., probable malingerers) were compared to the remainder. Slick and colleagues examined redundancy among the CVLT indicators by determining the proportion of patients with suboptimal performance who were identified by a score below the cutoff on one or more indicators. This boosted sensitivity to 58%,

while specificity fell to 87%. They concluded that the CVLT indicators are nonredundant but that consideration of any one or more of them as indicative of suboptimal performance may be associated with weaker than acceptable specificity.

Further analyses by Slick et al. revealed that, among the TBI patients with at least one positive CVLT indicator, those with negligible to mild injuries by objective indicators were more likely to have scored below cutoffs on three or four indicators, while those with moderate to severe injuries were more likely to have scored below the cutoff on only one or two indicators. Thus, while the presence of one positive CVLT indicator may carry an unacceptable risk of false positives, especially among patients with moderate to severe brain injury, the presence of more positive indicators makes suboptimal performance or malingering a more likely explanation than severe brain dysfunction. Similar conclusions have been drawn by Curtis and colleagues (2006).

Emphasizing that examinees may produce implausible scores for reasons other than malingering, Moore and Donders (2004) took a different methodological approach to investigating the relationship between neuropsychological measures and invalid test scores. They investigated factors associated with invalid performances on two malingering measures: CVLT-II forced-choice recognition and Trial 2 of the TOMM (Tombaugh, 1996). In the second edition of the CVLT, a 16-item forced-choice recognition task (List A words vs. foils) was added after the standard long-delay recognition trial for the purpose of assessing effort. Moore and Donders noted that 99% of the examinees in the normative standardization sample obtained scores of 15 or 16, resulting in a cutoff score of 14 or less for invalid effort (Delis, Kramer, Kaplan, & Ober, 2000). Moore and Donders examined 132 patients from a 3-year series of consecutive neuropsychological evaluations with TBI (various severity levels) and no prior neurological or special education history.

Some of the patients had financial incentives. The likelihood of malingering was not an independent variable; rather, the patients were subdivided according to whether they performed below a priori cutoffs on either of two malingering indices. Fifteen patients (11.4% of the sample) scored below the cutoff on CVLT forced-choice recognition, 11 patients (8.3%) scored below the cutoff on the TOMM, and 6 patients from these two groups (4.5% of the full sample) performed below the cutoff on both measures. Thus, of patients with invalid performances, 75% were identified by the CVLT index, and only 25% with an invalid performance failed to fall below the cutoff on CVLT forced-choice recognition.

The diagnostic accuracy of this measure could not be determined because the sample was not classified according to malingering status. However, patients with an invalid performance (on either measure) were significantly more likely to have a financial incentive compared to subjects without an invalid performance (40% versus 16%). The only other factor significantly associated with an invalid performance was the presence of premorbid psychiatric disturbance, which is consistent with the premise that patients

may produce implausible scores for reasons other than frank malingering. Moore and Donders noted that two of the patients with an invalid CVLT-II performance had had a moderate–severe injury (rather than mild TBI). Of these two, one had a history of antisocial factors, including long-standing truancy and lack of follow-through on physician's recommendations, and it was concluded that that patient performed poorly probably because of defiant noncompliance. They suggested that only 5% of individuals with an invalid CVLT-II score in their sample could reasonably be considered false positive. However, given the absence of any independent assessment of malingering and an inference of malingering based on the presence of mild TBI and possible financial incentives, it might be more accurate to say that the post hoc analysis suggests that the specificity of the CVLT-II measure may be as high as 95%.

In summary, investigation of the clinical utility of the CVLT for the identification of malingered or invalid performances has been characterized by multiple independent examinations of the Millis cutoffs. Unfortunately, no clear picture emerges regarding which of the frequently studied CVLT indicators is the most sensitive, and sensitivities in ostensibly similar clinical samples have varied widely. Interestingly, variability in the sensitivity of these indicators is accounted for more by the different investigations than by the different indicators: Sensitivities were consistently quite high in the study by Millis et al., uniformly weak in the study of Slick et al. (2000), and uniformly intermediate in the study of Sweet et al. (2000). The marked discrepancy between the sensitivities in the studies by Millis et al. and Slick et al. defy easy explanation, as both were groups of probable malingerers comprising patients with negligible to mild brain injuries, pursuit of financial compensation, and failure on symptom validity testing. Further studies in independent samples will help illuminate the sensitivity that might be expected with the Millis cutoffs. However, while the exact sensitivities of the Millis CVLT cutoffs are unclear, they typically have high specificities and, consequently, are preferable to other more liberal cutoffs that result in an unacceptable level of false positives.

Nonetheless, two approaches to the CVLT data warrant further comment. First, Demakis (1999) hypothesized that response inconsistency (within and across administrations of the CVLT) might help identify invalid performances, and the preliminary data are encouraging. As hypothesized, decreased consistency across learning trials was more characteristic of simulated malingerers than normal controls, and weaker performance on repeated administration of the CVLT (in contrast to the practice effect seen in normal controls) was sensitive to malingering. Although Demakis reported specificities in the 62–71% range for the absence of practice effects for learning, SDFR, and LDFR across administrations, the high level of sensitivities (67–81%) raises the question of whether a more conservative cutoff might identify a significant proportion of malingerers with an acceptable rate of false positives.

A second potentially useful approach involves the combining of CVLT indicators. Slick et al. (2000) noted that although the four frequently used indicators showed sensitivities of only 36–39% when applied individually, when all of the positive CVLT indicators were tallied together, this index had 58% sensitivity and 87% specificity (with a cutoff of one or more positive indicators). Furthermore, higher scores on this index were related to an increased likelihood of invalid performance.

Discussion

Of greatest concern with regard to the classification accuracy of the measurement techniques reviewed in this chapter are sensitivity and specificity values. For several of the measures we have discussed, the lack of both studies and consistency found for the proposed malingering cutoffs tested mean that we are unable to reach clear conclusions about the utility of these measures for malingering detection (Recognition Memory Test, Complex Figure Test, Trail-Making Test, Processing Speed Index of the WAIS-III). However, for some of these measures, stringent cutoffs that maximize specificity even across disparate studies can be identified (e.g., the Recognition Memory Test), although at major cost to sensitivity. However, even cutoffs that were found to have the most consistency in specificity vary widely in their sensitivity to malingering. For example, the Digit Span age-corrected scaled score of <5 ranged from 25% to 90% sensitivity (with at least 90% specificity across samples), while the Reliable Digit Span score of <8 ranged from 19.6% to 86% sensitivity (with the vast majority of studies showing a specificity of 90% or greater), and the California Verbal Learning Test delayed recognition score of <11 ranged from 36% to 48% sensitivity (with 90–100% specificity across studies).

Although we considered 90% specificity at least adequate in our review, more confidence should be placed in cutoffs with 95% or higher specificity, and several of the cutoffs we have discussed here obtain this, at least in reasonable clinical comparison groups. As is clear from our review, sensitivity will always suffer if attention is focused on specificity, but guarding against false positives is crucial (Greve & Bianchini, 2004).

Of course, in an individual clinical case, the classification accuracy of the reviewed cutoffs must be considered in the context of relevant additional information (e.g., base rates for malingering in samples of individuals with similar presenting concerns or diagnoses). The results of several studies reviewed in this chapter also support the argument that a multiprobabilistic interpretation of scores is far more accurate for the use of these measures in malingering detection. In an individual case, examining the level of sensitivity and specificity associated with various cutoff scores relative to appropriate comparison groups is likely to result in a more accurate understanding of the likelihood that the individual examinee's performance is invalid (Barrash

et al., 2004; Silverberg & Barrash, 2005; Slick et al., 2000). While space considerations precluded including this level of detailed information for each measure, several reviewed studies do take this approach (Barrash et al., 2004; Boone et al., 2005; Millis, 2002; Silverberg & Barrash, 2005), and it should be an aspirational goal for future studies that examine the value of these measures for malingering detection.

Most researchers recommend that multiple measures to assess malingering be employed concurrently to provide converging evidence regarding the presence of malingering, and we strongly agree with such a recommendation. However, the multiple measures should provide relatively independent sources of information in order to truly increase one's confidence in prediction by improving sensitivity without increasing error (Barrash et al., 2004; Boone & Lu, 2003; Iverson & Binder, 2000; Rosenfeld, Sands, & van Gorp, 2000). For example, the studies of Boone and colleagues and Barrash and colleagues suggest that indices within a given measure (the AVLT) can be combined to create malingering indices with considerably greater sensitivity than individual AVLT variables, while maintaining good levels of specificity. Combining information regarding (a) exceedingly low levels of performance (especially on recognition) and (b) patterns of performance atypical of bona fide memory impairment increases sensitivity while also providing information that is potentially useful for examining the risk of false positive determinations in individual cases (Silverberg & Barrash, 2005). Additionally, the inclusion of patterns of performance may enhance the clinical utility of malingering measures, as they have been found to be less vulnerable to coaching than level variables (Suhr, 2002; Suhr & Gunstad, 2000; Suhr et al., 2004).

Others have explored the value of examining relatively independent indicators across several different types of measures. Nelson, Boone, Dueck, Wagener, Lu, and Grills (2003) examined the relationships among eight malingering measures, some of which were derived from standard neuropsychological tests, in a sample of patients who were being evaluated for litigation/compensation reasons. Of the measures discussed in this chapter, CFT, AVLT recognition, Digit Span, and RMT words were included among their variables. For the most part, the scores on these measures were not highly related; the only two measures that shared more than 50% of their variance were Digit Span and the Dot Counting Test. Thus, the variables they compared provided relatively nonredundant information regarding potential malingering. This is particularly important given that several of these indices, when taken alone, have low sensitivity but high specificity. Aggregation of scores across relatively independent indicators is discussed in more detail in chapter 2 and chapter 13 of this volume. Thus, the use of the best-supported cutoffs described here, in combination with relatively independent information from other, more traditional malingering instruments, should enhance one's confidence in concluding that an individual's neuropsychological test performance is an invalid indicator of that person's cognitive abilities.

References

Ashendorf, L., O'Bryant, S. E., & McCaffrey, R. J. (2003). Specificity of malingering detection strategies in older adults using the CVLT and WCST. *The Clinical Neuropsychologist, 17,* 255–262.

Ashton, V. L., Donders, J., & Hoffman, N. M. (2005). Rey Complex Figure Test performance after traumatic brain injury. *Journal of Clinical and Experimental Neuropsychology, 27,* 55–64.

Axelrod, B. N., Fichtenberg, N. L., Millis, S. R., & Wertheimer, J. C. (2006). Detecting incomplete effort with Digit Span from the Wechsler Adult Intelligence Scale, third edition. *The Clinical Neuropsychologist, 20,* 513–523.

Babikian, T., Boone, K. B., Lu, P., & Arnold, G. (2006). Sensitivity and specificity of various Digit Span scores in the detection of suspect effort. *The Clinical Neuropsychologist, 20,* 145–159.

Backhaus, S. L., Fichtenberg, N. L., & Hanks, R. A. (2004). Detection of suboptimal performance using a floor-effect strategy in patients with traumatic brain injury. *The Clinical Neuropsychologist, 18,* 591–603.

Baddeley, A. D., & Warrington, E. K. (1970). Amnesia and the distinction between long- and short-term memory. *Journal of Verbal Learning and Verbal Behavior, 9,* 176–189.

Baker, R., Donders, J., & Thompson, E. (2000). Assessment of incomplete effort with the California Verbal Learning Test. *Applied Neuropsychology, 7,* 111–114.

Baldessarini, R. J., Finklestein, S., & Arana, G. W. (1983). The predictive power of diagnostic tests and the effect of prevalence of illness. *Archives of General Psychiatry, 40,* 569–573.

Barrash, J., Suhr, J., & Manzel, K. (1998). A brief, sensitive, and specific procedure for detecting malingered memory impairment. *Journal of the International Neuropsychological Society, 4,* 28.

Barrash, J., Suhr, J., & Manzel, K. (2004). Detecting poor effort and malingering with an expanded version of the Auditory Verbal Learning Test (AVLTX): Validation with clinical samples. *Journal of the International Neuropsychological Society, 26,* 125–140.

Bernard, L. C. (1990). Prospects for faking believable memory deficits on neuropsychological tests and the use of incentives in simulation research. *Journal of Clinical and Experimental Neuropsychology, 12,* 715–728.

Bernard, L. C. (1991). The detection of faked deficits on the Rey Auditory Verbal Learning Test: The effect of serial position. *Archives of Clinical Neuropsychology, 6,* 81–88.

Bernard, L. C., Houston, W., & Natoli, L. (1993). Malingering on neuropsychological memory tests: Potential objective indicators. *Journal of Clinical Psychology, 49,* 45–53.

Bigler, E. D., Johnson, S. C., Anderson, C. V., Blatter, D. D., Gale, S. D., Russo, A. A., et al. (1996). Traumatic brain injury and memory: The role of hippocampal atrophy. *Neuropsychology, 10,* 333–342.

Bigler, E. D., Rosa, L., Schultz, F., Hall, S., & Harris, J. (1989). Rey Auditory Verbal Learning Test and Rey-Osterreith Complex Figure Design performance in Alzheimer's disease and closed-head injury. *Journal of Clinical Psychology, 45,* 277–280.

Binder, L. M. (1993). Assessment of malingering after mild head trauma with the Portland Digit Recognition Test. *Journal of Clinical and Experimental Neuropsychology, 15,* 170–182.

Binder, L. M., Kelly, M. P., Villanueva, M. R., & Winslow, M. M. (2003). Motivation and neuropsychological test performance following mild head injury. *Journal of Clinical and Experimental Neuropsychology, 25,* 420–430.

Binder, L. M., & Rohling, M. L. (1996). Money matters: Meta-analytic review of the effects of financial incentives on recovery after closed-head injury. *American Journal of Psychiatry, 153,* 7–10.

Binder, L. M., Villanueva, M. R., Howieson, D., & Moore, R. T. (1993). The Rey AVLT recognition memory task measures motivational impairment after mild head trauma. *Archives of Clinical Neuropsychology, 8,* 137–147.

Boone, K. B., & Lu, P. (2003). Noncredible cognitive performance in the context of severe brain injury. *The Clinical Neuropsychologist, 17,* 244–254.

Boone, K. B., Lu, P., & Wen, J. (2005). Comparisons of various RAVLT scores in the detection of noncredible memory performance. *Archives of Clinical Neuropsychology, 20,* 301–319.

Butters, N., & Cermak, L. (1980). *Alcoholic Korsakoff's syndrome: An information-processing approach.* San Diego: Academic Press.

Cermak, L. S., & Butters, N. (1972). The role of interference and encoding in the short-term memory deficits of Korsakoff patients. *Neuropsychologia, 10,* 89–96.

Chouinard, M. J., & Rouleau, I. (1997). The 48-Pictures Test: A two-alternative forced-choice recognition test for the detection of malingering. *Journal of the International Neuropsychological Society, 3,* 245–252.

Cohen, N. J., & Eichenbaum, H. (1993). *Memory, amnesia, and the hippocampal system.* Cambridge, MA: MIT Press.

Coleman, R. D., Rapport, L. J., Millis, S. R., Ricker, J. H., & Farchione, T. J. (1998). Effects of coaching on detection of malingering with the California Verbal Learning Test. *Journal of Clinical and Experimental Neuropsychology, 20,* 201–210.

Curtis, K. L., Greve, K. W., Bianchini, K. J., & Brennan, A. (2006). California Verbal Learning Test indicators of malingered neurocognitive dysfunction: Sensitivity and specificity in traumatic brain injury. *Assessment, 13,* 46–61.

Delis, D. C., Kramer, J. H., Kaplan, E., & Ober, B. A. (2000). *California Verbal Learning Test* (2nd ed.). San Antonio: Psychological Corp.

Demakis, G. J. (1999). Serial malingering on verbal and nonverbal fluency and memory measures: An analog investigation. *Archives of Clinical Neuropsychology, 14,* 401–410.

Demakis, G. J. (2004). Application of clinically derived cutoffs on the California Verbal Learning Test and the Wechsler Adult Intelligence Test-Revised to an analog malingering study. *Applied Neuropsychology, 11,* 220–226.

Duncan, S. A., & Ausborn, D. L. (2002). The use of reliable digits to detect malingering in a criminal forensic pretrial population. *Assessment, 9,* 56–61.

Etherton, J. L., Bianchini, K. J., Ciota, M. A., & Greve, K. W. (2005). Reliable Digit Span is unaffected by laboratory-induced pain: Implications for clinical use. *Assessment, 12,* 101–106.

Etherton, J. L., Bianchini, K. J., Ciota, M. A., Heinly, M. T., & Greve, K. W. (2006). Pain, malingering, and the WAIS-III Working Memory Index. *Spine Journal, 6*(1), 61–71.

Etherton, J. L., Bianchini, K. J., Greve, K. W., & Heinly, M. T. (2005). Sensitivity and specificity of Reliable Digit Span in malingered pain-related disability. *Assessment, 12*, 130–136.

Etherton, J. L., Bianchini, K. J., Heinly, M. T., & Greve, K. W. (2006). Pain, malingering, and performance on the WAIS-III Processing Speed Index. *Journal of Clinical and Experimental Neuropsychology, 28*, 1218–1237.

Faust, D., Hart, K., & Guilmette, T. J. (1988a). Neuropsychologists' capacity to detect adolescent malingerers. *Professional Psychology: Research and Practice, 19*, 508–515.

Faust, D., Hart, K., & Guilmette, T. J. (1988b). Pediatric malingering: The capacity of children to fake believable deficits on neuropsychological testing. *Journal of Clinical and Consulting Psychology, 56*, 578–582.

Flowers, K. A., Sheridan, M. R., & Shadbolt, H. (1996). Simulation of amnesia by normals on Rey's Auditory Verbal Learning Test. *Journal of Neurolinguistics, 9*, 147–156.

Freed, D. M., Corkin, S., Growden, J. H., & Nissen, M. H. (1989). Selective attention in Alzheimer's disease: Characteristic cognitive subgroups of patients. *Neuropsychology, 27*, 325–339.

Gfeller, J. D., & Cradock, M. M. (1998). Detecting feigned neuropsychological impairment with the Seashore Rhythm Test. *Journal of Clinical Psychology, 54*, 431–438.

Glassmire, D. M., Bierley, R. A., Wisniewski, A. M., Greene, R. L., Kennedy, J. E., & Date, E. (2003). Using the WMS-III Faces subtest to detect malingered memory impairment. *Journal of Clinical and Experimental Neuropsychology, 25*, 465–491.

Goebel, R. A. (1983). Detection of faking on the Halstead-Reitan Neuropsychological Test Battery. *Journal of Clinical Psychology, 39*, 731–742.

Greiffenstein, M. F., Baker, W. J., & Gola, T. (1994). Validation of malingered amnesia measures with a large clinical sample. *Psychological Assessment, 6*, 218–224.

Greiffenstein, M. F., Gola, T., & Baker, W. J. (1995). MMPI-2 validity scales versus domain-specific measures in the detection of factitious traumatic brain injury. *The Clinical Neuropsychologist, 9*, 230–240.

Greve, K. W., & Bianchini, K. J. (2004). Setting empirical cutoffs on psychometric indicators of negative response bias: A methodological commentary with recommendations. *Archives of Clinical Neuropsychology, 19*, 533–541.

Guilmette, T. J., Faust, D., Hart, K., & Arkes, H. R. (1990). A national survey of psychologists who offer neuropsychological services. *Archives of Clinical Neuropsychology, 5*, 373–392.

Haines, M. E., & Norris, M. P. (2001). Comparing student and patient simulated malingerers' performance on standard neuropsychological measures to detect feigned cognitive deficits. *The Clinical Neuropsychologist, 15*, 171–182.

Heaton, R., Smith, H., Lehman, R., & Vogt, A. (1978). Prospects for faking believable deficits on neuropsychological testing. *Journal of Consulting and Clinical Psychology, 46*, 892–900.

Heinly, M. T., Greve, K. W., Bianchini, K. J., Love, J. M., & Brennan, A. (2006). WAIS Digit Span–based indicators of malingered neurocognitive dysfunction: Classification accuracy in traumatic brain injury. *Assessment, 12*, 429–444.

Hermann, B. P., Connell, B., Barr, W. B., & Wyler, A. R. (1995). The utility of the Warrington Recognition Memory Test for temporal lobe epilepsy: Pre- and postoperative results. *Journal of Epilepsy, 8*, 139–145.

Horton, A. M., & Roberts, C. (2002). Trail-Making Test and malingering among substance abusers. *International Journal of Neuroscience, 112,* 1489–1496.

Inman, T. H., & Berry, D. T. R. (2002). Cross-validation of indicators of malingering: A comparison of nine neuropsychological tests, four tests of malingering, and behavioral observations. *Archives of Clinical Neuropsychology, 17,* 1–23.

Iverson, G. L., & Binder, L. M. (2000). Detecting exaggeration and malingering in neuropsychological assessment. *Journal of Head Trauma Rehabilitation, 15,* 829–858.

Iverson, G. L., & Franzen, M. D. (1994). The Recognition Memory Test Digit Span and Knox Cube Test as markers of malingered memory impairment. *Assessment, 1,* 323–334.

Iverson, G. L., & Franzen, M. D. (1998). Detecting malingered memory deficits with the Recognition Memory Test. *Brain Injury, 12,* 275–282.

Iverson, G. L., Lange, R. T., Green, P., & Franzen, M. D. (2002). Detecting exaggeration and malingering with the Trail-Making Test. *The Clinical Neuropsychologist, 16,* 398–406.

Iverson, G. L., & Tulsky, D. S. (2003). Detecting malingering on the WAIS-III: Unusual Digit Span performance patterns in the normal population and in clinical groups. *Archives of Clinical Neuropsychology, 18,* 1–9.

Killgore, W. D. S., & DellaPietra, L. (2000). Using the WMS-III to detect malingering: Empirical validation of the Rarely Missed Index (RMI). *Journal of Clinical and Experimental Neuropsychology, 22,* 761–771.

King, J. H., Gfeller, J. D., & Davis, H. P. (1998). Detecting simulated malingering with the Rey Auditory Verbal Learning Test: Implications of base rates and study generalizability. *Journal of Clinical and Experimental Neuropsychology, 20,* 603–612.

Kneebone, A. C., Chelune, G. J., & Luders, H. O. (1997). Individual patient prediction of seizure lateralization in temporal lobe epilepsy: A comparison between neuropsychological memory measures and the intracarotid amobarbital procedure. *Journal of the International Neuropsychological Society, 3,* 159–168.

Lamberty, G. J., Putnam, S. H., Chatel, D. M., Bieliauskas, L. A., & Adams, K. M. (1994). Derived Trail-Making Test indices: A preliminary report. *Neuropsychiatry, Neuropsychology, and Behavioral Neurology, 7,* 230–234.

Lange, R. T., Senior, G., Douglas, L., & Dawes, S. (2003, October). *Base rates and clinical utility of the WMS-III Rarely Missed Index: Identifying cognitive exaggeration in a head-injury litigant sample.* Paper presented at the annual conference of the National Academy of Neuropsychology, Dallas.

Lange, R. T., Sullivan, K., & Anderson, D. (2005). Ecological validity of the WMS-III Rarely Missed Index in personal-injury litigation. *Journal of Clinical and Experimental Neuropsychology, 27,* 412–424.

Langeluddecke, P. M., & Lucas, S. K. (2003). Quantitative measures of memory malingering on the Wechsler Memory Scale, third edition, in mild head-injury litigants. *Archives of Clinical Neuropsychology, 18,* 181–197.

Larrabee, G. J. (2003). Detection of malingering using atypical performance patterns on standard neuropsychological tests. *The Clinical Neuropsychologist, 17,* 410–425.

Lees-Haley, P. R., Smith, H. H., Williams, C. W., & Dunn, J. T. (1996). Forensic neuropsychological test usage: An empirical survey. *Archives of Clinical Neuropsychology, 11,* 43–51.

Lezak, M. D., Howieson, D. B., & Loring, D. W. (2004). *Neuropsychological assessment* (4th ed.). New York: Oxford University Press.

Lu, P. H., Boone, K. G., Cozolino, L., & Mitchell, C. (2003). Effectiveness of the Rey-Osterreith Complex Figure Test and the Meyers and Meyers Recognition Trial in the detection of suspect effort. *The Clinical Neuropsychologist, 17,* 426–440.

Martin, T. A., Hoffman, N. M., & Donders, J. (2003). Clinical utility of the Trail-Making Test ratio score. *Applied Neuropsychology, 10,* 163–169.

Mathias, C. W., Greve, K. W., Bianchini, K. J., Houston, R. J., & Crouch, J. A. (2002). Detecting malingered neurocognitive dysfunction using the Reliable Digit Span in traumatic brain injury. *Assessment, 9,* 301–308.

Meyers, J. E., Bayless, J., & Meyers, K. (1996). The Rey Complex Figure: Memory error patterns and functional abilities. *Applied Neuropsychology, 3,* 89–92.

Meyers, J. E., & Diep, A. (2000). Assessment of malingering in chronic pain patients using neuropsychological tests. *Applied Neuropsychology, 7,* 133–139.

Meyers, J. E., & Meyers, K. (1995). *Rey Complex Figure and Recognition Trial: Professional manual.* Odessa, FL: Psychological Assessment Resources.

Meyers, J. E., Morrison, A. L., & Miller, J. C. (2001). How low is too low, revisited: Sentence repetition and AVLT recognition in the detection of malingering. *Applied Neuropsychology, 4,* 234–241.

Meyers, J. E., & Volbrecht, M. (1998). Validity of reliable digits for detection of malingering. *Assessment, 5,* 303–307.

Meyers, J. E., & Volbrecht, M. E. (1999). Detection of malingering using the Rey Complex Figure and Recognition Trial. *Applied Neuropsychology, 6,* 201–207.

Meyers, J. E., & Volbrecht, M. E. (2003). A validation of multiple malingering-detection methods in a large clinical sample. *Archives of Clinical Neuropsychology, 18,* 261–276.

Miller, L. J., Ryan, J. J., Carruthers, C. A., & Cluff, R. B. (2004). Brief screening indices for malingering: A confirmation of Vocabulary-Digit Span from the WAIS-III and the Rarely Missed Index from the WMS-III. *The Clinical Neuropsychologist, 18,* 327–333.

Millis, S. R. (1992). The Recognition Memory Test in the detection of malingered and exaggerated memory deficits. *The Clinical Neuropsychologist, 6,* 406–414.

Millis, S. R. (2002). Warrington Recognition Memory Test in the detection of response bias. *Journal of Forensic Neuropsychology, 2,* 147–166.

Millis, S. R., & Dijkers, M. (1993). Use of the Recognition Memory Test in traumatic brain injury. *Brain Injury, 7,* 53–58.

Millis, S. R., & Putnam, S. H. (1994). The Recognition Memory Test in the assessment of memory impairment after financially compensated mild head injury: A replication. *Perceptual and Motor Skills, 79,* 384–386.

Millis, S. R., Putnam, S. H., Adams, K. M., & Ricker, J. H. (1995). The California Verbal Learning Test in the detection of incomplete effort in neuropsychological evaluation. *Psychological Assessment, 7,* 463–471.

Moore, B. A., & Donders, J. (2004). Predictors of invalid neuropsychological test performance after traumatic brain injury. *Brain Injury, 18,* 975–984.

Naugle, R. I., Chelune, G. J. H., Schuster, J., Luders, H. O., & Comair, Y. (1994). Recognition memory for words and faces before and after temporal lobectomy. *Assessment, 1,* 373–381.

Nelson, N. W, Boone, K., Dueck, A., Wagener, L., Lu, P., & Grills, C. (2003). Relationships between eight measures of suspect effort. *The Clinical Neuropsychologist, 17,* 263–272.

O'Bryant, S. E., Hilsabeck, R. C., Fisher, J. M., & McCaffrey, R. J. (2003). Utility of the Trail-Making Test in the assessment of malingering in a sample of mild traumatic brain-injury litigants. The Clinical Neuropsychologist, 17, 69–74.

Paniak, C., Reynolds, S., Phillips, K., Toller-Lobe, G., Melnyk, A., & Nagy, J. (2002). Patient complaints within 1 month of mild traumatic brain injury: A controlled study. Archives of Clinical Neuropsychology, 17, 319–334.

Peaker, A., & Stewart, L. E. (1989). Rey's Auditory Verbal Learning Test: A review. In J. R. Crawford & D. M. Parker (Eds.), Developments in clinical and experimental neuropsychology (pp. 219–236). New York: Plenum.

Rogers, R., Harrell, E. H., & Liff, C. D. (1993). Feigning neuropsychological impairment: A critical review of methodological and clinical considerations. Clinical Psychology Review, 13, 255–274.

Rosenfeld, B., Sands, S. A., & van Gorp, W. G. (2000). Have we forgotten the base rate problem? Methodological issues in the detection of distortion. Archives of Clinical Neuropsychology, 15, 349–359.

Ross, S. R., Putnam, S. H., Gass, C. S., Bailey, D. E., & Adams, K. M. (2003). MMPI-2 indices of psychological disturbance and attention and memory tests in head injury. Archives of Clinical Neuropsychology, 18, 905–916.

Ross, S. R., Putnam, S. H., Millis, S. R., Adams, K. M., & Krukowski, R. A. (in press). Detecting insufficient effort using the Seashore Rhythm and Speech-Sounds Perception tests in head injury. The Clinical Neuropsychologist.

Ruffolo, L. F., Guilmette, T. J., & Willis, W. G. (2000). Comparison of time and error rates on the Trail-Making Test among patients with head injuries, experimental malingerers, patients with suspect effort on testing, and normal controls. The Clinical Neuropsychologist, 14, 223–230.

Rundus, D. (1971). Analysis of rehearsal processes in free recall. Journal of Experimental Psychology, 89, 63–72.

Sherman, D. S., Boone, K. B., & Razani, J. (2002). Re-examination of a Rey Auditory Verbal Learning Test/Rey Complex Figure discriminant function to detect suspect effort. The Clinical Neuropsychologist, 16, 242–250.

Silverberg, N., & Barrash, J. (2005). Further validation of the expanded Auditory Verbal Learning Test for detecting poor effort and response bias: Data from temporal lobectomy candidates. Journal of the International Neuropsychological Society, 27, 212–220.

Slick, D., Iverson, G. L., & Green, P. (2000). California Verbal Learning Test indicators of suboptimal performance in a sample of head-injury litigants. Journal of Clinical and Experimental Neuropsychology, 22, 569–579.

Slick, D. J., Sherman, E. M. S., & Iverson, G. L. (1999). Diagnostic criteria for malingered neurocognitive dysfunction: Proposed standards for clinical practice and research. The Clinical Neuropsychologist, 13, 545–561.

Spector, J., Lewandowski, A. G., Kelly, M. P., & Kaylor, J. A. (1994, November). The use of the Seashore Rhythm test as a forced-choice measure to detect malingering in a compensation-seeking mildly head-injured sample. Paper presented at the 14th annual conference of the National Academy of Neuropsychology, Orlando, FL.

Strauss, E., Slick, D. J., Levy-Bencheton, J., Hunter, M., MacDonald, S. W. S., & Hultsch, D. F. (2002). Intraindividual variability as an indicator of malingering in head injury. Archives of Clinical Neuropsychology, 17, 423–444.

Suhr, J. (2002). Malingering, coaching, and the serial position effect. *Archives of Clinical Neuropsychology, 17*, 69–77.

Suhr, J., & Gunstad, J. (2000). The effects of coaching on the sensitivity and specificity of malingering measures. *Archives of Clinical Neuropsychology, 15*, 415–424.

Suhr, J., Gunstad, J., Greub, B., & Barrash, J. (2004). Exaggeration Index for an expanded version of the Auditory Verbal Learning Test: Robustness to coaching. *Journal of Clinical and Experimental Neuropsychology, 26*, 416–427.

Suhr, J., Tranel, D., Wefel, J., & Barrash, J. (1997). Memory performance after head injury: Contributions of malingering, litigation status, psychological factors, and medication use. *Journal of Clinical and Experimental Neuropsychology, 19*, 500–514.

Sweet, J. J., Demakis, G. J., Ricker, J. H., & Millis, S. R. (2000). Diagnostic efficiency and material specificity of the Warrington Recognition Memory Test: A collaborative multisite investigation. *Archives of Clinical Neuropsychology, 15*, 301–309.

Sweet, J. J., Wolfe, P., Sattlberger, E., Numan, B., Rosenfeld, J. P., Clingerman, S., et al. (2000). Further investigation of traumatic brain injury versus insufficient effort with the California Verbal Learning Test. *Archives of Clinical Neuropsychology, 15*, 105–113.

Tombaugh, T. N. (1996). *Test of Memory Malingering (TOMM)*. Toronto: Multi-Health Systems.

Trueblood, W. (1994). Qualitative and quantitative characteristics of malingered and other invalid WAIS-R and clinical memory data. *Journal of Clinical and Experimental Neuropsychology, 16*, 597–607.

Trueblood, W., & Schmidt, M. (1993). Malingering and other validity considerations in the neuropsychological evaluation of mild head injury. *Journal of Clinical and Experimental Neuropsychology, 15*, 578–590.

van Gorp, W. G., Humphrey, L. A., Kalechstein, A., Brumm, V. L., McMullen, W. J., Stoddard, M., et al. (1999). How well do standard clinical neuropsychology tests identify malingering? A preliminary analysis. *Journal of Clinical and Experimental Neuropsychology, 21*, 245–250.

Warrington, E. K., & Weiskrantz, L. (1973). An analysis of short- and long-term memory deficits in man. In J. A. Deutsch (Ed.), *The physiological basis of memory* (pp. 365–395). New York: Academic Press.

Williams, J. M. (1998). The malingering of memory disorder. In C. R. Reynolds (Ed.), *Detection of malingering during head-injury litigation* (pp. 105–132). New York: Plenum.

8

Detection of Cognitive Malingering
With Tests of Executive Function

Kevin W. Greve and Kevin J. Bianchini

He is fitful, irreverent, indulging at times in the grossest profanity
(which was not previously his custom), manifesting but little
deference for his fellows, impatient of restraint or advice when it
conflicts with his desires, at times pertinaciously obstinate, yet
capricious and vacillating, devising many plans of future operation,
which are not sooner arranged than they are abandoned in turn for
others appearing more feasible. In this regard, his mind was radically
changed, so decidedly that his friends and acquaintances said he was
"no longer Gage."
—Harlow, 1868 (cited in Neylan, 1999, p. 280)

Background

It seems almost a requirement that a chapter on the frontal lobes and executive function begin with some mention of Phineas Gage, the 25-year-old
railroad construction supervisor who was wounded in 1848 when a prema-
ture explosive detonation propelled a steel tamping rod upward through his
left cheek and out the top of his skull. Damasio, Grabowski, Frank, Galaburda, and Damasio (1994), using Gage's skull and modern neuroimaging
techniques, reconstructed Gage's injuries, clearly demonstrating bilateral
frontal lobe involvement. Harlow noted the effect of this dramatic behavioral
change: "His contractors, who regarded him as the most efficient and capable
foreman in their employ previous to his injury, considered the change in his
mind so marked that they could not give him his place again" (Harlow, 1868,
cited in Neylan, 1999, p. 280).

The profoundly disabling effects of frontal lobe lesions illustrated so
clearly in Harlow's report, particularly as they involve judgment, planning,
problem solving, and other aspects of effective decision making, have also been
demonstrated in modern patients such as EVR (Eslinger & Damasio, 1984),
whose vocational problems related to his orbitofrontal meningioma are described in detail in Damasio and Anderson (2003). What was particularly
striking about EVR was the fact that, despite his functional difficulties, he

performed in the normal and often superior range on measures of cognitive ability, including measures of executive function.

The higher level cognitive abilities subserved by the frontal lobes and related structures (e.g., limbic system, anterior temporal lobes) may be considered under the rubric of "executive functions." Executive functions refer to those capacities that optimize and integrate the operation of a number of cognitive systems (e.g., Baddeley, 1986). These abilities may involve the regulation of arousal and behavior, responsiveness to changing contingencies, planning and sequencing, strategy application, and decision making (Damasio & Anderson, 2003). In practical terms, "the executive functions consist of those capacities that enable a person to engage successfully in independent, purposive, self-serving behavior" (Lezak, Howieson, & Loring, 2004, p. 35). The functional impact of executive impairment is also well stated by these authors:

> So long as the executive functions are intact, a person can sustain considerable cognitive loss and still continue to be independent, constructively self-serving, and productive. When executive functions are impaired, the individual may no longer be capable of satisfactory self-care, of performing remunerative or useful work independently, or of maintaining normal social relationships regardless of how well-preserved the cognitive capacities are (or how high the person scores on tests of skills, knowledge, and abilities. (ibid.)

In short, even when other cognitive abilities are intact, pathology of the frontal lobe systems and related executive dysfunction can be seriously disabling.

In the context of compensable brain injuries (e.g., personal-injury litigation, workers compensation claims) in the United States, disability pays (Bianchini, Greve, & Glynn, 2005). Specifically, compensation is based on loss of function, not necessarily the presence or absence of neuropathology. For example, one element in the valuation of damages involves the loss of future wages. This is generally determined by calculating the differences between the preinjury wage and the presumably lower, postinjury wage, multiplied by the number of years the patient is expected to work after the injury. The lower the post injury wage, the greater the reward.

Therefore, a patient who is able to work a job that requires a certain level of cognitive skill preinjury but is unable to return to work at that wage level because of the injury would potentially garner an award for wage loss. If the patient is unable to work at all, then the potential award would be greater still. The same logic applies to the issue of self-care because patients may demand awards to cover loss of the capacity for self-care. Thus, brain dysfunction that produces executive function deficits may garner a larger award than pathology that affects more discrete cognitive functions because executive deficits have a broader functional impact and are thus more disabling.

Because executive dysfunction is potentially so disabling and therefore highly compensable, there should be substantial motivation to fabricate or

exaggerate deficits in the realm of executive control. Evidence of this is found in the anosmia literature. While not an executive function per se, the structures subserving the sense of smell are immediately adjacent to the orbitalfrontal cortex, that region obliterated in EVR and other cases whose pathology was associated with executive deficits. Thus, disruptions in the sense of smell may serve as a risk factor for disability due to executive dysfunction. Early studies of anosmia (e.g., Varney, 1988) appeared to demonstrate a powerful association between self-reported anosmia and vocational dysfunction independent of externally defined injury severity.

Since then the methodology of those early reports has been strongly criticized (Greiffenstein, Baker, & Gola, 2002, 2003). More methodologically sound studies have failed to replicate the early findings (Correia, Faust, & Doty, 2001; Greiffenstein et al., 2002). More relevant to the present issue of malingering of executive dysfunction, however, is the work of Green and colleagues (Green & Iverson, 2001; Green, Rohling, Iverson, & Gervais, 2003), which demonstrated that olfactory deficits were associated with severity of brain injury but only in persons who had given good effort on cognitive testing as measured by the Word Memory Test (WMT). In the absence of a control for effort, no dose-response relationship between anosmia and injury severity was observed. Like many of Varney's patients, Green's patients who failed the WMT were much more likely to have suffered mild brain trauma. It thus appears that anosmia and associated functional executive problems are more likely to be exaggerated by persons with milder or more ambiguous injuries.

Such a conclusion is consistent with the literature on compensation. It is well established that financial incentive is related to outcome in traumatic brain injury (TBI) and that the effect of financial incentive is strongest at the mild end of the severity continuum (Binder & Rohling, 1996). Financial incentive similarly influences outcome in chronic pain (CP; Rohling, Binder, & Langhinrichsen-Rohling, 1995; Harris, Mulford, Solomon, van Gelder, & Young, 2005). Green, Rohling, Lees-Haley, and Allen (2001) found that effort, as measured by performance on the WMT, accounted for more variance in neuropsychological test results than did injury severity. Greiffenstein and Baker (2006) have demonstrated that evidence of symptom exaggeration increased with the ambiguity of the compensable condition.

These findings suggest that exaggeration of executive deficits would be more common in persons less likely to demonstrate the kinds of objective brain pathology that typically underlie such deficits. Of course, the question of malingering is not only whether a person is truly injured or malingering; truly injured persons can and do malinger (Bianchini, Greve, & Love, 2003; Bianchini, Etherton, & Greve, 2004; Franzen & Iverson, 1998; Iverson, 2003; Sweet, 1999). The potentially more important question is whether the nature and severity of disability attributed to the injury is inconsistent with what would be expected given the physical parameters of the injury. Thus, even patients with objectively documented neuropathology may malinger

functional impairment since greater functional impairment is associated with potentially greater compensation.

In other words, malingerers are not just faking or exaggerating brain damage (or other injury); they are also faking or exaggerating the degree of functional impairment (disability) attributable to brain injury as reflected in neuropsychological testing and other forms of evaluation (Bianchini, Greve, & Glynn, 2005). Because executive dysfunction can cause serious disability, neuropsychological evidence of executive dysfunction may be particularly valuable in the context of litigation because it may represent this disability. Therefore, there should be substantial motivation to fabricate or exaggerate deficits on measures of executive function. Moreover, in the Internet era, there is copious information that can be relied upon by those who wish to imitate (as an element of their approach to malingering) the kind of neurobehavioral and neurocognitive impairments (including impairments on neurocognitive tests) seen in patients with frontal systems pathology (see, for example, the entry on the Wisconsin Card Sorting Test [WCST] at wikipedia.org).

The methodology exists for accurately identifying malingered cognitive deficits and for developing effective indicators of malingering on tests of executive abilities. In fact, some of the earliest research on malingering detection has involved classic measures of executive functioning. These measures are generally considered to be most sensitive to lesions of the dorsolateral prefrontal cortex (e.g., Milner, 1963) relative to other prefrontal regions, although impaired performance is not specific to the frontal lobe pathology (see Anderson, Damasio, Jones, & Tranel, 1991). In the past 15 years several tests sensitive to dysfunction (or damage) of the orbitalfrontal cortex have been developed (e.g., Iowa Gambling task [Bechara, Damasio, Damasio, & Anderson, 1994]; Revised Strategy Application Test [Levine et al., 1998]). However, no studies of malingering have been reported for these instruments.

Therefore, this chapter focuses on the extensive malingering literature related to the two major frontal lobe or executive function tests (the Wisconsin Card Sorting Test and the Category Test [CaT]) and touches on findings related to other more obscure or experimental tasks. Before we delve into that specific research, it is important to review some of the conceptual and methodological issues in malingering research. This section is brief since these topics are covered in greater detail elsewhere in this volume.

Conceptual Issues in Malingering Research

Operationalizing Malingering

Research on malingering requires that malingering be clearly operationalized and that malingering groups be defined on the basis of external criteria derived from a systematic analysis and an integration of multiple sources of

clinical information encompassing behavior in multiple domains (Bianchini, Mathias, & Greve, 2001). Greiffenstein and colleagues (Greiffenstein et al., 1994, 1995) were among the first to make use of structured systems for classifying litigating patients into malingering versus nonmalingering groups.

In 1999 Slick, Sherman, and Iverson published comprehensive and well thought-out criteria for the diagnosis of malingered neurocognitive dysfunction (MND). These criteria now serve as the basis of classification in an increasing number of studies of malingering in the neuropsychological literature (Greve, Bianchini, Mathias, Houston, & Crouch, 2002; Greve, Bianchini, Mathias, Houston, & Crouch, 2003; Larrabee, 2003a, 2003b, 2003c, 2003d; Bianchini et al., 2003) and have also been applied in pain cases (Larrabee, 2003d; Etherton, Bianchini, Ciota, & Greve, 2005; Etherton, Bianchini, Greve, & Heinly, 2005; Greve, Bianchini, & Ameduri, 2003; Bianchini, Etherton, et al., 2004; Bianchini, Heinly, & Greve, 2004).

Bianchini et al. (2005) have developed a system for the diagnosis of malingered pain-related disability that broadens the Slick et al. criteria by allowing the diagnosis of malingering of specific pain-related physical and psychological complaints and deficits, as well as cognitive deficits. Overall, the last 10 years have seen the development and application of methods for operationalizing malingering for both clinical and research purposes. The systematic and objective nature of the Slick et al. (1999) criteria is illustrated by the decision tree presented by Millis (2004). The Bianchini et al. (2005) system could be similarly represented.

Accuracy Statistics

Second, empirical data concerning the accuracy of detection techniques are essential for their ongoing development, clinical application, and admissibility in legal proceedings. The relevant indices of classification accuracy are sensitivity, specificity, and predictive value (Gouvier, Hayes, & Smiroldo, 1998; Hennekens & Buring, 1987). *Sensitivity* (detecting a condition, in this case, malingering, when it is truly present) and *specificity* (not detecting malingering when it is truly absent) are characteristics of the test or indicator and are dependent on the decision rule or cutoff examined. *Predictive value* is a measure of confidence in the meaning of a test result and is dependent on sensitivity and specificity, as well as the base rate of the target condition in a given population. Predictive value can be positive (probability that a positive test result was produced by a malingerer, defined as the ratio of true positives to true positives plus false positives) or negative (probability that a negative test result was produced by a nonmalingerer, defined as the ratio of true negatives to true negatives plus false negatives). To contribute to an empirical science of malingering detection, the classification accuracy of malingering detection techniques must be clearly stated in terms of these indices.

The Importance of Specificity

The sensitivity of all individual indicators designed to detect malingering will always be less than perfect if one wishes to guard against excessive false positive errors. Perfect sensitivity is practically impossible for three reasons. First, for some tests (e.g., forced-choice symptom validity tests), patients may easily recognize the means of detecting negative response bias; the more obvious the detection strategy, the less likely a malingerer is to be detected by the task (Bianchini et al., 2001). Second, those who malinger may use different approaches to appearing impaired, and no indicators or tests are yet capable of detecting all of the approaches (Greve et al., 2003; Heaton, Chelune, Talley, Kay, & Curtiss, 1993; Larrabee, 2003a). Third, if a patient is provided with information about specific malingering tests (i.e., coaching), then that person may be more likely to avoid detection (Youngjohn, 1995; Allen & Green, 2001).

Thus, attempts to set cutoffs that detect all true malingerers will inevitably result in an unacceptably high number of false positive errors. Even attempts to establish cutoffs that maximize the overall classification accuracy must compromise specificity. In contrast, it is possible to identify performance levels associated with perfect or near perfect specificity. This means that one can likely be confident that the score reflects a suspect behavior pattern. Practically, it is better to detect some malingerers with few false positives than to try to achieve the impossible goal of complete discrimination of groups.

Research Designs in Malingering

Rogers (1997) outlined three different research designs used in the study of malingering: differential prevalence, simulation, and known groups. The *differential prevalence* design compares two groups that are expected to have very different rates of malingering (e.g., patients with and without an incentive for being impaired). While this design can provide estimates of base rates of malingering-related phenomena in a given population, it has significant weaknesses, the most important of which is the inability to provide meaningful classification accuracy data (ibid.; Bianchini, Mathias, Greve, Houston, & Crouch, 2001; Larrabee, 2005).

The *simulator* design asks uninjured subjects (and sometimes clinical patients) to intentionally feign impairment (Trueblood & Schmidt, 1993). The use of simulator designs is a necessary and valuable means of investigating malingering, especially in the early stages of test development (Bianchini, Mathias, & Greve, 2001), and simulator studies can also provide valuable convergent data when used in concert with a known-groups study. For a good example, see Etherton, Bianchini, Ciota, et al. (2005) and Etherton, Bianchini, Greve, and Ciota (2005).

However, while simulator data can be directly generalized to clinical patients under certain circumstances (Bianchini et al., 2005; Greve et al., 2005),

the application of data from these studies to clinical patients can be limited because simulators do not have the incentives (e.g., compensation) or disincentives (e.g., psychological distress) seen in clinical patients. Many simulator studies include nonmalingering clinical patients as a comparison group and thus may offer information regarding specificity. In certain circumstances simulator research can be applied clinically (Bianchini et al., 2005). However, sensitivity data derived from simulator studies may be inflated (see discussion below), so caution is needed in the application of findings from this type of mixed design.

The *known-groups* design is the best approach for the study of malingering because it requires strict operationalization of malingering (Greve & Bianchini, 2004) and also allows for the most important comparison of malingering with true clinical impairment. This design requires, at minimum, two criterion samples: a probable clinical malingering sample and a nonmalingering clinical control group. Because it uses clinical patients, the known-groups design has the capacity to address and control those factors that hamper the application of findings from simulator studies.

Evaluating Malingering With Measures of Executive Function

Wisconsin Card Sorting Test

Background
Card sorting tasks have been used to study cognitive function since the 1920s and 1930s, when researchers used them to study the so-called process of abstraction. The early sorting tests were weak in that the methods of evaluating test performance were very subjective and provided no objective, quantitative scores. In the 1940s many sorting tests were modified to provide more objective and reliable scores. The development of the Wisconsin Card Sorting Test (WCST) was part of this trend toward greater objectivity and quantifiability.

The Wisconsin Cart Sorting Test (Grant & Berg, 1948; Heaton, 1981; Heaton et al., 1993) is a well-established measure of executive function. Its value and popularity are illustrated by the ever-increasing number of studies incorporating the WCST and by a 2005 survey of clinical practice conducted by Rabin, Barr, and Burton, which shows that the WCST is the most frequently used measure of executive function. The first 40 years of the WCST's existence (1948 to 1988) saw its use in fewer than 100 published journal articles, more than half of which appeared in the 1980s alone. In contrast, the following 15 years witnessed the publication of hundreds of articles about use of the WCST.

The first 10 years of research with the WCST focused primarily on the study of learning and problem solving through the modification of factors inherent in the test and its administration. By the early 1960s the use of the WCST had extended beyond the study of normal problem-solving abilities

and had found its way into a variety of clinical and experimental settings. However, as the utilization of the WCST expanded, it became clear that many variations of the original administration and scoring procedures (Grant & Berg, 1948) were in use.

The proliferation of both minor and significant modifications of the WCST was so great that in 1981 Heaton suggested that there was not one WCST but many. The WCST methodology with which most neuropsychologists are familiar was formalized by Heaton with the publication of the first WCST manual by Psychological Assessment Resources (PAR) in 1981. The second edition of the manual (Heaton et al., 1993) provided users with more comprehensive norms and scoring instructions that took much of the mystery out of identifying perseverative responses. Among the scores normed by Heaton et al. were categories completed, perseverative responses, and perseverative errors (in this context, *perseveration* refers to continuing to match to the same dimension when it is no longer correct), nonperseverative errors, failure to maintain set (runs of five to nine consecutive correct responses), and percent conceptual level responses (the percentage of consecutive correct responses occurring in runs of three or more).

The following summary reviews the developmental history of the WCST. Beginning with the ancestral sorting tests and proceeding through the first 10 years of developmental research by the Wisconsin group (e.g., Grant and Berg), this review ends with an examination of the support for two assertions commonly made regarding the WCST: (a) that it is a test of frontal lobe pathology or dysfunction and (b) that it is a test of executive function or dysfunction. The first claim is addressed through a review of a wide variety of clinical syndromes and disorders in which the WCST has been used. The second is addressed via an examination of factor analytic studies that have sought to clarify the cognitive processes underlying WCST performance.

Early Sorting Tests   Early sorting tests, used extensively to study the process of abstraction and factors related to cognitive processing, existed in a variety of forms, including the Patch Test (Armitage, 1946), the Cube Test (Goldstein & Scheerer, 1941), the Block Sorting Test (Vigotsky, 1934; Hanfman & Kasanin, 1942), the Object Sorting Test (Goldstein & Scheerer, 1941; Weigl, 1941), an object sorting task different from the Goldstein-Scheerer test (Hebb, 1945), the Gelf-Goldstein Color Sorting Test (Goldstein & Scheerer, 1941), and the Color-Form Test (Goldstein & Scheerer, 1941). The earliest research with sorting tests (Vigotsky, 1934; Weigl, 1941) relied strictly on the qualitative descriptions of performances for comparing groups. Hanfman and Kasanin (1942) went one step further by assigning scores to three different types of performances and then comparing groups on the basis of these scores. Though a more objective approach, this method still relied on the qualitative evaluation of performance.

Despite the fact that the early sorting tests were commonly used both clinically and in research, all (with the exception of Armitage's [1946] Patch

Test and Hebb's [1945] Object Sorting Test) were limited in their applicability to research and clinical evaluation. Interpretations of test performances were typically restricted to a qualitative, two-dimensional evaluation (i.e., all of the performances on these tests were considered the result of either "abstract" or "concrete" thought processes), and no quantitative measures were developed or included for most of the tests (Berg, 1948; Goldstein, 1981). In an attempt to remedy this situation, new tests (or variations based on the old sorting tests) were devised that allowed for more objective and reliable quantitative scoring. The variation developed at the University of Wisconsin in the late 1940s (Grant & Berg, 1948) served as the model for successive versions.

The Early WCST   The test materials for the WCST formulated by Grant and Berg (1948) and the basic administrative procedure are well known to all neuropsychologists. Successful performance on the WCST requires the subject to recognize the three possible dimensions, determine which is the correct one to match on at the moment using feedback, maintain responding until the correct dimension shifts, then ignore the previously correct matching behavior, and repeat the process to find the next correct dimension.

Berg's (1948) study of the WCST in normal college students represented a departure from the use of qualitative analysis of performance on sorting tests to the use of objective and reliable scores. He administered the WCST to one large group of subjects and then identified three groups of subjects based on success on the WCST. He found significant differences among them, with the first group having fewer errors. The findings of this study led Berg to suggest that the WCST provided an objective and reliable method for assessing "abstraction" abilities. It also demonstrated the tremendous variability in the performance of clinically normal persons, which is characteristic of the WCST (Heaton, 1981; Heaton et al., 1993).

Development in Normal Populations   While the early WCST research in 1940s and 1950s focused mainly on questions of learning and problem solving, these studies provided important information about administration and potential procedural confounds. Among the factors investigated were the effects of varying the criterion number of consecutive correct responses required before the correct matching dimension was shifted (Grant & Berg, 1948; Grant & Cost, 1954); the relative difficulty of correctly matching each stimulus dimension (Grant, Jones, & Tallantis, 1949); the effect on learning efficiency produced by using a standard versus nonsystematic configuration of stimuli on each response card (Grant, 1951; Grant & Curran, 1952); the influence of "ambiguous" response cards (i.e., those cards that matched a stimulus card on more than one dimension) on learning the correct matching dimension (Gormezano & Grant, 1958); and the effects of various distractions on overall performance (Ross, Rupel, & Grant, 1952).

This research demonstrated the value and limitations of the WCST as a tool in the study of cognitive processes and produced three significant

findings regarding WCST administration. First, optimal performance in normals is produced by requiring 10 consecutive correct responses before changing category. Important in this finding is that requiring more than 10 correct responses does not result in additional improvement. Thus fewer than 10 correct responses may not allow an adequate test of learning, while more than that number is not beneficial. Second, the relative difficulty of the three dimensions (in order of increasing difficulty, number [N], form [F], color [C]) was clearly established. Additionally, this series of studies indicated that the systematic configuration of items on each response card made the number dimension easier, although the use of a nonsystematic configuration did not influence the overall order of difficulty sufficiently to warrant the general use of the nonsystematic cards. The significance of these findings is reflected in the fact that the number of consecutive correct responses required for a change of category and the order in which each dimension is correct (i.e., C, F, N) are the most stable administrative features of a test known for its large number of procedural modifications.

Finally, this series of studies indicates that increasing the number of ambiguous response cards increases the difficulty of learning the correct response set. Despite the methodological limitations of that study, removal of the ambiguous cards has become an important and increasingly popular modification for use with some populations (e.g., elderly people) (for a review of this variant see de Zubicaray & Ashton, 1996). Thus, the research of the Wisconsin group has been important in establishing administrative parameters that have been adopted by the neuropsychological research community and have doubtless contributed to the usefulness and popularity of the WCST as a clinical research instrument since the early 1960s.

Clinical Research in Brain Injury
Goldstein (1936) reported that sorting tests were sensitive to lesions of the frontal cortex in humans, that the frontal lobes were the seat of "abstract" processing, and that damage to this area would result in the loss of "abstract" ability. Heaton (1981) described the WCST as "one of the very few tests that has shown specific sensitivity to brain lesions involving the frontal lobes" (p. 7). The WCST has been used in numerous studies of non-brain-damaged and clinical populations. The following section discusses whether sufficient justification exists for concluding that the WCST has shown specific sensitivity to damage of the frontal lobes in humans.

Studies by Fey (1951), Malmo (1974), Parsons and Klein (1970), Benson, Stuss, Naeser, Weir, Kaplan, et al. (1981), and Stuss, Levine, Alexander, Hong, Palumbo, et al. (1983) indicate that people with schizophrenia performed better on the WCST than nonschizophrenic patients with major bilateral excision of the frontal lobes and generally performed worse than normal controls (or at least differently). The implications of these findings, however, are not clear. Due to the potential negative impact of hospitalization history,

medication history, current psychotic status, and other factors on neuro-psychological test performance in general, establishing whether the WCST performance of people with schizophrenia is a direct function of the disorder or a secondary effect resulting from the extraneous influences associated with schizophrenic disorders is difficult.

Positing that lesions of the frontal cortex and basal ganglia produce similar deficits in both humans and animals, Bowen, Kamieny, Burns, and Yahr (1975) investigated the effects of Parkinson's disease on WCST perfor-mance. Parkinson's patients who were receiving L-dopa treatment were com-pared to a nontreatment group and a nonpatient control group. Three find-ings were significant: (a) both Parkinson's groups completed fewer categories than the control group; (b) both Parkinson's groups made more errors than the controls, but the non-L-dopa group made more than the group being treated with L-dopa; and (c) both Parkinson's groups made more nonpersev-erative errors than the controls, and again the non-L-dopa group performed the worst. Interestingly, there were no group differences in perseverative er-rors. In fact, the deficit in the Parkinson's disease patients appeared to be in the maintenance of the correct response set sufficient to complete a category rather than a tendency toward perseveration.

Chronic alcoholics also show impairment on WCST performance. Tarter and Parsons (1971) and Tarter (1973) demonstrated that both short- and long-term alcoholics exhibited more difficulty in shifting categories and committed more perseverative errors than nonalcoholic control or student groups. Al-though the alcoholics made more perseverative errors, maintaining correct re-sponding was most problematic. As with the Parkinson's patients, they gen-erated significantly more runs of five consecutive correct matches followed by an incorrect match than the control groups. Longer histories of alcohol-ism were positively correlated with increased shifts from correct responding. Subcortical damage that is characteristic of Korsakoff's syndrome was hypoth-esized as the source of this behavior pattern.

Lesions of the human frontal lobes often produce a syndrome charac-terized by apathy, slowing, perseveration, deficient self-awareness, and con-crete attitude. With the exception of apathy, these characteristics resemble those often associated with antisocial personality disorder (Gorenstein, 1982). Assuming frontal lobe involvement, several researchers have investigated the relationship between the diagnosis of antisocial personality disorder and tests of frontal lobe function. While Gorenstein (ibid.) found that patients who had been diagnosed as having antisocial personality disorder committed sig-nificantly more perseverative errors on the WCST than comparison groups consisting of college students and persons who did not have the disorder, his studies have been criticized for their methodology, and his results have not been replicated in several attempts (Hare, 1984; Sutker, Moan, & Allain, 1983; Sutker & Allain, 1983). Hare (1984) argued that little support exists for the conceptualization of antisocial personality disorder as a problem with

frontal lobe functioning. With the exception of Gorenstein's study, subjects diagnosed as having antisocial personality disorder have shown no differences on measures of cognitive or frontal lobe functioning, including the WCST.

In the first published study of brain-damaged patients using the WCST, Teuber, Battersby, and Bender (1951) studied a group of men with penetrating missile wounds received during World War II. Group assignment was based on the location of the documented entrance wound (frontal, intermediate, and posterior). The subjects with posterior entrance wounds performed the worst, making more errors and correctly naming fewer of the possible sorting dimensions. The patients with frontal entrance wounds were also impaired but not as much as the posterior group, and the intermediate group did about as well as the controls. A number of factors may bear on the interpretation of these results. Teuber (1966) suggested that the subjects with frontal lesion may have performed more poorly if they had not been warned that the category was about to change. This and other modifications of administration procedure (i.e., enforced shifts) changed the nature of the task and limit its comparability to Heaton's version of the WCST. Additionally, the use of the entrance point of a bullet wound incurred in battle constitutes unreliable localization of the lesion.

Milner's (1963, 1964) landmark study is largely responsible for the current view of the WCST as a test of frontal lobe functioning. Her subjects were presurgical patients scheduled for excision of epileptogenic brain tissue. Using an incomplete, pretest-posttest design, a group of 74 patients was evaluated both before and after surgery, while another group of 23 patients was tested postoperatively only. Preoperative group differences were not significant; however, postoperatively, those patients with frontal excision performed significantly more poorly than those with excisions from other brain areas. Patients who were tested only postoperatively were likewise impaired on the WCST relative to the other groups. Additionally, lesion size was ruled out as a possible cause of this differential performance. Milner suggested that frontal lobectomy impairs the patients' ability to shift categories once the original category is no longer correct, producing perseveration. Thus, the perseverative performance is not the result of an impairment in abstract thinking because the patient may successfully identify the three possible matching dimensions.

Robinson, Heaton, Lehman, and Stilson (1980) and Heaton (1981) administered the Halstead-Reitan Battery (HRB) and the WCST to brain-damaged patients with lesions in various locations and normal controls. The control group performed significantly better than all of the brain-damaged groups (except the left nonfrontal group) on all measures derived from the WCST, with the exception of "learning to learn." Controlling for overall level of impairment, the focal frontal groups did worse than the focal nonfrontal groups; however, the diffuse damage subgroup did equally poorly. The perseverative response score was a good predictor of focal frontal lesions, but

it failed to discriminate persons with focal frontal lesions from those with diffuse lesions.

Wallesch, Kornhuber, Kollner, Haas, and Hufnagel (1983) studied a group of patients with unilateral, circumscribed medial, or dorsolateral frontal lobe lesions. Patients with multiple lesions, cerebral atrophy, or psychiatric disorders were excluded. The control group comprised nonaphasic patients with retrorolandic lesions of similar size and etiology. Those with frontal lesions were not successfully discriminated from those with retrorolandic lesions based on WCST performance. Thus, while both groups were impaired on the WCST, evidence supporting frontal lobe specificity was not found.

Wallesch, Kornhuber, Kunz, and Brunner (1983) studied patients with small, well-demarcated, unilateral thalamic lesions; small ischemic lesions of the white matter of the cerebral hemispheres; and non-brain-damaged non-psychiatric normal controls. Using a modification of the WCST, they demonstrated that patients with thalamic lesions made significantly fewer correct responses than the normal controls, but no differences in the number of categories achieved among the groups. While the WCST has been found to be sensitive to frontal lobe lesions, multiple functions contributing to a successful performance are distributed throughout the brain.

Up to this point, discussion has focused mainly on the ability of WCST performance to discriminate between frontal lobe lesions in general and lesions of other parts of the brain (i.e., the issue of specificity of the test to frontal lobe lesions). Of equal importance is whether all lesions to the frontal lobes result in the same type or level of deficit; in other words, is the WCST sensitive to frontal lobe lesions? Milner (1963, 1964) found that only one patient in seven with removal of the orbital surface of one frontal lobe showed deficits in WCST performance, while all excisions involving the superior frontal area resulted in impaired performance on the WCST.

Milner's findings are supported by Benson et al. (1981) and Stuss et al. (1983), who found that patients with schizophrenia with orbital lesions due to frontal leukotomies performed similar to most normals. Finally, Eslinger and Damasio (1984) reported a patient from whom a large orbitofrontal tumor was removed (essentially sparing only the dorsolateral surface of the frontal lobes) and who had completely normal performance on the WCST. That ventromedial/orbitofrontal lesions fail to cause an increase in perseveration (and may fail to cause general cognitive impairment) has since been replicated (Anderson et al., 1991; Cicerone & Tanenbaum, 1997). However, even more recently, Stuss, Levine, Alexander, Hong, Palumbo, et al. (2000) demonstrated that ventromedial/orbitofrontal lesions may produce higher levels of failure to maintain set.

Summary

Regarding the sensitivity of the WCST to frontal lobe pathology, it appears that pathology involving the dorsolateral prefrontal cortex results in increased

perseveration as measured by the WCST. In contrast, orbitofrontal lesions rarely produce perseveration, though they seem to have a subtle effect on the ability to sustain correct responding. Moreover, from reading the preceding evidence, it might at first appear that the test does not show good specificity to frontal lobe dysfunction. In fact, a number of clinical conditions that are not specifically associated with structural lesions of the frontal cortex (e.g., schizophrenia, Parkinson's disease, chronic alcoholism) are associated with poor specificity on the WCST. However, all of the areas of suspected dysfunction in these conditions have extensive connections with the frontal lobe (e.g., thalamus, striatum; Damasio, 1979), and the conditions themselves may also be associated with general dementing processes, both of which are sufficient to explain impaired performance on the WCST. Thus it is arguable that WCST impairment is a function of the dysfunction of the frontal lobes and/or *associated brain structures* and that any disorder that disturbs the normal information-processing role of the frontal lobes, even if they are intact, should result in reduced WCST performance, a finding that appears to be supported by the MRI and PET scan data provided by Lombardi, Andreason, Sirocco, Rio, Gross, et al. (1999).

Malingering Detection Research
The last 10 years have seen a large number of studies of the WCST's capacity to detect malingering in neuropsychological cases. The first published analyses (Bernard, McGrath, & Houston, 1996; Suhr & Boyer, 1999) were followed by both known-groups studies and investigations that were designed to test the limits of specificity of the WCST indicators but otherwise lacked simulator or malingering groups (specificity studies). Table 8.1 summarizes these studies, and the following section reviews them in detail.

The Early Studies   Bernard et al. (1996) developed a series of discriminant function equations that took advantage of a potential malingerer's lack of knowledge of how brain injury affects WCST performance. Specifically, they argued as follows:

> It is likely that an individual who wishes to perform poorly on the WCST would realize that completing few categories and/or making a lot of errors would indicate impaired performance. However, that same individual likely would not realize that elevated perseverative responses and perseverative errors are of great significance in indicating impaired brain function. (Bernard et al., 1996, p. 233)

Thus, their analyses focused on categories completed as an obvious indicator and perseverative errors as a subtle indicator. Their sample consisted of 24 college students who were asked to simulate brain damage in a compensation-seeking context, 21 college students who were asked to perform their best, 70 traumatic brain-injury patients with documented brain pathology, and 89 neurological patients with documented central nervous system pathology

Table 8.1.
Summary of WCST Malingering Studies

Study	Design	Sample	Variables	Diagnostic Statistics
Bernard et al. (1996)	simulator, specificity	college students, TBI, mixed neurological patients	total errors, perseverative responses, perseverative errors, categories completed, unique responses, discriminant function formulae	sensitivity, specificity
Suhr & Boyer (1999)	simulator, known groups	college students, TBI	categories completed, errors, perseverative errors, failure to maintain set, logistic regression formula	none
Donders (1999)	specificity	TBI	Bernard et al. discriminant function formula	false positive error rate
Greve & Bianchini (2002)	specificity	college students, TBI, substance abuse, CVA, mixed neurological	Bernard and Suhr formulae	false positive error rate
Greve et al. (2002)	known groups	TBI	Bernard and Suhr formulae, unique responses	sensitivity, specificity, predictive power
King et al. (2002), Study 1	known groups	TBI	standard WCST scores, new variables, Bernard and Suhr formulae, derived logistic regression formula	sensitivity, specificity

(*continued*)

Table 8.1.
(*continued*)

Study	Design	Sample	Variables	Diagnostic Statistics
King et al. (2002), Study 2	specificity/known groups	acute moderate–severe TBI with no known incentive	same as Study 1	sensitivity, specificity
King et al. (2002), Study 3	specificity/known groups	mild TBI with no known incentive	same as Study 1	sensitivity, specificity
Ashendorf et al. (2003)	specificity	healthy older adults	Bernard and Suhr formulae, unique responses, perfect matches missed	specificity
Larrabee (2003), Study 1	known groups	moderate–severe TBI, alleged pathology in malingerers not described	failure to maintain set, Suhr formula	sensitivity, specificity
Larrabee (2003), Study 2	known groups	TBI, toxic exposure, electrical injury, mixed neurologic, psychiatric	failure to maintain set	sensitivity, specificity
Heinly et al. (2006)	known groups	TBI (mild, moderate–severe), general clinical patients	standard WCST scores, Bernard, Suhr, and King et al. formulae	sensitivity, specificity, positive predictive power

without brain trauma. Three discriminant analyses were conducted on half of each group, randomly selected, comparing simulators to each of the other three groups. The second half of the sample was used for cross-validation.

Bernard et al.'s simulator-control analyses were highly accurate, correctly classifying 91% (0% false positive error rate) in the original analysis and 96% (8% false positive error rate) in the cross-validation. Of greater importance, however, is the ability to discriminate simulators from patients with brain pathology. When the simulators were compared to the TBI patients, the classification accuracy was again excellent, with 98% correctly classified in the original analysis with a 3% false positive error rate. The cross-validation was less accurate at 95% overall (6% false positive error rate) but still good.

Accuracy in the mixed neurological sample was poorer: 89% with a false positive error rate of 4% in the original analysis and 91% overall with a false positive error rate of 0% in the cross-validation. The authors then presented the classification function coefficients for each of the three analyses (see Table 6 on page 241 of the original article). Overall, the classification accuracy of their indicators was excellent, but clinical application may be limited because theirs was a simulator study.

Suhr and Boyer (1999) attempted to replicate the findings of Bernard et al. in a sample that included college students (including a simulated malingering group), patients with TBI, and a group of probable clinical malingerers (workers compensation litigants with at least two external indicators of malingering). Their overall experimental design was quite sophisticated in that they used actual clinical patients and multiple criteria in defining malingering. Because they found perseverative errors to be highly correlated with categories completed, Suhr and Boyer included failure to maintain set (FMS) as their "subtle" score to reduce the risk of multicolinearity and because of the reported relative insensitivity of FMS to brain injury (Heaton, 1981; Heaton et al., 1993).

Suhr and Boyer developed an equation utilizing logistic regression rather than discriminant analysis. Among the students (normal versus simulators), the logistic regression had an overall accuracy of 77.8% with sensitivity at 70.7% and a false positive error rate of 12.9%. In the patient sample, a new analysis correctly classified 87.5% of the nonmalingering TBI and Probable Malingerers, with sensitivity at 82.4% and a false positive error rate at 6.7%. In addition to reporting the beta weights for the patient equation (Table 2 on p. 705 of the original article), they also reported score cutoffs for probabilities of malingering ranging from 50% to 99%. These probabilities are the posttest odds that were produced as part of the logistic regression analysis (J. A. Suhr, personal communication, April 14, 2006) and thus reflect the pretest odds of the study sample.

Summary
Two essentially different formulae for detecting malingering on the WCST have been reported. Both have produced good specificity (less than a 10%

false positive error rate) relative to nonmalingering TBI and mixed neurological patients without TBI. The sensitivity of both methods was also very good, and the Bernard et al. formula continued to be accurate in crossvalidation. Despite cross-validation, the application of the Bernard et al. formula to clinical patients may be limited, however, because it was based on the performance of simulators, not a clinically diagnosed malingering group. The Suhr and Boyer formula, on the other hand, used a known-groups design, which should allow direct application to the clinical setting. Nevertheless, the findings were not cross-validated. Overall, the results of Bernard et al. (1996) and Suhr and Boyer (1999) indicate that both methods hold promise, but additional studies are needed to better understand the limits of their accuracy.

Specificity Studies   Donders (1999) examined the specificity of the Bernard equations in a sample of 130 traumatic brain-injury patients evaluated within 1 year of their injury. They ranged in age from 17 to 74, had no previous neurological history, and were absent any factors that might have invalidated the assessment such as severe uncorrected visual impairment or non–English language background. Patients were also excluded if they were seeking financial compensation for their injuries. In examining the accuracy of the Bernard et al. formula, Donders counted as positive any case in which the score for the malingering formula exceeded that of the brain-injury formula. Of these, 5% ($n = 7$) were positive. Those seven patients were well described, and all had significant complicating factors (e.g., severe brain injury, comorbid posttraumatic stress disorder, severe pain, premorbid substance abuse, or psychiatric history). Donders cautioned against the mechanistic use of this formula especially in older persons.

Greve and Bianchini (2002) examined the specificity of the Bernard and Suhr formulas in seven samples: (a) normal college students with no psychiatric or neurological history ($n = 133$); (b) unselected college students ($n = 76$); (c) patients in a 28-day inpatient substance abuse treatment program ($n = 44$); (d) survivors of chronic severe TBI living in a residential treatment facility ($n = 69$); (e) stroke patients in a subacute comprehensive inpatient physical rehabilitation facility ($n = 83$); and (f) two mixed neurological samples derived from a general outpatient practice and several inpatient rehabilitation facilities ($n = 128$ and 360). The Bernard et al. (1996) equation for controls was used with the two college student samples. Their equation for TBI was used for the severe TBI sample. Finally, the equation for the mixed neurological sample was used for the remaining samples. The Suhr and Boyer (1999) equation for undergraduates was used for the two college student samples, and the equation for patients was used for the other samples.

Table 8.2 illustrates that, with a few notable exceptions, both sets of equations produced an unacceptably high (greater than 10%; for previous use of this value, see Millis, Putnam, Adams, & Ricker, 1995, and Millis, Ross, &

Table 8.2.
False Positive Error Rate Reported by Greve and Bianchini (2002) for the Bernard and Suhr Formulas

	All Samples		
		False Positive Error Rate	
Sample	*N*	Bernard	Suhr
normal college students Sample 1	133	2.3[a]	.0
normal college students Sample 2	76	15.8[a]	1.3[b]
substance abusers	44	20.5	18.2
severe traumatic brain injury	69	41.7	26.1
cerebrovascular accident	83	12.0	26.5
mixed neurological Sample 1	128	7.8	14.1
mixed neurological Sample 2	360	13.3	20.3

	By Diagnostic Category for the Mixed Neurological Samples					
	Sample 1			Sample 2		
	N	Bernard	Suhr	*N*	Bernard	Suhr
TBI	71	7.0	11.3	157	8.9	14.6
stroke	37	5.4	21.6	117	12.0	24.8
anoxia	5	20.0	20.0	—	—	—
tumor	4	.0	.0	—	—	—
infection	1	.0	.0	—	—	—
dementia	9	22.2	11.1	35	22.6	28.6
seizure disorder	1	.0	.0	7	42.9	42.8
psychiatric	—	—	—	33	27.3	18.2
substance abuse	—	—	—	11	.0	22.2

Note. [a]The Bernard et al. TBI equation was actually more accurate for the college student sample (false positive error rate = .8 and 7.9, respectively) than was the control equation.
[b]The Suhr and Boyer undergraduate equation was only slightly better than the patient equation in Sample 2 (false positive rate with the patient equation was 3.9); the rates were identical for Sample 1.

Ricker, 1998) rate of false positive errors. With the Bernard equation, the extremely poor rates were as follows: for the substance abusers, 20.5; severe TBI patients, 41.7. With the Suhr formula, the rates were as follows: for the severe TBI patients, 26.1; cerebrovascular accident patients (CVA), 26.5; and mixed sample 2, 20.3. When used in the specific diagnostic subgroups of the mixed samples, the Bernard equation yielded good results for the TBI and CVA subsamples, while the Suhr equation resulted in false positive error rates of greater than 10% for all of the subsamples. Donders (1999)

reported a 5% false positive error rate in TBI patients who were less than 1 year postinjury. The majority of our TBI patients (two groups, $n = 71$ and $n = 157$, respectively, see Table 8.2B; excluding the chronic severe group, $n = 69$) were seen in this same time frame and had a false positive error rate of less than 10% using the Bernard et al. system, thus replicating Donders.

Two points are particularly relevant to the findings of this study, which seems to suggest marginal specificity. First, very poor specificity appears to be limited to patients with more severe neuropathology (e.g., those with dementia, stroke, and severe TBI) while their accuracy in the clinic-based TBI sample is actually adequate. Moreover, even in that sample, mild TBI patients are not separated from those with more severe injuries for purposes of specificity analysis. Since no single subject analysis was reported, it is not known whether more severe injuries were more frequent among those patients with positive scores. Given the clear injury severity effect in other patient groups, a similar effect in the TBI samples seems likely. Finally, it is possible that the method of excluding potential malingerers was too conservative and thus left some malingerers in the sample. Again, a careful examination of those TBI patients who were positive on either formula would probably have helped address this concern.

Ashendorf, O'Bryant, and McCaffrey (2003) have examined the specificity of the Bernard et al. and Suhr formulas along with unique responses and perfect matches missed, which had been reported by Greve, Bianchini, et al. (2002; see the following section on known-group studies) in a sample of 185 community-dwelling older adults (mean age = 64.57, range = 55–75). For unique responses, a cutoff of > 5 resulted in a false positive error rate of 8.6%, while more than one missed perfect match was associated with a false positive error rate of about 5%. Bernard's TBI formula resulted in a false positive error rate of almost 25%, while the false positive error rate for Suhr formula's was 52.4%. It appears that the Suhr formulas fared rather poorly in this study, with false positive error rates exceeding 50%.

Known-Group Studies   Miller, Donders, and Suhr (2000) examined the accuracy of the Bernard et al. and Suhr formulas in 90 TBI patients. Their sample comprised 30 patients in each of three groups: severe injury without incentive; mild injury without incentive; mild injury with incentive. Of these, 13 patients were identified as "likely malingerers" on the basis of failure on either the Recognition Memory Test (RMT) or the Test of Memory Malingering (TOMM). Ten came from the mild-incentive group, 2 from the severe group, and 1 from the mild–no incentive group. Since external incentive is a requirement for a diagnosis of malingering, the 3 patients from the two no-incentive groups could not be classified as malingering and should have been considered false positive cases relative to the external classification scheme (i.e., RMT, TOMM). That left 10 possible malingerers out of 30 patients with incentive, or a 33% base rate (not 14% or 13/90). This value is consistent with

the base rate of malingering reported by Mittenberg, Patton, Canyock, and Condit (2002).

Three patients were identified as possible malingerers by the Bernard et al. formula; those 3 and 1 more were identified by the Suhr formula. However, all of these were from the nonlitigating group, and none had scored below the cutoffs on either the RMT or the TOMM. These patients were clearly false positive cases. By Miller et al.'s count, these results represented false positive error rates of approximately 5% (3/77 and 4/77), which is equivalent to the false positive error rate that resulted from the TOMM and the RMT (3 no-incentive patients out of 60 failed one of those measures). The critical finding in this study, however, is that neither of the WCST formulas detected any of the patients who failed the TOMM or the RMT; sensitivity was 0%.

Thus, based on this study, these formulas are more likely to detect non-malingerers than malingerers, which is clinically unacceptable. It is interesting that the false positive rate associated with these indicators is acceptable and within the range of what one would expect. The 0% sensitivity may be more a consequence of limitations in the way that malingering was operationally defined rather than the insensitivity of the indicators themselves. As we will see, problems with sensitivity were not observed in others studies of the WCST.

Greve, Bianchini, et al. (2002) evaluated the accuracy of four methods for detecting malingering on the WCST (the Bernard et al. formula, the Suhr and Boyer formula, unique responses, and perfect matches missed) in a known-groups format. The sample of TBI patients was divided into four groups based on the Slick et al. criteria: (a) no-incentive control ($n = 17$); (b) probable MND ($n = 32$), those patients meeting the Slick et al. criteria for at least probable MND; (c) suspect ($n = 30$), positive on only one Slick et al. criterion; and (d) incentive only ($n = 10$), negative on all Slick et al. criteria.

The classification accuracy associated with two sets of cutoffs was examined. The first cutoff was the score that incorrectly classified two or fewer control subjects (i.e., produced a specificity of approximately .90). Those cutoffs are as follows: unique responses > 0; perfect matches missed > 0; Bernard > -3.00; Suhr > 1.90. The second set of cutoffs was more conservative: unique responses > 1; perfect matches missed > 1; Bernard > 0; Suhr > 3.68. Finally, classification accuracy was reported for combinations of the Bernard et al. formula, the Suhr and Boyer formula, and unique responses.

Unique responses and the formulas by Bernard et al. and by Suhr each correctly identified at least one third of the probable malingerers while maintaining a false positive rate of approximately 10%. The marker for perfect matches missed had perfect specificity but very limited sensitivity. The Suhr formula and unique responses were found to be sensitive to two different approaches to malingering on the WCST and together correctly identified as many as two thirds of the probable malingerers, although specificity suffered slightly. Under more conservative criteria, half of the probable malingerers were identified, and specificity was acceptable. The Bernard et al. formula shared a substantial degree of variance with the Suhr formula and did not

detect any malingerers that had not already been detected using one of the other methods. Its use in combination with the other methods therefore did not enhance diagnostic accuracy.

King, Sweet, Sherer, Curtiss, and Vanderploeg (2002) report three studies of the classification accuracy of three WCST composite scores designed to detect malingering: the Bernard et al. formula, the Suhr and Boyer formula, and a new logistic regression–based indicator developed in this study, employing categories completed, failure to maintain set, and percent conceptual level responses. The first study is a known-groups study, while the others are specificity studies designed to assess the influence of different TBI variables (acute moderate to severe TBI in Study 2, mild to severe TBI in Study 3) on WCST indicator performance.

Study 1 compared 33 nonmalingering moderate to severe TBI patients (who passed all of the malingering indicators and had no extratest evidence of malingering) with 27 TBI patients in the insufficient effort group who failed one or more malingering tests or indicators and met one or more extratest criteria for malingering. These criteria are similar to those of Greiffenstein et al. (1994), and the patients in the insufficient effort group likely would have met the Slick et al. (1999) criteria for MND. False positive error rates ranged from 6% (Bernard et al. formula) to 18% (new logistic regression formula). The Suhr and Boyer formula had a false positive error rate of 12%. Sensitivity ranged from 59% (Suhr and Boyer) to 70% (new formula).

Subjects in the second study were 75 moderate to severe TBI patients who were seen acutely shortly after emerging from posttraumatic amnesia. In this sample, the false positive error rates increased substantially for the Suhr and Bernard et al. formulas (to about 25%), but the new formula showed a dramatic improvement (to only 3%). The sample in the third study included 130 mild to severe TBI patients being treated in a Veterans Administration brain-injury program. These patients were seen farther postinjury than those from Study 2 and might be considered postacute but not yet chronic (like the ones in Study 1). The false positive error rates for the Bernard et al. formula and the new formula (5% and 1%, respectively) were excellent. The Suhr formula was less accurate, incorrectly classifying about 15% of these patients.

Overall, there was considerable variability in the false positive error rate across samples, though these were mostly within acceptable ranges ($< 15\%$) and would likely improve substantially had a range of cut scores been examined. The lowest false positive error rate was for the acute moderate to severe TBI patients, who would be expected to have more difficulty on cognitive testing in any case. Sensitivity was quite good even though it would most likely come down somewhat if the cut scores were adjusted to improve specificity.

Larrabee (2003a) examined the performance of two sets of malingering and nonmalingering patients on the WCST, as well as four other clinical indicators of malingering, in an effort to identify performance patterns that were atypical of legitimate brain-injured patients. Subjects in the derivation

sample were 26 patients who claimed brain damage in the absence of objective neurological findings and who performed significantly worse than chance on a forced-choice symptom validity test (SVT; definite MND) and 31 moderate–severe TBI patients, some of whom were in litigation. The litigating moderate–severe patients were considered not to be malingering in part because their clinical test results seemed consistent with trauma severity and did not differ from those of the nonlitigating patients.

While not the primary focus of this study, Larrabee (ibid.) examined the accuracy of the Suhr and Boyer formula. A cutoff of >0 detected 64% of definite MND patients but had a false positive error rate of 48.4. Increasing the cutoff to >2.41 resulted in a sensitivity of 40% with a false positive error rate of 12.9%. A cutoff of >1 failure to maintain set (FMS) resulted in a slightly (but not significantly) higher sensitivity (48%) and an identical specificity. No nonmalingering patient had more than three FMS, and only one had three. In contrast, 12% of the definite MND patients had more than three FMS, and 20% had more than two.

Importantly, Larrabee (ibid.) demonstrated that requiring two failures out of five tests (Benton Visual Form Discrimination, combined bilateral finger tapping speed, Reliable Digit Span, WCST FMS, and the Lees-Haley Fake Bad scale for the MMPI-2) resulted in a sensitivity of 87.5% with a false positive error rate of 11.1%. The FMS contributed to all of the false positive errors. When three failures were required, sensitivity dropped to 54.2%, but specificity rose to 100% (no false positive errors). This suggests that the cutoff for FMS may have been a little too low. An FMS >2 was associated with a false positive error rate of 4%, compared to 13% for FMS >1.

Results for FMS alone were not presented for the cross-validation sample (Study 2). However, on average about 20% of the patients who were claiming brain damage and had failed two SVTs failed on FMS and at least one other indicator. However, when FMS was used in combination with other indicators in the nonmalingering mixed neurological and psychiatric samples, no one was incorrectly identified as malingering. Larrabee pointed out that, while FMS was involved in the false positives in the derivation sample, all of those subjects were severe TBI patients, and none had more than three FMS. Thus, patients without severe injuries or with more than three FMS are unlikely to be false positives.

In the most comprehensive known-groups study of the WCST yet reported, Heinly, Greve, Love, & Bianchini (2006) examined the classification accuracy of all of the scores routinely output by the WCST scoring software, as well as scores previously reported as indicative of malingering (unique responses, FMS, Suhr formula, Bernard et al. formula, King formula). Sensitivity and false positive error rates (not just fixed cutoffs) were reported for a range of scores. Their sample included three groups of TBI patients (mild, $n = 137$; moderate–severe, $n = 139$; chronic severe in a residential facility, $n = 101$) and more than 1,000 general clinical patients. The mild and moderate-to-severe TBI samples were divided into malingering ($n = 47$ and

90) and nonmalingering ($n = 21$ and 118) groups based on the Slick et al. (1999) criteria. Of the standard scores, only categories completed, perseverative responses (PR), perseverative errors (PE), and FMS showed any value in differentiating malingering from nonmalingering patients; thus, only their results were reported. Data for the specialized indicators were reported regardless of their effectiveness.

At cutoffs associated with false positive error rates of between 5% and 10%, sensitivity was typically about 20% even among the malingering moderate to severe patients. One exception was the Bernard et al. formula, which was ineffective in the mild TBI patients but detected 15–20% of malingering moderate to severe patients with a false positive error rate of 5–10%. Unique responses appeared to be an ineffective discriminator. The false positive error rates for the chronic severe TBI patients, as well as the stroke and dementia patients, were very high, indicating two things: (a) that WCST indicators should not be used in persons with objectively documented severe neuropathology and (b) that the performance and motivations of persons with no, mild, or ambiguous neuropathology (e.g., mild TBI) who score at a level comparable to such patients are highly suspicious. In general, discrimination between malingering and nonmalingering TBI patients was more accurate for the mild group than the moderate to severe group.

Summary

Most studies of the capacity of the WCST to detect malingering have been of the known-group variety. Larrabee (2003a) used all definite MND, while the other studies used either all probable MND or a combination of probable and definite (to the extent that Miller et al.'s patients did not score below chance on the RMT or the TOMM, they are best classified as possible malingering). Three specificity-only studies were reported, two of which presented data for traumatic brain-injury patients. The only simulator studies were those by Bernard et al. and Suhr and Boyer (which also included a known-group component). Table 8.3 presents the classification accuracy for TBI patients from five known-group studies (Greve, Bianchini, et al., 2002; Heinly et al., 2005; King et al., 2002; Larrabee, 2003a; Miller et al., 2000) and the two specificity studies with TBI data (Greve & Bianchini, 2002; Donders, 1999) for a range of cutoffs for four WCST malingering indicators: Bernard et al. formula, Suhr and Boyer formula, FMS, and unique responses. This table also presents the classification accuracy aggregated across these studies for each cutoff. Table 8.4 presents those same aggregate rates along with 95% confidence intervals (95% CI) for those rates and positive predictive power (+PP).

Typically, the known-groups studies reported classification accuracy for only one or two cutoffs per indicator (a third was rarely reported). The exception was the study by Heinly et al. (2005), which presented false positive error rates and sensitivity for a range of scores across several indicators and patient groups. Consequently, the Heinly et al. data can help to evaluate the consistency of classification accuracy findings across studies for comparison

Table 8.3.
WCST Known-Groups Study Comparisons at Different Cut Scores

Study	Cutoff	Reported FP	Reported Sens	Aggregate Accuracy n/N	Aggregate Accuracy FP	Aggregate Accuracy n/N	Aggregate Accuracy Sens
Bernard et al. formula							
Greve et al.	> -3	11	38	33/225	15	34/100	34
Heinly et al., mild		13	32				
Heinly et al., mod/sev		16	34				
Greve et al.	> 0	6	16	58/746	8	39/127	31
King et al. #1		6	63				
King et al. #3		5	—				
Donders		5	—				
Greve & Bianchini #1		7	—				
Greve & Bianchini #2		9	—				
Heinly et al., mild		9	24				
Heinly et al., mod/sev		12	29				
Suhr & Boyer formula							
Larrabee	> 0	48	64	111/239	46	61/104	59
Heinly et al., mild		40	57				
Heinly et al., mod/sev		51	81				
Greve et al	> 1.90	11	47	44/225	20	43/100	43
Heinly et al., mild		12	37				
Heinly et al., mod/sev		26	53				
Larrabee	> 2.41	13	40	37/239	15	31/80	39
Heinly et al., mild		12	33				
Heinly et al., mod/sev		19	24				
King et al. #1	> 3.16	9	59	45/371	12	33/95	35
King et al. #3		8	—				
Heinly et al., mild		10	29				
Heinly et al., mod/sev		14	15				
Greve & Bianchini #1	> 3.68	11	—	50/453	11	22/100	22
Greve & Bianchini #2		15	—				
Heinly et al., mild		7	22				
Heinly et al., mod/sev		9	5				
Failure to maintain set							
Larrabee	> 1	13	48	51/239	21	35/94	37
Heinly et al., mild		15	35				
Heinly et al., mod/sev		28	34				
Larrabee	> 2	4	20	21/239	9	22/94	23
Heinly et al., mild		8	24				
Heinly et al., mod/sev		11	5				
Larrabee	> 3	0	12	6/239	3	11/94	12
Heinly et al., mild		0	16				
Heinly et al., mod/sev		5	0				

Table 8.4.
WCST Aggregate Classification Accuracy With Positive Predictive Power for Several Hypothetical Base Rates

Indicator	cutoff	FP (95% CI)	Sens (95% CI)	BR	.20	.30	.40	.50
		Aggregate Accuracy			+PP			
Bernard et al.	>−3	15 (10–20)	34 (25–44)		.36	.49	.60	.69
formula	>0	8 (6–10)	31 (23–40)		.49	.62	.72	.79
Suhr & Boyer	>0	46 (40–53)	59 (48–68)		.24	.35	.46	.56
formula	>1.90	20 (15–25)	43 (33–53)		.35	.48	.59	.68
	>2.41	15 (11–21)	39 (28–50)		.39	.53	.63	.72
	>3.16	12 (9–16)	35 (25–45)		.42	.56	.66	.74
	>3.68	11 (8–14)	22 (14–31)		.33	.46	.57	.67
Failure to	>1	21 (16–27)	37 (27–48)		.31	.43	.54	.64
maintain set	>2	9 (6–13)	23 (15–33)		.39	.52	.63	.72
	>3	3 (1–5)	12 (6–20)		.50	.63	.73	.80

and cross-validation. Data for mild and moderate to severe TBI patients are presented separately for each cutoff in order to clarify the behavior of the WCST scores as malingering indicators.

Bernard et al. Formula   Three false positive (FP) rates are reported for a cutoff of greater than −3 with an aggregate FP rate of 15%. All three individual values fall within the 95% CI for the aggregate value. Seven false positive error rates have been reported for a Bernard et al. cutoff of >0 ranging from 5% to 12% (aggregate FP rate = 8%). All individual FP rates except that of Heinly et al.'s moderate–severe TBI patients fell within the 95% CI for the aggregate value. At 12%, the Heinly et al. moderate to severe TBI FP rate is significantly higher than the aggregate rate ($p < .01$). In short, with the exception of the Heinly et al. moderate–severe sample, the FP data for these reported cutoffs is very consistent.

The meaning of the sensitivity data is less clear. Only two studies—Greve, Bianchini, et al. (2002) and Heinly et al. (2005)—provide sensitivity data for the >−3 cutoff. Similarly, those same two studies, plus that by King et al. (2002) , provide sensitivity data for the >0 cutoff. Sensitivity for the >−3 cutoff is consistent across the studies with an aggregate of 34%. However, at the >0 cutoff, the sensitivity reported by King et al. (63%) is more than double that reported by Heinly et al. and almost triple that reported by Greve et al. In fact, this value is almost twice the 38% reported by Greve, Bianchini, et al. (2002) for a much more liberal cutoff of >−3. Moreover, the King et al. value is well outside the 95% CI of the aggregate sensitivity for this cutoff (39%). Without King et al., sensitivity was almost 20

percentage points lower (22%). Using the one aggregate specificity value and the two sensitivity values leads to a +PP ranging from.54 to .79 for the hypothetical base rates of .30, .40, and .50. +PP for the two aggregate sensitivities that differed by less than 10% at all three levels.

In summary, for the Bernard et al. formula, estimates of the false positive error rate are generally consistent for the two cutoffs examined in multiple studies. The accuracy of the > -3 cutoff, as indicated by +PP, is arguably too low to justify interpreting a score at this level as an indication of malingering. On the other hand, the classification accuracy of scores greater than 0, as indicated by +PP, is good regardless of whether the King et al. data are included in the calculation of aggregate sensitivity. Nonetheless, it is likely that the King et al. sensitivity value (but not specificity) is an overestimate, given the overall findings for the Suhr and Boyer formula (see the following section). These data indicate that the Bernard et al. formula can serve as an indication of malingering especially in mild TBI and may be used with caution in moderate TBI. However, the Heinly et al. data suggest that it probably should not be used in objectively very severe cases. Additional research with clinical defined malingerers is important to better define the sensitivity of this indicator at multiple cutoffs.

Suhr and Boyer Formula   Five different studies have reported classification accuracy at several different cutoffs for this formula. The aggregate FP rates show a graded decline as scores become more extreme. Interestingly, this graded decline is due to the Heinly et al. moderate–severe TBI patients. When the Heinly et al. moderate–severe TBI data are excluded, the FP rates show very little variability even at different cutoffs. The aggregate false positive error rate is about 12% when combined across all cutoffs of 1.90 or greater. Unfortunately, at the most extreme cutoff for which there are data from more than one study, the FP error rate is still rather large (i.e., cutoff >3.68, aggregate FP rate $= 11\%$). Heinly et al.'s data indicate that in mild TBI an FP rate of 6% can be achieved at ≥ 4 (sensitivity $= 22\%$), and a 2% FP rate (sensitivity $= 9\%$) can be achieved at ≥ 4.5. The accuracy of the Suhr and Boyer formula in moderate–severe TBI is generally unacceptable at any level according to the Heinly et al. findings. Given those findings, it is probably best not to use this formula in patients with objectively documented brain pathology.

There seems to be less variability in the sensitivity of this formula than was seen in the Bernard et al. formula. However, sensitivity in the Heinly et al. mild TBI patients was lower than that reported in earlier studies, even at the same cutoff. As before, the sensitivity reported by King et al. is substantially higher than all other estimates, even at more conservative cutoffs, approaching triple the sensitivity reported by Heinly et al. in the mild TBI patients. Table 8.3 shows a clear drop in aggregate sensitivity as cutoffs become more conservative. However, at 3.68, King et al. report a sensitivity of 59%, a value that is little different from that reported by Larrabee and

Heinly et al. for a score of 0. Thus, since data from several studies show a clear sensitivity gradient as scores become more extreme and the King et al. sensitivity findings for a cutoff of 3.68 are well outside even the 99% CI for all cutoffs except 0, it is likely that their value for sensitivity (but not specificity) is an overestimate and should not be relied upon for clinical decision making.

In summary, the false positive error rate is fairly stable at 12% (from 1.90 up) across studies and cutoffs. However, sensitivity drops in a graded fashion from about 40% at a cutoff of > 1.90 to about 20% at a cutoff of 3.68. As Table 8.4 illustrates, +PP is marginal at best at all cutoffs when the hypothetical base rate is 30% or less and remain less than .75 at all reported cutoffs. The Heinly et al. data will allow the calculation of +PP at higher cutoffs. Again, these findings mean that caution should be exercised in concluding that a Suhr and Boyer score indicates malingering except when the score is extreme (e.g., >4.00 based on the Heinly et al. data). Moreover, the more severe the injury (based on acute characteristics), the more likely that a given score will be a false positive error, which means that, as with the Bernard et al. formula, it should probably not be used in cases of more severe TBI.

Failure to Maintain Set   FMS is a somewhat mysterious variable. Because it appears to be relatively insensitive to brain trauma (Heaton, 1981; Heaton et al., 1993), it has been used as a malingering indicator. Yet, FMS (in several variations) appears to be sensitive to ventromedial frontal pathology (Stuss et al., 2000). In any factor analysis of the WCST in which it was included, FMS always loaded on its own factor (for a review see Greve, Stickle, Love, Bianchini, & Stanford, 2005). Moreover, Greve, Love, Sherwin, Mathias, and Ramzinski (2002) identified a subgroup of chronic severe TBI patients whose performance was characterized by high FMS scores. For this reason Greve and Bianchini (2002) originally criticized the Suhr and Boyer formula (the Bernard et al. formula was criticized for a similar reason relative to nonperseverative errors).

Nonetheless, the classification accuracy data of Larrabee (2003a) and Heinly et al. (2005) for mild TBI are strikingly similar and are acceptable for the detection of malingering (see Table 8.3). The aggregate false positive error rate for cutoffs of >1, 2, and 3 are 21%, 9%, and 3%, respectively. Sensitivity at the same cutoffs was 37%, 23%, and 12%. Again, the Heinly et al. moderate–severe TBI patients scored much more poorly on this indicator than the mild TBI patients. When they are excluded, the FP rate for FMS >3 is 0%, and +PP is perfect. Importantly, about 15% of the Heinly et al. patients with a range of documented neuropathology including moderate–severe TBI, stroke, and dementia produced FMS scores above this cutoff; thus, consideration of the clinical facts of the case is important before applying FMS. When the base rate is 20%, +PP is notably lower at the lower cutoffs and below .50. The highest +PP was .80 using FMS >3 and a base rate of .50. Thus, FMS appears to have empirical value as a malingering indicator in mild TBI and can be applied in these cases.

Conclusions

Malingering indicators derived from the WCST have been examined in a number of known-groups studies. The data from these studies indicate that three of these indicators (Bernard et al. formula, Suhr & Boyer formula, and FMS) can be used to detect malingering in mild traumatic brain injury. The indicators should be used with great caution in moderate–severe TBI as the false positive error rates can be quite high. As the scores become more extreme, all three are stronger indicators of malingering. Only Heinly et al. report the classification accuracy for these more extreme scores. Given the general consistency of findings across studies at lower cutoffs, application of the Heinly et al. data is reasonable. However, replication in carefully designed known-groups studies by other laboratories will be important to clarify the limits of accuracy at those more extreme score levels.

Category Test

Background

Developed in the 1940s, the Category Test (CaT) is part of the same sorting test tradition that led to the WCST. In fact, the progenitor of the CaT was an object sorting test (Halstead, 1940), and modification led to the use of geometric designs (Halstead & Settlage, 1943). By 1950 the CaT had been further refined (Halstead & White, 1950) and remains in that form today. The modern CaT is a 208-item, seven-subtest instrument in which each item is projected onto a screen, and the patient/subject responds by pulling a lever or pushing a button. Feedback regarding the accuracy of the responses is provided in the form of different auditory tones.

The bulkiness of the original apparatus limited its clinical use, however. As a result, a number of modifications of the original setup have been offered (Boyle, 1986; Calsyn, O'Leary, & Chaney, 1980; Charter, Swift, & Bluzewicz, 1997; DeFillipis & McCampbell, 1991; Labreche, 1983; Russell & Levy, 1987; Wetzel & Boll, 1987). Sweet and King (2002) state that they did not differentiate among these various versions in their review of CaT malingering research because there has been little evidence of differences among them. Of these several versions, the Booklet Category Test (DeFillipis & McCampbell, 1991) is the most popular (Rabin et al., 2005). No CaT version is more widely used than the WCST, however (ibid.). For convenience, this chapter refers to all versions of the Category Test as "CaT."

The CaT appears to be multidimensional in nature (Allen, Goldstein, & Mariano, 1999; Donders, 2001; Nesbit-Greene & Donders, 2002), usually loading on three factors when individual subtest scores are examined. Interestingly, despite their comparable sensitivity to brain pathology (Lezak et al., 2004), the CaT and the WCST share little variance and are not clinically interchangeable (Bond & Buchtel, 1984; Goldberg, Kelsoe, Weinberger, Pliskin, Kirwin, et al., 1988; Golden, Kushner, Lee, & McMorrow, 1998; Greve, Farrrell, Besson, & Crouch, 1995; King & Snow, 1981; MacInnes, Golden,

McFadden, & Wilkening, 1983; Pendleton & Heaton, 1982; Perrine, 1993). Nonetheless, like the WCST, the CaT is a measure of higher level abstract thinking and problem-solving abilities (Allen et al., 1999).

Research seems to indicate that, although the CaT is considered to be a measure of executive function, it cannot be considered a measure of frontal lobe function per se. The test was originally intended to detect frontal lobe lesions, and the research by Shure and Halstead (1958) appeared to support this conclusion. However, a reanalysis of those data by Wang (1987) demonstrated poor performances in a substantial portion of the nonfrontal patients. In their review of the CaT, Sweet and King (2002) state that it is sensitive to diffuse cerebral dysfunction and that specific location, etiology, and duration are relevant factors in CaT performance. Conversely, like the WCST, not all frontal lobe lesions affect performance (Heck & Bryer, 1986). Conclusions about the nonspecificity of the CaT to frontal lobe damage has been supported more recently by the work of Anderson, Bigler, and Blatter (1995) and Demakis (2004).

Dikmen, Machamer, Winn, and Temkin (1995) found that only the most severely injured TBI patients (those unable to follow commands for 2 weeks or more) scored significantly worse than trauma controls on the CaT 1 year after injury. Those with less than an hour of unresponsiveness did not differ at all from the trauma controls (mean error scores of 24 in the trauma controls versus 22 for the TBI patients). This suggests that mild brain injury as it is normally defined does not have a lasting effect on CaT performance and that only the most severe brain injuries appear to affect performance significantly. Conversely, Heaton, Grant, and Matthews (1991) found that about 15% of their neurologically healthy normative sample scored in the impaired range (demographically corrected T score < 40) on the CaT with the percentages of impaired scores increasing with greater age and lower educational attainment.

Malingering Detection Research

The CaT is among the earliest neuropsychological tests that were used in the development of malingering indicators. Numerous studies of the CaT in malingering have been published. Table 8.5 summarizes these studies. Research on malingering with the CaT differs in several important ways from that with the WCST.

First, whereas the WCST was designed as an independent, stand-alone measure, the Halstead Category Test (HCT) is a standard component of the Halstead-Reitan Battery and therefore has been part of studies of malingering detection with the HRB. As a result, data related to the CaT's malingering detection accuracy alone may not be reported. The earliest studies reporting independent data on the CaT (e.g., Goebel, 1983; Heaton, Smith, Lehman, & Vogt, 1978) focused chiefly on the overall ability of the HRB to detect malingering but also reported on the results from individual tests.

The second difference between malingering research on the CaT and the WCST is that, unlike the WCST, where most of the studies are of the known-

groups variety, the CaT has been studied primarily with simulator designs. It is important to point out, however, that, in addition to evaluating sensitivity using the performance of neurologically normal persons asked to feign cognitive impairment, most of these simulator studies also included as their control group a sample of nonmalingering moderate to severe TBI patients whose scores can provide good estimates of specificity.

The Early Studies   Heaton et al. (1978) attempted to identify elements of the Halstead-Reitan Battery, including the CaT, that could differentiate malingering (simulating) subjects from nonmalingering patients with objectively defined brain pathology. The HRB performance of 16 severe traumatic brain-injury (TBI) patients was compared to that of 16 persons recruited from the community and paid $25 to fake in a believable manner, with the incentive of a $5 bonus if they were successful. The oft-quoted finding of this study is that the ability of the 10 neuropsychologists who were asked to accurately identify the malingered versus nonmalingered HRB protocols was "modest." Regarding CaT performance, the TBI patients actually scored worse than the simulators (total error mean = 46.1 and 67.4, respectively). When the classification accuracy was estimated from group means and standard deviations (Greve & Bianchini, 2003) using a cutoff of > 87 total errors (a recommendation of Tenhula & Sweet, 1996; see the following section on simulator studies), the sensitivity to simulators was 2%, while the false positive error rate in moderate to severe traumatic brain injury was 22%.

Goebel (1983) sought to extend Heaton et al.'s (1978) findings by substantially increasing the sample size and including a diverse group of patients with objective evidence of brain trauma. He also used a large sample of college students and community volunteers, 102 of whom were given one of four different sets of simulation instructions. Like Heaton et al. (ibid.), Goebel's simulators scored better than his patients on the CaT (total errors mean = 46.1 and 86.2, respectively, with controls committing 30.3 errors). No standard deviations were reported, so it is impossible to estimate sensitivity and specificity. Of course, as in the Heaton et al. (ibid.) study, since the patients actually did worse, the false positive error rate would be higher than the sensitivity.

Bolter, Picano, and Zych (1985) attempted to develop a validity scale for the CaT. Their results were reported at the annual meeting of the National Academy of Neuropsychology and have been summarized by Sweet and King (2002). Bolter et al. compared the results of 50 mixed brain-damage patients to those of 50 persons felt to have nonneurological symptoms (not necessarily malingerers). Eighteen items rarely missed by this group of patients were identified across the test. Of this group, 76% failed none of the items, and 97% failed two or fewer. A subsequent unpublished study resulted in the elimination of 4 of the original 18 items. Nonetheless, Sweet and King note that most subsequent studies of the Bolter Index or Bolter items actually use the original 18-item set.

Table 8.5.
Summary of Category Test Malingering Studies

Study	Design	Sample	Variables	Diagnostic Statistics
Heaton et al. (1978)	simulator, specificity	TBI, community normals, college students	total errors	none
Goebel (1983)	simulator, specificity	college students, mixed neurological patients	total errors	none
Trueblood & Schmidt (1993)	known groups	TBI	errors on subtest VII, Bolter items	none
Mittenberg et al. (1996)	simulator, specificity	normal volunteers, TBI	total errors	none
Tenhula & Sweet (1996) Study 1	simulator, specificity	college students, TBI	errors on each subtest, discriminant function score, Bolter, easy, and difficult items	sensitivity, specificity
Tenhula & Sweet (1996) Study 2	simulator, specificity	college students, TBI	same as study 1	sensitivity, specificity
Ellwanger et al. (1999) study 1	simulator	college students	Tenhula & Sweet decision rules and discriminant function score	sensitivity, specificity
DiCarlo et al. (2000)	simulator, specificity	college students, TBI	errors on subtests I and II, subtest VII, total errors, Easy items	sensitivity, specificity
Williamson et al. (2003)	differential prevalence	TBI	Tenhula & Sweet decision rules	none
Forrest et al. (2004), Study 1	specificity	structural brain damage, schizophrenia, non patients	errors on subtests I, II, VII, error proportions I–VI:VII and V:VI	specificity
Forrest et al. (2004), Study 2	simulator	college students, structural brain damage	same as Study 1	sensitivity, specificity
Greve et al. (2007)	known groups	TBI (mild, moderate–severe), general clinical patients		sensitivity, specificity, positive predictive power

Simulator Studies   Mittenberg, Rotholc, Russell, and Heilbronner (1996) examined CaT performance in 80 simulators and 80 nonlitigating patients with documented brain trauma. The sample was divided into an initial validation group and a cross-validation group. Like Heaton et al. (1978) and Goebel (1983), Mittenberg et al. actually examined the entire HRB. Unlike the two earlier studies, their simulators performed worse than the brain-injured subjects on total errors (mean = 81.18 and 63.75, respectively, in the validation study, and 85.20 and 61.63, respectively, in the cross-validation study). Because standard deviations were reported, the classification accuracy for the cut score recommended by Tenhula and Sweet could be calculated. In this case, like Heaton et al. (1978), the false positive error rate was 22%. However, sensitivity to simulated brain damage was nearly double that value at 41%.

Mittenberg et al. went on to examine the accuracy of their discriminant function score derived from the entire HRB in three clinical patients who were likely to be malingering. Of these three patients, only one would have been identified as malingering based on the Tenhula and Sweet recommendation (total errors = 99). One other was borderline (total errors = 84), but the third was not even close (total errors = 48).

In one of the most comprehensive CaT studies reported, Tenhula and Sweet (1996) examined the accuracy of a broad array of CaT variables, including a discriminant function-derived score and a range of individual scores (total errors, subtest scores, Subtest I + Subtest II errors, Subtest VII, errors on easy, difficult, and Bolter items) with cross-validation in a second sample. The initial sample consisted of 34 normal controls, 33 normal controls who were asked to simulate brain damage, and 29 TBI patients with objective evidence of brain damage. The cross-validation study included 24 normal controls, 18 simulators, and 25 TBI patients. Some of the TBI patients were in litigation related to their injuries.

As expected, the simulators performed significantly worse than both the control and the TBI samples. To determine malingering cutoffs and discriminant functions, the nonsimulating controls and the TBI patients were combined into a single nonmalingering group to be compared to the simulators. Seven discriminant functions were developed. The two including the difficult items produced the lowest overall classification accuracy—at 72.5%—with both sensitivity and specificity falling in that range. The remainder demonstrated sensitivity in the 75% range with specificity typically higher than 90% (see ibid., Table 3, p. 111, for the classification results of the combined sample).

When simple clinical decision rules were applied to the scores of interest, the sensitivity dropped by up to 25 percentage points, while the specificity improved, often to about 98% (2% false positive error rate). Generally, they reported sensitivity from 50% (total errors) to 75% (Subtests I + II errors) with false positive error rates of less than 3% except for the number of errors on Subtest VII (false positive error rate = 8.3%). The difficult items proved to be both insensitive and nonspecific.

In a novel study, Ellwanger, Tenhula, Rosenfeld, and Sweet (1999) attempted to enhance the identification of malingering by combining the CaT with event-related potentials. They also used a simulator design in which 29 college students were randomly assigned to either a control or a simulator group and then administered the CaT and the P3 Multi-Digit Memory Test (P3MDMT; an electrophysiological procedure; see Rosenfeld, Ellwanger, & Sweet, 1995). The CaT variables examined included total errors, errors on Subtest I + Subtest II, Subtest VII, and easy, difficult, and Bolter items. On the CaT alone there were no false positive errors by the college students (except for the difficult items), and sensitivity in student simulators ranged from as low as 30% (total errors) to as high as 90% (errors on Subtests I and II). The Tenhula and Sweet (1996) discriminant function rules produced similar specificity but a slight drop in sensitivity. There appeared to be no difference in the accuracy of the CaT and the P3MDMT, though the sample sizes were probably too small to make a meaningful comparison.

DiCarlo, Gfeller, and Oliveri (2000) reported on the accuracy of all but the Bolter items in nonmalingering TBI ($n = 30$), as well as coached ($n = 32$) and uncoached ($n = 30$) college student simulators, and optimal controls ($n = 30$). At the cutoffs reported by Tenhula and Sweet (1996), the false positive error rate ranged from 0% (Subtest I + II errors) to 30% (Subtest VII errors). The uncoached simulators were much more likely to be detected (mean sensitivity = 85%) compared to coached simulators (mean sensitivity = 55.5%). These findings, while replicating those of Tenhula and Sweet, also provide additional evidence that coaching can make malingering more difficult to detect.

Forrest, Allen, and Goldstein (2004) conducted two studies in an effort to identify CaT variables that effectively differentiated between real patients and those simulating the effects of brain damage. Their goal was to develop a number of indexes that do not differentiate between impaired and unimpaired persons but do distinguish between malingerers and impaired persons. They examined the accuracy of errors on Subtest I, Subtest II, Subtest I + II, Subtest VII, total errors, Subtest V errors minus Subtest VI errors (V − VI), and the difference between the weighted mean of Subtest I through VI errors and Subtest VII errors ([I to VI] − VII).

The results of their first study, which examined the performance of more than 600 clinical patients suggested that Subtest I + II and V − VI were potential malingering indicators. The second attempted to validate the findings in 25 college student controls, 75 college student simulators, and 177 brain-damaged patients. They generally reported specificity of 90% or higher at the cutoffs examined and also developed a discriminant function that included Subtest I errors, total errors, and Subtest II errors. This function differentiated between brain-damaged patients and simulators, correctly classifying 76% of simulators (sensitivity) and 94.9% of the brain-damaged group (false positive error rate = 5.1%).

Known-Groups Studies   Trueblood and Schmidt's (1993) study of the CaT is one of the earliest true known-groups studies of any malingering indicator. Trueblood and Schmidt classified patients as malingering based on significantly below-chance scores on a forced-choice symptom validity test (definite malingering; $n = 8$) or as questionably valid because of highly improbable findings (probable malingering; $n = 8$). The members of each group were carefully matched to nonmalingering traumatic brain-injury patients. They reported means for category key items (this may refer to the Bolter items), a "spike three" pattern reported by Wetzel and Boll (1987), and errors on Subtest VII. Unfortunately, this study did not report classification accuracy for CaT indicators, and the reported findings are insufficient to estimate sensitivity and specificity. In any case, the small sample size would mean that those estimates would be unstable. Despite the limited clinical usefulness of this study, it remains one of the first examples of the known-groups design in the neuropsychological literature.

In the only other known-groups study of malingering on the CaT, Greve, Bianchini, and Roberson (2007) used a known-groups design to determine the classification accuracy of variables from the CaT in the detection of cognitive malingering in traumatic brain injury. The TBI patients were divided by injury severity (mild versus moderate–severe). Malingerers met the Slick et al. (1999) criteria. Nonmalingerers completed at least one forced-choice test symptom validity test and the MMPI and had no evidence of suspect effort, including any positive findings on any indicator of negative response bias.

This study examined the classification accuracy of all of the CaT variables reported in the malingering research discussed earlier with the exception of Tenhula and Sweet's (1996) discriminant function scores since they had reported that those scores were no more accurate than the individual variables. Table 8.6 presents the false positive error rate, sensitivity, and positive predictive power for total errors (raw) at a range of hypothetical base rates and cutoffs for mild and moderate–severe TBI patients both separately and combined. This study demonstrated acceptable sensitivity at reasonable specificity levels for some of the variables. The total errors raw score was the most accurate indicator overall, while the effectiveness of others was related to injury severity.

Summary

Unlike the WCST, the majority of studies of the CaT have used a combined simulator-specificity design (often with nonmalingering, moderate–severe TBI controls). Only Trueblood and Schmidt (1993) and Greve et al. (in press) used a known-groups design, and only Greve et al. reported data that allow for a detailed examination of classification accuracy. The differences in classification accuracy between simulator and known-groups studies are striking. Table 8.7 presents the false positive error rates and sensitivity for the

Table 8.6.
False Positive Error Rate, Sensitivity, and Positive Predictive Power for Total Errors (Raw) at a Range of Hypothetical Base Rates and Cutoffs

	Cutoff	FP Rate	Sens	BR	Positive Predictive Power				
					.10	.20	.30	.40	.50
Mild TBI	≥ 83	16.3	46.5	.24	.42	.55	.67	.74
	≥ 85	9.3	46.5	.36	.57	.67	.76	.83
	≥ 104	4.7	20.9	.33	.57	.63	.78	.82
Mod/sev TBI	≥ 87	14.7	56.3	.30	.50	.62	.73	.78
	≥ 95	8.8	43.8	.33	.50	.70	.75	.85
	≥ 115	5.9	0.0	.00	.00	.00	.00	.00
All TBI	≥ 83	15.6	52.2	.27	.45	.58	.68	.76
	≥ 88	10.4	47.5	.35	.54	.66	.74	.82
	≥ 105	5.2	18.6	.33	.45	.62	.71	.76
	≥ 116	1.3	6.8	.33	.67	.75	.80	.83

Note. FP rate = false positive error rate; Sens = sensitivity; BR = hypothetical base rate or prevalence; TBI = traumatic brain injury.

Greve et al. patients at the cutoffs proposed by Tenhula and Sweet (1996). Generally, the indicators that Tenhula and Sweet (ibid.) identified as most effective were also found by Greve et al. to be effective. However, false positive error rates observed by Greve et al. were often higher. When the false positive error rates were comparable, the sensitivity was substantially lower.

Thus, part of the difference between the results of the two studies is that simulators performed substantially worse than clinical malingerers. Extremely poor performance by simulators was also reported by Etherton, Bianchini, Greve, and Ciota (2005) on the Test of Memory Malingering. In contrast, on the Reliable Digit Span, simulators performed at about the same level as the clinical malingerers (Etherton, Bianchini, Greve, & Heinly, 2005). It may be that simulator performance on some indicators is very extreme relative to clinical malingerers because the simulators do not have the same incentives to avoid detection. It may also be due to the fact that simulators have been instructed to perform poorly on a task that clinical malingerers might not consider to be relevant to their malingering presentation. This possibility is explored in more detail later. In any case, these findings emphasize the need to be cautious in applying the results of simulator studies to clinical cases when they have not been validated in a known-groups design.

Greve et al. (2007) also demonstrated the effect of injury-associated cognitive limitations on BCT-based validity indicators described by Williamson, Green, Allen, and Rohling (2003). The cutoffs generally had to be higher in moderate–severe TBI patients to achieve the same level of specificity as seen in the mild TBI patients. Even at cutoffs with good specificity as

Table 8.7.
False Positive Error Rates and Sensitivity for the Cutoffs Reported by
Tenhula and Sweet (1996)

| | | | | Greve et al. 2007 | | | | | |
| | | Tenhula & Sweet | | All TBI | | Mild TBI | | M/S TBI | |
	Cutoff	FP	Sens	FP	Sens	FP	Sens	FP	Sens
Total errors	> 87	2.8	51.1	10.4	47.5	9.3	44.2	11.8	56.3
Subtest I & II	> 1	1.9	75.6	3.9	15.3	4.7	16.3	23.5	12.5
Subtest VII	> 5	8.3	66.7	32.7	52.5	30.2	51.2	29.4	56.3
Bolter items	> 3	1.9	51.1	2.6	5.1	2.3	7.0	2.9	0.0
Easy items	> 2	1.9	55.6	7.8	28.8	9.3	37.2	5.9	6.3

Note. FP = false positive error rate; Sens = sensitivity; TBI = traumatic brain injury.

defined by the moderate–severe TBI patients, the mixed clinical group, which
included patients with stroke and dementia, had a still high false positive
error rate. The problem with capacity was also seen in the fact that the difference between the false positive error rate and the sensitivity decreased at
higher score levels; in fact, in some scores, the sensitivity reached 0% before
the false positive error rate did. Fortunately, this effect was not observed on
all of the variables, even in moderate–severe TBI. For example, 30 or more
errors on Subtest IV correctly detected 50% of malingerers with moderate–
severe TBI with only a 6% false positive error rate.

A conservative approach to using any indicator of response bias is best,
particularly when the indicator is also sensitive to actual cognitive capacity,
as is the case with the CaT (and the WCST). Sweet and King recommended
the following:

> Reduce the risk of false positives by considering the significant ef-
> fects that age and education are known to have on the CaT (cf. Garb &
> Lutz, 2001). With an individual who is older or less educated than the
> subjects of the Tenhula and Sweet (1996) and DiCarlo et al. (2000)
> studies, apply these criteria very cautiously. Do not apply the indica-
> tors at all in patients with very discrepant age and education or with
> very severe TBI. (2002, pp. 263–264)

Thus, if there is any doubt that a given patient's performance may reflect real
capacity issues, use extreme caution when interpreting the CaT as indicative
of malingering if the score is at a level that is associated with a false positive
error rate that is greater than zero. That is, greater caution is warranted in the
application of these indicators if a given patient has characteristics/attributes
(e.g., age, injury severity/neuropathology) that are empirically associated
with reduced specificity.

In short, some CaT variables have value in the detection of malingering in TBI, even in moderate–severe TBI. However, because of their sensitivity to real ability differences, they must be used with even greater care than is afforded other indicators that are less affected by the legitimate residual cognitive capacities of persons seen in the context of a brain-injury evaluation. Again, it is critical to emphasize that the interpretation of an individual patient's CaT scores should be based on comparisons with the appropriate nonmalingering control group.

Conclusions

The CaT is both a well-established measure of executive function and also one of the first standard clinical neuropsychological tests studied for its potential as an indicator of malingering in patients alleging disabilities due to brain trauma. Unlike the WCST, whose ability to accurately detect malingering has been studied using known-groups designs in several labs, most of the studies of malingering on the CaT have used a simulator design and thus are limited in their generalizability to clinical cases. Greve et al. (2007) is the only known-groups study to provide clinically useful data on the accuracy of the CaT in the detection of malingering in TBI. The results of that study indicate that, in certain TBI patient groups, some CaT scores are sufficiently accurate for this purpose. However, it is important to replicate these findings using known-groups studies in other laboratories. Doing so will allow the determination of the consistency of error rates and the computation of aggregate error rates that will be more precise and stable because of the larger sample sizes.

Progressive Matrices

Raven's Progressive Matrices (RPM; Raven, 1938, 1996) compose a conceptual thinking test that was developed in the 1930s (about the same time as the CaT and the early sorting tests that became the WCST). Unlike those two tasks, the Progressive Matrices are paper-and-pencil tasks that are designed to test one's ability to form perceptual relations and to reason by analogy. The matrices consists of 60 items grouped into five sets. Each item contains a pattern problem with eight possible solutions. Participants must select the correct solution. As the name of the test implies, the items become progressively more difficult. Lezak et al. (2004) indicate that success requires the ability to "conceptualize spatial, design, and numerical relationships ranging from the very obvious and concrete to the very complex and abstract" (p. 579). Other matrix reasoning tests are also available (e.g., Raven's Coloured Progressive Matrices [Raven, 1995]; Matrix Reasoning from the Wechsler Adult Intelligence Scale-III [Wechsler, 1997]).

Because of its conceptual thinking and reasoning requirements, the RPM test arguably measures aspects of executive function. Carpenter, Just,

and Shell's (1990) characterization of the core abilities tapped by the RPM support the idea that it is sensitive to impaired executive functioning. In Rabin et al.'s (2005) survey of neuropsychological test use, the RPM was rated number 22 among executive function measures. Interestingly, however, several functional brain-imaging studies (e.g., Haier, Seigel, Nuechterlein, Hazlett, Wu, et al., 1988; Risberg, Maximilian, & Prohovnik, 1977) show relatively greater activation of the posterior compared to the frontal cortex during performance of the RPM. In their reviews of the test, Spreen and Strauss (1998) and Lezak et al. (2004) suggest that it is most sensitive to the degree rather than the location of brain damage. In traumatic brain injury, scores decline with increases in the length of posttraumatic amnesia (Brooks & Aughton, 1979).

Malingering Detection Research

Three studies of the ability of the RPM to detect malingering were identified. The first (Gudjonsson & Shackleton, 1986) was inspired in part by a criminal case in which the low intelligence of the defendant was part of the defense. Opposing counsel presented a witness who testified that psychometric tests of intelligence were easily faked. Since one of the measures used to assess the defendant's intelligence was the RPM, the authors sought to determine its accuracy in detecting faking. They used a sophisticated simulator-specificity design.

Twenty-five soldiers and 27 forensic patients referred for neuropsychological evaluation took the test once with standard instructions. The forensic group included head injury and tumor patients and some who were suspected of organic impairment. A second group of 29 bright normals took the test twice, first with instructions to "fake substantially and convincingly" and the second time under normal instructions. Two variables were examined. First, a score that measures consistency across item sets was calculated by subtracting an individual's score for each set from the score expected, given that person's total test score. Any deviation of greater than 2 indicates inconsistency. The second score was a statistical formula measuring linear trends across different levels of performance consistency. Overall, these two measures are indices of the rate of decay (RD) of performance across the progressively more difficult subtests.

A figural presentation of the raw subtest scores demonstrated a fairly consistent pattern of decay across the three groups with standard instructions (see Figure 8.1). The decay trajectory of the simulators is nearly flat because they missed nearly as many easy items as more difficult ones. Group analyses bore out these differences, with the nonfaking groups showing greater decay than the faking group. The rate of decay was negatively correlated with the total score for the nonfaking groups but positively correlated in the faking group.

The authors also reported the individual classification accuracy for both indices. For Raven's consistency score, the sensitivity was 62% with a false

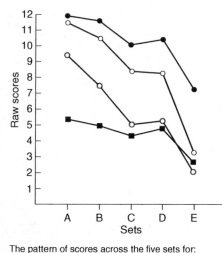

Figure 8.1. Performance on the subtests of the Raven's Standard Progressive Matrices from Gudjonsson and Shackleton (1986). Reproduced with permission from the *British Journal of Clinical Psychology*, © The British Psychological Society.

The pattern of scores across the five sets for:
o—o , group 1
●—● , group 2 ("non-fakers")
■—■ , group 2 ("faking bad")
o—o , group 3

positive error rate of 22%; this results in +PP of .54, assuming a base rate of 30%. In contrast, the RD formula was 83% sensitive with only a 5% false positive error rate. The positive predictive power is correspondingly larger at .89. Gudjonsson and Shackleton noted that faking reduces the rate of decay because simulators tend to miss too many of the easy items at the beginning of the test. They also point out that the performance of the organically impaired forensic patients was just as easily differentiated from that of the simulators, as was the performance of the bright normals, who were doing their best.

McKinzey, Podd, Krehbiel, and Raven (1999) cross-validated the RD formula in a simulator study. The participants were 427 community residents, 46 of whom were asked to simulate deficits due to a motor vehicle accident, for which they might receive a settlement. The 5% false positive error rate was replicated in this study. However, the sensitivity dropped from 83% to 74%. Thus, +PP based on the data from this study was .86 at a 30% base rate—still excellent. These authors, in fact, reported +PP and −PP (negative predictive power) of .63 and .97, respectively, assuming a 10% base rate. They recommended cross-validation in neurologically impaired patients and in children since, at the time, no measures of malingering had been designed for children.

McKinzey, Prieler, and Raven (2003) studied the RD in a sample of 44 children and adolescents in a simulator study. The simulator instructions

were far simpler than had been used with adults and seemed to be at a level appropriate for children: "We know that some people don't try their best on this test. We'd like to find a way to catch them. To help us, please do as badly on this test as you can, without getting caught" (p. 96). All of the children were first given the RPM with standard instructions, and then it was administered a second time with the simulator instructions included. The RD formula resulted in a sensitivity of 83%, but the false positive error rate rose substantially (relative to adults) to 17%. Three exceedingly easy items were identified from the first administration of the test. In later analyses, these items were missed very frequently. When the criterion for malingering was getting at least one of these items wrong, sensitivity was 95%, and the false positive error rate was 5%.

Summary

The Raven Progressive Matrices are often used as a measure of intelligence, but the test has properties like those of other tests traditionally considered to measure executive function, notably a conceptual thinking or problem-solving element. The results of three simulator studies of rate-of-decay indicators have been reported. In general, the accuracy of the indicators has stood up well to cross-validation, although the false positive error rate of the RD formula in children was higher than in adults. Nonetheless, the authors identified a set of easy items that were quite accurate in discriminating between valid and faked protocols. That indicator set should be cross-validated. Since the two most recent studies have been done by the same research group, a short report using the 1999 data set seems reasonable. In any case, the authors also point out that it is important to cross-validate the RPM indicators in patients with documented brain damage. If malingering indicators imbedded in the RPM are to be applied in a clinical setting with confidence, it is also necessary to test them using a known-groups design.

Overall Summary

The WCST and the CaT have both been the subject of research on the detection of malingering in patients who are presenting for neuropsychological evaluation. Special malingering indicators have been derived from the scores of both tests, and some individual scores have proven useful in the detection of malingering. Overall, the WCST has been more frequently examined than the CaT and, generally, there are more known-groups studies of the WCST. Examination of the results of these studies and specificity data (when available) has demonstrated that, in general, sensitivity of the WCST and the CaT to malingering in traumatic brain injury is only about 20% at cutoffs associated with a 5% false positive error rate. However, for CaT total errors, when a 10% false positive error rate cutoff is used, the sensitivity

Table 8.8.
False Positive (FP) Error Rate and Sensitivity in Mild TBI and Positive Predictive Power Using a Base Rate of 35%

FP Error Rate/Sensitivity	Approximate FP Error Rate			
	15	10	5	1
FMS	15/35	8/24	—	0/16
Suhr formula	12/37	10/29	6/22	2/9
Bernard formula	13/32	9/24	4/3	2/0
CaT total errors	16/51	9/47	7/26	2/21
PDRT total trials	14/79	12/74	3/71	0/66
TOMM Trial 2	15/77	7/70	4/53	2/40
CVLT hits	—	8/61	4/47	0/37
RDS	17/71	—	7/46	0/27
Positive Predictive Power				
FMS	.56	.62	—	1.00
Suhr formula	.62	.61	.66	.71
Bernard formula	.57	.59	.29	.00
CaT total errors	.63	.74	.67	.85
PDRT total trials	.75	.77	.93	1.00
TOMM Trial 2	.73	.84	.88	.92
CVLT hits	—	.80	.86	1.00
RDS	.69	—	.78	1.00

nearly doubles. With more liberal cutoffs on the WCST, the increases in sensitivity are more modest.

Not surprisingly, the highest accuracy regardless of cutoff is typically observed in mild TBI. Indicators derived from these measures often show sensitivity equal to or lower than the false positive error rate in more severe TBI, particularly at more extreme levels. Table 8.8 presents exact classification accuracy, including positive predictive power (assuming a base rate of .35) for WCST and CaT variables in mild TBI at false positive error rates of approximately .15, .10, .05. and .01.

Table 8.8 also allows a comparison of the accuracy of the WCST and the CaT to that reported for two well-known forced-choice symptom validity tests: the Portland Digit Recognition Test (PDRT; Binder, 1993) and the Test of Memory Malingering (Tombaugh, 1996). In an early known-groups study, Bianchini et al. (2001) reported 77% sensitivity with a 0% false positive error rate in mixed-severity TBI patients. In a replication, at cutoffs associated with a 5% false positive error rate, Greve and Bianchini (2006) demonstrated sensitivity in the 60–70% range in mild TBI and in the 50–60%

range in moderate–severe TBI. At similar false positive error rate levels, Greve, Bianchini, and Doane (2006) demonstrated sensitivity in the 50–60% range in mild TBI and in the 30% range for moderate–severe TBI. Generally, +PP was about 10 points better for the stand-alone measures at all FP levels.

It is true that the PDRT and the TOMM are stand-alone SVTs and the indicators from the WCST and CaT are embedded. It is possible that accuracy may be lower for embedded indicators. This hypothesis is not supported, however, by the finding that embedded effort measures on memory tests perform better than those derived from the WCST and the CaT, as shown by the findings of Curtis, Greve, Bianchini, and Brennan (2006) for the California Verbal Learning Test (CVLT).

Again, at similar false positive levels, sensitivity for recognition hit scores was in the 40% range for all TBI patients. For the linear shrinkage model described by Millis and Volinsky (2001), sensitivity was in the 50% range for mild TBI and the 40% range for moderate–severe TBI (overall it was 56% at the cutoff associated with a 6% false positive error rate. Even the Reliable Digit Span (Greiffenstein et al., 1994) is more sensitive than the most accurate WCST and CaT indicators (Heinly, Greve, Bianchini, Love, & Brennan, 2005). Thus, malingering indicators derived from these two well-known measures of executive function are substantially less accurate at a range of specificity levels than are indicators of malingered memory.

Why Is Sensitivity Low?

For the WCST and the CaT, the low sensitivity to malingering is likely a function of three factors related to these two tests. First, even in the absence of acquired brain dysfunction, large individual differences in performance are still found in the normal population. For the WCST, demographic factors accounted for as much as 20% of the observed variance. Age and education were particularly important factors (Heaton et al., 1993). Similar findings have been reported for the CaT (Heaton et al., 1991).

Second, measures of executive function in general and the WCST and CaT, specifically, are among the most sensitive neuropsychological tests of brain dysfunction. As a result, when studies use patients with documented brain pathology as the control, some of those patients will likely score in the range of persons who are malingering. The effects of genuine brain dysfunction are evident even on the CVLT indicators and the RDS (related to the higher cognitive demands of backward span). Williamson et al. (2003) demonstrated that cognitive ability influences performance on CaT indicators.

Third, it is possible that people who choose to malinger do not perceive these tasks as relevant. To illustrate this point, Greve et al. (2001) identified three approaches that malingerers applied to the WCST. The first was to avoid too many consecutive correct responses. The second approach was to avoid matching to any of the three dimensions. The third was to perform validly on the WCST, which seems to be what a third of the malingerers in

Greve et al. (ibid.) did. They may not have considered the WCST as a task that reflects the deficits they believed were associated with traumatic brain injury.

Thus, different patients may approach malingering in different ways. As a result, even indicators derived from the same test may detect slightly different subsets of malingerers, or indicators derived from a given test may fail to detect a specific malingering strategy. Moreover, people who are malingering do not necessarily choose to malinger on all tests. In that case, some tests would likely reflect their true ability. In the case of the executive function measures, their true ability may or may not be in the normal range. One could reasonably argue that whether and how someone malingers on a given test will depend on their beliefs about the effects of brain injury on behavior and what they think a given test measures. If the WCST and CaT do not look like tests that measure something the individual thinks should be affected by brain damage, then the probability of malingering on those tests would be lower, as would the probability of detecting malingering with those tests. Given the data we have reviewed here, the WCST and the CaT malingering indicators are better at ruling in than at ruling out malingering.

Applying WCST and CaT Results to the Slick et al. (1999) Criteria

Data on the classification accuracy of malingering indicators derived from the WCST and the CaT indicate that they can be used with caution at least in mild traumatic brain injury. Regardless of the classification accuracy of any single indicator of response bias, malingering detection techniques are not perfect and should not be used in isolation for the clinical diagnosis of malingering. As many articles, manuals, and book chapters have noted and as Slick et al. (1999) have pointed out, a formal diagnosis of malingering should be based on the integration of diverse clinical information. While questions of accuracy inform the decision of whether and under what circumstances an indicator should be used to indicate malingering, it is also necessary to determine how an indicator should be used in making such a diagnosis. In other words, where do the indicators from the WCST and CaT fit into the system developed by Slick et al.?

The Slick et al. approach divides evidence consistent with malingering into two broad categories or sets of criteria. Criterion B (criterion A is the presence of incentive) involves findings from neuropsychological testing, while criterion C involves evidence from self-report. Since they are derived from neuropsychological tests, the WCST and CaT indicators would be applied to criterion B, which is divided into six categories, referred to for convenience as criteria B1 through B6. The B criteria most relevant for the WCST and CaT are B2 ("performance on one or more *well-validated* psychometric tests or indices designed to measure exaggeration or fabrication of cognitive deficits is consistent with feigning"; ibid., p. 553) and B6 ("improbably poor performance on two or more standardized tests of cognitive func-

tion within a specific domain [e.g., memory] that is inconsistent with documented neurological or psychiatric history"; ibid., p. 554).

Thus, B2 refers to indicators that have been specifically designed to detect poor effort, suboptimal performance, and/or malingering. All SVTs and most internal validity indicators (such as RDS or Millis's indicators for the CVLT) were specifically designed to detect malingering. Thus, these indicators apply to the B2 criterion, and a positive finding on only one indicator is needed to meet this condition. With regard to whether published classification accuracy supports the actual clinical application of these criteria, from a conceptual perspective the Bernard et al. (1996), Suhr and Boyer (1999), and King et al. (2002) formulas for the WCST, as well as some of the indicators developed by Forrest et al. (2004) for the CaT, could be applied to B2. It is reasonable to conclude that the CaT Subtest I and II items, the Bolter items, and the easy items could be applied to B2 as well.

The remaining indicators (e.g., FMS from the WCST, total errors from the CaT) are scores originally to assess executive function and related cognitive functions, not malingering. Consequently, these variables should apply to criterion B6 (not B2), which requires extreme scores relative to an appropriate comparison group and requires findings from two separate tests of similar functions. Thus, results from both the WCST and the CaT would likely be needed to meet this criterion. It is possible that other tests often considered under the rubric of executive function (these are reviewed in other chapters of this book, e.g., Trail-Making Test, Controlled Oral Word Association, Similarities and Matrix Reasoning from the Wechsler Adult Intelligence Scale, Stroop Color-Word Test) could also be used in conjunction with the WCST and the CaT to meet criterion B6.

In addition, it is important to point out that conservative application requires that these variables be applied to only one B criterion. The Slick system allows a diagnosis of probable MND when either (a) two B criteria or (b) one B criterion and one C criterion are met. With regard to the second case, there are no applications problems relevant to malingering indicators derived from measures of executive function. However, the first case poses potential problems if the findings from these indicators are applied in a mechanistic fashion.

Theoretically, a person could be diagnosed as malingering based almost exclusively on WCST performance, with the Suhr and Boyer formula meeting B2 and FMS in part meeting B6. This would be particularly inappropriate because the Suhr and Boyer formula actually includes FMS. The same kind of outcome could occur with the CaT. Conservative application of detection data requires that indicators that are derived in whole or in part from an individual test performance be applied to only one B criterion. This conservative approach should also be followed within the B6 criterion. Specifically, indicators that are derived in whole or in part from either WCST or CaT performance should be applied to only one of the two "improbably poor performance[s]." This kind of usage ensures that a diagnosis of malingering

is actually based on multiple independent findings and is consistent with the conservative intent of the Slick et al. criteria.

Conclusions

The WCST and the CaT are useful in the detection and diagnosis of malingering in neuropsychological evaluations. At comparable levels of specificity, however, they are not as sensitive to malingering as many other indicators. Because performance is influenced by actual executive ability and because executive ability is influenced by a number of factors, the potential relevance of those factors (clinical cases, in particular) must be carefully considered before concluding that a score from these tests reflects malingering. In cases in which these factors are less likely to be an issue (e.g., mild or no brain injury, young, premorbidly high functioning), then one can be more confident about the interpretation of these scores and indicators. The more extreme the score, the more confident one can be that it reflects an effort to appear impaired. The use of these tests (particularly the CaT) would benefit substantially from additional known-groups and specificity research. Simulator studies alone add little of clinical value, although when used in conjunction with known-groups studies they provide valuable cross-validation. The WCST and the CaT will likely never carry the weight that memory-based indicators do. Nonetheless, they provide a means for detecting unusual or idiosyncratic approaches to malingering and can also provide information on the validity of WCST and CaT performance independent of the issues of malingering.

References

Allen, D. N., Goldstein, G., & Mariano, E. (1999). Is the Halstead Category Test a multidimensional instrument? *Journal of Clinical and Experimental Neuropsychology, 21,* 237–244.

Allen, L. M., & Green, P. (2001). Declining CARB failure rates over 6 years of testing: What's wrong with this picture? *Archives of Clinical Neuropsychology, 16,* 846.

Anderson, C. V., Bigler, E. D., & Blatter, D. D. (1995). Frontal lobe lesions, diffuse damage, and neuropsychological functioning in traumatic brain-injured patients. *Journal of Clinical and Experimental Neuropsychology, 17,* 900–908.

Anderson, S. W., Damasio, H., Jones, R. D., & Tranel, D. (1991). Wisconsin Card Sorting Test performance as a measure of frontal lobe damage. *Journal of Clinical and Experimental Neuropsychology, 13,* 909–922.

Armitage, S. G. (1946). An analysis of certain psychological tests used for the evaluation of brain injury. *Psychological Monographs, 60,* 1–48.

Ashendorf, L., O'Bryant, S. E., & McCaffrey, R. J. (2003). Specificity of malingering detection strategies in older adults using the CVLT and WCST. *The Clinical Neuropsychologist, 17,* 255–262.

Baddeley, A. (1986). *Working memory.* Oxford, UK: Clarendon.

Bechara, A., Damasio, A. R., Damasio, H., & Anderson, S. W. (1994) Insensitivity to future consequences following damage to human prefrontal cortex. *Cognition, 50,* 7–15.

Benson, D. F., Stuss, D. T., Naeser, M. A, Weir, W. S., Kaplan, E. F., & Levine, H. L. (1981). The long-term effects of prefrontal leukotomy. *Archives of Neurology, 38,* 165–169.

Berg, E. A. (1948). A simple objective technique for measuring flexibility in thinking. *Journal of General Psychology, 39,* 15–22.

Bernard, L. C., McGrath, M. J., & Houston, W. (1996). The differential effects of simulating malingering, closed-head injury, and other CNS pathology on the Wisconsin Card Sorting Test: Support for the "pattern of performance" hypothesis. *Archives of Clinical Neuropsychology, 11,* 231–245.

Bianchini, K. J., Etherton, J. L., & Greve, K. W. (2004). Diagnosing cognitive malingering in patients with work-related pain: Four cases. *Journal of Forensic Neuropsychology, 4,* 65–85.

Bianchini, K. J., Greve, K. W., & Glynn, G. (2005). On the diagnosis of malingered pain-related disability: Lessons from cognitive malingering research. *Spine Journal, 5,* 404–417.

Bianchini, K. J., Greve, K. W., & Love, J. (2003). Definite malingered neurocognitive dysfunction in moderate/severe traumatic brain injury. *The Clinical Neuropsychologist, 17,* 574–580.

Bianchini, K. J., Heinly, M. T., & Greve, K. W. (2004). Unnecessary cervical disc surgery in definite malingering. *Spine Journal, 4,* 718–719.

Bianchini, K. J., Mathias, C. W., & Greve, K. W. (2001). Symptom validity testing: A critical review. *The Clinical Neuropsychologist, 15,* 19–45.

Bianchini, K. J., Mathias, C. W., Greve, K. W., Houston, R. J., & Crouch, J. A. (2001). Classification accuracy of the Portland Digit Recognition Test in traumatic brain injury. *The Clinical Neuropsychologist, 15,* 461–470.

Binder, L. M. (1993). *Portland Digit Recognition Test manual* (2nd ed.). Beaverton, OR: Author.

Binder, L. M., & Rohling, M. L. (1996). Money matters: A meta-analytic review of the effects of financial incentives on recovery after closed-head injury. *American Journal of Psychiatry, 153,* 7–10.

Binder, L.M., Rohling, M. L., & Larrabee, G. (1997). A review of mild head trauma. Part 1: Meta-analytic review of neuropsychological studies. *Journal of Clinical and Experimental Neuropsychology, 19,* 421–431.

Bolter, J. F., Picano, J. J., & Zych, K. (1985, October). *Item error frequencies on the Halstead Category Test: An index of performance validity.* Paper presented at the annual meeting of the National Academy of Neuropsychology, Philadelphia.

Bond, J. A., & Buchtel, H. A. (1984). Comparison of the Wisconsin Card Sorting Test and the Halstead Category Test. *Journal of Clinical Psychology, 40,* 1251–1255.

Bowden, S. C., Fowler, K. S., Bell, R. C., Whelan, G., Clifford, C. C., Ritter, A. J., et al. (1998). The reliability and internal validity of the Wisconsin Card Sorting Test. *Neuropsychological Rehabilitation, 8,* 243–254.

Bowen, F. P., Kamieny, R. S., Burns, M. M., & Yahr, M. D. (1975). Parkinsonism: Effects of levodopa treatment on concept formation. *Neurology, 25,* 701–704.

Boyle, G. J. (1986). Clinical neuropsychological assessment: Abbreviating the Halstead Category Test of brain dysfunction. *Journal of Clinical Psychology, 42,* 615–625.

Brooks, D. N., & Aughton, M. E. (1979). Psychological consequences of blunt head injury. *International Rehabilitation Medicine, 1,* 160–165.

Calsyn, D. A., O'Leary, M. R., & Chaney, E. F. (1980). Shortening the Category Test. *Journal of Consulting and Clinical Psychology, 48,* 788–789.

Carpenter, P. A., Just, M. A., & Shell, P. (1990). What one intelligence test measures: A theoretical account of the processing in the Raven Progressive Matrices Test. *Psychological Review, 97,* 404–431.

Charter, R. A., Swift, K. M., & Bluzewicz, M. J. (1997). Age- and education-corrected standardized short form of the Category Test. *The Clinical Neuropsychologist, 11,* 142–145.

Cicerone, K. D., & Tanenbaum, L. N. (1997). Disturbance of social cognition after traumatic orbitofrontal brain injury. *Archives of Clinical Neuropsychology, 12,* 173–188.

Correia, S., Faust, D., & Doty, R. L. (2001). A re-examination of the rate of vocational dysfunction among patients with anosmia and mild to moderate closed-head injury. *Archives of Clinical Neuropsychology, 16,* 477–488.

Curtis, K. L., Greve, K. W., Bianchini, K. J., & Brennan, A. (2006). California Verbal Learning Test indicators of malingered neurocognitive dysfunction: Sensitivity and specificity in traumatic brain injury. *Assessment, 13,* 46–61.

Damasio, A. R., & Anderson, S. W. (2003). The frontal lobes. In K. M. Heilman & E. Valenstein (Eds.), *Clinical neuropsychology* (4th ed., pp. 404–446). New York: Oxford University Press.

Damasio, H., Grabowski, T., Frank, R., Galaburda, A. M., & Damasio, A. R. (1994). The return of Phineas Gage: Clues about the brain from the skull of a famous patient. *Science, 20,* 1102–1105.

de Zubicaray, G., & Ashton, R. (1996). A role for the hippocampus in card sorting? A cautionary note. A comment to Corcoran and Upton. *Cortex, 32,* 187–190.

DeFilippis, N. A, & McCampbell, E. (1979, 1991). *Manual for the Booklet Category Test.* Odessa, FL: Psychological Assessment Resources.

Demakis, G. J. (2004). Frontal lobe damage and tests of executive processing: A meta-analysis of the Category Test, Stroop Test, and Trail-Making Test. *Journal of Clinical and Experimental Neuropsychology, 26,* 441–450.

DiCarlo, M. A., Gfeller, J. D., & Oliveri, M. V. (2000). Effects of coaching on detecting feigned cognitive impairment with the Category Test. *Archives of Clinical Neuropsychology, 15,* 399–413.

Dikmen, S. S., Machamer, J. E., Winn, H. R., & Temkin, N. R. (1995). Neuropsychological outcome at 1-year post head injury. *Neuropsychology, 9,* 80–90.

Donders, J. (1999). Brief report: Specificity of a malingering formula for the Wisconsin Card Sorting Test. *Journal of Forensic Neuropsychology, 1,* 35–42.

Donders, J. (2001). Clinical utility of the Category Test as a multidimensional instrument. *Psychological Assessment, 13,* 592–594.

Ellwanger, J., Tenhula, W. N., Rosenfeld, J. P., & Sweet, J. J. (1999). Identifying simulators of cognitive deficit through combined use of neuropsychological test performance and event-related potentials. *Journal of Clinical and Experimental Neuropsychology, 21,* 866–879.

Eslinger, P. J., & Damasio, A. R. (1984). Severe disturbance of higher cognition after bilateral frontal lobe ablation: Patient EVR. *Neurology, 35,* 1731–1741.

Etherton, J. L., Bianchini, K. J., Ciota, M. A., & Greve, K. W. (2005). Reliable Digit Span is unaffected by laboratory-induced pain: Implications for clinical use. *Assessment, 12,* 101–106.

Etherton, J. L., Bianchini, K. J., Greve, K. W., & Ciota, M. A. (2005). Test of Memory Malingering performance is unaffected by laboratory-induced pain: Implications for clinical use. *Archives of Clinical Neuropsychology, 20,* 375–384.

Etherton, J. L., Bianchini, K. J., Greve, K. W., & Heinly, M. T. (2005). Sensitivity and specificity of Reliable Digit Span in malingered pain-related disability. *Assessment, 12,* 130–136.

Fey, E. T. (1951). The performance of young schizophrenics and young normals on the Wisconsin Card Sorting Test. *Journal of Consulting Psychology, 15,* 311–319.

Forrest, T. J., Allen, D. N., & Goldstein, G. (2004). Malingering indexes for the Halstead Category Test. *The Clinical Neuropsychologist, 18,* 334–347.

Franzen, M. D., & Iverson, G. L. (1998). Detecting malingered memory deficits with the Recognition Memory Test. *Brain Injury, 12,* 275–282.

Garb, H. N., & Lutz, C. (2001). Cognitive complexity and the validity of clinicians' judgments. *Assessment, 8,* 111–115.

Goebel, R. A. (1983). Detection of faking on the Halstead-Reitan Neuropsychological Test Battery. *Journal of Clinical Psychology, 39,* 731–742.

Goldberg, T. E., Kelsoe, J. R., Weinberger, D. R., Pliskin, N. H., Kirwin, P. D., & Berman, K. F. (1988). Performance of schizophrenic patients on putative neuropsychological tests of frontal lobe function. *International Journal of Neuroscience, 42,* 51–58.

Golden, C. J., Kushner, T., Lee, B., & McMorrow, M. A. (1998). Searching for the meaning of the Category Test and the Wisconsin Card Sort Test: A comparative analysis. *International Journal of Neuroscience, 93,* 141–150.

Goldstein, G. (1981). Some recent developments in clinical neuropsychology. *Clinical Psychology Review, 1,* 245–269.

Goldstein, K. (1936). The significance of frontal lobes for mental performance. *Journal of Neurological Psychopathology, 17,* 27–40.

Goldstein, K., & Scheerer, M. (1941). Abstract and concrete behavior: An experimental study with special tests. *Psychological Monographs, 53,* 1–151.

Gorenstein, E. E. (1982): Frontal lobe functions in psychopaths. *Journal of Abnormal Psychology, 91,* 368–379.

Gormezano, I., & Grant, D. A (1958). Progressive ambiguity in the attainment of concepts on the Wisconsin Card Sorting Test. *Journal of Experimental Psychology, 55,* 621–627.

Gouvier, W. D., Hayes, J. S., & Smiroldo, B. B. (1998). The significance of base rates, test sensitivity, test specificity, and subjects' knowledge of symptoms in assessing TBI sequelae and malingering. In C. R. Reynolds (Ed.), *Detection of malingering during head injury litigation* (pp. 55–79). New York: Plenum.

Grant, D. A (1951). Perceptual versus analytical responses to the number concept of a Weigl-type card-sorting test. *Journal of Experimental Psychology, 41,* 23–29.

Grant, D. A., & Berg, E. A. (1948). A behavioral analysis of degree of reinforcement and ease of shifting to new responses in a Weigl-type card-sorting problem. *Journal of Experimental Psychology, 38,* 404–411.

Grant, D. A., & Cost, J. R. (1954). Continuities and discontinuities in conceptual behavior in a card-sorting problem. *Journal of General Psychology, 50,* 237–244.

Grant, D. A., & Curran, J. F. (1952). The relative difficulty of the number, form, and color concepts of a Weigl-type problem using unsystematic number cards. *Journal of Experimental Psychology, 43,* 408–413.

Grant, D. A., Jones, O. R., & Tallantis, B. (1949). The relative difficulty of the number, form, and color concepts of a Weigl-type problem. *Journal of Experimental Psychology, 39*, 552–557.

Green, P., & Iverson, G. L. (2001). Effects of injury severity and cognitive exaggeration on olfactory deficits in head-injury compensation claims. *NeuroRehabilitation, 16*, 237–243.

Green, P., Rohling, M. L., Iverson, G. L., & Gervais, R. O. (2003). Relationships between olfactory discrimination and head-injury severity. *Brain Injury, 17*, 479–496.

Green, P., Rohling, M. L., Lees-Haley, P. R., & Allen, L. M. (2001). Effort has a greater effect on test scores than severe brain injury in compensation claimants. *Brain Injury, 15*, 1045–1060.

Greiffenstein, M. F., & Baker, W. J. (2006). Miller was (mostly) right: Head-injury severity inversely related to simulation. *Legal and Criminological Psychology, 11*, 131–145.

Greiffenstein, M. F., Baker, W. J., & Gola, T. (1994). Validation of malingered amnesia measures with a large clinical sample. *Psychological Assessment, 6*, 218–224.

Greiffenstein, M. F., Baker, W. J., & Gola, T. (2002). Brief report: Anosmia and remote outcome in closed-head injury. *Journal of Clinical and Experimental Neuropsychology, 24*, 705–709.

Greiffenstein, M. F., Baker, W. J., & Gola, T. (2003). Straw man walking: Reply to Varney (2002). *Journal of Clinical and Experimental Neuropsychology, 25*, 152–154.

Greiffenstein, M. F., Gola, T., & Baker, W. J. (1995). MMPI-2 validity scales versus domain-specific measures in detection of factitious traumatic brain injury. *The Clinical Neuropsychologist, 9*, 230–240.

Greve, K. W., & Bianchini, K. J. (2002). Using the Wisconsin Card Sorting Test to detect malingering: An analysis of the specificity of two methods in nonmalingering normal and patient samples. *Journal of Clinical and Experimental Neuropsychology, 24*, 48–54.

Greve, K. W., & Bianchini, K. J. (2003, October). Estimating the specificity and sensitivity of malingering indicators. *Archives of Clinical Neuropsychology, 18*, 783.

Greve, K. W., & Bianchini, K. J. (2004). Setting empirical cutoffs on psychometric indicators of negative response bias: A methodological commentary with recommendations. *Archives of Clinical Neuropsychology, 19*, 533–541.

Greve, K. W., & Bianchini, K. J. (2006). Classification accuracy of the Portland Digit Recognition Test in traumatic brain injury: Results of a known-groups analysis. *The Clinical Neuropsychologist, 20*, 816–830.

Greve, K. W., Bianchini, K. J., & Ameduri, C. J. (2003). The use of a forced-choice test of tactile discrimination in the evaluation of functional sensory loss: A report of 3 cases. *Archives of Physical Medicine and Rehabilitation, 84*, 1233–1236.

Greve, K. W., Bianchini, K. J., & Doane, B. M. (2006). Classification accuracy of the Test of Memory Malingering in traumatic brain injury: Results of a known-groups analysis. *Journal of Clinical and Experimental Neuropsychology, 28*, 1176–1190.

Greve, K. W., Bianchini, K. J., Mathias, C. W., Houston, R. J., & Crouch, J. A. (2002). Detecting malingered performance with the Wisconsin Card Sorting Test: A preliminary investigation in traumatic brain injury. *The Clinical Neuropsychologist, 16*, 179–191

Greve, K. W., Bianchini, K. J., Mathias, C. W., Houston, R. J., & Crouch, J. A. (2003). Detecting malingered performance on the Wechsler Adult Intelligence

Scale: Validation of Mittenberg's approach in traumatic brain injury. *Archives of Clinical Neuropsychology, 18,* 245–260.

Greve, K. W., Bianchini, K. J., & Roberson, T. (2007). The Booklet Category Test and malingering in traumatic brain injury: Classification accuracy in known groups. *The Clinical Neuropsychologist, 14,* 12–21.

Greve, K. W., Farrell, J. F., Besson, P.S., & Crouch J. A. (1995). A psychometric analysis of the California Card Sorting Test. *Archives of Clinical Neuropsychology, 10,* 265–278.

Greve, K. W., Love, J. M., Heinly, M. T., Doane, B. M., Uribe, E., Joffe, C. L., et al. (2005). Detection of simulated tactile sensory loss using a forced-choice test of tactile discrimination. *Journal of Occupational and Environmental Medicine, 47,* 718–727.

Greve, K. W., Love, J. M., Sherwin, E., Mathias, C. W., & Ramzinski, P. (2002). Wisconsin Card Sorting Test in chronic severe traumatic brain injury: Factor structure and performance subgroups. *Brain Injury, 16,* 29–40.

Greve, K. W., Stickle, T. R., Love, J. M., Bianchini, K. J., & Stanford, M.S. (2005). Latent structure of the Wisconsin Card Sorting Test: A confirmatory factor analytic study. *Archives of Clinical Neuropsychology, 20,* 355–364.

Gudjonsson, G., & Shackleton, H. (1986). The pattern of scores on Raven's Matrices during "faking bad" and "nonfaking" performance. *British Journal of Clinical Psychology, 25,* 35–41.

Haier, R., Seigel, B., Nuechterlein, K., Hazlett, E., Wu, J. C., Paek, J., et al. (1988). Cortical glucose metabolic rate correlates of abstract reasoning and attention studied with positron emission tomography. *Intelligence, 12,* 199–217.

Halstead, W. C. (1940). Preliminary analysis of grouping behavior in patients with cerebral injury by the method of equivalent and non-equivalent stimuli. *American Journal of Psychiatry, 96,* 1263–1294.

Halstead, W. C., & Settlage, P. H. (1943). Grouping behavior of normal persons and of persons with lesions of the brain. *Archives of Neurology and Psychiatry, 49,* 489–503.

Halstead, W. C., & White, J. (1950). *Manual for the Halstead Battery of Neuropsychological Tests.* Chicago: University of Chicago Press.

Hanfman, E., & Kasanin, J. (1942). Conceptual thinking in schizophrenia. *Nervous and Mental Disorder Monographs, 67.*

Hare, R. D. (1984). Performance of psychopaths on cognitive tasks related to frontal lobe function. *Journal of Abnormal Psychology, 93,* 133–140.

Harris, I., Mulford, J., Solomon, M., van Gelder, J. M, & Young, J. (2005). Association between compensation status and outcome after surgery: A meta-analysis. *Journal of the American Medical Association, 293,* 1644–1652.

Heaton, R. K. (1981). *A manual for the Wisconsin Card Sorting Test.* Odessa, FL: Psychological Assessment Resources.

Heaton, R. K., Chelune, G. J., Talley, J. L. Kay, G. G., & Curtiss, G. (1993). *Wisconsin Card Sorting Test manual* (Rev. and exp.). Odessa, FL: Psychological Assessment Resources.

Heaton, R. K., Grant, I., & Matthews, C. G. (1991). *Comprehensive norms for an expanded Halstead-Reitan Battery.* Odessa, FL: Psychological Assessment Resources.

Heaton, R. K., Smith, H. H., Lehman, R. A. W., & Vogt, A. T. (1978). Prospects for faking believable deficits on neuropsychological testing. *Journal of Consulting and Clinical Psychology, 46,* 892–900.

Hebb, D. O. (1945). Man's frontal lobes: A critical review. *Archives of Neurology and Psychiatry, 54,* 10–24.

Heck, E. T., & Bryer, J. B. (1986). Superior sorting and categorizing ability in a case of bilateral frontal atrophy: An exception to the rule. *Journal of Clinical and Experimental Neuropsychology, 8,* 313–316.

Heinly, M. T., Greve, K. W., Bianchini, K. J., Love, J. L., & Brennan, A. (2005). WAIS Digit Span–based indicators of malingered neurocognitive dysfunction: Classification accuracy in traumatic brain injury. *Assessment, 12,* 429–444.

Heinly, M. T., Greve, K. W., Love, J. M., & Bianchini, K. J. (2006, February). *Sensitivity and specificity of Wisconsin Card Sorting Test indicators of potential malingered neurocognitive dysfunction in traumatic brain injury.* Poster presented at the 34th annual meeting of the International Neuropsychological Society, Boston.

Hennekens, C. H., & Buring, J. E. (1987). *Epidemiology in medicine.* Boston: Little, Brown.

Iverson, G. L. (2003). Detecting malingering in civil forensic evaluations. In A. M. Horton & L. C. Hartlage (Eds.), *Handbook of forensic neuropsychology* (pp. 137–177). New York: Springer.

King, J. H., Sweet, J. J., Sherer, M., Curtiss, G., & Vanderploeg, R. D. (2002). Validity indicators within the Wisconsin Card Sorting Test: Application of new and previously researched multivariate procedures in multiple traumatic brain injury samples. *The Clinical Neuropsychologist, 16,* 506–523.

King, M. C., & Snow, W. G. (1981). Problem-solving task performance in brain-damaged subjects. *Journal of Clinical Psychology, 57,* 400–404.

Labreche, T. M. (1983). *The Victoria revision of the Halstead Category Test.* Victoria, British Columbia, Canada: University of Victoria.

Larrabee, G. J. (2003a). Detection of malingering using atypical performance patterns on standard neuropsychological tests. *The Clinical Neuropsychologist, 17,* 410–425.

Larrabee, G. J. (2003b). Detection of symptom exaggeration with the MMPI-2 in litigants with malingered neurocognitive dysfunction. *The Clinical Neuropsychologist, 17,* 54–68.

Larrabee, G. J. (2003c). Exaggerated MMPI-2 symptom report in personal-injury litigants with malingered neurocognitive deficit. *Archives of Clinical Neuropsychology, 18,* 673–686.

Larrabee, G. J. (2003d). Exaggerated pain report in litigants with malingered neurocognitive dysfunction. *The Clinical Neuropsychologist, 17,* 395–401.

Larrabee, G. J. (2005). Assessment of malingering. In G. J. Larrabee (Ed.), *Forensic neuropsychology: A scientific approach* (pp. 115–158). New York: Oxford University Press.

Levine, B., Stuss, D. T., Milberg, W. P., Alexander, M. P., Schwartz, M., & Macdonald, R. (1998). The effects of focal and diffuse brain damage on strategy application: Evidence from focal lesions, traumatic brain injury, and normal aging. *Journal of the International Neuropsychological Society, 4,* 247–264.

Lezak, M. D., Howieson, D. B., & Loring, D. W. (2004). *Neuropsychological assessment* (4th ed.). New York: Oxford University Press.

Lombardi, W. J., Andreason, P. J., Sirocco, K. Y., Rio, D. E., Gross, R. E., Umhau, J. C., et al. (1999). Wisconsin Card Sorting Test performance following head injury: Dorsolateral fronto-striatal circuit activity predicts perseveration. *Journal of Clinical and Experimental Neuropsychology, 21,* 2–16.

MacInnes, W. D., Golden, C. J., McFadden, J., & Wilkening, G. N. (1983). Relationships between the Booklet Category Test and the Wisconsin Card Sorting Test. *International Journal of Neuroscience, 2,* 257–264.

Malmo, H. P. (1974). On frontal lobe functions: Psychiatric patient controls. *Cortex*, *10*, 231–237.

McKinzey, R. K., Podd, M. H., Krehbiel, M. A., & Raven, J. (1999). Detection of malingering on Raven's Standard Progressive Matrices: A cross-validation. *British Journal of Clinical Psychology*, *38*, 435–439.

McKinzey, R. K., Prieler, J., & Raven, J. (2003). Detection of children's malingering on Raven's Standard Progressive Matrices. *British Journal of Clinical Psychology*, *42*, 95–99.

Miller, A., Donders, J., & Suhr, J. (2000). Evaluation of malingering with the Wisconsin Card Sorting Test: A cross-validation. *Clinical Neuropsychological Assessment*, *2*, 141–149.

Millis, S. R. (2004). Evaluation of malingered neurocognitive disorders. In M. Rizzo & P. J. Esslinger (Eds.), *Principles and practice of behavioral neurology and neuropsychology* (pp. 1077–1089). Philadelphia: Saunders.

Millis, S. R., Putnam, S. H., Adams, K. M., & Ricker, J. H. (1995). The California Verbal Learning Test in the detection of incomplete effort in neuropsychological evaluation. *Psychological Assessment,7*, 463–471.

Millis, S. R., Ross, S. R., & Ricker, J. H. (1998), Detection of incomplete effort on the Wechsler Adult Intelligence Scale-Revised: A cross-validation. *Journal of Clinical and Experimental Neuropsychology*, *20*, 167–173.

Millis, S. R., & Volinsky, C. T. (2001). Assessment of response bias in mild head injury: Beyond malingering tests. *Journal of Clinical and Experimental Neuropsychology*, *23*, 809–828.

Milner, B. (1963). Effects of different brain lesions on card sorting. *Archives of Neurology*, *9*, 90–100.

Milner, B. (1964). Some effects of frontal lobectomy in man. In J. M. Warren & K. Akert (Eds.), *The frontal granular cortex and behavior* (pp. 313–334). New York: McGraw Hill.

Mittenberg, W., Patton, C., Canyock, E.M., & Condit, D.C. (2002). Base rates of malingering and symptom exaggeration. *Journal of Clinical and Experimental Neuropsychology*, *24*, 1094–1102.

Mittenberg, W., Rotholc, A., Russell, E., & Heilbronner, R. (1996). Identification of malingered head injury on the Halstead-Reitan Battery. *Archives of Clinical Neuropsychology*, *11*, 271–281.

Nesbit-Greene, K., & Donders, J. (2002). Latent structure of the Children's Category Test after pediatric traumatic head injury. *Journal of Clinical and Experimental Neuropsychology*, *24*, 194–199.

Neylan, T. C. (1999). Frontal lobe function: Mr. Phineas Gage's famous injury. *Journal of Neuropsychiatry and Clinical Neurosciences*, *11*, 280–283.

Parsons, O. A. (1975). Brain damage in alcoholics: Altered states of unconsciousness. In M. M. Gross (Ed.), *Alcohol intoxication and withdrawal: Experimental studies II* (pp. 569–584). New York: Plenum.

Parsons, O. A., & Klein, H. P. (1970). Concept identification and practice in brain-damaged and process-reactive schizophrenic groups. *Journal of Consulting and Clinical Psychology*, *35*, 317–323.

Pendleton, M. G., & Heaton, R. K. (1982). A comparison of the Wisconsin Card Sorting Test and the Category Test. *Journal of Clinical Psychology*, *38*, 392–396.

Perrine, K. (1993). Differential aspects of conceptual processing in the Category Test and Wisconsin Card Sorting Test. *Journal of Clinical and Experimental Neuropsychology*, *15*, 461–473.

Rabin, L. A., Barr, W. B., & Burton, L. A. (2005). Assessment practices of clinical neuropsychologists in the United States and Canada: A survey of INS, NAN, and APA Division 40 members. *Archives of Clinical Neuropsychology, 20,* 33–65.

Raven, J. C. (1938, 1996). *Progressive matrices: A perceptual test of intelligence, individual form.* Oxford, UK: Oxford Psychologists Press.

Raven, J. C. (1995). *Coloured progressive matrices: Sets A, Ab, B (manual sections 1 and 2).* Oxford, UK: Oxford Psychologists Press.

Risberg, J., Maximilian, A. V., & Prohovnik, I. (1977). Changes of cerebral activation patterns during habituation to reasoning test. *Neuropsychologia, 15,* 793–798.

Robinson, A. L., Heaton, R. K., Lehman, R. A. W., & Stilson, D. W. (1980). The utility of the Wisconsin Card Sorting Test in detecting and localizing frontal lobe lesions. *Journal of Consulting and Clinical Psychology, 48,* 605–614.

Rogers, R. (1997). Researching dissimulation. In R. Rogers (Ed.), *Clinical assessment of malingering and deception* (pp. 398–426). New York: Guilford.

Rohling, M. L., Binder, L. M., & Langhinrichsen-Rohling, J. (1995). A meta-analytic review of the association between financial compensation and the experience and treatment of chronic pain. *Health Psychology, 14,* 537–547.

Rosenfeld, J. P., Ellwanger, J., & Sweet, J. J. (1995). Detecting simulated amnesia with event-related brain potentials. *International Journal of Psychophysiology, 19,* 1–11.

Ross, B. M., Rupel, J. W., & Grant, D. A. (1952). Effects of personal, impersonal, and physical stress upon cognitive behavior in a card-sorting paradigm. *Journal of Abnormal and Social Psychology, 47,* 546–551.

Russell, E. W., & Levy, M. (1987). Revision of the Halstead Category Test. *Journal of Consulting and Clinical Psychology, 55,* 898–901.

Shure, G., & Halstead, W. C. (1958). Developmental variability in frontal lobe functioning. *Psychological Monographs, 72*(465).

Slick, D. J., Sherman, E. M. S., & Iverson, G. L. (1999). Diagnostic criteria for malingering cognitive dysfunction: Proposed standards for clinical practice and research. *The Clinical Neuropsychologist, 13,* 545–561.

Spreen, O., & Strauss, E. (1998). *A compendium of neuropsychological tests: Administration, norms, and commentary* (2nd ed.). New York: Oxford University Press.

Stuss, D. T., Benson, D. F., Kaplan, E. F., Weir, W. S., Naeser, M. A, Ueberman, I., et al. (1983). The involvement of orbitofrontal cerebrum in cognitive tasks. *Neuropsychologia, 21,* 235–248.

Stuss, D. T., Levine, B., Alexander, M. P., Hong, J., Palumbo, C., Hamer, L., et al. (2000). Wisconsin Card Sorting Test performance in patients with focal frontal and posterior brain damage: Effects of lesion location and test structure on separable cognitive processes. *Neuropsychologia, 38,* 388–402.

Suhr, J. A., & Boyer, D. (1999). Use of the Wisconsin Card Sorting Test in the detection of malingering in student simulator and patient samples. *Journal of Clinical and Experimental Neuropsychology, 21,* 701–708.

Sutker, P. B., & Allain, A. N. (1983). Behavior and personality assessment in men labeled adaptive sociopaths. *Journal of Behavioral Assessment, 5,* 65–79.

Sutker, P. B., Moan, C. E., & Allain, A N. (1983). Assessment of cognitive control in psychopathic and normal prisoners. *Journal of Behavioral Assessment, 5,* 275–287.

Sweet, J. J. (1999). Malingering: Differential diagnosis. In J. J. Sweet (Ed.), *Forensic neuropsychology: Fundamentals and practice* (pp. 255–285). Exton, PA: Swets & Zeitlinger.

Sweet, J. J., & King, J. H. (2002). Category test validity indicators: Overview and practice recommendations. *Journal of Forensic Neuropsychology, 3,* 241–274.

Tarter, R. E. (1973). An analysis of cognitive deficits in chronic alcoholics. *Journal of Nervous and Mental Disease, 157,* 138–147.

Tarter, R. E., & Parsons, O. A. (1971). Conceptual shifting in chronic alcoholics. *Journal of Abnormal Psychology, 77,* 71–75.

Tenhula, W. N., & Sweet, J. J. (1996). Double cross-validation of the Booklet Category Test in detecting malingered traumatic brain injury. *The Clinical Neuropsychologist, 10,* 104–116.

Teuber, H.-L. (1966). The frontal lobes and their function: Further observations on rodents, carnivores, subhuman primates, and man. *International Journal of Neurology, 5,* 282–300.

Teuber, H.-L., Battersby, W. S., & Bender, M. B. (1951). Performance of complex visual tasks after cerebral lesions. *Journal of Nervous and Mental Disease, 114,* 413–429.

Tombaugh, T. (1996). *Test of Memory Malingering manual.* New York: Multi-Health Systems.

Trueblood, W., & Schmidt, M. (1993). Malingering and other validity considerations in neuropsychological evaluation of mild head injury. *Journal of Clinical and Experimental Neuropsychology, 15,* 578–590.

Varney, N. R. (1988). Prognostic significance of anosmia in patients with closed-head trauma. *Journal of Clinical and Experimental Neuropsychology, 10,* 250–254.

Vigotsky, L. S. (1934). Thought in schizophrenia. *Archives of Neurology and Psychiatry, 31,* 1063–1077. Trans. J. Kasanin.

Wallesch, C. W., Kornhuber, H. H., Kollner, C., Haas, H. C., & Hufnagel, J. M. (1983). Language and cognitive deficits resulting from medial and dorsolateral frontal lobe lesions. *Archiv für Psychiatrie und Nervenkrankheiten, 233,* 279–296.

Wallesch, C. W., Kornhuber, H. H., Kunz, T., & Brunner, R. J. (1983). Neuropsychological deficits associated with small unilateral thalamic lesions. *Brain, 106,* 141–152.

Wang, P. L. (1987). Concept formation and frontal lobe function. In E. Perecman (Ed.), *The frontal lobes revisited* (pp. 189–205). New York: IRBN Press.

Wechsler, D. A. (1997). *Wechsler Adult Intelligence Scale-III.* New York: Psychological Corp.

Weigl, E. (1941). Zur Psychologie sogenannter Abstraktionsprozesse [On the psychology of so-called processes of abstraction]. *Journal of Abnormal and Social Psychology, 36,* 3–33. Trans. M. J. Rioch from *Zeitschrift für Psychologie, 103,* 2–45, 1927.

Wetzel, L., & Boll, T. J. (1987). *Short Category Test, booklet format.* Los Angeles: Western Psychological Services.

Williamson, D. J., Green, P., Allen, L., & Rohling, M. L. (2003). Evaluating effort with the Word Memory Test and Category Test—or Not: Inconsistencies in a compensation-seeking sample. *Journal of Forensic Neuropsychology, 3,* 19–44.

Youngjohn, J. R. (1995). Confirmed attorney coaching prior to neuropsychological evaluation. *Assessment, 2,* 279–283.

9

Detection of Feigned Psychiatric Symptoms During Forensic Neuropsychological Examinations

David T. R. Berry and Lindsey J. Schipper

A recent National Academy of Neuropsychology position paper states that "symptom exaggeration or fabrication occurs in a sizable minority of neuropsychological examinees, with greater prevalence in forensic contexts" (Bush, Ruff, Troster, Barth, Koffler, et al., 2005, p. 425). Although the bulk of the document focuses on symptom validity testing, the authors also point out that "evidence of exaggerated or fabricated problems may be evident from the original and more recently developed validity scales of self-report psychological tests, such as the MMPI-2" (ibid., p. 422). Thus, it is important to assess for *both* feigned psychological complaints *and* inadequate effort in forensic neuropsychological evaluations. This chapter reviews objective techniques for the identification of false reports of psychiatric symptoms (broadly defined as disturbance in mood and affect, somatic experience, thought pattern or perception, etc.). We provide an overview of important background issues, a review of leading instruments for detecting feigned psychiatric symptom reports, and finally an evaluation of the available data as they bear on forensic neuropsychological examinations.

Background

Importance of Assessing the Accuracy of Self-Reported Psychiatric Symptoms

Feigned symptom reports are an important concern for forensic psychological evaluations of any type because the formal diagnosis of psychiatric disorders is heavily dependent on self-reported symptoms. Although the text for each Axis I diagnosis in *DSM-IV-TR* (APA, 2000) typically includes extensive sections on associated laboratory findings, as well as associated physical examination findings, leading academic psychiatrists have stated that, "despite many proposed candidates, not one laboratory marker has been found to be specific in identifying any of the *DSM*-defined syndromes" (Kupfer, First, & Regier, 2002, p. xviii). In the absence of pathognomonic physiological signs, symptom reports from patients (as well as clinician and collateral observations) must be a key component of the psychiatric diagnostic process. In forensic examinations, where important outcomes are contingent on diagnostic decisions, it should be clear that objective evaluation of the accuracy of self-reported psychiatric symptoms is imperative.

In the past decade, considerable progress has been made in the development and validation of techniques for detecting cognitive malingering (Bianchini, Mathias, & Greve, 2001; Larrabee, 2005a; Sweet, 1999; Vickery, Berry, Inman, Harris, & Orey, 2001). However, it is not at all clear that results from these procedures will generalize to the accurate identification of feigned psychiatric symptoms. Fortunately, there are several multiscale inventories of psychopathology that include well-established or newly identified embedded scales for assessing symptom overreporting, including the Minnesota Multiphasic Personality Inventory (2nd ed.), *F, Fp,* and FBS scales (MMPI-2; Butcher, Dahlstrom, Graham, Tellegan, & Kaemmer, 1989), the Personality Assessment Inventory NIM and MI scales (PAI; Morey, 1991), as well as dedicated tests for addressing this issue, such as the Structured Interview of Reported Symptoms (SIRS; Rogers, Bagby, & Dickens, 1992), the Miller Forensic Assessment of Symptoms Test (M-FAST; Miller, 2001), and the Structured Inventory of Malingered Symptomatology (SIMS; Widows & Smith, 2005). Given the need to discriminate fabricated or exaggerated symptom reports from valid ones in forensic cases, neuropsychologists may be interested in a review of current data on objective techniques for addressing the issue.

Diagnostic Framework for Evaluating False Symptom Reports

In the *DSM-IV-TR* diagnostic system, inaccurate or invalid symptom reports are an important feature of three conditions of interest. This nosology utilizes two factors to classify individuals who inaccurately report symptoms: whether conscious control is exerted over feigned symptom reports and whether

apparent goals are viewed as external (e.g., money, narcotics, avoidance of criminal prosecution) or intrapsychic (fulfill the sick role, resolve unconscious conflicts). The resulting hypothetical two-by-two table includes two mental disorders, one V code and one void. The mental disorders include factitious disorder (conscious feigning for internal goal; e.g., to achieve the sick role) and conversion disorder (unconscious production of symptoms to resolve internal psychological conflicts). The V code, malingering, is said to involve conscious feigning for external goals. The "void" in the grid involves unconscious feigning for external goals; little or no research exists on this topic. Consideration of this system reveals an important point: *Simply establishing the presence of exaggerated or fabricated symptom reports is necessary but not sufficient for identifying malingering.* The issues of conscious intent, as well as apparent goals, must also be evaluated.

Larrabee (2005a) and Iverson and Binder (2000) have elaborated on the previously mentioned two-by-two table of possible feigned symptom presentations. They have proposed a three-factor model indicating that malingering can occur in three ways: (a) intentionally poor performance on tests of ability, (b) gross exaggeration of symptoms, or (c) a combination of the first two factors. Thus, their conceptualization also highlights the need to assess for both types of feigning. Slick, Sherman, and Iverson (1999) proposed criteria for the identification of malingered neurocognitive disorder (MNCD). Although very useful for guiding the diagnosis of feigned neuropsychological impairment, these criteria were not intended to apply specifically to the detection of feigned psychiatric disorder.

Base Rates of Exaggerated or Fabricated Symptom Reports

As chapter 2 of this volume points out, knowledge or at least estimates of the base rates of the condition in question are fundamental to understanding the likely accuracy of a diagnostic technique. Unfortunately, because patients who provide invalid symptom reports almost invariably attempt to escape detection, it has proven challenging to establish reliable prevalence rates for this phenomenon. One approach to addressing this issue has been to ask clinicians to provide estimates of the base rates of malingering in their settings. This method was used in early work by Rogers, Sewell, and Goldstein (1994), as well as Rogers, Salekin, Sewell, Goldstein, and Leonard (1998). In the former report, forensic psychologists provided subjective estimates of the base rates of malingering as 7.4% of nonforensic and 15.7% of forensic evaluees. In the latter study, forensic experts estimated that malingering was occurring in 7.2% of nonforensic and 17.4% of forensic patients. Although important for establishing the nontrivial prevalence of malingering, these reports may have been limited by two factors. First, during the time frame in which these estimates must have been based, there were very few well-validated objective techniques available for the detection of feigned psychiatric symptoms. Second, logically, successful malingerers by definition escape

detection and would therefore be unavailable to enter into clinicians' impressions. Thus, it appears that these estimates are likely to constitute a "floor" of psychiatric malingering in about 7.3% of nonforensic patients and about 16.5% of forensic evaluees.

Another approach to estimating the base rates of feigned problems has been to administer objective, well-validated indicators of false psychiatric symptom reports to consecutive forensic patients. Using the Structured Interview of Reported Symptoms, Norris and May (1998) found that about 45% of 75 adult county jail inmates who complained of psychological problems were feigning. In a study of 51 men in a federal prison undergoing pretrial evaluations for competence to stand trial or mental state at the time of a crime, Lewis, Simcox, and Berry (2002) reported that about 31% produced SIRS results indicative of feigned symptoms. Miller (2004) indicated that 28% of a sample of male criminal defendants who had been placed in the forensic units of a state hospital because of a determination of incompetence to stand trial were classified as feigning by the SIRS.

In addition, Guy and Miller (2004) administered the SIRS to 50 males in a maximum-security prison who had requested mental health services and found that 42% were feigning symptoms. This general approach of using scales validated to detect false symptom reports in consecutive evaluees is limited by the fact that these techniques, in isolation, do not address patient volition and goals. Nevertheless, these objective data suggest that false psychiatric symptom reports may occur in approximately 28–45% of criminal evaluees with psychological complaints. Consistent with the earlier noted hypothesis that successful feigners are not incorporated in clinicians' base rate estimates, these reports suggest a somewhat higher base rate of feigning in criminal cases than that obtained in a recent survey of board-certified clinical neuropsychologists reported by Mittenberg, Patton, Canyock, and Condit (2002). These authors estimated that, adjusted for referral source, about 23% of criminal cases were thought to be exaggerating or fabricating symptoms.

One potential limitation of these feigning base rate estimates generated from consecutive patients (at least for the purposes of forensic neuropsychologists) is that most were derived from settings in which primarily psychiatric, rather than neuropsychological, examinations were administered. Thus, it is not entirely clear that another referral stream, such as compensation-seeking mild head-injury patients, would have a comparable prevalence of false claims of psychiatric symptoms. However, the 2002 survey of board-certified clinical neuropsychologists reported by Mittenberg et al. indicates estimates of feigning of various psychiatric symptom types during neuropsychological examinations, adjusted for referral source, as follows: fibromyalgia or chronic fatigue (38.6%); pain or somatoform disorders (33.5%); depressive disorders (16.1%); anxiety disorders (13.6%); and dissociative disorders (10.5%). Particularly if clinicians' estimates run below actual base rates of malingering, these findings suggest that, even in the context of forensic neuropsychological examinations, false reports of psychiatric

symptoms are common, with some types estimated to occur at levels comparable to those found in criminal forensic psychological contexts.

Coaching

In the last decade, forensic neuropsychologists have become increasingly concerned with the issue of the coaching of evaluees to avoid detection by established procedures for identification of invalid responses (Victor & Abeles, 2004). Coaching involves the provision of information to evaluees to assist in avoiding identification as a malingerer on various validity procedures. This raises complex problems for the identification of feigned symptom reports. In its extreme form (which hypothetically involves detailed description of all likely validity procedures to forensic evaluees), the ability of these instruments to detect feigning is likely to be severely compromised.

Perhaps more realistic is the possibility that a forensic clinician will utilize a regular battery of well-validated instruments to detect inadequate effort, as well as scales for the identification of false psychiatric symptom reports. In this situation, it seems likely that attorneys who practice in the area will become familiar with the battery. Those who coach clients on these tests may thus significantly attenuate the sensitivities of selected instruments for the detection of malingering. Even if only a subset of procedures is known to a coached evaluee, the decision rules for combining the results from multiple validity procedures may be adversely affected. For example, if the MMPI-2 Validity scales are used as a screen for determining whether the SIRS should be administered, evaluees who feign psychiatric symptoms but avoid detection using the former scales will go undetected when the latter test is not administered.

One potential defense against coaching is for forensic clinicians to identify multiple well-validated malingering detection procedures and to rotate their use across the evaluees in order to raise the bar for successful coaching. It is important for forensic clinicians to think through the implications of coaching on selected instruments for decision rules aimed at combining results from multiple validity procedures for the optimal detection of malingering. Chapter 11 of this volume provides further information on coaching and its implications for forensic neuropsychological assessment.

Techniques for Evaluating the Validity of Symptom Self-Reports

Various techniques have been suggested for the identification of invalid psychiatric symptom reports, although only a few have been extensively validated. The proposed techniques have included objective self-report psychological scales, structured interviews, projective psychological tests, analysis of nonverbal behavior, physiological testing, and drug-assisted interviews (Granhag & Strömwell, 2004; Rogers, 1997). Only the first three approaches are likely to be practical in most clinical neuropsychological settings, and of

these, only the first two have been extensively evaluated in the published empirical literature. Thus, this review is restricted to objective self-report psychological scales, as well as structured interviews validated for the detection of feigned psychiatric symptom reports. To focus attention on those instruments most likely to be useful to forensic neuropsychologists, we cover only those procedures that have been subjected to adequate scrutiny in the peer-reviewed published literature.

Methodologies for Assessing the Accuracy of Malingering Scales

The methodologies used to evaluate the accuracy of malingering detection scales are generally recognized as important in determining the generalizability of the resulting data (Rogers, 1997). Broadly speaking, the major methods for validating purported tests of false psychiatric symptom reports fall into four categories: case studies, differential prevalence designs, simulation studies, and known-groups studies. Case studies, which by definition involve a very limited number of participants selected for their unique qualities, are of unknown generalizability and thus not regarded as adequate tests of the accuracy of a malingering detection technique.

Informed evaluation of the remaining validation techniques requires an understanding of the major operating characteristic statistics used to evaluate diagnostic tests. Although chapter 2 of this volume addresses this topic in detail, it is useful here to briefly review the major statistics of interest. Given the usual situation of a continuous predictor variable for the identification of malingering, a cutting score must be identified to allow the dichotomization of results into those that are positive (i.e., predictive of the presence of malingering) and those that are negative (i.e., suggestive of the absence of malingering).

Prevalence, or base rate, is the percentage of the entire sample who have the condition. When this test and cutting score are applied to criterion groups known either to have or to be free of the condition in question, two basic accuracy parameters are generated. *Sensitivity* is the percentage of those in the group known to have the condition who are correctly classified using the test at the recommended cutting score. *Specificity* is the percentage of the group known to be free of the condition in question who are correctly classified by the test results.

At a given cutting score, sensitivity and specificity are the parameters typically used to compare the accuracies of two or more diagnostic procedures. These values are widely presumed to be invariant properties of the test at a given cutting score, although this assumption may be tenuous in some cases (Kraemer, 1992). Moreover, an overall *hit rate* (percentage of correct test classifications) may also be generated to quantify a test's accuracy. A major limitation of the hit rate as a descriptor of the operating characteristics of a test is that any given value for this variable may subsume a wide range of sensitivity and specificity levels. Thus, it is impossible to use hit rate

values to estimate the likely accuracy of positive or negative predictions by the test.

Sensitivity and specificity must be integrated with the prevalence (base rate) of the condition in question in order to determine the likely accuracy of test predictions of the presence or absence of the condition in question. *In the absence of at least estimates of the base rates of a condition in a referral stream, it is impossible to quantify the probable accuracy of a diagnostic test.* In combination with sensitivity and specificity, base rate estimates are used to determine positive predictive power (PPP; i.e., the likelihood that an individual with a positive test sign has the condition in question) and negative predictive power (NPP; i.e., the likelihood that an individual with a negative test sign is free of the condition). Because they reflect the accuracy of a diagnostic procedure in a clinical application, these two parameters are the most clinically relevant of the basic operating characteristic statistics.

As determined in part by the prevailing base rates, PPP and NPP at a given cutting score may be highly divergent. Thus, when choosing a malingering test and a cutting score, the clinician should carefully consider the primary purpose of the test (e.g., ruling in or ruling out presence of the condition in question). A test used to rule out a condition (i.e., a screening instrument) should possess high NPP at the base rate prevailing in the local setting (Berry, Baer, Rinaldo, & Wetter, 2002). A test intended to rule in a condition should possess high PPP at the base rate prevailing in the local setting. Failure to think through the desired purpose of the scale in question (e.g., to rule in or rule out a condition) may result in test choices that lack adequate predictive power for their intended purpose.

Turning to the application of these statistics to the three remaining methodologies for evaluating the accuracy of a malingering detection procedure, the first to be considered is the differential prevalence design. This methodology involves examining results from a malingering instrument administered to a group thought to have a high base rate of malingering and comparing them to the findings from a group thought to have a low base rate of malingering. For example, the results from such a scale used to evaluate subjects in a compensation-seeking situation could be compared with those of subjects who are not seeking compensation. If the scale in question is a valid predictor of malingering, the scores should be significantly higher in the compensation-seeking group.

Importantly, although such results potentially contribute to the validation of a procedure in a naturalistic setting, because the malingering status of individuals in the compensation-seeking and the non-compensation-seeking group is unknown, in differential prevalence designs it is usually impossible to calculate the key accuracy parameters of sensitivity and specificity. *Thus, the results from differential prevalence designs cannot be substituted for results from simulation and known-groups studies.*

Frederick (2000) has suggested that if the positive sign rate of a test at a given cutting score remains stable across samples and the approximate base

rates of the condition in the groups evaluated in a differential prevalence design are known, it is possible to estimate sensitivity and specificity in the absence of knowledge of the status of individuals. However, these assumptions may not tenable in all cases, and to date, the hypothesis has apparently not been empirically evaluated using ecologically valid data.

Simulation designs compare the results from a malingering detection procedure administered to a group instructed to malinger with those from a group instructed to answer honestly or thought to lack motivation to malinger. In the weaker version, college students or other convenience samples are randomly divided into groups receiving malingering or honest instructions and given the test. In the stronger variant, the honest group is a clinically relevant sample (such as non-compensation-seeking evaluees) who have received the procedure.

Rogers (1997) and Berry et al. (2002) have described numerous methodological safeguards to increase the validity of results from simulation studies (see the following paragraph for details). However, even with these methodological safeguards in place, simulation studies remain vulnerable to concerns about limited generalizability to real-world malingerers. Simulation studies do possess some important strengths, including the prospect of drawing causal inferences based on random assignment to groups and the instruction manipulation, the possibility of eliciting a wide range of malingering strategies and intensities, and the potential to serve as a controlled comparison of the accuracy rates of multiple procedures administered to the same samples. Results from the malingering group may be used to estimate sensitivity, whereas the results from an appropriate clinical control group may be used to assess specificity. However, Rogers (1997) recommends that results from simulation studies be cross-validated in known-groups designs prior to placing any confidence in a malingering procedure.

Known-groups designs involve the comparison of results from a malingering test in a clinically identified group of malingerers with those of a comparably identified group of honest patients. Methodological safeguards for this research design are also addressed as follows:

Simulation Designs

- Are the participants' characteristics similar to those with whom the test will be used in clinical practice?
- Are analog malingerers given a plausible scenario that they understand and may identify with?
- Are analog malingerers instructed to be believable in their feigning (try to avoid detection)?
- Are analog malingerers given sufficient time and resources to prepare to malinger successfully?
- Are analog malingerers provided with information on symptoms and detection strategies to reflect knowledge that is probably easily available to real-world malingerers?

- Are analog malingerers provided with an incentive powerful enough to motivate them to attempt to feign successfully?
- Are analog malingerers debriefed at the end of the study to determine whether they recalled, comprehended, and complied with their instructions?
- Are nonmalingering measures included in the experimental protocol, replicating clinical practice in which both malingering and standard tests are given?
- Is a clinically relevant patient control group included?
- Is the honesty of the patient control group verified through posttest debriefing or other independent means?
- Are the numbers of participants in the malingering and honest groups adequate to detect an effect?

Known-Groups Designs
- How valid is the criterion that is being used to assign group membership? (Criterion validity will place a ceiling on predictor validity.)
- How representative of malingerers are those assigned to the malingering group? (If only flagrant malingerers are "caught," the results may misrepresent the ability of the test to identify malingering.)
- Is the honesty of the patient control group verified through posttest debriefing or other independent means?
- How representative of honest patients are those assigned to the nonmalingering control group?

The strengths of the known-groups approach include the use of clinically relevant populations and ecologically valid procedures. Rarely considered weaknesses include the inability to infer a causal link between malingering and any observed test differences, the possibility of identifying only blatant or incompetent feigners in the malingering group with resulting limitations to generalizability, and the ceiling on accuracy placed by the standard or procedure used to assign patients to groups (Dearth, Berry, Vickery, Vagnini, Baser, et al., 2005).

Rogers (1997) has suggested that results from both simulation and known-groups designs would ideally be available to support the validity of a malingering test. An alternative perspective, proposed by Bianchini, Mathias, & Greve (2001), is that, given the importance of positive predictive power, establishing a low false positive rate across multiple nonlitigating clinical groups in association with demonstrated sensitivity in known-groups designs could provide strong support for a procedure in the absence of results from simulation studies.

Quality-Control Issues

Forensic neuropsychologists must be constantly mindful of the empirical evidence supporting the accuracy and appropriateness of the tests they use in

evaluating legal or potential legal cases (Greiffenstein & Cohen, 2005; Hom and Denney, 2002; Larrabee, 2005c). This concern applies just as much to indicators of feigned psychiatric symptoms as it does to any other technique. What factors bear on judging the quality of a putative test of psychiatric malingering? Beyond meeting the guidelines from *Standards for Educational and Psychological Testing* (APA, 1999), the recommendations for evaluating the quality of the malingering procedure in question are as follows:

1. There should be sufficient peer-reviewed publications on the operating characteristics of a test to allow an informed evaluation of its classification accuracy. More explicitly, sensitivity and specificity data using the procedure at the recommended cutting score should have been derived in well-characterized and appropriate samples and published in peer-reviewed outlets.
2. Reasonable convergence in sensitivity and specificity values at recommended cutting scores should be shown across published reports based on comparable samples.
3. Predictive power values in varying base rate environments should have been calculated and determined to provide support for the intended clinical application of the test.
4. Supportive results should have been based on both high-quality simulation and known-groups methodologies and published in peer-reviewed outlets.
5. Supportive results should have been published in peer-reviewed outlets by at least one research team independent of the test's original developers.
6. For use in neuropsychological settings, data on control groups of neurologic patients should be available.

Effects of Neurologic Disorders on Psychological Questionnaires

The final item in the preceding recommendations—that the results from neurologic control groups should be available for scales assessing the feigning of psychiatric symptoms in the context of forensic neuropsychological evaluations—merits elaboration. Although it is widely recognized that certain psychiatric conditions, such as schizophrenia or major depression, may significantly affect neuropsychological results, it is less commonly recognized that neurologic conditions may also affect the psychological experience of the patient and thus alter self-reported psychiatric symptoms.

Gass (2002) states that genuine head-injured patients tend to elevate MMPI-2 clinical scales 1, 2, 3, 7, and 8 apparently due, at least in part, to accurate reports of neurologic rather than psychiatric symptoms. Gass recommends that neuropsychologists consider the effect of neurologic, as well as psychiatric, symptoms on these scales (but also see Brulot, Strauss, & Spellacy, 1997, who found that correction items did not correlate with TBI injury severity indicators). Regarding the effects of head injury on validity scales,

Dearth et al. (2005) compared MMPI-2 results from demographically matched community volunteers and non-compensation-seeking TBI patients. Several validity scales were significantly higher in TBI patients than in controls, with Cohen's *d* scores of .74 for *F*, .48 for *Fb*, and .53 for FBS (these scales are described later).

Thus, some evidence exists that neurologic disorders affect responses to both clinical and validity scales derived from self-report psychological symptom inventories. It therefore seems important to obtain data on validity scales from control groups of patients with neurologic disorders prior to using them in settings serving individuals with these conditions. Should the psychiatric malingering techniques prove to be significantly affected by the presence of genuine neurologic disorder, it may be necessary to derive and validate new cutting scores that are optimal for use in forensic neuropsychological examinations. Further, optimal cutting scores on malingering scales might vary as a function of the context in which the tests are administered (e.g., criminal versus civil, or neuropsychological versus psychiatric evaluation).

Major Types of Instruments for the Detection of Feigned Psychiatric Symptoms

Broadly speaking, the major categories of instruments validated for the detection of feigned psychiatric symptoms include self-report tests and structured interviews. Self-report tests may be further divided into those possessing feigning scales embedded in longer, multiscale inventories such as the MMPI-2, as well as procedures that are dedicated solely to the detection of false psychiatric symptom complaints. As mentioned earlier, in order to focus attention on the best-validated instruments, only those that have been adequately evaluated in published empirical studies are reviewed in this chapter. Further, only those simulation studies that include patient controls are addressed here. Procedures that met or nearly met these criteria include the MMPI-2 (Butcher et al., 1989), the MCMI-III (Millon, Davis, & Millon, 1997), the PAI (Morey, 1991), the SIMS (Widows & Smith, 2005), the M-FAST (Miller, 2001), and the SIRS (Rogers et al., 1992).

Review of Major Objective Procedures for Detection of Feigned Psychiatric Symptoms: Multiscale Inventories

Minnesota Multiphasic Personality Inventory-2

The MMPI-2 (Butcher et al., 1989) is the updated version of the MMPI and is currently the most frequently administered test in forensic psychological evaluations (Pope, Butcher, & Seelen, 2000). Written at an eighth-grade reading level, the MMPI-2 includes 567 true/false items scored on multiple

clinical, content, and supplementary scales with generally acceptable psycho-metric characteristics. Additionally, one of the major strengths of the MMPI-2 for forensic applications is the presence of several well-validated scales for the assessment of various problematic response sets.

The original MMPI fake fad scale *(F)*, which consisted of items rarely endorsed in the MMPI normative sample, was carried over almost intact to the first part of the MMPI-2. Three additional validity scales were added to the MMPI-2 to increase accuracy in evaluating feigning. For example, *Fb* includes items rarely endorsed by the MMPI-2 normative sample. It is sensitive to the same effects as *F* (feigning, random responding, and severe psycho-pathology) but is located in the latter part of the test. Both the Variable Response Inconsistency Scale (VRIN) and the True Response Inconsistency Scale (TRIN) consist of content-linked item pairs that are sensitive to random responding and yea-saying/nay-saying, respectively. *These response consistency scales play a key role in evaluating profile validity as they serve to identify the presence of random responding, which may explain elevations on fake bad validity scales* (Wetter, Baer, Berry, Smith & Larsen, 1992).

A more recently developed MMPI-2 Fake Bad Scale is *Fp* (infrequency-psychopathology; Arbisi & Ben-Porath, 1995), which was constructed to include only items endorsed infrequently by *both* the normative sample and large samples of psychiatric inpatients. This developmental methodology makes *Fp* less sensitive to genuine psychopathology than *F* and *Fb*. Provided that random responding has been ruled out using VRIN and TRIN, significant elevations on *Fp* are thus thought to be due primarily to feigned psychiatric symptoms.

The MMPI and MMPI-2 Fake Bad Scales have been the focus of extensive empirical research, and several meta-analyses summarizing the published results have appeared (Berry, Baer, & Harris, 1991; Rogers, Sewell, & Salekin, 1994). The most recent such review (Rogers, Sewell, Martin, & Vitacco, 2003) suggests that the *F* and *Fp* Validity scales are the most effective for identifying psychiatric malingering on the MMPI-2. However, there is some discrepancy across publications regarding which of the many available MMPI-2 Validity scales is the most accurate for detecting psychiatric malingering; in addition, some variability exists in reported optimal cutting scores and associated sensitivity and specificity values (Berry et al., 2002).

The original MMPI-2 feigning scales were developed and validated to detect malingering in psychiatric settings and were only later applied to neuropsychological environments (Heaton, Smith, Lehman, & Vogt, 1978). Greiffenstein, Gola, and Baker (1995) questioned the use of these scales in civil (as opposed to criminal) forensic neuropsychological examinations and presented data suggesting that *F* was insensitive to feigned symptoms of traumatic brain injury.

Larrabee (1998) proposed that somatic malingering, which involves complaints of unusual physical dysfunction, was much more common than psychiatric feigning in civil neuropsychological examinations. He offered data

suggesting that traditional MMPI-2 Validity scales were relatively insensitive to somatic malingering. Larrabee (ibid.) also suggested that the Lees-Haley Fake Bad scale (FBS; Lees-Haley, English, & Glenn, 1991), originally developed to detect feigned symptoms in personal injury litigation, was useful for detecting somatic malingering and presented data supporting this conclusion. Several subsequent studies have found that, of the MMPI-2 Validity scales, the FBS is the most sensitive to malingering in civil forensic neuropsychological examinations (Greiffenstein, Baker, Axelrod, Peck, and Gervais, 2004; Larrabee, 2003; Ross, Millis, Krukowski, Putnam, & Adams, 2004).

In contrast, Butcher, Arbisi, Atlis, and McNulty (2003) have presented FBS results from a large database that encompasses several types of patient referrals and concluded that its false positive rate was unacceptable in psychiatric samples. This precipitated a lively exchange in the literature (Arbisi & Butcher, 2004; Greve & Bianchini, 2004; Lees-Haley & Fox, 2004), which unfortunately failed to entirely resolve the issues. However, a meta-analysis by Nelson, Sweet, and Demakis (2006) provides strong support for FBS as the most effective MMPI-2 Validity scale in civil forensic settings. Further research is needed to examine its use in psychiatric settings (ibid.). Despite the earlier controversy, the FBS clearly has significant published support for the detection of feigning in civil forensic neuropsychological examinations.

This review of available data on the accuracy of the MMPI-2 Fake Bad Validity Scales focuses on the traditional F scale, the more recently developed Fp scale, and the FBS (Fb was excluded due to its conceptual similarity to the F scale).

Table 9.1 provides results from patient-controlled evaluations of the MMPI-2 Validity scales that have addressed either psychiatric or neuropsychological malingering. With regard to quality-control issues, the extensive number of published evaluations of MMPI-2 Validity scales have included simulation and known-groups designs with provision of sensitivity and specificity characteristics and moderately high classification rates in general. Additionally, several studies including neurologic patients are available and provide support for the use of the MMPI-2 in neuropsychological settings. Although the published data on these scales meet most of the quality-control indices proposed earlier, one concern that arises from a review of the results in Table 9.1 involves the considerable variability in reported cutting scores and the associated sensitivity and specificity values across publications. Unless the examiner uses mean recommended cutting scores and associated classification parameters (Berry et al., 2002; Rogers et al., 2003), there is some risk of arbitrary selection of scales and cutting scores and possibly idiosyncratic inferred operating characteristics.

Due to the extensive published research on the MMPI-2, it is possible to evaluate the effects of different research designs on the results for the fake bad scales. Table 9.2 compares mean cutting scores, sensitivity, specificity, and Cohen's d's from simulation versus known-groups designs. Overall,

Table 9.1.
Results From Patient-Controlled Studies of the MMPI-2 Validity Scales

Study	Group	N	Sample	Control	Inpt/Outpt	Design	Scale	Cutoff	SN	SP	d^a
Graham (1991)	FB	30	M Student			Sim.	F	≥120T†	.90	.97	1.90
	Hon	30	M Pat.-Mixed	P	Inpt						
	FB	20	F Student			Sim.	F	≥120T†	.95	.95	1.98
	Hon	20	F Pat.-Mixed	P	Inpt						
Lees-Haley (1992)	Mal	55	Pers. Injury		Output	K-G***	F	≥62T†	.89	.98	2.03
	Hon	64	Pers. Injury-PTSD	P	Output		FBS	≥24M†	.75	.96	1.71
							FBS	≥26F†	.74	.92	1.71
Rogers (1993)	FBNC	15	Comm.		Inpt	Sim.	F	>120T†	.60	.97	.72
	Hon	37	Pat.-Schiz.	P							
	FBCS	15	Comm.		Inpt	Sim.	F	>120T†	.73	.97	.72
	Hon	37	Pat.-Schiz.	P							
	FBCV	14	Comm.		Inpt	Sim.	F	>120T†	.21	.97	.72
	Hon	37	Pat.-Schiz.	P							
	FBCB	15	Comm.		Inpt	Sim.	F	>120T†	.47	.97	.72
	Hon	37	Pat.-Schiz.	P							
Wetter (1993)	FB	20	Comm.		Output	Sim.	F	≥96T†	.85	.70	1.49
	Hon	20	Pat.-PTSD	P							
	FB	22	Comm.		Output	Sim.	F	≥104T†	1.00	.90	3.15
	Hon	20	Pat.-PASC	P							
Bagby (1994)	FB	58	Student		Inpt	Sim.	F	>104T†	.88	.81	1.73
	Hon	173	For. Pat.-Mixed	P							
Bagby (1994)	FB	58	Student		Inpt	Sim.	F	>89T†	.91	.81	2.28
	Hon	95	Pat.-Mixed	P							

(continued)

Table 9.1.
(*cont'nued*)

Study	Group	N	Sample	Control	Inpt/Outpt	Design	Scale	Cutoff	SN	SP	d^a
Berry (1996)	FB	30	Pat.-Mixed		Outpt	Sim	F	>108T†	.63	1.00	3.82
	Hon	30	Pat.-Mixed	P	Outpt		F(p)	>109T†	.60	1.00	2.49
Iverson (1995)	FB	28	Correc.		Inpt	Sim.	F	≥92T†	.89	.98	2.98
	Hon	51	Pat.-Mixed	P							
Rogers (1995)	FB	33	Pat.-Mixed		Output	Sim.	F	>120T†	.94	.92	.84
	Hon	38	Pat.-Mixed	P	Outpt		F(p)	>110T†	.88	.95	2.53
Sivec (1995)	FB	65	Student		Inpt	Sim.	F	>99T†	.95	.90	2.94
	Hon	40	Pat.-BPD	P							
Pensa (1996)	FB	20	S&C		Inpt	Sim.	F	≥95T†	.93	.98	2.35
	Hon	20	Pat.-Psychotic	P							
Arbisi (1998)	FB	33	Pat.-Mixed		Inpt	Sim.	F	≥100T*	.97	.80	2.17
	Hon	41	Pat.-Mixed	P	Inpt		F(p)	≥100T*	.97	.98	3.74
Bagby (2000)	FB	23	Experts		Inpt/Output	Sim.	F	≥80T†	.80	.85	2.12
	Hon	100	Pat.-Depressed	P			FBS	≥24†	.74	.73	1.54
Elhai (2000)	FB	79	Student		Output	Sim.	F	≥120T†	.75	.77	.93
	Hon	124	Pat.-PTSD	P							
Storm (2000)	FBNC	67	M Student			Sim.	F	>120T†	.67	.98	1.70
	Hon	192	M Pat.-Mixed	P	Inpt		F(p)	>106T†	.75	.95	2.68
	FBNC	124	F Student			Sim.	F	>120T†	.82	.97	1.84
	Hon	160	F Pat.-Mixed	P	Inpt		F(p)	>120T†	.86	.97	2.91
	FBCV	93	M Student			Sim.	F	>101T†	.54	.83	.99
	Hon	192	M Pat.-Mixed	P	Inpt		F(p)	>94T†	.59	.90	1.49
	FBCV	156	F Student			Sim.	F	>85T†	.78	.64	.97
	Hon	160	F Pat.-Mixed	P	Inpt		F(p)	>89T†	.69	.83	1.38

(continued)

Archer (2001)	FB	60	M S&C			Sim.	F	≥65T†	.62	.79	1.09
	Hon	329	M Pat.-Mixed	P	Inpt		F(p)	≥70T*	.53	.73	1.12
	FB	143	F S&C			Sim.	F	≥65T*	.50	.75	.69
	Hon	288	F Pat.-Mixed	P	Inpt		F(p)	≥70T*	.39	.83	.72
Bury (2002)	FBNC	35	Student			Sim.	F	>96T*	.34	.87	1.05
	Hon	61	Pat.-PTSD	P	Inpt		F(p)	>102T*	.31	.95	1.31
	FBCS	29	Student			Sim.	F	>96T*	.34	.87	1.05
	Hon	61	Pat.-PTSD	P	Inpt		F(p)	>102T*	.24	.95	1.24
	FBCV	30	Student			Sim.	F	>96T*	.27	.87	.68
	Hon	61	Pat.-PTSD	P	Inpt		F(p)	>102T*	.13	.95	.93
	FBCB	37	Student			Sim.	F	>96T*	.32	.87	.94
	Hon	61	Pat.-PTSD	P	Inpt		F(p)	>102T*	.27	.95	1.12
Greiffen (2002)	FB	159	Pat.-Pers. Injury		Outpt	K-G***	FBS	≥20†	.87	.53	1.13
	Hon	68	Pat.-Pers. Injury	N	Out						
Lewis (2002)	FB	24	Correc.-Mixed		Inpt	K-G*	F	≥107T*	.67	1.00	2.90
	Hon	31	Correc.-Mixed	P	Inpt		F(p)	≥100T*	.50	1.00	2.60
Heinze (2003)	FB	33	Pat.-Mixed		Inpt	K-G***	F	≥100T*	.73	.88	N/A
	Hon	33	Pat.-Mixed	P	Inpt		F(p)	≥100T*	.52	.85	N/A
Larrabee (2003)	FB	26	Pat.-TBI		Outpt	K-G**	F	>65T†	.35	.79	.54
	Hon	29	Pat.-TBI	N	Outpt		F(p)	>90T*	.04	1.00	.39
Greiffen (2004)	FB	26	M Pat.-PTS		Outpt	K-G***	FBS	>19†	.92	.79	1.81
	Hon	15	M Pat.-PTS	P	Outpt		FBS	≥21†	.88	.60	1.50
	FB	15	F Pat.-PTS		Outpt	K-G***	FBS	≥26†	.81	.88	3.41
	Hon	33	F Pat.-PTS	P	Outpt						
Ross (2004)	FB	59	Pat.-TBI		Inpt/Outpt	K-G***	F	≥65T†	.66	.64	.80
	Hon	59	Pat.-TBI	N	Inpt/Outpt		FBS	≥21†	.90	.90	2.84

Table 9.1.
(continued)

Study	Group	N	Sample	Control	Inpt/Outpt	Design	Scale	Cutoff	SN	SP	d^a
Dearth (2005)	FB	39	Pat.-TBI& Comm.		Outpt	Sim	F	$> 107T^*$	.41	1.00	1.50
	Hon	21	Pat.-TBI	N	Outpt		F(p)	$> 100T^*$	.28	1.00	.97
							FBS	$\geq 22^*$	.72	.76	1.01
Greve (2006)	FB	65	Pat.-mild TBI		Outpt	K-G**	F	$\geq 80T^{**}$	.31	.96	n/a
	Hon	97	Pat.-TBI	N	Outpt		F(p)	$\geq 95T^{**}$	.08	.99	n/a
							FBS	$\geq 23^{**}$	.66	.82	n/a

Note. For studies, only the first author is listed. Control = type of control group, Inpt = inpatient sample, Outpt = outpatient sample, SN = sensitivity, SP = specificity, ^{a} = d calculated using pooled SD. For grcup: FB = fake bad, Hon = honest, FBNC = fake bad no coaching, FBCS = fake bad with coaching on symptoms, FBCV = fake bad with coaching on validity scales, FBCB = fake bad with coaching on both symptoms and validity scales. For sample: F = female, M = male, Pat = patient, Experts = psychology professionals, Pers. Inj = personal injury litigant, Schiz. = schizophrenic, Comm. = community, Mixed = mixed psychiatric disorders, PTSD = posttraumatic stress disorder, PASC = paranoid schizophrenia, Psychot = psychotic, PTS = posttraumatic stress, TBI = traumatic brain injury, For. Pat. = forensic patient, Pers. Injury = personal-injury litigant, Correc. = correctional, S&C = student and community, Pat.-TBI & Comm. = TBI patients and community volunteers, BPD = Borderline Personality Disorder. For design: Sim = simulation, K-G = known groups. For K-G designs: * = K-G formed using SIRS criteria, ** = K-G formed using other criteria. For cutoff: † = cutoff optimal in study sample, * = cutoff determined a priori, ** = cutoff based on mean cutting scores found in below summary tables. F = Psychiatric control, N = Neurologic control.

Table 9.2.
Comparison of MMPI-2 Validity Scales Results From Simulation Versus Known-Groups Designs

	Validity Scale					
	F		F(p)		FBS	
Research Design	Sim	K-G	Sim	K-G	Sim	K-G
Cutting Score						
mean	104.3	79.8	98.3	96.3	23	22.5
SD	13.0	19.5	14.0	4.8	1.41	2.7
range	80–120	62–107	70–120	90–100	22–24	19–26
N	29	6	14	4	2	8
Sensitivity						
mean	.69	.60	.54	.29	.73	.82
SD	.24	.23	.27	.26	.01	.09
range	.21–1.00	.31–.89	.13–.97	.04–.52	.72–.74	.66–.92
N	29	6	14	4	2	8
Specificity						
mean	.88	.88	.92	.96	.75	.80
SD	.10	.14	.08	.07	.02	.16
range	.64–1.00	.64–1.00	.73–1.00	.85–1.00	.73–.76	.53–.96
N	29	6	14	4	2	8
Cohen's d						
mean	1.59	1.57	1.76	1.50	1.28	2.02
SD	.86	1.10	.92	1.56	.37	.81
range	.68–3.82	.54–2.90	.72–3.74	.39–2.60	1.01–1.54	1.13–3.41
N	29	4	14	2	2	7

Note. Cutting score = point at or above which scale value is interpreted as a positive test sign. Cutting scores given in T scores, except FBS, which is given in raw scores.

considerable consistency is evident in the Validity scale results across the two designs. However, two discrepancies across the methods are noteworthy. First, a fairly large difference is apparent between the mean cutting scores for F moving from simulation to known-groups designs (approximately 104T and 80T, respectively). Second, a substantial decline occurs in mean sensitivity for Fp moving from simulation to known-groups methodologies (.54 and .29, respectively), and the absolute level of sensitivity for this scale is rather low in known-groups designs. With these two exceptions, the two methodologies appear to produce relatively consistent results.

The published literature on the MMPI-2 also allows direct comparison of the accuracy of the validity scales in detecting feigning in studies using psychiatric versus neurologic control groups. Table 9.3 provides a summary of relevant operating characteristic variables. In general, FBS appears to have comparable results across psychiatric and neurologic control groups on all

of the parameters examined here. In contrast, F has notably different mean cutting scores across the two control groups (psychiatric controls: 103T; neurologic controls: 79T), as well as mean sensitivity values that drop considerably moving from psychiatric to neurologic controls (psychiatric controls: .70; neurologic controls: .43). The Fp scale has mean d values for neurologic controls (.68) that are about one third of those for psychiatric control groups (1.88).

Additionally, the mean sensitivity of Fp drops significantly moving from psychiatric (.55) to neurologic controls (.13), with the latter value unacceptably low. It should be noted that the decline in sensitivity of Fp must be due to some aspect of these studies other than the neurologic control group itself, as sensitivity is calculated based only on those known to have the condition in question. However, the data summarized in Table 9.3 provide overall support for the use of FBS in a forensic neuropsychological evaluation, which is consistent with Nelson et al. (2006). In contrast, the results in Table 9.3 raise questions about the effectiveness of both the F and Fp scales in forensic neuropsychological settings.

Clearly, the MMPI-2 Validity scales have a very substantial research base that supports their ability to detect feigned symptom reports, albeit with different operating profiles for different settings. For psychiatric evaluations, both F and Fp appear to be well supported and likely also useful for criminal forensic neuropsychological evaluations. In contrast, FBS appears at present to have the strongest support for use in civil forensic neuropsychological settings.

Millon Clinical Multiaxial Inventory III

The Millon Clinical Multiaxial Inventory has long been a popular instrument among psychologists who are particularly concerned with personality disorders. The newest version of the test is the MCMI-III (Millon, Davis, & Millon, 1997), which includes 175 true/false items summarized by 24 content scales that tap clinical personality patterns, severe personality pathology, basic clinical syndromes, and severe syndromes. These scales address both Axis I and II disorders from *DSM-IV*. To interpret these scales, the MCMI-III uses base rate (BR) scores that attempt to incorporate varying prevalences of psychiatric disorders, thus offering a potential advantage over the fixed base rates that most standard scores implicitly assume.

In addition to the content scales, the MCMI-III includes a Validity index (V) and three modifying indices: Disclosure (X), Desirability (Y), and Debasement (Z), all intended to address response sets. The Validity index consists of three items with highly skewed endorsement rates and is sensitive to random responding. The Disclosure index is said by Millon to assess the tendency of the test taker "to be frank and self-revealing or reticent and secretive" (ibid., p. 118). This inclination is determined "from the degree of positive or negative deviation from the midrange of an adjusted composite raw score for Scales 1 to 8B" (ibid.), which was apparently derived from the

Table 9.3.
Comparison of MMPI-2 Validity Scales Results From Psychiatric Versus Neurologic
Control Groups

	Validity Scale					
	F		F(p)		FBS	
Control Group	Psych	Neuro	Psych	Neuro	Psych	Neuro
Cutting score						
mean	102.8	79.0	98.4	95.0	24.2	21.0
SD	14.7	19.8	13.5	5.0	2.0	1.6
range	62–120	65–107	70–120	90–100	21–26	19–23
N	31	4	15	3	5	5
Sensitivity						
mean	.70	.43	.55	.13	.78	.81
SD	.23	.16	.25	.13	.06	.12
range	.21–1.00	.31–.66	.13–.97	.04–.28	.74–.88	.66–.92
N	31	4	15	3	5	5
Specificity						
mean	.89	.85	.92	.99	.82	.76
SD	.09	.17	.08	.01	.15	.14
range	.64–1.00	.64–1.00	.73–1.00	.99–1.00	.60–.96	.53–.90
N	31	4	15	3	5	5
Cohen's d						
mean	1.65	.95	1.88	.68	1.97	1.70
SD	.88	.50	.92	.41	.81	.84
range	.68–3.82	.54–1.50	.72–3.74	.39–.97	1.50–3.41	1.01–2.84
N	30	3	14	2	5	4

Note. Cutting score = point at which scale value is interpreted as a positive test sign. Cutting
scores given in T scores, except FBS, which is given in raw scores.

developmental patient sample. In addition to serving as a validity indicator,
the Disclosure index is used to adjust scores on most other scales. The Debasement index is the most directly applicable to the detection of overreporting of psychological problems. It assesses a tendency to "devalue
oneself by presenting more troublesome emotional and personal difficulties
than are likely" (ibid.). Finally, the Desirability index taps the "inclination to
appear socially attractive, morally virtuous, or emotionally well composed"
(ibid.) and thus should be sensitive to a "fake good" approach to the test.
However, this index is thought to be a "bipolar" scale and thus has been used
to detect faking bad in some work.

A number of issues arise for the MCMI-III Validity scales. Regarding the
V scale, it should be obvious that with only three items, it will likely miss
many random responders. A nonelevated V scale may indirectly lead to

erroneous conclusions by failing to alert the test interpreter to the presence of random responding as an explanation for elevated fake bad scales. Another potential problem is that the BR scores of 75 and 85 (interpretive thresholds) for the X, Y, and Z scales were set simply to cut off percentile rankings of 75 and 90 in the normative patient sample without reference to any independent determination of the presence or absence of response sets (ibid., pp. 61–62). Thus, no criterion-related information was incorporated into setting these cutting points.

Of further concern is the fact that scales Y and Z were developed for the previous edition of the test based on the responses of a small number of graduate students ($n = 12$; Millon, 1987) who were asked to respond under "fake good" and "fake bad" instructions, and little information (group means only) is provided regarding the results from two small-scale validation studies reported in the MCMI-II manual. No empirical evaluation of the new versions of the validity scales is reported in the manual for the newest version of the complete test. Furthermore, Rogers and Bender (2003) raise significant doubts about the MCMI-III Disclosure index by pointing out that 27 of the 46 items are new to the latest version of the test. This is potentially problematic, given that the recent version of the scale has undergone little or no study. A change in more than half of the items on the Disclosure index suggests that it would be unwise simply to assume complete compatibility between the present and previous versions of this scale.

Table 9.4 presents data on patient-controlled studies of the MCMI-III Validity scales. First, it is noteworthy that so few high-quality studies have been published to date on the characteristics of these scales. No data from neurologic control groups are available. Another issue is the variability in sensitivity and specificity values associated with cutting scores in the published data. The low sensitivity values reported by Schoenberg, Dorr, and Morgan (2003) also suggest that the NPP will likely be poor in most settings, meaning that failure to administer an additional malingering-specific measure will likely result in an inability to detect feigned symptom reports.

Another methodologically important concern is that no known-groups studies of the MCMI-III Validity scales have yet been published. Regarding the MCMI-III's major scale intended to detect the overreporting of psychiatric symptoms (Z), Rogers and Bender (2003) have stated that "more extensive research is needed before its use in forensic evaluations" is appropriate (p. 115). Given these serious concerns, it appears unwise at this time to use the MCMI-III in a forensic neuropsychological examination, particularly if no dedicated malingering detection instrument is administered to the evaluee.

Personality Assessment Inventory

The Personality Assessment Inventory (PAI; Morey, 1991) is a widely used multiscale instrument that has been the focus of a steadily increasing body of research since its publication. This 344-item questionnaire arranges re-

Table 9.4.
Results From Patient-Controlled Malingering Detection Studies Using the MCMI-III

Study	Group	N	Sample	Design	Scale	Cutoff	SN	SP	d^a
Daubert	FB	80	Psy. OutPt	Sim	X	≥ 85BR	.61	.81	1.13
(2000)	Hon	80	Psy. OutPt		Y	≤ 35BR	.58	.76	−.83
					Z	≥ 85BR	.55	.79	1.12
					X*	≥ 80BR	.76	.71	
					Y*	≤ 39BR	.64	.74	
					Z*	≥ 81BR	.64	.78	
Schoenberg	Mal	106	Student	Sim	X*	> 89BR	.35	.88	.81
(2003)	Hon	202	Psy. InPt		Y*	< 21BR	.33	.85	−.66
					Z*	> 82BR	.59	.66	.59
					X	> 178R	.00	1.00	

Note. For studies, only first author is listed. SN = sensitivity, SP = specificity, d = Cohen's d, [a] = d calculated based on pooled SD. For group: FB = fake bad, Hon = honest, Mal = malingering. For sample: Psy. OutPt = psychiatric outpatient, Psy. InPt = psychiatric inpatient. For design: Sim = simulation. For scale: X = disclosure, Y = desirability, Z = debasement, * = optimal cutting score in samples. For cutoff: BR = base rate score, R = raw score.

sponses to a 4-point Likert-type answer format into 22 scales within four broad classes: validity scales (4), clinical syndrome scales (11), treatment indicators (5), and 2 interpersonal-style scales with strong associated psychometric characteristics. Most relevant to this chapter are the 4 validity scales.

The original validity scales identify random responding, as well as positive and negative impression management. The Inconsistency scale (ICN) consists of pairs of highly correlated items, whereas the Infrequency scale (INF) comprises items that are either very rarely endorsed or nearly always endorsed in the normative sample but are not reflective of psychopathology. Both ICN and INF are sensitive to random responding, which tends to elevate indicators of feigned psychopathology because they are composed of items with skewed endorsement rates.

A third response bias scale on the PAI is the Positive Impression scale (PIM). The PIM consists of items with low overall endorsement frequencies in both clinical and nonclinical populations, although the endorsement frequencies are higher among nonclinical respondents (ibid.). The PIM elevations indicate that a test taker has a tendency to deny unfavorable items and thus are sensitive to denial of psychopathology.

The final original PAI Validity scale is the Negative Impression scale (NIM), which detects negative response bias, that is, a tendency to exaggerate or fabricate symptoms. In general, the NIM items were rarely endorsed by clinical, as well as nonclinical, subjects. As is typical of similar scales, however, the presence of genuine psychopathology tends to raise the NIM to

Table 9.5.
Results From Patient-Controlled Malingering Detection Studies Using the PAI

Study	Group	N	Sample	Design	Scale	Cut	SN	SP	d^a
Rogers (1996)	FB	182	Student	Sim	NIM	≥77T[†]	.56	.81	.68
	Hon	221	Psy. pt.		MI	≥3[†]	.32	.90	
Wang (1997)	Mal	15	Corr. Psy. Pt.	K-G*	NIM	≥77T*			1.08
	Hon	25	Corr. Psy. Pt.		MI	≥3*			.70
Liljequist (1998)	FB	27	Student	Sim	MI	≥3[†]	.59		
	Hon	29	Psy. Inpt.					.90	1.10
	Hon	30	Psy. Inpt.					.83	.70
Morey (1998)	FB	44	Student	Sim	NIM	≥77T[†]	.91	.87	1.63
	Hon	45	Psy. Pt.		RDF	≥57[†]	.96	.96	1.96
					MI	≥3[†]	.82	.93	1.75
Rogers, Ustad (1998)	Mal	16	Corr. Psy. Pt.	K-G*	NIM	>80T*	.63	.95	2.22
	Hon	43	Corr. Psy. Pt.						
Rogers, Sewell (1998)	Mal	57	Corr. Psy. Pt.	K-G*	NIM	≥77T[†]	.84	.74	
	Hon	58	Corr. Psy. Pt.		MI	≥3[†]	.47	.86	
					RDF	≥57[†]	.51	.72	
Scragg (2000)	Mal	25	Comm. Vol.	Sim	NIM	>84T*	.54	1.00	1.17
	Hon	19	Psy. Pt.		MI	≥3*	.45	.94	
					RDF	≥.06*	.63	.94	
Calhoun (2000)	Mal	23	Student	Sim	NIM	≥84T*	.43	.74	
	Hon	23	Psy. Outpt.		MI	≥3*	.56	.78	
Bagby (2002)	Mal	22	Student (uncoached)		NIM				.53
					RDF				1.55
					MI				.48
		23	Student (coached)		NIM				.44
					RDF				1.87
	Hon	75	Psy. Pt.		MI				.05
Blanchard 2003	Mal.	52	Student		NIM	≥110T[†]	.54	.99	2.48
	Hon	432	Psy. Inpt.		MI	≥5[†]	.48	1.00	2.61
					RDF	≥1.8[†]	.60	.99	2.48

Note. Group: For studies, only first author is listed unless additional authors are required to identify reference. SN = sensitivity, SP = specificity, d = Cohen's d, [a] = d calculated based on pooled SD. For group: FB = fake bad, Hon = honest, Mal = malingering. For sample: Psy. Pt. = psychiatric patient, Corr Psy. Pat. = correctional psychiatric patient, Psy. Inpt. = psychiatric inpatient, Psy. Outpt. = psychiatric outpatient. For design: Sim = simulation, K-G = known groups. * = K-G formed using SIRS criteria. For scales: MI = Malingering Index, NIM = Negative Impression Management, RDF = Rogers Discriminant Function. For cutoff: [†] = cutoff optimal in study sample, * = cutoff determined a priori.

some extent. Thus, clinical control groups are vital to the validation of this and similar malingering detection scales.

Subsequent to publication of the test, additional indices of faking bad on the PAI were described. Morey (1993) introduced the Malingering index (MI), which is a configurally based scale composed of eight specific components. Rogers, Sewell, Morey, and Ustad (1996) also identified a discriminant function derived from multiple PAI variables (Rogers Discriminant Function [RDF]).

Table 9.5 presents results from patient-controlled studies of the fake bad indices on the PAI. These data suggest a number of strengths, particularly for the NIM and MI scales. These feigning scales have been evaluated in multiple, appropriate samples with independent authors and both simulation and known-groups designs providing support. At the recommended cutting scores, reasonable consistency in operating characteristics is evident. Data on the RDF are mixed, particularly with regard to optimal cutting scores. As is often the case with malingering detection scales, specificity is generally much higher than sensitivity for NIM and MI. One implication of this pattern is that, at recommended cutting scores, these validity scales, in most settings, will have higher PPP than NPP, meaning that they are not ideal screens for deciding whether to administer another malingering detection instrument. Another limitation of the available data for the PAI from a forensic neuropsychological perspective is that no control groups of neurologic patients have been reported to date. The possible effect of neurologic disorder on the clinical and validity scales of the PAI should be a high-priority topic for future research on the instrument.

Review of Major Objective Procedures for Detection of Feigned Psychiatric Symptoms: Dedicated Self-Report Inventories

Structured Inventory of Malingered Symptomatology

Smith (1992) developed the SIMS with the goal of producing a brief, self-report malingering screening instrument that was easily administered, capable of high rates of detection, and written at a low reading level (fifth grade). The 75-item SIMS includes five scales sensitive to specific forms of malingering, including psychosis (P), amnesia (Am), neurologic impairment (N), affective disorder (Af), and low intelligence (Li) (Smith & Burger, 1997). These subscales potentially provide insight into the type of feigning exhibited. The total score (TS), summed across all of the scales on the SIMS, is the preferred summary variable for predicting the presence or absence of malingering. The SIMS was published by Psychological Assessment Resources (Widows & Smith, 2005), and reliability has been reported to be acceptable (Merckelbach & Smith, 2003).

Table 9.6.

Results From Patient-Controlled Malingering Detection Studies Using the SIMS

Study	Group	N	Sample	Design	Scale	Cutoff	SN	SP	d^a
Rogers (1996)	FB	53	Psy Inpt (Adol)	Sim	Tot. Sc.	>16	.44	.94	NA
	Hon	53	Psy Inpt (Adol)	W-G					
Lewis (2000)	Mal	20	Corr. Comp. Eval	K-G	Tot. Sc.	>16	1.00	.55	3.0
	Hon	31	Corr. Comp. Eval	K-G*					
Merckelbach (2003)	FB	57	Student	Sim	Tot. Sc.	>16	.95	NA	2.2
	Hon	10	Psy Inpt						

Note. For studies, only the first author is listed. SN = sensitivity, SP = specificity, d = Cohen's d, ^{a} = d is based on pooled SD. For group: FB = fake bad, Hon = Honest, Mal = Malingering. For sample: Psy Inpt (Adol) = adolescent psychiatric inpatient, Corr. Comp. Eval = correctional compensation evaluation, Psy Inpt = psychiatric inpatient. For design: Sim = simulation, W-G = Within groups, K-G = Known groups, * = K-G determined using SIRS criteria. For scale: Tot. Sc. = SIMS total score. For cutoff: † = cutoff optimal in study sample, * = cutoff determined a priori.

Table 9.6 presents the available published data on patient-controlled studies of the SIMS. The test has been successfully evaluated in both simulation and known-groups designs, and the available d scores are respectable. The recommended cutting score for use in a screening role has been fairly consistent across reports, although the associated sensitivity and specificity values have varied somewhat. Supportive research has been published by independent authors. Another strength of the test is that it has been evaluated in several different populations. Assuming high sensitivity at the recommended cutting score for adults, the SIMS total score has an excellent profile for use as a screening tool to determine whether additional malingering tests should be administered (e.g., high NPP).

At present, use of the SIMS in forensic neuropsychological examinations raises a few potential concerns. First, only three high-quality studies have been published to date. Second, Table 9.6 reveals a fair amount of variability in sensitivity and specificity values at the recommended cutting score, although this may be partly attributable to the unique characteristics of adolescent responders reported by Rogers, Hinds, and Sewell (1996). Another possible issue is that the test does not have a scale for identifying random responding. A totally random approach to the test would likely cause midrange raw scores on all of the malingering scales, a potentially misleading result. A final concern is the lack of data from neurologic controls. It is not clear what specificity rates would be expected in genuine head-injury patients, for example. Overall, the SIMS is an only moderately strong candidate for use in forensic neuropsychological evaluations at present. However, it is

quite possible that additional publications will provide sufficiently supportive data for the use of this test in forensic neuropsychological examinations.

Review of Major Objective Procedures for Detection of Feigned Psychiatric Symptoms: Dedicated Structured Interviews

Miller Forensic Assessment of Symptoms Test

The Miller Forensic Assessment of Symptoms Test (M-FAST; Miller, 2001) is a brief (5 m) structured interview designed to provide a screen for malingered psychiatric symptoms. The test includes 25 items that were based on seven malingering detection strategies identified by Rogers (1997) in his development of the SIRS. The strategies used on the M-FAST include unusual hallucinations (UH), reported versus observed symptoms (RO), extreme symptoms (ES), rare combinations of symptoms (RC), negative image (NI), unusual symptom course (USC), and suggestibility (S). An overall summary indicator is the total score (TS), which is the sum of all of the items answered in the keyed direction.

Reliability has been strong (Miller, 2001). A cutting score of TS ≥ 6 has been recommended for interpretation and shown to have high sensitivity (>.90) and moderate specificity (>.80) in initial work (Miller, 2004). This profile of high sensitivity and moderate specificity results in high NPP in most settings, a desirable characteristic in a screening instrument (Berry et al., 2002). Additionally, the structured-interview format of the M-FAST provides an additional modality for gathering converging evidence on the possibility of feigned symptom reports.

Table 9.7 presents available published data on patient-controlled studies of the M-FAST. Several high-quality studies are available, and they show that Cohen's d is quite strong (1.86–2.80). Sensitivities ranged from moderate to very high (.76–.93), whereas specificities ranged from moderately high to high (.83–.90). Samples are all clinically relevant, as they were derived from legal settings (either pretrial defendants judged incompetent to stand trial or inmates of jails or prisons). The results were relatively consistent across the simulation and known-groups designs. The test has been cross-validated by investigators independent of the original author.

Overall, the available data on the M-FAST are quite supportive. However, one potential limitation from the standpoint of a forensic neuropsychological examination is that none of the available published studies utilized primarily neuropsychological evaluees or neurologic controls, although it is possible that subsets of the available control samples had neurologic conditions. Data from neurologic controls would thus be desirable prior to using the M-FAST in a forensic neuropsychological examination.

Table 9.7.

Results From Patient-Controlled Malingering Detection Studies Using the M-FAST

Study	Group	N	Sample	Design	Scale	Cutoff	SN	SP	d^a
Guy (2004)	Mal	21	Corr. Psy Pt	KG*	Total	≥ 6	.86	.83	2.06
	Hon	29	Corr. Psy Pt						
Miller (2004)	Mal	14	Psy ICST	KG*	Total	≥ 6	.93	.83	2.76
	Hon	36	Psy ICST						
Jackson (2005)	Mal	43	Corr. Prisoners	Sim.	Total	≥ 6	(.76)	(.90)+	1.86
	Hon	96	Corr. Prisoners						
	Mal	8	Psy ICST	KG*	Total	≥ 6	(.76)	(.90)+	2.80
	Hon	41	Psy ICST						
Veazey (2005)	Mal	5	Psy Inpt	KG~	Total	≥ 6	.80	.85	NA
	Hon	39	Psy Inpt						

Note. For studies, Only first author is listed. SN = sensitivity, SP = specificity, d = Cohen's d, ^{a} = d based on pooled SD. For group: Mal = malingering, Hon-honest. For sample: Corr. Psy Pt = correctional sample receiving psychiatric services, Psy ICST = defendants determined incompetent to stand trial and receiving inpatient mental health services, Corr. Prisoners = correctional prisoners, Psy Inpt = psychiatric inpatient. For design: Sim. = simulation design, KG = known-groups design. For KG designs, * = group status determined by SIRS. + = sensitivity and specificity in Jackson et al. (2005) study collapsed across KG & Sim. samples. ~ = Malingering status determined using PAI Mal index ≥ 3 as malingering.

Structured Inventory of Reported Symptoms

The Structured Inventory of Reported Symptoms (Rogers, Kropp, Bagby, & Dickens, 1992) was developed to assess malingered psychological symptoms, as well as other response sets, in a structured-interview format. The 172 items are organized into eight primary scales that have consistently shown the ability to discriminate between malingerers and honest responders, and five supplementary scales that have not proven as effective in detecting malingering or are intended to assess other response sets (inconsistency, defensiveness).

Three of the primary scales focus on very unusual symptom presentations (rare symptoms, symptom combinations, improbable symptoms, and absurd symptoms), four assess the range and severity of symptoms (blatant symptoms, subtle symptoms, selectivity of symptoms, severity of symptoms), and the final primary scale examines discrepancies between self-reports of overt symptoms and interviewer observations (reported versus observed symptoms). As with the M-FAST, the structured-interview format adds an additional dimension to data considered for identification of malingering beyond self-report testing. Finally, structured clinical interviews have

facilitated improved reliability and validity of psychiatric diagnoses and offer the same potential for the detection of malingering (Rogers, 1995).

Raw scores from each of the SIRS scales are classified as honest, indeterminate, probable feigning, or definite feigning based on extensive data from patients, prisoners, analog malingerers, and independently identified malingerers (Rogers et al., 1992). The overall results are interpreted as suggestive of feigned psychological symptoms if one or more primary scales are in the definite feigning range, if three or more primary scales are in the probable feigning range, or if the total raw score exceeds 76. Reports published by the test's authors, as well as independent investigators, have supported the accuracy of the SIRS for the detection of malingering. Interrater reliability, a key concern for interview-based data, has been reported to be quite strong (mean reliability = .96). Although the SIRS includes a supplementary consistency scale (INC), it does not appear to have been extensively validated for detection of random responding. Presumably however, the interviewer would detect random answers.

Table 9.8 presents summaries from publications that have evaluated the SIRS (the Rogers et al. [1992] manual incorporates results from several previous peer-reviewed publications on the instrument). The SIRS has been validated using both simulation and known-groups designs. Although several independent evaluations of the SIRS are available, many of the available publications unfortunately do not present data in a form easily amenable to summarizing the operating characteristics or d scores.

However, Luis (2003) has completed an unpublished meta-analysis of the SIRS for his dissertation. This analysis provides results from 13 contrasts

Table 9.8.
Results From Patient-Controlled Malingering Detection Studies Using the SIRS

Study	Group	N	Sample	Design	Scale	Cutoff	SN	SP	d^a
Rogers+	Mal.	206	Mixed	K-G*	PS	≥3 Feign	.48	.99	
1992	Hon	197	Pt/Cor/Com	Sim					
Gothard	Mal.	37	For/Cor	K-G*	PS	≥3 Feign	.97	.97	3.88
1995	Hon	78	For/Cor	Sim.					
Heinze	Mal.	33	ICST	K-G*	PS	>2 Feign	.58	.79	
2003	Hon.	33	ICST						

Note: For studies, only first author is listed. + data from several publications summarized in manual. SN = sensitivity, SP = specificity, d = Cohen's d, [a] = d calculated based on pooled SD. For Group: Mal-malingering, Hon-honest. For Sample: Mixed = forensic, correctional, community, & student, Pat = patient, Cor = correctional, Com = community, ICST = found incompetent to stand trial and hospitalized. For Design: KG Sim = includes both known groups and simulation designs. For Scale: PS = Primary Scales. For Cutoff: Feign = in probable feigning range. * = feigning status clinically-determined.

and includes both published articles and unpublished works such as conference presentations, theses, and dissertations. After culling outliers, Luis calculated a mean d of 1.62 with a 95% confidence interval of 1.47–1.78 for the SIRS primary scales. This effect size is large and consistent with those for the best validated instruments in this area.

According to the manual (Rogers et al., 1992), the specificity of the SIRS using the recommended cutting score is .99, whereas the sensitivity is .49. The specificity value is roughly confirmed by the independent work of Gothard, Viglione, Meloy, and Sherman (1995), who used the criteria recommended by Rogers et al. (1992) even though Heinze (2003) reported a somewhat lower specificity value. The high specificity for the SIRS should ensure a high PPP in most base rate environments, making it a good choice for ruling in a condition. However, the only moderate sensitivity at this cutting score will likely result in a low NPP for ruling out feigned symptom reports in most settings.

The SIRS is also one of the very few instruments evaluated for the detection of feigned psychiatric symptoms in adolescent populations (Rogers, Hinds, & Sewell, 1996). Moreover, evidence suggests that the test has only limited vulnerability to coaching (Rogers, Gillis, Bagby, & Monteiro, 1991). Additionally, in terms of neurologic control data, Hayes, Hale, and Gouvier (1998) found the SIRS accurate for use in samples of subjects with mental retardation who were being evaluated for competency to stand trial.

Overall, the SIRS appears to be among the best validated procedures for the detection of feigned psychiatric symptoms and should be carefully considered by forensic neuropsychologists. However, for use in forensic neuropsychological examinations, additional data on neurologic controls are desirable.

Evaluation of Forensic Neuropsychological Application of Instruments for the Detection of Feigned Psychiatric Symptoms

Table 9.9 summarizes the current status of the major psychiatric feigning-detection scales described in this chapter with regard to the quality-control indicators reviewed earlier and their application to forensic neuropsychological examinations. These data suggest that the two leading instruments for forensic neuropsychological purposes should be the MMPI-2 and the SIRS. Overall, the validity scales from the MMPI-2 are the most thoroughly studied of all of these procedures. Forensic neuropsychologists who use the MMPI-2 may consult the evaluations provided by multiple independent reports on the operating characteristics of validity scales with regard to varied populations. In particular, the MMPI-2 also has support from several studies that have included neurologic populations.

Table 9.9.
Quality Control Indicators for Scales for Detection of Feigned Psychiatric
Symptoms During Forensic Neuropsychological Examinations

	MMPI-2			MCMI-3		PAI			SIRS	SIMS	M-FAST
	F	F(p)	FBS	X	Z	NM	MI	RD	PS	TS	TS
Adequate # publications	Y	Y	Y	N	N	Y	Y	Y	Y	N	Y
Oper. char. from approp. samp.	Y	Y	Y	Y	Y	Y	Y	Y	Y	Y	Y
Convergence in oper. char.	?	?	Y	N	N	Y	Y	?	Y	?	Y
Appropriate predictive power	?	?	Y	N	N	Y	Y	?	Y	?	Y
Both sim. & K-G results supp.	Y	Y	Y	N	N	Y	Y	Y	Y	Y	Y
Independent cross-validation	Y	Y	Y	Y	Y	Y	Y	Y	Y	Y	Y
Neurologic control groups	Y	Y	Y	N	N	N	N	N	Y	N	N

Note: See text for definition of test acronyms and scales as well as elaboration on quality
control indicators.

The results reviewed here, as well as those presented by Nelson et al.
(2006), suggest that if false symptom complaints of injury or illness manifested in physical complaints are suspected in civil forensic cases, FBS is the
leading contender. However, if false psychiatric complaints in criminal cases
are of concern, F and Fp appear to be effective. One caveat should be carefully
considered by forensic clinicians using the MMPI-2. Reviewing all of the
available fake bad scales from the test, which potentially include F, Fp, and
FBS, as well as several indicators not reviewed in this chapter (Fb, Ds2, F–K,
O–S, etc.) and treating positive results on any one of them as indicative of
false symptom reports will elevate the overall false positive rate far beyond
that for any scale considered alone.

The other leading candidate for detection of false psychiatric symptom
reports in forensic neuropsychological examinations is the SIRS, which also
has extensive supporting published research. Two issues regarding this instrument should be noted. First, the recommended cutting score for the SIRS
(≥3 primary scales in the probably feigning range) has specificity closely
approaching 1.00 but only moderate sensitivity. This means that the PPP will
be higher than the NPP at most base rates, a profile that suggests that this
instrument is better at ruling in than ruling out feigned psychiatric symp-

toms. The second issue is that only a single work has evaluated the SIRS in a neurologic population (Hayes et al., 1998), and this sample consisted of defendants with mental retardation. Although these patients obviously experience brain dysfunction, it would be reassuring to have SIRS data available from a wider range of neurologic populations.

Two scales from the PAI are also rather strong candidates for use in detecting feigned psychiatric symptoms. Both NIM and MI meet all of the quality-control recommendations made in this chapter with the exception of evaluations in neurologic populations. Research investigating the effect of brain dysfunction on these PAI Validity scales should be a high priority and will likely provide much needed support for the use of this instrument in forensic neuropsychological evaluations.

Another very promising instrument for identifying feigned psychiatric symptoms is the M-FAST, which also meets all of the quality-control standards proposed here except for the availability of neurologic control data. Given the brevity of the M-FAST, as well as its operating characteristic profile, which lends itself to ruling out feigning (high NPP), research on the effects of brain dysfunction on responses to this instrument should be a high priority. Once these data are available, the M-FAST will likely also prove to be a very useful resource for forensic neuropsychologists.

The presently available data on the SIMS are somewhat less supportive than for several other instruments. The SIMS needs additional independent evaluations in appropriate populations, including neurologic patients in particular, before it may be recommended for forensic neuropsychological examinations. However, given the SIMS's Low Intelligence, Amnesia, and Neurologic Symptom subscales, this test could be very useful in neuropsychological settings after additional supportive published data become available.

The MCMI-III had the weakest support of all of the instruments reviewed here. The validity scales featured on this test clearly require more extensive evaluation before potentially becoming appropriate for forensic neuropsychological examinations. However, given the popularity of this test in certain settings, further research on the MCMI-III's Validity scales, especially in neurologic samples, seems urgent.

Conclusions

Because psychiatric disorders are an important consideration in forensic neuropsychological examinations and their diagnosis is heavily dependent on accurate patient self-reports of symptoms, examiners should use objective instruments for the assessment of feigned symptom reports in *all* such evaluations. This chapter has reviewed the major instruments currently available for such purposes and proposed a framework for evaluating their quality. The

presently available data point to the MMPI-2 and the SIRS as the best choices for evaluating the possibility of feigned symptom reports during forensic neuropsychological evaluations. Additionally, the PAI, SIMS, and M-FAST appear likely to become strong contenders once supporting data derived from neurologic samples become available. Finally, at present the MCMI-III does not appear to be a viable choice for detecting feigned psychiatric symptom reports during forensic neuropsychological examinations.

References

American Psychiatric Association. (2000). *Diagnostic and statistical manual of mental disorders* (4th ed., text rev.). Washington, DC: Author.

American Psychological Association. (1999). *Standards for educational and psychological testing*. Washington, DC: Author.

Arbisi, P. A., & Ben-Porath, Y. S. (1995). An MMPI-2 infrequent response scale for use with psychopathological populations: The Infrequency-Psychopathology scale, *F(p)*. *Psychological Assessment, 4,* 424–431.

Arbisi, P. A., & Ben-Porath, Y. S. (1998). The ability of the Minnesota Multiphasic Personality Inventory-2 Validity scales to detect fake-bad responses in psychiatric inpatients. *Psychological Assessment, 10,* 221–228.

Arbisi, P. A., & Butcher, J. N. (2004). Failure of the FBS to predict malingering of somatic symptoms: Response to critiques by Greve and Bianchini and Lees-Haley and Fox. *Archives of Clinical Neuropsychology, 19,* 341–345.

Archer, R. P., Handel, R. W., Greene, R. L., Baer, R. A., & Elkins, D. E. (in press). An evaluation of the usefulness of the MMPI-2 *F(p)* scale. *Journal of Personality Assessment.*

Bagby, R. M., Nicholson, R. A., Bacchiochi, J. R., Ryder, A. G., & Bury, A. S. (2002). The predictive capacity of the MMPI-2 and PAI Validity scales to detect coached and uncoached feigning. *Journal of Personality Assessment, 78,* 69–86.

Bagby, R. M., Nicholson, R. A., Buis, T., & Bacchiochi, J. R. (2000). Can the MMPI-2 Validity scales detect depression feigned by experts? *Assessment, 7,* 55–62.

Bagby, R. M., Rogers, R., & Buis, T. (1994). Detecting malingered and defensive responding on the MMPI-2 in a forensic inpatient sample. *Journal of Personality Assessment, 62,* 191–203.

Bagby, R. M., Rogers, R., Buis, T., & Kalemba, V. (1994). Malingered and defensive response styles on the MMPI-2: An examination of validity scales. *Assessment, 1,* 31–38.

Berry, D. T. R., Adams, J. F., Clark, C. D., Thacker, S. R., Burger, T. L., Wetter, M. W., et al. (1996). Detection of a cry for help on the MMPI-2: An analog investigation. *Journal of Personality Assessment, 67,* 26–36.

Berry, D. T. R., Baer, R. A., & Harris, M. J. (1991). Detection of malingering on the MMPI: A meta-analytic review. *Clinical Psychology Review, 11,* 585–598.

Berry, D. T. R., Baer, R. A., Rinaldo, J. C., & Wetter, M. W. (2002). Assessment of malingering. In J. N. Butcher (Ed.), *Clinical personality assessment: Practical approaches* (2nd ed., pp. 269–302). New York: Oxford University Press.

Bianchini, K. J., Mathias, C. W., & Greve, K. W. (2001). Symptom validity testing: A critical review. *The Clinical Neuropsychologist, 15,* 19–45.

Blanchard, D. D., McGrath, R. E., Pogge, D. L., & Khadivi, A. (2003). *Journal of Personality Assessment, 80,* 197–205.

Brulot, M. M., Strauss, E., & Spellacy, F. (1997). Validity of the Minnesota Multiphasic Personality Inventory-2 correction factors for use with patients with suspected head injury. *The Clinical Neuropsychologist, 11,* 391–401.

Bury, A. S., & Bagby, R. M. (2002). The detection of feigned uncoached and coached posttraumatic stress disorder with the MMPI-2 in a sample of workplace accident victims. *Psychological Assessment, 14,* 472–484.

Bush, S. S., Ruff, R. M., Troster, A. I., Barth, J. T., Koffler, S. P., Pliskin, N. H., et al. (2005). Symptom validity assessment: Practice issues and medical necessity. *Archives of Clinical Neuropsychology, 20,* 419–426.

Butcher, J. N., Arbisi, P. A., Atlis, M. M., & McNulty, J. L. (2003). The construct validity of the Lees-Haley Fake Bad scale: Does this measure somatic malingering and feigned emotional distress? *Archives of Clinical Neuropsychology, 18,* 473–485.

Butcher, J. N., Dahlstrom, W. G., Graham, J. R., Tellegen, A., & Kaemmer, B. (1989). *MMPI-2: Manual for administration and scoring.* Minneapolis: University of Minnesota Press.

Calhouns, P. S., Earnst, K. S., Tucker, D. D., Kirby, A. C., & Beckham, J. C. (2000). Feigning combat-related posttraumatic stress disorder on the PAI. *Journal of Personality Assessment, 73,* 338–350.

Daubert vs. Merrell, Dow Pharmaceuticals, Inc., 113 S. Ct. 2786 (1993).

Daubert, S. D., & Metzler, A. E. (2000). The detection of fake-bad and fake-good responding on the Millon Clinical Multiaxial Inventory III. *Psychological Assessment, 12,* 418–424.

Dearth, C. D., Berry, D. T. R., Vickery, C. D., Vagnini, V. L., Baser, R. E., Orey, S. A., et al. (2005). Detection of feigned head-injury symptoms on the MMPI-2 in head-injured patients and community controls. *Archives of Clinical Neuropsychology, 20,* 95–110.

Elhai, J. D., Gold, P. B., Frueh, B. C., & Gold, S. N. (2000). Cross-validation of the MMPI-2 in detecting malingered posttraumatic stress disorder. *Journal of Personality Assessment, 75,* 449–463.

Frederick, R. I. (2000). Mixed-group validation: A method to address the limitations of criterion group validation in research on malingering detection. *Behavioral Sciences and the Law, 18,* 693–718.

Gass, C. S. (2002). Personality assessment of neurologically impaired patients. In J. N. Butcher (Ed.), *Clinical personality assessment: Practical approaches* (2nd ed., pp. 208–224). New York: Oxford University Press.

Gothard, S., Viglione, D. J., Meloy, J. R., & Sherman, M. (1995). The detection of malingering in competency to stand trial evaluations. *Law and Human Behavior, 19,* 493–505.

Graham, J. R., Watts, D., & Timbrook, R. E. (1991). Detecting fake good and fake bad MMPI-2 profiles. *Journal of Personality Assessment, 57,* 264–277.

Granhag, P. A., & Strömwell, L. A. (2004). *The detection of deception in forensic contexts.* New York: Cambridge University Press.

Greiffenstein, M. F., Baker, W. J., Axelrod, B., Peck, E. A., & Gervais, R. (2004). The Fake Bad scale and MMPI-2 F-family in detection of implausible psychological trauma claims. *The Clinical Neuropsychologist, 18,* 573–590.

Greiffenstein, M. F., Baker, W. J., Gola, T., Donders, J., & Miller, L. (2002). The Fake Bad Scale in atypical and severe closed head injury litigants. *Journal of Clinical Psychology, 58,* 1591–1600.

Greiffenstein, M. F., & Cohen, L. (2005). Neuropsychology and the law: Principles of productive attorney-neuropsychologist relations. In G. J. Larrabee (Ed.), *Forensic neuropsychology: A scientific approach* (pp. 29–91). New York: Oxford University Press.

Greiffenstein, M. F., Gola, T., & Baker, W. J. (1995). MMPI-2 Validity scales versus domain-specific measures in detection of factitious traumatic brain injury. *The Clinical Neuropsychologist, 3,* 230–240.

Greve, K. W., & Bianchini, K. J. (2004). Response to Butcher et al., the construct validity of the Lees-Haley Fake Bad Scale: Does this measure somatic malingering and feigned emotional distress? *Archives of Clinical Neuropsychology, 19,* 337–339.

Greve, K. W., Bianchini, K. J., Love, J. M., Brennan, A., & Heinly, M. T. (2006). Sensitivity and specificity of MMPI-2 Validity scales and indicators to malingered neurocognitive dysfunction in traumatic brain injury. *The Clinical Neuropsychologist, 20,* 491–512.

Guy, L. S., & Miller, H. A. (2004). Screening for malingered psychopathology in a correctional setting: Utility of the Miller-Forensic Assessment of Symptoms Test (M-FAST). *Criminal Justice and Behavior, 31,* 695–716.

Hayes, J. S., Hale, D. B., & Gouvier, W. D. (1998). Malingering detection in a mentally retarded forensic population. *Applied Neuropsychology, 5,* 33–36.

Heaton, R. K., Smith, H. H., Lehman, R. A., & Vogt, A. J. (1978). Prospects for feigning believable deficits on neuropsychological testing. *Journal of Consulting and Clinical Psychology, 46,* 892–900.

Heinze, M. C. (2003). Developing sensitivity to distortion: Utility of psychological tests in differentiating malingering and psychopathology in criminal defendants. *Journal of Forensic Psychiatry and Psychology, 14,* 151–177.

Hom, J., & Denney, R. L. (2002). Preface. *Journal of Forensic Neuropsychology, 2,* xv–xx.

Iverson, G. L., & Binder, L. M. (2000). Detecting exaggeration and malingering in neuropsychological assessment. *Journal of Head Trauma Rehabilitation, 15,* 829–858.

Iverson, G. L., Franzen, M. D., & Hammond, J. A. (1995). An examination of inmates' ability to malinger on the MMPI-2. *Psychological Assessment, 7,* 118–121.

Jackson, R. L., Rogers, R., & Sewell, K. W. (2005). Forensic applications of the Miller Forensic Assessment of Symptoms Test (MFAST): Screening for feigned disorders in competency to stand trial evaluations. *Law and Human Behavior, 29,* 199–210.

Kraemer, H. C. (1992). *Evaluating medical tests: Objective and quantitative guidelines.* Newbury Park, CA: Sage.

Kupfer, D. J., First, M. B., & Regier, D. E. (2002). Introduction. In D. J. Kupfer, M. B. First, & D. E. Regier (Eds.), *A research agenda for DSM-V* (pp. xv–xxviii). Washington, DC: American Psychiatric Association.

Larrabee, G. J. (1998). Somatic malingering on the MMPI and MMPI-2 in personal injury litigants. *The Clinical Neuropsychologist, 12,* 179–188.

Larrabee, G. J. (2003). Detection of symptom exaggeration with the MMPI-2 in litigants with malingered neurocognitive dysfunction. *The Clinical Neuropsychologist, 17,* 54–68.

Larrabee, G. J. (2005a). Assessment of malingering. In G. J. Larrabee (Ed.), *Forensic neuropsychology: A scientific approach* (pp. 115–158). New York: Oxford University Press.

Larrabee, G. J. (2005b). *Forensic neuropsychology: A scientific approach.* New York: Oxford University Press.

Larrabee, G. J. (2005c). A scientific approach to forensic neuropsychology. In G. J. Larrabee (Ed.), *Forensic neuropsychology: A scientific approach* (pp. 3–28). New York: Oxford University Press.

Lees-Haley, P. R. (1992). Efficacy of MMPI-2 Validity scales and MCMI-II Modifier scales for detecting spurious PTSD claims: F, F-K, Fake Bad Scale, ego strength, subtle-obvious subscales, DIS, & DEB. *Journal of Clinical Psychology, 48,* 681–688.

Lees-Haley, P. R., English, L. T., & Glenn, W. J. (1991). A Fake Bad Scale on the MMPI-2 for personal-injury claimants. *Psychological Reports, 68,* 203–210.

Lees-Haley, P. R., & Fox, D. D. (2004). Commentary on Butcher, Arbisi, Atlis, & McNulty (2003) on the Fake Bad Scale. *Archives of Clinical Neuropsychology, 19,* 333–336.

Lewis, J. L., Simcox, A. J., & Berry, D. T. R. (2002). Screening for feigned psychiatric symptoms in a forensic sample by using the MMPI-2 and the structured inventory of malingered symptomatology. *Psychological Assessment, 14,* 170–176.

Liljequist, L., Kinder, B. N., Schinka, J. A. (1998). An investigation of malingering posttraumatic stress disorder on the Personality Assessment Inventory. *Journal of Personality Assessment, 71,* 322–336.

Luis, J. (2003). Efficacy of the Structured Inventory of Reported Symptoms (SIRS): A meta-analysis. *Dissertation Abstracts International, 63,* 10B. (UMI No. AAI3067819)

Merckelbach, H., & Smith, G. P. (2003). Diagnostic accuracy of the Structured Interview of Malingered Symptomatology (SIMS) in detecting instructed malingering. *Archives of Clinical Neuropsychology, 18,* 145–152.

Miller, H. A. (2001). *Miller-Forensic Assessment of Symptoms Test (M-FAST): Professional manual.* Odessa, FL: Psychological Assessment Resources.

Miller, H. A. (2004). Examining the use of the M-FAST with criminal defendants incompetent to stand trial. *International Journal of Offender Therapy and Comparative Criminology, 48,* 268–280.

Millon, T. (1987). *Manual for the MCMI-II.* Minneapolis: National Computer Systems.

Millon, T., Davis, R., & Millon, C. (1997). *Millon Clinical Multiaxial Inventory III, manual* (2nd ed.). Minneapolis: National Computer Systems.

Mittenberg, W., Patton, C., Canyock, E. M., & Condit, D. C. (2002). Base rates of malingering and symptom exaggeration. *Journal of Clinical and Experimental Psychology, 24,* 1094–1102.

Morey, L. C. (1991). *Personality Assessment Inventory professional manual.* Odessa, FL: Psychological Assessment Resources.

Morey, L. C. (1993, August). Defensiveness and malingering indices for the PAI. Paper presented at the meeting of the American Psychological Association, Toronto.

Morey, L. C., & Lanier, V. W. (1998). Operating characteristics of six response distortion indicators for the Personality Assessment Inventory. *Assessment, 5,* 203–214.

Nelson, N. W., Sweet, J. J., & Demakis, G. J. (2006). Meta-analysis of the MMPI-2 Fake Bad scale: Utility in forensic settings. *The Clinical Neuropsychologist, 20,* 39–58.

Norris, M. P., & May, M. C. (1998). Screening for malingering in a correctional setting. *Law and Human Behavior, 22,* 315–323.

Pensa, R., Dorfman, W. J., Gold, S. N., & Schneider, B. (1996). Detection of malingered psychosis with the MMPI-2. *Psychotherapy in Private Practice, 14,* 47–62.

Pope, K. S., Butcher, J. N., & Seelen, J. (2000). Some final thoughts. In J. N. Butcher & K. S. Pope (Eds.), *The MMPI, MMPI-2, and MMPI-A in court: A practical guide for expert witnesses and attorneys* (2nd ed., pp. 225–231). Washington, DC: American Psychological Association.

Rogers, R. (1995). *Diagnostic and structured interviewing: A handbook for psychologists.* Odessa, FL: Psychological Assessment Resources.

Rogers, R. (Ed.). (1997). *Clinical assessment of malingering and deception* (2nd ed.). New York: Guilford.

Rogers, R., Bagby, R. M., & Chakraborty, D. (1993). Feigning schizophrenic disorders on the MMPI-2: Detection of coached simulators. *Journal of Personality Assessment, 60,* 215–226.

Rogers, R., Bagby, R. M., & Dickens, S. E. (1992). *SIRS, Structured Interview of Reported Symptoms: A professional manual.* Odessa, FL: Psychological Assessment Resources.

Rogers, R., & Bender, S. D. (2003). Evaluation of malingering and deception. In A. Goldstein (Ed.), *Handbook of psychology: Vol. 11. Forensic psychology* (pp. 109–129). Hoboken, NJ: Wiley.

Rogers, R., Gillis, J. R., Bagby, R. M. & Monteiro, E. (1991). Detection of malingering on the Structured Interview of Reported Symptoms (SIRS): A study of coached and uncoached simulators. *Psychological Assessment, 3,* 673–677.

Rogers, R., Hinds, J. D., & Sewell, K. W. (1996). Feigning psychopathology among adolescent offenders: Validation of the SIRS, MMPI-A, and SIMS. *Journal of Personality Assessment, 67,* 244–257.

Rogers, R., Kropp, P. R., Bagby, R. M., & Dickens, S. E. (1992). Faking specific disorders: A study of the Structured Interview of Reported Symptoms (SIRS). *Journal of Clinical Psychology, 48,* 643–648.

Rogers, R., Salekin, R. T., Sewell, K. W., Goldstein, A., & Leonard, K. (1998). A comparison of forensic and nonforensic malingerers: A prototypical analysis of explanatory models. *Law and Human Behavior, 22,* 353–367.

Rogers, R., Sewell, K. W., & Goldstein, A. (1994). Explanatory models of malingering: A prototypical analysis. *Law and Human Behavior, 18,* 543–552.

Rogers, R., Sewell, K. W., Martin, M. A., & Vitacco, M. J. (2003). Detection of feigned mental disorders: A meta-analysis of the MMPI-2 and malingering. *Assessment, 10,* 160–177.

Rogers, R., Sewell, K. W., Morey, L. C., & Ustad, K. L. (1996). Detection of feigned mental disorders on the Personality Assessment Inventory: A discriminant analysis. *Journal of Personality Assessment, 67,* 626–640.

Rogers, R., Sewell, K. W., & Salekin, R. T. (1994). A meta-analysis of malingering on the MMPI-2. *Assessment, 1,* 227–237.

Rogers, R., Sewell, K. W., & Ustad, K. L. (1995). Feigning among chronic outpatients on the MMPI-2: A systematic examination of fake-bad indicators. *Assessment, 2,* 81–89.

Rogers, R., Ustad, K. L., & Salekin, R. T. (1998). Convergent validity of the Personality Assessment Inventory: A study of emergency referrals in a correctional setting. *Assessment, 5,* 3–12.

Ross, S. R., Millis, S. R., Krukowski, R. A., Putnam, S. H., & Adams, K. M. (2004). Detecting incomplete effort on the MMPI-2: An examination of the Fake Bad Scale in mild head injury. *Journal of Clinical and Experimental Neuropsychology, 26,* 115–124.

Schoenberg, M. R., Dorr, D., & Morgan, C. D. (2003). The ability of the Millon Clinical Multiaxial Inventory, third edition, to detect malingering. *Psychological Assessment, 15,* 198–204.

Scragg, P., Bor, R., & Mendham, M. C. (2000). Feigning post-traumatic stress disorder on the PAI. *Clinical Psychology and Psychotherapy, 7,* 155–160.

Sivec, H. J., Hilsenroth, M. J., & Lynn, S. J. (1995). Impact of simulating borderline personality disorder on the MMPI-2: A cost-benefits model employing base rates. *Journal of Personality Assessment, 64,* 295–311.

Slick, D. J., Sherman, E. M. S., & Iverson, G. L. (1999). Diagnostic criteria for malingered neurocognitive dysfunction: Proposed standards for clinical practice and research. *The Clinical Neuropsychologist, 13,* 545–561.

Smith, G. P. (1992). *Detection of malingering: A validation study of the SLAM test.* Unpublished doctoral dissertation, University of Missouri, St. Louis.

Smith, G. P., & Burger, G. K. (1997). Detection of malingering: Validation of the Structured Inventory of Malingered Symptomatology (SIMS). *Journal of the American Academy of Psychiatry and the Law, 25,* 183–189.

Storm, J., & Graham, J. R. (2000). Detection of coached general malingering on the MMPI-2. *Psychological Assessment, 12,* 158–165.

Sweet, J. J. (1999). *Forensic neuropsychology.* Exton, PA: Swets and Zeitlinger.

Ustad, K. L. (1996). *Assessment of malingering on the SADS in a jail referral sample.* Unpublished doctoral dissertation, University of North Texas, Denton.

Veazey, C. H., Hays, J. R., Wagner, A. L., & Miller, H. A. (2005). Validity of the Miller Forensic Assessment of Symptoms Test in psychiatric inpatients. *Psychological Reports, 96,* 771–774.

Vickery, C. D., Berry, D. T. R., Inman, T. H., Harris, M. J., & Orey, S. A. (2001). Detection of inadequate effort on neuropsychological testing: A meta-analytic review of selected procedures. *Archives of Clinical Neuropsychology, 16,* 45–73.

Victor, T. L., & Abeles, N. (2004). Coaching clients to take psychological and neuropsychological tests: A clash of ethical obligations. *Professional Psychology: Research and Practice, 35,* 373–379.

Wang, E. W., Rogers, R., Giles, C. L., Diamond, P. M., Herrington-Wang, L. E., & Taylor, E. R. (1997). A pilot study of the Personality Assessment Inventory (PAI) in corrections: Assessment of malingering, suicide risk, and aggression in male inmates. *Behavioral Sciences and the Law, 15,* 469–482.

Wetter, M. W., Baer, R. A., Berry, D. T. R., Robeson, L. H., & Sumpter, J. (1993). MMPI-2 profiles of motivated fakers given specific symptom information: A comparison to matched patients. *Psychological Assessment, 5,* 317–323.

Wetter, M. W., Baer, R. A., Berry, D. T. R., Smith, G. T., & Larsen, L. H. (1992). Sensitivity of MMPI-2 Validity scales to random responding and malingering. *Psychological Assessment, 4,* 369–374.

Widows, M. R., & Smith, G. P. (2005). *Structured Inventory of Malingered Symptomatology: Professional manual.* Odessa, FL: Psychological Assessment Resources.

Wiener, D. W. (1948). Subtle and obvious keys for the MMPI. *Journal of Consulting Psychology, 12,* 164–170.

10

Evaluation of Exaggerated Health and Injury Symptomatology

Glenn J. Larrabee

Persons who undergo neuropsychological evaluation because of claimed injuries from a traumatic accident or because of alleged deficits resulting from illness in the context of a disability claim commonly report symptoms in three general clusters: (a) somatic concerns such as pain and fatigue, (b) cognitive concerns such as reduced concentration and poor memory, and (c) emotional concerns such as depression, anxiety, and irritability.

These symptoms are not specific to a particular condition, such as concussion or neurotoxic exposure, but are also seen in patients claiming primary psychiatric disability (Lees-Haley and Brown, 1993). Moreover, pain patients without neurologic dysfunction frequently complain of cognitive symptoms similar to those reported by patients with postconcussion syndrome (Iverson and McCracken, 1997; Muñoz & Esteve, 2005). Additionally, patients who allege disability due to pain disorder show a high frequency of failure on symptom validity tests (Gervais, Russell, Green, Allen, Ferrari, et al., 2001; Meyers & Diep, 2000). The recent extension of the Slick, Sherman, and Iverson (1999) criteria for malingered neurocognitive dysfunction (MND) to malingered pain-related disability by Bianchini, Greve, and Glynn (2005) includes measures of both effort and symptom exaggeration as part of the criteria for response bias. Financial incentive effect sizes based on performance measures for traumatic brain injury (.47; Binder & Rohling, 1996) are essentially identical to those based on pain rating scales for chronic pain (.48; Rohling, Binder, & Langhinrischen-Rohling, 1995). These data support the importance of assessing exaggerated health and injury symptomatology.

Detection of symptom exaggeration in relation to legitimate symptom reporting differs from detection of invalid effort in relation to legitimate neuropsychological impairment. Measures of symptom validity used to evaluate effort do not show strong correlations with actual measures of neuropsychological function in non-compensation-seeking patients (Larrabee, 2003a). Typically, patients with objectively demonstrated memory impairment can perform nearly perfectly on tasks such as the Test of Memory Malingering (TOMM; Tombaugh, 1996). This is because the tasks comprising procedures such as the TOMM are actually quite easy to do. By contrast, it is not possible to create symptom report validity measures that are not correlated with scales related to actual legitimate symptom reporting. Thus, the *F, Fb,* and *Fp* scales of the MMPI-2 (Butcher, Graham, Ben-Porath, Tellegen, Dahlstrom, et al., 2001) all correlate with scales *Pa* and *Sc* (ibid.), just as the Lees-Haley Fake Bad Scale (FBS; Lees-Haley, English, & Glenn, 1991) correlates with scales *Hs, D, Hy, Pt,* and *Sc* (Larrabee, 2003b). These validity scales are useful in defining ranges of symptom reporting that do not occur in non-compensation-seeking patients but occur only in litigants/compensation seekers showing other evidence for malingering.

The *accuracy-of-knowledge* model proposed by Lanyon (1997) provides a framework for developing measures of symptom exaggeration for symptom-report-based scales such as the MMPI-2 and the Personality Assessment Inventory (PAI; Morey, 1991). The accuracy-of-knowledge model holds that, for deception to succeed, the deceiver must have accurate knowledge of the target condition. Successful deceivers know both the *facts* about the condition and how to *behave* like a person who has the target characteristic. Three ways in which deception can be detected are (a) lack of uncommon knowledge (e.g., the Subtle subscale items on the MMPI-2), (b) erroneous stereotype (e.g., reporting total loss of childhood memories in feigned amnesia); and (c) overendorsement (e.g., endorsing more pain symptomatology, pain disability, and showing more somatic preoccupation than the typical pain patient; Larrabee, 2003d).

Lanyon (2001) has also demonstrated the occurrence of at least three types of self-serving misrepresentation in forensic assessment. Based on a large sample of forensic cases including child-custody cases, personal-injury litigation, sex offenses, and other criminal offenses, Lanyon identified three factors: (a) report of extreme virtue (e.g., elevated MMPI-2 *L* scale); (b) exaggeration of psychopathology (e.g., elevations on MMPI-2 *F* scale); and (c) overreporting of health concerns (e.g., elevations on MMPI-2 *Hs* and *Hy* scales). Consistent with Lanyon's findings, I (Larrabee, 2003c) have described two types of symptom overreporting on the MMPI-2: (a) exaggerated psychopathology (represented by elevations on *F* and MMPI-2 scales *Pa* and *Sc;* see Graham, Watts, & Timbrook, 1991) and (b) exaggerated health and injury symptoms (represented by elevations on the FBS and on scales *Hs, D,* and *Hy;* Larrabee, 2003b, 2003c; Ross, Millis, Krukowski, Putnam, & Adams, 2004).

This chapter focuses on the detection of overreporting of health and injury symptomatology on the MMPI-2, as well as on specialized measures of pain and health concerns. The overreporting of psychiatric symptoms is covered by Berry and Schipper in chapter 9.

Overreporting of Health Concerns on the MMPI-2

In a review of the MMPI, Butcher and Harlow (1987) concluded that elevations on *Hs* and *Hy* were the most predictive of malingering in personal-injury settings, in comparison to all other MMPI scales. Subsequently, Sivec, Lynn, and Garske (1994) found that college students simulating somatoform disorder on the MMPI-2 produced high scores on scales *Hs* and *Hy* and also had an elevated *F* scale. These somatoform dissimulators produced slightly higher scores on *Hs* and *Hy* than a group of paranoid dissimulators, although the mean scores were not significantly different.

By contrast, the somatoform dissimulators produced significantly lower scores on *F, Pa,* and *Sc* compared to college students simulating paranoid psychosis. Lees-Haley (1997) also found that the most common 2-point MMPI-2 code type was *Hs* and *Hy* for both male and female personal-injury litigants. Lanyon and Almer (2002) found that litigating personal-injury claimants produced higher scores on *Hs, D,* and *Hy* than did nonlitigants. Of interest, *Hs* and *Hy* discriminated between litigants alleging physical injury and nonlitigants, as well as between litigants alleging psychological injury alone and nonlitigating psychologically injured persons.

Recognizing a different pattern of symptom reporting in personal-injury litigants than was captured by overendorsement on the *F* scale, Lees-Haley and colleagues (Lees-Haley et al., 1991; Lees-Haley, 1992) developed a scale that would be sensitive to personal-injury symptom exaggeration, the FBS. The FBS was constructed on a rational content basis, taking into consideration unpublished frequency counts of probable malingerers' MMPI-2 test data and responses that fit a model of goal-directed behavior focused on (a) appearing honest, (b) appearing psychologically normal except for the influence of the alleged cause of injury, (c) avoiding admitting preexisting psychopathology, (d) attempting to minimize the impact of previously disclosed preexisting complaints, (e) minimizing or hiding preinjury antisocial or illegal behavior, and (f) presenting a degree of injury or disability within perceived limits of plausibility.

The FBS contains 18 items scored in the "true" direction and 25 items scored in the "false" direction. Content analysis (Butcher, Arbisi, Atlis, & McNulty, 2003) suggests five groups of items: (a) somatic symptoms, (b) sleep disturbance, (c) tension or stress, (d) low energy/anhedonia, and (e) denial of deviant attitudes or behaviors.

In the initial FBS study Lees-Haley et al. (1991) found that the optimal FBS cutoff was 20 or higher. This limit correctly identified 96% of

personal-injury litigants suspected of malingering (based on factors such as surveillance video) and 90% of personal-injury litigants believed to be making a valid presentation of psychological injury. This investigation also utilized groups of noninjured simulators and found that 88% of the motor-vehicle-accident simulation group were correctly identified, compared with 53% of a group simulating emotional distress to toxic exposure and 83% of a group simulating emotional reaction to employment stress.

Subsequently, Lees-Haley (1992) recommended cutoffs of 24 or higher for males and 26 or higher for females for discriminating litigants with pseudo-PTSD from litigants with legitimate psychological claims. Of male and female pseudo-PTSD claimants, 75% and 74%, respectively, were identified. By contrast, 96% of males and 92% of females who had legitimate psychological claims were correctly identified.

Using the FBS cutoffs of 24 or higher for males and 26 or higher for females, I (Larrabee, 1998) found that 11 of 12 litigants with independent objective evidence of malingering on procedures such as the Rey 15-item Test (Rey, 1964, as cited in Lezak, Howieson, & Loring, 2004) and the Portland Digit Recognition Test (PDRT; Binder, 1993) produced elevated scores, compared to only 3 of 12 with F scores greater than T 69 for the MMPI or T 64 for the MMPI-2. Additionally, the sample of probable malingerers produced scores on scale Hy that exceeded those produced by noninjured persons simulating a somatoform disorder on the MMPI-2 (Sivec et al., 1994).

Miller and Donders (2001) found that litigating patients with mild TBI produced higher FBS scores than nonlitigating patients with mild TBI. Moreover, the litigating mild TBI patients were twice as likely to produce FBS scores greater than 23 for males and 25 for females. Miller and Donders also found that the mild TBI litigants and nonlitigants both produced higher FBS scores than a group of patients with moderate or severe TBI, leading them to advise caution if relying solely on the FBS as an indicator of symptom exaggeration.

Martens, Donders, and Millis (2001) replicated the Miller and Donders (2001) finding of higher FBS scores for litigating subjects with mild TBI compared to the FBS scores of patients with moderate and/or severe TBI. Prior psychiatric history was associated with elevations on the FBS in both litigating and nonlitigating mild TBI patients. Additionally, Martens et al. found an association between the FBS and measures of invalid effort derived from the California Verbal Learning Test (CVLT; Delis, Kramer, Kaplan, & Ober, 1987). Not a single patient with moderate or severe TBI produced invalid scores on both the FBS and the CVLT, demonstrating that the use of multiple independent criteria to determine invalid response set improved the diagnostic accuracy for malingering.

Greiffenstein, Baker, Gola, Donders, and Miller (2002) have correctly identified 57% of litigants with atypical symptom history/outcome following mild TBI and 96% of nonlitigating patients with moderate-to-severe TBI using an FBS cutoff above 23. These authors found an association between

the FBS and the presence of anosmia and residual motor impairment in their litigating moderate-to-severe TBI patients. The FBS correlated with a Symptom Improbability Rating Scale and with measures of invalid neuropsychological test performance, including the PDRT-27, the Rey 15-ItemTest, and Rey's Word Recognition List in the litigating mild TBI sample with atypical outcome but did not correlate with these variables in the litigating group with moderate-to-severe TBI.

Meyers, Millis, and Volkert (2002) developed a composite weighted validity index for the MMPI-2 based on the T score for F, the raw F minus K difference, Fp, Dissimulation scale (Revised), Ego Strength (ES), sum difference of Subtle minus Obvious scores, and the FBS. The empirically derived cutoff score for this index was set to have 100% specificity (i.e., none of 100 nonlitigating chronic-pain patients were identified) and identified 36% of litigating chronic pain patients, as well as 86% of noninjured persons attempting to simulate chronic pain impairment. The FBS scores greater than 24 identified 42% of the litigating patients with chronic pain and correctly identified 84% of the nonlitigants. No nonlitigating chronic pain patient scored more than 29 on the FBS.

I (Larrabee, 2003c) found that the FBS was significantly more sensitive to the detection of symptom exaggeration than F, Fb, or Fp in 33 litigants with definite or probable malingered neurocognitive dysfunction (Slick et al., 1999). Additionally, the MMPI-2 profiles of the definite/probable malingerers were characterized by significantly higher elevations on scales Hs, Hy, and Pt than scores produced by several clinical groups, including nonlitigating severe TBI, multiple sclerosis, spinal-cord injury, chronic pain, and depression. The definite/probable malingerers also produced significantly higher elevations on scales D and Sc than all of the other clinical groups, with the exception of the depressed patient group. These data, showing elevations on the FBS and scales Hs, D, Hy, Pt, and Sc for personal-injury definite/probable malingerers were contrasted with the Graham et al. (1991) profile for students who were simulating psychosis, characterized by significant elevations on F and on scales Pa and Sc, showing at least two patterns of malingering on the MMPI-2: malingered injury and malingered severe psychiatric disturbance.

In a subsequent investigation, I (Larrabee, 2003b) found that the FBS was superior to F, Fb, Fp, Meyer's Weighted Validity Index, F minus K, Dissimulation scale (Revised), Subtle minus Obvious difference, and ES in discriminating 26 litigants with definite MND (scoring worse than chance on the PDRT) from 29 patients with moderate or severe TBI. In a larger sample that combined the definite MND, moderate or severe TBI, and additional litigants with probable MND, the FBS was the only MMPI-2 validity scale that correlated significantly with the PDRT. The FBS correlated most strongly with ES and the Meyers Index and showed the strongest correlations with Hs, D, Hy, and Pt. Consistent with my earlier investigation showing that scales Hs, D, Hy, Pt, and Sc were higher in probable malingerers compared to other clinical groups (Larrabee, 2003c), these five clinical scales correlated

significantly with the PDRT. By contrast, *F*, *Fb*, and *Fp* did not correlate significantly with the PDRT. Interestingly, scales *Hs* and *Hy* did not add any additional discriminative variance to group separation when contrasted with the discrimination provided by the FBS alone, but the FBS added significant discriminative variance to that provided by either *Hs* or *Hy* in differentiating between the definite MND and moderate or severe TBI. A cutting score above either 20 or 21 provided optimal discrimination between the definite MND and moderate-to-severe TBI, with a sensitivity of .808 and specificity of .862. No moderate or severe TBI patient scored above 30 on the FBS, and only one scored higher than 25.

Ross et al. (2004) found that an FBS cutting score above either 20 or 21 was effective in discriminating 59 probable malingerers from 59 nonlitigating patients with moderate-to-severe TBI, which is the exact same score established in the Larrabee (2003c) investigation. This score yielded a 90% specificity and a 90% sensitivity. None of their nonlitigating moderate-to-severe TBI patients scored higher than 26 on the FBS.

In an investigation that included subjects from my other studies (Larrabee, 1998, 2003b, 2003c), plus additional clinical and malingering subjects, the FBS was the single most sensitive measure for discriminating between definite MND and moderate-to-severe TBI when compared to other measures of motivational impairment derived from Benton Visual Form Discrimination, Finger Tapping, Reliable Digit Span, and Wisconsin Card Sorting Test Failure to Maintain Set (Larrabee, 2003a). The FBS remained the most frequently failed validity indicator in a cross-validation that discriminated litigants with probable MND from groups of nonlitigating neurologic and psychiatric patients.

Dearth, Berry, Vickery, Vagnini, Baser, et al. (2005) compared the MMPI-2 results of four groups of college students: (a) history of mild TBI taking the MMPI-2 honestly, (b) history of mild TBI taking the MMPI-2 under instructions to feign head-injury symptoms, (c) no history of mild TBI taking the MMPI-2 honestly, and (d) no history of mild TBI taking the MMPI-2 under instructions to feign head-injury symptoms. Large effect sizes were obtained for the instructional set (malingered vs. honest) for all clinical scales, with the largest effect sizes for Scale 7 (1.74) and Scale 1 (1.52). The instructional set effect sizes were 2.00 for *F*, 1.38 for *Fb*, 1.26 for *Fp*, 1.69 for *Ds-2*, and 1.39 for the FBS. Head-injured malingerer versus head-injured control contrasts showed combined hit rates of .69 for *F* (T > 107), .72 for *Fb* (T > 108), .64 for *Fp* (T > 100), .67 for *Ds-2* (> 35 raw score), and .72 for FBS ($\geq$ 22 raw score). Dearth et al. stated that the FBS did not show the clear superiority over the *F* scale family in their investigation that others had found and conjectured that this result might have been the consequence of using a simulation rather than a known-groups design.

Greve, Bianchini, Love, Brennan, and Heinly (2006) used a known-groups design based on the Slick et al. (1999) diagnostic criteria for malingered neurocognitive dysfunction to contrast malingering and nonmalingering

traumatic brain injury and neurologic and psychiatric clinical patients. These authors present numerous tables for various MMPI-2 Validity scales, including the *F* scale family, *Ds-r*, and the FBS, as well as the score distributions for these scales for various subject classifications, including those without malingered neurocognitive dysfunction, those with incentive only, and those with suspected MND, and probable and/or definite MND. An FBS score of 27 or greater had a sensitivity of .46 and specificity of .96, whereas a score of 25 or greater had a sensitivity of .52 and specificity of .89. By contrast, an *F* scale of T 80 or higher had a sensitivity of .30 and specificity of .96, and an *F* scale of T 70 or higher had a sensitivity of .50 and specificity of .91. An *Fb* score of T 70 or higher had a sensitivity of .54 and specificity of .87. The authors concluded that *Fb*, *Ds-r*, and ES showed the best overall positive predictive power. The FBS had its best positive predictive power in mild TBI, where it detected 40% of probable/definite malingerers with no false positives at a score of 30 or higher. Greve et al. noted that these data were consistent with several other studies in demonstrating that FBS scores of 30 or greater were quite specific to malingering.

Others have also found the FBS to be sensitive to the presence of symptom exaggeration in mixed personal-injury samples. Posthuma and Harper (1998) found that the FBS was elevated in a sample of personal-injury litigants contrasted with FBS scores produced by a child-custody litigant sample. Tshushima and Tshushima (2001) found that only the FBS significantly discriminated a sample of personal-injury litigants from a sample of clinical patients. The FBS also had the largest effect size contrasting the personal-injury group with a group of job applicants undergoing employment screening.

Several investigations have reported on correlations of the FBS with other measures of symptom validity, supporting the construct validity of the FBS. Slick, Hopp, Strauss, and Spellacy (1996) reported more significant correlations of the FBS with the Victoria Symptom Validity Test than were found for the *F* scale. Martens et al. (2001) reported a significant association between the FBS and performance invalidity measures derived from the California Verbal Learning Test. Greiffenstein et al. (2002) found significant associations between the FBS and a Symptom Improbability Rating Scale, Grip Strength, Finger Tapping Speed, PDRT-27, Rey 15-Item Test, and Rey Word List in a sample of probable malingerers showing atypical outcome for mild TBI. I reported a significant association between the FBS and the PDRT (Larrabee, 2003b), and the FBS was frequently associated with other performance invalidity measures based on the Benton Visual Form Discrimination Test, Finger Tapping, Reliable Digit Span, and the Wisconsin Card Sorting Failure to Maintain Set in samples of probable and definite malingerers (Larrabee, 2003a). The FBS was also significantly associated with the Reliable Digit Span in a sample of probable pain malingerers (Larrabee, 2003d).

The sensitivity and specificity of the FBS decline when investigated in psychiatric settings. Rogers, Sewell, and Ustad (1995) found that *F*, *Fb*, *F*

minus K, and Fp were superior to the FBS in the correct identification of psychiatric outpatients taking the MMPI-2 under honest or simulated malingering conditions. The FBS had a 21.1% false positive rate in the honest condition but only a 48.5% sensitivity in the malingered condition. Berry and Schipper, in chapter 9 of the current volume, report more positive data on the utility of the FBS in psychiatric settings.

Iverson, Henrichs, Barton, and Allen (2002) have found that an FBS cutoff of 20 or higher misclassified 30% of medical outpatients and 24% of substance abusers as malingerers. Raising the cutoff to 24 misclassified 15% of the medical outpatients and 8% of the substance abusers. Sixty percent of inmates instructed to malinger (simulate disturbance on the MMPI-2) were identified by a cutoff of 20 or higher, but the number decreased to 24% using a cutoff of 24 or higher. Ninety-six percent of inmates taking the MMPI-2 under conditions of straightforward responding were correctly identified at a cutoff of 20 or higher, and the number increased to 100% using a cutoff of 24 or higher.

Two works have appeared that are highly critical of the FBS. One, by Butcher et al. (2003), reports what the authors believe to be unacceptably high false positive rates in litigants, as well as in various clinical groups; the other, by Bury and Bagby (2002), reports poor sensitivity and specificity in discriminating simulating PTSD subjects from subjects with clinical PTSD.

Butcher et al. (2003) studied six subject samples. Four were obtained from the National Computer Systems (NCS) database (i.e., profiles sent in by clinicians for NCS scoring and interpretation) and included psychiatric inpatients, individuals in a correctional facility, general medical patients, and persons with chronic pain. Another sample was from a large tertiary-care Veterans Affairs medical center, and a sixth sample included personal-injury litigants. The authors concluded that the FBS had an unacceptably high false positive rate and poor internal consistency. Butcher et al. did not, however, report the percentage of subjects involved in compensation or litigation actions in the psychiatric, chronic pain, general medical, or Veterans Affairs samples, nor did they report the context in which the MMPI-2 tests were conducted in the correctional facility (e.g., competency to proceed to trial, criminal responsibility, consideration for early release). Moreover, Butcher et al. did not utilize *any* measures of exaggeration and symptom validity that were independent of the MMPI-2, to evaluate presence of malingering in their correctional facility or personal injury samples.

Thus, specificity values based on true false positives cannot be computed; sensitivity values, absent independent assessment of malingering in the correctional facility and personal-injury samples, also cannot be computed. At best, elevated FBS scores in the personal-injury sample can serve as base rate indications of the frequency of malingering, assuming the FBS is a valid indicator of symptom exaggeration. Consequently, the rates of persons exceeding the cutoff score of FBS > 23 for males (24.1%) and exceeding the FBS score of 25 for females (37.9%) are well within the 30–40% average base

rate of malingering in personal-injury samples (Larrabee, 2003a; Mittenberg, Patton, Canyock, & Condit, 2002) and the 35–42% rate of excess claims in support of auto-injury claims (Carroll, Abrahamse, & Vaiana, 1995).

Data from Butcher et al. (2003) actually support the validity of the FBS. Although these authors have criticized the internal consistency of the FBS, the median Cronbach alpha of .62 for all six subject samples is quite similar to the Cronbach alpha of .64 for males and .63 for females for the F scale, as reported in the MMPI-2 manual (Table D-7, p. 97; Butcher, Dahlstrom, Graham, Tellegan, & Kaemmer, 1989). As Lees-Haley and Fox (2004) have observed, it is significant that the Cronbach alpha of .85 reported for the FBS in the Butcher et al. (2003) personal-injury sample is higher than Cronbach alphas for nearly every MMPI-2 scale, as reported in the manual (Butcher et al., 1989). The FBS Cronbach alpha of .85 for the personal-injury sample is substantially higher than the FBS alphas reported for chronic pain (.47) and general medical patients (.58), contradicting Butcher et al.'s claim that the FBS measures legitimate somatic concerns in these two patient groups. Last, Butcher et al. (2003), in their Table 4, show that the FBS correlated most strongly with MMPI-2 scales *Hs, D, Hy, Pt,* and *Sc,* which are the MMPI-2 scales most likely to be elevated in personal-injury probable malingerers (Boone & Lu, 1999; Larrabee, 1998, 2003b, 2003c; Ross et al., 2004).

Lees-Haley and Fox (2004) note, among other problems, that the absence of determination of the base rate of malingering and of an independent measure of exaggeration in the Butcher et al. (2003) investigation makes it impossible to evaluate the accuracy of the FBS with their methodology. Lees-Haley and Fox also find it remarkable that Butcher et al. criticize the FBS as biased simply because men and women responded differently in their sample, despite the fact that different norms have been used for men and women on the MMPI for more than half a century.

In their criticism of Butcher et al. (2003) Greve and Bianchini (2004) state that, without a clearly determined malingered and a clearly determined nonmalingered sample, Butcher et al. cannot know either the sensitivity or the specificity of the FBS. Greve and Bianchini highlight the importance of relying on multiple indicators in coming to a conclusion of malingering and point out that, among the psychometric data, empirical research clearly supports the value of the FBS.

Bury and Bagby (2002) compared the MMPI-2 Validity scales of a sample of patients diagnosed with PTSD to the scores produced by samples of university students taking the MMPI-2 under both standard instructions and conditions of exaggeration. They found that the family of F scales, particularly *Fb* and *Fp,* consistently produced the highest overall classification rates. In contrast, they found that the FBS was ineffective and failed to produce significant group differences between the PTSD claimants and research participants.

As I have previously observed (Larrabee, 2005), the Bury and Bagby study suffered from a "fatal" research design error: Their *entire* clinical PTSD

sample was seeking continuation or reinstatement of compensation from the Workplace Safety and Insurance Board of Toronto, Ontario, Canada, and Bury and Bagby did not assess their clinical sample on measures of symptom exaggeration and performance validity that were independent of the MMPI-2. Indeed, Bury and Bagby acknowledged that their clinical PTSD sample showed evidence that some of the claimants were likely exaggerating their symptoms. As I noted (ibid.), the mean FBS of 26.31 obtained for the Bury and Bagby clinical PTSD sample was well within the range of FBS values produced by analogue, as well as by suspected, malingerers (Table 4.3 of ibid., p. 141).

Greiffenstein, Baker, Axelrod, Peck, and Gervais (2004) found that the FBS had good sensitivity, specificity, and positive predictive power in discriminating 48 nonlitigating patients suffering psychological trauma (primarily from workplace robberies) from 57 litigants with atypical symptom reports seeking compensation for psychological damages following relatively minor events that did not reach *DSM-IV* gatekeeper criteria for major trauma. By contrast, the *F* family showed poor discrimination. Logistic regression yielded cutting scores of 21 for males and 26 for females, while scores greater than 29 for males and 30 for females were associated with 100% positive predictive power.

Nelson, Sweet, and Demakis (2006) have published a meta-analysis of the Fake Bad scale in civil forensic practice. The FBS had the largest grand effect size (.96), followed by Obvious-Subtle (.88), Dissimulation (Revised-2) (.79), *F* minus *K* (.69), and the *F* scale (.63). The authors concluded that the FBS performs as well as (if not superior to) other MMPI-2 validity scales in discriminating overreporting and comparison groups. Nelson et al. observed that the preponderance of the present literature supports the use of the FBS within forensic settings.

Greiffenstein, Fox, and Lees-Haley (in press) reviewed the use of the FBS in the detection of noncredible brain-injury claims. They concluded that the FBS appears to be a valid measure of exaggerated disability and physiological suffering, most of all in the context of litigated minor head injury. As part of their review, they compiled FBS frequency distribution data for 1,052 nonlitigating clinical and nonclinical subject samples, including severe TBI, psychiatric patients, medically ill and substance-abusing male patients, nontraumatic brain diseases, criminal probationers, and job applicants. An FBS score of 23 or higher had a specificity of .903. Greiffenstein et al. recommended an FBS score of ≥ 23 as a universal cutting score justifying preliminary suspicions about symptom validity. They also stated that scores of 30 and above have a 99–100% probability of indicating the promotion of suffering, providing the greatest confidence irrespective of medical or psychiatric context and gender.

Other recently developed validity scales are sensitive to exaggeration of health and injury symptomatology on the MMPI-2, including the Response Bias Scale (RBS; Gervais, Ben-Porath, Wygant, & Green, in press; Nelson,

Sweet, & Heilbronner, 2007), Henry-Heilbronner index (Henry, Heilbronner, Mittenberg, & Enders, 2006); and the *Fs* scale (Wygant, Ben-Porath, & Arbisi, 2004).

The RBS was developed by selecting those MMPI-2 items that discriminated between non-head-injury disability claimants who passed or failed the Word Memory Test (WMT; Green, 2003), the Computerized Assessment of Response Bias (CARB; Allen, Conder, Green, & Cox, 1997), and/or the Test of Memory Malingering (TOMM; Tombaugh, 1996) (Gervais et al., in press). Twenty-eight items were identified through multiple regression as predictors of failure on the WMT, CARB, or TOMM. The RBS correlated significantly with the FBS, $r = .65$, *F* and *Fb*, $r = .67$, and with *Fp*, $r = .36$. The RBS added significant incremental variance when entered following the *F*-family and FBS scores, but none of the other response exaggeration scales added significant incremental variance when the RBS was entered first in regression equations that predicted failing performance on the WMT, TOMM, or CARB.

Scores of 17 or higher on the 28-item scale were reported to have a specificity of .95 to 1.00 for various clinical groups and a PPP of .77 to 1.00, but sensitivity was low (.25 to .29). In their investigation Gervais et al. (ibid.) found a larger Cohen's *d* for the RBS (.92) than for the FBS (.61). Cohen's *d* was .63 for *F*, 1.00 for *Fb*, and .57 for *Fp*. Gervais et al. note that the RBS may be very sensitive to cognitive symptom exaggeration because it was developed on the basis of passing or failing cognitive symptom validity tests. They also report that somewhat less than 40% of the items are directly cognitive in nature, while the remaining items reflect content, including somatic symptoms, denial of antisocial behaviors, and mistrustful attitudes. Consequently, the RBS may have a broader application to cases in which symptoms other than or in addition to cognitive complaints are exaggerated.

Nelson et al. (2007) contrasted samples with secondary gain and no secondary gain (differential prevalence design) on several MMPI-2 Validity scales, including the FBS and an older version of the RBS. The RBS yielded the largest effect size ($d = .65$), followed closely by the FBS ($d = .60$), and the RBS correlated highly with the FBS ($r = .74$). By contrast, the effect sizes were .22 for *F*, .01 for *Fb*, and .05 for *Fp*. Nelson et al. suggested that the RBS and the FBS may represent a similar construct of symptom validity and may outperform other MMPI-2 Validity scales in discriminating patient groups with and without secondary gain.

The Henry-Heilbronner index (HHI) is a 15-item MMPI-2 subscale that was empirically derived from both the 43-item FBS and the 17-item Pseudoneurologic scale (PNS) of Shaw and Matthews (1965; Henry et al., 2006). Using logistic regression, the authors compared the ability of the FBS, PNS, and a combined FBSPNS scale to discriminate a group of 45 litigation/compensation-seeking subjects defined as meeting the Slick et al. (1999) criteria for either definite or probable malingered neurocognitive dysfunction from a group of 74 nonlitigating, non-compensation-seeking traumatic brain-injury patients, most of whom (85%) had mild traumatic brain injury.

All three scales discriminated between the head-injured and probable malingering groups, with the FBS and combined FBSPNS performing better than the PNS.

Henry et al. then performed an item analysis, in which they conducted phi correlations of each of the FBS and PNS items with group membership, to select 15 items that best discriminated the two groups. The resulting HHI scale, comprising nine FBS items, four PNS items, and two items shared by FBS and PNS, outperformed the FBS, PNS, and combined FBSPNS scales. A score of 8 or higher on the HHI had a sensitivity of .80 and specificity of .89. A principal components analysis of the HHI showed that it comprised one dominant factor, including mostly physical items, leading Henry et al. to suggest that the HHI is best considered a "pseudosomatic index" and that elevated HHI scores may be a purer measure of "somatic malingering" than the FBS and MMPI-2 scales 1 and 3 as identified by Larrabee (1998).

Last, Wygant et al. (2004) describe the *Fs* scale as a new MMPI-2 scale consisting of 16 items that reflect various somatic complaints that were endorsed by less than 20% of men and women in two large medical samples, one including general medical patients and the other a group of chronic pain patients. These items were also infrequently endorsed by the MMPI-2 normative sample. Wygant et al. (ibid.) describe the *Fs* as the somatic complaining equivalent of *Fp*. Consequently, an individual who scores high on *Fs* presents with a combination of somatic complaints that is unlikely to be characteristic of persons who have genuine medical problems.

In summary, the MMPI-2 appears to detect at least two types of malingering. The first is exaggerated psychopathology, manifested by elevations on *F*, *Fb*, and *Fp* and by extreme elevations on scales *Pa* and *Sc* (see Graham, 2006; Greene, 2000; Greiffenstein et al., in press, and chapter 9, by Berry and Schipper, in the current volume). The second type represents exaggerated cognitive, health, and injury concerns, as well as nonpsychotic emotional distress occurring in the context of personal-injury litigation for neuropsychological claims, manifested by elevations on the FBS and on scales *Hs*, *D*, *Hy*, *Pt*, and *Sc*. More recently developed MMPI-2 Validity scales such as the *RBS*, *HHI*, and *Fs* also show promise for the detection of exaggerated health and injury symptoms.

The preceding MMPI-2 malingering patterns should be supported by the presence of abnormal scores on other measures of performance validity and symptom exaggeration in order to minimize the chance of false positive errors. According to the work of Donders and colleagues (Martens et al., 2001; Miller & Donders, 2001), preexisting psychiatric history can be a mitigating factor in FBS elevations in nonlitigating mild TBI patients, and Greiffenstein et al. (2002) state that the presence of anosmia or residual motor impairment can be a mitigating factor in evaluating the FBS scores of litigating patients with moderate and severe TBI. The sensitivity of the FBS may decline in psychiatric settings (Rogers et al., 1995). In neurological settings, optimal FBS cutoffs are in the low to mid-20s, and false positives are highly unlikely

above raw scores of 30. Greiffenstein et al. (in press) offer similar interpretive guidelines.

Overreporting of Health Concerns on Other Self-Report Inventories

Other personality inventories and health behavior questionnaires such as the Symptom Checklist 90-Revised (SCL-90-R; Derogatis, 1992) and the Illness Behavior Questionnaire (Pilowsky & Spence, 1975) have been evaluated specifically for sensitivity to malingered pain symptomatology. The SCL-90-R was administered by Wallis and Bogduk (1996) to whiplash patients with chronic pain and to a group of noninjured persons who were asked to simulate chronic pain resulting from a whiplash injury. They found that the genuine whiplash group produced elevations on the Somatization, Obsessive-Compulsive, and Depression scales, whereas the simulating group produced greater elevations on these scales than those produced by the genuine group, as well as elevations across the range of clinical scales on the SCL-90-R.

McGuire and Shores (2001b) compared the SCL-90-R endorsements of chronic pain patients (primarily back pain) with the SCL-90-R scores of noninjured first-year undergraduate psychology students who were asked to simulate pain disorder in the context of a vignette regarding a compensation evaluation. Similar to the results of Wallis and Bogduk (1996), they found that the pain patients produced their highest elevations on Somatization, Obsessive, and Depression scales, whereas the simulators produced elevations on all of the SCL-90-R scales that were higher than those produced by the pain patients. McGuire and Shores also evaluated the utility of the Positive Symptom Total (PST) score and found optimal discrimination at 77 for males and 84 for females (these score cutoffs were much higher than those recommended by Derogatis of > 50 for males and > 60 for females). Wallis and Bogduk (1996) did not evaluate the Positive Symptom Total in their investigation. McGuire and Shores (2001) concluded that their results were consistent with those of Wallis and Bogduk in demonstrating that simulators overestimate the degree of psychopathology experienced in people with chronic pain.

Pilowsky and Spence (1975) developed seven scales from the Illness Behavior Questionnaire (IBQ) to measure abnormal illness behavior, a construct that includes malingering. Pilowsky, Murrell, and Gordon (1979) used these scales to screen patients presenting at pain clinics in the United States and Australia.

Clayer, Bookless, and Ross (1984) administered the IBQ to 164 noninjured persons employed at a public utility, half of whom completed the IBQ normally, and half of whom completed it under instructions to simulate injury in the context of financial compensation. The IBQ was also administered

to 82 persons at a pain clinic in whom the complaint of pain was considered to be neurotically determined. The responses of the normals and the simulators to the 62 items of the IBQ were contrasted to identify 46 discriminating items. The responses of the simulators and the neurotics to these 46 items were then compared to identify 21 items discriminating the simulating and the neurotic groups. These 21 items were identified as constituting a Conscious Exaggeration (CE) scale.

Clayer, Bookless-Pratz, and Ross (1986) had two psychiatrists each rate 10 litigating/compensation-seeking patients with physical complaints following injury as to conscious exaggeration on a 0 to 100 scale (0 = no exaggeragageration, 100 = complete fabrication of signs and symptoms). The CE scale correlated significantly ($r = .64$) with the conscious exaggeration ratings of the psychiatrists.

Mendelson (1987) compared the CE responses of litigating/compensation-seeking chronic pain patients to the scores produced by nonlitigants and found no significant CE score differences. Moreover, he found that CE scores correlated significantly with trait anxiety, hostility, state anxiety, and McGill pain descriptors. Mendelson concluded that the CE scale was not useful in detecting deception.

Fishbain, Cutler, Rosomoff, and Steele-Rosomoff (2002) reported CE results that generally questioned the validity of the CE as a measure of malingering in chronic pain. The CE scores of 34 nonlitigating/non-compensation-seeking chronic back pain patients were compared to the CE scores of 62 patients receiving or seeking compensation (54 through Workers' Compensation, 37 through a lawyer, and 20 in litigation). The CE scores were the lowest for the non-compensation-seeking group compared to the compensation-seeking/receiving groups, and the highest scores were produced by those patients in litigation. Indeed, the effect sizes computed from Fishbain et al.'s Table 1, which contrasts the nonlitigating/non-compensation-seeking pain patients with those pain patients in litigation are d (pooled SD) = .86 ($p < .0038$) at pretreatment base line and $d = .64$ ($p < .0276$) posttreatment, representing large and moderate effect sizes, respectively.

While these findings appear to support the CE as a measure of malingering, there was no difference in the magnitude of change of pre- to posttreatment CE scores for any of the groups. Moreover, the CE scores were not predicted by the subgroups of compensation-seeking status, nor was the CE predictive of return to work. Last, the CE was significantly correlated with the Beck Depression Inventory and State-Trait Anxiety. Of course, if these measures of depression and anxiety are also exaggerated, this positive correlation would be expected. Unfortunately, the authors did not report the means and standard deviations for the non-compensation-seeking versus the compensation seekers on the Beck Depression Inventory and the State-Trait Anxiety scales. Fishbain et al. concluded that the CE scale is simply measuring emotional distress and arousal.

Pain Scales and Pain Symptom Exaggeration

Dirks, Wunder, Kinsman, McElhinny, and Jones (1993) reported on the development of a Pain Rating Scale and a Pain Behavior Checklist. A sample of 395 chronic pain patients, most with compensation issues (63.3% with a work-related injury; 30.9% with motor vehicle accident injuries; 73.2% represented by an attorney), was administered a visual analog Pain Rating Scale (PRS) ranging from 0 (absolutely no pain) to 100 (extreme pain, i.e., producing instant suicide) and a Pain Behavior Checklist (PBC) based on 16 rateable behaviors (e.g., limping, grimacing).

The PRS was rated for worst pain, least pain, and present pain, and scores were generated for difference (worst to least). The PBC scores had a maximum potential range of 0 to 24 (8 items had frequency ratings). The PRS and PBC scores were combined to yield a total pain score and a consistency score based on PRS and PBC comparisons (difference score of 0 = mean consistency). Of the 395 patients, 127 (32%) were judged to be consciously exaggerating pain symptoms (or pain effects) by an interdisciplinary evaluation team, based on gross inconsistencies in pain behavior across evaluations, nonorganic findings on physical examination, and so on. This group, labeled conscious exaggerators, was compared against the remaining pain patients. The conscious exaggerators differed significantly from the other pain subjects on PRS worst, least, and present, on the total pain score (PRS and PBC), and on consistency (between PRS and PBC). The authors concluded that, for the chronic pain patients studied, the results argue for the use of both pain ratings and pain behavior scores.

McGuire and Shores (2001a) evaluated the sensitivity of the Pain Patient Profile (P3; Tollison & Langley, 1995) to malingered pain. They compared 40 patients with a pain condition who completed the P3 under normal instructions with 20 students who completed it under instructions to feign a pain disorder but to attempt to avoid detection. The simulators did not differ on the P3 Validity scale compared with the pain group but scored significantly higher on the Depression, Anxiety, and Somatization subscales. The simulators were more likely to obtain a T score over 55 on all three clinical scales, and the Depression scale had the highest positive and negative predictive power, correctly classifying 80% of the participants.

In a second investigation, McGuire, Harvey, and Shores (2001) compared the P3 scores of three groups of subjects: (a) 62 chronic pain patients who took the test under standard instructions, (b) 34 clinical non-pain-rehabilitation patients who were instructed to simulate malingered pain, and (c) 26 chronic pain patients who were instructed to exaggerate the extent of their pain and related problems. Both groups of simulators scored significantly higher on P3 Anxiety, Depression, and Somatization scales contrasted with the nonsimulating pain patients. The P3 Validity scale differentiated the chronic pain

simulators from the pain control group, but the rehabilitation pain simulators did not score differently from the pain control group on P3 Validity.

I (Larrabee, 2003d) compared the scores of 29 litigants with pain complaints who met the Slick et al. (1999) criteria for definite or probable malingered neurocognitive dysfunction (who also would have met the Bianchini et al. [2005] criteria for definite or probable malingered pain-related disability) to published pain patient data on the McGill Pain Questionnaire (MPQ; Melzack, 1975; Mikail, Dubreuil, & D'Eon, 1993), Pain Disability Index (PDI; Tait, Chibnall, & Krause, 1990), and Modified Somatic Perception Questionnaire (MSPQ; Main, 1983).

Using Lanyon's (1997) model for the evaluation of malingering and focusing on overendorsement of symptoms, cutting scores were set that misidentified 10%, 5%, or 1% of pain patients based on the preceding published data (e.g., 90%, 95%, or 99% of these patients were identified as nonmalingering, below the given cutting score). At 90% specificity, the MPQ, PDI, and MSPQ had sensitivities of 21%, 59%, and 90%, respectively. Using a base rate of malingering of 36% (Meyers et al., 2002), the positive predictive power (PPP) for the MSPQ at the 99% specificity cutoff was .97, while the negative predictive power (NPP) was .85. By contrast, the PPP was .63 and the NPP was .64 for the MPQ, and the PPP was .85 with NPP of .66 for the PDI at the 99% specificity cutoff. The PDI correlated significantly (.43) with minimum pain ratings using a 0 to 100 scale and correlated $-.43$ with pain range (maximum minus minimum on the 0 to 100 scale). Minimum pain correlated significantly (.60) with the MSPQ. The MSPQ was the only one of the three pain scales that correlated significantly with the FBS (at .37). The MSPQ also correlated at $-.35$ with the Rey 15-Item Test, just short of the traditional values for significance, $p < .06$.

My investigation of pain malingering (Larrabee, 2003d) clearly demonstrates the sensitivity, specificity, and predictive power of the MSPQ. These results are interesting when considered in reference to an investigation by Main, Wood, Hollis, Spanswick, and Waddell (1992), who found that MSPQ scores greater than 12 were indicative of somatic distress related to poor outcome for treatment of low-back-pain patients. In my study (ibid.), MSPQ scores greater than 12 had a positive predictive power of malingering greater than .91. In this vein, it is noteworthy that a recent meta-analysis has found an association between compensation status and poor outcome after surgical intervention (Harris, Mulford, Solomon, van Gelder, & Young, 2005).

Summary and New Directions

Various measures of symptom report were reviewed in the context of exaggerated health and injury detection. First reviewed was research on the MMPI-2 that supports the utility of the Lees-Haley Fake Bad Scale in detecting

exaggerated health and injury concerns for persons with neuropsychological claims, with the strongest support for the discrimination of malingering following traumatic brain injury. The finding of elevations on MMPI-2 scales *Hs, D, Hy, Pt,* and *Sc* in persons with probable malingered neuropsychological dysfunction is consistent with research on the SCL-90-R in chronic pain patients, demonstrating significantly higher scores on the Somatization, Depression, and Obsession scales for simulating pain patients compared to patients with clinical chronic pain, as well as a pattern of general overendorsement on the SCL-90-R (McGuire & Shores, 2001b; Wallis & Bogduk, 1996). These data are also consistent with the presence of significant elevations for noninjured dissimulators on the Somatization, Anxiety, and Depression scales of the P3 (McGuire & Shores, 2001a; McGuire et al., 2001). The preceding data conform to Lanyon's (1997) accuracy of knowledge model of malingering in demonstrating overendorsement of symptoms by malingerers relative to the endorsement patterns of clinical patients.

Data on the relationship of the Illness Behavior Questionnaire Conscious Exaggeration scale to malingering are mixed (Clayer et al., 1984, 1986; Mendelson, 1987; Fishbain et al., 2002). One study that claims to show the insensitivity of the scale to malingered pain (Fishbain et al., 2002) actually contains data supporting the Conscious Exaggeration scale as a measure of pain malingering, when nonlitigating/non-compensation-seeking chronic pain patients are contrasted with chronic pain patients in litigation.

A simple pain severity rating questionnaire, in combination with a structured pain behavior rating scale, showed good discrimination of probable pain malingerers from persons not thought to be malingering chronic pain (Dirks et al., 1993). A study that compared three self-report scales frequently employed to evaluate chronic pain patients—the McGill Pain Questionnaire (MPQ), Pain Disability Index (PDI), and Modified Perception Questionnaire (MSPQ)—showed poor diagnostic utility for the MPQ, intermediate utility for the PDI, and strong diagnostic utility for the MSPQ (Larrabee, 2003d) for the detection of probable malingering.

The study by Bianchini et al. (2005) specifying diagnostic criteria for malingered pain-related disability (MPRD) will greatly enhance research in the area of malingered chronic pain. The majority of the studies conducted to date rely on comparisons of noninjured persons simulating pain impairment to actual pain patients. This is problematic because data exist showing that simulators may overplay their symptom reports, particularly those related to psychopathology, compared to known groups of malingerers (e.g., Sivec et al. [1994] found elevations on *F* and *Pa* in noninjured simulators, patterns that were not seen in Larrabee, 1998). The MPRD criteria of Bianchini et al. will allow the formation of known groups of probable malingerers to compare and contrast with nonmalingering chronic pain samples and consequently provide a greater generalizability of findings.

Of equal importance is the definition of nonmalingering chronic pain comparison groups. Typically, these groups are themselves in either Workers'

Compensation actions or personal-injury litigation (Keller & Butcher, 1991). This is problematic given the substantial compensation effect size in chronic pain samples demonstrated by Rohling et al. (1995). Application of the Larrabee (2003b) regression formula for the estimation of FBS to the mean primary MMPI-2 scores of the Keller and Butcher (1991) chronic pain sample yielded an estimated mean FBS of 21.46. Using the Greiffenstein et al. (in press) omnibus FBS cutoff of 23 or higher, the estimated FBS mean of 21.46, and an FBS standard deviation of 4.0 (Greene, 2000) yields a z score of .14 for an FBS of 23 in the Keller and Butcher (1991) chronic pain sample.

Assuming a symmetric distribution of FBS, 44% of the Keller and Butcher chronic pain sample have FBS scores of 23 or more. This value, in a chronic pain sample that is 91.2% of males and 77.9% of females who are seeking compensation and/or litigating, is within the range of the base rates of malingering discussed in chapter 1 of this volume. Consequently, efforts should focus on collecting chronic pain samples that are not in settings where external incentives are a factor. Alternatively, chronic pain patients in compensation and litigation settings could be utilized if carefully screened for absence of the Bianchini et al. (2005) criteria, although one always runs the risk of including cases that are false negative for malingering when using samples of subjects who have external incentives with potential for symptom reinforcement.

Application of the Bianchini et al. (2005) MPRD criteria and careful attention to defining nonmalingering chronic pain contrast groups can yield valuable information on measures of invalid effort and exaggerated symptomatology in future research on pain malingering. The present review has focused on symptom report measures, but other research on pain malingering has concentrated on physical examination findings, functional capacity evaluation, and formal measures of symptom validity currently used in neuropsychological settings (ibid.; Gervais et al., 2001; Meyers & Diep, 2000).

More carefully controlled research utilizing the MPRD criteria and contrast groups represented by patients with bona fide problems could be applied to answer questions about controversial measures such as the Waddell signs (Waddell, McCulloch, Kummel, & Venner, 1980). To date, several, including Waddell himself, have argued that the signs he devised are not measures of malingering (Fishbain et al., 1999; Main & Waddell, 1998). With effective study design, it is conceivable that certain of these signs (or a total number of these signs) may be found useful in the detection of malingered pain-related disability.

References

Allen, L., Conder, R. L., Green, P., & Cox, D. R. (1997). *CARB '97 manual for the Computerized Assessment of Response Bias*. Durham, NC: CogniSyst.

Bianchini, K. J., Greve, K. W., & Glynn, G. (2005). On the diagnosis of malingered pain-related disability: Lessons from cognitive malingering research. *Spine Journal, 5,* 404–417.

Binder, L. M. (1993). Assessment of malingering after mild head trauma with the Portland Digit Recognition Test. *Journal of Clinical and Experimental Neuropsychology, 15,* 170–182.

Binder, L. M., & Rohling, M. L. (1966). Money matters: A meta-analytic review of the effects of financial incentives on recovery after closed-head injury. *American Journal of Psychiatry, 153,* 7–10.

Boone, K. B., & Lu, P. H. (1999). Impact of somatoform symptomatology on credibility of cognitive performance. *The Clinical Neuropsychologist, 13,* 414–419.

Bury, A. S., & Bagby, R. M. (2002). The detection of feigned uncoached and coached post-traumatic stress disorder with the MMPI-2 in a sample of workplace accident victims. *Psychological Assessment, 14,* 472–484.

Butcher, J. N., Arbisi, P. A., Atlis, M. M., & McNulty, J. L. (2003). The construct validity of the Lees-Haley Fake Bad Scale: Does this scale measure somatic malingering and feigned emotional distress? *Archives of Clinical Neuropsychology, 18,* 473–485.

Butcher, J. N., Dahlstrom, W. G., Graham, J. R., Tellegan, A., & Kaemmer, B. (1989). *Manual for administration and scoring of the MMPI-2.* Minneapolis: University of Minnesota Press.

Butcher, J. N., Graham, J. R., Ben-Porath, Y. S., Tellegen, A., Dahlstrom, W. G., & Kaemmer, B. (2001). *MMPI-2: Manual for administration, scoring, and interpretation* (Rev. ed.). Minneapolis: University of Minnesota Press.

Butcher, J. N., & Harlow, T. C. (1987). Personality assessment in personal-injury cases. In I. B. Weiner & A. K. Hess (Eds.), *Handbook of forensic psychology* (pp. 128–154). New York: Wiley-Interscience.

Carroll, S., Abrahamse, A., & Vaiana, M. (1995). *The costs of excess medical claims for automobile personal injuries.* Santa Monica: RAND.

Clayer, J. R., Bookless, C., & Ross, M. W. (1984). Neurosis and conscious symptom exaggeration: Its differentiation by the Illness Behavior Questionnaire. *Journal of Psychosomatic Research, 28,* 237–241.

Clayer, J. R., Bookless-Pratz, C. L., & Ross, M. W. (1986). The evaluation of illness behaviour and exaggeration of disability. *British Journal of Psychiatry, 148,* 296–299.

Dearth, C. S., Berry, D. T. R., Vickery, C. D., Vagnini, V. L., Baser, R. E., Orey, S. A., et al. (2005). Detection of feigned head injury symptoms on the MMPI-2 in head-injured patients and community controls. *Archives of Clinical Neuropsychology, 20,* 95–110.

Delis, D. C., Kramer, J. H., Kaplan, E., & Ober, B. A. (1987). *California Verbal Learning Test: Adult version.* San Antonio: Psychological Corp.

Derogatis, L. R. (1992). *SCL-90-R: Administration, scoring, and procedures manual II for the revised version.* Towson, MD: Clinical Psychometric Research.

Dirks, J. F., Wunder, J., Kinsman, R., McElhinny, J., and Jones, N. F. (1993). A pain rating scale and a pain behavior checklist for clinical use: Development, norms, and the consistency score. *Psychotherapy and Psychosomatics, 59,* 41–49.

Fishbain, D. A., Cutler, R. B., Rosomoff, H. L., & Rosomoff, R. S. (1999). Chronic pain disability exaggeration/malingering and submaximal effort research. *Clinical Journal of Pain, 15,* 244–274.

Fishbain, D. A., Cutler, R. B., Rosomoff, H. L., & Steele-Rosamoff, R. (2002). Does the Conscious Exaggeration scale detect deception within patients with chronic pain alleged to have secondary gain? *Pain Medicine, 3,* 39–46.

Gervais, R. O., Ben-Porath, Y. S., Wygant, D. B., & Green, P. (in press). Development and validation of a Response Bias scale (RBS) for the MMPI-2. *Assessment.*

Gervais, R. O., Russell, A. S., Green, P., Allen, L. M., Ferrari, R., & Pieschl, S. D. (2001). Effort testing in patients with fibromyalgia and disability incentives. *Journal of Rheumatology, 28,* 1892–1899.

Graham, J. R. (2006). *MMPI-2: Assessing personality and psychopathology* (4th ed.). New York: Oxford University Press.

Graham, J. R., Watts, D., & Timbrook, R. E. (1991). Detecting fake-good and fake-bad MMPI-2 profiles. *Journal of Personality Assessment, 57,* 264–277.

Green, P. (2003). *Green's Word Memory Test for Windows: User's manual.* Edmonton, Alberta, Canada: Green's Publishing.

Greene, R. L. (2000). *The MMPI-2: An interpretive manual* (2nd ed.). Needham Heights, MA: Allyn and Bacon.

Greiffenstein, M. F., Baker, W. J., Axelrod, B., Peck, E. A., & Gervais, R. (2004). The Fake Bad scale and MMPI-2 F-family in detection of implausible psychological trauma claims. *The Clinical Neuropsychologist, 18,* 573–590.

Greiffenstein, M. F., Baker, W. J., Gola, T., Donders, J., & Miller, L. (2002). The Fake Bad scale in atypical and severe closed-head injury litigants. *Journal of Clinical Psychology, 58,* 1591–1600.

Greiffenstein, M. F., Fox, D., & Lees-Haley, P. R. (in press). The MMPI-2 Fake Bad scale in detection of noncredible brain-injury claims. In K. B. Boone (Ed.), *Assessment of feigned cognitive impairment. A neuropsychological perspective.* New York: Guilford.

Greve, K. W., & Bianchini, K. J. (2004). Response to Butcher et al., The construct validity of the Lees-Haley Fake Bad Scale. *Archives of Clinical Neuropsychology, 19,* 337–339.

Greve, K. W., Bianchini, K. J., Love, J. M., Brennan, A., & Heinly, M. T. (2006). Sensitivity and specificity of MMPI-2 Validity scales and indicators to malingered neurocognitive dysfunction in traumatic brain injury. *The Clinical Neuropsychologist, 20,* 491–512.

Harris, I., Mulford, J., Solomon, M., van Gelder, J. M., & Young, J. (2005). Association between compensation status and outcome after surgery: A meta-analysis. *Journal of the American Medical Association, 293,* 1644–1652.

Henry, G. K., Heilbronner, R. L., Mittenberg, W., & Enders, C. (2006). The Henry-Heilbronner index: A 15-item empirically derived MMPI-2 subscale for identifying probable malingering in personal-injury litigants and disability claimants. *The Clinical Neuropsychologist, 20,* 786–797.

Iverson, G. L., Henrichs, T. F., Barton, E. A., & Allen, S. (2002). Specificity of the MMPI-2 Fake Bad Scale as a marker for personal-injury malingering. *Psychological Reports, 90,* 131–136.

Iverson, G. L., & McCracken, L. M. (1997). "Postconcussive" symptoms in persons with chronic pain. *Brain Injury, 11,* 783–790.

Keller, L. S., & Butcher, J. N. (1991). *Assessment of chronic pain patients with the MMPI-2.* Minneapolis: University of Minnesota Press.

Lanyon, R. I. (1997). Detecting deception: Current models and directions. *Clinical Psychology: Science and Practice, 4,* 377–387.

Lanyon, R. I. (2001). Dimensions of self-serving misrepresentation in forensic assessment. *Journal of Personality Assessment, 76,* 169–179.

Lanyon, R. I., & Almer, M. D. (2002). Characteristics of compensable disability patients who choose to litigate. *Journal of the American Academy of Psychiatry and Law, 30,* 400–404.

Larrabee, G. J. (1998). Somatic malingering on the MMPI and MMPI-2 in personal-injury litigants. *The Clinical Neuropsychologist, 12,* 179–188.

Larrabee, G. J. (2003a). Detection of malingering using atypical patterns of performance on standard neuropsychological tests. *The Clinical Neuropsychologist, 17,* 410–425.

Larrabee, G. J. (2003b). Detection of symptom exaggeration with the MMPI-2 in litigants with malingered neurocognitive dysfunction. *The Clinical Neuropsychologist, 17,* 54–68.

Larrabee, G. J. (2003c). Exaggerated MMPI-2 symptom report in personal-injury litigants with malingered neurocognitive deficit. *Archives of Clinical Neuropsychology, 18,* 673–686.

Larrabee, G. J. (2003d). Exaggerated pain report in litigants with malingered neurocognitive dysfunction. *The Clinical Neuropsychologist, 17,* 395–401.

Larrabee, G. J. (2005). Assessment of malingering. In G. J. Larrabee (Ed.), *Forensic neuropsychology: A scientific approach* (pp. 115–158). New York: Oxford University Press.

Lees-Haley, P. R. (1992). Efficacy of MMPI-2 Validity scales and MCMI-II Modifier scales for detecting spurious PTSD claims: F, F-K, Fake Bad Scale, Ego Strength, Subtle-Obvious subscales, DIS, and DEB. *Journal of Clinical Psychology, 48,* 681–689.

Lees-Haley, P. R. (1997). MMPI-2 base rates for 492 personal-injury plaintiffs: Implications and challenges for forensic assessment. *Journal of Clinical Psychology, 53,* 745–755.

Lees-Haley, P. R., & Brown, R. S. (1993). Neuropsychological complaint base rates of 170 personal-injury claimants. *Archives of Clinical Neuropsychology, 8,* 203–209.

Lees-Haley, P. R., English, L. T., & Glenn, W. J. (1991). A Fake Bad Scale for the MMPI-2 for personal-injury claimants. *Psychological Reports, 68,* 203–210.

Lees-Haley, P. R., & Fox, D. D. (2004). Commentary on Butcher, Arbisi, Atlis, and McNulty (2003) on the Fake Bad scale. *Archives of Clinical Neuropsychology, 19,* 333–336.

Lezak, M. D., Howieson, D. B., & Loring, D. W. (2004). *Neuropsychological assessment* (4th ed.). New York: Oxford University Press.

Main, C. J. (1983). The Modified Somatic Perception Questionnaire (MSPQ). *Journal of Psychosomatic Research, 27,* 503–514.

Main, C. J., & Waddell, G. (1998). Behavioral responses to examination: A reappraisal of the interpretation of "nonorganic signs." *Spine, 23,* 2367–2371.

Main, C. J., Wood, P. L. R., Hollis, S., Spanswick, C. C., & Waddell, G. (1992). The distress and risk assessment method: A simple patient classification to identify distress and evaluate the risk of poor outcome. *Spine, 17,* 42–52.

Martens, M., Donders, J., & Millis, S. R. (2001). Evaluation of invalid response sets after traumatic head injury. *Journal of Forensic Neuropsychology, 2,* 1–18.

McGuire, B. E., Harvey, A. G., & Shores, A. E. (2001). Simulated malingering in pain patients: A study with the Pain Patient Profile. *British Journal of Clinical Psychology, 40,* 71–79.

McGuire, B. E., & Shores, E. A. (2001a). Pain Patient Profile and the assessment of malingered pain. *Journal of Clinical Psychology, 57*, 401–409.

McGuire, B. E., & Shores, E. A. (2001b). Simulated pain on the Symptom Checklist 90-Revised. *Journal of Clinical Psychology, 57*, 1589–1596.

Melzack, R. (1975). The McGill Pain Questionnaire: Major properties and scoring methods. *Pain, 1*, 277–299.

Mendelson, G. (1987). Measurement of conscious symptom exaggeration by questionnaire: A clinical study. *Journal of Psychosomatic Research, 31*, 703–711.

Meyers, J. E., & Diep, A. (2000). Assessment of malingering in chronic pain patients using neuropsychological tests. *Applied Neuropsychology, 7*, 133–139.

Meyers, J. E., Millis, S. R., & Volkert, K. (2002). A Validity index for the MMPI-2. *Archives of Clinical Neuropsychology, 17*, 157–169.

Mikail, S. F., DuBreuil, S., & D'Eon, J. L. (1993). A comparative analysis of measures used in the assessment of chronic pain patients. *Psychological Assessment, 5*, 117–120.

Miller, L. J., & Donders, J. (2001). Subjective symptomatology after traumatic head injury. *Brain Injury, 15*, 297–304.

Mittenberg, W., Patton, C., Canyock, E. M., & Condit, D. C. (2002). Base rates of malingering and symptom exaggeration. *Journal of Clinical and Experimental Neuropsychology, 24*, 1094–1102.

Morey, L. C. (1991). *The Personality Assessment Inventory: Professional manual.* Lutz, FL: Psychological Assessment Resources.

Muñoz, M., & Esteve, R. (2005). Reports of memory functioning by patients with chronic pain. *Clinical Journal of Pain, 21*, 287–291.

Nelson, N. W., Sweet, J. J., & Demakis, G. J. (2006). Meta-analysis of the MMPI-2 Fake Bad Scale: Utility in forensic practice. *The Clinical Neuropsychologist, 20*, 39–58.

Nelson, N. W., Sweet, J. J., & Heilbronner, R. L. (2007). Examination of the new MMPI-2 Response Bias scale (Gervais): Relationship with MMPI-2 Validity scales. *Journal of Clinical and Experimental Neuropsychology, 29*, 67–72.

Pilowsky, I., Murrell, T. G. C., & Gordon, A. (1979). The development of a screening method for abnormal illness behavior. *Journal of Psychosomatic Research, 23*, 203–207.

Pilowski, I., & Spence, N. D. (1975). Patterns of illness behaviour in patients with intractable pain. *Journal of Psychosomatic Research, 19*, 279–287.

Posthuma, A. B., & Harper, J. F. (1998). Comparison of MMPI-2 responses of child custody and personal-injury litigants. *Professional Psychology: Research and Practice, 29*, 437–443.

Rey, A. (1964). *L'examen clinique en psychologie* [The clinical examination in psychology]. Paris: Presses Universitaires de France.

Rogers, R., Sewell, K. W., & Ustad, K. L. (1995). Feigning among chronic outpatients on the MMPI-2: A systematic examination of fake-bad indicators. *Assessment, 2*, 81–89.

Rohling, M. L., Binder, L. M., & Langhinrischen-Rohling, J. (1995). Money matters: A meta-analytic review of the association between financial compensation and the experience and treatment of chronic pain. *Health Psychology, 14*, 537–547.

Ross, S. R., Millis, S. R., Krukowski, R. A., Putnam, S. H., & Adams, K. M. (2004). Detecting incomplete effort on the MMPI-2: An examination of the Fake-Bad Scale in mild head injury. *Journal of Clinical and Experimental Neuropsychology, 26*, 115–124.

Shaw, D. J., & Matthews, C. G. (1965). Differential MMPI performance of brain-damaged versus pseudoneurologic groups. *Journal of Clinical Psychology, 21,* 405–408.

Sivec, H. J., Lynn, S. J., & Garske, J. P. (1994). The effect of somatoform disorder and paranoid psychotic role-related dissimulations as a response set on the MMPI-2. *Assessment, 1,* 69–81.

Slick, D. J., Hopp, G., Strauss, E., & Spellacy, F. J. (1996). Victoria Symptom Validity Test: Efficiency for detecting feigned memory impairment and relationship to neuropsychological tests and MMPI-2 Validity scales. *Journal of Clinical and Experimental Neuropsychology, 18,* 911–922.

Slick, D. J., Sherman, E. M. S., & Iverson, G. L. (1999). Diagnostic criteria for malingered neurocognitive dysfunction: Proposed standards for clinical practice and research. *The Clinical Neuropsychologist, 13,* 545–561.

Tait, R. C., Chibnall, J. T., & Krause, S. (1990). The Pain Disability index: Psychometric properties. *Pain, 40,* 171–182.

Tollison, D. C., & Langley, J. C. (1995). *Pain patient profile manual.* Minneapolis: National Computer Services.

Tombaugh, T. N. (1996). *TOMM: Test of Memory Malingering.* Tonawanda, NY: Multi-Health Systems.

Tsushima, W. T., & Tsushima, V. G. (2001). Comparison of the Fake Bad Scale and other MMPI-2 Validity scales with personal-injury litigants. *Assessment, 8,* 205–212.

Waddell, G., McCulloch, J. A., Kummel, E., Venner, & R. M. (1980). Nonorganic physical signs in low-back pain. *Spine, 5,* 193–203.

Wallis, B. J., & Bogduk, N. (1996). Faking a profile: Can naive subjects simulate whiplash responses? *Pain, 66,* 223–227.

Wygant, D.B., Ben-Porath, Y.S., & Arbisi, P.A. (2004, May). *Development and Initial Validation of a Scale to Detect Infrequent Somatic Complaints.* Poster presented at the 39th Annual Symposium on Recent Developments of the MMPI-2/MMPI-A, Minneapolis, MN.

11

Coaching and Malingering: A Review

Julie A. Suhr and John Gunstad

Although many neuropsychologists administer tests to assess for malingering of cognitive impairment, they mistakenly believe that patients will have little knowledge of malingering tests or how they work. However, there is growing evidence that motivated clients have easy access to information that may help them appear cognitively impaired when they are not or more impaired than they truly are. The provision of such information is what we term "coaching." As Rogers (1997) indicates, the goal of coaching research is to develop malingering detection strategies that are robust to various coaching methods. Ben-Porath (1994) describes the cyclical history of coaching research, with attempts by researchers to develop malingering measures that are robust to coaching, followed by attempts by malingerers to combat the new measures, followed by further malingering test development and refinement. This chapter reviews coaching research (with a focus on malingered neuropsychological impairment), describes the robustness of malingering detection methods to coaching, and discusses areas in need of continued research.

Sources of Coaching Information

Access to information to be used in the coaching of malingering is available from multiple sources. One source is repeated neuropsychological evaluations. During the course of litigation, patients often complete several neuropsychological evaluations. Contact with physicians and psychologists who provide feedback about symptom presentation and how it matches with

a particular diagnosis may allow malingerers to refine their symptom presentation in subsequent evaluations. In addition, participation in support groups and other meetings with patients who have symptoms of neurological impairment may provide information to help refine a malingerer's presentation of a particular constellation of symptoms and impairments (Franzen, Iverson, & McCracken, 1990; Trueblood & Schmidt, 1993).

Another common source of coaching-related information is the Internet, where one can find information on the symptoms that are common for particular disorders, specifics on how to present oneself in a particular manner, and even information on how to answer questions or test items to create a convincing presentation of a specific disorder. Test catalogues are also accessible online and provide information about psychological tests (what they measure and what they look like), which allows malingerers to recognize the test stimuli during evaluation.

Ruiz, Drake, Glass, Marcotte, and van Gorp (2002) conducted an Internet search for information about psychological and neuropsychological tests and procedures and asked a group of experts to evaluate the degree of threat that information posed to the validity of the tests. Of the websites they identified, 70–85% were judged to be of minimal assistance for coaching since they included information only about typical symptoms of various psychological or neuropsychological disorders and/or general information on test instructions or test purposes. Another 20–25% of sites were labeled as an indirect threat to test validity because they provided the actual names of malingering instruments, details about independent medical examination (IME) procedures, specific signs of malingering, or discussion of general ways to avoid detection. These also included sites for bookstores that sold protected psychological assessment materials to nonprofessionals, but most of the sites were posted by psychologists and legal professionals.

Only 2–5% of sites were judged to be a direct threat to test security. These sites provided details about the tests used in medicolegal evaluations, displayed or described actual test stimuli, and/or provided explicit instructions for how to respond to test items or present with symptoms in order to obtain disability status. Although much of the coaching information was for "faking good," some was specifically geared toward malingering of impairment. Of concern, much of the available information was provided by psychologists and/or attorneys.

In another Internet study, Bauer and McCaffrey (2006) used the Google search engine to see how easy it was to find information that would threaten the test security of three popular malingering measures (Test of Memory Malingering, Victoria Symptom Validity Test, Word Memory Test). Of the sites they identified, 26% posed a moderate to high threat to security because they provided enough information to allow someone to avoid detection on these instruments.

Yet another source of information for coaching of malingerers is attorneys themselves. Attorneys who have experience with neuropsychological tests

can inform clients on how to present and respond to test items or what to watch for during a neuropsychological evaluation. Wetter & Corrigan (1995) conducted a survey of 70 attorneys and 150 law students. The vast majority of the survey respondents (79–87% of attorneys and 65% of students) believed an attorney should discuss psychological testing with a client prior to evaluation. Another 22% of students and 42% of attorneys believed an attorney should provide as much specific information as possible about psychological testing. Only 8% of students and 0–3% of attorneys said that no information should be provided to clients prior to evaluation. Nearly 36% of students and about 47% of attorneys believed an attorney should usually or always inform clients about validity scales, while about one third of each group believed such information should never be provided.

Other researchers have also found that attorneys are a common source of coaching information. Lees-Haley (1997) reviewed evidence that attorneys learn skills to prepare clients for both psychological and neuropsychological evaluations via their continuing education classes and articles published in their journals. Gutheil (2003) provides an example of a leaflet given out by attorneys to potential examinees that indicates how to answer specific questions and respond to test stimuli (in this case, pain stimulation) so as to appear believable. Victor and Abeles (2004) have reported on a National Academy of Neuropsychology and Association of Trial Lawyers survey that shows that 75% of attorneys spend 25–60 minutes preparing clients for psychological evaluation by providing information about the tests they will take and how they should respond to test items. In their survey, 44% of attorneys indicated that they wanted to know which specific neuropsychological tests were going to be given during an evaluation, and most reported receiving an answer from the psychologist when they asked for this information.

Ethical Issues in Coaching

The coaching of patients and/or research participants about malingering detection involves the intersection of multiple ethical demands. Many attorneys believe that clients with a valid illness or injury should be prepared prior to clinical evaluation and should be provided information about the nature of tests to be administered. However, Gutheil (2003) notes the difficulty in distinguishing appropriately preparing a client from outright coaching. Furthermore, some attorneys believe coaching is part of attorney-client privilege, meaning that the clinician will be unable to discover the extent to which the client was prepared for the evaluation (Lees-Haley, 1997). For psychologists, the ethical code of the American Psychological Association (APA, 2002) indicates that clients should not be coached, as such instruction harms test security, invalidates test results, and leads to the potential misinterpretation of test findings.

Although most psychologists would not directly coach a client, the provision of information to a client's attorney about the battery of tests to be used during an evaluation may be a violation of this ethical principle. A position statement by the National Academy of Neuropsychology (NAN, 2003) recommends that nonspecific information be provided in such circumstances (for example, a list of domains to be assessed rather than specific instruments to be used). Furthermore, as our psychological opinions should be based on reliable and valid methods, we must consider whether our clients may have been coached by others (or even found this information on their own), when interpreting the results of our evaluations.

Many ethical issues must also be considered when conducting research on the effects of coaching. Berry, Lamb, Wetter, Baer, and Widiger (1994) refer to the "fundamental tension" between the need to understand the effects of coaching on instruments designed to detect malingering and the risks of providing effective strategies to avoid detection. This risk is relevant not just to study participants, who are directly provided with potential ways to malinger successfully. A much larger risk exists when study results are published, as these provide easy access for patients and/or attorneys to discover strategies to avoid detection.

Several researchers have offered suggestions to balance test protection with the provision of enough information for others to replicate study findings. Rogers (1997) recommends that coaching studies utilize strategies that involve information likely to be easily obtained only by real-world malingerers. However, as mentioned earlier, virtually any type of coaching information can be publicly obtained by motivated individuals through the Internet. Berry and colleagues (1994) recommend that researchers not directly reveal the specific coaching strategies used in their studies but limit release of that information to individuals known to be bound by the APA Ethical Code. Researchers can then document both the reason for the request (e.g., independent replication of study findings) and the identity of the requester.

To respect these ethical concerns, this chapter discusses general methods of coaching when reviewing the existing literature but does not provide specific details about the coaching methods used. Interested readers are referred to the original articles and their authors for such information.

Methodological Issues in Coaching Research

Given the nature of coaching research, the most common method used is the simulated malingering design. Much of this research has been conducted in undergraduate samples, and researchers have expressed concern about its generalizability to real-world malingering (see the review by Rogers [1997]). The specific forms of coaching used in these studies influence their external validity, and some authors suggest that the simulated malingering design should include detailed information for the simulators (in other words, coach

them) in order to increase generalizability (ibid.; Sullivan, Keane, & Deffenti, 2001).

However, as Ruiz et al. (2002) point out, real-world malingerers have greater motivation to locate testing-related information, more time to prepare their presentation, and access to and contact with more individuals with potentially useful information (e.g., physicians, support group leaders and members, attorneys). On the other hand, the ethical concerns described earlier become even more pronounced when conducting coaching research on patients with real-world secondary gain issues. Thus, most coaching studies have used simulated malingering designs in nonpatient populations.

In addition to sampling methods, many other methodological issues can affect the generalizability of coaching study results. An important methodological decision is whether malingering tests were administered alone or as part of a full neuropsychological battery. If one wants to determine whether a malingering test is easy to detect, particularly by a coached malingerer, it would be best to include the malingering test as part of a standard battery of neuropsychological tests. However, as our review shows, many coaching studies have not assessed the robustness of malingering instruments within a full test battery.

Another methodological issue is the knowledge base of the group asked to malinger. In the early years of malingering research, it was common for researchers to argue that malingering studies should use individuals who have specific knowledge about the disorder of interest. These individuals, they maintained, would have knowledge of and/or be better able to find out how to access such information when preparing to malinger, making the results of such studies more generalizable to actual patient malingerers. Comparisons have been made of various knowledgeable groups, including members of neuroscience classes, psychology graduate students or faculty, psychologists in practice, attorneys, and physicians. Although this approach is not coaching per se, many studies have examined the effects of other types of coaching in concert with being a member of a more knowledgeable group. Thus, in the following review the effect of knowledgeable group membership is also discussed.

A final methodological issue of particular relevance to coaching research is whether participants are given time to prepare to implement the coaching strategies. Tan, Slick, Strauss, and Hultsch (2002) provide data suggesting that, given at least a day to prepare for their role as malingerers, undergraduates are motivated to seek helpful information to prepare for the simulation. Of the undergraduates who were asked to simulate brain damage in their study, 44% spent at least 1 hour finding information to assist them in their simulator role. When asked about the information they accessed, 36% of the malingerers reported surfing the Internet, 16% read books or articles to assist them, 28% talked with friends about how to portray themselves as having brain damage, 24% talked with family members, and 8% spoke with psychologists or doctors. No one reported consulting with an attorney. Thus,

when undergraduates were given time to prepare, a majority accessed information that would be useful to a patient malingerer. However, as our review points out, very few studies provide more than a few minutes for their coached malingerers to prepare for their role.

We have provided a comprehensive but succinct overview of these methodological issues so that readers can judge the quality of each study for themselves. Thus, in the summary tables, the participant samples are noted in a separate column, as is the assessment design (whether the malingering tests were stand-alone—that is, given either by themselves or with other malingering tests—or whether they were administered as part of a larger neuropsychological battery). Whether a study used a knowledgeable group and/or provided preparation time is noted together with other coaching methods.

Methods of Coaching Used in Research

Coaching studies can be grouped into three broad categories based upon the nature of the information provided to participants: (a) typical symptoms of the disorder to be simulated, (b) details about the tests to be administered and test-taking strategies to avoid detection and/or validly simulate a disorder, and (c) a warning about the use of malingering detection methods during the battery of tests to be administered.

Many coaching studies involve the provision of information about typical symptoms of head injury and commonly consist of describing the requested simulation or providing a brief article or handout that lists typical consequences of head injury. Many of these studies indicate that the information used to coach the participants was taken from information readily available to the public (e.g., brochures from local head-injury associations), in response to the ethical concerns noted earlier. The level of detail of this information, however, varies considerably across studies and ranges from merely listing typical symptoms (e.g., memory problems) to providing great detail about symptoms (e.g., specific patterns of memory performance in head-injured persons).

Many studies have also tested the effect of providing test-taking strategies as a way to avoid detection on malingering instruments. Again, the level of coaching varies greatly in these studies. For example, some studies suggest a particular number to get correct on a given task, whereas others give specific information about how malingering tests are developed and how one should respond to malingering test items to avoid detection.

In a survey of experts' practices in malingering detection, Slick et al. (2004) found that 54% of clinicians never warn about the presence of malingering detection tests in their evaluations, and 37.5% always do. More recently, coaching studies have included warnings about the presence of malingering detection in the instructions to the simulated malingerers. It is likely that this method tests the "face validity" of the malingering instrument.

In other words, how easy is it for a malingerer to identify the malingering test as easier than it first may appear, if warned that some tests are measuring effort?

Effects of Coaching on Forced-Choice Tests

Table 11.1 summarizes studies that examine the effects of coaching on forced-choice test performance. The majority of these studies have been conducted with undergraduate simulators, using only malingering instruments in their assessment battery. In six of the seven studies that used knowledgeable groups, there was no evidence that groups with knowledge of head injury were better able to avoid detection. Preparation time was assessed in two studies, though persons receiving additional time were not more effective at avoiding detection.

The effects of symptom coaching were examined in five studies, with seven different outcomes. In three of the seven, forced-choice tests were robust to symptom coaching; coached malingerers were just as easily detected and/or had average scores similar to the uncoached malingerers. In two of the seven, the coached participants were better able to avoid detection, and in the other two the coached participants actually performed worse than the uncoached participants on the forced-choice tasks. Of the two studies that found malingerers were better able to avoid detection (Martin, Bolter, Todd, & Gouvier, 1993; Suhr & Gunstad, 2000), both used a combination of symptom coaching and a warning about malingering detection as coaching strategies. In fact, in this set of studies, warning coaching was used only in combination with other types of coaching, with the exception of Greub and Suhr (2006), and thus its unique effect on forced-choice task performance is unknown.

The effects of providing information about test-taking strategies were assessed in four studies. However, since some of the studies utilized more than one forced-choice method, this approach resulted in eight different outcomes. In six of the eight, the forced-choice task was relatively robust to coaching and led to no difference in the detection rates between coached and uncoached malingerers. In one of the eight, the coached participants were better able to avoid detection by performing better than the uncoached participants (Warrington Recognition Memory Test; Cato, Slick, Strauss, & Hultsch, 2002), while in another study the coached group actually performed worse than the uncoached participants (Multidigit Memory Test; Martin, Hayes, & Gouvier, 1996).

A final set of studies assessed combinations of coaching methods and typically provided both information about symptoms and test-taking strategies to participants. This method appeared to produce sophisticated malingerers, as coached malingerers were generally able to avoid detection (5 studies, 10 outcome measures, only 1 of which showed resistance to coaching).

Table 11.1.
Review of Studies Assessing the Effects of Coaching on Forced-Choice Malingering Tests

Study	Forced-Choice Task; SA or B Administration	Participants	Coaching Methods	Results
Frederick & Foster (1991)	FC task created for study (modified TONI) (SA)	1	TTS	No difference in detection of C and UC
Martin et al. (1993)	MDMT (SA)	1, 2	SX, W	C worse than TBI performance but scored higher than UC
Hiscock et al. (1994)	Digit Memory Test (B)	1,4	KG, SX, TTS	C scored better than UC; inmates scored better than students
Rose et al. (1995)	PDRT (SA)	1, 2	SX, TTS	C still worse than TBI but scored higher than UC; more C escaped detection using cutoff score
Hayes et al. (1995)	MDMT (SA)	1, 1*	KG	KG not related to performance or ability to detect malingering
Martin et al. (1996)	MDMT (SA)	1, 1*, 2,	TTS, KG	KG did not change detection rates; C performed worse than UC
Franzen & Martin (1996)	FC recognition of WMS-R LM (SA)	5	KG	KG no effect; 32 of 37 still classified as malingerers
Rees et al. (1998)	TOMM (B)	1, 2	KG	KG no effect
Inman et al. (1998)	VSVT, LMT (SA)	1	TTS	No difference in performance between C and UC; replicated in second study in same article

Study	Test			Results
Rose et al. 1998	PRDT and a nonverbal, forced-choice test (SA)	1, 2, 3	SX, TTS	C better than UC on both; C still worse than TBI on PDRT but similar to TBI on other task
Ju & Varney (2000)	PDRT (SA)	2, 3	KG	Both groups worse on PDRT when asked to malinger, but TBI C no better at escaping detection than TBI UC
Suhr & Gunstad (2000)	PDRT (B)	1	SX, W	C better able to avoid detection than UC
Cato et al. (2002, 2003)	WRMT, abbreviated Hiscock FC (SA)	1, 2	TTS	C avoided detection on WRMT; C not different from UC on the abbreviated Hiscock
Tan et al. (2002)	TOMM, VSVT, WMT (SA)	1	prep time	Even those who reported spending at least 1 hour preparing were still detected at high rates on all tests
Dunn et al. (2003)	WMT and CARB (SA)	1	TTS, SX	C harder to detect than UC on both measures, though just SX info actually did worse on tasks
Glassmire et al. 2003	WMT Faces I	6, 2	KG	No effect of KG in avoiding detection
Vickery et al. (2004)	Digit memory test, TOMM, LMT (B)	1*, 3,	KG, SX, TTS	C better at avoiding detection than UC; KG did not have an effect
Shum et al. (2004)	MDMT (SA)	1, 2	SX, prep time	Prep time did not have an effect
Powell et al. (2004)	TOMM (B)	1	SX, TTS	Detection rates of SX C no different from TTS C (no UC group)

(continued)

Table 11.1.
(continued)

Study	Forced-Choice Task; SA or B Administration	Participants	Coaching Methods	Results
Gorny et al. (2005)	ASTM, WCMT, MSVT	3	SX, W, TTS	Detection rates declined with level of C information provided; ASTM still detected all malingerers
Greub & Suhr (2006)	LMT	1*	W	No significant difference between C and UC participants

Note. Malingering tests: TOMM = Test of Memory Malingering, MDMT = Multi-Digit Memory Test, LMT = Letter Memory Test, WMT = Word Memory Test, CARB = Computerized Assessment of Response Bias, WMS-R LM = Wechsler Memory Scale-Revised Logical Memory Subtest, VSVT = Victoria Symptom Validity Test, FC = Forced Choice, WRMT = Warrington Recognition Memory Test, PDRT = Portland Digit Recognition Test, ASTM = Amsterdam Short-Term Memory Test, WCMT = Word Completion Memory Test, MSVT = Medical Symptom Validity Test, SA = stand-alone (only malingering tests given in the study), B = battery (malingering tests given in the context of other neuropsychological tests), TONI = Test of Nonverbal Intelligence. Participants: 1 = undergraduate simulators, 1* = undergraduates with head injury history, 2 = patients with head injury, 3 = community volunteers, 4 = inmates, 5 = graduate students/psychologists, 6 = military personnel. Coaching methods: SX = coaching by provision of typical symptoms of head injury, W = coaching by warning about malingering detection methods, TTS = coaching by provision of test-taking strategies, KG = assumption that groups with more knowledge and/or more access to knowledge about head injury will be more sophisticated malingerers, C = coached malingerers, UC = uncoached malingerers, TBI = traumatic brain injury participants.

Overall, in about 46% of the findings, coached malingerers were better able to avoid detection on forced-choice tasks, while in about 42% of the findings no differences in performance were evident between coached and uncoached malingerers. In only 12% of cases did coached malingerers actually perform worse than the uncoached malingerers. In general, more detailed coaching (i.e., using a combination of coaching strategies) resulted in greater ability to avoid detection on the forced-choice measures, suggesting that they are not very robust to coaching.

However, as mentioned earlier, a primary limitation of these studies is that most of the forced-choice measures were presented alone or only in combination with other malingering tests. Thus, it is unknown whether forced-choice tests, when embedded in a full neuropsychological battery, are more or less vulnerable to coaching; we believe that they would be even more vulnerable to coaching because they may be easier to identify as malingering tests within that context due to the contrast in task difficulty between malingering and standard neuropsychological tests. Future studies that assess the robustness of forced-choice methods to coaching techniques should increase the external validity of their studies by including the malingering test of interest within a full, clinically relevant neuropsychological battery.

Effects of Coaching on Other Malingering Tests

Several studies have examined the effects of coaching on traditional non-forced-choice malingering detection tests, such as the Dot Counting Test, the 15-Item Test, the 16-Item Test, and the 21-Item Test. These studies are reviewed in Table 11.2. The majority of these coaching studies are consistent with other literature on these tests, which suggests that, in general, they are not sensitive to malingering regardless of whether the malingerers are coached or uncoached. For example, of the 10 coaching studies using the Dot Counting Test, 5 found that it was insensitive to malingering. Another 4 studies reported no differences between coached and uncoached malingerers, although malingering detection rates were low for both groups. Interestingly, in the final study, the coached malingerers actually performed worse than the uncoached malingerers under the conditions of symptom and warning coaching, being a member of a knowledgeable group, and receiving compensation for malingering (Erdal, 2004). Of the 8 studies using the 15-, 16-, and/or 21-item tests, 5 showed a lack of sensitivity to malingering regardless of whether the malingerers were coached.

In two outcomes reported in one article (Inman, Vickery, Berry, Lamb, Edwards, et al., 1998), test-taking strategy coaching did not affect performance on these tests. In another work (Rose, Hall, Szalda-Petree, & Bach, 1998), a combination of test-taking strategy and symptom coaching made the coached malingerers harder to detect, but Erdal (2004) found that a combination of symptom and warning coaching in a knowledgeable group

Table 11.2.
Effects of Coaching on Traditional Non-Forced-Choice Malingering Tests

Study	Tests	Participants	Coaching Method	Results
Hiscock et al. (1994)	DC, 15IT (B)	1, 4	KG, SX, TTS	Not sensitive to malingering, whether C or UC
Frederick et al. (1994)	15IT, DC, 21IT, 16IT (SA)	1, 2	TTS	DC, 15IT, 21IT not sensitive to malingering; C less likely to be detected on 21IT, 15IT
Hayes et al. (1995)	DC (SA)	1, 1*	KG	KG no effect on performance
Martin et al. (1996)	DC (SA)	1, 1*, 2	TTS, KG	C no different from UC; KG no effect
Franzen & Martin (1996)	21IT, 15IT, DC (SA)	5	KG	21IT, 15IT, DC not sensitive to malingering
Binks et al. (1997)	DC(SA)	1, 2	TTS	C no different from UC in detection
Inman et al. (1998)	21IT (SA)	1	TTS	C no different from UC; replicated in second study reported in same article
Rose et al. (1998)	DC, 21IT, (SA)	1, 2, 3	SX, TTS	C better than UC on 21IT; DC not sensitive to malingering
Cato et al. (2002, 2003)	15IT, DC (SA)	1, 2	TTS	Measures not sensitive to malingering, whether C or UC
Erdal (2004)	15IT, DC (B)	1	KG, SX, W	C interacted with provision of compensation; KG made easier to detect when compensation; SX plus W tended to avoid detection, except when compensation
Shum et al. (2004)	15IT (SA)	1, 2	SX, prep time	On 15IT, long prep time led to more detection
Suhr et al. (2004)	FIT (B)	1*	W	15IT not sensitive to malingering

Note. Malingering tests: DC = Dot Counting Test, 15IT = 15-Item Test, 21IT = 21-Item Test, 16IT = 16-item Test, B = full test battery, SA = only malingering tests administered. Participants: 1 = undergraduate simulators, 1* = undergraduates with head injury history, 2 = patients with head injury, 3 = community volunteers, 4 = inmates, 5 = graduate students/psychologists. Coaching methods: SX = coaching by provision of typical symptoms of head injury, W = coaching by warning about malingering detection methods, TTS = coaching by provision of test-taking strategies, KG = assumption that groups with more knowledge and/or more access to knowledge about head injury will be more sophisticated malingerers, C = coached malingerers, UC-uncoached malingerers.

actually made the coached malingerers easier to detect, as they performed worse than the uncoached malingerers on the 15-Item Test.

The primary conclusions from the coaching studies that investigated these traditional instruments further demonstrate their insensitivity to malingering. This is all the more notable in that the vast majority of these coaching studies tested the effectiveness of these instruments without including them as part of a comprehensive neuropsychological battery, where they may be easier for an individual to identify (even without coaching) as malingering tests.

Coaching and Patterns of Test Performance on Standard Neuropsychological Tests

In the early 90s, researchers suggested that standard neuropsychological tests were not useful in the detection of malingering, as no typical malingering profiles had emerged from the existing studies. This prompted the development of many stand-alone malingering tests, for which a convincing number of validity data exist at the present time. However, as noted earlier, stand-alone malingering tests that are used exclusively for malingering may be more vulnerable to coaching. For malingerers who wish to learn about such tests, information is more readily available about the traditional malingering instruments.

Lezak (in Lezak, Howieson, & Loring, 2004) provides an anecdotal account of a patient she evaluated who said, "Oh, the TOMM," when this test was presented, despite having never been administered it in a prior evaluation. Allen and Green (2001) documented the decline in sensitivity of the CARB over several years and speculated that the deterioration may have been due to the test's growing familiarity to attorneys during that time. Tests with a ceiling effect such as the 15-Item Test are obviously easy, which makes them generally insensitive to malingering, whether coached or not. Furthermore, symptom validity tests have a specific look to them that may make it easier for malingerers to recognize the nature of the task when being evaluated. Developing malingering indices embedded within standard neuropsychological tests presents many potential advantages, only one of which may be the increased robustness to the effects of coaching. Altering performance on patterns of tests in order to simulate an injury requires remembering information about the appropriate presenting pattern on two or more indicators at once, which in theory would be much harder to simulate convincingly, relative to simply having to pay attention to the number of correct responses to give.

Table 11.3 summarizes the results of coaching studies that have examined patterns of test performance for detection of malingering. Most of these studies have simply determined whether standard neuropsychological tasks exhibit group differences as a result of coaching. The findings for memory tests suggest an interesting pattern. Several studies have shown better or more

Table 11.3.

Effects of Coaching on Neuropsychological Test Performance and Test Patterns

Study	Tests	Participants	Coaching Method	Results
Martin et al. (1993)	Multi-Digit Memory Test pattern over trials (SA)	1, 2	SX, W	C showed performance decline over blocks of trials (increase in delay); UC and TBI patients showed no change over time
Frederick et al. (1994)	FC modified TONI patterns, word recognition vs. recall on AVLT (SA)	1, 2	TTS	Word recall/recognition not sensitive to malingering; C less likely to be detected on FC patterns of performance
Rosenfeld et al. (1995)	recall of autobiographical information (SA)	1	SX, TTS	C showed improved recognition of autobiographical information but still only 50% correct, while autobiographical responses were closer to 100% in amnesics
Martin et al. (1996)	Digit Span (SA)	1, 1*, 2	TTS, KG	C no different from UC; KG no effect
Franzen & Martin (1996)	Digit Span (SA)	5	KG	Digit Span forward detected 29 of 37 malingerers.
Johnson & Lesniak-Karpiak (1997)	Grooved Pegboard Test, WMS-R	1	W	C better than UC on all WMS-R indices; C no different from UC on Grooved Pegboard.
Schwartz et al. (1998)	WMS, WAIS-R (B)	2, 3, 8	KG, SX	Lawyers performed more like actual TBI patients than physicians.
Wong et al. (1998)	Grooved Pegboard Test, TMT, LM 1 and II, Digit Span, VR 1 and II (B)	1	W	C no different from UC on any of the measures

Study	Test			Findings
Rose et al. (1998)	PDRT response latencies, non-verbal FC test patterns (SA)	1, 2, 3	SX, TTS	C no different from UC in response latency on PDRT and on patterns on nonverbal FC test; C better than UC on patterns on nonverbal FC test
Rapport et al. (1998)	Grip Strength, Finger Tapping, Grooved Pegboard Test (SA)	1	SX, TTS	When assessing overall motor performance profile, UC consistent with TBI; C inconsistent with TBI
Gfeller & Cradock (1998)	Seashore Rhythm Test (SA)	1, 2	SX	C no different from UC
Coleman (1998)	CVLT (SA)	1	SX, TTS	C better than UC on learning across trials; C no different from UC on recognition hits, slope, and discriminability
Kurtz et al. (1999)	Olfactory test (SA)	1, 7	TTS	Whether C or UC, pattern of olfactory discrimination not consistent with true anosmia
Suhr & Gunstad (2000)	AVLT patterns (B)	1	W	Having at least one AVLT pattern indicator detected both C and UC at a relatively high rate.
DiCarlo et al. (2000)	Category test (SA)	1, 2	TTS	C better able to avoid detection than UC
Sullivan et al. (2001)	AVLT (SA)	1, 8	SX, W, KG	No effect of C methods on performance
Haines & Norris (2001)	AVLT, implicit memory test, TMT (B)	1, 2	KG	No effect of KG
Sullivan et al. (2002)	AVLT patterns (SA)	1, 8	SX, W, KG	No difference in C or UC
Suhr (2002)	AVLT serial position effect (B)	1	SX, W	No difference in C or UC
Dunn et al. (2003)	CARB reaction time (SA)	1	SX, TTS	C and UC no different on reaction time
Borckarat et al. (2003)	Cognitive Behavioral Driver's Inventory (SA)	1	SX, TTS	C and UC no different on any of the subtests

(continued)

Table 11.3.
(*continued*)

Study	Tests	Participants	Coaching Method	Results
Shum et al. (2004)	Digit Span, visual memory span of WMS-R (SA)	1, 2	SX, prep time	Long prep time meant better performance and was harder to detect
Powell et al. (2004)	TOMM patterns (B)	1	SX, TTS	TTS C did better across trials of TOMM than SX C
Suhr et al. (2004)	EIAVLTX (B)	1*	W	No difference in detection rates between C and UC
Bender & Rogers (2004)	Test of Cognitive Abilities (B)	1, 2, 3	W, TTS	C did not affect detection rates on the effort measures
Gorny et al. (2005)	Reliable Digit Span, TMTA/TMTB, CFT	3	SX, W, TTS	TMTA/B relatively insensitive to malingering; C easier to detect on CFT; Reliable Digit Span robust to C
Greub & Suhr (2006)	LMT difference in easy versus hard items	1*	W	Relatively robust to C

Note. Malingering measures: FC = forced choice, TONI = Test of Nonverbal Intelligence, AVLT = Auditory Verbal Learning Test, WMS-R = Wechsler Memory Scale-Revised, WAIS-R, Wechsler Adult Intelligence Scale-Revised, TMT = Trail-Making Test, LM = logical memory, VR = visual reproduction, PDRT = Portland Digit Recognition Test, CARB = Computerized Assessment of Response Bias, TOMM = Test of Memory Malingering, CFT = Complex Figure Test, LMT = Letter Memory Test, B = full test battery, SA = only malingering tests administered, EIALTX = Effort Index AVLT Extended. Participants: 1 = undergraduate simulators, 1* = undergraduates with head-injury history, 2 = patients with head injury, 3 = community volunteers, 4 = inmates, 5 = graduate students/psychologists, 7 = other neurological patients, 8 = attorneys/physicians. Coaching methods: SX = coaching by provision of typical symptoms of head injury, W = coaching by warning about malingering detection methods, TTS = coaching by provision of test-taking strategies, KG = assumption that groups with more knowledge and/or more access to knowledge about head injury will be more sophisticated malingerers, C = coached malingerers, UC-uncoached malingerers, TBI = traumatic brain injury.

realistic performances in coached malingerers (using various methods of coaching) on the Wechsler Memory scale indices or subtests when comparing coached and uncoached malingerers (Johnson & Lesniak-Karpiak, 1997; Shum, O'Gorman, & Alpar, 2004; Schwartz, Gramling, Lawson Kerr, & Morin, 1998); an exception is Wong, Lerner-Poppen, and Durham (1998), who found no effect of warning coaching on subtests of the Wechsler Memory scale.

On the other hand, in studies that examined group differences on serial list learning tasks, the results typically indicate that coached and uncoached malingerers are not distinguishable in their performance on variables such as recognition hits, slope, discriminability, and serial position in learning trials even when using combinations of coaching strategies (Coleman, Rapport, Millis, Ricker, & Farchione, 1998; Haines & Norris, 2001; Suhr, 2002; Sullivan, Deffenti, & Keane, 2002).

Relatively fewer studies have created cutoff scores based on standard neuropsychological test results in order to use them as malingering detection indices. Frederick, Sarfaty, Johnston, and Powell (1994) used a simple index to code for malingering when recall performance was better than recognition memory performance on a list learning task; the index was not sensitive to malingering, whether coached or uncoached. Barrash, Suhr, and Manzel (2004) developed an exaggeration index for the Auditory Verbal Learning Test (AVLT) based on several patterns of performance that are not likely to occur in neurologically based memory disorders but are seen in malingerers. Suhr, Gunstad, Greub, and Barrash (2004) tested the robustness of the AVLT exaggeration index to coaching in two separate, simulated malingering samples. No differences in detection rates were observed among coached and uncoached malingerers in either sample, which suggests that the index was relatively robust to coaching.

The vast majority of malingering measures to date focus on malingered memory deficits. Fewer studies have analyzed nonmemory neuropsychological tests; even fewer of those have explored whether coaching affects the accuracy of the proposed malingering indicators. Overall, studies that have examined nonmemory tests (e.g., motor speed, abstract reasoning, attention, intellect) have found no clear effect of coaching, regardless of the strategy type (Gfeller & Cradock, 1998; Gorny, Merten, Henry, & Brockhaus, 2005; Rapport, Farchione, Coleman, & Axelrod, 1998; Wong et al., 1998). A couple of studies have analyzed computerized test batteries and reported that they are generally robust to coaching (Borckardt, Engum, Lambert, Nash, Bracy, et al., 2003; Bender & Rogers, 2004), though neither battery has been tested in more than one study. Finally, although a smattering of other coaching studies have looked for patterns of test performance in very specific cognitive domains (based on what one would expect in normal head-injury autobiographical information, such as implicit memory and olfactory skills), more work needs to be done to replicate these findings in other labs to make these patterns useful for malingering detection.

Patterns of Performance on Forced-Choice Tests

Several recent studies have examined patterns of performance on forced-choice malingering tests, including performance over items and trials that may on the surface appear to grow more difficult, consistency in performance on equally difficult items, and adding reaction time to the forced-choice task. Thus far, the results are relatively promising. For example, Martin et al. (1993) demonstrated that changes in performance over item difficulty level are robust to symptom and warning coaching, while Powell, Gfeller, Hendricks, and Sharland (2004) demonstrated that performance over item difficulty level is vulnerable to symptom and test taking strategy coaching.

In addition, Frederick and Foster (1991; Frederick et al., 1994) developed a pattern of performance index based on both performance over item difficulty and consistency in performance over equally difficult items, as applied to a nonverbal forced-choice test. Using that index, they successfully detected approximately 94% of uncoached malingerers and 74% of coached malingerers (Frederick & Foster, 1991); however, in a replication study (Frederick et al., 1994), the detection rates declined, particularly for the coached participants (81.75 of uncoached malingerers, 49.1% of coached malingerers).

Greub and Suhr (2006) have described an index for the Letter Memory Test (LMT) by using performance on the easiest-item set relative to the hardest set. Overall, the proposed index was moderately sensitive to malingering (though less so than the standard LMT cutoffs) and relatively robust to warning coaching. Although the addition of reaction time to forced-choice measures has shown some promise with regard to robustness to coaching (Rose et al., 1998; Dunn, Shear, Howe, & Ris, 2003), the usefulness of reaction time as a measure of malingering detection is unclear; whether coached malingerers perform faster or slower depends on the comparison group utilized (e.g., uncoached malingerers or patients with traumatic brain injury). Future studies should continue to examine patterns of performance, including reaction time, as an added component to forced-choice measures to determine whether they make such measures more robust to the effects of coaching.

Effects of Coaching on Self-Report Data

Few studies have examined the effects of coaching on self-reported symptoms in head injury or other neuropsychological conditions. Our review is limited to studies that focus on self-reports of head-injury symptoms rather than general malingering of psychopathology, injury, or illness on self-report instruments such as the MMPI, which are reviewed in chapter 9 by Berry and Schipper and chapter 10 by Larrabee in this volume. Relevant coaching

studies are reviewed in Table 11.4. We have included the Wong et al. (1998) MMPI study because the participants were specifically asked to malinger head injury when completing the instrument.

Overall, the data in this research area are limited by the use of primarily undergraduate simulator samples, and the only methods of coaching that have been tested are the provision of typical symptoms of head injury, use of knowledgeable groups, and warning about the use of malingering detection techniques during testing. None of the reviewed studies reported any different patterns of self-report symptoms based on coaching. For the most part, coached malingerers reported just as many symptoms as naïve malingerers and were no more difficult to detect on self-report validity indices. No study examined patterns of symptom report that might distinguish malingerers

Table 11.4.
Effects of Coaching on Self-Reported Symptoms of Head Injury

Study	Sample	Measures	Coaching Method	Results
Sullivan & Richter (2002)	1	Neuropsychological Symptoms Checklist	SX, W	No effect of C
Haines & Norris (2001)	1, 2, 9	Memory Self-Efficacy Questionnaire	SX	No group differences
Martin et al. (1996)	1, 1*	Postconcussion Symptom Checklist	TTS, W, KG	No effects for KG; no differences for U or UC
Hayes et al. (1995)	1, 1*	Postconcussion Symptom Checklist	KG	No main effect for KG; no interaction of KG with malingering status
Wong et al. (1998)	1	102-item version of MMPI-2 (including all items from standard validity scales)	SX, W	C detected by F scale as often as UC

Note. Participants: 1 = undergraduate simulators, 1* = undergraduates with head injury history, 2 = patients with head injury, 9 = other patients. Measures: MMPI-2 = Minnesota Multiphasic Personality Inventory (2nd ed.). Coaching methods: SX = coaching by provision of typical symptoms of head injury, W = coaching by warning about malingering detection methods, TTS = coaching by provision of test-taking strategies, KG = assumption that groups with more knowledge and/or more access to knowledge about head injury will be more sophisticated malingerers, C = coached, UC = uncoached, F = frequency scale.

from individuals with neuropsychological impairment; however, related re-search suggests that such a pattern may be difficult to demonstrate, given the high base rate of purported "postconcussive syndrome" symptom report in non-head-injured groups (Dunn, Lees-Haley, Brown, Williams, & English, 1995; Fox, Lees-Haley, Earnest, & Dolezal-Wood, 1995; Gunstad & Suhr, 2004) and the evidence that individuals with knowledge of neuroscience are unable to pick out symptoms of traumatic brain injury from among a list of common psychological symptoms (Lees Haley & Dunn, 1994). However, given the frequent use of self-report instruments to identify symptoms of mild head injury, there is a crucial need for more research on the robustness of symptom report measures to coached malingering.

Summary and Discussion

The coaching literature is still fraught with methodological concerns, which makes it difficult to draw many conclusions from the existing research. In deference to the many ethical concerns, most coaching studies employ a sim-ulated malingerer design. Knowledgeable participants do not appear better at avoiding detection and at times were actually easier to detect on malingering measures. However, the exact nature of the knowledge may be important; Schwartz et al. (1998) found that lawyers (who are likely as knowledgeable about test-taking strategies as they are of head-injury symptoms) were best able to perform in a manner consistent with traumatic brain-injury patients, while physicians (who are likely to be more knowledgeable about symptoms rather than tests) performed worse than traumatic brain-injury patients. In any event, it behooves future researchers to make the simulation as convincing as possible, provide preparation time for the simulation, and assess the ef-fectiveness of malingering instruments within the context of a full neuro-psychological battery in order to best simulate actual clinical conditions and make the results more externally valid.

Although it is difficult to draw conclusions about any particular type of coaching strategy from the existing literature, a few final words about the use of warning seem warranted. In 1997 Johnson and Lesniak-Karpiak reported that warning simulators about malingering detection resulted in the nor-malization of neuropsychological data. They interpreted these findings as indicating that clinicians should warn clients about the use of malinger-ing detection, as this would make the test results more valid. In fact, they maintained that psychologists may be ethically obligated to include such a warning as part of informed consent. However, Youngjohn, Lees-Haley, and Binder (1999) took the opposing view, arguing that such a warning simply results in more sophisticated malingering; rather than making the test results more valid, warning just makes the malingerers harder to detect.

The debate over whether clinicians should notify patients about ma-lingering detection continues today. Slick and Iverson (2003) contend that it

would be good clinical practice to include a general warning about malingering detection as part of informed consent prior to an evaluation. However, Victor and Abeles (2004) maintain that, if coaching can distort the accuracy of an evaluation (which our review suggests a warning can do), then clients should simply be advised to perform honestly and to do their best; any additional information would be improper. As we have shown, clinicians are quite split on this issue; the results of the Slick et al. (2004) survey suggest that, even though more than half of all clinicians never warn about malingering detection, more than a third of them always do. A position statement by the National Academy of Neuropsychology (NAN, 2003) offers an example of a consent procedure that balances concerns about the effects of warning with the need to provide informed consent. The organization recommends instructing patients to answer accurately by not minimizing problems but also by not exaggerating. It also recommends instructing patients to give their best effort in testing and informing them that the examination procedures include assessment of the accuracy of their responses, as well as the effort they give on the tests.

Our review suggests that, in general, standard forced-choice indices are vulnerable to coaching, particularly if more than one coaching strategy is used. Research on patterns of performance (both on traditional neuropsychological measures and on forced-choice based measures) can help make malingering indices more robust, but overall this area of research is still in its infancy. Understanding the effects of various forms of coaching on malingering measures remains a critical clinical issue.

References

Allen, L. M., & Green, P. (2001). Declining CARB failure rates over 6 years of testing: What's wrong with this picture? *Archives of Clinical Neuropsychology, 16,* 846.

American Psychological Association. (2002). Ethical principles of psychologists and code of conduct. *American Psychologist, 57,* 1060–1073.

Barrash, J., Suhr, J., & Manzel, K. (2004). Detecting poor effort and malingering with an expanded version of the Auditory Verbal Learning Text (AVLTX): Validation with clinical samples. *Journal of Clinical and Experimental Neuropsychology, 26,* 125–140.

Bauer, L., & McCaffrey, R. J. (2006). Coverage of the Test of Memory Malingering, Victoria Symptom Validity Test, and Word Memory Test on the Internet: Is test security threatened? *Archives of Clinical Neuropsychology, 21*(1), 121–126.

Bender, S. D., & Rogers, R. (2004). Detection of neurocognitive feigning: Development of a multistrategy assessment. *Archives of Clinical Neuropsychology, 19,* 49–60.

Ben-Porath, Y. S. (1994). The ethical dilemma of coached malingering research. *Psychological Assessment, 6,* 14–15.

Berry, D. T. R., Lamb, D. G., Wetter, M. W., Baer, R. A., & Widiger, T. A. (1994). Ethical considerations in research on coached malingering. *Psychological Assessment, 6,* 16–17.

Binks, P. G., Gouvier, W. D., & Walters, W. F. (1997). Malingering detection with the Dot Counting Test. *Archives of Clinical Neuropsychology, 12,* 41–46.

Borckardt, J. J., Engum, E. S., Lambert, E. W., Nash, M., Bracy, O., & Ray, E. C. (2003). Use of the CBDI to detect malingering when malingerers do their "homework." *Archives of Clinical Neuropsychology, 18,* 57–69.

Coleman, R. D., Rapport, L. J., Millis, S. R., Ricker, J. H., & Farchione, T. J. (1998). Effects of coaching on detection of malingering on the California Verbal Learning Test. *Journal of Clinical and Experimental Neuropsychology, 20,* 201–210.

Dunn, J., Lees-Haley, P., Brown, R., Williams, C., & English, L. (1995). Neurotoxic complaint base rates of personal-injury claimants: Implications for neuropsychological assessment. *Journal of Clinical Psychology, 51,* 577–581.

Dunn, T. M., Shear, P. K., Howe, S., & Ris, M. D. (2003). Detecting neuropsychological malingering: Effects of coaching and information. *Archives of Clinical Neuropsychology, 18,* 121–134.

Erdal, K. (2004). The effects of motivation, coaching, and knowledge of neuropsychology on the simulated malingering of head injury. *Archives of Clinical Neuropsychology, 19,* 73–88.

Fox, D., Lees-Haley, P., Earnest, K., & Dolezal-Wood, S. (1995). Nonspecificity of postconcussive symptoms: Base rates and etiology in psychiatric patients. *The Clinical Neuropsychologist, 9,* 89–92.

Franzen, M. D., Iverson, G. L., & McCracken, L. M. (1990). The detection of malingering in neuropsychological assessment. *Neuropsychology Review, 1,* 247–279.

Franzen, M. D., & Martin, N. (1996). Do people with knowledge fake better? *Applied Neuropsychology, 3,* 82–85.

Frederick, R. I., & Foster, H. G. (1991). Multiple measures of malingering on a forced-choice test of cognitive ability. *Psychological Assessment, 3,* 596–602.

Frederick, R. I., Sarfaty, S. D., Johnston, J. D., & Powell, J. (1994). Validation of a detector of response bias on a forced-choice test of nonverbal ability. *Neuropsychology, 8,* 118–125.

Gfeller, J. D., & Cradock, M. M. (1998). Detecting feigned neuropsychological impairment with the Seashore Rhythm test. *Journal of Clinical Psychology, 54,* 431–438.

Glassmire, D. M., Bierley, R. A., Wisniewski, A. M., Greene, R. L., Kennedy, J. E., & Date, E. (2003). Using the WMS-III Faces subtest to detect malingered memory impairment. *Journal of Clinical and Experimental Neuropsychology, 25,* 465–481.

Gorny, I., Merten, T., Henry, M., & Brockhaus, R. (2005, July). *Information, warning, coaching: How much do they need? An analogue study on feigned cognitive symptoms.* Poster presented at the joint meeting of the International Neuropsychological Society, British Neuropsychological Society, and Division of Neuropsychology of the British Psychological Society, Dublin, Ireland.

Greub, B. L., & Suhr, J. A. (2006). The validity of the Letter Memory Test as a measure of memory malingering: Robustness to coaching. *Archives of Clinical Neuropsychology, 21,* 249–254.

Gunstad, J., & Suhr, J. A. (2004). Cognitive factors in postconcussive syndrome symptom report. *Archives of Clinical Neuropsychology, 19,* 391–405.

Gutheil, T. G. (2003). Reflections on coaching by attorneys. *Journal of the American Academy of Psychiatry and Law, 31,* 6–9.

Haines, M. E., & Norris, M. P. (2001). Comparing student and patient simulated malingerers' performance on standard neuropsychological measures to detect feigned cognitive deficits. *The Clinical Neuropsychologist, 15,* 171–182.

Hayes, J. S., Martin, R., & Gouvier, W. D. (1995). Influence of prior knowledge and experience on the ability to feign mild head-injury symptoms in head-injured and non-head-injured college students. *Applied Neuropsychology, 2,* 63–66.

Hiscock, C. K., Branham, J. D., & Hiscock, M. (1994). Detection of feigned cognitive impairment: The 2-alternative forced-choice method compared with selected conventional tests. *Journal of Psychopathology and Behavioral Assessment, 16,* 95–110.

Inman, T. H., Vickery, C. D., Berry, D. T. R., Lamb, D. G., Edwards, C. L., & Smith, G. T. (1998). Development and initial validation of a new procedure for evaluating adequacy of effort given during neuropsychological testing: The Letter Memory Test. *Psychological Assessment, 10,* 128–139.

Johnson, J. L., & Lesniak-Karpiak, K. (1997). The effect of warning on malingering on memory and motor tasks in college samples. *Archives of Clinical Neuropsychology, 12,* 231–238.

Ju, D., & Varney, N. R. (2000). Can head-injury patients simulate malingering? *Applied Neuropsychology, 7,* 201–207.

Kurtz, D. B., White, T. L., Hornung, D. E., & Belknap, E. (1999). What a tangled web we weave: Discriminating between malingering and anosmia. *Chemical Senses, 24,* 697–700.

Lees-Haley, P. R. (1997). Attorneys influence expert evidence in forensic psychology and neuropsychology cases. *Assessment, 4,* 321–324.

Lees-Haley, P. R., & Dunn, J. T. (1994). The ability of naïve subjects to report symptoms of mild brain injury, posttraumatic stress disorder, major depression, and generalized anxiety disorder. *Journal of Clinical Psychology, 50,* 252–256.

Lezak, M. D., Howieson, D. B., & Loring, D. W. (2004). *Neuropsychological assessment* (4th ed.). New York: Oxford University Press.

Martin, R. C., Bolter, J. F., Todd, M. E., & Gouvier, W. D. (1993). Effects of sophistication and motivation on the detection of malingered memory performance using a computerized forced-choice task. *Journal of Clinical and Experimental Neuropsychology, 15,* 867–880.

Martin, R. C., Hayes, Y., & Gouvier, W. D. (1996). Differential vulnerability between postconcussion self-report and objective malingering tests in identifying simulated mild head injury. *Journal of Clinical and Experimental Neuropsychology, 18,* 265–275.

National Academy of Neuropsychology. (2003). *Independent and court-ordered forensic neuropsychological examinations: Official statement of the National Academy of Neuropsychology.* Accessed February 23, 2007, at http://www.nanonline.org/downloads/paio/Position/NANIMEpaper.pdf.

Powell, M. R., Gfeller, J. D., Hendricks, B. L., & Sharland, M. (2004). Detecting symptom- and test-coached simulators on the Test of Memory Malingering. *Archives of Clinical Neuropsychology, 19,* 693–702.

Rapport, L. J., Farchione, T. J., Coleman, R. D., & Axelrod, B. D. (1998). Effects of coaching on malingered motor function profiles. *Journal of Clinical and Experimental Neuropsychology, 20,* 89–97.

Rees, L. M., Tombaugh, T. N., Gansler, D. A., & Moczynski, N. P. (1998). Five validation experiments of the Test of Memory Malingering (TOMM). *Psychological Assessment, 10,* 10–20.

Rogers, R. (Ed.). (1997). *Clinical assessment of malingering and deception* (2nd ed.). New York: Guilford.

Rose, F. E., Hall, S., & Szalda-Petree, A. D. (1995). Portland Digit Recognition Test-Computerized: Measuring response latency improves the detection of malingering. *The Clinical Neuropsychologist, 9,* 124–134.

Rose, F. E., Hall, S., Szalda-Petree, A. D., & Bach, P. J. (1998). A comparison of four tests of malingering and the effects of coaching. *Archives of Clinical Neuropsychology, 13,* 349–363.

Rosenfeld, J. P., Ellwagen, J., & Sweet, J. (1995). Detecting simulated amnesia with event-related brain potentials. *International Journal of Psychophysiology, 19,* 1–11.

Ruiz, M. A., Drake, E. B., Glass, A., Marcotte, D., & van Gorp, W. G. (2002). Trying to beat the system: Misuse of the Internet to assist in avoiding the detection of psychological symptom dissimulation. *Professional Psychology: Research and Practice, 33,* 294–299.

Schwartz, S. M., Gramling, S. E., Lawson Kerr, K., & Morin, C. (1998). Evaluation of intellect and deficit-specific information on the ability to fake memory deficits. *International Journal of Law and Psychiatry, 21,* 261–272.

Shum, D. H. K., O'Gorman, J. G., & Alpar, A. (2004). Effects of incentive and preparation time on performance and classification accuracy of standard and malingering-specific memory tests. *Archives of Clinical Neuropsychology, 19,* 817–823.

Slick, D. J., & Iverson, G. L. (2003). Ethical issues arising in forensic neuropsychological assessment. In I. Z. Schultz and D. O. Brady (Eds.), *Psychological injuries at trial* (CD). Chicago: American Bar Association Press.

Slick, D. J., Tan, J. E., Strauss, E. H., & Hultsch, D. F. (2004). Detecting malingering: A survey of experts' practices. *Archives of Clinical Neuropsychology, 19,* 465–473.

Suhr, J. A. (2002). Malingering, coaching, and the serial position effect. *Archives of Clinical Neuropsychology, 17,* 69–77.

Suhr, J. A., & Gunstad, J. (2000). The effects of coaching on sensitivity and specificity of malingering measures. *Archives of Clinical Neuropsychology, 15,* 415–424.

Suhr, J. A., Gunstad, J., Greub, B., & Barrash, J. (2004). Exaggeration index for an expanded version of the Auditory Verbal Learning Test: Robustness to coaching. *Journal of Clinical and Experimental Neuropsychology, 26,* 416–427.

Sullivan, K., Deffenti, C., & Keane, B. (2002). Malingering on the RAVLT, Part II: Detection strategies. *Archives of Clinical Neuropsychology, 17,* 223–233.

Sullivan, K., Keane, B., & Deffenti, C. (2001). Malingering on the RAVLT, Part 1: Deterrence strategies. *Archives of Clinical Neuropsychology, 16,* 627–641.

Sullivan, K., & Richer, C. (2002). Malingering on subjective complaint tasks: An exploration of the deterrent effects of warning. *Archives of Clinical Neuropsychology, 17,* 691–708.

Tan, J. E., Slick, D. J., Strauss, E., & Hultsch, D. F. (2002). How'd they do it? Malingering strategies on symptom validity tests. *Clinical Neuropsychologist, 16,* 495–505.

Trueblood, W., & Schmidt, M. (1993). Malingering and other considerations in the neuropsychological evaluation of mild head injury. *Journal of Clinical and Experimental Neuropsychology, 15,* 578–590.

Vickery, C. D., Berry, D. T. R., Dearth, C. S., Vagnini, V. L., & Baser, R. E. (2004). Head injury and the ability to feign neuropsychological deficits. *Archives of Clinical Neuropsychology, 19,* 37–48.

Victor, T. L., & Abeles, N. (2004). Coaching clients to take psychological and neuropsychological tests: A clash of ethical obligations. *Professional Psychology: Research and Practice, 35,* 373–379.

Wetter, M. W., & Corrigan, S. K. (1995). Providing information to clients about psychological tests: A survey of attorneys' and law students' attitudes. *Professional Psychology: Research and Practice, 26,* 474–477.

Wong, J. L., Lerner-Poppen, L., & Durham, J. (1998). Does warning reduce obvious malingering on memory and motor tasks in college samples? *International Journal of Rehabilitation and Health, 4,* 153–165.

Wong, J. L., Regennitter, R., & Barrios, F. (1994). Base rate and simulated symptoms of mild head injury among normals. *Archives of Clinical Neuropsychology, 9,* 411–425.

Youngjohn, J. R., Lees-Haley, P. R., & Binder, L. M. (1999). Comment: Warning malingerers produces more sophisticated malingering. *Archives of Clinical Neuropsychology, 14,* 511–515.

12

Features of the Neurological Evaluation
That Suggest Noncredible Performance

James W. Albers and Randolph Schiffer

Clinical neurologists have always known that a functional disconnection exists between the structural neuropathology of disease or injury and the functional impairment that it produces. Neurological disease or injury, including the way in which it affects one's functional performance, is unique for every person who experiences it. This phenomenon has at times been described as the disconnection between "disease," which is the neurobiological process itself, and "illness," which is the lived experience of the disease (Ensalada, 2000). Litigants are understandably pressured to exploit this gap in forensic proceedings, where financial awards are linked to the severity of illness behavior. It is the responsibility of the court to determine the degree of illness behavior, which is reasonably attributable to the disease or injury at issue in any given case. However, the forensic neurologist is obliged to advise the court about the major medical issues at play in any particular case. In this chapter we review the issue of exaggerated illness behavior in legal settings and the ways in which neurologists determine that it is excessive.

We use the term *noncredible* in this chapter for illness behavior or clinical neurological findings that are exaggerated or unrelated to any underlying neurobiological injury or disease. We are writing for a forensic audience, for whom "believability" is a fundamental criterion for evidence or testimony; hence our selection of the term *noncredible*, which does not commit an expert witness to any specific psychological motivation for the production of the behavior or findings. A variety of conditions can produce such behaviors, ranging from those that produce neurological symptoms based on misinterpretation of normal physiological or psychological events to blatant

malingering in a conscious attempt to mislead the clinician. The following items are recognized psychiatric disorders that produce behaviors that mimic medical or neurological disease (Schiffer, 2006):

conversion disorder

factitious disorder

malingering

psychological pain disorder

somatoform disorder

In forensic proceedings it is not necessary (and is frequently difficult, if not impossible) to distinguish among these various psychiatric syndromes. Exceptions exist, such as observing patients with a neurological impairment functioning normally when they believe they are not being observed.

> **Case vignette 1.** A disabled laborer was referred for neurological evaluation as part of his litigation involving a car accident that had occurred 3 years earlier. During the accident, the car that he was driving was struck from behind, resulting in minor damage to both vehicles. At the time of the accident, he experienced immediate low back pain but did not seek evaluation or treatment, and he drove home. Over several days, his back pain increased, and within a few weeks he experienced difficulty walking because of pain and weakness in his legs. Despite numerous evaluations and studies, all of which produced normal results, he eventually became confined to a wheelchair. He could transfer from his wheelchair only with great difficulty and assistance. His wife confirmed that he had not walked since a few weeks after the accident, and he required increasing amounts of medications to control his pain. He sat rigidly in his wheelchair and resisted any attempts to evaluate his back because movement exacerbated the pain. Examination of his legs was limited by pain, and all of his movements were slow and deliberate with give-away weakness. During the examination, he stood with assistance briefly but said he could not walk. His sensation and reflexes were intact, and a review of previous imaging and electrodiagnostic studies produced normal results.
>
> Following the evaluation, one of the resident physicians who had participated in this individual's evaluation observed him entering his car in the hospital parking structure. The patient's wife was in the passenger seat, and the patient was loading the wheelchair into the trunk, bending and moving without difficulty or hesitation. He then walked around the car with no evidence of impairment, entered the driver's seat, and drove away.

*Details of the history for each of the clinical vignettes presented in this chapter have been modified to preserve the anonymity of the individual and the individual's family.

This case vignette leaves little doubt that portions of the history provided by the patient and his wife were untrue and that the performance was feigned in what appeared to be a blatant attempt to deceive the examiners. More often, however, distinguishing between feigned and physiologically or psychologically based conditions is challenging, and establishing volitional intent for the feigned behavior may be quite difficult, if not impossible.

Of course, the fundamental reason that a chapter such as this needs to be written is that the reward systems of clinical medicine are reversed in forensic settings. Most patients in practice settings have intrinsic motivation to get better, and in that sense they are aligned with their physicians' motivation to help them. Exceptions occur, such as when disability or Workers' Compensation issues intrude into clinical medicine, but these are side issues in most of general medicine and neurology. In forensic proceedings, however, whether criminal or civil, there is often substantial gain to be realized by the plaintiff or defendant for an exaggeration of illness behavior.

The sections that follow are separated into the evaluation of information obtained directly from the patients in terms of their particular complaints or history and the clinical evaluation of performance on the conventional neurological examination. Although the history provided by each patient is generally considered subjective, the patient's neurological performance can be observed and evaluated as the history is presented, as well. In contrast, the more objective neurological examination also includes a subjective interpretation of noncredible performance by the clinician, particularly as reflected in clinical experience and understanding of normal and abnormal performance related to underlying neuropathology or neurophysiology.

Features of the Clinical History That Raise Suspicion for Noncredible Performance

Following damage to the nervous system by injury or disease, a finite set of symptoms and signs (examination findings) emerge. Each domain of illness or injury has its own characteristic pattern of symptoms and clinical course. When the alleged set of symptoms from the clinical history deviates from that generally observed in clinical practice, the examiner is alerted to the possibility of noncredible symptomatology.

The clinical history is fundamentally the story of illness or injury that is told by the patient. During the taking of the history, the patient is also asked to describe the chief symptoms, past medical information (including results of evaluations and medications), family history, occupational history, social history (including educational achievements), and review of systems. Previous medical records are usually available for review as well. One clue to noncredible performance is the occurrence of substantial discrepancies between the patient's report of problems and those documented in the available records. Minor or fleeting medical or psychological problems are often

forgotten, particularly when they resolve without residual deficits or the need for follow-up evaluations. On the other hand, in the absence of substantial cognitive problems, it is unusual to forget severe or chronic disorders. In the context of litigation, minimizing past problems or failing to report the results of relevant negative evaluations suggests that the patient's history may not be trustworthy.

Vague and nonspecific complaints also suggest a psychological basis rather than a neurological basis as the source of the complaints. Vague symptoms such as occasional forgetfulness, nonspecific muscle aches or pains, intermittent weakness, or fleeting numbness and tingling are more likely due to normal physiological and psychological factors (including response to the stress of everyday life) than to neurological impairment. These symptoms are common among the general population, including those with no known neurological problems. For this reason, complaints such as the following have been referred to as "symptoms of life," emphasizing their high prevalence and generally benign nature among the general population (Angell, 1994; Lees-Haley & Brown, 1993):

dizziness	occasional muscle aches	generalized fatigue
occasional headache	lightheadedness	forgetfulness
trouble concentrating	intermittent numbness	blurred vision
weakness	forgetting names	muscle twitching
occasional tingling	daily headache	neck or low back pain
irritability	anxiety	faint feeling
ringing in ears	daytime drowsiness	giving out of the leg
trouble sleeping	generalized malaise	occasional stumbling
lump in throat	moving spots in eyes	muscle cramps

These high base rates of nonspecific complaints indicates that such complaints are unlikely to reflect a neuropsychological impairment and should be viewed with skepticism in the context of litigation (ibid.).

Imprecision about the time of symptom onset or whether the symptoms are improving or worsening is not characteristic of actual neurological disease or injury. Difficulty in determining when symptoms first appeared or whether they are improving or worsening raises questions about the credibility of the complaint, although it is sometimes difficult to describe the temporal profile of very mild disorders that have insidious onset and progression.

Furthermore, in our experience, another feature of the clinical history provided by some litigants (as opposed to patients with known neurological disorders) is the propensity to deny preceding medical disease or injury that could contribute to the person's complaints. In contrast, all symptoms including those that are unlikely to reflect a common cause are attributed to the single event that is at issue in the lawsuit. Such behavior raises questions about the veracity of the patient's report. In forensic settings, responses that appear practiced or rehearsed raise uncertainty about the legitimacy of the complaint or its description. Clues that suggest coaching or suggestion include

the use of medical terms or expressions that are inconsistent with the patient's general fund of knowledge or vocabulary.

> **Case vignette 2.** A young woman who was undergoing evaluation complained of "short-term memory loss but normal remote memory" following exposure to a noxious cleaning product. The memory loss, which had not changed since onset more than a year earlier, interfered with her ability to work. When asked what she meant by short-term memory loss, she said that she could not remember anything she was told for a few hours but that after a few hours (or certainly by the next day) she could remember everything without difficulty.

Memory loss patterns due to neurologic disease or injury generally follow predictable patterns, depending upon the type of disease. This pattern of memory loss described in the clinical vignette is atypical of known memory disorders and raises the possibility that the complaint of "short-term memory loss but normal remote memory" had been suggested to her, despite her having little or no understanding of its actual meaning. Further, in the context of this evaluation, the complaint appeared unnatural and contrived compared to other information provided during the evaluation. The woman repeated this complaint several times during the interview, using nearly identical words, in a manner atypical of complaints provided by patients with known memory deficits or early dementia. A detailed description of neurologically based memory disorders is beyond the scope of this chapter; for a recent review of amnesic disorders, see Bauer, Grande, and Valenstein (2003).

Unwillingness or inability to answer questions about one's clinical history is another feature suggestive of exaggeration in litigation settings.

> **Case vignette 3.** A patient (who had no apparent secondary gain) with a complaint of memory loss after hitting his head in a fall responded that he was unable to remember anything about the complaint he had just reported or, for that matter, even reporting it, saying this was an example of his "memory loss." When asked to further describe his memory problem, he responded that he had never been asked to do so before and refused to provide additional information. He seemed oblivious of the absurdity of his refusal to describe his problems or of the incongruity of his complaint and his otherwise clinically normal neurological performance.

Several months after the evaluation, records from the evaluation were requested for use in ongoing litigation related to the fall.

Inappropriate affect while presenting complaints or describing neurological problems may also suggest a psychologically based disorder. The term *la belle indifférence* describes a relative apathy or disinterest expressed by a patient in the setting of describing what should be an alarming or threatening problem. The absence of emotion associated with what most people would consider a devastating condition raises concern, just as does a dramatic

presentation of a seemingly trivial complaint. Similarly, noncredible symptoms are often refractory to modification based on feedback from the examiner.

> **Case vignette 4.** A patient complained that she could stay awake
> no longer than 2 hours during the day before becoming so fatigued that
> she had to take a 30–40 minute nap. When, after about 5 hours of
> examination (without a break at her request and with no indication of
> fatigue), the patient was asked whether she preferred to stop and come
> back another time to finish or to go on for another few hours and fin-
> ish, she without hesitation elected to complete the testing. When
> the apparent inconsistency between her complaint and her behavior was
> pointed out, the patient said simply that "today is not characteris-
> tic of my usual day."

Unwillingness to modify or retract a seemingly irrational complaint can at times be a reflection of behavioral pathology. The psychological principle of "cognitive dissonance" predicts not only that commitment to a position will motivate a person to maintain a particular position but also that the effect is so strong that it will influence or alter the person's perceptions and interpretations of reality in order to support the chosen viewpoint (Festinger, 1957).

With regard to the clinical history of cognitive impairment, the examiner should pay attention to the alleged consequences of the cognitive loss. Some individuals, when asked to explain their cognitive symptoms, include examples of behaviors or situations that represent completely normal absentmindedness or forgetfulness, which is unlikely to interfere with normal activities. Such complaints have little credibility in situations of obvious secondary gain. The following types of memory complaints, for example, do not represent examples of definitely abnormal performance:

needing to make a list before grocery shopping

needing reminders for scheduled events such as dental appointments

being able to remember details of important events from the distant past but being unable to remember what one had for breakfast

going into a room and looking for something and then forgetting to retrieve it

going about repetitive daily activities but remembering few of the details related to the events that were accomplished (e.g., "I drive to work but don't remember anything about the drive")

forgetting what I was going to say if I don't pay attention

seeing an old movie on TV that I have seen before but not remembering many of the scenes or the ending

being unable to remember the names of familiar people at social events

forgetting things my spouse told me and being told that I don't listen well

having difficulty reading now compared to the past, although I have rarely read for the past 20 years (failing to recognize the lack of practice)

In fact, the patient who denies ever experiencing any of these complaints is less credible than the patient who reports them. Normative data reflecting common memory complaints have been reported by Crook and Larrabee (1992). When symptoms reflecting memory complaints common among the general population constitute the patient's primary complaints and are presented as evidence of dementia or brain injury, they should be considered noncredible.

Features of the Neurological Examination That Suggest Noncredible Performance

The neurologic examination is composed of the following five domains (and subdomains) of functional assessment:

mental status
arousal and attention

mood and affect

language

personality and behavioral style

cognition

cranial nerves

motor
gait

coordination

strength

tone

involuntary movements

sensory
station

vibration, fine touch, joint position

pain, temperature

discriminatory

reflexes
muscle stretch

pathological

The assessment of each of these domains involves a standard set of interactive maneuvers on the part of the examiner, combined with careful observations of the patient's responses by the examiner (DeJong, 1979). There is a neurobiological base for the functional domains described in the preceding list, so that, when assessing these functions, the examiner is "inventorying" the anatomic and functional networks of the nervous system (Schiffer and Lajara, 2003). Considerable skill and experience are called for in this neurological evaluation, and for many of the assessments, cooperation and effort on the part of the patient are also required.

Other portions of the examination, such as the pupillary reflexes (light and accommodation), extraocular movements, evaluation for nystagmus, and corneal, atavistic, and gag reflexes require little voluntary effort from the patient. Similarly, the examination of muscle stretch reflexes is objective and relatively independent of motivation, cooperation, education, concentration, or fatigue. Other parts of the neurological examination are intermediate between the extremes since they require some volitional cooperation or activation on the part of the subject. Much of the motor examination falls within this category. The patient must initiate the response, but the evaluations of the individual components are objective in terms of identifying abnormal or pathological function.

Since the neurological examination, including the mental status examination, assesses functionally integrated neural networks in the brain, there are certain general, expectable patterns of abnormality that are produced by injury or disease, depending upon location. Illness behaviors (i.e., neurologic findings on the examination that deviate from expected patterns) raise suspicion of nonneurologically based dysfunction. For example, difficulty in performing simple cognitive, memory, or motor tasks, yet performing more challenging tasks with little difficulty, is unexpected for a disease- or injury-based neurological problem. Isolated slowness in initiation of responses is generally not a true neurologic finding. A patient who complains of sensory loss but who, when touched or asked to distinguish between one or two stimuli, pauses for a very long time and then responds with 100% accuracy is unlikely to have a peripheral nervous system explanation for this behavior. Similarly, a patient who denies feeling a sharp pin but who jumps when unexpectedly touched with the pin is likely receiving some sensory information. Variability in performance on standard tests in the neurological examination or responses that are strongly influenced by suggestion or distraction also argue against a neurological impairment. Other neurological findings suggestive of noncredible performance are discussed in the following sections related to specific examination domains.

Not all neurological signs reflect underlying neuropathology or neurological disease. Some are of no importance (or at least of uncertain importance) in terms of neuropathology. The following list presents some signs that are of limited clinical importance in isolation:

unsustained lateral gaze nystagmus

give-away weakness

mild postural or physiological tremor

palmomental reflexes

hyperactive reflexes

diffusely hypoactive reflexes

physiological postural tremor

fasciculations

withdrawal versus true Babinski signs

absence of ankle reflexes after the age of 60

absence of abdominal reflexes

increased sway on Romberg testing (without breaking stance)

Mental Status Examination

The manner in which the mental status examination is conducted may reflect variability and flexibility, but generally the categories of behavior listed earlier in the five subdomains of functional evaluation are assessed. In neurological disease or injury, there should be consistency with the pattern of impairment demonstrated. Examination of mental status occurs during all parts of the neurologic evaluation. A patient with memory complaints who interrupts to insert information that could not be remembered earlier demonstrates intact short-term memory and concentration, as does a patient who interrupts to tell the examiner that a certain question was already asked or discussed. The patient who notices a play on words, responds to or contributes humorous comments, or unconsciously participates in repartee with the examiner demonstrates a relatively high level of interpersonal functioning, which requires substantial cognitive abilities. Such performance can be compared to results obtained during the formal examination. Substantial discrepancies should not appear between informally and formally assessed neuropsychiatric function.

Cranial Nerve Examination

As noted earlier, many parts of the cranial nerve examination, such as the pupillary reflexes (light and accommodation), extraocular movements, evaluation for nystagmus, and corneal and gag reflexes, require little voluntary effort from the patient and are not influenced by motivation. Other parts of the examination (e.g., testing of visual or auditory acuity) use standardized psychometric procedures, which are often supervised by specialists in ophthalmology, neuroophthalmology, or otolaryngology. Some of these tests are highly precise and reproducible, which makes it relatively easy to identify performance that is neither credible nor attributable to neuro-

logical dysfunction. Consider, for example, a complaint of visual impairment reflecting constricted visual fields. Visual field constriction that does not appropriately change in size as the subject is moved farther from the target does not have a physiological explanation and does not reflect credible performance (Gale, 1983).

Motor Examination

The motor examination includes an evaluation of several dimensions of motor function, including strength, muscle tone and bulk, and coordination. The clinical motor examination includes a mixture of isolated muscle or movement evaluations and an evaluation of complex integrated movements, such as walking. The evaluation of the individual motor components is important in the context of identifying noncredible performance. Whereas it is not difficult for a patient to feign weakness for a specific integrated activity, such as arising from a chair, lifting a heavy object, or gripping a dynamometer, it is especially difficult to feign weakness of individual muscles short of complete paralysis. When muscles or peripheral nerves have been injured, the examiner expects to find certain signs such as atrophy and weakness. In this context of disease or injury to the peripheral nervous system, weakness is uniform during testing, as opposed to the sudden give-away weakness associated with some central nervous system disorders, pain inhibition, or poor volitional effort.

Certain test maneuvers encourage the patient to produce maximum effort. Requiring the patient to overcome the force exerted by the examiner (rather than the examiner trying to overcome the patient) requires the patient to apply increasing levels of force. In this setting, it is difficult to feign weakness, and either the sudden release of force or discontinuous force on the part of the patient suggests poor volitional effort. This discontinuous force is sometimes called "give-away weakness" and in the absence of pain suggests inconsistent effort.

Weakness from central nervous system injury or disease presents in a characteristic pattern with associated reflex changes. Unilateral cortical lesions involving the motor pathways produce contralateral signs that include hemiparesis with a characteristic pattern of abnormality, with weakness of arm extension and leg flexion, circumducting gait (with characteristic shoe wear), decreased alternate motion rate, hyperreflexia, and pathological reflexes (e.g., Babinski and Chaddock signs). More subtle arm weakness is associated with posture changes, such as pronator drift of the outstretched arms, reduced dexterity of fine finger movements, and reduced involuntary arm swing while walking. The absence of these characteristic patterns in the setting of alleged central nervous system damage raises doubt about a neurological explanation for the weakness. Patterns of motor and reflex signs that violate these general neurobiological principles cannot be attributed to central nervous system lesions. When only some components of these collective

patterns of abnormality are present, it is difficult to determine their importance, particularly when the abnormal signs involve only those parts of the examination under volitional control (e.g., slow alternate motion rate as opposed to pathological reflexes). Certain additional findings suggest noncredible performance, such as the coactivation of opposing muscle groups during the clinical examination of a single muscle (e.g., activation of the triceps and biceps during examination of arm extension). Similarly, slow alternating motion rate on one side that appears normal when both sides are tested together also suggests a noncredible result in the context of some underlying neuropathology.

The evaluation of integrated motor activities should confirm a performance pattern that is consistent with the performance of the individual parts. An example of failed confirmation is the juxtaposition of weak grip strength (measured clinically or quantitatively with a grip dynamometer) and normal strength of individual muscles that participate in grip (flexor digitorum profundus, flexor digitorum superficialis, extensor carpi radialis, opponens, flexor digitorum longus, and flexor pollicis longus). Similarly, the inability or unwillingness to activate a specific muscle in isolation but the ability to use the same muscle in other integrated activities suggests noncredible performance. As an example, a patient who cannot activate the quadriceps muscles in isolation but who can rise from a chair (or vice versa) is unlikely to have a neurological explanation for the alleged problem.

Some complex motor performances that appear to reflect underlying neurologic damage actually require an intact nervous system. The term *astasia abasia* describes an erratic and ataxic gait with difficulty standing that actually requires exquisite strength, sensation, and coordination. Patients to whom this description is applied demonstrate a somewhat theatrical appearance of ambulation difficulty by assuming strange positions that approach the threshold of falling but do not cross it. A related clinical phenomenon concerns the individual with alleged impairment of sensation and difficulty standing who nonetheless easily maintains stance with the eyes closed. The combined neurological signs are difficult to reconcile, as visual cues are needed to maintain balance in the absence of intact proprioception.

The core neurologic issue here is that it is difficult to maintain a consistent appearance of partial weakness across various maneuvers unless that weakness has a neurologic basis. Complete paralysis is easier to feign than is partial paralysis, but similarly, complete paralysis usually cannot be maintained throughout an entire neurologic examination.

> **Case vignette 5.** An electrician was evaluated for complete paralysis of his right leg, which had developed after an electrical shock to the leg and had persisted unchanged for almost a year. The skin had not been injured or burned in association with the electrical shock, and no other symptoms were reported. Electrophysiological evaluations of the limb were normal, other than an absence of motor units under

volitional control, and the limb paralysis was believed to have a psychological, not a neurological, explanation.

The neurological examination was normal other than completed paralysis of the leg. Despite the paralysis, the leg showed normal muscle bulk and tone, normal reflexes, and no pathological reflexes. Certain maneuvers, such as repositioning the patient on the examination table, produced brief reflex activation of the supposedly paralyzed leg muscles. Other maneuvers, such as asking the patient to raise the weak leg while supine, did not activate the extensor muscles of the normal leg (positive Hoover sign).

The most effective way to evaluate limb paralyses thought to reflect noncredible performance (conversion or malingering) is to combine the clinical examination with a needle EMG examination of the involved limb muscles. As in the preceding case vignette, it is difficult (if not impossible) to avoid brief, inadvertent activation of the limb muscles when one is asked to change position. Such activation can be objectively identified during the EMG evaluation in the form of normal motor unit recruitment in the "paralyzed" muscle, something that was not commented on by the electromyography in the case vignette. Just as it is difficult to maintain a certain level of weakness across different maneuvers, it also is difficult to feign a consistent level of reduced speed or impaired coordination during tests of rate and rhythm of performance, such as testing alternate motion rate or finger-to-nose coordination tests. Clinicians experienced in the evaluation of a spectrum of neurological impairments (mild to severe) are familiar with the relative neurological deficits across different clinical tests. Such experience is important in recognizing inconsistent or noncredible performance during the clinical examination.

Sensory Examination

The peripheral nervous system is composed of a fixed network of roots, plexus, and peripheral nerves, whose injury produces predictable patterns of sensory loss. These patterns cannot usually be reproduced in noncredible performance. The sensory examination is substantially dependent on the subjective reports of the patient, however, and is therefore especially liable to the production of noncredible performance in forensic settings. Some components of the sensory examination produce observable response behaviors, such as pain responses, but even here the examiner's judgment plays a central role in interpretation.

Variability in response reports is inherent in the sensory examination, but exaggerated variability suggests noncredible performance. The sensory examination has substantial internal organization that is based on the underlying neural networks that subserve sensory experience. Some sensory modalities are linked to peripheral nervous system networks (fine touch, pin

pain, temperature, joint position, vibration), and some are linked to central nervous system networks (discriminative sensory functions such as localization, two-point discrimination, dual simultaneous stimulation, stereognosis, baragnosis, and directional discrimination). The response interplay across these various sensory modalities follows certain organizational patterns in disease or injury of the nervous system. Noncredible performance is suggested whenever these patterns are violated. For example, noncredible performance on the sensory examination does not usually localize properly across specific levels of the nervous system (peripheral, spinal cord, or cerebral levels) because the patient has difficulty with consistent responses to a mix of superficial and interpretive stimuli. The problem with the sensory examination in forensic proceedings is that even patients with actual disease or injury to the nervous system are sometimes inconsistent on these tests.

> **Case vignette 6.** A woman with an arm injury reported profound circumferential sensory loss distal to the midarm. Aside from sensory testing, her neurological examination was normal. This included intact coordination testing and an ability to manipulate small objects in her hand using her fingers while her eyes were closed, despite her report that she was unable to feel or identify the objects. During the sensory examination with her eyes closed, she initially correctly identified touch in the anesthetic region after being asked to indicate whether she was being touched on the right side, the left side, or both sides at once. Her sensory impairment was nearly complete, with a sharp circumferential demarcation to touch and pin-prick sensation. Nevertheless, during coordination testing with her eyes closed, when one of her anesthetic fingers was lightly touched by the examiner and she was asked to touch that finger to her nose, she did so readily without hesitating. There was no evidence of pseudoathetosis, the random movement of the fingers and hand observed among patients with severe sensory loss.

This woman's sensory complaints did not respect the anatomic patterns of the peripheral nervous system, and her response pattern was inconsistent across different sensory modalities, producing the overall impression of a noncredible performance. The ability to manipulate coins, paper clips, and other objects in her hand while claiming she could not identify or feel the objects indicated intact neural networks for sensation since the performance of this test with the eyes closed requires intact superficial and discriminative sensations. She also showed inconsistent sensory responses, such as incorrectly answering fine touch questions on individual finger testing, while answering such questions correctly during coordination testing. The absence of pseudoathetosis further reduced the likelihood that the reported sensory loss reflected a credible abnormality.

In a similar way, if superficial and deep sensations are substantially impaired, it is not possible for more complex, discriminative functions to be performed accurately. For example, the combination of markedly impaired

superficial sensation involving light touch or touch pressure cannot coexist with intact two-point discrimination and dual simultaneous discrimination.

A last point of neurological reasoning has to do with the interconnectedness of the domains of the neurological examination. Although we have discussed them separately, there are interconnections in function between the sensory systems and the other domains of the neurological examination, and severe sensory deficits inevitably produce functional changes in the motor and reflex systems. As an example, profound large fiber sensory loss (touch, joint position, and vibration sensations) in the legs is almost always associated with imbalance and postural abnormalities, as well as with impaired coordination of the limbs. Similarly, it is difficult to reconcile impaired vibration, joint position, and touch sensations if muscle stretch reflexes are intact since the large sensory axons subserving these sensory modalities also compose the afferent limb of this reflex arc.

Reflex Examination

Reflex responses are under limited conscious influence. Patterns of pathological reflexes should generally accompany injuries or diseases affecting the nervous system, and when they do not, noncredible performance is suggested. Disorders that affect the peripheral nervous system generally reduce or abolish certain reflexes, and disorders of the central nervous system augment them and produce other discrete pathological reflexes. The preservation of normal muscle stretch reflexes in case vignettes 5 and 6 argued against a central or peripheral nervous system explanation for the apparent clinical abnormalities.

Special Examination Maneuvers to Identify Noncredible Sensory Performance

Several types of special maneuvers are sometimes used during the neurological examination to determine the presence of noncredible deficits. These maneuvers must be used with discretion because they are designed to "lead" the patient, and they sometimes produce false positive results in patients who are just suggestible, yet have disease of the nervous system.

One way to confirm neurological impairments is to make observations of neurological function outside the context of the direct examination, when the appearance of being tested is no longer evident. The inadvertent observation of the patient described in case vignette 1 is such an example. Another example follows.

> **Case vignette 7.** A patient who was undergoing evaluation for memory complaints attributed to a closed-head injury provided a slow, labored history. He apologized frequently, attributing the slowness to his memory loss and difficulty concentrating, problems that interfered with his daily life. He described making notes for everything, including

reminders to eat meals and even reminders to read his notes. He was unable to remember any of the items on the minimental status examination. After the evaluation, he was accompanied by his wife to the waiting room. As he departed, he was asked whether he was planning to watch an upcoming sporting event, as his home team was contending for the title. The comment unexpectedly elicited an enthusiastic, animated exchange during which he described minute details of a preceding game, the consequences of an officiating error, the coach's comments, and descriptions of a player's injury, the team's standing the preceding year, and a reminder that the scheduled start time had been changed to accommodate television. The wife ended our conversion by saying, "He remembers what he wants to remember."

This patient's maximal performance, based on this interchange after the evaluation was complete, exceeded expectations based on the more formal evaluation, indicating that the earlier performance was noncredible in terms of reflecting disease or injury to the nervous system. For a description of the anticipated neuropsychological consequences of closed-head injury, see Levin, Benton, and Grossman (1982).

Pain in Forensic Settings

Perhaps the most difficult condition for the neurologist to evaluate in a forensic setting is the complaint of pain since pain always remains a subjective complaint on the part of the patient (Fields, 2003). There may or may not be objective evidence of neurologic disease or injury in such cases, and the "value" of the case to plaintiffs is generally higher when such objective evidence of damage exists. The most common pain syndromes in forensic settings are back pain, neck pain, and headache.

In the evaluation of low back or neck pain, a key forensic issue is whether there is evidence of objective injury to one of the cervical, lumbar, or sacral roots. Various clinical, imaging, and neurophysiological techniques are available to help make this determination. Chronic pain syndromes are generally accepted as sequelae of such injuries, and financial recognition of these injuries must be accorded to plaintiffs. When pain syndromes occur in the absence of evidence of root injury, however, they can be downgraded in terms of legal value through the argument that objective evidence of neurologic injury is lacking, but they cannot simply be dismissed. One has to look for evidence of noncredibility within the pattern of pain behaviors that the patient presents, and these behaviors must be measured against the hypothetical standard of "reasonable pain behavior" in the context of the injury or disease involved in the litigation at hand.

Consider, for example, the first case vignette, which involves a man with severe back pain and a complaint of leg weakness after a motor vehicle

accident. One clinical sign of nerve root compression is a positive straight-leg-raising test. This test involves passive elevation of the symptomatic leg in the supine position, a maneuver that stretches the ipsilateral lumbosacral nerve roots. A positive test, characterized by the reproduction of radicular leg pain with elevation of the symptomatic limb, suggests nerve root pathology. Most patients with chronic low back pain are familiar with this test, although some variations of this test are less well known.

In one variation, the examiner asks the patient to extend the leg while seated, in the context of examining the foot. This maneuver produces a 90° leg extension, similar to the supine straight-leg-raising test. If a patient who has a markedly positive supine straight-leg-raising test performs the test seated without hesitation, the former results may not be credible. Patients with compressive radiculopathy commonly show a restricted lumbar spine range of motion and paraspinal muscle spasm. The painful spasm typically involves muscles contralateral to the radiculopathy. The spasm is elicited by tilting toward the lesion, a maneuver that produces involuntary guarding to prevent further compression of the root. A subjective complaint of increased pain (without palpable paraspinal muscle spasm) on the ipsilateral side when tilting away from the lesion is a less credible finding. None of these examples definitively disproves a nerve root compression, but neither do any of these behaviors conform to the anticipated findings. They merely represent findings that should encourage a search for alternative explanations for the patient's complaints.

A few of the sensory tests reported for case vignette 6 involving the patient with an anesthetic limb reflect special maneuvers to identify noncredible performance, and this patient, who was thought to be embellishing her sensory signs, showed intact sensation under altered test conditions. Asking patients to acknowledge randomly delivered fine touch stimuli with their eyes closed is one means of verifying previously identified anesthesia (e.g., "Say 'touch' when you feel me touch you"). When the touches are performed rapidly with random timing and to random sites on the skin, an initial response of "touch" in the anesthetic area, followed by hesitation after beginning to respond, indicates at least some sensory perception of the stimuli. Occasionally patients initially respond "no" when touched in the anesthetic region despite random timing of the stimuli, again indicating perception of the stimulus and indicating noncredible performance.

Migraine and related headache syndromes are difficult to assess and explain in forensic settings because all such disorders have an innate behavioral dimension (Gorman, 2003). These chronic pain disorders are difficult to treat, are often compounded by a propensity to addiction, and are widely known to worsen after concussive head trauma. Sometimes there is such a departure from the generally expectable symptom patterns in headache complaints that noncredibility can be suspected (see case vignette 8). We have found that, as in the radiculopathy syndromes described earlier, searching for objective evidence of injury to nervous system structures either on the

neurologic examination, through imaging, or through neurophysiological tests (see below) is a useful way to approach head pain syndromes in the setting of legal proceedings. The legal "value" of a headache case is much higher if such objective evidence of injury exists.

The Use of Neurophysiological and Imaging Tests in Detecting Noncredible Performance

Nerve conduction studies performed during an EMG examination represent the gold standard for identifying peripheral large-fiber sensory dysfunction. Normal sensory responses recorded during EMG testing are inconsistent with a large-fiber sensory neuropathy, suggesting that a finding of substantial peripheral sensory loss is noncredible. The most effective way to evaluate limb paralyses that are potentially due to peripheral nervous system disease or injury is to combine the clinical examination with a needle EMG examination of the involved limb muscles, as described in case vignette 5. It is difficult (if not impossible) to avoid brief, inadvertent activation of the nonparalyzed limb muscles when a patient is asked to change position. When the examination is performed without auditory EMG feedback to the patient (i.e., thereby not conveying information about the muscle to the patient), the neurologist can usually evaluate motor unit recruitment in the "paralyzed" muscle by assessing the motor units inadvertently activated by the patient. Normal recruitment, however brief, is inconsistent with a peripheral nervous system explanation for the patient's weakness.

With respect to brain imaging, severe cognitive disorders that produce substantial dementia or chronic encephalopathy are associated with imaging evidence of cerebral atrophy or white matter abnormalities. Consider, for example, the extensive list of disorders or conditions that produce leuko-encephalopathy (Filley & Kleinschmidt-DeMasters, 2001). Among patients diagnosed with mild leukoencephalopathy, MRI evidence of periventricular white matter hyperintensity is present independently of the underlying cause at the earliest level of clinically apparent dysfunction. Failure to show imaging evidence of white matter abnormality suggests that a diagnosis of leukoencephalopathy is noncredible.

Complaints of Cognitive Loss and Neuropsychological Testing

Complaints involving cognition or memory are among the most difficult neurologic problems to evaluate in forensic settings. Typically, neurologists must review and analyze the results of neuropsychological testing in addition to the results of their own cognitive examinations. The principles described

previously regarding the interpretation of the clinical history also apply to the history of cognitive impairment. The magnitude of cognitive loss by history should bear some reasonable relationship to the severity of the injury or disease (Larrabee, 1990; Slick, Sherman, & Iverson, 1999; and chapter 13 in the present volume). For example, consider the relationship that exists between cognitive decline observed among patients with Alzheimer-type dementia and decreased cortical volume and perfusion in dementia of Alzheimer type (Obara, Meyer, Mortel, & Muramatsu, 1994). Certain archetypal symptom patterns should apply, such as the presence of retrograde and anterograde amnesia surrounding the period of a head injury, with the anterograde usually lasting longer than the retrograde. A pattern of improvement over time in all such complaints should be evident.

The results of neuropsychological testing are frequently used as evidence in legal settings because the testing can readily show "deficits" when in fact these poor scores can be accounted for by explanations other than brain damage or dysfunction (Larrabee, 1990). The results are used in plaintiff's evidence or by defense attorneys in criminal cases because of the sensitivity of such test results to motivation and effort on the part of the plaintiff or defendant. Indeed, the "objectivity" of such testing is no greater than that of the neurological examination, and the results of neuropsychological testing should never be considered in isolation from the remainder of the neurological examination. The most effective confirmation or disconfirmation of neuropsychological test results is the neurologist's own observations of the patient or plaintiff during the entire evaluation, including during mental status testing, often in concert with the results of a second, independent examination by a qualified neuropsychologist who employs the symptom validity procedures discussed in the present volume. Clinical neurology has a long tradition of examining the mental state, and most forensic neurological experts must be capable of projecting their own credibility concerning the mental status examination.

Features of the Neurological Diagnosis That Suggest Noncredible Interpretation of Findings

To this point, the emphasis on noncredible neurological performance has been discussed in terms of the patient's performance. At times, the physician's ready attribution of a patient's symptoms or signs to an underlying neurological disease or to a specific antecedent event or injury facilitates an underlying psychogenic disorder (Schaumburg & Albers, 2005). This form of iatrogenesis is particularly problematic when a physician or a psychologist misdiagnoses one of the common everyday phenomena listed earlier as a sign of brain injury. Patients with premorbid excessive health concerns may focus on these common symptoms and become increasingly anxious, with further worsening of their condition, a mechanism described as a key feature in

somatoform disorder (Mittenberg, DiGiulio, Perrin, & Bass, 1992; Putnam & Millis, 1994; Watson & Pennebaker, 1989).

> **Case vignette 8** (modified from Schaumburg et al., 2005). A woman with a history of migraine headaches was exposed to a pesticide at work. Shortly thereafter, she experienced nausea and developed a unilateral throbbing headache that gradually became more intense. In a local emergency department, a physician described her presentation as "histrionic." She was diagnosed with a respiratory reaction to a "toxic exposure" and given a bronchodilator. She made repeated visits to her physicians with increasing headache frequency and numerous other somatic symptoms, resulting in a diagnosis of "chemical exposure sensitivity." Despite numerous comprehensive neurological examinations documenting excellent memory function, diagnoses of "toxic brain syndrome and chronic hyperventilation" were established. Over a period of months, the headaches were reported to occur daily and were associated with poor concentration and signs of depression. Thrice-weekly parenteral opiate agonists provided transient improvement. Over the following 5 years, the woman consulted many neurologists, who suggested diagnoses including "chronic toxin-aggravated migraine syndrome" and "analgesic rebound syndrome." She continued treatment with a varying regimen of triptans, antidepressants, and opiates. She wore sunglasses "to avoid light" and responded slowly, appeared preoccupied and withdrawn, and requested the examiner to repeat most of the questions. Her examination was otherwise normal.

Headache is common among individuals (particularly those with preexisting migraine) following exposure to a variety of substances and numerous situations. However, there are no substances known to cause continuous or recurrent headaches in the absence of ongoing or recurrent exposure. The woman's symptoms, which differed only in frequency from her long-standing migraine syndrome, intensified after she was diagnosed with "toxic brain syndrome," which gradually evolved into a daily headache syndrome, augmented by analgesic rebound.

Any patient, with or without preexisting anxiety or depression, can become concerned that nonspecific symptoms represent early signs of a degenerative disease or reflect an injury to the nervous system from some cause. Being told that neurological abnormalities are consistent with "brain injury" is undoubtedly frightening, causes increased worry and anxiety, and possibly reinforces or precipitates underlying psychogenic illness. The importance of misinformation provided by a physician or other authority figure is often underestimated. The effect of the misinformation on the patient's psychological well-being can be harmful, and the consequences can be difficult to reverse. The neurological signs listed earlier include some that are of limited clinical importance in isolation but are sometimes used in the context of litigation to suggest the presence of an underlying disease or injury to the

nervous system, a potentially noncredible neurological interpretation (mis-interpretation). Physicians who provide preposterous and unsubstantiated diagnoses based on noncredible interpretation of neurological information, while ignoring information suggesting an intact nervous system or ignoring the consequences of medication use or other information, can promote a patient's psychological decline, as in this case vignette.

Summary

The divide between a neurological impairment resulting from disease or injury to the nervous system and the way in which the impairment influences performance may be altered in forensic proceedings if the results or financial awards are linked to the severity of illness behavior. In a medical or a legal context, it is the neurologist's responsibility to identify neurological impairments and to determine when illness behavior is exaggerated or noncredible in terms of its relationship to the underlying neurobiological injury or disease. In this chapter we have reviewed conditions associated with noncredible illness behaviors ranging from those that represent misinterpretation of normal physiological or psychological events to those that reflect blatant malingering in an attempt to mislead the clinician. We recognize that it is unnecessary and quite difficult (if not impossible) to distinguish among the various syndromes that produce these behaviors, particularly in terms of determining motivation or intent. Examples of different illness behaviors have been included in a case vignette format to highlight information obtained from the history and from the neurological examination indicative of exaggerated illness behaviors. Often, recognition of exaggerated or noncredible performance helps identify a psychological, rather than a neurological, explanation for behavior.

The nervous system has a limited repertoire of responses to injury or disease. Familiarity with the possible response patterns, including knowledge about which responses reflect underlying neuropathology or neurological disease and which ones are under volitional control, helps identify behaviors unlikely to have a neurological explanation. The neurological examination has substantial redundancy, which permits evaluation of consistency across seemingly different measures of performance. Similarly, in the context of identifying noncredible performance, comparison of integrated functional activities to the evaluation of their individual components is important in ensuring that the performance pattern is consistent with the presence or absence of underlying impairments.

Cognitive complaints are frequently at issue in forensic proceedings, and the results of neuropsychological testing are commonly used to document subtle impairments. Yet, neuropsychological tests are influenced by motivation and cooperation, and their "objectivity" is no greater and potentially less than that of the neurological examination and related neurological measures such as imaging and electrophysiological studies. As such, the results

of neuropsychological testing should never be considered in isolation from the neurological examination results. The most effective confirmation of neuropsychological test results by opposing experts reflects the results of the cognitive examination conducted by the neurologist integrated with the results of a second, independent neuropsychological evaluation by a qualified neuropsychologist. Finally, the importance and influence of an examiner's interpretation of a patient's symptoms or signs in the identification of neurological damage due to disease or injury have been shown to potentially facilitate or precipitate underlying psychogenic illness.

References

Angell, M. (1994). Do breast implants cause systemic disease? Science in the courtroom. *New England Journal of Medicine, 330,* 1748–1749.

Bauer, R. M., Grande, L., & Valenstein, E. (2003). Amnestic disorders. In K. M. Heilman & E. Valenstein (Eds.), *Clinical neuropsychology* (4th ed., pp. 495–573). New York: Oxford University Press.

Crook, T. H., & Larrabee, G. J. (1992). Normative data on a self-rating scale for evaluating memory in everyday life. *Archives of Clinical Neuropsychology, 7,* 41–51.

DeJong, R. N. (1979). *The neurologic examination.* Hagerstown, MD: Harper.

Ensalada, L. H. (2000). The importance of illness behavior in disability management. *Occupational Medicine, 15,* 739–754.

Festinger, L. (1957). *A theory of cognitive dissonance.* Stanford, CA: Stanford University Press.

Fields, H. L. (2003). Evaluation and treatment of neuropathic pain. In R. B. Schiffer, S. M. Rao, & B. S. Fogel (Eds.), *Neuropsychiatry* (2nd ed., pp. 395–404). Philadelphia: Lippincott Williams and Wilkins.

Filley, C. M., & Kleinschmidt-DeMasters, B. K. (2001). Toxic leukoencephalopathy. *New England Journal of Medicine, 345,* 425–432.

Gale, D. (1983). Visual field defects in medico-legal cases. *Transactions of the Ophthalmological Societies of the United Kingdom, 103,* 347–350.

Gorman, J. M. (Ed.). (2003, June). Migraines: Neurological and psychiatric perspectives. *CNS Spectrums, 8*(6), 406.

Larrabee, G. J. (1990). Cautions in the use of neuropsychological evaluation in legal settings. *Neuropsychology, 4,* 239–247.

Lees-Haley, P. R., & Brown, R. S. (1993). Neuropsychological complaint base rates of 170 personal-injury claimants. *Archives of Clinical Neuropsychology, 8,* 203–209.

Levin, H. S., Benton, A. L., & Grossman, R. (1982). *Neurobehavioral consequences of closed head injury.* New York: Oxford University Press.

Mittenberg, W., DiGiulio, D. V., Perrin, S., & Bass, A. E. (1992). Symptoms following mild head injury: Expectation as etiology. *Journal of Neurology, Neurosurgery, and Psychiatry, 55,* 200–204.

Obara, K., Meyer, J. S., Mortel, K. F., & Muramatsu, K. (1994). Cognitive declines correlate with decreased cortical volume and perfusion in dementia of Alzheimer type. *Journal of the Neurological Sciences, 127,* 96–102.

Putnam, S. H., & Millis, S. R. (1994). Psychosocial factors in the development and maintenance of chronic somatic and functional symptoms following mild traumatic brain injury. *Advances in Medical Psychotherapy, 7,* 1–22.

Schaumburg, H. H., & Albers, J. W. (2005). Pseudoneurotoxic disease. *Neurology, 65,* 22–26.

Schiffer, R. B. (in press). Psychiatric disorders in medical practice. In L. Goldman & D. Ausiello (Eds.), *Cecil textbook of medicine* (23rd ed.). Philadelphia: Saunders Elsevier.

Schiffer R. B., & Lajara, W. A. (2003). The neuropsychiatric examination. In R. B. Schiffer, S. M. Rao, & B. S. Fogel (Eds.), *Neuropsychiatry* (2nd ed., pp 3–19). Baltimore: Lippincott Williams and Wilkins.

Slick, D. J., Sherman, E. M. S., & Iverson, G. L. (1999). Diagnostic criteria for malingered neurocognitive dysfunction: Proposed standards for clinical practice and research. *The Clinical Neuropsychologist, 13,* 545–561.

Watson, D., & Pennebaker, J. W. (1989). Health complaints, stress, and distress: Exploring the central role of negative affectivity. *Psychological Review, 96,* 234–254.

13

Refining Diagnostic Criteria for Malingering

Glenn J. Larrabee, Manfred F. Greiffenstein,
Kevin W. Greve, and Kevin J. Bianchini

The preceding chapters in this volume have covered (a) freestanding symptom validity tests (SVTs; chapter 3 by Boone and Lu, and chapter 4 by Grote and Hook), (b) procedures that are embedded in or derived from standard psychological and neuropsychological tests (chapter 5 by Larrabee, chapter 6 by Greiffenstein, chapter 7 by Suhr and Barrash, and chapter 8 by Greve and Bianchini), and (c) measures pertinent to the overreporting of symptoms (chapter 9 by Berry and Schipper, and chapter 10 by Larrabee). Chapter 12 by Albers and Schiffer reviews the procedures employed in the course of standard neurological evaluation to evaluate the credibility of the results of the examination.

A common theme across the chapters is the consistency of test performance, behavioral presentation, and historical self-report relative to a (a) well-understood target conditions or (b) neuroanatomical fundamentals. By *target conditions* we mean the unequivocal neurological, developmental, or psychiatric problems that clinical patients show. This analytical approach of detecting feigned disorder by measuring deviation of presentation from reasonable expectations may be termed the *discrepancy method*. The operationalization of discrepancy analysis served as the methodological basis of some of the most influential early known-groups studies of malingering detection (e.g., Greiffenstein, Baker, & Gola, 1994; Trueblood & Schmidt, 1993).

Slick, Sherman, and Iverson (1999) comprehensively formalized the discrepancy method with their multilayered criteria for diagnosing malingered neurocognitive dysfunction (MND). Their system supplied a framework for

malingering classification that was relied upon in subsequent malingering research, much of which is reviewed in this volume. Nonetheless, while still conceptually sound, research and clinical application of the Slick et al. criteria have revealed limitations and weaknesses that limit the potential value of the system. The purpose of this chapter is to review the conceptual basis of the Slick et al. system, address its strengths and weaknesses, and propose potential modifications to the guidelines for future malingering research.

Discrepancy Method Explained

The *discrepancy method* has a long history in the evaluation of the credibility of medical and psychometric performance. As used in medicine, it refers to a subjective appraisal of the distance between observed findings and prototypic findings expected with a claimed disease. The greater the subjective distance (discrepancy), the greater the clinician's confidence in a nonorganic diagnosis.

In the history of neuropsychology, the discrepancy method dates to the writings of Zangwill (1943) on the interpretation of measures of memory impairment. More recently, attempts to quantify discrepancies include Wiggins and Brandt's (1988) demonstration of atypical memory performance in simulators relative to subjects who were suffering alcoholic Korsakoff amnesia. For example, simulators gave more incorrect answers to autobiographical questions than did the amnesic patients. In a second study, Wiggins and Brandt (ibid.) found that simulators performed more poorly on forced-choice word recognition than did patients with memory disorder.

Larrabee (1990) proposed consistency analysis in qualitative, intuitively impressionistic terms that were not specific to malingered memory impairment. He put forward five forms of discrepancy to be analyzed before one considers diagnosing genuine problems: internal consistency/inconsistency of neurobehavioral domains; disease-deficit compatibility (concurrent validity); inconsistency with severity of injury; inconsistency between test scores and observed behaviors from the same domain (ecological validity); and violations of performance curves. These forms of discrepancy are reviewed here.

Internal Consistency/Inconsistency
of Neurobehavioral Domains

This refers to grossly divergent performance on tests that should be highly correlated. The computational theory of mind (Pinker, 1999) dictates that human cognition is modular and depends on enriched input from computation processes earlier in the information-processing chain; a defective module should affect computation that is "downstream." This is the case with

acute confusional state, in which amnesia is secondary to poor attention. Thus a finding of defective attention but good recall on formal testing would represent divergent performance. The reasoning is that this pattern diverges from the requirement that initial deep encoding (necessary for effective delayed retrieval) presumes adequate attentional focus. Mittenberg, Azrin, Millsaps, and Heilbronner (1993) provided empirical evidence for this inference by demonstrating that noninjured persons who were simulating memory disturbance performed more poorly on the Wechsler Memory Scale-Revised (WMS-R; Wechsler, 1987) Attention/Concentration index relative to General Memory, a pattern *opposite* that produced by their genuine traumatic brain-injury sample.

Disease-Deficit Compatibility

Production of impairments not considered primary symptoms of a claimed disorder also represents discrepancy. For example, focal motor impairments are not expected in mild TBI, even in the acute state (Alexander, 1997). Greiffenstein, Baker, and Gola (1996b) showed disease-deficit incompatibility in the motor domain in a study of motor skills profiles in late postconcussion patients. They found that subjectively disabled litigants with remote but minor head injury produced a group motor skills profile opposite that seen in clinic patients with TBI and genuine upper motor neuron signs. The disease-deficit incompatibility took the form of subjectively disabled litigants who showed poorer scores on simple motor tasks (Grip Strength) but better performance on complex, fine motor tasks (Grooved Pegboard). The genuine neurology patients showed the expected gradient of worsening scores with the task demands of increasing sensorimotor integration. Another illustrative example is probable malingerers who perform more poorly on recognition than on recall on the California Verbal Learning Test (CVLT; Delis, Kramer, Kaplan, & Ober, 1987), while the reverse pattern (i.e., poorer recall than recognition) is the expected pattern in genuine neurological dysfunction (Millis, Putnam, Adams, & Ricker, 1995).

Inconsistency With Severity of Injury

A first principle of clinical medicine is dose-response relations, that is, the greater the magnitude of the pathogen, the greater the symptoms and impairment. Second, diagnosis not only involves the application of symptom checklists but also requires temporal anchors (e.g., duration and timing of symptoms). Any compelling violations of these considerations are grounds for considering alternate, nonorganic explanations (Greiffenstein & Baker,

2006). In neuropsychology, abnormal scores of greater magnitude than expected, given initial severity or postincident latency, raise an issue of disease-deficit incompatibility—for example, performing at the level consistent with that of patients suffering more than 30 days of coma when records show the test respondent did not suffer loss of consciousness (Larrabee, 1990; Rohling, Meyers, & Millis, 2003) or scoring three or four SD units below the appropriate comparison means (Greiffenstein et al., 1994, 1995). Larrabee (1990) has referred to this as "indexing" or "referencing" of performance to biological markers and temporal anchors of injury severity.

Ecological Validity Discrepancy

An *ecological validity discrepancy* refers to inconsistency between test scores and observed behaviors from the same domain; this is a subjective judgment that the deficits implied by poor scores are not manifested in observed behavior (for example, WMS-III scores that imply a dense organic amnesia but good capacity to give a detailed history during interview). Other examples include the ability to handle finances despite impaired performance on measures of simple calculation or the ability to drive a stick-shift car in a litigant who can tap the dominant index finger only five times in 10 seconds on the Finger Tapping Test.

Violations of Performance Curves

The test performances of both brain-injured and neurologically normal persons are affected by item difficulty level; gross violations of the difficulty hierarchy signal noncompliance or variable effort. A good example of performance curve expectations comes from the Symbol Digit Modalities Test (SDMT; Sheridan, Fitzgerald, Adams, Nigg, Martel, et al., 2006). This test of psychomotor speed (a clerical substitution task) has separately scored written and oral conditions. Both controls and heterogeneous neurologically impaired patients perform better on the oral than the written sections, which is consistent with the fact that we all speak faster than we write. However, oral SDMT scores equivalent to or poorer than written scores suggest exaggerated speech defect, exclusive of persons with premorbid stuttering. Other examples of performance curve violations include failure on the simplest Category Test items (Sweet & King, 2002), the Validity Indicator Profile (VIP; Frederick, 2000), and errors on rarely failed Wechsler Memory Scale items (Killgore & DellaPietra, 2000; Langeluddecke & Lucas, 2004), as well as the atypical motor dysfunction pattern described earlier in the disease-deficit incompatibility example (Greiffenstein et al., 1996b).

Formal Criteria for the Diagnosis of Malingering

Background

In a landmark paper Slick et al. (1999) applied the discrepancy method to develop formal diagnostic criteria for malingering (hereinafter referred to as Slick). The Slick system offered a set of criteria for the diagnosis of malingered neurocognitive dysfunction (MND) with rules for assigning a general confidence level to the diagnosis (i.e., definite, probable, or possible). Slick et al. (ibid.) defined MND as "the volitional exaggeration or fabrication of cognitive dysfunction for the purpose of obtaining substantial material gain, or avoiding or escaping formal duty or responsibility. Material gain includes money, goods, or services" (p. 552).

The Slick criteria were strongly influenced by a number of considerations. First, the logic and methodology of Greiffenstein et al. (1994) and Nies and Sweet (1994) were relied upon, namely by employing a multidimensional, multimethod approach to validate the detection of malingering. Second, the Slick system was also formatted to parallel the *DSM-IV* (American Psychiatric Association, 1994) template of a general definition, followed by various necessary and sufficient criteria to support (or reject) a conclusion of malingering. The publication of the Slick criteria for MND incorporated operational definitions employed in earlier research on malingering and thus allowed for the creation of "known groups" necessary for the validation of malingering measures. The Slick et al. criteria have been adapted by the third and fourth authors of this chapter for the definition of the criteria for malingered pain-related disability (MPRD; Bianchini, Greve, & Glynn, 2005).

Neither the Slick criteria for MND nor the Bianchini et al. (2005) criteria for MPRD require the clinician to determine whether a specific/single behavior is indicative of intentional exaggeration. Instead, the ultimate determination of intent is dealt with in a more comprehensive manner by considering multiple, highly improbable events as indicative of intent. This is a clear departure from past attempts to define malingering, which have frequently placed the clinician in the position of inferring intention from a single event. Rather, it is not necessary to rely on single events that unequivocally demonstrate intent because the MND and MPRD criteria are based on behaviors and symptom reports that are atypical for and not representative of expected clinical findings in legitimate, unequivocal neurological, psychiatric, or developmental disorders. Thus intent is inferred from the combined improbability of events rather than a single definitive indication of intent. Although it is not necessary to rely on a single event with the Slick system, a single definitive finding of below-chance SVT performance is a key feature of the identification of definite malingering. The Bianchini et al. (2005) system also includes the designation of "compelling inconsistency" as indicating definite malingering.

The Slick Criteria

In determining the presence of MND, the clinician must evaluate the case on the basis of four criteria: (A) presence of substantial external incentive; (B) evidence from neuropsychological testing; (C) evidence from self-report; and (D) the ability of psychiatric, neurological, or developmental factors to fully account for behaviors that meet the necessary B and C criteria. Table 13.1 summarizes these criteria. Under this system, all diagnoses of malingering require the presence of an external incentive (criterion A) plus criterion B and/or C evidence as noted in Table 13.1.

If external incentives are present, criterion B behaviors are sufficient for a diagnosis of malingering on their own; a finding of definite response bias alone is sufficient for a diagnosis of definite MND. A diagnosis of probable MND can be made with two types of criterion B evidence or one type of criterion B evidence and one or more types of criterion C evidence. Criterion

Table 13.1.
Summary of the Slick, Sherman, and Iverson (1999) Criteria for Malingered Neurocognitive Dysfunction

A. Presence of substantial external incentive. At least one clearly identifiable and substantial incentive for exaggeration or fabrication of symptoms is present at the time of examination.

B. Evidence from neuropsychological testing
1. definite negative response bias
2. probable response bias
3. discrepancy between test data and known patterns of brain functioning
4. discrepancy between test data and observed behavior
5. discrepancy between test data and reliable collateral reports
6. discrepancy between test data and documented background history

C. Evidence from self-report
1. self-reported history is discrepant with documented history
2. self-reported symptoms are discrepant with known patterns of brain functioning
3. self-reported symptoms are discrepant with behavioral observations
4. self-reported symptoms are discrepant with information obtained from collateral informants
5. evidence from exaggerated or fabricated psychological dysfunction

D. Behaviors meeting necessary criteria from groups B and C are not *fully* accounted for by Psychiatric, Neurological, or Developmental factors. Behaviors meeting necessary criteria from groups B and C are the product of an informed, rational, and volitional effort aimed *at least in part* toward acquiring or achieving external incentives as defined in Criterion A.

Adapted from Slick, Sherman, and Iverson (1999).

C evidence is not sufficient for a diagnosis in the absence of criterion B evidence. Possible MND is diagnosed when the criteria for probable MND have been met but criterion D factors are present. Table 13.2 summarizes the definitions for the three probability levels for an MND diagnosis.

Slick Criterion A

The first criterion refers to the presence of a substantial external incentive; it is he gatekeeper criterion. Any diagnosis of MND must involve at least one clearly identifiable and substantial external incentive for exaggeration or fabrication of symptoms at the time of examination. Examples include the following:

- prospects for jury award or personal-injury settlement
- disability pension
- evasion of criminal prosecution
- release from military service
- narcotics access
- avoidance of death penalty

Evidence of noncredible psychological or neuropsychological presentation in the absence of clear incentive or for the fulfillment of psychological needs ("primary gain") may meet the criteria for factitious disorder (American Psychiatric Association, 1994) but not necessarily for malingering. The *DSM* rules for distinguishing malingering from factitious presentations have conceptual problems that are beyond the scope of this chapter (see Cunnien, 1997, for further discussion). For our present purposes, all that is necessary is that external incentive be present; it need not be definitively shown to be motivating noncredible behavior (Greve, Bianchini, & Ameduri, 2003; Eisendrath, 1996).

Slick Criteria B1–B6

Criteria B1–B6 (hereinafter B) are test centered. They rely on poor performance on specialized validity tests (B1 and B2) or on discrepancies between

Table 13.2
Probabilistic Classification of Malingering Within the Slick et al. Criteria

Definite	Meets Criterion A *and* Criterion B1 *and* Criterion D.
Probable	Meets Criterion A *and* two or more B Criteria (excluding B1); or, meets one B Criterion (excluding B1) *and* one or more C Criteria. Meets Criterion D.
Possible	Meets Criterion A *and* one or more C Criteria *but not* Criterion D; or, meets all criteria for Definite or Probable *but does not* meet Criterion D.

test data and known patterns of brain functioning (B3); behavioral observations (B4); information from collaterals (B5); and postincident documented history (B6).

Criteria B1 and B2   The most powerful evidence meeting B is documentation of negative response bias on simple, forced-choice measures of cognitive function. Both B1 (definite) and B2 (probable) are distinguished by below-chance performance and unusually poor performance, respectively, on a *well-validated* response bias measure. Examples include the Test of Memory Malingering (TOMM) and the Word Memory Test (WMT). The B2 (but not B1) criteria can also be met by specialized SVTs that rely on simplicity but not a forced-choice format (see chapter 3, by Boone and Lu, in the current volume; examples include the Rey 15-Item Test [Boone, Salazar, Lu, Warner-Chacon, & Razani, 2002]; the Dot Counting Test [Boone, Lu, Back, King, Lee, et al., 2002]; the Harbor-UCLA *b* Test [Boone, Lu, Sherman, Palmer, Back, et al., 2000]) and indicators derived from standard tests (e.g., Reliable Digit Span [RDS; Greiffenstein et al., 1994]; Millis's composite scores for the CVLT [Millis & Volinksy, 2001]; the Bernard, McGrath, & Houston, 1996, and Suhr & Boyer, 1999, formulas for the Wisconsin Card Sorting Test [WCST; Heaton, Chelune, Talley, Kay, & Curtiss, 1993]; and the Bolter items for the Category Test [Bolter, Picano, & Zych, 1985]). Forced-choice SVTs are reviewed by Grote and Hook in the present volume and have also been reviewed by Bianchini, Mathias, and Greve (2001; see also Slick, Tan, Strauss, & Hultsch, 2004, for the results of a survey of B2 indicators commonly used in clinical practice).

Criterion B3   Criteria B3–B6 include subjective judgments in addition to objective test scores. Criterion B3 requires scores that are markedly discrepant from the fundamental principles of normal and abnormal neurological function. The key element is claimants who are behaving in a qualitatively different fashion from persons with normal brain function or those with documented brain disease. Slick et al. (1999) provide the examples of poor attention but average memory scores or failing items on recognition testing that were spontaneously recalled on earlier free recall trials. Lu, Boone, Jimenez, and Razani (2004) describe normal interference effects on the Stroop Test in persons claiming posttraumatic alexia; the Stroop effect (dysfluency caused by conflicting task demands) requires normal reading. Because many forensic cases involve serial neuropsychological assessments, particularly good evidence for B3 is a marked decline in performance when a nondementing condition is claimed (Babikian, Boone, Lu, & Arnold, 2006; Boone et al., 2002; Curtis, Greve, Bianchini, & Heinly, 2005; Greiffenstein et al. 1996a, 1996b; Lange, Iverson, Sullivan, & Anderson, 2006; Mittenberg, Azrin, Millsaps, & Heilbronner, 1993; Mittenberg, Theroux-Fichera, Zielinski, & Heilbronner, 1995; Ord, Greve, & Bianchini, 2006).

Criterion B4   Criterion B4 requires a discrepancy between the test data and observed behavior. For example: a well-educated patient who presents with fluent speech and no paraphasias or word-finding difficulties during the interview but performs in the severely impaired range on verbal fluency and confrontation naming tests.

Criterion B5   Criterion B5 refers to a discrepancy between at least two neuropsychological test scores and reliable collateral reports. Obvious examples that we frequently encounter are claimants who produce diffusely abnormal scores but by all accounts live independently, handle their own finances, and drive. Reliable collateral sources should not be limited to family (who may have great self-interest) but reasonably include outside records (e.g., medical doctors; speech, physical, or occupational therapists) and surveillance video (see for example, Boone et al., 2002). Babikian et al. (2006) mention a plaintiff who was supposedly unable to compute simple calculations but was shown on surveillance tape completing store and bank transactions unassisted. We are not aware of any psychometric indicators or standardized rating systems for quantifying B5.

Criterion B6   Criterion B6 is defined as "improbably poor performance on two or more standardized tests of cognitive function within a specific domain (e.g., memory) that is inconsistent with documented neurological or psychiatric history" (Slick et al., 1999, p. 554). Their example involved a person who, in the absence of any history of brain pathology or dysfunction, performed in the severely impaired range on verbal memory tests after a motor vehicle accident that resulted in mild brain injury at worst. Another example that met this criterion described by Greiffenstein et al. (1995) was a woman who was "stunned" following head trauma and who scored 4 SD below her age group on the Stroop Test and Halstead Grip Strength. The operationalization of this criterion is relatively easy. Greiffenstein et al. (1994) used z scores of < -3 in the context of remote mild injury as evidence for pseudo-abnormality.

Some tests that have been examined with the known-groups design include the Wechsler Adult Intelligence Scale-III (Wechsler, 1997a; Working Memory Index, Processing Speed Index), Wechsler Memory Scale-III (Wechsler, 1997b), California Verbal Learning Test (Delis et al., 1987; e.g., recognition hits), Wisconsin Card Sorting Test (Failure to Maintain Set [FMS]; unique responses), the Category Test (Reitan & Wolfson, 1993; total errors, Sweet & King, 2002), and the Finger Tapping Test (Reitan & Wolfson, 1993; Arnold, Boone, Dean, Wen, Nitch, et al., 2005; see also the chapters by Greiffenstein; Suhr and Barrash; and Greve and Bianchini in the present volume). This is not a comprehensive list, and any standard clinical measure may apply to this criterion with proper validation. It is important to point out that, unlike B2, this criterion refers to performance on tests originally

designed to clinically assess cognitive function, not those designed to detect malingering.

The fact that specialized indicators have been derived from some of these same tests creates a potential problem. Theoretically, a person could be diagnosed as malingering based largely if not exclusively on findings from a single test (RDS for B2 or Digit Span scaled score for B6; Suhr & Boyer WCST formula for B2; FMS for B6; CVLT linear shrinkage model for B2; recognition hits for B6). Conservative application of detection data requires that indicators that are derived in whole or in part from an individual test performance be applied to only one B criterion. This kind of usage ensures that a diagnosis of malingering is actually based on multiple independent findings and is consistent with the conservative intent of the Slick et al. criteria. For a detailed discussion of this issue, see chapter 8 by Greve and Bianchini in the present volume.

Slick Criteria C1–C5

The C1–C5 criteria weight self-report and historical evidence with respect to consistency and validity. These are the most subjective elements of the Slick system, although they are easily amenable to quantification or rating. The following are discrepancies in self-report and other considerations such as behavioral observations and expected symptom evolution for the claimed disease.

Criterion C1   This criterion is met when the patient's self-reported history is discrepant with documented medical or psychosocial history. The self-report can be discrepant in a way that exaggerates the severity of the injury (e.g., exaggerated severity of physical injury or length of loss of consciousness and posttraumatic amnesia [LOC/PTA]) or overstates the baseline against which the current function is compared (e.g., exaggerated premorbid educational or occupational achievement; denial of previous head injury or previous psychiatric history). Also meeting this criterion would be a report of total disability in a major social role following a concussion (Greiffenstein et al., 1994). The criterion used by Boone and colleagues (Boone, Lu et al. 2002; Boone, Salazar et al., 2002)—major contradictions between self-report of symptoms, medical records, and observed behavior including surveillance— would be consistent with C1 if the index suspect behavior is self-reported history rather than test performance (which would be B5) or symptoms/ complaints (which would be C4; see below).

Criterion C2   Like B3, C2 refers to self-reported symptoms that are inconsistent with known patterns of brain functioning or, like B6, are inconsistent with expectations for the type or severity of the documented injury or pathology. Particularly useful are self-reported symptoms absurd on their face. A good example involves dual claims of neurogenic amnesia and reexperiencing

symptoms (nightmares, flashbacks) for the same trauma (Greiffenstein, Baker, Axelrod, Peck, & Gervais, 2004). Boone, Lu et al. (2002), and Boone, Salazar et al. (2002) provide the example of seeing letters upside down and backward and the inability to see through glass. More common examples include remote memory loss (e.g., autobiographical information; Greiffenstein et al., 1994), extended retrograde memory loss with good recall of the alleged causal accident (Greiffenstein et al., 1995), and atypical symptom evolution after ambiguous neurological trauma (Greiffenstein, Baker, Gola, Donders, & Miller, 2002). At present there are no psychometric indicators or standardized rating scales by which to quantify evidence that applies to this criterion.

Criterion C3   To meet C3, self-reported symptoms (as opposed to test scores, B4) are inconsistent with observed behavior. Slick et al. (1999) described examples of findings that meet this criterion, including complaints of severe episodic memory deficits in a patient who is able to drive independently and arrives on time for an appointment in an unfamiliar area or a patient who complains of severely slowed mentation and concentration problems yet easily follows complex conversations. At this time there are no psychometric indicators or standardized rating scales by which to quantify evidence applying to this criterion.

Criterion C4   Self-reported symptoms are discrepant with information obtained from collateral informants. This is essentially the same criterion as B5, except that the suspect behavior is now a self-report. Criterion C4 includes nonorganic findings on physical examinations (Boone, Lu et al. 2002; Boone, Salazar et al., 2002). At this time there are no psychometric indicators or standardized rating scales by which to quantify evidence that applies to this criterion. For more detailed discussions of nonorganic physical signs see Bianchini et al. (2005), Albers and Schiffer (this volume), and Greve, Bianchini, Black, et al., 2006.

Criterion C5   This refers to evidence of exaggerated or fabricated symptoms. Specifically, "self-reported symptoms of psychological dysfunction are substantially contradicted by behavioral observation and/or reliable collateral information" (Slick et al., 1999, p. 554). Included under this heading are the following:

- deviant elevations on MMPI-2 Validity scales such as the Fake Bad scale (FBS) or F-Family (e.g., Greve, Bianchini, Love, et al., 2006)
- Meyers Index (Meyers, Millis, & Volkert, 2002)
- grossly elevated Modified Somatic Perception Questionnaire and Pain Disability Index (Larrabee, 2003c)
- invalid Personality Assessment Inventory and Millon Multiaxial Clinical Inventory-III

However, PAI and MMCI-3 validity have not been studied with known-groups designs, unlike the MMPI-2 and other validity scales.

Slick Criterion D

This criterion describes exclusionary rules, that is, conditions under which findings that are sufficient for an MND diagnosis would not be classified as malingering. Specifically, behaviors that meet the necessary criteria from B and C that can be *fully* accounted for by genuine psychiatric, developmental, or neurological disorders should not be labeled as malingering. Hence, evidence for a significantly diminished capacity to appreciate the laws or mores against malingering or an inability to conform one's behavior to such standards that correlates with a strong history of treatment-resistant schizophrenia in association with suspiciously poor scores should not be deemed MND. This criterion makes it clear that malingering cannot be ruled out unless it can be reasonably demonstrated that positive B and/or C criteria are fully accounted for by psychological or neurological disturbance and are not at all motivated by any identifiable external incentives. For example, the mere fact of having mild mental retardation is not automatic grounds for ruling out MND. There has to be a clear demonstration of how the retardation in these persons explains their particular test scores. A death penalty candidate with documented mild retardation can still be labeled MND if the person scores below chance on a two-alternative test. Mental retardation cannot *fully* explain a score that implies sufficient cognitive control to inhibit correct answers in favor of wrong ones (see Hayes, Hale, & Gouvier, 1997, for other examples).

The motivating role of potential financial compensation is discussed in the next section.

Validity of the Slick et al. Criteria

An important issue regarding the Slick et al. or any diagnostic criteria for that matter is their validity. In this case, the question is, what is the evidence that persons who meet the MND criteria are in fact malingering? The definition of malingering includes three fundamental evidentiary elements: (a) the behavior in question is exaggerated or fabricated; (b) the exaggeration or fabrication is intentional; and (c) the exaggeration or fabrication is motivated by a recognizable external incentive.

Data from a range of clinical conditions in which there is no incentive help identify the point at which behaviors (cognitive/physical deficits, subjective symptoms) become meaningfully inconsistent with those seen in genuine illness and thus reflect exaggeration or fabrication. Thus, determining the presence of exaggeration is not difficult, and this volume is replete with examples. However, inferring intent and motivation are more complicated. This section reviews evidence that the psychometric findings that support a diagnosis of malingering reflect an intentional effort to appear impaired and that those same findings are motivated by clear external incentives.

Validity of the Definite MND Definition

Bianchini et al. (2005) have stated, "At the heart of the issue of malingering is the question, 'is the patient *intentionally* performing below their true capacity or manifesting more disability/symptoms than is actually the case?' Intent is something that generally has to be inferred from the facts of the case in the form of the quantity, magnitude and pattern of inconsistencies in a patient's presentation" (p. 407). Short of an admission or compelling videotape evidence, how does one ever know that a clinical patient has intentionally underperformed?

Forced-choice SVTs make a unique contribution to the neuropsychologist's ability to infer intent (Bianchini et al., 2001). Specifically, because of the forced-choice format of these tasks, scores can be compared to the appropriate binomial distribution, and the probability of that score occurring by chance (i.e., guessing in someone with no previous knowledge or memory of the stimuli) can be determined. Scores significantly below the level expected by chance factors alone ($p < .05$ according to the Slick et al. criteria) are considered definitive evidence of intentional exaggeration and, along with the presence of incentive, meet the criteria for definite MND in the Slick et al. system. What is the basis for this inference?

The interpretation of a significantly below-chance result as definitive evidence of *intentional* exaggeration of cognitive deficits even in the context of objective pathology has become well established in the neuropsychological literature (ibid.; Bianchini, Greve, & Love, 2003; Tombaugh, 1996; Reynolds, 1998; Binder, 2000). For example, Tombaugh (1996) pointed out that significantly below-chance scores "imply that the person knew some of the pictures were correct, but intentionally picked the incorrect picture" (p. 19). Similarly, Reynolds (1998) stated that "SVT theory argues that the [below-chance] score is not a random or chance occurrence, but represents a purposive distortion by the examinee" (p. 272). Binder (2000), one of the pioneers of this method, has noted that "authorities agree that performance on a forced-choice test that is significantly worse than chance indicates that the patient deliberately provided wrong answers" (p. 35). That is, below-chance performance on an SVT requires *active* avoidance of the correct response. Pankratz has characterized worse-than-chance performance as "the smoking gun of intent" (p. 385) (Pankratz & Erickson, 1990).

Beyond this theoretical argument, there is concrete evidence that supports the contention that below-chance performances are intentional. This evidence is the convergence of findings from clinical patients who perform below chance on a forced-choice SVT with those of persons asked to intentionally underperform for experimental purposes (simulators). Several studies have provided comparisons between patients scoring at below-chance levels (definite malingerers) and simulators on scores from the WAIS and MMPI.

The performance of definite malingerers and simulators can be compared on Reliable Digit Span, one of the best studied clinical malingering

indicators. Three studies (Inman & Berry, 2002; Etherton, Bianchini, Greve, & Ciota, 2005; Strauss, Slick, Levy-Bencheton, Hunter, MacDonald, et al., 2002) reported RDS data for 138 combined simulators (mean = 6.89, SD = 3.03), while four studies (Etherton, Bianchini, Ciota, Heinly, & Greve, 2006; Etherton, Bianchini, Heinly, & Greve, 2006; Heinly, Greve, Bianchini, Love, & Brennan, 2005; Larrabee, 2003a) reported data on 77 definite malingerers (mean = 7.11, SD = 2.47). These means are not significantly different.

Three studies (Etherton et al., 2005; Rees, Tombaugh, Gansler, & Moczynski, 1998; Tombaugh, 1997) reported Test of Memory Malingering data (Tombaugh, 1996) for 115 simulators (Trial 2 mean = 31.3, SD = 9.8). These data were compared to the nine definite malingerers (Trial 2 mean = 33.4, SD = 14.4) reported by Greve, Bianchini, and Doane (2006). These two groups did not differ significantly.

Similarly, Bianchini, Etherton, Greve, Heinly, and Meyers (under review), in a direct comparison of simulators and definite malingerers on the MMPI-2, found no group differences on MMPI-2 Validity scales F, Fp, FBS, DS-r, O-S, F minus K, and the Meyers Index. There was a difference on Fb, but on that scale the clinical malingerers actually scored worse than the simulators. Moreover, two studies (Dearth, Berry, Vickery, Vagnini, Baser, et al., 2005; Bianchini et al., in preparation) reported FBS data on 72 simulators ($M = 25.7$, $SD = 6.4$) while three studies (Bianchini et al., under review; Greve et al., 2006; Larrabee, 2003b) reported FBS data for 72 definite malingerers (mean = 28.5, SD = 4.66). These two groups differed significantly ($p < .01$), with the definite malingerers scoring worse than the simulators.

Etherton, Bianchini, Ciota, et al. (2006) reported WAIS Working Memory Index (WMI) data for simulators (mean = 74.40, SD = 12.5) and definite malingerers (mean = 74.94, SD = 16.44) and found no significant group differences on either the WMI or its constituent subtests (Arithmetic, Digit Span, and Letter-Number Sequencing). The rates of positive findings (defined as less than or equal to 70, the 5% false positive error rate cutoff) were almost identical (47% and 45% for definite malingerers and simulators, respectively). The most divergent results were seen for the WAIS Processing Speed Index (PSI; Etherton, Bianchini, Heinly, et al., 2006) on which the definite malingerers scored significantly higher on average (mean = 71.25, SD = 10.17) than the simulators (mean = 65.85, SD = 7.33). Moreover, 63% of definite MND patients scored less than or equal to 70 (the 5% false positive error rate cutoff) compared to 80% of simulators. The results were similar for the constituent subtests of PSI (Digit Symbol-Coding, Symbol Search).

Thus, these data demonstrate that two groups of persons whose faking is known to be intentional (but for different reasons) are indistinguishable (particularly on specifically designed validity indicators). The fact that definite clinical malingerers do not differ from persons known to be fabricating their deficits because they have been instructed to do so in an experimental context supports the theoretically defined position that a below-chance SVT finding indicates an intentional effort to appear impaired. In summary, the

inference that significantly below-chance performance is due to a conscious effort to appear impaired is supported statistically, theoretically, and empirically. The result is that persons who are classified as definite malingerers can be used to test the hypothesis that clinically diagnosed probable malingerers are also intentionally exaggerating.

Validity of the Probable MND Definition

A diagnosis of probable malingering is made on the basis of a combination of suspect behavior patterns (e.g., test scores and other findings, B2–B6 and C criteria) that together imply conscious intent or awareness of inconsistency. Conceptually, the more inconsistencies, the less likely the patient is unaware of being inconsistent. "As clinicians find incongruities in the patient's total presentation (history, presentation, progress in recovery, and so on), the probability of malingering likewise increases" (Reynolds, 1998, p. 281).

It has been the convention in the study of cognitive malingering to require two positive findings for a diagnosis of malingering (Slick et al., 1999; Greiffenstein et al., 1994, 1995; Millis, Ross, & Ricker, 1998; Mittenberg et al., 2001; Boone et al., 2002). This approach has been justified on statistical grounds as well (Larrabee, 2003a; Boone & Lu, 2003). What evidence supports the assertion that such findings imply intentional efforts to appear impaired? Several studies demonstrate that persons who are classified as probable malingerers do not differ significantly from those classified as definite malingerers (Curtis, Greve, Bianchini, & Brennan, 2006; Greve, Bianchini, Love, Brennan, & Heinly, 2006; Heinly, Greve, Bianchini, Love, & Brennan, 2005; Larrabee, 2003a).

The studies of Curtis et al. (2006) and Heinly et al. (2005) have focused on single cognitive tests (the California Verbal Learning Test [CVLT] and Digit Span and related scores, respectively). In these two studies patients who met B2 and C5 criteria were classified as probable MND. Criterion B2 was met with a positive finding on *either* the Portland Digit Recognition Test (PDRT; Binder, 1993) *or* the TOMM (Tombaugh, 1996) *or* by two or more positive findings on embedded indicators. Criterion C5 was met with positive MMPI findings. Of the CVLT raw scores examined (total trials 1–5, recognition hits, Discriminability Index, Long-Delay Cued Recall), the definite and probable MND cases differed only on recognition hits. However, the effect size (eta^2) for the difference between these two groups was only .09. The Heinly et al. (2005) study showed no differences on Digit Span–based scores, including the Digit Span scaled score and the Reliable Digit Span. These studies demonstrate that malingering groups defined on the basis of psychometric evidence of cognitive malingering did not differ on measures of cognitive ability or cognitive effort.

In the MMPI study of Greve et al. (2006), the probable malingering subjects, like those of Curtis et al. and Heinly et al., were defined almost completely on the basis of inconsistencies related to cognitive symptoms

and performance. Like the previous studies, the probable group generally did not differ from the definite malingerers. Moreover, there tended to be a dose-response relationship between the magnitude or significance of the malingering findings and the percentage of malingerers scoring above the 95% specificity level for the nonmalingering control group on the MMPI-2 Validity scales. In addition to demonstrating the comparability of definite malingerers and probable malingering groups, this study demonstrates that a finding of cognitive malingering predicts to a noncognitive behavioral domain.

These findings are consistent in supporting the validity of the standard Slick et al. criteria for probable MND. Additionally, the original B criteria specified by Slick et al., by which a patient can fail multiple B2 criteria (e.g., symptom validity tests such as the TOMM and the WMT) but receive a diagnosis of only possible MND if no other B or C criteria are met, require revision, as is discussed in the next section of this chapter.

Validity of Alternative Definitions of Probable MND

A number of studies suggest that the Slick et al. system might be too rigid in how psychometric indicators are combined. Three detection studies (Larrabee, 2003a; Vickery, Berry, Dearth, Vagnini, Baser, et al., 2004; Victor, Boone, Serpa, & Buehler, 2006) indicate that multiple positive findings on independent psychometric indicators, regardless of the specific criterion to which they apply, may be sufficient for a diagnosis of probable MND.

Using a known-groups design, Larrabee (2003a) examined the detection accuracy of one B2 indicator (Reliable Digit Span, Greiffenstein et al., 1994), three B6 indicators (Benton Visual Form Discrimination, Benton et al., 1994; B6: Finger Tapping, Reitan & Wolfson, 1993; Wisconsin Card Sorting Test Failure to Maintain Set, Heaton et al., 1993), and one C5 indicator (FBS, Lees-Haley et al. 1991). Larrabee (2003a) found that, although the average *sensitivity* of the five different derived or embedded indicators of malingering was .536, with an average *specificity* of .907 (similar to the meta-analytic results of Vickery, Berry, Inman, Harris, & Orey, 2001), *sensitivity increased* to .857, with no appreciable change in *specificity* (.889) when any two of the five indicators were positive. When any three of five indicators were positive, sensitivity dropped to .542, but specificity was 1.00.

Similarly, as part of an investigation of classification accuracy, Vickery et al. (2004) found a specificity of .952 for any two of three B2 indicators (Letter-Memory Test, TOMM, and the Digit Memory Test) and 1.00 for all three indicators. Sensitivity decreased from .891 at ≥ 1 indicator positive to .652 at ≥ 2 positive indicators and further still to .326 for all 3 indicators positive. This decrease in sensitivity may be due to the fact that Vickery et al. (ibid.) used malingering indicators that were all from one domain (free-standing, memory-paradigm symptom validity tests; B2 indicators), whereas Larrabee (2003a) used embedded or derived indicators from four performance

domains and one symptom report domain, thereby tapping three different Slick et al. criteria (B2, B6, C5).

In their known-groups study, Victor, Boone, Serpa, and Buehler (2006) contrasted the performance of a probable MND group with the performance of a group of nonlitigating psychiatric and neurologic patients on three embedded B2 indicators (Reliable Digit Span, Greiffenstein et al., 1994; Rey-Osterrieth [RO] Complex Figure Effort Equation, Lu, Boone, Cozolino, & Mitchell, 2003; RO/Rey Auditory Verbal Learning Test discriminant function, Sherman, Boone, Lu, & Razani, 2002) and one B6 indicator (dominant hand Finger Tapping, Arnold et al., 2005). A positive finding on any two of the four indicators was associated with sensitivity of .875 and specificity of .961. With any three indicators positive, sensitivity dropped to .542, but specificity was nearly perfect at .98. Strikingly, the Victor et al. (2006) two- and three-indicator models produced values nearly identical to those obtained by Larrabee (2003a), who in his combined derivation and cross-validation samples, found sensitivity of .878 and specificity of .944 for any two failed validity indicators, as well as sensitivity of .512 and specificity of 1.00 for any three failed validity indicators.

The benefits of aggregating across multiple indicators is explained by the low correlation between malingering indicators in nonmalingering clinical comparison groups. Larrabee (2005) showed that the average intercorrelation among the five malingering indicators from Larrabee (2003a) was .175, such that a nonlitigating patient who scored above the cutoff of 1.57 SD from the mean (an invalid score) had a predicted score of .274 SD above the mean on any second indicator, a value substantially below the value of 1.57 SD for invalid effort. Boone and Lu (2003) made a similar point, arguing that if validity indicators are essentially uncorrelated in nonmalingering clinical samples and each has a false positive rate of .10, then the false positive rate of six out of six failed indicators would be 0.1^6, or as low as 1 in 1 million.

The formula for the binomial allows for the determination of the probability of occurrence by chance alone of subsets of a particular size taken from a larger population with a given false positive rate (e.g., .1). The formula (Glass & Stanley, 1970) is the following:

$$\binom{n}{n_1} p^{n_1} q^{n - n_1}$$

Where p is the probability of a false positive on any one trial, q is the probability of a true negative and equals $1 - p$, while $n_1 = 0, 1, 2, \ldots n$. For two of five indicators, each with a false positive rate of .1, this becomes the combination of two things taken from five things, or $5!/(2!)(3!)$ multiplied by $.1^2 \times .9^3$ for a probability of .073. For three of five indicators this becomes $5!/(3!)(2!)$ multiplied by $.1^3 \times .9^7$ for a probability of .008.

A third way to examine the relationship of multiple SVT failure to increased probability of malingering relies on the use of Likelihood Ratios

(LR; Straus, Richardson, Glasziou, & Haynes, 2005). Positive LR (LR+) can be computed for the likelihood of the presence of a particular diagnosis, whereas negative LR (LR−) can be computed for the likelihood of the absence of a particular diagnosis. In this case, we are interested in the LR+ for the presence of malingering. LR+ represents the ratio of the sensitivity of a particular test/ cutting score to the false-positive rate associated with the particular test/ cutting score. This ratio can be multiplied by the pretest odds (odds of the condition, derived from the baserate, defined as base rate/1 − base rate), to yield the posttest odds of the condition. These posttest odds can then be transformed by the formula odds/odds + 1 to yield the posttest probability. Moreover, if individual SVTs are independent (uncorrelated), multiple LR+ can be "chained" (ibid.) such that the posttest odds after application of the first test become the pretest odds for application of the subsequent SVT.

We provide an example of chaining of LR+, using the data from Larrabee (2003a), The average sensitivity of the five embedded/derived SVTs in this study was .53, with an average specificity of .91, and average intercorrelation of .175 in the non-malingering clinical subjects which was not significantly different than zero. At a base rate of malingering of .40, the pretest odds become .40/1 − .40 or .67. These are then multiplied by .53/.09 or 5.89 to yield posttest odds of malingering of 3.95, for a probability of malingering of 3.95/ 4.95 or .80. If a second test is then conducted (that matches the average sensitivity of .53 and specificity of .91), the LR+ remains 5.89 which is now multiplied by the previous posttest odds of 3.95 to yield new posttest odds of 23.27, associated with a posttest probability of malingering of .96 for two failed SVTs. Adding failure of a third independent SVT with matching sensitivity and specificity characteristics increases the posttest odds to 137.1, to yield a posttest probability of malingering of .99.

Thus, chaining of LR+ demonstrates nicely why aggregating across multiple failed independent indicators dramatically increases the probability that the conclusion that a patient is malingering is correct. Straus et al. (ibid.) caution that the posttest probabilities are overestimated, if the individual tests used in chaining of LR+ are correlated. The above results, however, with posterior probabilities approaching 1.0, are nearly identical to the actual PPP for three indicators found by Larrabee (2003a); Vickery et al. (2004), and Victor et al. (2006), This suggests that for the Larrabee (2003a) sample, the assumption of SVT independence was tenable, consistent with the average SVT intercorrelation of .175 that was not significantly different than zero. Last, generalizability of these LR+ results is supported by the close similarity of the average sensitivity and specificity of .53 and .91 obtained by Larrabee (2003a), to the average sensitivity of .56 and specificity of .96 found by Vickery et al. (2001) in their meta-analysis of SVTs,

Overall, these findings suggest that two and certainly three positive findings on multiple independent psychometric measures *regardless of the specific Slick criterion to which they apply* should be sufficient for a diagnosis of probable MND. How this type of criterion compares to the conventional

definitions of MND proposed by Slick et al. is addressed in studies by Larrabee (2003a) and Greve et al. (2006).

Larrabee (2003a) examined litigants defined as definite MND based on worse-than-chance performance on the PDRT (Binder, 1993) and also those defined as probable MND on the basis of (a) a PDRT score in the bottom 2% of a nonlitigating severe traumatic brain-injury group and (b) failure on at least one other B2 measure of symptom validity such as the TOMM or Rey 15-Item Test. These two groups were compared on the malingering indicators noted earlier, as well as four sensitive neuropsychological tests (Controlled Oral Word Association, Benton, Hamsher, & Sivan, 1994; Trail-Making Test Part B, Reitan & Wolfson, 1993; Verbal Selective Reminding Test, Buschke, 1973; Larrabee, Trahan, Curtiss & Levin, 1988; Continuous Visual Memory Test, Trahan & Larrabee, 1988). As Table 13.3 indicates, there are *no* significant differences on either the malingering indicators or the sensitive neuropsychological tests.

Table 13.3.
Neuropsychological Malingering Indicators and Other Selected Scores for Definite and Probable MND

	Definite MND[a]		Probable MND[b]	
	Mean	(SD)	Mean	(SD)
RDS	7.37	(1.92)	6.82	(1.67)
VFD	25.58	(5.16)	27.53	(3.45)
FT	70.97	(26.72)	66.86	(30.27)
FMS	1.42	(1.53)	1.12	(1.11)
FBS	26.41	(5.16)	26.71	(5.70)
COWA	−.76	(1.18)	−.88	(.93)
TMT-B	−.93	(1.30)	−1.03	(.94)
VSRT	−2.26	(1.51)	−2.23	(.98)
CVMT	−1.95	(.55)	−1.37	(.93)

Note. [a] $n = 24$
[b] $n = 17$ for RDS, VFD, FT, FMS, and FBS, with $n = 14$ for COWA,
TMT-B, VSRT, and CVMT
MND = malingered neurocognitive dysfunction
RDS = Reliable Digit Span (raw score)
VFD = Visual Form Discrimination (raw score)
FT = Finger Tapping Combined (raw score)
FMS = failure to maintain set (raw score)
FBS = Fake Bad scale (raw score)
COWA = Controlled Oral Word Association (z score)
TMT-B = Trail-Making Test B (z score)
VSRT = Verbal Selective Reminding Test Consistent Long-Term Retrieval (z score)
CVMT = Continuous Visual Memory Test (z score).
Adapted from G.J. Larrabee, Detection of Malingering Using Atypical Performance Patterns on Standard Neuropsychological Tests. *The Clinical Neuropsychologist, 17*, 410–425, 2003.

In addition to their conventionally defined probable MND group, Greve et al. (2006) also created a group based on the logic described in Larrabee (2005), which they called "statistically likely" MND. Members of this group did not meet the conventional Slick et al. criteria for probable MND, but were positive on at least two B2 indicators. The statistically likely group did not differ from the probable MND group on either the WAIS Full-Scale IQ or any of the eight MMPI-2 validity scales examined. Moreover, this statistically likely group also did not differ from the definite MND group on six of those scales.

Overall, the findings of Larrabee (2003a) and Greve et al. (2006) support the conclusion that multiple failures on malingering indicators at levels not worse than chance characterizes the same degree of motivated performance deficit as does significantly worse-than-chance performance. These findings also indicate that multiple positive B2 findings have similar diagnostic power as the use of multiple B and C criteria used in the studies by Greve and colleagues described earlier. Altogether the studies described in this section demonstrate that the exaggerated behavior reflected in a range of malingering indicators is intentionally produced. It is now necessary to examine whether the goal of that intentional symptom/deficit production can be linked to recognizable external incentives.

External Incentives Motivate Intentional Exaggeration

A diagnosis of malingering implies that symptoms/deficits are intentionally fabricated or exaggerated in order to obtain some easily recognizable incentive (Bianchini et al., 2005; *DSM-IV*, 1994; Slick et al., 1999). What is the evidence that the suspicious behaviors outlined in the Slick et al. criteria are so motivated? While a number of potential incentives may motivate malingering, the effect of a financial incentive (e.g., Workers' Compensation or personal-injury claim) is the easiest to document and the most well studied. Numerous studies published in the past 20 years address this question.

It is well established that financial incentive is related to outcome in brain injury in general, and the effect of money is strongest at the mild end of the severity continuum (Binder & Rohling, 1996; Paniak, Reynolds, Toller-Lobe, Melnyk, Nagy, et al., 2002; Price & Stevens, 1997; Reynolds, Paniak, Toller-Lobe, & Nagy, 2003; Youngjohn, Burrows, & Erdal, 1995). The specific influence of financial compensation on the severity of symptoms was assessed in a meta-analysis conducted by Binder and Rohling (1996), who found that the strength of the association between outcome measures, including neuropsychological test results and financial incentive (d), was 0.47 overall (.89 for mild TBI). By contrast, the mild traumatic brain-injury effect size in nonlitigants was not significant (generally less than .10; Binder, Rohling, & Larrabee, 1997). Binder and Rohling (1996) reported finding an incentive by injury severity interaction, with MTBI patients with incentive performing worse on neuropsychological measures than individuals with more severe injuries or without incentive.

Hill (1965) posited nine criteria for judging whether an association is causal. Among these is the idea that a strong association is more likely than a weak one to reflect a causal relationship. A second criterion is evidence of consistency in that the effect occurs across studies and populations. Binder and Rohling (1996) demonstrated that the incentive effect is both strong and consistent. Moreover, subsequent research has supported their findings (Bernstein, 1999; Boone & Lu, 2003; Cato, Brewster, Ryan, & Giuliano, 2002; Iverson & Binder, 2000; Reynolds et al., 2003; Youngjohn et al., 1995). Carroll, Cassidy, Peloso, Borg, von Holst, et al. (2004) have published a comprehensive review of mild TBI and concluded that, "where symptoms persist, compensation/litigation is a factor" (p. 84). This conclusion has been echoed by Belanger, Curtiss, Demery, Lebowitz, and Vanderploeg (2005) in their meta-analysis of outcome in mild TBI. Thus, this strong and consistent incentive effect indicates that some aspect of the medicolegal context leads to an exaggeration of deficit and raises the possibility that some patients with persistent symptoms are motivated by potential financial compensation to intentionally exaggerate their cognitive deficits (i.e., malinger). However, a problem with these studies is that they do not disentangle the influence of financial compensation and that of processes inherent in the medicolegal context (e.g., litigation itself, delay in receiving treatment, unemployment).

One way of disentangling the effects of these two interrelated factors is to establish what is effectively a dose-response relationship between the magnitude of potential compensation and failure on tests sensitive to malingering. The dose-response relationship is another of Hill's criteria for causality (Hill, 1965). If potential external incentive were indeed motivating poor performance in some TBI patients, one could hypothesize that greater potential incentive should result in a higher frequency of exaggerated test results and possibly in the report of a greater variety of subjective symptoms because a broader symptom presentation would produce greater disability, which is more "valuable" in the medicolegal context (Bianchini et al., 2003; Bianchini, Etherton, & Greve, 2004; Bianchini et al., 2005).

Bianchini, Curtis, and Greve (2006) tested this hypothesis by examining the rates of malingering test failures and diagnosable malingering in three groups of TBI patients with different levels of potential financial compensation: (a) no incentive; (b) limited incentive as provided by Louisiana Workers' Compensation law; and (c) high incentive as provided by federal law. The effects of compensation were examined in the overall TBI sample and in mild and moderate–severe TBI separately. As in previous studies, the presence of financial compensation was positively associated with failures on a range of validity indicators. In general, both groups showed an increased likelihood of being positive when incentive was present, but mild TBIs were substantially more likely to be positive than moderate–severe TBIs. These results replicate and expand upon past research on monetary impact on disability exaggeration (Binder & Rohling, 1996; Paniak et al., 2002; Price & Stevens, 1997; Reynolds et al., 2003; Youngjohn, Burrows, & Erdal, 1995).

Beyond the simple incentive/no incentive comparison, the magnitude of potential compensation as represented by the legal jurisdiction under which Workers' Compensation claims are handled was clearly associated with malingering test failures. For *every* indicator, individuals covered by federal law showed considerably higher rates of positive findings and diagnosable malingering than individuals covered by state law. Interestingly, the moderate–severe TBI patients consistently showed a general incentive effect. They did not, however, generally show a dose-response relationship like that seen in the mild TBI patients. Interestingly, while this finding may reflect sample size issues, those who would be most impaired and possibly most vulnerable to the adverse effects of litigation-related stressors did not appear to be affected by the magnitude of potential compensation. Thus, when combined with previous research, this study reinforces the notion that financial incentive motivates intentional symptom exaggeration.

Strengths and Weakness of the Slick et al. Criteria

Published in 1999, the Slick et al. criteria represent a formal integration of the thinking on malingering diagnosis at that time. Since then they have been used in numerous studies and have been the subject of formal (e.g., NAN symposium) and informal debate, discussion, and critique among neuropsychologists. This process has led to clarifications of both their strengths/advantages and weaknesses/limitations. With regard to the former, when the specific criteria are properly operationalized, their application is objective, systematic, organized, and structured. Millis (2004) has developed a diagnostic flow chart (reproduced in Figure 13.1) that illustrates the orderliness of this approach.

The Slick criteria are comprehensive and flexible in that they allow the use of information from multiple domains without requiring any specific type of finding. The comprehensiveness is not absolute because Slick applies only to cognitive malingering; moreover, findings that are indicative or suggestive of malingering in other domains carry less weight than those that involve cognitive testing (for a discussion and an alternative approach, see the modification of the Slick criteria for the diagnosis of malingered pain-related disability in Bianchini et al., 2005). The focus on cognitive malingering likely results in false negative cases.

The Slick criteria have several advantages. First, they represent a tool belt rather than a single tool. Second, they define different classes of behavior reflective of malingering. This allows for the flexible development and refinement of indicators applicable to a variety of functional illnesses or fabricated presentations. Third, the operationalization of the Slick criteria is not static and can benefit from scientific advances. Tools can be added, removed, or refined based on future science. Fourth, the criteria are multimodal. The "criterion problem" in psychology is an old issue and refers to insufficient consideration of a criterion's construct validity. The only cure for this is aggregated, multimodal data that are uninfluenced by the dependent variable

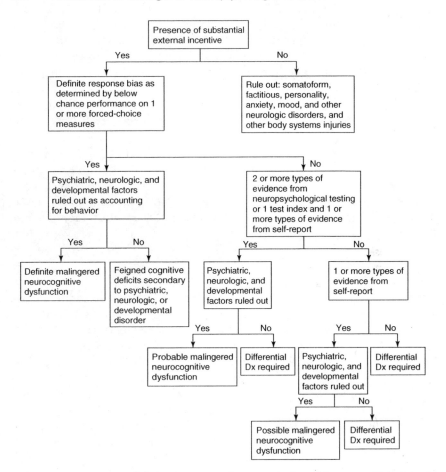

Figure 13.1. Diagnostic decision tree. Dx = diagnosis. (Adapted from D. J. Slick, E. M. S. Sherman, & G. L. Iverson, Diagnostic criteria for malingered neurocognitive dysfunction: Proposed standards for clinical practices and research. *The Clinical Neuropsychologist, 13,* 545–561, 1999.) Reprinted from *Principles and practice of behavioral neurology and neuropsychology,* M. Rizzo & P. Eslinger (eds.), S. R. Millis, *Evaluation of malingered neurocognitive disorders* (pp. 1077–1089), 2004, with permission from Elsevier.

(Hunsley & Meyer, 2003). Finally, the Slick et al. criteria are conservative. They are designed to substantially reduce prospects for false positive identification due to genuine cerebral dysfunction in the noncredible index group (see Arnold et al., 2005; Bianchini et al., 2003, for good examples).

Over the past 7 years, much work with the Slick et al. criteria has also demonstrated their weaknesses and limitations. First, as already noted, their focus on cognitive malingering tends to ignore or minimize important evidence of malingering in other behavioral domains (emotional, physical, self-report). Second, certain combinations of variables may predict malingering

with a very high degree of specificity (nearly perfect), but because they all represent the same B criterion (usually either B2 or B6), they are not sufficient for a probable MND diagnosis. From a practical standpoint there is an over-reliance on cognitive test findings (particularly B1, B2, and B6 findings), while nontest or noncognitive test findings (e.g., C5), although potentially strongly indicative of malingering, are given less weight. Third, the C criteria are very operator dependent. The reliability of clinical judgments of atypical self-report or an implausible-sounding symptom evolution (e.g., worsening complaints after mTBI) depends heavily on the depth and breadth of fundamental neuro-logical knowledge of the individual neuropsychologist. A clinician who does not know that monocular diplopia (double vision with one eye closed) is neuro-anatomically inconsistent may miss MND, while the clinician who does not know that repetition deficit is central to conduction aphasia may misdiagnose MND because of failure on the Greiffenstein Reliable Digit Span. For this rea-son, development of atypical symptom rating scales will reduce operator depen-dence. Finally, in some ways the Slick criteria are too conservative (e.g., re-quiring two B6 hits for a positive B6). Given what we now know about the strengths and weakness of the Slick et al. criteria, certain modifications may be justified.

Proposed Modifications of Slick

1. Allow Multiple Psychometric Findings to Define Probable MND

The data on the effects of aggregating across multiple diagnostic indicators support modifications to the Slick et al. (1999) criteria. In the original B cri-teria Slick et al. specified, a patient can fail multiple B2 criteria (e.g., symptom validity tests such as the TOMM and the WMT) but receive a diagnosis of only possible MND if no other B criteria or C criteria are met. The findings of Larrabee (2003a), Vickery et al. (2004), Victor et al. (2006), and Greve et al. (2006) indicate that failure on three well-validated indicators is associated with essentially no false positives (i.e., a specificity of 1.00). Per the discussion of classification statistics in chapter 2, specificities of 1.00 result in a positive predictive power of 1.00 (true positives/true positives + 0 false positives). Hence, failure of three well-validated indicators appears to be associated with 100% probability of malingering and is statistically equivalent to definite MND (as discussed in chapter 2, scores falling at 100% PPP are not concep-tually equivalent to the active avoidance of the correct alternative associated with significantly worse-than-chance performance on two-alternative, forced-choice testing). Additional validation of the group defined by this modified criterion will be important as will additional specification of appropriate cutting scores and, where possible, classification accuracy of the aggregated indicators, as has been done by Larrabee (2003a) and Victor et al. (2006). As Meyers and Volbrecht (2003) have stated, the preceding data regarding no

false positives in persons with three or more well-validated indicators apply to persons who do not require a 24-hour supervised living setting.

2. Require Only One B6 Hit to Meet the B6 Criterion

Many studies have attempted to validate tests and indicators that would meet the B2 criterion. Also the subject of considerable recent study are scores and indicators that meet the B6 criterion: "improbably poor performance on two or more standardized tests of cognitive function within a specific domain (e.g., memory) that is inconsistent with documented neurological or psychiatric history" (Slick et al., 1999, p. 554). To meet this criterion, index scores must be extreme relative to an appropriate comparison group and requires findings from two separate tests of similar functions. "Extreme" may be defined in terms of standard deviation units (see, for example, Greiffenstein et al., 1994).

However, the known-groups methodology has been applied to numerous scores from a number of standard neuropsychological tests. Much of this research has been reviewed in the preceding chapters of this volume. These studies have often demonstrated classification accuracy that is comparable to that seen in specialized B2 indicators. See, for example, the accuracy of the Digit Span scaled score relative to RDS (Heinly et al, 2005; Babikian et al., 2006). These findings raise a simple question: If one hit on a well-validated, specialized (B2) indicator is sufficient to meet B2, then why would a single well-validated B6 score not be sufficient to meet B6? In short, if B6 indicators have been and are being subjected to the same rigorous known-groups studies as have been done with B2 indicators, allowing one B6 hit to meet this criterion is justified.

3. Require Multiple Qualitative, Subjective Criteria

Criteria B4, B5, and C1 through C4 (and to some extent B3) require subjective, qualitative judgments that increase the risk of bias influencing what is for all the other criteria an objective decision. Clear objective standards for the evaluation of inconsistencies between behavioral clinical presentation and evidence of capacities outside the clinical setting should be developed. In the absence of such standards, the determination that such inconsistencies reflect an intentional effort to appear impaired should be cautious and conservative and in some cases may be left to the trier of fact rather than the clinician (Bianchini et al., 2005).

In the case of these criteria, "conservative" may mean that at least two of the criteria must be positive (based on independent findings) in order to increase the likelihood that the inconsistencies are real and reflective of a pattern of misrepresentation. Moreover, those findings would not be sufficient for a diagnosis of MND in the absence of at least one positive finding on a psychometric criterion (B1–3, B6, C5). Again, this recommendation follows the conceptual logic behind the discriminative power of aggregated malingering indicators and is consistent with previous research (e.g., Boone

et al., 2002; Greiffenstein et al., 1994, 1995). However, this does not eliminate the need for a standardized method of evaluating nonpsychometric findings (e.g., through the development of behaviorally anchored rating scales) but instead serves as a method of reducing the risk of false positive errors while still allowing the use of information that might prevent false negative errors in some cases until such methods are developed.

4. Give C Criteria Equal Weight

Unlike the B criteria, which are test-centered inconsistencies or discrepancies, the C criteria involve significant discrepancies in the patient's self-reported symptoms that suggest a deliberate attempt to exaggerate or fabricate cognitive deficits. The Slick criteria are asymmetric in that failure of multiple B criteria is sufficient for determination of probable MND, but without the presence of positive B criteria, failure of multiple C criteria can reach the level of only possible MND. This means that, in the absence of cognitive test data consistent with an effort to exaggerate or fabricate deficits or disabilities, even compelling extratest evidence of malingering is not sufficient for a diagnosis of MND.

Greve, Bianchini, Love, et al. (2006), Greve, Bianchini, Black, et al. (2006), and Bianchini et al. (2005) have argued that, because of its focus on test findings and cognitive malingering, the Slick et al. criteria are insensitive to some (maybe many) cases of true malingering. The difficulty with this modification is that, with the exception of the "well-validated validity scales or indices on self-report measures of psychological adjustment" (Slick et al., 1999, p. 553), the C criteria are not easily quantifiable and require subjective judgment. The problem with subjective judgment is the same for C1 through C4 (and even parts of C5) as for B4 and B5.

However, if this modification is implemented, it would be possible for someone to be diagnosed as MND without demonstrating "exaggeration or fabrication of *cognitive* dysfunction" (ibid., p. 552; italics added). For example, a person could have a 33 on the FBS (C5) and be caught on videotape riding a motorcycle after claiming disabling balance problems (C1). This person would arguably be malingering but would not be malingering cognitive dysfunction. However, even if there were C evidence of cognitive malingering (e.g., a report of remote memory loss, C2, instead of the video evidence contradicting balance claims), that person would not be diagnosed as MND according to the Slick criteria.

This modification does not on its face reduce the conceptual purity of the malingering neurocognitive dysfunction diagnosis because it is possible that C criteria could be met with observations relevant to cognition (e.g., a report of 6 weeks of coma by someone when documents demonstrate that they had a Glasgow Coma Scale [GCS] of 15 at the accident scene). Thus, the asymmetry actually puts more weight on cognitive *test* scores rather than giving equal weight to evidence of cognitive symptom malingering. Practically, giving equal weight to the C criteria would probably reduce the

conceptual purity of the Slick criteria but to the benefit of identifying more true malingerers.

General Recommendations for Future Research

1. Objectively Define the Qualitative Criteria

Bianchini et al. (2005) have argued that clear objective standards for the evaluation of congruity between behavior in the clinic and behavioral capacity outside the clinic should be established. This would both improve the accuracy of clinical decision making and facilitate the operationalization of malingering for research purposes. One approach is to develop a broad set of examples of behavior meeting a given criterion against which the behavior of a clinical patient could be compared. Alternatively, a rating scale that allows the behavior to be compared against a set of descriptors could be developed. In any case, such research would increase the confidence one has in their assessment of suspicious behavior.

2. Continue Validation Studies

General recommendations for future research on measures of invalid performance and symptom exaggeration include the use of known-group research designs using the diagnostic criteria reviewed in this chapter, combined with a broad sampling of nonlitigating patients with bona fide neurologic, developmental, and psychiatric disorders (e.g., stroke, dementia, mental retardation). This is critical to clearly define the specificity of the particular validity indicator. The full range of score distributions should also be published for these groups so that clinicians can compute the positive predictive power and LR+ associated with the scores they are interpreting (see Greve & Bianchini, 2004). Recent examples of this type of data presentation are available in the published literature (Larrabee, 2003b; Ross, Millis, Krukowski, Putnam, & Adams, 2004).

3. Identify Nonmalingering Patients With Incentive (the Problems of Primary Gain and Somatization Behaviors)

Not all patients with exaggerated symptoms and/or evidence for reduced effort who are claiming a compensable injury are malingering, but there is reason to believe that psychosocial complications in some of these patients have an impact on test performance and treatment outcomes. The use of control groups without incentive does not address these potential nonspecific psychosocial effects of the litigation context. In the study of the accuracy of malingering indicators it is necessary to differentiate intentional

exaggeration associated with malingering from the nonintentional exaggeration seen in the psychologically complicated nonmalingering patient. This is particularly true in mild TBI, toxic exposure, and chronic pain, where somatization is likely to lead to persisting problems that are aggravated by the litigation context. Thus, it is important to develop and study methods for screening compensation-seeking patients to identify those who are very likely not malingering.

Nobody disputes the fact that mental illness or cognitive impairment can be disabling conditions that justify compensation. Hence, persons with genuine neuropsychiatric disorders will also seek compensation and be examined in settings involving secondary gain. A related problem is enmeshment in difficult psychosocial complications that potentially impact test performance and treatment outcomes; this concern is termed the problem of *primary gain*. Primary gain means a personal, idiosyncratic motivation to produce symptoms (e.g., exaggerating pain behavior to avoid sexual relations). The use of control groups without incentive does not address these potential nonspecific psychosocial effects of the litigation context.

This is a difficult methodological and conceptual problem. Several issues make the identification of exaggerated (even very exaggerated) but not malingered presentations difficult. Primary gain takes many nonmonetary forms, such as dependency tactics toward regressive ends, release from adult expectations, avoidance of mental illness stigma, and validation of the sick role. Ideally, the study of malingering indicators may require the differentiation of intentional from nonintentional exaggeration in the psychologically complex patient.

One commonly cited differential diagnosis is ruling out somatization disorder (SD; Binder & Campbell, 2004). This is particularly true in mild TBI, toxic exposure, and chronic pain, where putative somatization defenses mislead examiners into diagnosing psychological injuries or further aggravate the stress of the litigation process (and potentially are further aggravated by the litigation process, in turn). To show the conceptual problems of treating somatization as a genuine disorder, consider the fact that the clinical validity of SD and similar somatoform presentations have been seriously questioned (Brown, 2004). Of special interest is the repeated finding of antisocial personality and substance abuse in the male relatives of females who present with SD (Guze, 1993; Martin, Cloninger, & Guze, 1982). Some have conjectured that SD represents a sex-modified phenotypic variant of psychopathy (Harpending & Sobus, 1987; Mealy, 1995). Hence, the theory is that SD represents false illness signaling to manipulatively influence others' perception.

Ideally, it will eventually be important to develop and study methods for screening compensation-seeking patients with false symptom presentations due to primary gain to identify those who are likely not malingering. This is a difficult undertaking, as nonmalingering status has to be determined clinically and independently of the dependent malingering measures. One method is scaling of stressor intensity (independent of plaintiff self-report) or the

absence of implausible features. Greiffenstein et al. (2004) have identified persons bringing lawsuits in connection with undeniably severe psychological trauma (e.g., torture, mutilation); they produced elevated MMPI-2 Fake Bad scale scores relative to a pure clinical group but lower scores than litigants who experienced minor stressors (who were likely malingering).

4. Analyze False Positives

It is also important to identify the characteristics of patients identified as false positive at a particular cutting score. For example, Larrabee (2003a) reported that the three persons erroneously identified as noncredible had Wisconsin Card Sorting Test (Heaton et al, 1993) failure-to-maintain-set errors and structural abnormalities on CT scan in common; two had documented prolonged coma. Moreover, no traumatic brain-injury patient had more than three failures to maintain set, so that if a particular litigant had (a) no loss of consciousness, (b) no CT abnormality, and (c) a failure to maintain set score of 4, this litigant was in all likelihood a true positive rather than false positive according to the Larrabee (2003a) malingering formula.

Similarly, the Meyers and Volbrecht (2003) false-positive analysis showed a misclassification only of clinical patients showing either (a) the need for 24-hour residential care, (b) demonstrably large vascular lesions, (c) failure on simple mental status tests, or (d) histories of advanced dementia or mental retardation. By contrast, community-dwelling clinical patients who were suffering a variety of neurological disorders did not show elevated failure rates on the malingering indicators, compared to the high frequency of failure in litigating subjects with minor injuries. Greiffenstein et al. (1996b) showed improved malingering hit rates when global amnesic patients were removed. Further examples include Curtis et al., 2006; Greve et al., 2006; and Heinly et al., 2005).

5. Describe in Detail the Pathology of the Critical Control Groups

A required property of an SVT is proven insensitivity to genuine cerebral disruption. Hence it is important that SVT research rely on unambiguously impaired, neuropsychiatric control groups. To fully characterize the referent medical groups, objective neurological and neuroimaging abnormalities should be quantified and reported. Several easily available measures are specific to the neurological disease being claimed. Clinical measures include (by way of illustration, not exclusion) latency to follow commands in severe TBI (Dikmen, Machamer, Winn, & Temkin, 1995), focal neurological findings (e.g., hemiparesis, ataxia), and lowest Glasgow Coma Scale on admission (Jennett & Teasdale, 1977). Quantifiable neurodiagnostic variables include CT/MRI findings that describe the location and severity of brain disruption (Levin, Williams, Eisenberg, High, Guinto, et al., 1992) and video and EEG monitoring for seizure (Binder, Salinsky, & Smith, 1994).

For example, Greiffenstein and Baker (2006) quantified the percentage of claimants at various GCS levels and with abnormal CT scans. In the case of pain, it is important to describe the specific nature of the pathology (e.g., strain versus herniated disc), laboratory findings, and surgeries. In toxic exposure cases it would be helpful to describe the alleged substances and findings of appropriate laboratory tests, if available, including environmental air samples and blood/urine levels (Lees-Haley, Greiffenstein, Larrabee, & Manning, 2004). In cases of alleged posttraumatic stress disorder (PTSD), quantification of deaths, severity of physical injury (Blanchard & Hickling, 2004), or the number of confirmed combat episodes (Dohrenwend, Turner, Turse, Adams, Koenen, et al. 2006) may be considered. Some recent literature tentatively suggests that heart rate and blood pressure shortly after trauma are biological markers of stressor severity (Bryant, Harvey, Guthrie, & Moulds, 2000). Essentially, PTSD analysis requires methods of scaling stressor toxicity that are independent of self-report.

6. Describe the Operationalization of the Classification Criteria

It is insufficient to offer mere conclusory statements such as "malingering group members met the Slick et al. criteria." All psychometric criteria that control malingering group inclusion should be specified. In the case of criteria B1 and B2, the selected cutting scores must be appropriately referenced or logically justified. In the case of the more subjective criteria (B3–B6, all of C), it is important to describe and/or quantify the nature of excessive test errors or atypical complaints. These can be quantified either in nominal form (specific atypical symptom present or absent) or in terms of interrater concordance for atypicality. For example, Greiffenstein et al (2004) reported the percentage of respondents claiming *delayed* onset of PTSD who were reexperiencing symptoms. It is not necessary to present those data in the final published paper, and some would argue against such publication on ethical grounds (Ben-Porath, 1994), though a review of the literature indicates that it is fairly common. If the qualitative criteria are used, the decision-making rules regarding their application should be described. One approach to presenting qualitative behavioral criteria can be seen in the works of Greiffenstein and colleagues and Boone and colleagues, which are referenced throughout this chapter.

Summary and Conclusions

In the past two decades neuropsychology has addressed many of the methodological and conceptual problems associated with the detection of malingered cognitive deficits in the context of brain injury. In 1999 Slick et al. proposed a systematic method for organizing observations of suspect behavior and decision rules leading to a diagnosis of cognitive malingering. The Slick et al. system continues to serve as a framework for empirical research

and as a practical tool for the clinical diagnosis of malingering of cognitive deficits. Its use over the past 7 years has demonstrated its strengths and highlighted its limitations. The purpose of this chapter has been to review the Slick et al. criteria and underscore those assets and weaknesses. Several modifications to the system have been suggested to remedy some of those limitations and ensure the clinical and research value of the criteria into the future.

References

Alexander, M. P. (1997). Minor traumatic brain injury: A review of physiogenesis and psychogenesis. *Seminars in Clinical Neuropsychiatry, 2,* 177–187.

American Psychiatric Association. (1994). *Diagnostic and statistical manual of mental disorders* (4th ed.). Washington, DC: Author.

Arnold, G., Boone, K., Dean, A., Wen, J., Nitch, S., Lu, P., et al. (2005). Sensitivity and specificity of finger-tapping test scores for the detection of suspect effort. *The Clinical Neuropsychologist, 19,* 105–120.

Ashendorf, L., Constantinou, M., & McCaffrey, R. J. (2004). The effect of depression and anxiety on the TOMM in community-dwelling older adults. *Archives of Clinical Neuropsychology, 19,* 125–130.

Babikian, T., Boone, K. B., Lu, P., & Arnold, G. (2006). Sensitivity and specificity of various digit-span scores in the detection of suspect effort. *The Clinical Neuropsychologist, 20,* 145–159.

Belanger, H. G., Curtiss, G., Demery, J. A., Lebowitz, B. K., & Vanderploeg, R. D. (2005). Factors moderating neuropsychological outcomes following mild traumatic brain injury: A meta-analysis. *Journal of the International Neuropsychological Society, 11,* 215–227.

Ben-Porath, Y. S. (1994). The ethical dilemma of coached malingering research. *Psychological Assessment, 6,* 14–15.

Benton, A. L., Hamsher, K. deS., & Sivan, A. B. (1994). *Multilingual Aphasia Examination* (3rd ed.). Iowa City, IA: AJA.

Benton, A. L., Sivan, A. B., Hamsher, K. deS., Varney, N. R., & Spreen, O. (1994). *Contributions to neuropsychological assessment: A clinical manual* (2nd ed.). New York: Oxford University Press.

Bernard, L. C., McGrath, M. J., & Houston, W. (1996). The differential effects of simulating malingering, closed-head injury, and other CNS pathology on the Wisconsin Card Sorting Test: Support for the "pattern of performance" hypothesis. *Archives of Clinical Neuropsychology, 11,* 231–245.

Bernstein, D. M. (1999). Recovery from mild head injury. *Brain Injury, 13,* 151–172.

Bianchini, K. J., Curtis, K. L., and Greve, K. W. (2006). Compensation and malingering in traumatic brain injury: A dose-response relationship? *The Clinical Neuropsychologist, 20,* 831–847.

Bianchini, K. J., Etherton, J. L., & Greve, K. W. (2004). Diagnosing cognitive malingering in patients with work-related pain: Four cases. *Journal of Forensic Neuropsychology, 4,* 65–85.

Bianchini, K. J., Etherton, J. L., Greve, K. W., Heinly, M. T., & Meyers, J. E. (under review). Classification accuracy of MMPI-2 Validity scales in the detection of pain-related malingering: A known-groups approach.

Bianchini, K. J., Greve, K. W., & Glynn, G. (2005). On the diagnosis of malingered pain-related disability: Lessons from cognitive malingering research. *Spine Journal, 5,* 404-417.

Bianchini K. J., Greve K. W., & Love, J. (2003). Definite malingered neurocognitive dysfunction in moderate/severe traumatic brain injury. *The Clinical Neuropsychologist, 17,* 574-580.

Bianchini, K. J., Mathias, C. W., & Greve, K. W. (2001). Symptom validity testing: A critical review. *The Clinical Neuropsychologist, 15,* 19-45.

Binder, L. M. (1993). Assessment of malingering after mild head trauma with the Portland Digit Recognition Test. *Journal of Clinical and Experimental Neuropsychology, 15,* 170-182.

Binder, L. M. (2000). The Portland Digit Recognition Test: A review of validation data and clinical use. *Journal of Forensic Neuropsychology, 2,* 27-41.

Binder, L. M., & Campbell, K. A. (2004). Medically unexplained symptoms and neuropsychological assessment. *Journal of Clinical and Experimental Neuropsychology, 19,* 432-457.

Binder, L. M., & Rohling, M. L. (1996). Money matters: A meta-analytic review of the effects of financial incentives on recovery after closed-head injury. *American Journal of Psychiatry, 153,* 7-10.

Binder, L. M., Rohling, M. L., & Larrabee, G. J. (1997). A review of mild head trauma. Part I: Meta-analytic review of neuropsychological studies. *Journal of Clinical and Experimental Neuropsychology, 19,* 421-431.

Binder, L. M., Salinsky, M. C., & Smith, S. P. (1994). Psychological correlates of psychogenic seizures. *Journal of Clinical and Experimental Neuropsychology, 16,* 524-530.

Blanchard, E. B., & Hickling, E. J. (2004). *After the crash: Psychological assessment and treatment of survivors of motor vehicle accidents* (2nd ed.). Washington, DC: American Psychological Association.

Bolter, J. F., Picano, J. J., & Zych, K. (1985, October). *Item error frequencies on the Halstead Category Test: An index of performance validity.* Paper presented at the annual meeting of the National Academy of Neuropsychology, Philadelphia.

Boone, K. B., and Lu, P. H. (2003). Noncredible cognitive performance in the context of severe brain injury. *The Clinical Neuropsychologist, 17,* 244-254.

Boone, K. B., Lu, P. H., Back, C., King, C., Lee, A., Philpott, L., et al. (2002). Sensitivity and specificity of the Rey Dot Counting Test in patients with suspect effort and various clinical samples. *Archives of Clinical Neuropsychology, 17,* 625-642.

Boone, K. B., Lu, P., Sherman, D., Palmer, B., Back, C., Shamieh, E., et al. (2000). Validation of a new technique to detect malingering of cognitive symptoms: The *b* Test. *Archives of Clinical Neuropsychology, 15,* 227-241.

Boone, K. B., Salazar, X., Lu, P., Warner-Chacon, K., & Razani, J. (2002). The Rey 15-Item Recognition Trial: A technique to enhance sensitivity of the Rey 15-Item Memorization Test. *Journal of Clinical and Experimental Neuropsychology, 24,* 561-573.

Brown, R. J. (2004). Psychological mechanisms of medically unexplained symptoms: An integrative conceptual model. *Psychological Bulletin, 130,* 793-812.

Bryant, R. A., Harvey, A. G., Guthrie, R. M., & Moulds, M. L. (2000). A prospective study of psychophysiological arousal, acute stress disorder, and posttraumatic stress disorder. *Journal of Abnormal Psychology, 109,* 341-344.

Buschke, H. (1973). Selective reminding for analysis of memory and learning. *Journal of Verbal Learning and Verbal Behavior, 12,* 543-550.

Carroll, L. J., Cassidy, J. D., Peloso, P. M., Borg, J., von Holst, H., Holm, L., et al. (2004). Prognosis for mild traumatic brain injury: Results of the WHO Collaborating Centre Task Force on Mild Traumatic Brain Injury. *Journal of Rehabilitation Medicine, 43* (suppl.), 84–105.

Cato, M. A., Brewster, J., Ryan, T., & Giuliano, A. J. (2002). Coaching and the ability to simulate mild traumatic brain-injury symptoms. *The Clinical Neuropsychologist, 16,* 524–535.

Cunnien, A. (1997). Psychiatric and medical syndromes associated with deception. In R. Rogers (Ed.), *Clinical assessment of malingering and deception* (2nd ed., pp. 23–46). New York: Guilford.

Curtis, K. L., Greve, K. W., Bianchini, K. J., & Brennan, A. (2006). California Verbal Learning Test indicators of malingered neurocognitive dysfunction: Sensitivity and specificity in traumatic brain injury. *Assessment, 13,* 46–61.

Curtis, K. L., Greve, K. W., Bianchini, K. J., & Heinly, M. (2005, October). *Sensitivity and specificity of WAIS indicators to malingered neurocognitive dysfunction in traumatic brain injury.* Poster presented at the 25th annual meeting of the National Academy of Neuropsychology, Tampa, FL.

Dearth, C. S., Berry, D. T. R., Vickery, C. D., Vagnini, V. L., Baser, R. E., Orey, S. A., et al. (2005). Detection of feigned head-injury symptoms on the MMPI-2 in head-injured patients and community controls. *Archives of Clinical Neuropsychology, 20,* 95–110.

Delis, D. C., Kramer, J. H., Kaplan, E., & Ober, B. A. (1987). *California Verbal Learning Test: Adult version.* San Antonio: Psychological Corp.

Dikmen, S. S., Machamer, J. E., Winn, H. R., & Temkin, N. R. (1995). Neuropsychological outcome at 1-year post head injury. *Neuropsychology, 9,* 80–90.

Dohrenwend, B. P., Turner, J. B., Turse, N. A., Adams, B. G., Koenen, K. C., & Marshall, R. (2006). The psychological risks of Vietnam for U.S. veterans: A revisit with new data and methods. *Science, 313,* 979–982.

Eisendrath, S. J. (1996). When Munchausen becomes malingering: Factitious disorder that penetrates the legal system. *Bulletin of the American Academy of Psychiatry and the Law, 24,* 471–481.

Etherton, J. L, Bianchini, K. J., Ciota, M. A., Heinly, M. T., & Greve, K. W. (2006). Pain, malingering, and the WAIS-III Working Memory Index. *Spine Journal, 6,* 61–71.

Etherton, J. L., Bianchini, K. J., Greve, K. W., & Ciota, M. A. (2005). Test of Memory Malingering performance is unaffected by laboratory-induced pain: Implications for clinical use. *Archives of Clinical Neuropsychology, 20,* 375–384.

Etherton, J. L., Bianchini, K. J., Heinly, M. T., & Greve, K. W. (2006). Pain, malingering, and performance on the WAIS-III Processing Speed Index. *Journal of Clinical and Experimental Neuropsychology, 28,* 1218–1237.

Frederick, R. I. (2002). Review of the Validity Indicator Profile. *Journal of Forensic Neuropsychology, 2,* 125–145.

Glass, G. V., & Stanley, J. C. (1970). *Statistical methods in education and psychology.* Englewood Cliffs, NJ: Prentice-Hall.

Green, P. (2003). *Green's Word Memory Test user's manual.* Edmonton, Alberta, Canada: Green's Publishing.

Greiffenstein, M. F., & Baker, W. J. (2006). Miller was (mostly) right: Head-injury severity inversely related to simulation. *Legal and Criminological Psychology, 11,* 131–145.

Greiffenstein, M. F., Baker, W. J., Axelrod, B., Peck, E. A., & Gervais, R. (2004). The Fake Bad Scale and MMPI-2 F-family in detection of implausible psychological trauma claims. *The Clinical Neuropsychologist, 18,* 573–590.

Greiffenstein, M. F., Baker, W. J., & Gola, T. (1994). Validation of malingered amnesia measures with a large clinical sample. *Psychological Assessment, 6,* 218–224.

Greiffenstein, M., Baker, W. J., & Gola, T. (1996a). Comparison of multiple scoring methods for Rey's malingered amnesia measures. *Archives of Clinical Neuropsychology, 4,* 283–293.

Greiffenstein, M. F., Baker, W. J., & Gola, T. (1996b). Motor dysfunction profiles in traumatic brain injury and postconcussion syndrome. *Journal of the International Neuropsychological Society, 2,* 477–485.

Greiffenstein, M. F., Baker, W. J., Gola, T., Donders, J., & Miller, L. (2002). The Fake Bad Scale in atypical and severe closed-head-injury litigants. *Journal of Clinical Psychology, 58,* 1591–1600.

Greiffenstein, M. F., Gola, T., & Baker, W. J. (1995). MMPI-2 Validity scales versus domain-specific measures in detection of factitious traumatic brain injury. *The Clinical Neuropsychologist, 9,* 230–240.

Greve, K. W., & Bianchini, K. J. (2004). Setting empirical cutoffs on psychometric indicators of negative response bias: A methodological commentary with recommendations. *Archives of Clinical Neuropsychology, 19,* 533–541.

Greve, K. W., Bianchini, K. J., & Ameduri, C. J. (2003). Use of a forced-choice test of tactile discrimination in the evaluation of functional sensory loss: A report of three cases. *Archives of Physical Medicine and Rehabilitation, 84,* 1233–1236.

Greve, K. W., Bianchini, K. J., Black, F. W., Heinly, M. T., Love, J. M., Swift, D. A., et al. (2006). The prevalence of cognitive malingering in persons reporting exposure to occupational and environmental substances. *Neurotoxicology, 27,* 940–950.

Greve, K. W., Bianchini, K. J., & Doane, B. M. (2006). Classification accuracy of the Test of Memory Malingering in traumatic brain injury: Results of a known-groups analysis. *Journal of Clinical and Experimental Neuropsychology, 28,* 1176–1190.

Greve, K. W., Bianchini, K. J., Love, J. M., Brennan, A., & Heinly, M. T. (2006). Sensitivity and specificity of MMPI-2 Validity scales and indicators to malingered neurocognitive dysfunction in traumatic brain injury. *The Clinical Neuropsychologist, 20,* 491–512.

Guze, S. B. (1993). Genetics of Briquet's syndrome and somatization disorder: A review of family, adoption, and twin studies. *Annals of Clinical Psychiatry, 5,* 225–230.

Harpending, H. C., & Sobus, J. (1987). Sociopathy as an adaptation. *Ethology and Sociobiology, 8,* 63–72.

Hayes, J. S., Hale, D. B., & Gouvier, W. D. (1997). Do tests predict malingering in defendants with mental retardation? *Journal of Psychology: Interdisciplinary and Applied, 131,* 575–576.

Heaton, R. K., Chelune, G. J., Talley, J. L., Kay, G. G., & Curtiss, G. (1993). *Wisconsin Card Sorting Test manual.* Odessa, FL: Psychological Assessment Resources.

Heinly, M. T., Greve, K. W., Bianchini, K. J., Love, J. L., & Brennan, A. (2005). WAIS Digit Span–based indicators of malingered neurocognitive dysfunction: Classification accuracy in traumatic brain injury. *Assessment, 12,* 429–444.

Hill, A. B. (1965). The environment and disease: Association and causation. *Proceedings of the Royal Society of Medicine, 58,* 295–300.

Hunsley, J., & Meyer, G. J. (2003). The incremental validity of psychological testing and assessment: Conceptual, methodological, and statistical issues. *Psychological Assessment, 15,* 446–455.

Inman, T. H., & Berry, D. T. R. (2002). Cross-validation of indicators of malingering: A comparison of nine neuropsychological tests, four tests of malingering, and behavioral observations. *Archives of Clinical Neuropsychology, 17,* 1–23.

Iverson, G. L., & Binder, L. M. (2000). Detecting exaggeration and malingering in neuropsychological assessment. *Journal of Head Trauma Rehabilitation, 15,* 829–858.

Jennett, B., & Teasdale, G. (1977). Aspects of coma after severe brain damage. *Lancet,* Apr. 23, 1(8017), 878–881.

Killgore, W. D. S., & DellaPietra, L. (2000). Using the WMS-III to detect malingering: Empirical validation of the Rarely Missed Index (RMI). *Journal of Clinical and Experimental Neuropsychology, 22,* 761–771.

Lange, R. T., Iverson, G. L., Sullivan, K., & Anderson, D. (2006). Suppressed working memory on the WMS-III as a marker for poor effort. *Journal of Clinical and Experimental Neuropsychology, 28,* 294–305.

Langeluddecke, P. M., & Lucas, S. K. (2004). Validation of the Rarely Missed Index (RMI) in detecting memory malingering in mild head-injury litigants. *Journal of Forensic Neuropsychology, 4,* 49–64.

Larrabee, G. J. (1990). Cautions in the use of neuropsychological evaluation in legal settings. *Neuropsychology, 4,* 239–247.

Larrabee, G. J. (2003a). Detection of malingering using atypical performance patterns on standard neuropsychological tests. *The Clinical Neuropsychologist, 17,* 410–425.

Larrabee, G. J. (2003b). Detection of symptom exaggeration with the MMPI-2 in litigants with malingered neurocognitive dysfunction. *The Clinical Neuropsychologist, 17,* 64–68.

Larrabee, G. J. (2003c). Exaggerated pain report in litigants with malingered neurocognitive dysfunction. *The Clinical Neuropsychologist, 17,* 395–401.

Larrabee, G. J. (2005). Assessment of malingering. In G. J. Larrabee (Ed.), *Forensic neuropsychology: A scientific approach* (pp. 115–158). New York: Oxford University Press.

Larrabee, G. J., Trahan, D. E., Curtiss, G., & Levin, H. S. (1988). Normative data for the Verbal Selective Reminding Test. *Neuropsychology, 2,* 173–182.

Lees-Haley, P. R., English, L. T., & Glenn, W. J. (1991). A Fake Bad scale for the MMPI-2 for personal-injury claimants. *Psychological Reports, 68,* 203–210.

Lees-Haley, P. R., Greiffenstein, M. F., Larrabee, G. J., & Manning, E. L. (2004). Methodological problems in the neuropsychological assessment of the effects of exposure to welding fumes and manganese. *The Clinical Neuropsychologist, 18,* 449–464.

Levin, H. S., Williams, D. H., Eisenberg, H. M., High, W. M., & Guinto, F. C., Jr. (1992). Serial MRI and neurobehavioural findings after mild to moderate closed-head injury. *Journal of Neurology, Neurosurgery, and Psychiatry, 55,* 255–262.

Lu, P. H., Boone, K. B., Cozolino, L., & Mitchell, C. (2003). Effectiveness of the Rey-Osterrieth Complex Figure Test and the Meyers and Meyers Recognition Trial in the detection of suspect effort. *The Clinical Neuropsychologist, 17,* 426–440.

Lu, P. H., Boone, K. B., Jimenez, N., & Razani, J. (2004). Failure to inhibit the reading response on the Stroop Test: A pathognomonic indicator of suspect effort. *Journal of Clinical and Experimental Neuropsychology, 26,* 180–189.

Martin, R. L., Cloninger, C. R., & Guze, S. B. (1982). The natural history of somatization and substance abuse in women criminals: A six-year follow-up. *Comprehensive Psychiatry, 23*, 528–537.

Mealy, L. (1995). The sociobiology of sociopathy: An integrated evolutionary model. *Behavioral and Brain Sciences, 18*, 523–599.

Meyers, J. E., Millis, S. R., & Volkert, K. (2002). A validity index for the MMPI-2. *Archives of Clinical Neuropsychology, 17*, 157–169.

Meyers, J. E., & Volbrecht, M. E. (2003). A validation of multiple malingering detection methods in a large clinical sample. *Archives of Clinical Neuropsychology, 18*, 261–276.

Millis, S. R. (2004). Evaluation of malingered neurocognitive disorders. In M. Rizzo & P. Eslinger (Eds.), *Principles and practice of behavioral neurology and neuropsychology* (pp. 1077–1089). Philadelphia: Saunders.

Millis, S. R., Putnam, S., Adams, K., & Ricker, J. (1995). The California Verbal Learning Test in the detection of incomplete effort in neuropsychological evaluation. *Psychological Assessment, 7*, 463–471.

Millis, S. R., Ross, S. R., & Ricker, J. H. (1998). Detection of incomplete effort on the Wechsler Adult Intelligence Scale-Revised: A cross-validation. *Journal of Clinical and Experimental Neuropsychology, 20*, 167–173.

Millis, S. R., & Volinsky, C. T. (2001). Assessment of response bias in mild head injury: Beyond malingering tests. *Journal of Clinical and Experimental Neuropsychology, 23*, 809–828.

Mittenberg, W., Azrin, R., Millsaps, C., & Heilbronner, R. (1993). Identification of malingered head injury on the Wechsler Memory Scale-Revised. *Psychological Assessment, 5*, 34–40.

Mittenberg, W., Theroux, S., Aguila-Puentes, G., Bianchini, K. J., Greve, K. W., & Rayls, K. (2001). Identification of malingered head injury on the Wechsler Adult Intelligence Scale-3. *The Clinical Neuropsychologist, 15*, 440–445.

Mittenberg, W., Theroux-Fichera, S., Zielinski, R. E., & Heilbronner, R. L. (1995). Identification of malingered head injury on the Wechsler Adult Intelligence Scale-Revised. *Professional Psychology: Research and Practice, 26*, 491–498.

Nies, K., & Sweet, J. (1994). Neuropsychological assessment and malingering: A critical review of past and present strategies. *Archives of Clinical Neuropsychology, 9*, 501–552.

Ord, J., Greve, K. W., & Bianchini, K. J. (2006, October). *Detection of malingering in traumatic brain injury with the Wechsler Memory Scale-III.* Poster presented at the 26th annual meeting of the National Academy of Neuropsychology, San Antonio.

Paniak, C., Reynolds, S., Toller-Lobe, G., Melnyk, A., Nagy, J., & Schmidt, D. (2002). A longitudinal study of the relationship between financial compensation and symptoms after treated mild traumatic brain injury. *Journal of Clinical and Experimental Neuropsychology, 24*, 187–193.

Pankratz, L., & Erickson, R. D. (1990). Two views of malingering. *The Clinical Neuropsychologist, 4*, 379–389.

Pinker, S. (1999). How the mind works. In D. C. Grossman & H. Valtin (Vol. Eds.), *Annals of the New York Academy of Sciences: Vol. 882. Great issues for medicine in the twenty-first century: Ethical and social issues arising out of advances in the biomedical sciences* (pp. 119–127). New York: New York Academy of Sciences.

Price, J. R., & Stevens, K. B. (1997). Psycholegal implications of malingered head trauma. *Applied Neuropsychology, 4*, 75–83.

Rees, L. M., Tombaugh, T. N., & Boulay, Luc. (2001). Depression and the Test of Memory Malingering. *Archives of Clinical Neuropsychology, 16,* 501–506.

Rees, L. M., Tombaugh, T. N., Gansler, D., & Moczynski, N. (1998). Five validation experiments of the Test of Memory Malingering (TOMM). *Psychological Assessment, 10,* 10–20.

Reitan, R. M., & Wolfson, D. (1993). *The Halstead-Reitan Neuropsychological Test Battery: Theory and clinical interpretation* (2nd ed.). South Tucson, AZ: Neuropsychology Press.

Reynolds, C. R. (1998). Common sense, clinicians, and actuarialism. In C. R. Reynolds (Ed.), *Detection of malingering during head-injury litigation* (pp. 261–286). New York: Plenum.

Reynolds, S., Paniak, C., Toller-Lobe, G., & Nagy, J. (2003). A longitudinal study of compensation-seeking and return to work in a treated mild traumatic brain-injury sample. *Journal of Head Trauma Rehabilitation, 18,* 139–147.

Rohling, M. L., Meyers, J. E., & Millis, S. R. (2003). Neuropsychological impairment following traumatic brain injury: A dose-response analysis. *The Clinical Neuropsychologist, 17,* 289–302.

Ross, S. R., Millis, S. R., Krukowski, R. A., Putnam, S. H., & Adams, K. M. (2004). Detecting incomplete effort on the MMPI-2: An examination of the Fake-Bad scale in mild head injury. *Journal of Clinical and Experimental Neuropsychology, 26,* 115–124.

Sheridan, L. K., Fitzgerald, H. E., Adams, K. M., Nigg, J. T., Martel, M. M., Puttler, L. I., et al. (2006). Normative symbol digit modalities test performance in a community-based sample. *Archives of Clinical Neuropsychology, 21,* 23–28.

Sherman, D. S., Boone, K. B., Lu, P., & Razani, J. (2002). Re-examination of the Rey Auditory Verbal Learning Test/Rey Complex Figure discriminant function to detect suspect effort. *The Clinical Neuropsychologist, 16,* 242–250.

Slick, D. J., Sherman, E. M. S., & Iverson, G. L. (1999). Diagnostic criteria for malingered neurocognitive dysfunction: Proposed standards for clinical practice and research. *The Clinical Neuropsychologist, 13,* 545–561.

Slick, D. J., Tan, J. E., Strauss, E. H., & Hultsch, D. F. (2004). Detecting malingering: A survey of experts' practice. *Archives of Clinical Neuropsychology, 19,* 465–473.

Straus, S. E., Richardson, W. S., Glasziou, P., & Haynes, R. B. (2005). *Evidence-based medicine. How to practice and teach EBM* (3rd ed.). Edinburgh, UK: Elsevier Churchill Livingston.

Strauss, E., Slick, D. J., Levy-Bencheton, J., Hunter, M., MacDonald, S. W., & Hultsch, D. F. (2002). Intraindividual variability as an indicator of malingering in head injury. *Archives of Clinical Neuropsychology, 17,* 423–444.

Suhr, J. A., & Boyer, D. (1999). Use of the Wisconsin Card Sorting Test in the detection of malingering in student simulator and patient samples. *Journal of Clinical and Experimental Neuropsychology, 21,* 701–708.

Sweet, J. J., & King, J. H. (2002). Category Test validity indicators: Overview and practice recommendations. *Journal of Forensic Neuropsychology, 3,* 241–274.

Sweet, J. J., Wolfe, P., Sattlberger, E., Numan, B., Rosenfeld, J. P., Clingerman, S., & Nies, K. J. (2000). Further investigation of traumatic brain injury versus insufficient effort with the California Verbal Learning Test. *Archives of Clinical Neuropsychology, 15,* 105–113.

Tombaugh, T. N. (1996). *TOMM: Test of Memory Malingering.* Tonawanda, NY: Multi-Health Systems.

Tombaugh, T. N. (1997). The Test of Memory Malingering (TOMM): Normative data from cognitively intact and cognitively impaired individuals. *Psychological Assessment, 9*, 260–268.

Trahan, D. E., & Larrabee, G. J. (1988). *Continuous Visual Memory Test.* Odessa, FL: Psychological Assessment Resources.

Trueblood, W., & Schmidt, M. (1993). Malingering and other validity considerations in the neuropsychological evaluation of mild head injury. *Journal of Clinical and Experimental Neuropsychology, 15*, 578–590.

Vickery, C. F., Berry, D. T. R., Dearth, C. S., Vagnini, V. L., Baser, R. F., Cragar, D. F., et al. (2004). Head injury and the ability to feign neuropsychological deficits. *Archives of Clinical Neuropsychology, 19*, 37–48.

Vickery, C. D., Berry, D. T. R., Inman, T. H., Harris, M. J., & Orey, S. A. (2001). Detection of inadequate effort on neuropsychological testing: A meta-analytic review of selected procedures. *Archives of Clinical Neuropsychology, 16*, 45–73.

Victor, T. L., Boone, K. B., Serpa, J. G., & Buehler, M. A. (2006, February). *Using multiple measures of effort.* Paper presented at the 34th annual meeting of the International Neuropsychological Society, Boston.

Wechsler, D. (1987). *Wechsler Memory Scale-Revised manual.* San Antonio: Psychological Corp.

Wechsler, D. (1997a). *WAIS-III: Administration and scoring manual.* San Antonio: Psychological Corp.

Wechsler, D. (1997b). *WMS-III: Administration and scoring manual.* San Antonio: Psychological Corp.

Wiggins, E. C., & Brandt, J. (1988). The detection of simulated amnesia. *Law and Human Behavior, 12*, 57–78.

Youngjohn, J. R., Burrows, L., & Erdal, K. (1995). Brain damage or compensation neurosis? The controversial post-concussion syndrome. *The Clinical Neuropsychologist, 9*, 12–123.

Zangwill, O. (1943). Clinical tests of memory impairment. *Proceedings of the Royal Society of Medicine, 36*, 576–580.

Index

Page numbers followed by "t" denote tables; those followed by "f" denote figures.